History of Popular Music - From Edison to the 21st Century

Frank Hoffmann

Paw Paw Press

2015

Acoustic Era Recording Studio

TABLE OF CONTENTS

THE EVOLUTION OF NATIVE STYLES

Introduction	11
Popular Music and Its Fundamentals	11
Prelude to 20th Century Popular Music	12
Leading Acoustic Era Recording Artists	16
Table 1: James Reese Europe	55
The Top Acoustic Era Recording Artist	55
Table 2: Billy Murray's Recordings Classified By Humor Genres	56
Jazz	63
Table 3: Acid Jazz	67
Table 4: Smooth Jazz	67
Table 5: Ornette Coleman	68
Table 6: Mahavishnu Orchestra	69
Table 7: Pat Metheny	70

THE ROOTS OF ROCK MUSIC

The Blues	72
Table 8: Lonnie Johnson	75
Table 9: Albert King	76
Table 10: Freddie King	77
Table 11: Victoria Spivey	78
Rhythm and Blues	78
Table 12: Willie Dixon	84
Table 13: Louis Jordan	85
Table 14: Ike Turner	86
Table 15: Big Joe Turner	88
Table 16: Vee-Jay Records	89
Table 17: Jackie Wilson	91
Doo-Wop	91
Table 18: Drifters	97
Table 19: Platters	98
Table 20: A Cappella	99
Country and Western Music	100
Table 21: Brooks and Dunn	110
Table 22: Fiddlin' John Carson	111
Table 23: Dixie Chicks	112
Table 24: Faith Hill	112

Table 25: The Judds	113
Table 26: Loretta Lynn	114
Table 27: LeAnn Rimes	116
Table 28: Hank Snow	117
Table 29: Randy Travis	117
Crooners & The Tin Pan Alley Pop Tradition	119
Table 30: The Coming of the Crooners	124
Table 31: Gene Austin	159
Table 32: Bing Crosby	204
Table 33: Russ Columbo	265

THE CLASSIC ROCK 'N' ROLL ERA

Rockabilly	278
Table 34: Dorsey and Johnny Burnette	281
Table 35: Roy Orbison	282
Table 36: Carl Perkins	284
The Rise of Rock 'n' Roll	285
Table 37: Everly Brothers	291
Table 38: Little Richard	293
Table 39: Ritchie Valens	294

THE BRILL BUILDING ERA

Overview	295
The Teen Idols	296
Table 40: Christina Aguilera	298
Table 41: Frankie Avalon	299
Table 42: Pat Boone	300
Table 43: Brenda Lee	301
Table 44: Monkees	302
Table 45: 'N Sync	303
Dance Crazes	304
Table 46: Chubby Checker	308
Rock Instrumentals	309
Table 47: Ventures	312
Novelty Songs	312
The Payola Scandal	316
Table 48: Alan Freed	317
Commercial Folk Music	318
Table 49: Phil Ochs	321

Table 50: Tom Rush	322
The Spector Sound	322
Table 51: Ellie Greenwich	325
The Girl Groups	327

THE BRITISH INVASION

Historical Survey	332
Table 52: Animals	338
Table 53: Bee Gees	339
Table 54: Dave Clark Five	341
Table 55: Herman's Hermits	341
Table 56: Searcher	342
Table 57: Shadows	343
Table 58: 10cc	344
Table 59: Yardbirds	345

AMERICAN RENAISSANCE

Surf Music	347
Car Songs/Hot Rod Music	349
Folk Rock	350
Table 60: Byrds	352
Table 61: Donovan	354
Table 62: Pentangle	355
Table 63: Turtles	356
Protest Music	357
Soul Music	360
Table 64: Booker T. & the MGs	368
Table 65: Otis Redding	369
Table 66: Righteous Brothers	370
Table 67: Sam and Dave	372
Table 68: Percy Sledge	372
Table 69: Sly and the Family Stone	373
Table 70: Wilson Pickett	374

REGIONAL STYLES

Defining Statements	376
New Orleans Sound	377

Table 71: Fats Domino	379
The Calypso Craze	380
Reggae	381
San Francisco Sound	383
Table 72: Country Joe and the Fish	386
Table 73: Janis Joplin	386
Southern Rock	387
Salsa	389

HYBRID CHILDREN OF ROCK

Genealogical Outline	391
Christian Rock/Christian Contemporary	392
Punk/Garage Rock	392
Psychedelia	394
Progressive Rock/Classical Rock	396
Table 74: Band	399
Table 75: Jeff Beck	400
Table 76: Creedence Clearwater Revival	402
Table 77: Emerson, Lake and Palmer	403
Table 78: Procol Harum	404
Table 79: Spirit	405
Table 80: Traffic	406
Country Rock	407
Table 81: Eagles	409
Latin Rock	410
Big Band Rock	411
Table 82: Blood, Sweat & Tears	413
Glitter Rock	414
Heavy Metal	415
Table 83: Black Sabbath	416
Table 84: Deep Purple	418
Euro-pop/Euro-rock	419
Rock and Roll Revival	421
Blues Revival	422
Table 85: Michael Bloomfield	425
Bubblegum Sound	426
Table 86: Bell Records	427
Table 87: Buddah/Kama Sutra	428
Table 88: Tommy James and the Shondells	429
Singer/Songwriter Tradition	430
Table 89: Joni Mitchell	432

Table 90: Randy Newman	433
Table 91: Neil Sedaka	434
Table 92: Carly Simon	435
Soft Rock, MOR and Related Styles	436
Table 93: Herb Alpert (and the Tijuana Brass)	442
Table 94: Lovin' Spoonful	444
Power Pop	445
Album Oriented Rock (AOR)	447
Table 95: Boston	450
Table 96: Dire Straits	451
Table 97: Doobie Brothers	453
Table 98: John "Cougar" Mellencamp	454
Funk	455
Table 99: Ohio Players	458
Table 100: War	459
Disco	460
Table 101: Donna Summer	463
Rap/Hip Hop	464
Table 102: Africa Bambaataa	466
Table 103: EazyE	466
Table 104: Will Smith	467
Black Contemporary	468
Table 105: Anita Baker	471
Table 106: Boyz II Men	471
Table 107: Luther Vandross	472
Avant-Garde Rock	473
Table 108: Klaus Schulze	475
Table 109: Tangerine Dream	476
Table 110: John Zorn	477
New Age Music	478
Table 111: William Ackerman	480
World Beat: Conjunto	481

PUNK/NEW WAVE/POSTPUNK

New Wave	483
Table 112: The Clash	485
Table 113: Police	486
Table 114: The Ramones	487
No Wave	488
Postpunk Music	489
Table 115: Beggars Banquet	492

Table 116: DIY	493
Hardcore	494
Table 117: Jello Biafra/Dead Kennedys	495
Table 118: Henry Rollins	496
Table 119: SST	497
Thrash	498
Oi	498
Industrial Music	499
White Noise and Its Stylistic Offshoots	500
Techno-Pop	502
New Romantics	505
Ska/Bluebeat Revival	506
Table 120: Mighty Mighty Bosstones	507
Table 121: UB40	508
Goth Rock	509
Alternative Rock	509
Table 122: Beck	512
The Manc Sound	513
Ambient	514
Table 123: Massive Attack	516
Table 124: Orb	517
Riot Grrrl Movement	518
No Depression	518

OTHER NOTABLE TOPICS

Pop Music Video Clips	520
Table 125: Video Clips On Television, 1985	525
Table 126: Video Clip Categories	527
Trade Publications	
Table 127: Billboard	529
Record Producers	
Table 128: Lou Adler	531
Table 129: Milt Gabler	532
Table 130: Bill Laswell	533
Record Company Executives	
Table 131: Clive Davis	534
Recording Session Musicians	
Table 132: Hal Blaine	535
Table 133: Russ Titelman	536

APPENDICES

I.	Acoustic Era Song Lyrics	538
II.	Artist Recordings In Victor Catalog	542
III.	Pioneer Recording Artist Ratings	545

1955 Film Poster

THE EVOLUTION OF NATIVE STYLES

Introduction

The predominant theme in early American popular music—one also prominent in the other arts—was the clash between European models and rapidly evolving indigenous styles. The enfranchised classes were generally committed to importing Old World genres, ranging from Protestant hymns to opera, orchestral works, song lieder, and other vestiges of the art music tradition. While these forms all found a place in American society, distinctly homegrown variants had already appeared during the Colonial Era, including Appalachian folk music, Negro spirituals, patriotic airs and marches, and work songs of every imaginable stripe.

The victory of native popular culture was assured when minstrelsy achieved institutional status in the 1840s. Minstrelsy's ability to assimilate the full spectrum of American popular songs—from sentimental ballads composed by the likes of Stephen Foster to the coon and ragtime songs penned by early Tin Pan Alley tunesmiths—made it the preeminent theatrical tradition until the rise of vaudeville shortly before the turn of the twentieth century.

At the same time, rural southern cultures were responsible for nurturing those genres central to the rise of rock 'n' roll—Anglo-Saxon-derived country music, and the blues, performed by blacks while at work in the fields as well as in social settings. By the time jazz, the Broadway musical, bluegrass, western swing, rhythm and blues, and other indigenous styles had appeared in the twentieth century, the richness and vitality of American music would be acknowledged worldwide.

Popular Music and Its Fundamentals

Popular music is generally defined as either works created by the masses--i.e., modified by a series of contributors over time as in the case of the folk tradition--or material created by specific composers with the aim of achieving widespread acceptance (large record sales, high television ratings or large concert turnouts when performed, etc.). In contrast, serious music (also termed art or classical music) represents work created to please the specific needs of the particular composer rather than to please the general listening public. Most classical composers would readily admit that they have nothing against commercial success; however, this popularity must never come at the expense of artistic expression. The differing circumstances at the core of the music-making process don't necessarily have any bearing on the quality of the music produced. Excellent popular music can result from the initial impulse to generate a best-selling record, whereas the finest instincts to leave a masterpiece for posterity may lead to nothing more than an empty academic exercise unappreciated by anymore other than, perhaps, the composer.

All music is comprised of certain elements which can be discerned by any listener who possesses a basic understanding of the art form. Recognition of how these elements are employed by composers and musicians can further enhance one's appreciation of music.

Individual notes, whatever their pitch or volume, vary in general quality of sound, depending on the instruments producing them. This concept is known as "tone color" or "timbre," and can be described through the use of terms like warm, vibrant, brittle, brassy, muddy, etc.

Rhythm designates the time strictures of a musical work. Time is comprised of a succession of beats; the particular arrangements of long and short notes represent rhythms. An "accent" denotes those beats which are more emphatic than others. With most popular forms of music, a recurring rhythmic pattern can be discerned; each occurrence of a repeated pattern--consisting of a principal strong beat and one or more weaker beats—is known as a "measure" or "bar."

The performing of a succession of musical pitches according to a particular rhythm results in "melody." Of all musical elements, melody is likely to interest listeners to the greatest degree, often evoking strong emotions and sentiments. Melody can be effectively used to maintain interest in a work, as the listener waits to find out how the melody line works out. Groupings of simultaneous pitches are referred to as "chords." A melody is considered to be "harmonized" when supplied with a successive array of chords.

Music is also comprised of thematic material that varies in length and other characteristics. In a speech, the "themes" would be the main points elaborated on by the speaker. Musical notation can be developed in much the same way.

The blend of various sounds and melodic lines occurring simultaneously in a piece of music is called "texture." Whereas melody is perceived in the horizontal dimension, texture exists in a vertical framework.

These musical elements will be noted throughout the text in reference to particular qualities of the popular music styles being discussed. It is the unique combination of these elements which gives each musical genre--and, more specifically, each song--its own identity.

Prelude to 20th Century Popular Music

As far back as the Colonial Era, American popular music has been a rich stew comprised of many styles. The intermingling of these styles has resulted in the unique features characterizing our musical heritage. These pop styles have long been the most lucrative--and universally admired-- U.S. export.

The prevalent musical styles prior to 1900 tended to represent Americanized derivatives of popular European strains. The most notable included:

Protestant church music. Congregational music was undergoing a renaissance in Northern Europe during the settlement of the original colonies. Two diverse influences played a major role in the evolution of this genre: Martin Luther's compositions tried to emulate the beauty of the Catholic ritual (e.g., liberal use of organ and choir), while John Calvin, a bitter opponent of the fine arts, argued that music shouldn't attract attention to itself, but rather function as a peg upon which to hang the rhythmic recitation of psalms. The Englis Separatists (e.g., the Pilgrims, the Puritans) followed the Calvinist lead in advocating severe, ascetic musical forms. When the Pilgrims arrived in New England, in 1620, their music consisted of a small volume of Psalmody compiled by the Rev. Henry Ainsworth. It consisted of tunes, without any harmony, which paraphrased the Psalms.

The poetry of the originals often suffered from the exact character of the setting as typified by Psalm 1:

SCRIPTURAL TEXT

Blessed is the man that walketh not in the
counsel of the ungodly, nor standeth in the way
of sinners, nor sitteth in the seat of the scornful.
Therefore the ungodly shall not stand in the
judgment, nor sinners in the congregation of
the righteous.

AINSWORTH TEXT

O Blessed man that doth not in
The wicked's counsell walk;
Not stand in sinners' way, nor sit
In seat of scornful folk.
Therefore the wicked shall not in
The judgment stand upright:
And in th' assembly of the Just
Not any sinfull-wight.

Patriotic airs. These were frequently adapted, like the nation's art music of that time, from European songs. Primary examples include "Yankee Doodle" (originally sung in satirical fashion during the Colonial Era, its appeal to Revolutionary troops enabled it to spread far beyond its regional roots), "The Star-Spangeled Banner" (composed during the War of 1812), "Dixie" (written by Dan Emmett, it was first sung on Broadway at Dan Bryant's Minstrel Show a year or so before the Civil War), "Hail Columbia," and "The Battle-Hymn of the Republic." The latter work, considered the chief Northern song of the Civil War, had a rather complicated history. It started out as a Methodist camp-meeting song, sung in many Negro churches in the South. It was remade into a firemen's song in Charleston and, still later, appeared as a camp-song of rather ribald style, made famous by the Twelfth Massachusetts Regiment. Next revived as an abolition ode by Edna Dean Proctor, it was finally immortalized in Julia Ward Howe's 1861 version.

By the late 1800s, the march became the primary form of American patriotic music. The leading American march composer, John Philip Sousa, was the conductor of the world renown U.S. Marine Band prior to forming his own ensemble. His march recordings are reputed to have outsold all other releases during the 1890-1895 period.

Sea-songs. The ship environment, with its stultifying routine, proved conducive to singing. Lacking talented composers, sailors tended to appropriate foreign melodies and set American subjects to them. Primary examples of these songs, which typically employed a rough and ready style, included "Columbia, the Gem of the Ocean" (which referred to Washington rather than Lord Nelson, the subject of the English version, "Britannia, the Pride of the Ocean") and "The Constitution and Guerriere" (or "Hull's Victory"; based on the old English melody, "The Landlady's Daughter of France," it commemorates a famous naval battle from the War of 1812).

Folk songs. Material disseminated among the common people, compositional credits typically are either unknown or shared by many contributors over a period a time. Built on such musical traits as simplicity, directness, and musical imagery, folk songs often provided a more graphic picture of the subject matter at hand than was the case with journalistic overage, formal histories, etc. American output, as a result of our nation's focus on commerce and cultural amalgamation, has tended to be sectional (e.g., Old West, Appalachian, Southern blacks) rather than national in scope. The genre's vitality informed the work of formal composers; e.g., the *New World Symphony* of European art music composer Dvorak, Stephen Foster's parlor songs such as "Oh! Susannah," "My Old Kentucky Home," "Massa's in de Cold, Cold Ground," "The Old Folks at Home," and "Way Down Upon de Swanee River."

Sentimental songs. They flowered in a domestic setting due to the inclination of the American middle and upper classes to keep a piano in the parlor and the widespread availability of sheet music (which wasn't supplanted by sound recordings as the prime source of pop music for Americans until the World War I era).

Minstrel tradition. After the War of 1812, many Americans expressed the need for native forms, symbols, and institutions that would assert the nation's cultural distinctiveness as clearly and emphatically as the war had reaffirmed its political independence. Elite groups looked forward to a cultural renaissance in which American artists and subjects would push European forms and concepts to new heights of achievement. However, new forces were emerging which demanded that the American masses be permitted to shape the country in their own image. The mass migration of rural citizens to the cities had led to severe "culture shock." This disruption meant more than the mere loss of longtime amusements--stories, songs, tales, jokes, etc.--because, in folk societies, the verbal arts taught values and norms, invoked sanctions against transgressors, and provided vehicles for fantasy and outlets for social criticism. Through a process of trial and error, the popular arts emerged to fill this void.

Minstrelsy ultimately arrived at the most successful entertainment formula geared to the masses. In the 1830s, theater-goers still attended the same venue for cultural sustenance; a typical evening's entertainment consisted of a full-length play, whose acts were interspersed with variety specialties--dances, popular songs, black-faced acts, jugglers, acrobats, trained animals, and various novelties (e.g., freaks of nature). The Astor Place Riot (New York, 1849) rendered the by then unbridgeable cultural gap between common folk and elith society all too obvious, causing stage entertainment to divide into specialized forms. The 1850s saw major market areas offering different types of productions, including legitimate theater, opera, symphonic music, melodrama, variety, the circus, and minstrelsy.

Every part of the minstrel show--its features, form, and content--was hammered out in the interaction between performers and the vocal audiences they sought only to please. In addition to their entertainment value, blackfaced performers played a key role in helping white America come to grips with the changing role of blacks within society. Beginning in the 1820s, traveling blackfaced performers grew in popularity and continued to augment their repertoires. In February 1843, four blackfired white men took the stage billed as the Virginia Minstrels to perform for the first time an entire evening of the "oddities, peculiarities, and comicalities of that Sable Genus of Humanity." They left in their wake a minstrel-mad public and a bevy of imitators that reshaped American popular entertainment
.

Broadway musical theater. This genre represented the sum of many evolutionary influences: (a) British and Viennese operetta, (b) minstrelsy, (c) continental variety shows, (d)immigrant humor, and (e) Manhattan's songwriting factory, Tin Pan Alley. It arose out of the interaction of cultures in New York City during the last quarter of the nineteenth century. The folk traditions of blacks, Irish, and Eastern European immigrants mixed with each other as well as established American traditions and more entrenched music theater forms, resulting in a heightened degree of experimentation. Many dramatic works of the era used music and lyrics as elements in their productions. Songs were not integral to revealing plot and character; rather, they enhanced the atmosphere and gave the actors another outlet for their talents.

Ragtime. A dance-based vernacular style, it featured a syncopated melody against an even accompaniment (i.e., oom-pah or march-style bass). It was comprised of self-contained sections or strains, usually sixteen measures each, which were often repeated. Ragtime--which arose in the 1890s and faded by the late 1910s in the wake of dixieland jazz--comprised four main categories:

   a. Instrumental rags, which were usually play on the piano. They generally used conventional European harmonies and possessed a typical formal structure of "AA BB A CC DD" (where each letter indicated a separate strain with its own melody, rhythm, and harmony). The distinctiveness of the genre was largely rhythmic in nature; untied syncopations predominated to around 1900, after which tied syncopations came to dominate. After 1906 a melodic motif called "secondary rag" became a staple (this device is prominent in George Botsford's "Grizzly Bear Rag").

b. Ragtime songs. While the best piano rags--featuring more syncopation and musical elaboration--have better stood the tests of time and modern critical judgment, the turn-of-the-century public liked songs much better than piano rags. This variant evolved from the syncopated "coon songs" of the late 1890s. The word "ragtime" became so marketable that it became widely applied to songs that were either lightly syncopated or not syncopated at all. The label was also applied to songs whose only connection with ragtime was the mention of it in the lyrics. The tremendous popularity of Irving Berlin's "Alexander's Ragtime Band" (1911) caused the term to be increasingly applied to rhythmic, but not necessarily syncopated, popular songs.

c. Ragtime or syncopated waltzes.

d. "Ragging" of the classics or other preexisting pieces. The origins of ragtime go back to the practice of ragging an existing melody (examples of which have been ascertained as early as the 1870s). Only later were new compositions--i.e., banjo and piano rags and ragtime songs--written in a "raggy" style, with the syncopations an inherent, not an "added-on," part of the music. By 1886, George W. Cable described the rhythm of a black dance in New Orleans' Congo Square as "ragged." The first substantiated use of the words "rag" and "rag-time" occurred in August 1896 with the copyrighting of Ernest Hogan's "All Coons Look Alike to Me," which possessed an optional chorus labeled "Negro Rag Accompaniment."

Leading Acoustic Era Artists

Anthony, Harry (r.n.: John Young; d. 1954; 84)

He recorded successfully under many guises--solo artist; part of the gospel team, Harry Anthony and James F. Harrison; tenor with the Criterion Quartet--prior to joining the American Quartet in 1915. His hits included "When the Mists Have Rolled Away" (Edison 9105, 1905), "Meet Me Tonight In Dreamland" (with Elizabeth Wheeler, Edison 10290, 1910), and "Love Never Dies" (with Inez Barbour, Victor 17042, 1912).

Ash, Sam (d. October 21, 1951; 67)

This tenor split his time between Broadway musicals and recording. He later acted in several films. His hits included "Hello, Frisco!" (with Elida Morris, Columbia 1801, 1915), "America, I Love You" (Columbia 1842, 1916), and "Tears" (Columbia 2700, 1919).

Atlee, John Yorke (d. April 1, 1910; 68)

The "artistic whistler" was one of the earliest recording stars. His bestsellers included "The Mocking Bird" (Columbia, 1891), "Home, Sweet Home" (Columbia, 1891), and "After the Ball" (Columbia, 1893).

Austin, Gene (June 24, 1900-January 24, 1972)

Allegedly the most popular singer of the late 1920s, Austin started out as a vaudeville performer. His easygoing vocal and piano style enabled him to capitalize on the crooner craze fueled by the rise of both radio and electronic recording.

Baker, Elsie (d. April 28, 1958; 71)

The contralto frequently recorded under the pseudonym "Edna Brown." Her run as a first-line hitmaker ran from mid-1912 to mid-1922, and included solo work, various duo pairings (e.g., James F. Harrison, Reed Miller, Charles Harrison, Frederick Wheeler, Elliott Shaw, Olive Kline) and a stint with the Victor Light Opera Co. She had two top selling discs--"I Love You Truly" (Victor 17121, 1912) and "Hush-A-Bye Ma Baby" (Victor 18214, 1917)--and collaborated successively with Billy Murray on several occasions: "When You're Away" (with the American Quartet, Victor 17139, 1912), "Some Sort of Somebody" (Victor 17992, 1916), and "Simple Melody" (Victor 18051, 1916).

Ballard, George Wilton (d. April 6, 1950; 72)

The tenor recorded 15 years with Edison in the early years of the century. His biggest hit was "M-O-T-H-E-R (A Word That Means the World To Me) (Edison 50325, 1916).

Baur, Franklyn (d. February 24, 1950; 46)

Baur doubled as a solo artist and first tenor of the Revelers during the latter half of the 1920s. He was also the original "Voice of Firestone" on the radio. His biggest hits were "Deep In My Heart" (Victor 19378, 1924) and "Tonight You Belong To Me" (Brunswick 3319, 1926/27).

Bayes, Nora (r.n.: Dora Goldberg; d. March 19, 1928; 47)

Following her Broadway debut in 1901, she rose to stardom through shows teaming her with husband Jack Norworth. They wrote many popular songs, including "Shine On, Harvest Moon." She had two top-selling recordings: "Over There" (Victor 45130, 1917) and "Make Believe" (Columbia 3392, 1921).

Belmont, Joe (r.n.: Joseph Walter Fulton; d. August 28, 1949; 73)

The whistling soloist, known as "The Human Bird," had a recording career reaching back to the nineteenth century. He recorded with such luminaries as Murray and Ada Jones, and sang with the Columbia Male Quartet. Belmont had a top-selling recording, "Tell Me, Pretty Maiden" (with Byron G. Harlan, Frank C. Stanley, and the Florodora Girls, Columbia 31604, 1901).

Bernard, Al (d. March 9, 1949; 60)

A vaudeville comedy singer known as "the boy from Dixie, "Bernard was a throwback to an earlier era, often appearing onstage in blackface. His biggest hit was "I Want To Hold You In My Arms" (with Ernest Hare, Edison 50558, 1919).

Bieling, John (d. March 30, 1948; 79)

Bieling first made his mark as first tenor of the Manhansett Quartet in the 1890s. He was frequently teamed with Harry Macdonough on record; the pairing enjoyed a one top-selling hit, "In the Sweet Bye and Bye" (Victor 1855, 1903). He went on to become a member of both the Haydn and American Quartets during the first decade of the twentieth century.

Biese, Paul, Trio

Led by tenor saxophonist Paul Biese, the group had seven bestsellers in 1920-1921, four of which featured Frank Crumit as lead vocalist.

Big Four Quartet

This short-lived ensemble--comprised of Arthur Collins, Byron G. Harlan, Joe Natus, and A.D. Madeira--had a top-selling hit, "Good-Bye, Dolly Gray" (Edison 7728, 1901).

Brown, Edna (see: Elsie Baker)

Burr, Henry (r.n.: Harry H. McClaskey; January 15, 1882-April 6, 1941)

Like Billy Murray, he began recording for national labels in 1903. He is considered to have been the top balladeer of the pioneer era. He is reputed to have appeared on approximately 12,000 recordings, as a solo (often employing the pseudonym "Irving Gillette"), in duets with countless partners (most notably, Albert Campbell), and as a member of the Columbia Male Quartet, Peerless Quartet, and Sterling Trio. When his recordings stopped selling in the late 1920s, he shifted his energies to radio. He was part of the regular cast on NBC's National Barn Dance show at the time of his death. His top-selling recordings included "Come Down, Ma Ev'ning Star" (Columbia 1405, 1903), "In the Shade of the Old Apple Tree" (Edison 8958, 1905), "Love Me and the World Is Mine" (Columbia 3499, 1906), "I Wonder Who's Kissing Her Now" (Columbia 707, 1909), "Meet Me To-Night In Dreamland" (Columbia 905, 1910).

Campbell, Albert (d. January 25, 1947; 74)

The tenor balladeer began recording in 1897, achieving his greatest success in duets with Henry Burr and as a member of the Columbia Male Quartet, Peerless Quartet, and Sterling Trio. He also had several top-selling hits as a soloist: "My Wild Irish Rose" (Berliner 0139, 1899), "Ma Blushin' Rosie" (Gram-o-Phone 219, 1900), and "Love Me and the World Is Mine" (Victor 4823, 1906).

Cantor, Eddie (r.n.: Eddie Israel Iskowitz; January 31, 1892-October 10, 1964)

Cantor rose to stardom in the "Ziegfeld Follies of 1917" and remained a national figure for four decades, moving from vaudeville to radio, movies, and TV. His greatest successes as a comic singer spanned the 1917-1925 period, including three top-selling discs: "Margie" (Emerson 10301, 1921), "No, No, Nora" (Columbia 3964, 1923), and "If You Knew Susie" (Columbia 364, 1925).

Caruso, Enrico (February 27, 1873-August 2, 1921)

Probably the most renown singer ever, he came to America in 1902 following almost a decade of critical acclaim in Europe. His decision to record for Victor at that time has come to be viewed as one of the most important developments in the history of the phonograph; for the first time recordings came to be seen as an acceptable vehicle for serious music. His ability to compete with popular music artists on the bestselling charts has never been even remotely rivalled by a classical performer. The tenor had several top-selling recordings: "I Pagliacci--Vesti La Giubba" (Victor 88061, 1907), "Love Is Mine" (Victor 87095, 1912), and "Over There" (Victor 87294, 1918).

Casey, Michael (Pseudonym for Russell Hunting)

Clark, Helen

The New York-born contralto made many popular recordings between 1910-1930, as a soloist, in duets, and as a member of Victor Light Opera Company. Her collaboration with Murray, "Come On Over Here" (Victor 17441, 1913), was a major hit. "Sympathy" (Victor 17270), a duet with Walter Van Brunt, was a top seller in early 1913.

Cohan, George M. (July 3, 1878-November 5, 1942)

Cohan rose from the Four Cohans family vaudeville act to create a brash new style of American musical comedy which placed a greater emphasis on the dramatic dimension. He wrote, managed, and starred in a series of Broadway successes from the turn of the century to 1937. He recorded a number of his compositions prior to World War I (ironically, though, none of his more famous songs); his biggest seller was "Life's A Funny Proposition, After All" (Victor 60042, 1911).

Collins, Arthur (February 7, 1864-August 3, 1933)

A direct product of the minstrel tradition, Collins was considered the leading dialect comedy singer of the pioneer recording era. He was surpassed only by Burr and Murray as a hitmaker; his duo collaboration with Byron G. Harlan was one of the most successful in recording history. He was also a member of the Peerless Qaurtet (1906-1917) and the Big Four Quartet. His top-selling solo hits included "The Preacher and the Bear" (Edison 9000, 1905), allegedly the first recording to sell two million and the biggest hit of all time until 1920. Collins and Harlan also had approximately a dozen top sellers, most notably the most popular version of the Irving Berlin classic, "Alexander's Ragtime Band" (Victor 16908, 1911).

Columbia Comedy Trio

Comprised of Murray, Byron G. Harlan, and Steve Porter, this spontaneous studio lineup had one bestseller, "At the Village Post Office" (Columbia 3704).

Columbia Male Quartet

The forerunner to the Peerless Quartet, members included Henry Burr, Albert Campbell, Steve Porter, and Frank C. Stanley. Stanley also managed the group. Tom Daniels appears to have substituted for Stanley on a number of recordings.

Columbia Mixed Quartet

Built around Grace Kerns, Mildred Porter, Charles Harrison, and Frank Croxton, the ensemble had two big sellers, "The Battle Hymn of the Republic" (Columbia 1155, 1912) and "Hark! The Herald Angels Sing" (Columbia 2104, 1916).

Columbia Orchestra

Directed by Charles A. Prince, the ensemble backed many of Columbia's stable of singers as well as recording its own hits (the biggest being "Hiawatha," Columbia 1155; 1903).

Columbia Stellar Quartet

The group's original personnel included Charles Harrison, John Barnes Wells, Frank Croxton, and Andrea Sarto. In 1915, Wells was briefly replaced by Henry Burr, who then gave way to Reed Miller. The Quartet was often paired with guest vocalists in the studio; e.g., Oscar Seagle, Margaret Keyes, Lucy Gates. It had a top-selling recording, "The Battle Hymn of the Republic" (Columbia 2367), in 1918.

Confrey, Zez, and His Orchestra   (r.n.: Edward Elzear Confrey; d. 1972; 77)

An influential composer (Murray recorded his "Stumbling") as well as instrumentalist, his biggest hit was "Kitten On the Keys" (Brunswick 2082, 1921; new version, Victor 18900, 1922).

Connolly, Dolly

The wife of songwriter Percy Wenrich (e.g., "Rainbow"), she specialized in MOR versions of ragtime and minstrel material (e.g., "Red Rose Rag," 1911; "Waiting For the Robert E. Lee," 1912).

Conway's Band

This pops concert band, directed by Patrick Conway, had a string of bestsellers during the second decade of the century, most notably the "Spirit of Independence March" (Victor 18559, 1919).

Coon-Sanders Orchestra

This Kansas City band, led by Carleton Coon (d. May 3, 1932; 38) and Joe Sanders (d. May 14, 1965; 70), achieved popularity through its NBC radio show. The ensembled also had many hit records during the twenties, most notably "Some Little Bird" (Columbia 3403, 1921).

Croxton, Frank (d. September 3, 1949; 71)

Best known as the bass singer for the Columbia Stellar Quartet and Peerless Quartet (1919-1925), he also had a number of solo hits, most notably "On the Road to Mandalay" (Columbia 5441, 1913).

Crumit, Frank (d. September 7, 1943; 53)

Crumit had a very successful run as a recording artist in the 1920s even though his "small" voice has not felt to be suited to acoustic recording. He was perhaps best remembered for his work in Broadway musicals and the radio show he co-hosted with wife Julia Sanderson from 1929-1943. His biggest records included "Oh! By Jingo! Oh! By Gee! (Columbia 2935, 1920), "Sweet Lady" (Columbia 3475, 1921), and "A Gay Caballero" (Victor 21735, 1928/29).

Dalhart, Vernon (r.n.: Marion Try Slaughter; April 6, 1883-September 15, 1948)

Originally a light opera tenor, Dalhart started recording in 1916. His transformation into a hillbilly interpreter of narrative dirges such as "The Wreck of the Old 97" and "The Death of Floyd Collins" resulted in phenomenal sales spanning some 30 labels and dozens of pseudonyms (e.g., Al Craver, Mack Allen). His hit, "The Prisoner's Song" (Victor 19427, 1925) was allegedly the biggest-selling non-holiday record of the pre-1955 era, accounting for more than seven million units.

Deleath, Vaughn (r.n. Leonore Vonderleath; May 28, 1943; 46)

Considered to be the first woman to sing on radio, Deleath performed more than 15,000 songs on 2,000 broadcasts from the early 1920s to the mid-1930s. Also recognized by some to be the first "crooner," his biggest hit recordings were "Ukelele Lady" (Columbia 361, 1925) and "Are You Lonesome Tonight?" (Edison 52044, 1927).

Denny, Will (d. October 2, 1908; 48)

The Boston native had a number of top sellers during the early years of recording, most notably "The Pretty Red Rose" (New England cylinder, 1892) and "Any Old Place I Hang My Hat Is `Home, Sweet Home' To Me" (Gram-o-Phone 956, 1901).

Dockstader, Lew (d. October 26, 1924; 68)

Vaudeville and minstrel show comedian who was a star from the 1870s to the early 1900s. He had one notable hit record, "Everybody Works But Father" (Columbia 3251, 1905). Al Jolson toured with his company prior to becoming a major Broadway star.

Dudley, S.H. (r.n.: Samuel Holland Rous; d. June 6, 1947; 81)

After a career singing opera (1886-1898), Dudley became the baritone of the Edison Male Quartet and Haydn Quartet. With the disbanding of the latter group, he went on to become a Victor executive. He became famous as the editor of the Victor record catalogs and **Book of the Opera**. His biggest sellers as a soloist were "When Reuben Comes to Town" (Victor A-519/Victor 3001, 1900), "Whistling" (Victor A-706, 1901), and "Meet Me In St. Louis, Louis" (Victor 2807, 1904).

Edison Male Quartette

Comprised of Harry Macdonough, John Bieling, S.H. Dudley, and William F. Hooley, this group is best known as the predecessor to the Haydn Quartet. The ensemble had a top-selling rendition of the classic, "My Old Kentucky Home" (Edison 2223), in early 1898.

Edwards, Cliff (d. July 18, 1972; 76)

Better known as "Ukelele Ike," Edwards' amiable, jazz-inflected approach stimulated a nationwide craze for the ukelele in the mid-1920s. He appeared in more than 50 film musicals, and achieved immortality as the voice of Jiminy Cricket in the Disney animated feature, **Pinocchio**. His long list of hits included two top sellers: "I Can't Give You Anything But Love" (Columbia 1471, 1928) and "Singin' in the Rain" (Columbia 1869, 1929).

Farrell, Marguerite (September 16, 1888-January 26, 1951)

This multi-faceted performer was successful in vaudeville (comic acting, dancing, singing) as well as operetta and grand opera. Her recording career was comprised of two phases: 1916-1917, when she worked for Columbia and Victor, and 1921-1922, when her name appeared in the Edison lists. She had a top seller, "If I Knock the `L' Out of Kelly (It Would Still Be Kelly to Me)" (Victor 18105) in 1916.

Favor, Edward M. (d. January 10, 1936)

A comic singer popular in vaudeville and on Broadway, Favor appears to have been influential in the development of Murray's recording style (and, perhaps ironically, found his career in that medium eclipsed by the latter's meteoric success). He had two top sellers, "Say Au Revoir, But Not Goodbye" (North American 858, 1894) and "My Best Girl's A New Yorker" (Columbia 2107, 1895).

Fields, Arthur (d. March 29, 1953; 64)

A professional singer at eleven, Fields was successful in vaudeville, radio, and recording. His career peaked during the period of U.S. involvement in World War I, composing as well as singing on a string of hits of a topical nature (including the very politically incorrect "Would You Rather Be a Colonel With an Eagle on Your Shoulder or a Private With a Chicken on Your Knee?"). His only top-selling disc was the Irving Berlin-penned "Oh, How I Hate to Get Up in the Morning" (Victor 18489, 1918).

Florodora Girls

Their names are lost in the past; however, they were the first cast members of a Broadway musical to record a song from their show: i.e., "Tell Me, Pretty Maiden" (Columbia 31604, 1901), along with Byron G. Harlan, Frank C. Stanley, and Joe Belmont.

Fuller's Novelty Orchestra, Earl

Led by trumpeter/trombonist Earl Fuller, the ensemble helped popularize the dance band trends of the 1920s. The group's biggest hit was "Sand Dunes" (Columbia 2697, 1919).

Gallagher and Shean

Ed Gallagher and Al Shean comprised one of the leading vaudeville comedy teams between 1910-1925. Their song, "Mr. Gallagher and Mr. Shean" (Victor 18941), culled from the Broadway revue, *Ziegfeld Follies of 1922*, became one of the biggest selling comedy records of all time.

Gaskin, George J. (d. circa 1920)

Known as "the Silver-Voiced Irish Tenor," Gaskin's stature as a recording artist in the 1890s was rivaled only by Dan Quinn and Len Spencer. His top selling recordings included "Drill, Ye Terriers, Drill" (North American, 1891), "Slide, Kelly, Slide" (North American, 1892), "O Promise

Me" (New Jersey, 1893), "After the Ball" (New Jersey, 1893), "Sweet Rosie O'Grady" (Edison 1551, 1897), "On the Banks of the Wabash" (Columbia 4130, 1897), and "When You Were Sweet Sixteen" (Columbia 4281, 1900).

Georgia Minstrel Co.

A studio concoction built around tenors Harry Macdonough and S.H. Dudley, bass singer William F. Hooley, and piano accompanist Frank Banta, the ensemble had two hits in 1901, "Minstrel Record No. 3" (Victor 508) and "Minstrels: First Part, No. 5" (Victor 3039). Both attempted to simulate the variety show approach employed in minstrel shows.

Gibbs, Arthur, and His Gang

The pianist-bandleader had a number one bestseller, "Charleston" (Victor 19165, 1924), which set off the biggest dance craze of that decade.

Gilmore's Band

Patrick S. Gilmore first achieved fame for co-writing "When Johnny Comes Marching Home" in 1863 while bandleader of the Union Army. He had several bestselling cylinders during the first decade of commercial recording, most notably "Volunteers' March (New York, 1892) and "The Star-Spangled Banner" (New Jersey, 1892).

Glantz, Nathan, and His Orchestra

The alto and tenor saxophonist was widely recorded during the 1920s. His biggest disc was "Romany Love" (Gennett 4888, 1922).

Golden, Billy (d. January 30, 1926; 67)

The popular vaudeville comedian had a number one cylinder, "Turkey in the Straw" (Columbia, 1891) during the infancy of the record industry.

Great White Way Orchestra

The studio aggregate's biggest seller, "Yes! We Have No Bananas" (Victor 19068, 1923), was notable for the presence of Billy Murray's guest vocal and whistling.

Greene, Gene (d. April 5, 1930; 52)

Known as "the Ragtime King" on the vaudeville circuit, Greene's most popular recording was "King of the Bungaloos" (Columbia 994, 1911).

Hall, Wendell

The ukelele-playing Hall became an overnight sensation when "It Ain't Gonna Rain No Mo'" (Victor 19171), adapted from a nineteenth century Kentucky folk song, become the top-selling hit in early 1924, eventually selling more than two million copies. He continued to be popular for many years in radio and vaudeville.

Halley, William J. (r.n.: William J. Hanley; d. November 14, 1961; 68)

Allegedly the only bestselling artist to become a state legislator (New Jersey Assembly, 1917-1918) and a judge (Hoboken District Court Judge, 1923-1933), his biggest hits were "You Made Me Love You" (Victor 17381, 1913) and "Do You Take This Woman For Your Lawful Wife?" (Columbia 1497, 1914). Halley's willingness to abandon a promising career at a relatively tender age illustrates the low esteem accorded the recording profession.

W.C. Handy's Orchestra (November 16, 1873-March 29, 1958)

The cornetist, bandleader, music teacher first achieved success with his composition of "The Memphis Blues" in 1913. "The St. Louis Blues" (1914) went on to become the most recorded American song in history. The "Livery Stable Blues" (Columbia 2419, 1918) was the biggest seller for his own performing ensemble.

The Happiness Boys (see: Ernest Hare and Billy Jones)

Happy Six

The band, featuring Phil Ohman (piano) and George Hamilton Green (xylaphone), had a couple of hits, "My Sahara Rose" (Columbia 2934, 1920) and "Do You Ever Think of Me?" (Columbia 3372, 1921).

Harding, Roger (d. 1901)

An original member of the Edison Male Quartet (1894) who also produced some of the first children's recordings, Harding had a couple of best sellers, "Bye and Bye You Will Forget Me" (with Len Spencer, Columbia 8404, 1897) and "On the Banks of the Wabash" (Edison 2042, 1898).

Hare, Ernest, and Billy Jones (d. March 9, 1939, 55; November 23, 1940, 51)

The baritone Hare and tenor Jones formed a team popular on radio in the 1920s and 1930s. The duo also had many hit recordings in the 1920s, most notably "In the Little Red School House" (Edison 50962, 1922), Mr. Gallagher and Mr. Shean (Okeh 4608, 1922), "Barney Google" (Columbia 3876, 1923), and "I Miss My Swiss (My Swiss Miss Misses Me)" (Victor 19718, 1925).

Harlan, Byron G. (August 29, 1861-September 11, 1936)

In addition to his success as part of the ragtime and minstrel comedy team, Collins and Harlan, he was extremely successful as a soloist, specializing in sentimental ballads. His top sellers included "Tell Me, Pretty Maiden" (with Frank C. Stanley, Joe Belmont, and the Florodora Girls, Columbia 31604, 1901), "Hello Central, Give Me Heaven" (Edison 7852, 1901), "The Mansion of Aching Hearts" (Edison 8093, 1902), "Blue Bell" (with Stanley, Edison 8655, 1904), "All Aboard for Dreamland" (Edison 8700, 1904), "Where the Morning Glories Twine Around the Door" (Columbia 3282, 1905), "Wait Till the Sun Shines, Nellie" (Columbia 3321, 1906), "The Good Old U.S.A." (Columbia 3463, 1906), "My Gal Sal" (Victor 4918, 1907), "School Days" (Victor 5086, 1907), "Nobody's Little Girl" (Victor 5147, 1907), and "Tramp! Tramp! Tramp!" (with Stanley, Victor 16531, 1910).

Harris, Marion (d. April 23, 1944; 48)

Harris was a veteran of Broadway musicals in addition to being perhaps the leading female singer in the last decade of the acoustic era. Her top-selling recordings included "After You've Gone" (Victor 18509, 1919), "St. Louis Blues" (Columbia 2944, 1920), "Look for the Silver Lining" (Columbia 3367, 1921), and "Tea For Two" (Brunswick 2747, 1925).

Harrison, Charles (d. February 2, 1965; 74)

In addition to being a member of the Columbia Stellar Quartet, Columbia Mixed Quartet, Revelers, and American Singers, the tenor balladeer had many hits as a solo artist, including the following top sellers: "Peg O' My Heart" (Victor 17412, 1913), "Ireland Must Be Heaven, For My Mother Came From There" (Victor 18111, 1916), and "I'm Always Chasing Rainbows" (Victor 18496, 1918).

Harrison, James F. (r.n.: Frederick Wheeler; d. August 7, 1951; 73)

Harrison rose to prominence as part of the gospel duo, James F. Harrison and Harry Anthony, and enjoyed a string of hits as a soloist, paired with James Reed (real name: Reed Miller), and as a member of the Knickerbocker Quartet. The baritone balladeer's top-selling recordings included "Keep the Home Fires Burning" (Victor 17881, 1915/16), "My Little Dream Girl" (with Reed, Victor 17789, 1915), and "There's A Long, Long Trail" (with Reed, Victor 17882, 1915/16).

Hart, Charles

A veteran of opera, vaudeville, and stage acting, Hart had a series of hit recordings both as a solo artists and as first tenor in the Shannon Four (1917-1923). "Till We Meet Again" (Victor 18518, 1919), a duet with Lewis James, was his only top seller.

Harvey, Morton

Discovered in a minstrel show by Billy Murray, he had a number of bestselling discs during the World War I era, most notably the top-selling hit, "I Didn't Raise My Boy To Be a Soldier" (Victor 17716, 1915).

Haydn Quartet/Hayden Quartet (1910-1914)

Considered to be one of three great vocal groups of the pionner era (along with the American and Peerless), the Haydn Quartet was a consistent hitmaker from 1898 to 1914. The original members were tenors John Bieling and Harry Macdonough, baritone S.H. Dudley, and bass William F. Hooley; they recorded for Edison as the Edison Male Quartet. During the aggregate's later years Billy Murray often sang lead and Reinald Werrenrath was frequently substituted for Dudley. When the Haydn disbanded in 1914, Macdonough, Hooley, Werrenrath, and tenor Lambert Murphy formed the Orpheus Quartet. The group's top-seeling recordings included "Because" (Gram-o-Phone 105, 1900), "In the Good Old Summer Time" (Victor 1793, 1903), "Bedelia" (Victor 2559, 1904), "Toyland" (with Corrine Morgan, Victor 2721, 1904), "Blue Bell" (Victor 2750, 1904), "Sweet Adeline" (Victor 2934, 1904), "Dearie" (with Morgan, Victor 4396, 1905), "How'd You Like to Spoon With Me?" (with Morgan, Victor 4532, 1906), "Take Me Out to the Ball Game" (with Murray, Victor 5570, 1908), "Sunbonnet Sue" (Victor 5568, 1908), "Put On Your Old Gray Bonnet" (Victor 16377, 1909), and "By the Light of the Silv'ry Moon" (Victor 16460, 1910).

Hayman, Joe

This comedian specialized in skits built around the use of Jewish dialect. His chart topper, "Cohen on the Telephone" (Columbia 1516, 1914), may well have been the first million-selling spoken comedy recording.

Henderson, Fletcher, and His Orchestra (d. December 29, 1952; 54)

This pianist led one of the 1920s most important jazz ensembles; in the 1930s he was an arranger for Benny Goodman and other bands. His biggest recordings were "Charleston Crazy" (Vocalion 14726, 1924) and "Sugar Foot Stomp" (Columbia 395, 1925).

Hickman, Art, and His Orchestra (d. January 16, 1930; 43)

The West Coast dance band leader had many popular discs in the early 1920s, including a couple of top sellers, "Hold Me" (Columbia 2899, 1920) and "The Love Nest" (Columbia 2955, 1920).

Hickman, Mina

This Broadway musical interpreter had about a half dozen bestselling recordings during the 1901-1904 period, most notably the top seller, "Come Down, Ma Evening Star" (Columbia 955, 1903).

Hill, Murry K. (r.n.: Joseph T. Pop, Jr.; d. October 23, 1942)

The vaudeville comedian had one bestseller, "In the Good Old Steamboat Days" (Edison 9619, 1907).

Hindermyer, Harvey (d. October 22, 1957; 75)

The tenor was an original member of the Shannon Four (until 1918), and became popular on radio in the 1920s as one of the "Gold Dust Twins." His biggest solo hit was "Take Me Out to the Ballgame" (Columbia 586, 1908).

Hooley, William F. (d. October 12, 1918; 57)

The bass singer anchored the sound of both the Haydn Quartet (1898-1914) and American Quartet (1909-1918). He enjoyed a top seller in 1899, "Gypsy Love Song" (Edison 7163).

Hopper, DeWolf (d. September 23, 1935; 77)

Although popular in musical comedy for years, he was best known for the monologue, "Casey at the Bat" (Victor 31559, 1906), first performed onstage in 1888 and reprised by Hopper an estimated 10,000 times.

Hunting, Russell (d. February 20, 1943; 78)

Hunting began as a dramatic actor in the Boston Theatre Co. After becoming famous for his "Casey" Irish comedy recordings (where he frequently assumed multiple parts and supplied a variety of sound effects), he became an Edison Bell executive and the recording head of the Pathe company. His top selling cylinders included "Michael Casey as a Physician" (New York, 1891), "Michael Casey at the Telephone" (Columbia, 1892), "Michael Casey Taking the Census" (Columbia, 1892), "Casey as Insurance Agent" (New Jersey, 1894), and "Casey at Denny Murphy's Wake" (Columbia 1894).

International Novelty Orchestra

The studio ensemble, directed by Nat Shilkret, was notable for backing Billy Murray on several recordings (including the hit, "Charley, My Boy," Victor 19411, 1924) as well as Vernon Dalhart on what was allegedly the first electrically-recorded disc to be released ("Let It Rain, Let It Pour," Victor 19624, 1925).

Irwin, May

The leading vaudeville performer of the 1890s, Irwin introduced such classics as "Ta-ra-ra-Boom-Der-e" and "The Bully" (both top sellers for Len Spencer) to stage audiences. Early film viewers were scandalized by her role in *The Kiss* (1895).

Issler, Edward, and His Orchestra

The pianist was one of the first musicians to record on a commercial basis, recording for North American in 1889. His band was the first to become famous through the recordings they made. His biggest hit was "Dream of Passion Waltz" (New Jersey, 1897).

James, Lewis (d. February 19, 1959; 66)

James was popular as a solo artist and as a member of the Shannon Four, the Revelers, and the Criterion Trio. He is reputed to have made about 3,000 recordings from 1917 through the 1930s. He had a top selling hit, "Till We Meet Again" (with Charles Hart, Victor 18518, 1919).

Jaudas' Society Orchestra

The ensemble was headed by violinist Eugene A. Jaudas, for many years Edison's orchestra leader. Its hits included "Missouri Waltz" (Edison Blue Amberol 2950, 1916) and "The Darktown Strutters' Ball" (Edison 50469, 1918).

Johnson, George Washington (d. circa 1910; approx. 64)

One of the first entertainers to make recordings (on tin foil in 1877), the formaer slave had two seminal top-selling cylinders, "The Laughing Song" (Columbia, 1891) and "The Whistling Coon" (Columbia, 1891). The former was reputed to be the largest selling cylinder of the 1890s; due to the absence of mass production techniques, Johnson was required to to re-recorded the song around 40,000 times.

Johnson, James P. (d. November 17, 1955; 64)

The influential jazz pianist had one hit, "Carolina Shout" (Okeh 4495, 1922).

Jolson, Al (r.n.: Asa Yoelson; March 26, 1886-October 23, 1950)

Beginning with minstrel shows and vaudeville, Jolson conquered Broadway in 1911 and dominated the American musical for two decades on the strength of his dramatic vocal style and onstage personal rapport with fans. **The Jazz Singer**, which featured him in a singing role, stimulated the rise of sound in films. After a decade of decline, the 1946 motion picture, **The Jolson Story**, resurrected his career. Among his many hit recordings were the following top sellers: "That Haunting Melody" (Victor 17037, 1912), "Ragging the Baby to Sleep" (Victor 17081, 1912), "The Spaniard That Blighted My Life" (Victor 17318, 1913), "You Made Me Love You, I Didn't Want To Do It" (Columbia 1374, 1913), I Sent My Wife to the Thousand Isles" (Columbia 2021, 1916), "I'm All Bound Round With the Mason Dixon Line" (Columbia 2478, 1918), "Hello Central, Give Me No Man's Land" (Columbia 2542, 1918), "Rock-A-Bye Your Baby With a Dixie Melody" (Columbia 2560, 1918), "I'll Say She Does" (Columbia 2746, 1919), "I've Got My Captain Working For Me Now" (Columbia 2794, 1919/20), "Swanee" (Columbia 2884, 1920), O-H-I-O (O-My! O!)" (Columbia 3361, 1921), "April Showers" (Columbia 3500, 1922), "Angel Child" (Columbia 3568, 1922), "Toot Toot Tootsie (Goo'bye)" (Columbia 3705, 1922/23), "California, Here I Come!" (Brunswick 2569, 1924), "When the Red, Red Robin Comes Bob-Bob-Bobbin' Along" (Brunswick

3222, 1926), "Sonny Boy" (Brunswick 4033, 1928), "There's a Rainbow Round My Shoulder" (Brunswick 4033, 1928), and "Little Pal" (Brunswick 4400, 1929).

Jones, Ada (June 1, 1873-May 22, 1922)

Regarded as leading female recording artist of the acoustic era, the contralto was unsurpassed in her sense of comic timing and use of ethnic and national dialects. Her long string of hits was augmented her popularity in duets with Len Spencer and Murray (the Jones/Murray pairing may well may been the most successful in recording history). Her solo top-selling discs included "I Just Can't Make My Eyes Behave" (Columbia 3599, 1907), "The Yama Yama Man" (with the Victor Light Opera Co., Victor 16326, 1909), "I've Got Rings On My Fingers" (Columbia 741, 1909), "Call Me Up Some Rainy Afternoon" (with the American Quartet, Victor 16508, 1910), "Come, Josephine, In My Flying Machine" (with the American Quartet, Victor 16844, 1911), "Row! Row! Row!" (Victor 17205, 1913), and "By the Beautiful Sea" (with Billy Watkins, Columbia 1563, 1914).

Jones, Billy (d. November 23, 1940; 51)

Jones started out in vaudeville and later gained renown on radio and recordings as part of the Happiness Boys together with Ernest Hare. He also had a string of hits as a solo artist, sometimes employing the pseudonym "Victor Roberts." One disc, "Yes! We Have No Bananas" (Edison 51183), was a top seller in 1923.

Jones, Isham, and His Orchestra (d. October 19, 1956; 62)

Tenor saxophonist Jones led one of the finest dance bands of the 1920s as well as writing many of its hits. The ensemble's top selling recordings included "Wabash Blues" (Brunswick 5065, 1921), "On the Alamo" (Brunswick 2245, 1922), "Swingin' Down the Lane" (Brunswick 2438, 1923), "Spain" (Brunswick 2600, 1924), "It Had To Be You" (Brunswick 2614, 1924), "I'll See You In My Dreams" (Brunswick 2788, 1925), "Remember" (Brunswick 2963, 1925), and "Star Dust" (Brunswick 4586, 1930).

Jose, Richard (d. October 20, 1941; 72)

Jose, a counter-tenor popular in vaudeville beginning in the 1890s, had a half dozen bestsellers, including the top-selling hit, "Silver Threads Among the Gold" (Victor 2556, 1904).

Kaufman, Irving (d. January 3, 1976; 85)

Reputed to be most prolific band singer ever (said to have recorded with 62 different orchestras between 1923-1933), Kaufman was also a member of the Avon Comedy Four, an extremely popular vaudeville act during the World War I era. He recorded many of the same songs identified with Billy Murray from 1914 to the late 1920s. He had one top seller, "Hail! Hail! The Gang's All Here" (with the Columbia Quartet, Columbia 2443, 1918).

Kaufman, Jack (d. February 27, 1948; 65)

Kaufman was often paired with his brother, Irving, in recordings. Their biggest hit was "Nobody Knows (And Nobody Seems To Care)" (Columbia 2795, 1920).

Kay, Dolly

Kay had a number of big hits in the early 1920s, most notably "You've Got To See Mama Ev'ry Night (Or You Can't See Mama At All) (Columbia 3808, 1923) and "Hard-Hearted Hannah" (Columbia 151, 1924).

Kelly, Dan

After performing with Christy's and other minstrel companies in 1870s and 1880s, he became one of the leading comic recording artists during the 1890s. He had one top seller, "Pat Kelly as a Police Justice" (Ohio, 1891).

Kerns, Grace (d. September 10, 1936; 50)

The concert soprano had close to a dozen hits between 1911-1917, most notably "Love Has Wings" (with Charles Harrison, Columbia 5574, 1914) and "Chinatown, My Chinatown" (with John Barnes Wells, Columbia 1624, 1915).

King, Charles (d. January 11, 1944; 49)

A veteran of many Broadway musicals from 1911 to 1930, King also recorded a series of bestsellers during that period, including "Let Me Live and Stay In Dixieland" (Victor 5843, 1911) and "My Own Iona" (Columbia 2059, 1916).

Kline, Olive

The concert soprano was a member of the Lyric Quartet and regularly featured in the Victor Light Opera Company. Among her top selling discs were "Hello Frisco!" (with Reinald Werrenrath, billed as "Alice Green and Edward Hamilton, Victor 17837, 1915) and "They Didn't Believe Me" ("Alice Green and Harry Macdonough", Victor 35491, 1915).

Landry, Art, and His Orchestra

The violinist bandleader had a number of hits during 1923-1927, including the top seller, "Dreamy Melody" (Gennett 5052, 1923).

Lanin, Sam, and His Orchestra

Also musical director of the star recording group, the Ipana Troubadors, Lanin was one of the most heavily-recorded bandleaders between the early 1920s and early 1930s. The orchestra's biggest seller was "The Blue Room" (billed as the "Melody Sheiks", Okeh 40603, 1926).

Lauder, Harry (d. February 25, 1950; 79)

The Scottish comedian and folk interpreter was popular in English-speaking countries around the world during the decade prior to World War I. His biggest selling discs were "I Love a Lassie" (Victor 52002, 1907) and "She Is My Daisy" (Victor 58007, 1909).

Leachman, Silas (d. April 28, 1936; 76)

This minstrel singer was one of the most popular artists during the first decade of commercial recording. Based in Chicago, he abruptly stopped recording activities in 1902 when faced with the imperative of moving East (where the studios of the major labels were located). He had one top seller, "Dem Golden Slippers" (Columbia, 1894).

Levy, Jules (d. November 28, 1903; 45)

Widely considered "the world's greatest cornet player" during the latter decades of the nineteenth century, Levy was also the first prominent musician to be recorded on a regular basis. He had several bestsellers, most notably "My Country 'Tis Of Thee" (North American 470, 1893).

Lewis, Ted, and His Band (r.n.: Theodore Friedman; August 25, 1971, 79)

The multi-talent bandleader--clarinetist, singer, songwriter, and entertainer whose delivery was a product of his formative years in vaudeville--enjoyed great success as a recording artist in the 1920s and 1930s. His top-selling discs included "When My Baby Smiles At Me" (Columbia 2908, 1920), "All By Myself" (Columbia 3434, 1921), "O! Katharina" (Columbia 295, 1925), "Just a Gigolo" (Columbia 2378, 1931), "In a Shanty in Old Shanty Town" (Columbia 2652, 1932), and "Lazybones" (Columbia 2786, 1933).

Libbey, J. Aldrich

This successful vaudeville performer was perhaps best known for introducing "After the Ball." His biggest selling recordings were "On a Sunday Afternoon" (Edison 8018, 1902) and "In the Sweet Bye and Bye" (Edison 8300, 1903).

Lyman, Abe, and His California Orchestra (r.n.: Abraham Simon; d. October 23, 1957, 60)

The drummer-songwriter-bandleader had a lengthy run as a successful recording artist (1923-1945). His biggest hits included "Mary Lou" (Brunswick 3135, 1926) and "Little Old Lady" (Decca 1120, 1937).

Lyric Quartet

The group--formed in 1910--was originally comprised of Harry Macdonough, Frank C. Stanley, Elise Stevenson, and Corrine Morgan. Its membership from 1913 on consisted of Macdonough, Reinald Werrenrath, Olive Kline, and Elsie Baker. Its best-selling recordings were "Winter" (Victor 5814, 1911) and "Down Among the Sheltering Palms" (Victor 17778, 1915).

MacDonald, Christie (d. July 25, 1962; 87)

MacDonald starred in a string of Broadway musicals between 1898-1920. Her biggest hits were "The Angelus" (with Reinald Werrenrath and the Victor Male Chorus, Victor 70099, 1913) and "Sweethearts" (written specifically for her by Victor Herbert; Victor 60101, 1913).

Macdonough, Harry (r.n.: John S. MacDonald; March 30, 1871-September 26, 1831)

The tenor was surpassed in popularity only by Henry Burr as a balladeer during the acoustic era. His solo career was complemented by widespread recording activity as a member of the Victor Light Opera Co. and the Edison, Haydn, Lyric, and Orpheus Quartets. He was employed as a record company executive after World War I. Macdonough's top sellers included "Tell Me, Pretty Maiden" (with Grace Spencer, Edison 7758, 1901), "Absence Makes the Heart Grow Fonder" (Victor 907, 1901), "The Tale of the Bumble Bee" (Victor 908, 1901), "The Mansion of Aching Hearts" (Victor 1415, 1902), "In the Sweet Bye and Bye" (with John Bieling, Victor 1855, 1903), "Hiawatha" (Edison 8425, 1903), "Shine On, Harvest Moon" (Victor 16259, 1909), "Down By the Old Mill Stream" (Victor 17000, 1911/12), "The Girl on the Magazine" (Victor 17945, 1916).

MacFarlane, George (d. February 22, 1932; 54)

The baritone, who performed on Broadway and in operettas, had one top-selling disc, "A Little Bit Heaven (Shure, They Call It Ireland)" (Victor 60132, 1915).

Mahoney, Jere

In addition to a stint with the Edison Male Quartet (1896-1900), Mahoney's top-selling solo recordings included "When You Were Sweet Sixteen" (Edison 7410, 1900) and "A Bird in a Gilden Cage" (Edison 7440, 1900).

Manhansett Quartette

The first vocal group to receive recognition for its recorded work, it was comprised of George J. Gaskin, Gilbert Girard, Joe Riley, and a gentleman named "Evans" (John Bieling joined in 1894). Among the aggregate's hits were two top sellers, "The Picture Turned Toward the Wall" (North American, 1892) and "Sally in Our Alley" (North American, 1892).

Marsh, Lucy Isabelle (d. January 20, 1956; 77)

In addition to working with the Victor Light Opera Co., the soprano had many bestsellers of her own between 1908-1922, including the top sellers, "The Glow-Worm" (Columbia 3791, 1908) and "Every Little Movement" (Victor 5784, 1910).

Marvin, Johnny (d. December 20, 1944; 47)

Very popular as a band vocalist in the late 1920s, Marvin went on the compose songs for Gene Autry films in the 1930s. He had one top-seller, "Breezin' Along With the Breeze" (Columbia 699, 1926).

McCormick, John (June 14, 1884-August 16, 1945)

The Irish tenor began recording in 1904 for Edison Bell. However, it was his operatic debut in Italy shortly thereafter which elevated him to superstardom. His popularity spread to America in 1910; by 1915, he found it necessary to concentrate on concert performances and recordings. Like Caruso, he did much to elevate the prestige of the latter medium. His top-selling hits included "I'm Falling In Love With Someone" (Victor 64174, 1911), "Mother Machree" (Victor 64181, 1911), "It's a Long, Long Way to Tipperary" (Victor 64476, 1915), "Somewhere a Voice Is Calling" (Victor 64405, 1916), "The Sunshine of Your Smile" (Victor 64622, 1916), "The Star-Spangled Banner" (Victor 64664, 1917), "Send Me Away With a Smile" (Victor 64741, 1917/18), and "All Alone" (Victor 1067, 1927).

Meeker, Edward (d. April 19, 1937; 63)

Better known to pioneer recording afficionados as Edison's song announcer and sound effects specialist from the early years of the century to the 1920s, Meeker enjoyed a couple of bestsellers as a solo artist: "Harrigan" (Edison 9616, 1907) and "Take Me Out to the Ball Game" (Edison 9926, 1908).

Metropolitan Orchestra

Reputed to be the first orchestra to record regularly in the studio, its top hit was "Creole Belles" (Victor 1023, 1902).

Meyer, John (d. May 3, 1949; 71)

Meyer sang bass for both the Peerless Quartet (1911-1925) and American Quartet (1921-1925). He also recorded two hits as a duo with Henry Burr, "Carolina Sunshine" (Okeh 4006, 1920) and "I Never Knew" (Okeh 4043, 1920).

Miller, Reed (d. December 29, 1923; 43)

The concert and operatic tenor had a string of hits with Frederick Wheeler (billed as "James Reed and James F. Harrison") and as a member of the Columbia Stellar Quartet. His biggest hits as a solo artist were "It's Always June When You're In Love" (Columbia 924, 1911) and "A Stein Song" (with Frank Croxton, Columbia 5386, 1912).

Montgomery and Stone (d. April 20, 1917; 46 and March 6, 1959; 85)

The musical comedy duo, Dave Montgomery and Fred Stone--popular in Broadway shows, vaudeville, and minstrel shows--had one bestseller, "Moriah-Scotch Medley" (Victor 70044, 1911).

Moran and Mack (r.n.: George Moran and Charles Sellers, aka Charles Mack; 1881-1949 and 1888-1934)

The vaudeville comedy team's first release, the politically incorrect "Two Black Crows--Parts 1 & 2 (The Early Bird Catches the Worm)" (Columbia 935, 1927), is reputed to have been one of that decade's biggest sellers. This disc was followed by a series of successful sequals; e.g., "Two Black Crows--Parts 3 & 4 (All About Lions)," "Two Black Crows--Part 5 (Curiosities on the Farm)," "Two Black Crows--Part 7 (No Matter How Hungry a Horse Is, He Cannot Eat a Bit)."

Morgan, Corrine (r.n.: Corrine Morgan Welsh; d. 1945; est. 70)

A steady hitmaker during the first decade of the century, the contralto is perhaps best remembered for her duets with Frank C. Stanley. Her top sellers included "Toyland" (with the Haydn Quartet, Victor 2721, 1904), "Dearie" (Victor 4396, 1905), "How'd You Like to Spoon With Me?" (Victor 4532, 1906), and "So Long, Mary" (Victor 4590, 1906).

Morris, Elida

A veteran of minstrel shows and opera, Morris recorded with Billy Murray and enjoyed a series of hits between 1910-1915, most notably "I've Got Your Number" (with Walter Van Brunt, Columbia 3191, 1911), "If I Had Someone at Home Like You" (Columbia 1523, 1914), and "Hello, Frisco!" (with Sam Ash, Columbia 1801, 1915).

Morton, Eddie (d. April 11, 1938; 67)

While the vaudeville comedian's most popular recording was "You Ain't Talking Me" (Columbia 777, 1910), his "Oceana Roll" (Victor 16908, 1911) achieved far wider distribution in that it appeared on the flip side of Collins and Harlan's mega-seller, "Alexander's Ragtime Band."

Murphy, Lambert (d. July 24, 1954; 69)

The tenor was a member of the Orpheus Quartet and performed with the Metropolitan Opera. His hits included "Goodbye, Girls, I'm Through" (Victor 17715, 1915), "Have a Heart" (with Olive Kline, billed as "Alice Green and Raymond Dixon"; Victor 18104, 1916), "Will You Remember?"

("Alice Green and Raymond Dixon", Victor 18399, 1918), and "Roses of Picardy" (Victor 45130, 1918).

Myers, J.W. (d. circa 1919; early 50s)

Originally a theatrical manager, Myers was considered the leading baritone balladeer of the acoustic era. A consistent hitmaker between 1892-1907, his top-selling recordings included
"Two Little Girls in Blue" (New Jersey, 1893), "The Sidewalks of New York" (Columbia, 1895), "Just Tell Them That You Saw Me" (Columbia 6009, 1895), "In the Shade of the Palm" (Columbia 31620, 1901), "On a Sunday Afternoon" (Columbia 106, 1902), "Way Down in Old Indiana" (Victor 1228, 1902), and "In the Good Old Summer Time" (Columbia 940, 1902).

Natus, Joe (d. April 26, 1917; 57)

A member of the Big Four Quartet, Natus had one top-selling cylinder as a solo artist, "The Song That Reached My Heart" (North American, 1892).

Nielsen, Alice (d. March 8, 1943; 66)

A performer with the Metropolitan Opera (1909-1913), the soprano's bestsellers included a number one hit, "Home, Sweet Home" (Columbia 5283) in 1915.

Norworth, Jack (d. September 1, 1959; 80)

A veteran of vaudeville and Broadway musicals, Norworth was also a successful recording artist and songwriter (e.g., "Shine On, Harvest Moon", "Take Me Out to the Ball Game"). His bestselling disc--which teamed him with his wife, Nora Bayes--was "Come Along, My Mandy" (Victor 70016, 1910).

Oakland, Will (r.n.: Herman Hinricks; d. May 15, 1956, 76)

Oakland parlayed his high counter-tenor voice to a lengthy career ranging from vaudeville in the early 1900s to television work in the 1950s. He worked extensively with Murray; in duets, in front of the American Quartet, and as a member of the Heidelberg Quintet. He also enjoyed a string of top-selling solo recordings, "Mother Machree (Edison Amberol 583, 1911), "I Love the Name of Mary" (Columbia 969, 1911), and I'm On My Way to Mandalay" (with Henry Burr and Albert Campbell, Victor 17503, 1914).

O'Connell, M.J.

O'Connell had about a half dozen hits during the World War I era, most notably a duet with Ada Jones, "Some Sunday Morning" (Columbia 2330, 1917).

O'Connor, George (d. September 28, 1946; 72)

This minstrel-show comedian was reputed to have been the favorite White House entertainer of every president from McKinley through Franklin D. Roosevelt. Walsh has written that no important social event in the Capitol was considered complete without O'Connor. His biggest selling recordings were "Everybody Rag With Me" (Columbia 1706, 1915) and "Pray For the Lights to Go Out" (Columbia 2143, 1917).

O'Hara, Geoffrey (d. 1965; 73)

Considered an expert on American Indian music, the singer-songwriter had two major hits, "All I Want Is a Cottage, Some Roses, and You" (Victor 18022, 1916) and "They Made It Twice As Nice As Paradise (And They Called It Dixieland)" (flip side of "Simple Melody", by Murray and Elsie Baker; Victor 18051, 1916).

Olcott, Chauncey (d. March 18, 1932; 74)

The tenor began his career in 1890s minstrel shows prior to achieving sucess in Broadway musicals. He also won acclaim as composer of Irish ballads (e.g., "When Irish Eyes Are Smiling," "My Wild Irish Rose," "Mother Machree"). Among his bestsellers were a couple of number one hits, "When Irish Eyes Are Smiling" (Columbia 1310, 1913) and "Too-Ra-Loo-Ra-Loo-Ral (That's An Irish Lullaby)" (Columbia 1410, 1913/14).

Oliver, King, and His Jazz Band (r.n.: Joseph Oliver, d. April 8, 1938)

The "king" of New Orleans jazz cornet during the post-World War I period, his sessions with protege Louis Armstrong in Chicago remain the seminal recordings of the dixieland genre. His was first black jazz band to record commercially; their biggest sellers were "Dipper Mouth Blues" (Okeh 4918, 1924) and "St. James' Infirmary" (Victor 22298, 1930).

Olsen, George, and His Orchestra (March 18, 1893-March 18, 1971)

This sweet-band leader had many hits during the first two decades of electronic recording, including the top sellers "Who?" (Victor 19840, 1926), "Always" (Victor 19955, 1926), "At Sundown (When Love Is Calling Me Home)" (Victor 20476, 1927), "A Precious Little Thing Called Love" (Victor 21832, 1929), "Lullaby of the Leaves" (Victor 22998, 1932), "Say It Isn't So" (Victor 24124, 1932), and "The Last Round-Up" (Columbia 2791, 1933).

Original Dixieland Jazz Band

Comprised of leader Nick LaRocca (cornet, composer of "Tiger Rag" and "Livery Stable Blues"), clarinetist Larry Shields, trombonist Eddie Edwards, pianist Harry Ragas, and drummer Tony Sbarbaro, the ODJB was both the first jazz group to be commercially recorded as well as the first to popularize jazz. "Tiger Rag" was its biggest seller (Victor 18472, 1918).

Orpheus Quartet

The group--whose members included tenors Harry Macdonough and Lambert Murphy, baritone Reinald Werrenrath, and bass William F. Hooley--had a string of hits during the World War I era, most notably "Turn Back the Universe and Give Me Yester Day" (Victor 18112, 1916).

Ossman, Vess (r.n.: Sylvester Louis Ossman; August 21, 1868-December 8, 1923)

The most recorded ragtime musician from the original ragtime era, Ossman was also known as "the King of the Banjo" from the 1890s to World War I. His lengthy run as a hitmaker included the following top sellers: "Yankee Doodle" (North American 905, 1894), "Cocoanut Dance" (Columbia 1069, 1895), and "A Hot Time on the Levee" (Columbia 7200, 1896).

Peerless Quartet

The most commercially successful vocal group ever, the Peerless remained popular despite frequently changes in personnel. The earliest edition--known as the Columbia Male Quartet--consisted of tenors Henry Burr and Albert Campbell, baritone Steve Porter, and bass Tom Daniels. In 1906 Daniels was replaced by Frank C. Stanley, who assumed lead singing and managing responsibilities. Arthur Collins then filled Porter's slot in 1909 and, with Stanley's death in 1910, John Meyer became bass and Burr took over as leader. When Collins left in late 1918 to be succeeded by Frank Croxton, the lineup remained stable through 1925. At this time Burr changed the personnel to include himself, Carl Mathieu, Stanley Baughman, and James Stanley; this version stayed in place until the ensemble was disbanded in 1928. Among the Quartet's many top sellers were "You're the Flower of My Heart, Sweet Adeline" (Columbia 32584, 1904), "Let Me Call You Sweetheart" (Columbia 1057, 1911), "I Didn't Raise My Boy To Be a Soldier" (Columbia 1697,

1915), "My Bird of Paradise" (Victor 17770, 1915), "The Lights of My Home Town" (Victor 17943, 1916), "Over There" (Columbia 2306, 1917), and "I Don't Know Where I'm Going But I'm On My Way" (Victor 18383, 1918).

Philadelphia Orchestra, conucted by Leopold Stokowski

The orchestra, led by the flamboyant Stokowski between 1912-1938, recorded close to a dozen bestsellers during the decade following World War I, including "A Midsummer Night's Dream--Scherzo" (Victor 74560, 1918), "Peer Gynt Suite No. 1 (Anitra's Dance)" (Victor 64768, 1919), "Invitation to the Waltz" (Victor 74598, 1920), "Hungarian Rhapsody No. 2" (Victor 74647, 1921), "The Young Prince and the Young Princess" (Victor 74691, 1921), and "The Firebird, Parts 1 & 2" (Victor 6492, 1925).

Porter, Steve (d. January 13, 1946; 81)

The baritone started out as a vaudeville comedian in the 1890s and went on to become a member of the Columbia Male (1904-1905), Peerless (1906-1909), and American Quartets (1909-1919). A consistent hitmaker between 1898-1910, his top selling recordings included "On the Banks of the Wabash" (Berliner 1784, 1898), "She's More To Be Pitied Than Censured (Columbia 4576, 1898), A Picture No Artist Can Paint (Columbia 4599, 1899), and "A Bird in a Gilded Cage" (Columbia 4608, 1900).

Price, Georgie (d. May 10, 1964; 64)

While the singer-comedian found his greatest success on vaudeville, he also had several hits in the early 1920s, the biggest being "California, Here I Come" (Victor 19261, 1924).

Prince's Orchestra (r.n.: Charles Adams Prince; d. October 10, 1937; 68)

Originally a pianist and celesta player, Prince served as musical director of Columbia Records from the turn of the century to the early 1920s. In that capacity his band backed virtually every vocalist recording for that label. The aggregate also was one of the leading hit producers of the acoustic period on its own. Among its successes were the following top selling discs: "Ballin' the Jack" (Columbia 5595, 1914), "Hello, Hawaii, How Are You?" (Columbia 5780, 1916), and "The Star-Spangled Banner" (Columbia 1991, 1916).

Arthur Pryor's Band (d. June 18, 1942; 71)

Pryor first won acclaim as first trombonist in John Philip Sousa's band; due to the latter's dislike of the recording medium, he also served as conductor on most of the Sousa releases. In the early years of the century, Pryor guided his own outfit to great success both on discs and as a concert attraction. His biggest hits included "Bedelia" (Victor 1558, 1904), "Meet Me In St. Louis Medley" (Victor 2960, 1904), "Hearts and Flowers" (Victor 31371, 1905), "You're a Grand Old Flag" (Victor 31539, 1906), and "On the Rocky Road to Dublin" (Victor 4842, 1906).

Quinn, Dan (d. November 7, 1938; 79)

Reputed to have recorded 2,500-odd songs over a 20-year career, Quinn was one of three major vocal recording stars of the 1890s (the others were George J. Gaskin and Len Spencer). His top selling hits included "Daddy Wouldn't Buy Me a Bow-Wow" (New Jersey, 1892), "The Bowery" (New Jersey, 1893), "Daisy Bell" (New Jersey, 1893), "Lindley, Does You Love Me?" (Columbia, 1894), "My Pearl Is a Bowery Girl" (Columbia, 1894), "And Her Golden Hair Was Hanging Down Her Back" (Columbia, 1894), "The Sidewalks of New York" (Columbia, 1895), "The Band Played On" (Columbia 2045, 1895), "The Little Lost Child" (Columbia 2048, 1895), In the Baggage Coach Ahead" (US Phonograph Co., 1896), "A Hot Time in the Old Town" (Edison 1038, 1896), "My Mother Was a Lady" (Columbia 5093, 1897), "There's a Little Star Shining For You" (Edison 1098, 1897), "She Was Happy Till She Met You" (Columbia 5354, 1898), "At a Georgia Camp Meeting" (Columbia 5353, 1898), "Curse of the Dreamer" (Columbia 5822, 1899), and "Good Evening, Carrie" (Victor 920, 1901).

Rainey, Ma (r.n.: Gertrude Malissa Pridgett; d. December 22, 1939, 53)

The pioneer blues singer (who married vaudeville performer William "Pa" Rainey) exerted a strong influence on Bessie Smith. Her only pop bestseller was the standard, "See See Rider Blues" (Paramount 12252, 1925).

Harry Reser's Orchestra (d. September 27, 1965)

Considered the leading banjo player of the 1920s, Reser was also the musical director of the Clevelanders and Clicquot Club Eskimos. His half dozen hits included "Yearning" (Columbia 319, 1925) and "Someone Is Losin' Susan" (Columbia 1378, 1926).

Rice, Gladys (r.n.: Gladys Hilberg; d. September 7, 1983, 92)

A popular interpreter of Broadway material, Rice had a series of hits paired with Billy Murray: "After You've Gone" (Edison Blue Amberol 3666, 1919), "Marion" (Victor 18671, 1920), "When My Baby Smiles At Me" (Edison 50651, 1920), "Oh! How I Laugh When I Think That I Cried

Over You" (Edison Blue Amberol 4048, 1920), and "I Gave You Up Just Before You Threw Me Down" (Victor 19023, 1923).

Ring, Blanche (d. January 13, 1961; 83)

During her long career on Broadway (1902-1938), she introduced many classics ("In the Good Old Summer Time"). Her top sellers included "I've Got Rings on My Fingers" (Victor 5737, 1909) and "Come, Josephine, In My Flying Machine" (Victor 60032, 1911).

Robbins, Will

Robbins had several hits during the World War I era, most notably "By Heck" (with Byron G. Harlan, Columbia 1722, 1915).

Roberts, Bob (d. January 21, 1930; 51)

The baritone specialized in the type of novelty material also interpreted by Billy Murray. Among his string of hits was a top-selling disc, "Ragtime Cowboy Joe" (Victor 17090, 1912).

Robison, Carson (d. March 24, 1957; 66)

This country and western performer was responsible for composing a number of classics (e.g., "My Blue Ridge Mountain Home," "Carry Me Back to the Lone Prairie"). His most popular recording was "When Your Hair Has Turned to Silver" (with Frank Luther, billed as "Bud and Joe Billings," Victor 22588, 1931).

Robyn, William

The tenor balladeer's only notable hit was "I'm In Heaven When I'm In My Mother's Arm" (Victor 18686, 1920).

Rodeheaver, Homer (d. December 18, 1955; 75)

Renown for singing hymns at Billy Sunday's revival meetings, Rodeheaver's most successful release was "The Old Rugged Cross" (Victor 18706, 1921).

Rogers, Walter B. (d. December 24, 1939; 74)

Rogers was the featured cornet player in Sousa's band and conducted on some of famed bandleader's recordings. He was also director of the Victor Light Opera Co. and Victor Military Band as well as orchestral conductor for virtually all Victor artists between 1908-1916.

Rogers, Will (d. August 1935; 55)

The stage and screen star recorded a number of hits, the biggest of which was "Will Rogers' First Political Speech" (Victor 45374, 1924).

Romain, Manuel (d. December 22, 1926; 56)

The tenor balladeer starred in vaudeville and minstrel shows during the first two decades of the century. He recorded about a dozen bestsellers, most notably "When I Lost You" (Columbia 1288, 1913), "I Miss You Most of All" (Columbia 1454, 1914), and "You're More Than the World To Me" (Columbia 1577, 1914).

Rose, Julian

The Jewish sketch comedian had one notable hit, "Levinsky at the Wedding, Parts 3 & 4" (Columbia 2366, 1918).

Sarto, Andrea

The bass singer was a founding member of the Columbia Stellar Quartet; he generally employed pseudonyms for the release of his solo material. His biggest seller was "There's a Girl in the Heart of Maryland," billed as by "Henry Burr and Edgar Stoddard" (Columbia 1360, 1913).

Seagle, Oscar (d. December 19, 1945; 68)

The concert baritone recorded several hits during the World War I era, most notably "There's A Long, Long Trail" (with Columbia Stellar Quartette, Columbia 245, 1918), "Calling Me Home to You" (Columbia 2452, 1918), and "Pack Up Your Troubles In Your Old Kit Bag" (with Columbia Stellar Quartette, Columbia 6028, 1918).

Seeley, Blossom (d. April 17, 1974; 82)

The singer-dancer starred on vaudeville and on Broadway in the 1920s. Her biggest selling discs were "Alabamy Bound" (Columbia 304, 1925) and "Yes Sir, That's My Baby" (Columbia 386, 1925).

Selvin, Ben, and His Orchestra (d. July 15, 1980; 82)

Originally a violinist, he cut more records (over 2,000) than any other bandleader. His extensive inventory of hits included the following top sellers: "I'm Forever Blowing Bubbles" (Victor 18603, 1919), "Dardanella" (the first recording to sell in excess of five million copies; Victor 18633, 1920), "Yes! We Have No Bananas" (guest vocal by Irving Kaufman, Vocalion 14590, 1923), "Oh, How I Miss You Tonight" (Columbia 359, 1925), "Manhattan" (Columbia 422, 1925), "Blue Skies" (Columbia 860, 1927), "Happy Days Are Here Again" (Columbia 2116, 1930), and "When It's Springtime in the Rockies" (Columbia 2206, 1930).

Shannon Four

The vocal group was originally comprised by tenoors Charles Hart and Harvey Hindermyer, baritone Elliott Shaw, and bass Wilfred Glenn. Lewis James took over for Hindermyer in 1918, and the ensemble had evolved into the Revelers by 1926. Its biggest sellers included "Hail! Hail! The Gang's All Here" (Victor 18414, 1918), "Sweet Little Buttercup" (with Elizabeth Spencer, Victor 18427, 1918), and "Mandy" (Victor 18605, 1919).

Shaw, Elliott

In addition to handling the baritone slot for both the Shannon Four and the Revelers, Shaw recorded under his own name. His most popular recording was a duet with Edna Brown, "Ka-Lu-A" (Victor 18854, 1922).

Shilkret, Jack, and His Orchestra (d. June 16, 1964; 67)

The pianist-bandleader had his biggest hit backing Billy Murray, "If You Knew Susie (Like I Know Susie)" (Victor 19675, 1925).

Shilkret, Nat, and the Victor Orchestra

Following stints as clarinetist with the New York Philharmonic and various concert bands (including Sousa's), he served as Victor's Director of Light Music, providing the accompaniment for many of the label's acts. He worked with Billy Murray, most notably on the hit, "Charley, My Boy" (Victor 19416, 1924). Among his many popular discs, he had one top seller, "Dancing With Tears In My Eyes" (guest vocal by Lewis James, Victor 22425, 1930).

Sissle, Noble (d. December 17, 2975)

The singer-bandleader is best remembered for his collaborations with pianist-composer Eubie Blake (lyricist), one of which proved to be his biggest hit, "Arkansas Blues" (Emerson 10443, 1922).

Smalle, Ed (d. November 23, 1968; 81)

Smalle's career consisted largely of associations with other artists, most notably Billy Murray, Vaughan Deleath, Johnny Marvin, and the Revelers. "That Old Gang of Mine" (with Murray, Victor 19095), which was a top seller in late 1923, was far and away his biggest hit.

Smith, Bessie (April 15, 1895-September 26, 1937)

Considered the best blues singer ever, Smith began her career touring with the legendary Ma Rainey. Her debut release was the million-selling "Down-Hearted Blues" (Columbia 3844, 1923); an amazing scenario for a "race" record. Her hits were concentrated between 1923-1929; together, they played a key role in saving Columbia from bankruptcy. These recordings remain vital to the present day; in addition to the unrivalled depth and power of her voice, she was frequently accompanied by the leading jazz musician of her generation (e.g., Louis Armstrong).

Joseph C. Smith's Orchestra

This seminal dance band was a consistent hitmaker between 1917-1922. Its biggest sellers were "Smiles" (guest vocal by Harry Macdonough; VIctor 18473, 1918), "Hindustan" (Victor 18507, 1918/19), "The Vamp" (with Murray and Macdonough on vocals; Victor 18594, 1919), "Yearning" (Victor 18603, 1919), "That Naughty Waltz" (Victor 18650, 1920), and "Sally--Medley" (Victor 35706, 1922).

Smith, Mamie, and Her Jazz Hounds (d. October 30, 1946; 56)

As the first blues vocalist to record, she blazed a trail followed by Bessie Smith, Ma Rainey, and others. Smith's first hit, "Crazy Blues" (Okeh 4169, 1920/21), was her biggest seller.

Smith, "Whispering" Jack (d. May 1951; 52)

Smith found it necessary to develop his intimate half-singing, half-talking style following an injury caused by an exploding gas shell in World War I. He enjoyed more than a dozen hit recordings during the first few years of the electronic era, including the top sellers "Gimme A Lil' Kiss, Will Ya, Huh?" (Victor 19978, 1926) and "Me and My Shadow" (Victor 20626, 1927).

Sousa's Band (November 6, 1854-March 5, 1932)

John Philip Sousa played violin in a number of orchestras prior to assuming the post of U.S. Marine Band director (1880-1891). His reputation rested with the memorable marches he composed during the last quarter of the nineteenth century. Due to his lack of interest in recorded music, his band was largely conducted by trombonist Arthur Pryor, with additional support from cornetists Walter B. Rogers and Herbert L. Clarke, in the studio. Sousa preferred the concert medium; his band is reputed to have given more than 10,000 concerts around the world. His lengthy hit run included the following top sellers: "El Capitan March" (Columbia, 1895), "Washington Post March" (Columbia, 1895), "The Stars and Stripes Forever" (Columbia 532, 1897; new version, Gram-o-Phone 306, 1901), and "In the Good Old Summer Time" (vocal refrain by Harry Macdonough and S.H. Dudley; Victor 1833, 1903).

Specht, Paul, and His Orchestra (d. 1954; about 59)

Specht enjoyed more than a dozen bestsellers in the 1920s, most notably "Roses of Picardy" (Columbia 3870, 1923) and "Waltz of Long Ago" (Columbia 13, 1924).

Spencer, Elizabeth (d. April 1930; about 54)

Spencer was a steady hit-maker between 1911-1923. Her most popular recordings were "When the Morning Glories Grow" (with the Sterling Trio; Victor 18403, 1918) and "Sweet Little Buttercup" (with the Shannon Four; Victor 18427, 1918).

Spencer, Grace

Spencer, a soprano, specialized in Broadway material. She was the first woman to record for Victor; however, she had greater success on the Edison label, including the top seller "Tell Me, Pretty Maiden" (with Harry Macdonough, Edison 7758, 1901).

Spencer, Len (r.n.: Leonard Garfield Spencer; February 12, 1867-December 15, 1914)

Reputed to have benn America's first nationally-known recording star, Spencer's career embraced a dizzying array of styles; sentimental ballads, minstrel songs, dramatic recitations, and comic duets (with Murray, Cal Stewart, Ada Jones, and others) which enabled him to assume many ethnic roles. His extensive inventory of hits included the following top sellers: "Little 'Liza Loves You" (Columbia, 1891), "Ta-Ra-Ra-Boom Der E" (Columbia, 1892), "The Old Folks At Home" (New Jersey, 1892), "Near It" (New Jersey, 1893), "Mamie, Come and Kiss Your Honey Boy" (New Jersey, 1893), "Little Alabama Coon" (Columbia 7156, 1895), "Dat New Bully" (Columbia 2107, 1895), "A Hot Time in the Old Town" (Columbia 7266, 1897), "Oh, Mr. Johnson, Turn Me Loose" (Columbia 7239, 1897), "My Gal Is a Highborn Lady" (Columbia 7252, 1897), "I Don't Like No Cheap Man" (Columbia 7440, 1898), "Hello! Ma Baby" (Berliner 05, 1899), "Ma Tiger Lily" (Columbia 7502, 1900), and "Arkansaw Traveler" (remake of 1900 Columbia hit; biggest seller of pre-1905 era; Victor 1101, 1902).

Stanley, Aileen (d. March 24, 1982; 89)

Stanley projected an blues-influenced sensuality that was rare in white female vocalists of that era. One of Billy Murray's regular singing partners in the 1920s, Stanley also recorded many hits with other collaborators and as a solo artist, most notably "Sweet Indiana Home" (Victor 18922, 1922) and "When My Sugar Walks Down the Street" (with Gene Austin; Victor 19585, 1925).

Stanley, Frank C. (r.n.: William Stanley Grinsted; d. December 12, 1910; 41)

Considered the major bass singer of the acoustic era, Stanley began his career playing the banjo, accompanying such luminaries at Arthur Collins on late-1890s cylinders. He went on to fame as leader--and manager--of the Peerless Quartet. He also had many hits as a soloist and via collaborations with other stars. His top selling recordings included "Blue Bell" (Edison 8655, 1904), "Good Evening, Caroline" (with Elsie Stevenson, Victor 5627, 1909), and "Tramp! Tramp! Tramp! (Victor 16531, 1910). During the latter years of his life, Stanley served as elected alderman and public school commissioner of Orange, New Jersey.

Steel, John (d. June 24, 1971; 71)

In addition to starring in several Broadway musicals, the tenor enjoyed over a dozen hits between 1919-1924, including two top sellers, "A Pretty Girl Is Like a Melody" (Victor 18588, 1919) and "The Love Nest" (Victor 18676, 1920).

Sterling Trio

Comprised of three members of the Peerless Quartet (Henry Burr, Albert Campbell, and John Meyer), the ensemble performed regularly as part of the Eight Victor Artists troupe and had a steady run of bestsellers between 1916-1922, most notably "Hawaiian Butterfly" (Victor 18272, 1917), "Where the Morning Glories Grow" (with Elizabeth Spencer, Victor 18403, 1918), and "That Tumble-Down Shack in Athlone" (Columbia 2698, 1919).

Stevenson, Elsie

In addition to very successful solo career, Stevenson was a member of the Lyric Quartet and Trinity Choir, sang on the early Victor Light Opera discs, and enjoyed duet hits with a number of partner (most frequently with her manager, Frank C. Stanley). She recorded the following top sellers: "Because You're You" (Victor 5020, 1907), "Are You Sincere?" (Victor 5467, 1908), "Good Evening, Caroline" (with Stanley; Victor 5627, 1909), and "Shine On, Harvest Moon" (billed as "Harry Macdonough and Miss Walton", the latter believed to be a pseudonym for Stevenson; Victor 16259, 1909).

Stewart, Cal (d. December 7, 1919; 63)

Stewart was close to 40 before he began recording; his early life was spent working on trains and in circuses, medicine shows, and vaudeville. His cylinders and discs made fictional New England farmer, "Uncle Josh Weathersby", and the town of Pumpkin Center (allegedly created by another vaudeville performer) leading symbols of Americana in the years immediately prior to and following the turn of the century. His droll humor has been compared to that of Mark Twain and Will Rogers, both of whom were personal friends. His lengthy inventory of bestsellers spanned the years 1898-1921, including the following top selling hits: "Uncle Josh's Arrival in New York" (Columbia 14000, 1898), "I'm Old But I'm Awfully Tough (Laughing Song)" (Edison 3903, 1898), "Jim Lawson's Horse Trade With Deacon Witherspoon" (Edison 7847, 1901), "Uncle Josh's Huskin' Bee Dance" (Edison 7861, 1901), and "Uncle Josh on an Automobile" (Columbia 1518, 1903).

Wilbur Sweatman's Original Jazz Band (d. March 9, 1961; 79)

Sweatman started out as a clarinetist in circus bands at the turn of the century. He enjoyed popularity in the twilight of the World War I era doing mainstream interpretations of then current fads (e.g., the blues, jazz, Broadway musicals), including "Everybody's Crazy 'Bout the Doggone Blues (But I'm Happy)" (Columbia 2548, 1918) and "I'll Say She Does" (Columbia 2752, 1919).

Tally, Harry (d. August 16, 1939; 73)

A member of the Empire City Quartet (which had no recording success of note, but was acclaimed on vaudeville) during the first two decades of the century, the tenor had about a dozen best-sellers, most notably the top seller, "Wait Till the Sun Shines, Nellie" (Victor 4551, 1906).

"That Girl" Quartet

Comprised of Harriet Keys, Allie Thomas, Precis Thompson, and Helen Summers, it was one of the first female vocal groups to make recordings. While "Honey Love" (Victor 16648, 19911) was probably the Quartet's most popular disc, "My Little Persian Rose" (Victor 17270, 1913; the flip side, "Sympathy", by Helen Clark and Walter Van Brunt, was a top-selling disc) was more widely distributed.

Trix, Helen (d. November 18, 1951; early 60s)

Trix was a popular vaudeville performer whose career peaked when she teamed with her sister Josephine in Great Britain during the 1920s. Her biggest seller was "The Bird on Nellie's Hat" (Victor 4904, 1907).

Tucker, Sophie (r.n.: Sonia Kalish; d. February 9, 1966; 81)

Billed as "The Last of the Red-Hot Mamas," Tucker parlayed a bold, sassy style to rise to the top of the vaudeville pantheon. She played an influential role in introducing many successful songs, some of which she never recorded herself. Her most popular recording (her theme song), "Some of These Days," was a bestseller on two different occasions (Edison Amberol 691, 1911; new version with Ted Lewis and His Band, Columbia 826, 1927).

U.S. Marine Band

Directed by John Philip Sousa in the early 1890s, "the President's band" is recognized as the first commercially successful recording act. Its top selling cylinders included the following marches: "Semper Fidelis" (Columbia, 1890), "Washington Post" (Columbia, 1890), "The Thunderer" (Columbia, 1890), and "The Liberty Bell" (Columbia, 1894).

Van and Schenck (r.n.: Gus Van and Joe Schenck; d. March 12, 1968, 80, and June 28, 1930, 39)

The musical comedians were a popular team in vaudeville, radio, and Broadway shows. They enjoyed a long string of hits between 1917-1928, most notably the top sellers, "For Me and My

Gal" (Victor 18258, 1917), "Ain't We Got Fun?" (Columbia 3412, 1921), and "Carolina in the Morning" (Columbia 3712, 1923).

Van Brunt, Walter

The precocious Van Brunt was turning out hits as early as age 17. Walsh related that he was Thomas Edison's favorite tenor; he allegedly sold more Edison Diamond Discs than any artist save Billy Murray. He changed his last name to Scanlan in 1917. Some sources have attributed this decision to Edison's advice so that the singer might avoid the anti-German backlash building up at that time. Others indicate that Victor Herbert suggested that Van Brunt take on a more "Irish" name for his leading role in the composer's 1917 operetta, Eileen. Van Brunt was frequently associated with Billy Murray during his career; he started out subbing for him in the American Quartet and in duets with Ada Jones for Columbia when Murray signed an exclusive contract with Victor and Edison. Later, from 1929-1933, they hosted a radio show and recorded together as a team. He had some 40 hits between 1909-1916, the biggest of which was "Sympathy" (with Helen Clark; Victor 17270, 1913).

Van Eps, Fred (d. November 22, 1960; 81)

Following in Vess Ossman's footsteps as "king of the banjo," Van Eps often recorded as part of a trio with pianist Felix Arndt and saxophonist Nathan Glantz. His hits included "Blaze Away" (Edison 8025, 1902) and "Red Pepper--A Spicy Rag" (Victor 17033, 1912).

Victor Light Opera Co.

The majority of Victor singing stars allegedly participated at one time or another in its sessions. Rogers conducted its records through 1916, and Nat Shilkret took over during the latter years. The group was a successful hitmaker between 1909-1926.

Waldorf-Astoria Dance Orchestra

The orchestra, directed by Joseph Knecht, recorded several bestsellers, including "Beautiful Ohio" (Victor 18526, 1919).

Fred Waring's Pennsylvanians (d. July 29, 1984; 84)

The dance band enjoyed a lengthy hit run spanning the years 1923-1954. Perhaps best remembered for his "glee club" featured on radio shows during the 1930s and 1940s, Waring also hosted a television show in the early 1950s. He was frequently referred to as "America's Singing Master" and "The Man Who Taught America How to Sing."

Weber & Fields (r.n.: Joe Weber and Moses Schanfield, aka Lew Fields; May 10, 1942, 74, and July 20, 1941, 75)

The beloved vaudeville comedy team was active from the 1880s through World War I. The twosome also starred in several Broadway productions and released several bestsellers, most notably "The Baseball Game" (Columbia 2092, January 13, 1917).

Werrenrath, Reinald (d. September 12, 1953; 70)

Werrenrath was associated with the New York Metropolitan Opera between 1919-1921 and allegedly headlined in more than 3,000 concerts. The featured baritone on many Victor Light Opera Co. recordings, he was a member of the Orpheus Quartet and also had many hits as a solo artist, most notably "As Long As the World Rolls On" (Edison 9662, 1908), "The Angelus" (with Christie MacDonald and the Victor Male Chorus; Victor 70099, 1913), and "Hello, Frisco!" (Victor 17837, 1915).

Wheeler, Elizabeth

The soprano enjoyed close to a dozen hits, many of which were duets (some with husband William Wheeler). Her most popular recordings included "When I Marry You" (with Harry Macdonough; Victor 16433, 1910), "Meet Me To-Night In Dreamland" (with Harry Anthony; Edison 10290, 1910), and "At the End of a Beautiful Day" (billed as "Jane Kenyon"; Victor 18065, 1916).

Whiteman, Paul, and His Orchestra (March 28, 1890-December 29, 1967)

While his right to the 1920s appellation, "king of jazz," has been discredited by hindsight, Whiteman was undoubtedly the most acclaimed bandleader of the pre-swing era. His band, formed in 1919 after stints as a violinist and violist in the Denver and San Francisco Symphony Orchestras, included such luminaries as Henry Busse (trumpet), Ferde Grofe (piano/arranger), Bix Beiderbecke (trumpet), and Bing Crosby. It gained further recognition for premiering George Gershwin's "Rhapsody in Blue". Second only to Crosby as a hitmaking entity, Whiteman was produced many top sellers, including "Whispering" (sold over two million copies; Victor 18690, 1920).

Williams, Bert (November 12, 1874-March 4, 1922)

Criticized in his time for helping to perpetuate certain African American stereotypes, Williams was nevertheless the first of his race to become a Broadway headliner. He and partner George Walker debuted in that venue in 1896, remaining a popular comedy team until the latter's death in 1910. Williams continued to work in vaudeville, the Ziegfield Follies (1910-1918), and as a recording artist. His hits included the following top-selling discs: "Good Morning, Carrie" (Victor 997, 1902), "Nobody" (co-written by Williams; Columbia 3423, 1906), "Let It Alone" (Columbia 3504, 1906), "He's a Cousin of Mine" (Columbia 3536, 1907), "Play That Barber-Shop Chord" (Columbia 929, 1910), "O Death, Where Is Thy Sting?" (Columbia 2652, 1919), and "It's Nobody's Business But My Own" (Columbia 2750, 1919).

Clarence Williams' Blue Five (d. November 6, 1965; 67)

The multi-talented Williams won acclaim as a jazz composer (e.g., "West End Blues"), pianist, combo leader, and musical director (Okeh Records). He also accompanied blues singers such as Bessie Smith and Ethel Waters. He had several bestsellers, most notably "Tain't Nobody's Bus'ness If I Do" (Okeh 4966, 1924) and "Everybody Loves My Baby (But My Baby Don't Love Nobody But Me)" (Okeh 8181, 1925).

Williams, Billy (r.n.: William Banks; 1877-1915)

The Australian singer-comedian, known as "The Man in the Velvet Suit," began his career with a small variety company in 1895. He then graduated to pantomime and musical comedy. Williams moved to London in 1900 and found work as the assistant-manager of a music hall. He moved into performing while also developing his skills as a songwriter. He began recording two-minute Edison Standard cylinders in 1907, his first (No. 13539) being the self-penned "John, John, Go and Put Your Trousers On" (which became one of his most popular records). He remained successful ("Great Britain's all-time most sensational performer for the phonograph"-- Jim Walsh, *Hobbies Magazine*) up until his death at 36 or 37.

Wills, Nat (July 11, 1873-December 9, 1917)

Wills started out in the 1890s as end man of the Ideal Minstrels in Washington; by 1900 he was a very popular vaudeville comedian. He alternated between theatrical stage shows (typically melodramas) and vaudeville performances throughout his life. He was best known as the "gentlemanly tramp" and went on to become, in Walsh's words (*Hobbies*, June 1951, p. 20), "the greatest master of parody writing and singing of his day." His first release, "No News" or "What Killed the Dog" (Victor 5612, 1909) was his biggest seller and one of the most consistently popular talking numbers ever recorded.

Table 1

James Reese Europe, February 22, 1880-May 9, 1919

Son of a former slave, Europe's family relocated from his birthplace of Mobile, Alabama to Washington, D.C. when he was nine. Continuing music lessons on piano, violin, and mandolin, he lived for a time just houses away from John Philip Sousa, whose march compositions and U.S. Marine Corps Band dominated American musical tastes. Moving to New York City around 1903, he began directing black dance ensembles and—when opportunities presented themselves—working in musical comedy.

In 1913 Europe achieved renown in New York society when his Exclusive Society Orchestra—one of the earliest jazz bands to perform at public venues—was frequently employed by the highly popular dance team of Vernon and Irene Castle. Collaborating with the Castles in early 1914, he played a key role in creating and popularizing the fox-trot. Hoping to capitalize on the popularity of the Castles, Victor signed Europe to record four titles on December 29, 1913 and February 10, 1914, respectively. His best-selling disc appears to have been "The Castles in Europe One-Step"/"Congratulations Waltz" (Victor 35372; 1914), issued in the twelve-inch configuration and retained in the company's monthly catalog for five years.

Enlisting in the 15th New York Infantry on September 18, 1916, Europe was induced to organize and lead a military band to boost troop morale. After the Armistice, he signed a recording contract with the New York-based Pathe Freres Phonograph Company. Four sessions—three in March and one in May 1919—produced eleven discs in the military band tradition, albeit punctuated by syncopation and other jazz effects. Their popularity, however, was limited because Pathe employed the vertical-cut process (often termed " hill-and-dale"), as opposed to lateral-cut technology, which was soon to dominate the marketplace. Actively collaborating with such major talents as Noble Sissle and Eubie Blake, Europe's promising career was prematurely ended when one of his drummer's stabbed him in the neck backstage during a Boston concert, just two days after recording his last six sides for Pathe.

The Top Acoustic Era Recording Artist

Billy Murray is unknown to the majority of Americans, including those professing to know something about popular music. Therefore, it is understandable that Murray would receive few votes in any poll attempting to name the twentieth century's most influential entertainers. After all, his career was effectively over by the time of the stock market crash of 1929. Moreover, there has never been any concerted effort to revive his recordings since the period of his peak popularity. Even during the time when he was a highly successful artist, between 1903-1927 (the span when his recordings were recognized to be best sellers), his name was curiously absent from the mainstream mass media as well as most entertainment publications.

But one of the greatest entertainers in this century he was. Murray's influence was centered within the recording industry; his impact manifested itself from a wide variety of perspectives. During an era dominated by a formal, operatically-influenced style of singing, he was a pivotal figure in ushering in a more natural approach, especially through the witty interplay of his duets with Ada Jones. The utilization of many dialogue-like features lead some contemporary observers such as singer William Robyn to wrongly dismiss Murray as a "talker."

It is notable that Victor, the company with which Murray is most closely identified, referred to him primarily as a comedian. The accomplishments of such notables as Cal Stewart, Arthur Collins and Byron G. Harlan, Billy Jones and Ernest Hare (The Happiness Boys), Spike Jones, Ray Stevens, and Al Yankovic notwithstanding, Murray left a greater body of comedy recordings than any other artist in the history of the medium. Like all great comedians, he often transcended his material through his mastery of dialect, nuance, and characterization. His range in the interpretation of humorous material was awesome. Whereas most comedians tended to focus on one subcategory such as satire or nonsense verse, Murray's body of recorded work suggested a talent for all comic forms (see: Table 2).

Table 2

BILLY MURRAY'S RECORDINGS CLASSIFIED BY HUMOR GENRES

Allegory

The War In Snider's Grocery Store (1914)

Black Humor

Some Little Bug Is Going To Find You (1915)

Blue Humor/Double Entendre

Hinky Dinky Parley Voo (1924)
If You Talk In Your Sleep Don't Mention My Name (1912)
You've Got To See Mama Ev'ry Night (Or You Can't See Mama At All) (1923)

Caricature

He's A Devil In His Own Home Town (1914)
They Start The Victrola (And Go Dancing Around The Floor) (1914)
This Is The Life (1914)

Comic Sketches

At The Village Post Office (1907)
An Evening At Mrs. Clancy's Boarding House (1907)

Ethnic/Racial Humor

Hi Lee Hi Lo (1923)
Indianola (1918)
The Irish Were Egyptians Long Ago (1942)
That Tango Tokio (1913)
When Tony Goes Over The Top (1919)

Nonsense Verse

Can You Tame Wild Wimmen? (1920)
Humpty Dumpty (1922)
Story Book Ball (1918)
What Does the Pussycat Mean When She Says "Me-ow"? (1923)
Whistle It (1907)
Yes, We Have No Bananas (1923)

Nut Songs

My Little 'Rang Outang (1903)
Up In A Cocoanut Tree (1903)

Parody

Africa (1924)
I'm Looking For The Man That Wrote The Merry Widow Waltz (1908)

K-K-K-Katy (1918)
My Cousin Caruso (1909)
Where Did Robinson Crusoe Go With Friday On Saturday Night? (1916)

Rube Sketches (See: Comic Sketches)

Satire

He Goes To Church On Sunday (1907)
In The Old Town Hall (1920)
My Old New Jersey Home (1920)
Over On The Jersey Side (1909)

Situational Comedy

Any Ice Today, Lady? (1923)
Do You Take This Woman For Your Lawful Wife? (1914)
Don't Bring Lulu (1925)
Everybody Works But Father (1905)
He Went In Like A Lion And Came Out Like A Lamb (1920)
I Don't Like Your Family (1907)
I Love Me (1921)
I'm Afraid To Come Home In The Dark (1907)
I've Got My Captain Working For Me Now (1919)
If War Is What Sherman Said It Was (1915)
Keep Your Skirts Down, Mary Ann (1926)

Topical Humor

The Alcoholic Blues (1919)
He'd Have To Get Under--Get Out And Get Under (To Fix Up His Automobile) (1914)
I Think I Oughtn't Auto Any More (1907)
The Little Ford Rambled Right Along (1915)
On The 5:15 (1915)
Take Your Girlie To The Movies (If You Can't Make Love At Home) (1919)
They Were All Out Of Step But Jim (1918)
Wait Till You Get Them Up In The Air, Boys (1920)

Word Play

And He'd Say Oo-La-La! Wee Wee! (1919)
Fido Is A Hot Dog Now (1915)
Sister Susie's Sewing Shirts For Soldiers (1918)
The Whole Damm Family (1907)

Murray was far more than a brilliant comedian, though; he was an incredibly versatile artist who was comfortable working within a variety of styles. His career was a testament to the fact that a multi-faceted recording artist could thrive without being compartmentalized. Murray's contemporaries were not always successful in avoiding the pigeon-holes provided for them by the record companies. Henry Burr and Harry Macdonough--the artists whose record sales came closest to equalling Murray's during the first two decades of the century--felt the need to change their names (from Harry McClaskey and John Scantlebury Macdonald, respectively) as well as to specialize in ballads and sentimental fare. Collins and Harlan were identified almost exclusively with coon songs and novelty items. Virtuoso instrumentalists were channeled into playing seemingly endless rounds of either short bravurapieces (e.g., violinist Charles D'Almaine) or time tested minstrel fare (e.g., banjo players Vess Ossman and Fred Van Eps). Even the industrious and well-connected Len Spencer found it hard to shake the label of rube impersonator for the remainder of his career after the hitherto unprecedented success of his comic sketch, "The Arkansaw Traveler."

Murray's career, however, served to shatter such precedents. After starting out as an interpreter of the sentimental ballads, vaudeville comedy, and novelty items popular at the time, he kept on top singing ragtime and other dance numbers. Despite some diminution of his popularity following World War I, he adapted well to jazz and band-oriented numbers from a stylistic point of view. Murray was still regarded highly enough that the majority of American record companies attempted to get him into the studio after the electronic recording process was implemented beginning in mid-1925.

The new technology helped bring into vogue a softer, crooning form of delivery. Murray was able to adjust yet again to this new style, despite mixed results at the outset. During the Great Depression his recorded output consisted largely of spoken dialogue to children's stories and film cartoons. He managed a singing comeback in the early 1940s, however, concentrating this time on Irish numbers which steered clear of the schlocky approach typifying the output of many other practitioners within this genre.

But above all else, Murray was born to legitimize the acoustical sound process which employed recording horns rather than the electronic microphone. He was endowed with a particular set of qualities--powerful lungs which enabled him to project his voice to maximum effect, excellent intonation, the bility to sing long phrases in rapid-fire material without taking a breath, and an unerring sense for mastering the basics of a song prior to the first take--which made him a virtuoso in that setting. His ability to cut clean, vibrant records gave that fledging industry the credibility--and sales impact--necessary to carry it to the next technological phase; i.e., electronic sound reproduction.

Perhaps of greatest importance to the recording industry, Murray was one of the first artists--and certainly the most successful of this group--to focus his energies on the studio environment. Whereas many of his contemporaries concentrated on live performance venues such as vaudeville and opera as well as other professions (e.g., artist management, executive slots with record companies, politics, education), Murray made a living largely from the accumulated receipts of his recording sessions. He considered himself a professional recording artist, a significant point in an era when such work was not widely respected. Even many of the recording artists of that era had reservations about the aesthetic value of the medium. Concerning the liberties taken by record companies at the outset of his career, Harry Macdonough commented,

> "That didn't matter, because I was completely indifferent to what they called me. I thought then that record-making was a sort of lowdown business, anyway."

Sammy Herman, a xylaphonist who performed with Murray and Burr as part of the Victor Eight during the mid-1920s, had negative feelings upon hearing the results of his first recording for Clear Tone, recalling, "It didn't sound the way I expected it to sound. I didn't like it."

While a measure of this ill repute was a result of the poor sound reproduction characterizing pioneer era records and cylinders, certain artists were simply endowed with poor recording voices. Sophie Tucker's reaction upon hearing her first takes represented evidence that sensational live performers did not always translate well to the studio (as well as justifying the existence of a cadre of professional record makers who possessed the voices, diction, and techniques necessary to produced good records):

> "I made the songs "The Lovin' Rag" and "That Lovin' Two-Step Man." I worked a whole morning on them. When I heard the playback I turned to the boys and let out a yell: 'My Gad, I sound like a foghorn!' I was terrible."

Classical music artists held similar reservations about the new industry. Arturo Toscanini, the most famous conductor of the first half of the twentieth century, spent little time in the studio prior to the 1930s. He only began recording heavily when he was convinced that the technology was sufficiently advanced to permit reasonably decent sound reproduction and he given complete control over the process. Caruso, whose name is virtually synonymous with early recording, also became involved with extreme misgivings, remaining highly selective regarding his sessions right up to his death.

Murray also deserves credit for his role in either introducing or popularizing countless pop music standards, including the more notable compositions of the leading American songwriters of that era such as Irving Berlin, George M. Cohan, and the von Tilzer brothers, Al and Harry. The monographs and reference sources available to the present generation tend to emphasize the role played by Broadway and other stage performers in putting across a song to the public. However, few Americans of that day had the opportunity to take in a stage show featuring the leading performing artists unless they were financially well off and resided near the cultural centers generally located on the Eastern seaboard (e.g., Boston, New York, Philadelphia, Washington, D.C.). But many rank-and-file Americans did own cylinder players and Victrolas. Popular recordings, sold in a wide variety of retail outlets honeycombing the nation as well as via mail order, often sold millions of units at a time when radio and television were not available in the home. Murray and his chief rivals were household names on a par with sport celebrities like Babe Ruth and movie stars such as Charlie Chaplin. Composers worked hard to get their material recorded by these artists; in turn, their interpretations became the ones most widely imprinted in the American mind. It was no accident that Warren Beatty included the American Quartet's rendition of "Oh, You Beautiful Doll" as part of the aural backdrop to a social gathering of intellectuals at home during the World War I era in his film, *Reds*.

The roll call of song classics Murray made his own is a lengthy one, including

--Alexander's Ragtime Band
--By The Beautiful Sea
--By the Light of the Silvery Moon
--Casey Jones
--Come, Josephine, In My Flying Machine
--Everything Is Peaches Down In Georgia
--For Me And My Gal
--Give My Regards To Broadway
--The Grand Old Rag (Flag)
--If You Knew Susie (Like I Know Susie)
--In My Merry Oldsmobile
--It's A Long, Long Way To Tipperary
--Meet Me In St. Louis, Louis
--Moonlight Bay
--Oh, You Beautiful Doll
--Over There
--Pretty Baby
--Shine On, Harvest Moon
--Yankee Doodle Boy

So why is Murray's name curiously absent from most chronicles of the music of the early part of the century? First and foremost, it should be noted that most music historians have exhibited a greater interest in genres other than mainstream pop music, especially classical forms and rural-based indigenous American forms such as country and western and the blues. Coverage of popular music has revealed a bias toward the performing artist in the case of Broadway musicals and the songwriter regarding Tin Pan Alley material.

Part of the reason behind this lack of coverage would appear to be the result of the negative stereotyping found in much of the era's music. Staunch advocates of political correctness would be alienated by the ethnic slurs of songs such as "That Tango Tokio" (Edison 2026; 1913) and "Indianola" (Victor; 1918). Likewise, feminists would find little humor in material like "When the Grown-Up Ladies Act Like Babies" (Victor 17678; 1915), "There's a Little Bit of Bad in Every Good Little Girl" (Victor 18143; 1916), and "Wait Till You Get Them Up In the Air, Boys" (Columbia 2794; 1919/20).

An even greater downside to the pre-World War I repertoire was the popularity of the coon song. The last stage of the minstrel song, the genre--almost always written and performed by whites--began with songs such as "Coonville Guards" (1881), ("The Coon Dinner" (1882) and "New Coon in Town" (1883) and peaked with Barney Fagan's "My Gal Is a Highborn Lady" (1886) and Ernest Hogan's "All Coons Look Alike to Me" (1886). Hamm defined it in the following manner:

> The 'coon' song is usually in dialect, with a
> text somewhat less than complimentary to blacks.
> Musically, it takes on the verse-solo form of
> contemporary Tin Pan Alley song, with the chief
> melodic material in the chorus, and is sung at a
> lively tempo, usually with some bits of simple
> syncopation. It is, in fact, nothing more or
> less than a slightly deviant offspring of Tin
> Pan Alley song, difficult to distinguish in
> style from the classics of the ragtime song.

In addition, the recording industry has been largely ignored in studies of early popular music. This situation is largely due to the primitive audio properties of acoustic recordings. the limited frequency range, preponderance of surface noise, and other features of early recordings have severely limited the output of reissued material in contemporary configurations such as the compact disc.

It is notable that even legendary artists whose output reaches back to the acoustic era--e.g., Al Jolson, Bing Crosby, Paul Whiteman, Louis Armstrong, and Duke Ellington--have had their later recordings receive far greater attention than their oftentimes superior early work. The potential for "cleaning up" and enhancing the sound quality of pioneer recordings via new technological advances such as the CEDAR 2 system could eventually improve the public's access to this material and ultimately stimulate greater attention on the part of researchers.

Jazz

Jazz, commonly referred to as "jass" until the latter stages of World War I, emerged at around the turn of the century. During the nineteenth century, distinctions between "pure" and "mixed" African ancestry were increasingly ignored. In the pre-Civil War era, the latter group-- known as "Creoles" in the tolerant, cosmopolitan climate of New Orleans--had tended to hold themselves aloof from black culture, sometimes even passing as whites. The entrenchment of segregated society during the Reconstruction caused whites to regard anyone with a percentage of African ancestry (no matter how small) as black. The interaction of Creoles--who tended to be well-schooled in white culture--and blacks facilitated the blending of European and African musical traditions.

A number of preconditions assured New Orleans' central role in the rise of jazz: (1) the presence of more musical organizations by the late 1700s than in any other American city; (2) the festive French tradition; (3) the brothel district (designated "Storyville" in 1897) generated work for musicians of all types; (4) its role as a magnet for freed and escaped slaves throughout the 1800s (due to the city's employment opportunities, social activity, diverse ways of life, convenient location, and influence on black culture as a result of the proportionately high number of resident African Americans); and (5) the considerable amount of sex and marriage between blacks and whites prior to the mid-1800s.

New Orleans provided the setting for the emergence of ragtime in the last decade of the nineteenth century. The role of ragtime in the development of early jazz has been debated by music historians for most of the twentieth century; some consider it to be the first jazz style, while others feel that it was just one of many American pop music genres which influenced the formation of jazz. What is certain, however, is that the term was being employed by the mass media during the World War I years when the New Orleans jazz style achieved astounding success across the nation through performers such as the Original Dixieland Jazz Band, the first jazz act to produce bestselling recordings.

Jazz is now recognized to be perhaps America's greatest indigenous art form. It embraces a number of well-defined subgenres, including

Dixieland. An innovative style from the World War I years to the late 1920s, its leading exponents included Kid Ory, Louis Armstrong, and the Original Dixieland Jazz Band.

Transitional/Dance. The musical accompaniment to the dance crazes of the Roaring Twenties, performers such as Paul Whiteman, Count Basie, Duke Ellington, and Fletcher Henderson utilized a slightly larger group performers than had been the norm with dixieland. However, the emphasis on tight ensemble playing remained.

Big Band/Swing. The small jump combos of the early 1930s evolved into large bands often including at least a half dozen of each major instrumental grouping; i.e., brass, winds, strings.

First the first time, solo breaks featuring headline performers (e.g., drummers like Buddy Rich and Gene Krupa) were widely employed. Major bandleaders included Benny Goodman, Glenn Miller, Artie Shaw, Cab Calloway, Tommy Dorsey, Jimmy Dorsey, and Harry James.

Bebop/Bop. The first jazz style to elevate concertizing above dancing, its stringent intensity precluded any aspirations for mainstream acceptance. The jazz vanguard from the mid- 1940s to the mid-1950s, the focus was now on scaled down bands whch featured virtuoso soloists such as saxophonist Charlie Parker, trumpeter Dizzie Gillespie, and pianist Thelonius Monk.

Modern/Cool Jazz. This strain, popular from the mid-1950s to the mid-1960s, featured a more restrained, reflective form of ensemble playing. Top artists included Miles Davis, Dave Brubeck, and Stan Getz. Stylistic offshoots included West Coast/Third Stream.

Fusion. This form, which arose in the mid-1960s and remains commercial viable to the present day, represents the intermingling of jazz values with one or more additional styles (e.g., Latin, funk). Jazz-rock was the most popular fusion style; notable interpreters included Miles Davis, Chick Corea's Return to Forever, Weather Report, the Mahavishnu Orchestra, and various collaborations involving guitarist Carlos Santana. Many consider the jazz-pop idiom--ranging from the soft soul excursions of Stanley Turrentine, Grover Washington, and others in the 1970s to the easy listening material of the likes of Kenny G. in the 1990s--to be the nadir of the genre.

Free Form/Avant-Garde. This category encompasses a wide variety of cutting edge experiments reaching back as far as the 1950s. Notable proponents have included Ornette Coleman (originator of the harmolodic system of improvisation), Sun Ra, and John Coltrane during the 1960s.

Despite the diversity of sounds found within jazz, certain features can be discerned which typify the genre as a whole. These traits (and probable ancestry) include:

1. Improvisation; i.e., simultaneously composing and playing a fresh melody or accompaniment. This technique appears to have been appropriated from both European (e.g., the Baroque period) and West African (e.g., drum ensembles) models.

2. Syncopation; i.e., the occurrence of accent at times when it is not normally anticipated. The most common rhythmic trait found in jazz, it has occasionally been employed in classical music (e.g., compositions by Mozart and Haydn), although it's far more prevalent in West African music.

3. Harmony; i.e., multiple melodic textures. While two- and three-part melodic textures are not unknown in Africa, they are generally conceived as simultaneous melodies rather than as a progression of chords. On the other hand, European music has had chord progressions like those employed by jazz at least since the 1500s.

4. A collective approach. Some African music allows each member of an ensemble to spontaneously vary his part while performing. While informal European dance and parade music

also employs this approach, with most formal concert works the improvisation is solo, not collective.

5. Call and response format. Although common in European church music, it has a greater predominance in African vocal music.

6. Choice of instruments. West Africa provided the banjo, the flute, and the xylophone; Europe, the trumpet, the trombone, the clarinet, the saxophone (as employed by military and concert bands), the piano, the bass viol, and the guitar.

7. Infrequency of loudness changes. This is typical of African music and European folk material; however, European concert music has long explored the dramatic effects of volume changes.

8. Counterpoint; i.e., the simultaneous sounding of several different melodic lines. Although examples can be discerned, this feature is not common to West African music. A longstanding European tradition, the Sousa variant of counterpoint became the model for early jazz recordings.

9. Prominent role of percussion. In formal European concert music it is used primarily for emphasis and dramatic effect rather than being a continuous element as in African music. It is important, however, in some European military and folk dance music.

10. Rigid maintenance of tempo. Passages without discernable tempo changes are the norm in European marching band and folk dance music, the West African heritage, and pre-1960s jazz. On the other hand, much European symphonic music required speeding and slowing.

11. An attraction for altering sounds by roughenings, buzzes, and ringings. This appears to be a uniquely African quality; jazz manifestations include mutes for brass instruments, simultaneously humming and blowing on a flute or trombone, the rasping texture employed by saxophonists, the electronic altering of tone quality, and the use of devices by drummers to produce ringings (e.g., the insertion of rivets in a cymbal to create a sizzle sound while vibrating).

12. Extensive use of short-term repetition. This approach has been employed by boogie woogie pianists such as Meade Lux Lewis, the Kansas City big band style popularized by Count Basie in the 1930s, and jazz rock as exemplified by Herbie Hancock and Weather Report in the 1970s. It is far more prevalent in African practice than in the full spectrum of European music.

13. Polyrhythmic construction; i.e., the simultaneous sounding of several rhythms. This is more common in African music than in the concert music of pre-20th century Europe. It appears to have filtered into jazz by way of ragtime.

14. Ways in which tones are decorated. These practices, which are African in origin, include: (a) the tendency of jazz singers and some jazz instrumentalists to start vibrato slowly and then increase its rate so that it is fastest at the end of the note (the employment of vibrato can help differentiate

styles--e.g., "hot" jazz players tended to use quicker vibratos than "cool" players of the 1940s and 1950s); (b) the use of a "fall-off" (a drop in pitch during a tone's decay) by many jazz singers and some jazz instrumentalists; (c) the cultivation of an assortment of "attacks" (decorations which precede a tone's fullness, also called "pitch bending"; illustrated in Bessie Smith's "St. Louis Blues") by jazz performers (the different types include the "scoop," starting the sound near the tone's pitch, going below it, and then working back up to it before giving the tone its full duration; the "smear," approaching the desired pitch from a pitch well below it, then gradually rising to the desired pitch; and the "doit," a rise in pitch at the end of a tone); and (d) manipulations of tone quality (e.g. beginning a tone with a smooth texture, then making it rough or hoarse, and ending smooth; a "whisper>robust>whisper" quality, best exemplified by Sarah Vaughan, Sidney Bechet, and John Coltrane).

15. Use of the blue note; i.e., sound achieved by playing a few critical notes out-of-tune or "off-key." It is likely that when Africans performed European-style music, they probably sang using their own pitch system, and it came out as though they were "playing in the cracks between the piano keys." The device has been widely used in jazz horn work (e.g., Miles Davis on the fluegelhorn for "Strawberries," from *Porgy and Bess*).

16. The tendency for jazz pieces and improvisations which are in a major key to sound as though they are minor.

17. An attitude of informality during performance (e.g., solos often continue long after climaxes instead of stopping, as they would in European compositions).

Some music critics and historians argue that the key to defining jazz lies in the performing arena. Mark C. Gridley, in *Jazz Styles*, provides four widely disseminated views of the ingredients necessary to be considered a jazz musician:

1. For some, a musician need only *be associated with the jazz tradition* to be considered a jazz player; he may neither improvise nor swing.

2. For others, a musician must *play with jazz swing feeling* in order to be called a jazz musician.

3. Still others feel a musician need only *be able to improvise* (however, Indian, rock, and selected pop musicians can also improvise).

4. The most common definition is that requiring the musician both to *improvise and swing in the jazz sense* in order to qualify as a jazz player.

Given the richness and diversity of jazz history, in addition to the conventions employed by its exponents, it would seem to be virtually impossible to deploy a definitive definition of this art form. Nevertheless, it could safely be posited that the more one listens to jazz, the more likely it is that this individual will possess a lucid understanding of exactly what the genre is all about.

Table 3

Acid Jazz

Acid jazz represents a synthesis of jazz fusion, funk, hip-hop, and urban dance music. Its improvisational, percussion-heavy, and predominantly live orientation came largely from jazz, whereas its dedication to an ongoing rhythmic groove were borrowed from the latter three genres.

The term entered the vernacular in 1988 when adopted as the name of a U.S.-based independent record company and, at the same time, employed as the title of an English-compilation series consisting of reissued 1970s jazz-funk material. The evolution of the form is closely aligned with the continuing cross-fertilization of a wide range of related styles, most notably alternative dance, ambient house, bass and drums, club/dance music, house, jazz-rap, soul-jazz, trip-hop, and trip jazz.

Due to this ongoing cross-pollenization, acid jazz artists bring many differing perspectives to their recorded work. One of the most popular bands within the genre, the Stereo MC's, moved from the British hip-hop in the late 1980s to a more organic, jazz-inflected amalgam of hip-hop and soul-funk with the release of their most popular LP, *Connected* (4th & Broadway 514061; 1992; #2 UK, #92 US). Courtney Pine came from the opposite side of the fence, bringing his hardcore jazz sensibilites directly into African American dance culture; his *Underground* (Talkin' Loud; 1997) melded steamy live grooves with a battery of technological effects.

Other important recording artists associated with acid jazz include the Brand New Heavies, the Coolbone Brass Band, Corduroy, Count Basic, D'Influence, D*Note, DJ Greyboy, Dread Flimstone, Galliano, the Grassy Knoll, Greyboy, Greyboy Allstars, Groove Collective, Incognito, Jamiroquai, the Jazz Warriors, Jhelisa, Ronny Jordan, A Man Called Adam, Marden Hill, Mondo Grossom Outside, Palm Skin Productions, Gilles Peterson, Red Snapper, Sandals, Slide Five, James Taylor (Quartet), and United Future Organization.

Table 4

Smooth Jazz

The aging of the Baby Boomers has played a major role in the development of a number of genres, most notably Adult Contemporary, new age music, and smooth jazz. While jazz has always possessed a softer side, smooth jazz evolved out of the fusion movement of the 1960s and 1970s. From fusion—built on the intermingling of jazz and a wide range of styles, from the bossa nova to progressive rock—smooth jazz appropriated the rhythmic groove and instrumental riffing (as opposed to improvisation). The gritty, funkier aspects of many such hybrids, however, have been de-emphasized in favor of more polished arrangements. The dance-oriented sensibilities of the generation accustomed to disco and funk undoubtedly contributed to the notion that a steady backbeat could be tamed. Many smooth jazz recordings possess multi-layered textures typically featuring synthesizers, guitars, and horns (saxophones, trumpets, etc.) to create a sound geared more to the subconscious rather than the intellectual domain.

The pop crossover success enjoyed by guitarist George Benson in the mid-1970s—particularly *Breezin'* (Warner Bros. 2919; 1976; #1), *Weekend in L.A.* (Warner Bros. 3139; 1978; #5), and *Give Me the Night* (Warner Bros. 3453; 1980; #3)—provided the template for the newly emerging genre. Kenny G is arguably the style's major star; hit albums such as *Duotones* (Arista 8427; 1986; #6), *Silhouette* (Arista 8457; 1988; #8), and *Breathless* (Arista 18646; 1992; #2) drew legions of new fans to smooth jazz. Other notable artists whose work falls—at least in part—within this field include Fattburger (*Livin' Large*; 1994), Fourplay (*Fourplay*; Warner Bros. 26656; 1991; #97), George Howard (*A Nice Place To Be*; MCA 5855; 1986; #109), and the Yellowjackets (*Mirage A Trois*; Warner Bros. 23813; #145).

Table 5

Ornette Coleman, March 9, 1930-

Ornette Coleman is one of the most innovative—and controversial—figures in jazz history. An early proponent of free jazz, his recordings led the way in illustrating how both musicians, and listeners, could resist the traditional laws of harmony, melody, rhythm, and pitch. He would formalize his techniques in the early 1970s under the heading of "harmolodics," in which harmonies, rhythms, and melodies—assigned equal importance—function independently.

Born in Fort Worth, Texas, Coleman began playing tenor and alto sax in R&B and jazz bands while still in his teens. Following more than a decade of experimentation and study, he burst upon the scene with a quartet comprised of kindred spirits including trumpeter Don Cherry, bassist Charlie Haden, and drummer Billy Higgins. In *Something Else!* (Contemporary 7551; 1958) and *Tomorrow Is the Question!* (Contemporary 7569; 1959) his basic group, augmented with additional veteran players, remained tied to established chordal and structural formats. However, his Atlantic albums released between 1959-1961—most notably, *The Shape of Jazz to Come* (Atlantic 1317; 1959), *Change of the Century* (Atlantic 1327; 1959), *This Is Our Music* (Atlantic 1353; 1960), *Free Jazz* (Atlantic 1364; 1960), *Ornette!* (Atlantic; 1961), and

Ornette on Tenor (Atlantic; 1961)—were milestones in the development of a more natural jazz form.

After several years outside the public eye, Coleman entered a new phase of productivity during the latter half of the 1960s, characterized by a more directed lyricism. While his solos on violin, trumpet, and musette—on which he produced individual, unorthodox sounds—were highly controversial, his work as a whole revealed a more directed lyricism, best exemplified on *At the "Golden Circle" Stockholm, Volume 1* (Blue Note 84224; 1965) and *At the "Golden Circle" Stockholm, Volume 2* (Blue Note 84225; 1965).

Coleman's theory of harmolody was introduced in his extended compositions, *Skies of America* (Columbia 31562; 1972), performed with the London Symphony Orchestra. He then embarked upon another of his frequent sabbaticals, studying world music, the rock scene, and electrified instruments such as the guitar. These experiences were all integrated into the funk-fusion album, *Dancing In Your Head* (Horizon 722; 1977), featuring his new band, Prime Time. Later versions of the band would vary in configuration, reflecting Coleman's far-ranging interests over the last decades of the twentieth century. In addition to reunions with old associates—the most acclaimed being his duet project with Haden, *Soapsuds, Soapsuds* (Artists House; 1977)—he has collaborated with a diverse array of artists, including Pat Metheny—*Song X* (Geffen; 1986)—and Jerry Garcia in *Virgin Beauty* (CBS Portrait; 1988).

As the world has gradually caught up with Coleman's innovations, an increasing number of reissued albums and retrospectives have been issued. Notable examples of the latter include *Broken Shadows* (Columbia; 1979), a collection of unissued material from the early 1970s, and *Beauty Is A Rare Thing* (Atlantic/Rhino; 1993), a six-CD compilation of his entire Atlantic oeuvre.

Table 6

Mahavishnu Orchestra

The Mahavishnu Orchestra was a primary recording and performing outlet for guitar virtuoso John McLaughlin. Born January 4, 1942, in Yorkshire, England, McLaughlin initially made his name performing in area blues bands, most notably units headed by Graham Bond and Brian Auger. Matriculating to the U.S. after recording the highly regarded *Extrapolation* (Verve/Polydor PD-5510; 1969), he recorded six jazz-rock albums with Miles Davis and the Tony Williams' Lifetime between 1969-1971.

McLaughlin experimented with various fusion lineups in his early U.S. solo releases: *Devotion* (Douglas 4; 1971) featured Jimi Hendrix's Band of Gypsys rhythm section

Lifetime organist Larry Young, and *My Goal's Beyond* (Douglas 30766; 1972) included drummer Billy Cobham, violinist Jerry Goodman, and Indian tabla player Badal Roy. He then formed the Mahavishnu Orchestra by adding two European jazz-oriented musicians, bassist Rick Laird and keyboardist Jan Hammer, while retaining Cobham and Goodman. Choosing a name provided by his guru, Sri Chimnoy, McLaughlin further refined the fusion formula by adding his own East-West synthesis, melding the stop-and-start melodies and rhythms of Indian ragas with the rock's power and the improvisational options of jazz. Despite its unprecedented success—the second album, *Birds of Fire* (Columbia 31996; 1973) reached number fifteen on the pop charts—he disbanded the group after the release of the third LP, the live *Between Nothingness & Eternity* (Columbia 32766; 1973), due to conflicts over composer credits (generally claimed by him).

McLaughlin retained the Mahavishnu Orchestra moniker for various recording projects; releases included *Apocalypse* (Columbia 32957;1974), *Visions of the Emerald Beyond* (Columbia 33411; 1975), and *Inner Worlds* (Columbia 33908; 1976). In 1976, however, he gave up the name after renouncing Sri Chimnoy; he briefly formed a group as the Mahavishnu Orchestra from 1984-1986, featuring drummer Danny Gottlieb, keyboardist Mitch Foreman, and saxophonist Bill Evans. Throughout, McLaughlin has continued to explore new musical directions both as a solo artist and in a number of group settings, most notably Shakti and Free Spirits. His charting albums have included *Love Devotion Surrender* (with Carlos Santana) (Columbia 32034; 1973), *Electric Guitarist* (Columbia 35785; 1979), and *Friday Night in San Francisco* (Columbia 37152; 1981).

Table 7

Pat Metheny, August 12, 1954-

Metheny was the dominant jazz guitarist of the last two decades of the twentieth century; the winner of thirteen Grammy awards through 2000, he has enjoyed commercial success while never compromising his constantly evolving artistic vision. He was influential in freeing the guitar of the technical and stylistic limitations which kept it from becoming one of the genre's leading solo instruments.

Emerging in the late 1970s, when fusion guitarists dominated the jazz field, Metheny has, from the start, embodied a blend of bop formalism and lyricism based on elements of contemporary pop music songcraft, including rich melodicism, harmonic sophistication, and country and rock embellishments. Working professionally in Kansas City by age sixteen, he was invited by vibist Gary Burton to teach at Boston's Berklee College of Music and play in his band. His earliest solo albums—*Bright Size Life* (ECM; 1975) and *Watercolors* (ECM; 1977)—which teamed him with bassist Jaco Pastorius and drummer Bob Moses, only hinted at his emerging talent.

Pat Metheny Group (ECM 1114; 1978; #123) signaled the beginning of the highly arranged, synthesizer-based quartet sound developed along with keyboardist Lyle Mays. Its breezy, engaging tone—which struck a responsive chord with the record-buying public—was continued with the solo outing, *New Chautauqua* (ECM 1131; 1979; #44), and collaborative efforts such as *American Garage* (ECM 1155; 1980; #53) and *As Falls Wichita, So Falls Wichita Falls* (ECM 1190; 1981; #50). In contrast to the rock band format employed in these releases, Metheny also experimented with more traditional jazz approach; most notably, *80/81* (ECM 1180; 1980; #89), a wide-ranging set featuring bassist Charlie Haden, drummer Jack DeJohnette, and saxophonists Dewey Redman and Michael Brecker, and *Song X* (Geffen; 1986), with avant garde saxophonist Ornette Coleman.

Metheny continued to excel in new venues during the 1980s, supplying the soundtrack to John Schlesinger's popular film, *The Falcon and the Snowman* (EMI America 17150; 1985; #54) and technological experimentation, including guitar effects and new instrument designs. He also explored world music, expanding his group to accommodate African-based polyrythms and sitting in on studio sessions by Brazilian singer/songwriter Milton Nascimento.

Metheny has consolidated his growth in the 1990s and beyond. The poetically reflective *Beyond the Missouri Sky, A Map of the World* (Verve 537130; 1997), another collaboration with Haden, represented a triumphant return to film scoring. On the other hand, albums like *Question and Answer* (Geffen 24293; 1990); #154, featuring bassist Dave Holland and drummer Roy Haynes, and *Trio 99>00* (Warner Bros.; 2000), with bassist Larry Grenadier and drummer Bill Stewart, demonstrated his continued technical and improvisational prowess within a small jazz combo.

THE ROOTS OF ROCK MUSIC

The Blues

The blues is a style characterized by a melancholy mood (particularly evident in the lyrics, which typically feature a second line repeat of the first line followed by the punch line or lines) and a standard chord progression generally comprised of twelve measures. The genre evolved out of the call-and-response work songs and spirituals of southern black culture during the mid-nineteenth century.

The first hit blues recordings were instrumental renditions of the W.C. Handy composition, "Memphis Blues," by Prince's Orchestra (Columbia) and the Victor Military Band (directed by Walter Rogers), both of which were released in the fall of 1914. "Memphis Blues" also became the first vocal blues recording in a treatment by Morton Harvey with accompaniment by the New York Philharmonic Orchestra (Victor), released in January 1915. However, none of these records were considered to constitute authentic blues interpretations; the earliest such recording may well have been Al Bernard's "Hesitation Blues" (Edison Diamond Disc, 1919), albeit by a white performer. The first black blues vocal was cut by Mamie Smith, backed by the Rega Orchestra, "That Thing Called Love"/"You Can't Keep a Good Man Down" (Okeh), released in July 1920. Smith would go on to achieve considerable success with a succession of Okeh recordings, most notably "Crazy Blues" (1920).

The major record labels were not aggressive in signing black blues artists; Victor and Edison ignored the field altogether. As a result, newly established independents such as Okeh, Paramount, and Black Swan were allowed to dominate the blues sector in the early 1920s. The industry employed the term "race records" to designate blues music and any other material interpreted by African Americans for an African American audience.

Columbia's signing of Bessie Smith in 1923 represented a watershed event. Smith immediately established herself as the top-selling blues singer, stimulating many other labels--even Victor and Edison--to enter the race market. Brunswick established a Race Record Division in 1926, and Paramount began recording notable black male singers such as Charlie Jackson (1924), Blind Lemon Jefferson (1926), and Charley Patton (1927).

Blues recordings peaked in popularity between 1927-1930, before the Great Depression nearly destroyed the record industry altogether. The Memphis Jug Band achieved great success with "Sun Brimmer's Blues"/"Stingy Woman Blues" on Victor in early 1927 and followed up with over 70 more records until 1934. Leroy Carr, the first blues pianist of note, as well as a singer, went on to become the leading blues artist up through the early 1930s.

As the blues matured in the 1930s, a series of stylistic offshoots also made considerable impact within the recording medium, including the piano-based barrelhouse and boogie woogie genres and urban blues. The latter idiom arose in Depression-era Chicago, its prime distinguishing features being a more aggressive delivery and a group setting to put it across. Leading performers in this style included Tampa Red and Big Bill Broonzy.

The Depression Era also saw many talented blues musicians continue to ply their trade in a more traditional vein. These artists, most notably the visionary Robert Johnson, chose to perform close to home in dance halls and drinking establishments located in rural hamlets throughout the Deep South.

The Decca label, established in 1934, made a substantial impression in the race market with its low-priced discs (thirty-five cents as compared with the standard seventy-five cents) and active pursuit of blues talent, including Sleepy John Estes, Rosetta Howard, Louis Jordan, the Norfolk Jubilee Quartet, Ollie Shepard, Johnnie Temple, and Peetie Wheatstraw. Decca retained its industry lead into the post-World War II years, at which time the style had evolved into electrified rhythm and blues. In recognition of this change, the music business retired the "race" and "sepia blues" terms, opting for the r & b moniker.

The older blues styles, most notably the acoustic-oriented country blues, were now followed primarily by folk music enthusiasts. Artists such as Leadbelly, Mississippi John Hurt, Furry Lewis, and Lightnin' Hopkins continued to record for retro specialty labels such as Arhoolie and Bluesville which catered almost exclusively to whites interested in the history of indigenous American music. Urban "electric" blues purists still active in the post-World War II era--most notably Albert King, B.B. King, John Lee Hooker, and the Chess Records stable--also performed and recorded largely for a white audience, particularly after the revival of interest in the genre during the 1960s.

Top Artists and Their Recordings

<u>Blues Pioneers</u>

Big Bill Broonzy--"Romance in the Dark" (1940)

Alberta Hunter--"Beale Street Blues" (1927)

Lonnie Johnson--"Tomorrow Night" (1948)

Bessie Smith--"Down Hearted Blues"/"Gulf Coast Blues" (1923); "Baby Won't You Please Come Home Blues" (1923); "T'aint Nobody's Biz-Ness If I Do" (1923); "The St. Louis Blues" (1925); "Careless Love Blues" (1925); "I Ain't Gonna Play No Second Fiddle" (1925); "I Ain't Got Noboody" (1926); "Lost Your Head Blues" (1926); "After You've Gone" (1927); "A Good Man Is Hard to Find" (1928); "Nobody Knows You When You're Down and Out" (1929)

Clara Smith--"Chicago Blues" (1924)

Mamie Smith (and Her Jazz Hounds)--"Crazy Blues" (1920/1); "Fare Thee Honey Blues" (1921); "Royal Garden Blues" (1921); "You Can't Keep a Good Man Down" (1921); "Dangerous Blues" (1921); "Lonesome Mama Blues" (1922); "You Can Have Him, I Don't Want Him Blues" (1923); "You've Got to See Mama Ev'ry Night (or You Can't See Mama At All)" (1923)

Pine Top Smith--*Pine Top's Boogie Woogie* (1929)

Roosevelt Sykes--"I Wonder" (1945); "The Honeydripper" (1945); "Sunny Road" (1946)

Tampa Red and His Chicago Five--"Let's Get Drunk and Truck" (1936)

<u>Modern Blues Performers</u>

Willie Dixon--"Walking the Blues" (1955)
John Lee Hooker--"Boogie Chillen'" (1949); "Hobo Blues" (1949); "Hoogie Boogie" (1949); "Crawling King Snake Blues" (1949); "I'm in the Mood" (1951); "Boom Boom" (1962)

Lightnin' Hopkins--"'T' Model Blues" (1949); "Shotgun Blues" (1949); "Give Me Central 209" (1952); "Coffee Blues" (1952)

Howlin' Wolf--"Moanin' at Midnight" (1951); "How Many More Years" (1951); "Smoke Stack Lightning" (1956); "I Asked For Water" (1956)

Elmore James--"Dust My Broom" (1952); "I Believe" (1953); "The Sky Is Crying" (1960); "It Hurts Me Too" (1965)

Albert King--"Don't Throw Your Love on Me So Strong" (1961); "That's What the Blues Is All About" (1974)

B.B. King--"Three O'Clock Blues" (1951/2); "You Know I Love You" (1952); "Woke Up This Morning" (1953); "Please Love Me" (1953); "Please Hurry Home" (1953); "You Upset Me Baby" (1954); Every Day I Have the Blues" (1955); "Bad Luck" (1956); "On My Word of Honor" (1956); "Please Accept My Love" (1958); "Sweet Sixteen, Pt. 1" (1960); "Partin' Time" (1960); "Peace of Mind" (1961); "Don't Answer the Door, Pt. 1" (1966); "The Thrill Is Gone" (1970); Chains and Things" (1970); "I Like to Live the Love" (1973/4); *Riding With the King* (w/Eric Clapton; 2000)

Freddy King--"Hide Away" (1961); "Lonesome Whistle Blues" (1961); "San-Ho-Zay" (1961); "I'm Tore Down" (1961)

Sonny Boy Williamson (r.n. Aleck Ford)—"Shake the Boogie" (1947); "Don't Start Me Talkin'" (1955)

Table 8

Lonnie Johnson, February 8, 1889-June 16, 1970

Alonzo "Lonnie" Johnson's accomplishments are legion. He was the creator of the guitar solo played note for note with a pick, now a standard device in blues, country, jazz, rock and other popular music styles. He inspired many twentieth century innovators—including jazz guitar creators Django Reinhardt and Charlie Christian, modern blues pioneers T-Bone Walker and B.B. King—as well as many other musicians who copied his style (e.g., the St. Louis school exemplified by Henry Townsend and Clifford Gibson) and repertoire (most notably, Skip James' rendition of "I'm So Glad").

Born and raised in New Orleans (he worked the Storyville district from 1910-1917), Johnson also spent a considerable amount of time in St. Louis, Texas, New York, and Chicago while performing in theaters and on riverboats, strongly influencing the musicians based in each of these areas. He was very active recording during the first wave of blues recording, producing 130 sides between 1925-1932 as a session player for Okeh, including collaborations with Louis Armstrong ("Hotter Than That"; Okeh 8535; 1928) and Duke Ellington. A conflict with powerful Chicago producer Lester Melrose temporarily halted his studio work, but he became active again between 1937-1942 for Columbia, Decca, Bluebird, Disc, and various other labels. Following World War II, he revived his career with a series of hits featuring his electric guitar playing, including "Tomorrow Night" (King 4201; 1948; #1 R&B, #19 pop), "Pleasing You" (King 4245; 1948; #2 R&B), "So Tired" (King 4263; 1949; #9 R&B), and "Confused" (King 4336; 1950; #11 R&B).

Dropping out of sight in the early 1950s, he was rediscovered at the beginning of the blues-folk revival in 1959, working as a porter in a Philadelphia hotel. Although consistently touring during the 1960s, his artistic and commercial impact did not approach that of many of his peers, primarily because his sophisticated, urban-based style—rooted in 1930s popular music—did not translated well with an audience most interested in the ethnic roots of the blues. Nevertheless, compact disc reissues of his work are widely available, including *Blues By Lonnie* Johnson Prestige Bluesville 502-2; 1991), *Blues & Ballads* (Prestige Bluesville 531-2; 1990; *Another Night to Cry* (Prestige Bluesville 550-2; 1992), *Stompin' at the Penny* (Columbia Legacy CK 57829; 1994), *The Complete Folkways Recordings* (Smithsonian Folkways 40067; 1993), and *Steppin' on the Blues* (CBS/Sony 467252-2). [Herzhaft. 1997]

Table 9

Albert King, April 25, 1923-December 21, 1992

At a time when even B.B. King adopted a more soulful pop sound in order to achieve commercial success, Albert King was instrumental in keeping a traditional blues sound on the R&B charts. His raw, rootsy style—modeled on blues shouters like Big Joe Turner and Jimmy Witherspoon and bottleneck guitar specialists Elmore James and Robert Nighthawk—was a primary influence on a large number of late twentieth century blues musicians, including Robert Cray, Joe Louis Walker, and Donald Kinsey.

Born Albert Nelson in Indianola, Mississippi, he performed live in Memphis area clubs as well as with the Harmony Kings gospel group between 1949-1951. By the early 1950s he had relocated to the Gary, Indiana-Chicago area, where he played occasionally on recording sessions for Chess. He would cut a series of tracks as a soloist for the label in the late 1950s and early 1960s, adhering closely to the prevailing Chicago blues style then being popularized by the likes of Muddy Waters and Howlin' Wolf. His first sessions as a leader, however, were recorded in St. Louis for the Parrot label (purchased by Chess in 1959); the surviving tracks—currently available *Door To Door* (MCA 9322; 1990)—include the self-penned "Bad Luck" (master #U53-177), "Merry Way" (#U53-178), and "Murder" (#U53-179). He was based in St. Louis by the mid-1950s, where his recordings for Bobbin brought him increased stature, but little commercial success.

King's first hit came in 1962 in the King/Federal firm (which owned his contract after purchasing Bobbin) with "Don't Throw Your Love on Me So Strong" (King 5575; #14 R&B). As a result, the Memphis-based Stax label added him to its roster. Accompanied by members of the company's renowned house band, Booker T. and the MGs as well as the Bar-Kays and Memphis Horns, he enjoyed a long string of chart successes, including "Laundromat Blues" (Stax 190; 1966; #29 R&B), "Crosscut Saw" (Stax 201; 1967; #34 R&B), ""Cold Feet" (Stax 241; 1968; #20 R&B, #67 pop), "Everybody Wants to Go to Heaven" (Stax 0101; 1971; #38 R&B), "I'll Play the Blues for You" (Stax 0135; 1972; #31 R&B), "Breaking Up Somebody's Home" (Stax 0147; 1972; #35 R&B), and "That's What the Blues Is All About" (Stax 0189; 1974; #15 R&B). Many of his Stax albums—most notably, *Born Under a Bad Sign* (MFSL/ Atlantic 577; c1967), *King Does the King's Things* (Stax 8504; 1991), Wednesday *Night in San Francisco* (Stax 8536; c1968), *Thursday Night in San Francisco* (Stax 8537; c1968), *Years Gone By* (Stax 2010; 1969), I'll *Play the Blues For You* (Stax 8513; c1972), *Blues at Sunrise* (Stax 8546; c1973)—are still considered classics today.

King landed with Utopia/Tomato following Stax's descent into bankruptcy in 1974. His output, however, was marred by unsympathetic supporting players, bland arrangements, and a preponderance of brass and strings. His fortunes improved somewhat when he signed with Fantasy in the early 1980s. However, he was better appreciated live than on record during the decade preceding his death.

Table 10

Freddie King, September 30, 1934-December 28, 1976

While overshadowed by namesakes, Albert and B.B., Freddie King was an emerging star at the time of his premature death from a heart attack. His stinging guitar style, anchored by a propulsive rhythmic intensity and flawless technique, reflected the years spent perfecting his craft in the gritty clubs of Chicago's black districts.

Born Freddie Christian in Gilmer, Texas, he moved to Chicago in 1950. Shortly thereafter, he began playing in area venues with bands headed by the likes of Little Sonny Cooper and Hound Dog Taylor. He also did session work for the local Parrot and Chess labels during the early 1950s. He eventually formed his own band, the Every Hour Blues Boys.

King's first solo recordings, more for El-Bee Records in 1956, failed to have any commercial impact. By early 1961, however, he achieved success with the King/Federal label due in no small part to the sure-handed guidance of producer-piano player Sonny Thompson. His biggest hits were divided between instrumental workouts—"Hide Away" (Federal 12401; 1961; #5 R&B, #29 pop) and "San-Ho-Zay" (Federal 12428; 1961; #4 R&B)—and searing vocal renditions—"Lonesome Whistle Blues" (Federal 12415; 1961; #8 R&B), "I'm Tore Down" (Federal 12432; 1961; #5 R&B). By the mid-1960s King had recorded an impressive body of work for the Cincinnati-based firm; nevertheless, he signed on with Atlantic which issued two LPs produced by the legendary saxophonist King Curtis.

Attempting to reach a mainstream audience in the early 1970s, he recorded three albums for Leon Russell's Shelter label. Although full of rock nuances, the raw vitality of classic cuts such as "Goin' Down" and "Big Leg Woman" revealed King at the height of his powers. His later work followed the then current vogue of placing American blues giants within a British framework (e.g., producer Mike Vernon and guitarist Eric Clapton), a formula already tried by Muddy Waters, Howlin' Wolf, and Bo Diddley, among others. The results were rather tepid, and any hopes of an artistic rebirth were dashed by his untimely death.

King is well represented on compact disc reissues. Both *Takin' Care of Business* (Charly 30) and *Texas Sensation* (Charly 242) compile the highlights of his

King/Federal period. Also available are *Just Pickin'* (Modern Blues 721)—a compilation of his instrumental tracks, *Texas Cannonball* (Shelter) and *Getting Ready* (Shelter 8003).

Table 11

Victoria Spivey, 1906-1976

Although not the most revered female blues recording artist to emerge in the 1920s, Texas native Victoria Spivey had the distinction of remaining musically active—both as a composer (e.g., "Big Black Limousine," "Mr. Cab") and singer—virtually her entire life. She was a vital force in the 1960s blues revival, creating her own record label, Spivey, which helped revive the careers of many classic blue artists in addition to nurturing new talents, including Olive Brown, Luther Johnson, Lucille Spann, Sugar Blue, and Bob Dylan.

A child singer/actor in vaudeville, Spivey's acidic blues vocals earned her a recording contract with Okeh in 1926. Her debut release, "Black Snake Blues" (Okeh; 1926), a hit in the blues market, would be recorded by countless artists over the years. Often backed by legendary musicians such as Louis Armstrong, Lonnie Johnson, and Tempa Red, she would produce definitive versions of "T.B. Blues," "Dope Head Blues," and :Murder in the First Degree." While many blues artists were not recruited to cut records after 1929, she developed an aggressive, modern style which kept her in demand as recording artist during the Depression until 1937.

In addition to running Spivey Records during the blues revival, her Greenwich Village folk connections enabled her to perform on many Prestige/Bluesville albums. Following her death, many LPs containing her work were still in print, including the solo releases *Blues Is Life* (Folkways 3541), *Queen and Her Nights* (Spivey 1006), *Recorded Legacy of the Blues* (Spivey 2001), *Victoria Spivey and Her Blues* (Spivey 1002), and *Victoria Spivey and the Easy Riders Jazz Band* (GHB 17).

Rhythm and Blues

The term "rhythm and blues" emerged as the most acceptable designation for the music that had developed out of pre-World War II blues styles, for the most distinctive new element in this genre was the addition of a dance beat. The expression first appeared in formal usage in the late 1940s as the name of RCA's division that served the American audience; other alternatives at the time included "ebony" (MGM) and sepia" (Decca and Capitol). Prior to the rise of rock 'n' roll, r & b had already evolved into a wide variety of subgenres, including:

(1) the self-confident, assertive dancehall blues which, in turn, encompassed (a) big band blues (e.g., Lucky Millinder, Tiny Bradshaw); (b) shout, scream, and cry blues (e.g., Wynonie Harris, Joe Turner, Big Maybelle, Ruth Brown, LaVern Baker, Roy Brown); and (c) combo blues or jump blues. Combo blues had a number of regional strains in addition to the cosmopolitan style exemplified by Louis Jordan: West Coast (e.g., Roy Milton, Amos Milbern, T-Bone Walker), Mississippi Delta (e.g., Ike Turner's Kings of Rhythm), New Orleans (e.g., Fats Domino, Professor Longhair), and Eastern Seaboard (e.g., Chuck Willis, Wilbert Harrison).

(2) The quieter, more despondent club blues (e.g., Charles Brown, Cecil Gant, Ivory Joe Hunter).

(3) The country-tinged bar blues (usually centered in either the Mississippi Delta or Chicago). Chief exponents included Muddy Waters, Howlin' Wolf, Elmore James, and John Lee Hooker.

(4) Vocal group singing, which was subdivided into (a) the cool style (e.g., The Orioles, the Cardinal, the Spaniels); (b) the dramatic style (e.g., the Moonglows, the Flamingos, the Platters); (c) the romantics (e.g., the Harptones); (d) the cool style with a strong blues emphasis (e.g., the Clovers, the Drifters); and (e) the song-along novelty approach geared to mainstream pop acceptance (e.g., the Crows, the Penguins, Frankie Lymon and the Teenagers).

(5) Gospel-based styles, which possessed three major strains: (a) spiritual singing, with the focus upon the quality of the voice (e.g., Mahalia Jackson); (b) gospel singing, with its concentration on the interplay between voices, which were often deliberately coarsened to stress the emotional conviction of the singers (e.g., Rosetta Tharpe, the Dixie Hummingbirds); and (c) preacher singing, with its tendency to speak the message in an urgent near-shout which often revealed the phrasing and timing of singing minus the melodic dimension.

It soon became evident, musically speaking, that "rhythm and blues" was a less than satisfactory name for at least two of the most important stylistic innovations of the 1950s, the various vocal group styles and the gospel-based styles, which were to become increasingly popular as rock 'n' roll began to siphon off the unique spirit of previous r & b forms. For instance, the new vocal groups invariably based their approach on the style of two black ballad-singing aggregates who had long been successful with the easy listening audience, the Mills Brothers and the Ink Spots. Both groups sang in the close harmony "barbershop" style, accompanied by a light rhythm section. They were similar in the ease with which they timed their harmonies, and the purity of their voices.

Of course, these characteristics were a far cry from those comprising the classic r & b style. Therefore, the term "rhythm and blues" became most useful as a market designation; i.e., an indication that the performer was black, recording for the black audience. As noted noted by Charlie Gillett, author of *The Sound of the City* (1970), there was ample justification--at least until 1956--for classifying the black market separately. The black audience was interested almost exclusively in African American performers; only five recordings by white acts reached the r & b Top Ten between 1950 and 1955, and three of those were rock 'n' roll records (Bill Haley's "Dim the Lights" and "Rock Around the Clock," and Boyd Bennett's "Seventeen"). Few white singers had either the interest or the cultural experience necessary to appeal to the black audience's taste--until rock 'n' roll changed the equation, resulting in a new type of white performer.

Motown Records played a pivotal role in the development of r & b into a mainstream genre. The product of the vision of one man, owner and founder Berry Gordy, the label sculpted a mainstream pop sound out of gospel and blues roots which reflected the vision of upward mobility and wholesome fun held by African American youth in the 1960s. Motown's stars were groomed to offend no one; the songs they sang had romantic lyrics that could appeal to practically anyone; and the music itself was rarely demanding, or even aggressive in the tradition of Southern soul.

Although the assembly-line approach employed by Motown led to criticism for monotony, the label released a remarkably diverse array of recordings, varying in sound, arrangement and feel. This diversity--reinforced by Motown's mainstream commercial success-- proved to be the launching pad for many of the black music styles that evolved after the mid-1960s.

A host of regional independent labels producing soul music in the 1960s sought to control production values and nurture available talent with an eye to the long-term payoff, including Vee-Jay and Chess/Checker (Chicago), Stax/Volt/Enterprise, Goldwax, and Hi (Memphis), Philadelphia International, Philly Groove, and Avco (Philadelphia), and Fame (Muscle Shoals, Alabama). Funk, disco, and the dance-oriented styles of the 1980s such as go-go music also owed much to Motown.

The rich diversification of styles and comparatively rapid rate of change characteristic of African American popular music in the post-World War II era stands in bold contrast to the chief white-dominated genre indigenous to the United States, country music. Gillett offers the following rationale for this situation:

> This is partly because several white southern styles have never been widely
> popular with the national American audience, so that singers did not
> continually have to invent styles that would be special to their local
> audiences--those invented [sixty or seventy] years ago were still special
> to a local area, or to the white south. In contrast, almost every black
> southern style has proved to have universal qualities that attract national
> and international audiences, and this situation has placed continual pressure
> on singers to come up with new styles that are not already widely known
> and that the local audience can feel to be its own. And invariably, musicians
> and singers have responded positively to such pressure.

This predisposition for change has proven to be at once a strength and a weakness. It has enabled African American music styles to remain dynamic, ever responsive to the needs and interests of its core audience. However, it has also tended to discourage participation on the part of the uninitiated, who are confused by the rapid succession of fads and fashions.

A Rhythm and Blues Chronology

1946. *Billboard* begins charting the sale of records in the "Negro" market, employing the heading, "Harlem Hit Parade." The weekly listing is eventually renamed "Race Records."

1948. Atlantic Records is formed. The label has shown a flair for assessing performing styles and audience tastes that has been unmatched in the post-World War II era of popular music. Signing a succession of performers from various sources and with various styles, Atlantic's mid-1950s rosters included Joe Turner, Ruth Brown, LaVern Baker, Clyde McPhatter, Ray Charles, Chuck Willis, Ivory Joe Hunter, The Cardinals, The Clovers, The Drifters, The Coasters, and Bobby Darin. With these performers the company's share of the r & b market grew from three Top Ten records in 1950 to seventeen (out of eighty-one) in 1956. Though no longer an independent, Atlantic continues to thrive as part of the WEA family.

June 17, 1949. *Billboard*, without any editorial comment, begins employing the term "rhythm and blues" in reference to the black charts.

March 6, 1959. "There Goes My Baby" is recorded by the Drifters (Atlantic #2025). It is considered the first high-profile r & b disc to use a string accompaniment. Its combined artistic and commercial success inspired an upsurge in the development of sophisticated recording techniques for African American music, culminating in the "Golden Age of Soul" (1964-1968).

March 12, 1960. *Cash Box* combines its pop and r & b charts. In an editorial appearing on the front page of that issue, the magazine justifies this decision by noting the similarity between the pop and r & b charts; that is, the r & b listing was at the time almost ninety percent pop in nature. *Cash Box* evidently had second thoughts about this policy, and reinstated the separate r & b compilation on December 17, 1960 ("Top 50 in Locations"). *Billboard* used the same reasoning in deleting its r & b singles charts between November 23, 1963 and January 30, 1965. On the latter date, *Billboard* ultimately returned to the two-chart system.

February 16, 1961. The Miracles' "Shop Around" (Tamla #54034) reaches number one, remaining three weeks. It was Motown's first major hit.

August 26, 1961. The Mar-Keys' "Last Night" becomes the first Stax production to reach number one. Stax--and later in the decade, the Muscle Shoals, Alabama, studio headed by Rick Hall--both offered a rawer, more spontaneous, gospel-influenced alternative to the Motown Sound. The Mar-Keys (whose rhythm section also recorded as Booker T. & the MGs) backed most of the label's artists, including Sam and Dave, Otis Redding, Eddie Floyd, Rufus Thomas, Carla Thomas, and Johnnie Taylor.

May 26, 1962. Ray Charles' country-influenced "I Can't Stop Loving You" (ABC #10330) begins the first of its eleven consecutive weeks at the top of the r & b charts. The song typified--in dramatic fashion due to its incredible commercial success--the inclination of talented black performers to favor sweet and sentimental sounds over personal expression in order to achieve mainstream pop impact. Similar career moves were taken by Sam Cooke, Jackie Wilson, Brook Benton, and others. By the late 1960s, however, African American singers like Wilson Pickett and Aretha Franklin were able to attain pop music success while remaining true to their cultural roots.

October 12, 1963. "Cry Baby," by Garnett Mimms and the Enchanters (United Artists #629) begins the first of two weeks at number one. "Cry Baby" was among the earliest--and certainly the most success- commercially--of the gospel-styled songs to have an accompaniment that was not slightly adapted from some other genre of music. Unlike most records, with their slow, gentle, lilting arrangements, "Cry Baby" offered an uncompromising expression of ecstasy. On other "gospel revivalist" records, the strong rhythms meant that the impact was absorbed physically by the listener and not on a purely emotional level as was the case with the Mimms track. In short, the song possessed all the prime ingredients characterizing the classic soul genre.

March 11, 1967. Dyke and the Blazers' "Funky Broadway" (Original Sound #64) enters the r & b charts, remaining there 27 weeks, peaking at number 11. The word "funk" didn't become part of the legitimate radio jargon until the song had "bubbled under" for so long that disc jockeys were forced to play it and say the word. Though nobody knows who coined the term, "funk" simply was not a word used in polite society. "Funky Broadway," however, changed all that.

March 11, 1967. Aretha Franklin's "I Never Loved a Man" (Atlantic #2386) reaches number one, remaining there for seven weeks. In a kind of soul-waltz time, the record built up from a quiet but dramatic opening organ figure into a hammering, screaming, but always firmly controlled yell of delight, as a brilliantly organized band fed more and more to support the singer's emotion. It was the first of Franklin's eighteen number one songs on the r & b charts, more than any other artist between 1960 and 1985. Noteworthy commercial success combined with impeccable artistry earned her the sobriquet, "Queen of Soul."

February 10, 1968. Sly and the Family Stone's first hit, "Dance to the Music" (Epic #10256) enters the r & b charts, eventually peaking at number three. The song shook off the assumptions about the separate roles of voices and instruments as sources of rhythm and harmony, alternating them and blending them yet never losing either melody or dance beat. The adventurousness of the sound was mainstream critics who had tended to deride soul arrangements as being overly simple. As Sly began employing increasingly personal lyrics, the social consciousness school of funk was created.

October 12, 1968. "Say It Loud, I'm Black and I'm Proud" (King #12715) by "Soul Brother Number One," James Brown, tops the charts. "Say It Loud" was merely the most successful of the wave of political slogan songs exploiting black pride. Much of this material would fall within the funk genre in the 1970s.

August 23, 1969. *Billboard* declares rhythm and blues officially dead by renaming its chart for that market "Best-Selling Soul Singles." Ironically, there was every sign that the new euphemism for "black"--which had been widely used during most of the 1960s-- would soon be musically outdated, and its successor defied prophesy.

June 9, 1973. Manu Dibango's "Soul Makossa" (Atlantic #2971) enters the r & b charts, eventually reaching the Top Twenty. Recorded by an African in Paris, "Soul Makossa" was imported into the U.S. when its enormous popularity in discos made domestic release seem like a good business proposition, Thus, the first disco pop hit was born.

July 29, 1978. "Soft and Wet," the first hit by Prince (Warner #8619), enters the charts, eventually reaching number nine. Prince's combination of street-level hipness and musical inventiveness propelled him to the vanguard of black music in the 1980s. He pioneered a new genre, funk punk, and nurtured many exponents of that sound (e.g., The Time, Vanity, Andre Cymone, Sheila E.).

April 10, 1982. *Cash Box* first employs a new term for the black charts, "Top 100 Black Contemporary Singles." The term gained nearly universal acceptance during the 1980s, encompassing the full range of African American pop music (jazz fusions, dance music, easy listening, and so forth) as well as white releases expected to appeal to the black audience. By the 1990s, however, the trade charts had reverted back to the term "rhythm and blues."

Top R & B Hits*

(1) Joe Liggins and His Honeydrippers--"The Honeydripper" (1945)
(2) Louis Jordan--"Choo Choo Ch'Boogie" (1946)
(3) Louis Jordan--"Ain't Nobody Here But Us Chickens" (1947)
(4) Lionel Hampton--"Hey! Ba-Ba-Re-Bop" (1946)
(5) Charles Brown Trio--"Trouble Blues" (1949)
(6) Paul Williams--"The Hucklebuck" (1949)
(7) The Dominoes--"Sixty-Minute Man" (1951)
(8) Erskine Hawkins--"Don't Cry, Baby" (1943)
(9) Charles Brown--"Black Night" (1951)
(9) Louis Jordan--"Boogie Woogie Blue Plate" (1947)
(11) Guitar Slim--"Things That I Used to Do" (1954)
(12) Bill Doggett--"Honky Tonk (Parts 1 & 2)" (1956)
(13) Joe Liggins and His Honeydrippers--"Pink Champagne" (1950)
(14) The Coasters--"Searchin'" (1957)
(15) Julia Lee and Her Boyfriends--"Snatch and Grab It" (1947)
(16) Louis Jordan--"Saturday Night Fish Fry (Part I)" (1949)
(17) Fats Domino--"Ain't That a Shame" (1955)
(18) Ruth Brown--"Teardrops From My Eyes" (1950)
(19) Fats Domino--"Blueberry Hill" (1956)
(20) Ella Fitzgerald/Ink Spots--"Into Each Life Some Rain Must Fall" (1944)
(20) Clyde McPhatter and the Drifters--"Money Honey" (1953)

(22) The Platters--"The Greater Pretender" (1956)
(23) Chuck Berry--"Maybellene" (1955)
(24) Marvin Gaye--"Sexual Healing" (1982)
(25) King Cole Trio--"Straighten Up and Fly Right" (1944)
(26) Faye Adams--"Shake a Hand" (1953)
(27) The Dominoes--"Have Mercy Baby" (1952)
(28) Johnny Ace--"Pledging My Love" (1955)
(28) Bobby Lewis--"Tossin' and Turnin'" (1961)
(30) Dinah Washington and Brook Benton--"Baby (You've Got What It Takes)" (1960)
(31) Ray Charles--"I Can't Stop Loving You" (1962)
(32) Julia Lee and Her Boyfriends--"King Size Papa" (1948)
(33) Michael Jackson--"Billie Jean" (1983)
(34) Little Esther/Johnny Otis Orchestra--"Double Crossing Blues" (1950)
(35) Stevie Wonder--"That Girl" (1982)
(36) Johnny Ace/The Beale Streeters--"My Song" (1952)
(36) Fats Domino--"I'm in Love Again" (1956)
(38) The Charms--"Hearts of Stone" (1954)
(39) Four Tops--"I Can't Help Myself" (1965)
(40) Al Green--"Let's Stay Together" (1972)
(41) Brook Benton--"It's Just a Matter of Time" (1959)
(42) Brook Benton--"Kiddio" (1960)
(43) Louis Jordan--"Buzz Me" (1946)
(44) Savannah Churchill--"I Want to Be Loved (But Only By You)" (1947)
(44) Mtume--"Juicy Fruit" (1983)
(44) Joe Turner--"Honey Hush" (1953)
(47) The Drifters featuring Clyde McPhatter--"Honey Love" (1954)
(48) Larry Darnell--"For You, My Love" (1949)
(49) Earth, Wind and Fire--"Let's Groove" (1981)
(50) Roy Hamilton--"You'll Never Walk Alone" (1954)
(50) Little Walter and His Night Cats--"Juke" (1952)
(50) Lucky Millinder--"Who Threw the Whiskey in the Well?" (1945)
(50) Prince--"When Doves Cry" (1984)

*Based upon weeks in the number one position on the *Billboard* R & B singles chart. Ties were broken by comparing total weeks charted.

Table 12

Willie Dixon, July 1, 1915-January 29, 1992

As a house producer for Chess Records beginning in 1954—responsible for writing, arranging, producing, and playing bass on the recordings of Chuck Berry, Buddy Guy, Howlin' Wolf, Little Walter, Otis Rush, Muddy Waters, Sonny Boy Williamson, and others—he was a key force in the development of the post-World War II Chicago blues scene. Many of his compositions have become blues standards, including "Back Door Man," "I Can't Quit You Baby," "I Just Want to Make Love to You," "I'm Ready," "I Ain't Superstitious," The Red Rooster," "The Seventh Son," and "Wang Dang Doodle."

Born in Vicksburg, Mississippi, Dixon revealed an aptitude for writing poetry as well as deep, rich voice developed in church prior to moving to Chicago in 1937. He first made his mark as a professional boxer before becoming a singer/bassist with a jazz-pop combo, the Five Breezes, in 1940. The group would record for Bluebird that year without commercial success; sessions with Mercury in the early 1940s, as a member of the Four Jumps of Jive, also failed to produce any hits. Together with pianist Leonard Caston and guitarist Bernardo Dennis, he then founded the Big Three Trio, whose jazz-R&B-pop amalgam was waxed by Columbia in the late 1940s. Their most popular recording, "You Sure Look Good to Me" (Columbia 38093; 1948), reached number ten on the *Billboard* R&B charts.

He began working as a producer for Chess Records in 1951, proving his worth on a series of tracks with guitarist Robert Nighthawk. While producing Chess sessions well into the 1970s, Dixon found time to pursue many other activities, including production work for the Chicago-based Cobra label, recording as the featured artist, promoting new talent (e.g., Little Wolf, Margie Evans), managing a record company (Yambo), and live performing, first with Memphis Slim in the early 1960s and, beginning in 1967, as head of his own band, the Chicago Blues All-Stars. Dixon's only solo hit, "Walking the Blues" (Checker 822; 1955) reached number six on the R&B charts.

Following the 1987 settlement of a two-decade dispute with Led Zeppelin over the failure to credit his contribution to the composition of "Whole Lotta Love" (based largely on his "You Need Love"), Dixon established the Blues Heaven Foundation, an organization dedicated to preserving blues music and culture as well as helping secure copyrights and ensuing royalties for other songwriters and recording artists. Despite a relative lack of success as a recording artist, much of his work has been reissued on compact disc, from the Big Three Trio to 1970s albums by the Chicago Blues All-Stars. His most enduring legacy, however, remains the classic Chess tracks he helped create in a supporting role. Many of them are available in a three-CD compilation, *The Willie Dixon Chess Box* (Chess 316500).

Table 13

Louis Jordan, July 8, 1908-February 4, 1975

Louis Jordan proved more successful than any other black artist in crossing over to the pop charts in the 1940s. Equally adept at jazz, blues, R&B, and pop music, his experiments in melding these styles played a major role in the emergence of rock 'n' roll.

Mastering the saxophone during his formative years in rural Arkansas, he went on to accompany Ida Cox, Ma Rainey, Bessie Smith, and other major blues singers as a member of the legendary Rabbit Foot Minstrels revue. He first recorded with the Jungle Band for Brunswick in 1929, then moving to New York to play with Clarence Williams, among others, in the early 1930s. Joining Chick Webb's swing band on alto sax in 1936, he would also contribute vocals on blues and novelty material.

In 1938 Jordan struck out on his own, forming the Elks Rendez-Vous Band. Inking a record contract with Decca the following year, he changed the group's name to the Tympany Five. Mining the jump style of R&B, Jordan's sassy humor, punning, and driving rhythmic approach (further accentuated by his wordplay) were responsible for a long string of hits, including the following R&B chart toppers: "What's the Use of Getting Sober" (Decca 8645; 1942), "Ration Blues" (Decca 8654; 1943), "G.I. Jive" (Decca 8659; 1944; #1 pop), "Mop Mop" (Decca 8668; 1945), the crossover success "Caldonia" (Decca 8670; 1945; #6 pop), "Buzz Me"/"Don't Worry 'Bout That Mule" (Decca 18734; 1946; #9 pop), "Stone Cold Dead in the Market" (Decca 23546; #7 pop), "Choo Choo Ch'Boogie" (Decca 23610; 1946; #7 pop), "Ain't That Just Like A Woman" (Decca 23669; 1946), "Ain't Nobody Here But Us Chickens" (Decca 23741; 1946; #6 pop), "Texas and Pacific" (Decca 23810; 1947), "Jack, You're Dead" (Decca 23901; 1947), "Boogie Woogie Blue Plate" (Decca 24104; 1947), "Run, Joe" (Decca 24448; 1948), "Beans and Corn Bread" (Decca 24673; 1949), and "Saturday Night Fish Fry (Part 1)" (Decca 24725; 1949).

The rise of rock 'n' roll rendered his sound passe. Although no longer an important recording artist, he was still active performing—particularly around his home base of Los Angeles—until suffering a fatal heart attack. His classic recorded work remains widely available today, must notably the monumental box set, *Louis Jordan: Let the Good Times Roll (1938-1954)* (Bear Family 15557).

Table 14

Ike Turner, November 5, 1931-December 12, 2007

Although generally mentioned in relation to his one-time wife, Tina, Ike was one of the early pioneers of rock 'n' roll in his own right. His talents—which spanned many aspects of the music industry—also play a key role in furthering the careers of many other African American artists.

Turner formed a band while still in high school, the Top Hatters. Later known as the

Kings of Rhythm, they worked the small clubs throughout the Mississippi delta. He secured a recording session at Sam Phillips' legendary Sun Studios in Memphis; his band cut the R&B chart-topper, "Rocket 88," cited by many experts as the earliest rock 'n' roll recording. Due to obscure contractual considerations, however, Chess gave label credit to saxophonist Jackie Brenston and the Delta Cats, thereby denying him a notable footnote in pop music history. He also alleged that the company paid him only forty dollars for writing, producing, and recording the disc.

Turner continued as a highly regarded session guitarist, producer, and talent scout during the 1950s. His collaborations with the likes of Johnny Ace, Bobby "Blue" Band, Roscoe Gordon, Howlin' Wolf, B.B. King, and Otis Rush were released on Chess, Modern, and RPM. By the mid-1950s, he was high profile club attraction based in St. Louis. One night in 1956, Annie Mae Bullock—who'd moved from Knoxville, Tennessee to St. Louis to try to build a career as a vocalist—was given a chance to sing with his band during a club date. Impressed with her performance, Turner asked her to join the group; they would get married in 1958.

The couple's recording breakthrough came unexpectedly in 1959 when a singer tapped to record Ike's composition, "A Fool in Love," failed to appear for the scheduled session. Tina (her adopted stage name) was substituted and the track (Sue 730) reached number two on the R&B charts (#27 pop) the following year. As a result, Ike decided to focus the act on Tina, bringing in a female backing group (the Ikettes), and working out arrangements and choreography to take advantage of her dynamic voice and stage presence. They recorded a long string of R&B hits for a variety of labels—including Kent, Loma, Modern, Philles, Warner Bros., Innis, Blue Thumb, Minit, and Liberty—in the 1960s, though few performed well on the pop charts. Producer Phil Spector had been particularly interested in packaging the duo for a wider audience through his renown "wall-of-sound," but the commercial failure of his reputed masterpiece, "River Deep, Mountain High" (Philles 131; 1966; #88 pop)—though it did reach number one in England—reputedly led to his decision to retire from the music business.

The late 1960s, however, brought a change of fortune as roots-based sounds once again began dominating mainstream pop. They received invaluable exposure by touring with the Rolling Stones and performing on major television programs and Las Vegas venues. Among their best-selling singles were "I Want to Take You Higher" (Liberty 56177; 1970; #34), "Proud Mary" (Liberty 56216; 1971; #4), and "Nutbush City Limits" (United Artists 298; 1973). Their albums also regularly made the charts, most notably *Outta Season* (Blue Thumb 5; 1969), *In Person* (Minit 24018; 1969), *River Deep-Mountain High* (A&M 4178; 1969; recorded 1966), *Come Together* (Liberty 7637; 1970), *Workin' Together* (Liberty 7650; 1970), *Live at Carnegie Hall/What You Hear Is What You Get* (United Artists 9953; 1971), *'Nuff Said* (United Artists 5530; 1971), *Feel Good* (United Artists 5598; 1972), and *Nutbush City Limits* (United Artists 180; 1973).

Despite their commercial success, the couple's marriage was in trouble. Tina ultimately decided to leave the act in Dallas during a 1975 tour; she obtained a divorce the following year. While she went on to both commercial and artistic success as a solo performer in the 1980s, Ike found nothing but problems. Not only did his recording activities fail to go anywhere, but he was dogged by a rash of drug and other personal problems. The one bright spot was the public's continued interest in the classic work of the Ike and Tina Turner Revue, which has led to the release of many recorded anthologies as well as original albums such as *Dance* (Collectibles 5759; 1996), *Don't Play Me Cheap* (Collectibles 5763; 1996), *Dynamite* (Collectibles 5298; 1994), and *It's Gonna Work Out Fine* (Collectibles 5137; 1994). He would finally receive a measure of recognition late in life when his album, *Risin' With the Blues*, earned a Grammy for Best Traditional Blues Album.

Table 15

Big Joe Turner, May 18, 1911-November 14, 1985

One of the leading shout blues interpreters of the 1930s and 1940s, Big Joe Turner—he was six feet, two inches in height, and weighed 300 pounds—would later find a whole new audience as a rock 'n' roll trailblazer. Taken in its entirety, his career represented a synthesis of most major twentieth century styles, including gospel, blues, swing, rhythm and blues, jazz, and rock 'n' roll.

Turner grew up in Kansas City, absorbing gospel singing in church, and folk, blues, and pop songs from local performers and sound recordings. In addition to selling papers and junk as a youth, he earned money singing with a blind guitarist in the streets. By the late 1930s, he had become a highly regarded blues singer though limited to performing in rundown bars and theaters in the Midwest. He was also garnering attention as a songwriter; his compositions included "Cherry Red," "Hold 'Em Pete," "Lucille," "Piney Brown Blues," and "Sun Risin' Blues." His earliest known recordings—done in a boogie-woogie style which was back in vogue following his success at the December 23, 1938 Carnegie Hall "Spirituals To Swing" concert—were made for Vocalion on December 30, 1938, with Pete Johnson: "Goin Away Blues" and "Roll 'Em Pete."

The duo would work together at Café Society and Café Society Uptown in New York City for the next five years as well as recording for Decca in 1940. Turner continued to make records for the label's Race and Sepia series for the next four years, both solo and with Willie "The Lion" Smith, Art Tatum, Sam Price, and the Freddie Slack Trio. Turner cut eleven singles for National Records between 1945-1947, but with limited success. He spent the next few years recording for a wide variety of companies—

including Freedom, MGM, Down Beat/Swingtime, Modern/RPM, Aladdin, Rouge, Imperial, and DooTone—but making little impact due to declining interest in the blues.

Sensing his potential as an updated R&B belter, Atlantic Records added him to their roster in 1951. Now referred to as the "boss of the blues," Turner enjoyed his greatest success as a recording artist with hits such as "Chains of Love" (Atlantic 939; 1951; #2 R&B, #30 pop), "The Chill Is On" (Atlantic 949; 1951; #3 R&B), "Sweet Sixteen" (Atlantic 960; 1952; #3 R&B), "Don't You Cry" (Atlantic 970; 1952; #5 R&B), "Honey Hush" (Atlantic 1001; 1953; #1 R&B, #23 pop), "Shake, Rattle, and Roll" (Atlantic 1026; 1954; #1 R&B, #22 pop), "Flip Flop and Fly" (Atlantic 1053; 1955; #2 R&B), "Hide and Seek" (Atlantic 1069; 1955; #3 R&B), and "Corrine Corrina" (Atlantic 1088; 1956; #2 R&B, #41 pop). When the singles stopped charting after 1958, he shifted his focus to albums, proving equally adept at classic blues, jazz, and R&B-inflected rock 'n' roll. Notable releases included *The Boss of the Blues* (Atlantic 1234; 1956), *Joe Turner* (Atlantic 8005; 1957), *Rockin' the Blues* (Atlantic 8023; 1958), *Big Joe Is Here* (Atlantic 8033; 1959), and *Big Joe Rides Again* (Atlantic 1322; 1960).

He continued to record up to his death for many labels, including Arhoolie, United Artists, MCA, Black and Blue, Big Town, Spivey, Muse, Savoy, and Pablo. Many of his classic recordings have been reissued on compilations such as *His Greatest Recordings* (Atco 376; 1971), The *Big Joe Turner Anthology* (Rhino 71550; 1994), and *Volume 1: I've Been to Kansas City* (Decca/MCA 42351).

Table 16

Vee-Jay Records

According to Old Town Records executive Sam Weiss, "Vee-Jay came the closest to being the number one black-owned pop label….They penetrated the white market like a cannonball going through butter. Had they overcome the family and financial problems that ultimately destroyed them, they would have become as big as Motown."

Vee-Jay was founded by deejay Vivian Carter and her husband, Jimmy Bracken, in Gary, Indiana, in 1953, in order to provide an outlet for the kin of black rhythm and blues that was still hard to find on records. The label's first two singles, Jimmy Reed's "High and Lonesome"/"Roll and Rhumba" (Vee-Jay 100; 1953) and the Spaniels' "Baby It's You"/"Bounce" (Vee-Jay 101; 1953; #10 R&B; the A-side was the first song recorded by the company), sold well, enabling Vee-Jay to adopt a more ambitious recording agenda. In addition to Reed and the Spaniels, the label found success in the 1950s with R&B acts such as the El Dorados, Jerry Butler, the Dells, Dee Clark, the Magnificents, John Lee Hooker, and Wade Flemons.

By 1955, Vee-Jay was successful enough to have established its own house band for use in the studio; key members included Lefty Bates on guitar, Quinn B. Wilson on bass, Paul Gusman and Vernel Fournier in drums, Horace Palm on piano, Red Holloway, Lucias Washington, and McKinley Easton on sax, Harlen Floyd on trombone, arrangers Von Freeman and Riley Hampton, and bandleader Al Smith. In 1957, the label began issuing albums and founded its first subsidiary, Falcon, in order to garner a greatly broadcast share (the threat of a lawsuit from a southern label led Vee-Jay to rename it Abner; another subsidiary, Tollie, would be created in the early 1960s). In 1958, the company formed a jazz department (signees would include Eddie Harris, Bill Henderson, Lee Morgan, Wynton Kelly, and Wayne Shorter), and substantially expanded its slate of gospel releases the following year, the first group of LPs featuring the Staple Singers, Swan Silvertones, Five Blind Boys, and Highway QC's.

By 1960, Vee-Jay had its own headquarters building at 1449 Michigan Avenue, Chicago, and had adopted its distinctive label design: a rainbow-colored band around a black and silver background which featured an inset red and white oval logo. In an attempt to garner a greater share of the mainstream pop market, the company issued Butler's "Moon River" (Vee-Jay 405; 1961; #11 pop, #14 R&B, #3 easy listening), the first time it scored on three national charts simultaneously.

Vee-Jay was recognized as a major force within the record industry by early 1963, having scored number one hits with Gene Chandler's "Duke of Earl" (Vee-Jay 416; 1961) and the Four Seasons' "Sherry" (Vee-Jay 456; 1962), "Big Girls Don't Cry" (Vee-Jay 465), and "Walk Like A Man" (Vee-Jay 485; 1963). Furthermore, they were given U.S. distribution rights to EMI artists Frank Ifield and the Beatles. Ifield's "I Remember You" (Vee-Jay 457; 1962) reached number five, but a succession of releases by the soon-to-be famous Fab Five all flopped.

By late 1963, however, the label was threatened by a rash of lawsuits, many of which were instigated by artists such as the Four Seasons due to poor bookkeeping practices and the failure to keep up with royalty payments. Ultimately, the loss of its leading artists—and the failure to find new talent at the height of the British Invasion—caused Vee-Jay to close its offices and file for bankruptcy in May 1966. Beginning in the early 1990s, the company's classic material was being reissued by the New York-based Vee-Jay Limited Partnership.

Table 17

Jackie Wilson, June 9, 1934-January 21, 1984

Jackie Wilson rivaled James Brown as one of the most dynamic performers of his generation, exuding a sexy athleticism capable of working his audience into a frenzy.

He was also one of the most versatile vocalists in the rock era, ranging from the soulful, gritty style of a Wilson Pickett to the smooth, gospel-inflected pop associated with Sam Cooke and Clyde McPhatter.

Born and raised in a blue collar section of Detroit, Wilson would win his Golden Gloves weight division in the late 1940s. After high school, he began singing in local nightclubs. In 1953, Wilson joined Billy Ward and His Dominoes as a replacement for McPhatter, who'd departed to found the Drifters. During his tenure the group recorded "St. Therese of the Roses" (Decca 29933; 1956), which reached number thirteen on the pop charts.

Wilson went solo in late 1956, signing with Brunswick Records. Between 1957-1972 he recorded forty-nine charting singles, including the Top Ten hits "Lonely Teardrops" (Brunswick 55105; 1958), "Night" (Brunswick 55166; 1960), "Alone At Last" (Brunswick 55170; 1960), "My Empty Arms" (Brunswick 55201; 1961), "Baby Workout" (Brunswick 55239; 1963), and "(Your Love Keeps Lifting Me) Higher and Higher" (Brunswick 55336; 1967). When record sales dropped off, he was relegated to playing the oldies circuit. On September 25, 1975, as part of the Dick Clark revue at the Latin Casino in Cherry Hill, New Jersey, he suffered a major heart attack while singing "Lonely Teardrops." Emerging from a coma with considerable brain damage, he never performed again. He was inducted into the Rock and Roll Hall of Fame in 1987.

Doo-Wop

Doo-wop represents a subcategory of vocal group harmony that includes the following musical qualities: group harmony, a wide range of vocal parts, nonsense syllables, a simple beat, light instrumentation, and simple music and lyrics. Above all, the focus is on ensemble singing. Single artists fit only when backed by a group (the possibility that the group may not be mentioned on the record label is immaterial). Typically solo billing simply means that this individual is more prominently placed in the musical arrangement (e.g., Dion, Bobby Day, Thurston Harris) as opposed to typical group productions.

Group Harmony

In doo-wop vocal harmonies echo--or, more commonly--run underneath the lead vocalist. Generally, the second tenor and baritone blend together as one sound, with the high tenor (or falsetto) running over the lead and the bass reverberating on the bottom end. The group harmony does not usually lead throughout; however, it may occasionally alternate with a tenor in this capacity (e.g., the Channels--"The Closer You Are").

In the early 1950s, groups like the Ravens and Five Keys pushed vocal blending techniques from the r & b realm to doo-wop with the use of "blow harmonies." This practice, wherein sounds like "ha-oo" resulted by abruptly forcing air out of the mouth, replaced humming as the predominant form of background support.

The genre sometimes utilized the device of progressive entrances by different voices. In most cases, the bass would begin, with others entering one at a time, until full harmony was achieved. Two notable 1958 releases, Dion and the Belmonts' "Tell Me Why" and Danny and the Juniors' "At the Hop," employed this technique as a primary hook.

In short, doo-wop harmonies evolved to a more complicated level than that reflected in the call-and-response format found in gospel. However, the genre lacked the musical depth—obtained through use of the minor keys--typifying the mature work of the Beach Boys.

The Wide Range Of Vocal Parts

The lead singer was usually a tenor, although sometimes a high tenor (or child castrato, the archtype being Frankie Lymon). Occasionally the bass will take the lead for at least part of a song, typically uptempo numbers (e.g., El Dorados--"Bim Bam Boom"). The lead in early doo-wop ballads frequently employed melisma, a gospel-derived vocal technique in which syllables are elongated to fit the meter of the song (e.g., "O-o-only You" in the Platters' "Only You").

Most song arrangements had a distinctive bass part, frequently it provided the introduction and/or punctuated the song between choruses. In some cases, the bass contributed a talking bridge in the middle of a song (e.g., the Diamonds' "Little Darling") or a percussive beat. All-female groups would substitute a contrasting lower voice for the bass part.

Falsetto parts were often used, typically at the end of a song, in conjunction with the lead's dramatic fade-out (e.g., "Tell Me Why," by Norman Fox and the Rob Roys; "Since I Don't Have You," by the Skyliners). In ballads, the falsetto part echoes the lead voice, is part of the background harmony, or runs above the vocal blend. The lead singer may move in and out of falsetto (e.g., the Channels' "The Closer You Are") or use it throughout (e.g., the Paragons' "Florence").

Nonsense Syllables

Nonsense syllables were derived from bop and jazz styles, traditional West African chants, a cappella street corner singing (in place of the instrumental bass line), and doo-wop-styled r & b songs during the 1950-1951 period (e.g., the Dominoes' "Harbor Lights"). They were commonly used in the bass and harmony parts; their use tends to be more restrained, simple, and somber when employed in ballads ("doh-doh-doh," "doo-wah," etc.). The Chips' "Rubber Biscuit" (1956) represented a virtuostic application of this technique:

Gow gow hoo-oo,
Gow gow wanna dib-a-doo,
Chick'n hon-a-chick hole-a-hubba,
Hell fried cuck-a-lucka wanna jubba,
Hi-low 'n-ay wanna dubba hubba,
Day down sum wanna jigga-wah,
Dell rown ay wanna lubba hubba,
Mull an a mound chicka lubba hubba,
Fay down ah wanna dip-a-zip-a-dip-a,
Mm-mh, do that again! (bass exclamation)
Gow gow lubba 'n a-bubba lubba,
Ow rown hibb'n 'n a-hibba-lu,
How low lubbin 'n a-blubba-lubba,
Hell fried ricky ticky hubba lubba,
Dull ow de moun' chicky hubba lubba,
Wen down trucka lucka wanna do-uh,
How low a zippin 'n a-hubba-lu,
Hell fried ricky ticky blubba-lu,
How low duh woody woody pecka pecka. (BMI)

During the doo-wop revival (1960-1963), nonsense lyrics became more complicated, almost baroque in style. These lyrical contortions sometimes became the main focus; e.g., the Edsels' "Rama Lama Ding Dong" (1961), the Marcels' "Blue Moon" (1961).

Simple Beat/Light Instrumentation

Since doo-wop rhythms were originally provided by the snapping of fingers and clapping of hands, background beats are usually simple and heavy (with an emphasis on the second and fourth beats). Instruments such as the piano, guitars, saxes, and drums were often used to accompany vocalist but remained very much in the background. An instrumental break usually appeared after two verses. Those rare songs without a break included the Charts' "Deserie" (1958) and the Flamingos' "I Only Have Eyes For You" (1959). In both of these instances, the choral refrain is repeated throughout the song.

Simple Chorus and Lyrics

Doo-wop music is often comprised of four-chord progressions. Even uptempo renditions of old standards generally flatten out the melody line; i.e., rendering it in a more simplified form (e.g., "A Sunday Kind of Love," "Stormy Weather"). The lyrics tend to be repetitive, simple, dialectical, and awkwardly-phrased. Some are even grammatically incorrect. Nevertheless, many transcend these limitations to convincingly express such complex feelings as disillusionment, desire, and love.

Evolution of the Genre

Doo-wop emerged in the urban ghettos from the blending of rhythm and blues, gospel, and popular black vocal group music in the post-World War II era. The style represented the culmination of many hours spent by teens--usually black males--practicing vocal harmonies in school gyms, street corners, and subway entrances. These young groups sought a piece of the American Dream via cross-over success in the music business. From their perspective, the more direct route to success meant adapting white pop standards to contemporary black vocal styles. In other words, they attempted to replicate the formula employed a generation earlier by black groups like the Mills Brothers and the Ink Spots. The pronounced gospel and r & b traits within their work reflected the influences from childhood (church, social activities, etc.) which formed the core of their music education. Doo-wop features began emerging in African American pop music during the 1948-1951 period. They can be discerned in r & b hits like the Orioles' "It's Too Soon To Know" (1948) and the Dominoes' "Sixty-Minute Man" (1951). The doo-wop era began around 1952--a time when the key musical qualities of the genre were all clearly in evidence--and remained artistically and commercially viable until the early 1960s. This time frame can be subdivided into several phases of stylistic development:

Paleo-Doo-Wop (1952-1954)

This subgenre retains many visible features of its stylistic ancestors; e.g., r & b in the Drifters' "Money Honey"; gospel in "The Bells of St. Mary's," by Lee Andrews and the Hearts; black pop vocal groups in the Platters' "Only You." These traits had yet to be synthesized into a truly singular style. Other notable records from this period included The Cadillacs--"Gloria" (1954) The Chords--"Sh-Boom" (1954; the cover by the Crewcuts became one of the biggest hits of that year), The Crows--"Gee" (1954), The Drifters--"Honey Love" (1954), The Harptones--"A Sunday Kind of Love" (1954), The Jewels--"Hearts of Stone" (1954), The Orioles--"Crying in the Chapel" (1953), and The Penguins--"Earth Angel" (1954).

Classical Doo-Wop (1955-1959)

This phase featured tight and sweet harmonies; however, the lead singers lost much of the smoothness typifying paleo-doo-wop recordings. Bass singers were given a more prominent role; in the past they had tended to function merely as part of the background harmony.

The performers were generally quite young, featuring lyrics primarily concerned with young, idealistic love. Nonsense syllables were employed in the majority of songs. Instrumentation remained in the background, albeit with a heavy backbeat. Key recordings included The Cleftones--"Little Girl of Mine" (1956), The Del Vikings--"Come Go With Me" (1957), The El Dorados--"At My Front Door" (1955), The Five Satins--"In the Still of the Night" (1956), The Flamingos--"I Only Have Eyes For You" (1959), The Heartbeats--"A Thousand Miles Away" (1956), The Monotones--

"Book of Love" (1958), The Rays--"Silhouettes" (1957), The Silhouettes--"Get a Job" (1958), and The Willows--"Church Bells May Ring" (1956).

The classical period saw the development of a wide array of spinoff styles, in part a response to newly devised marketing strategies:

(a) Schoolboy doo-wop. The focal point here was an ultra-high tenor, usually a male in his early teenage years. While Frankie Lymon was the definitive interpreter from the standpoint of both commercial success and singing prowess, he has many imitators, including brother Lewis Lymon (the Teenchords), the Kodaks, the Schoolboys, and the Students. Among the notable hits were Little Anthony and the Imperials--"Two People in the World" (1958), Frankie Lymon and the Teenagers-"Who Do Fools Fall in Love" (1956), and The Schoolboys--"Shirley" (1957).

(b) Gang doo-wop. Lead singers studiously avoided being smooth; rather, they seemed to swagger as they sang. Likewise, harmonies, though intricate, were rough in approach. Major hits included The Channels--"That's My Desire" (1957), The Charts--"Desiree" (1958), and The Collegians--"Zoom Zoom Zoom" (1957).

(c) Italo-doo-wop. Like African Americans, Italian Americans accorded music a prime place in their upbringing (through church). Although isolated white groups had appeared in the early 1950s (e.g., the Bay Bops, the Neons, the Three Friends), the first major wave of white doo-wop acts surfaced in 1958. This variant was distinguished by even tighter group harmonies, roughly-hewn tenors pushing their upper registers to produce a "sweet" sound, and the prominence of bass singers (the latter a premonition of the neo-doo-wop phase). Notable recordings included The Capris--"There's a Moon Out Tonight" (1958; 1961), The Classics--"Till Then" (1963), The Elegants--"Little Star" (1958), and The Mystics--"Hushabye" (1959).

(d) Pop doo-wop. Heavily influenced by the commercial mainstream going as far back as turn-of-the-century barbershop quartets, this style had little in common with classic doo-wop other than tight harmony. Practitioners developed a number of ploys geared to making inroads into the pop market, most notably (1) cover records, (2) softening the doo-wop sound in order that it might reach a broader range of age groups, and (3) jazzing up adult-oriented standards so as to appeal to youth. Among the more popular records in this vein were The Duprees--"You Belong to Me" (1962), The Echoes--"Baby Blue" (1961), The Fleetwoods--"Come Softly to Me" (1959), The Temptations (white group)--"Barbara" (1960), and The Tymes--"So Much in Love" (1963).

Neo-Doo-Wop (1960-1963)

The impetus for this phase was the oldies revival (largely focused on doo-wop) which began in 1959. Although neo-doo-wop maintained the simple melody lines and preoccupation with love lyrics typifying the classical phase, the distinctive features of doo-wop were greatly exaggerated; e.g., a greater preponderance of falsetto leads, heavier and more pronounced bass singing. Instruments also figured more prominently in song arrangements. Notable hits included Gene

Chandler with the Dukays--"Duke of Earl" (1961), The Devotions--"Rip Van Winkle" (1961; 1964), Dion with the Del Satins--"Runaround Sue" (1961), Curtis Lee With the Halos--"Pretty Little Angel Eyes" (1961), The Paradons--"Diamonds and Pearls" (1960), The Reflections--"(Just Like) Romeo and Juliet" (1964), The Regents--"Barbara Ann" (1961), and The Stereos--"I Really Love You" (1961).

The absorption of new talent from a variety of backgrounds spurred the development of new stylistic subcategories:

(a) Tin Pan Alley Doo-Wop. Exposed to doo-wop as well as schooled in music composition, young songwriters (e.g., Gerry Goffin/Carole King, Barry Mann/Cynthia Weil, Jeff Barry/Ellie Greenwich) and producers (Phil Spector) created their own formula. They melded doo-wop conventions (e.g., tight harmony, pronounced bass, nonsense syllables) with more complex melodies, augmented instrumentation, and thoroughgoing production values. Key recordings included The Chiffons--"He's So Fine" (1963), The Crystals--"Da Doo Ron Ron" (1963), The Raindrops--"The Kind of Boy You Can't Forget" (1963), Randy and the Rainbows--"Denise" (1963), and The Tokens--"Tonight I Fell in Love" (1961)

(b) Distaff Doo-Wop. With few exceptions (e.g., the Chantels, the Bobbettes, the Shirelles, and fronting male groups such as the Platters), women didn't play a prominent role in doo-wop until the Tin Pan Alley variant achieved popularity. Notable hits included Patti LaBelle and the Blue Belles--"You'll Never Walk Alone" (1963), The Cookies--"Don't Say Nothin' Bad About My Baby" (1963), and Reperata and the Delrons--"Whenever a Teenager Cries" (1964)

(c) Garage Band Doo-Wop. Denotes material recorded on substandard equipment. Representative examples included the Laddins' "Did It" and the Contenders' "The Clock."

(d) Novelty Doo-Wop. Almost without exception, this genre encompasses humorous, uptempo material. Themes covered include fantasy (e.g., the Eternals' "Rockin' in the Jungle," the Cadets' "Stranded in the Jungle"), rebellion (e.g., the Coasters' "Yakety Yak"), fads (e.g., the Royal Teens' "Short Shorts," the Sparkletones' "Black Slacks), and media heroes (e.g., Dante and the Evergreens' "Alley Oop").

(e) Pseudo-Doo-Wop. This category refers to the doo-wop style minus the vocal group format. Major strains have included solo efforts (e.g., Ron Holden and the Thunderbirds' "Love You So," Rosie and the Originals' "Angel Baby") and duos (e.g., Skip and Flip's "Cherry Pie," Don and Juan's "What's Your Name," Robert and Johnny's "Over the Mountain").

Post Doo-Wop (1964-)

For all practical purposes, the genre ceased to function in a creative sense as elements associated with it virtually disappear from recordings. With few exceptions, words replaced nonsense syllables as background responses, harmony receded into the background, falsetto appeared less frequently, the bass was used less as a separate voice, instrumentation took on much greater importance, and melodies exhibited a much greater degree of variation. A number of groups--most notably the Drifters, the Four Seasons, and Little Anthony and the Imperials--crossed over into the pop mainstream. The primary innovations in vocal group singing now took place within the a cappella genre.

Table 18

The Drifters

With the possible exception of the Dells, the Drifters were more successful in adapting to stylistic changes within the pop music scene than any other doo-wop group. Beginning as a rhythm and blues act in the early 1950s, they shifted to a more pop-oriented sound to remain leading hitmakers throughout the classic rock 'n' roll era, and were still regularly denting the charts at the peak of the British Invasion, folk rock, and Motown Soul.

Clyde McPhatter, formerly lead singer with Billy Ward's Dominoes, formed the Drifters in 1953 with second tenor Gerhard Thrasher, baritone Andrew Thrasher, and bass Bill Pinkney. Before McPhatter entered the Army in the mid-1950s, the group enjoyed a strong of R&B hits featuring his smooth, sexy tenor voice, most notably "Money Honey" (Atlantic 1006; 1953; #1 R&B 11 weeks), "Such A Night"/"Lucille" (Atlantic 1019; 1954; #2/#7 R&B), "Honey Love" (Atlantic 1029; 1954; #1 R&B 8 weeks, #21 pop), "Bip Bam" (Atlantic 1043; 1954; #7 R&B), "White Christmas" (Atlantic 1048; 1954/1955/1956; #2/#5/#12 R&B), "What 'Cha Gonna Do" (Atlantic 1055; #2), "Adorable"/"Steamboat" (Atlantic 1078; 1955; #1/#5 R&B), and "Ruby Baby" (Atlantic 1089; 1956; #10).

Following a period of diminished record sales—and various personnel changes—the group disbanded in 1958. Because the Drifters had signed a multi-year contract with New York's Apollo Theater, their manager recruited another group, the Five Crowns, to fill the void. Assisted by the songwriting/production team of Leiber and Stoller, the new Drifters quickly outstripped their predecessors with releases like "There Goes My Baby" (Atlantic 2025; 1959; #2), reputedly the first R&B recording to utilize a sophisticated string arrangement, "Dance with Me" (Atlantic 2040; 1959; #15), "This Magic Moment" (Atlantic 2050; 1960; #16), "Save the Last Dance for Me" (Atlantic 2071; 1960; #1), and "I Count the Tears" (Atlantic 2087; 1960; #17).

When lead singer Ben E. King—who would record the solo hits "Spanish Harlem" (Atlantic 6185; 1960-1961; #10) and "Stand By Me" (Atlantic 6194; 1961; #4)—departed, the Drifters remained successful with recordings such as "Up On the Roof" (Atlantic 2162; 1962; #5) and "On Broadway" (Atlantic 2182; 1963; #9), which featured Rudy Lewis singing lead. Following his death in 1963, Johnny Moore became the frontman for bestsellers such as "Under the Boardwalk" (Atlantic 2237; 1964; #4) and "Saturday Night at the Movies" (Atlantic 2260; 1964; #18).

By 1967 the hits had stopped coming, although the group continued to perform well into the 1970s. The act was revived in the mid-1970s to capitalized on the oldies circuit. Releases of both new material and updated versions of the group's old hits, however, failed to compete with regular reissues of the classic Drifters recordings.

Table 19

The Platters

At the height of their career, the Platters were an anachronism, performing classic Tin Pan Alley material updated slightly to fit the rhythmic framework of the rock 'n' roll era. Founded by Herbert Reed in 1953, the group—which also included David Lynch, Paul Robi, and lead singer Tony Williams—initially recorded in a doo-wop style for the Federal label. Failing to achieve a hit record, members were working as parking lot attendants in Los Angeles when they met music business entrepreneur Buck Ram. Initially using them to make demonstration discs of his own compositions (which tended to fall within the crooning genre), Ram insisted that Mercury Records sign them as part of a package deal involving another of his clients, the Penguins, then on the verge of stardom with the recording, "Earth Angel" (Dootone 348; 1954-1955). In one of the supreme ironies in recording history, the Penguins faded from the public eye without another pop hit, while the Platters (adding Zola Taylor in late 1955) became the top-selling vocal group of the second half of the 1950s. Their Top Ten singles included "Only You" (Mercury 70633; 1955), "The Great Pretender" (Mercury 70753; 1955-1956; #1), "(You've Got) The Magic Touch" (Mercury 70819; 1956), "My Prayer" (Mercury 70893; 1956; #1), "Twilight Time" (Mercury 71289; 1958; #1), "Smoke Gets In Your Eyes" (Mercury 71383; 1958-1959; #1), and "Harbor Lights" (Mercury 71563; 1960).

The group's decline in the early 1960s has been attributed to a number of causes, most notably the morals arrest of the male members on August 10, 1959, the departure of Williams (one of the most gifted vocalists in pop) for a solo career in 1960, and changing consumer tastes. The Platters continued to enjoy steady album sales with the release of titles such as *Encore of Golden Hits* (Mercury 20472; 1960; 174 weeks on pop charts) and *More Encore of Golden Hits* (Mercury 20591; 1960).

By the early 1970s, the group—by then recording for Musicor—was considered a nostalgia act, sometimes performing in Richard Nader's rock 'n' roll revival shows. As copyright holder of the Platters' name, Ram continued to manage the official version of the group well into the 1980s. However, he was continuously forced to file lawsuits to keep pseudo groups from using the name. Greatest hits packages featuring the

Mercury material have remained popular; Rhino issued a two-disc anthology and the German Bear Family label released a nine-CD box set in the late 1980s. [Stambler. 1989.]

Table 20

A Cappella

A cappella is generally believed to mean voices without instrumental accompaniment. The term is actually of Italian derivation, translating literally as "in the chapel style." In its original usage, it referred to the singing done in church without instrumental accompaniment.

Within a modern context, a cappella is generally associated with the doo-wop tradition of the 1950s and early 1960s. The first hits in this style were recorded by a New Haven-based group, the Nutmegs, in 1955: "Story Untold" and "Ship of Love." Once doo-wop proved its commercial potential, the record labels which possessed sufficient financial resources began employing instrumental backups during studio sessions. As a result, by the late 1950s, a cappella was limited to amateur groups who practiced largely on street corners and in apartment hallways.

Since the late 1960s, the genre has been dominated by two acts, the Persuasions--whose albums have included *A cappella* (1968), *Street Corner Symphony* (1972), and *Chirpin'* (1977)--and 14 Karat Soul. The Black Contemporary group, Boyz II Men, revived interest in the genre by utilizing its conventions on a string of hit singles in the early 1990s.

Country and Western Music

Country music developed out of the folk traditions brought to North America by Anglo-Celtic immigrants and gradually absorbed influences from other musical sources until it emerged as a force strong enough to survive—and ultimately thrive—in an urban-industrial-oriented society. However, to explain the genre solely in terms of its British background would be a limited and incomplete approach. Settlers of pre-revolutionary America, throughout the 13 colonies, came out of essentially the same ethnic and social backgrounds. Malone points out that southern history must be studied in order to explain how the area east of the Mississippi River and below the Mason-Dixon line produced a diversity of and the cross-fertilization of musical styles—can be traced back to the earliest days of colonization in the deep South. The extreme pride typifying the region was in large part a result of a cultural inferiority complex which, in turn, arose out of the censure of the civilized world with respect to the institution of slavery and the lagging pace of urbanization and industrialization. This situation undoubtedly heightened the cultural isolationism already based on geographical and climatological factors. However, reference to the cultural isolationism of the South is perhaps should not be overemphasized. The South provided the setting for the melding of many cultures—particularly British, French, Spanish, and African elements—as well as the impetus for the settlement of much of the West. The steadfastly conservative stance adopted by southerners to ward off potentially disruptive external influences was concentrated largely within the socio-economic sphere (particularly with respect to the influx of influences from the North); in the face of the region's prejudices relatively few barriers existed to impede the exchange of musical ideas between cultures. While this musical cross-fertilization changed all of the genres concerned, country music continued to maintain its own sense of identity. Malone succinctly outlines the development of this phenomenon:

Not only are certain songs transmitted from generation to generation, but the manner of performing them, both vocally and instrumentally, is also passed on through the years. A folk style, created by the interchange of musical ideas and techniques among folk musicians and singers, proves to be a very tenacious factor. A folk style will persist long after the folk songs are forgotten. With the coming of urbanization the old rustic-based songs are discarded and the new ones become largely devoid of rural settings; however, in the style of its performance and in its basic construction the song is, in point of origin, rural in nature. A rural inhabitant or an urban dweller who has formerly lived in the country will likely render a song in a country manner even though the words of the song describe an urban scene or event. This is significant in view of the fact that migration from southern rural areas to southern and northern urban centers has been a steady factor in southern life. Southern cities have been populated largely by individuals of rural origin who carry with them their musical appreciation and tastes. These cities, then, to a great extent continue to be affected by rural attitudes and values. This in great measure explains why country music has endured in an urbanizing south, and why its lyric content has changed to fit the needs of a rural people who no longer live in rural surroundings. That music which thrives in a honky-tonk atmosphere or depicts the problems inherent in an urban existence can accurately be termed country music since it sprang from a rural origin. (Malone 1968, p. 10.)

The spread of country music in an era devoid of mass media outlets such as radio and television was rendered possible by territorial mobility, cultural exchange, and other forces set into motion by the socio-economic climate of the late 19th and early 20th centuries. The process involved the slow but steady evolution of the country genre via the assimilation of minor traits and styles.

When southern people moved into new areas, their music acquired new characteristics from the cultures with which they came in contact. Still, a distinct southern backwoods style predominated and provided the basis for other styles that ultimately arose. It is for this reason that such urban-oriented styles as "western swing" and "honky-tonk" music developed when rural people adapted their older music to new environments. Western swing, specifically, is the product of the change that took place when southerners moved to Texas and Oklahoma and adapted the rural- or mountain-based music to new developments and surroundings. (Malone 1968, p. 11.)

The rise of radio and the record industry were of inestimable importance in broadening the audience for country music. Long before country headliners began criss-crossing the nation in customized buses, these media brought the performers into the living rooms of fans in the large northern cities. However, the genre was long known by the somewhat derogatory term "hillbilly music." The cultural pride of the antebellum South was updated in the campaign of leading apologists for the genre to have the more dignified heading "country and western" employed (see 1949 below). Others sought mainstream acceptance via the aesthetically misguided strategy of diluting country recordings with pop orchestral arrangements.

A Country Chronology

June 30, 1922. "Uncle" Eck Robertson and Henry Gilliand record two fiddle tunes—"Sallie Goodin" and "The Arkansas Traveller" for Victor in New York. Scholars are largely in agreement that these were the first country recordings.

August 14, 1922. The Jankins Family, a gospel group from Georgia, become the first "old time" performers to be heard on the radio (WSB, Atlanta).

January 4, 1923. WBAP, Forth Worth, broadcast the first radio "barn dance" program.

June 14, 1923. Ralph Peer records Fiddlin' John Carson's "Little Old Log Cabin in the Lane," considered to be country's earliest hit. The Carson recording proved that country records could sell.

April 19, 1924. The debut of the *Chicago Barn Dance* (WLS), which went on to become the highly successful *National Barn Dance*. The program, which ran continuously until 1970, and launched such stars as Gene Autry, Red Foley, George Gobel, Grandpa and Ramona Jones, and Bradley Kincaid.

August 13, 1924. Vernon Dalhart records "The Prisoner's Song," backed with "The Wreck of the Old 97," the first country record to sell a million copies. Technically, Dalhart was the first singer to change from pop to country, having specialized in light opera and parlor songs prior to recording "The Prisoner's Song."

November 28, 1925. The *WSM Barn Dance,* later renamed the *Grand Ole Opry*, first broadcast from WSM's Studio A in Nashville. Uncle Dave Macon, credited with being the *Opry's* initial star, began appearing during the first year.

August 1927. The Carter Family and Jimmie Rodgers cut their first records for Ralph Peer of Victor, in Bristol, Tennessee/Virginia. These sessions mark the beginning of commercial country music.

September 28, 1928. Technically, the first record ever made in Nashville is a Victor field recording of early *Opry* string bands. The real start of regular recording in Nashville did not begin until 1945.

October 9, 1929. Gene Autry, who would become America's most popular "Singing Cowboy," makes his first record. His first movie role was a cameo in Ken Maynard's *In Old Santa Fe*. Later that same year Autry starred in *The Phantom Empire.*

1929. *The Singing Brakeman*, a 15-minute short starring Jimmie Rodgers, is made; it is probably the earliest country music movie.

1930. Ken Maynard, starring in *Song of the Saddle*, becomes Hollywood's first singing cowboy.

1930. Dr. J.R. Brinkley, the infamous "goat gland doctor," begins broadcasting country music from radio station XERA in Villa Acuna, Mexico, just across the border from Del Rio, Texas. XERA was instrumental in establishing country music on the West Coast via the migrants who left Oklahoma's dust bowl for California.

1933. Bob Wills forms his Texas Playboys, the definitive Western swing band in America.

1933. WLS's *National Barn Dance* joins NBC's Blue Network, the first country barn dance show to be aired nationally.

August 16, 1935. Patsy Montana records "I Want To Be A Cowboy's Sweetheart," the earliest country release by a female singer to sell a million copies.

1935. Juke boxes are introduced to truck stops and restaurants in the South. The juke box had a profound effect on the kinds of music that country performers recorded, and helped influence the development of the honky-tonk style.

May 1939. Red River Dave sings his composition "The Ballad of Amelia Earhart" on television, from the RCA Pavilion at the 1939 World's Fair in New York, and proclaims himself to be "the world's first television star."

October 1939. Bill Monroe makes his initial appearance on the Opry stage, singing "Muleskinner Blues," thereby giving birth to bluegrass music.

1940. Clell Summey, of Pee Wee King's Golden West Cowboys, plays the electric guitar on the Opry stage, claiming to be the first musician to do so; however, the priority is also claimed by Sam McGee and Paul Howard.

1941. Bing Crosby records "You Are My Sunshine" and "New San Antonio Rose." These were probably the first country "crossover" hits, popular with a national, not merely country, audience.

1941. An electric guitar is used for the first time on a country music record. According to the story, juke box operators complained to Ernest Tubb that his records could not be heard over the din of their noisy honky tonks. Tubb proceeded to employ Fay (Smitty) Smith, staff guitarist for KGKO in Fort Worth, to play electric guitar on one of his recording sessions.

1943. Elton Britt's "There's A Star-Spangled Banner Waving Somewhere, " a song about a crippled boy who wants to help with the war effort, becomes country music's first gold record (awarded by his label).

1943. Fred Rose and Roy Acuff form Acuff-Rose, the first song publishing firm located in Nashville. Acuff-Rose became an outlet for country songwriters like Hank Williams, who probably could not have obtained songwriting contracts in Northern urban centers.

1944. *Billboard*, the music industry's leading trade publication, introduces the first country music popularity charts, under the heading "Most Played Juke Box Folk Records," thereby further legitimizing the country music business.

March/April 1945. Red Foley records at WSM's Studio B; he is considered to be the first performer to record officially in Nashville, aside from the 1928 Victor field recordings.

September 11, 1945. Ernest Tubb makes "It Just Don't Matter Now" and "When Love Turns to Hate," under the direction of Decca's Paul Cohen, Nashville's first major producer; many date the real start of commercial recording in Nashville to this session. By 1960, less than 15 years after the first recording studio had been built, most of the major recording companies were doing all of their country recording in Nashville, and by 1963 Nashville had 10 studios, 10 talent agencies, four recording-pressing plants, 26 record companies, and nearly 2,000 musicians and writers.

September 18/19, 1947. Ernest Tubb and Ray Acuff headline New York's Carnegie Hall, the first country music show ever presented in that venue; people had to be turned away from the doors.

1947. Harold "Sticks" McDonald, of Pee Wee King's Golden West Cowboys, plays drums on the stage of the *Grand Ole Opry* His claim to have been the first to do so is disputed by Smokey Dacus, of Bob Wills and his Texas Playboys, who says that he played drums at the Opry in 1946—behind the curtains. Even today, nothing more than a simple set of snare drums is allowed on the Opry stage.

January 13, 1948. *Midwestern Hayride*, the first country music show to be broadcast regularly on television, debuts on WLW, Cincinnati.

1949. *Billboard* changes the name of its country music charts from "Most Played Juke Box Folk Records" to "Country and Western," thereby legitimizing the term in the business.

September 30, 1950. The *Opry* is broadcast by television for the first time.

1951. Patti Page and Tony Bennett record "Tennessee Waltz" and "Cold, Cold Heart," respectively, and achieve mass popularity for country songs for the first time since 1941. The Bennett recording is Hank Williams' first crossover hit and does much to make the latter's name known nationally.

1952. Eddy Arnold becomes the first country star to host a network television show when he is chosen to be Perry Como's summer replacement on NBC-TV.

1954. The pedal steel guitar is first used on record, played by Bud Isaacs on Webb Pierce's "Slowly."

1955. George Jones has his first hit, "Why Baby Why?" Johnny Cash makes his earliest recordings (on the Sun label).

1957. The Country Music Association, the oldest country music trade organization, is formed.

1958. The Kingston Trio's "Tom Dooley" wins the initial country music Grammy award. The group's growing popularity was an early signal that rockabilly was already entering a decline; "Tom Dooley" helped spark the folk music revival of the early 1960s.

July 19, 1960. Loretta Lynn's first hit, "Honky Tonk Girl," enters the *Cash Box* country music charts.

November 3, 1961. Fred Rose, Hank Williams, and Jimmie Rodgers are installed as the first members of the Country Music Hall of Fame.

December 13, 1961. Jimmy Dean's album, *Big Bad John*, becomes the first country music record to receive the gold certification (signifying sales of a million dollars) from the Recording Industry Association of America.

1964. Johnny Cash records "It Ain't Me, Babe," becoming the first country singer to cut a Bob Dylan song.

1966. Bob Dylan becomes the first of the new generation of rock singers to make a major album in Nashville, *Blonde on Blonde.*
October 1967. The first Country Music Association Awards show is held.

1967. The first country rock album— *Safe At Home* by the International Submarine Band, featuring Gram Parsons—is released. One year later, Parsons joins the Byrds and the group produces *Sweetheart of the Rodeo*, a milestone in that genre.

1969. *Hee Haw*, the highly popular syndicated country television show, makes its debut.

1971. The first annual Fan Fair is held in Nashville's Municipal Auditorium.

March 1972. The first Dripping Springs, Texas, "Picnic" is held; the three-day redneck-meets-hippie festival includes Willie Nelson, who began sponsoring the event the following year. Thus begins outlaw music's dominance of the genre.

1972. Loretta Lynn is elected the Country Music Association's "Entertainer of the Year," the first woman to be so honored.

1973. The Opryland amusement park opens for business.

March 19, 1974. The *Grand Ole Opry's* first show at the new Opry House, on the grounds of Opryland, U.S.A., takes place.

1974. George Hamilton IV becomes the first country performer to tour the U.S.S.R.

1976. *Wanted: The Outlaws* (RCA), featuring Waylon Jennings, Willie Nelson, Jessi Colter, and Tompall Glaser, becomes the first country music record to be awarded the platinum designation (signifying sales of 1,000,000 copies of an album) by the RIAA.

1980. The Mandrell sisters—Barbara, Louise, and Irlene—become the first female country singers to host a regularly scheduled network television show.

1980. Paramount releases the film, *Urban Cowboy*, starring John Travolta. The movie is largely responsible for making country music a bankable commodity with Middle America in the early 1980s. Prime growth areas include honky tonks (particularly Gilley's, a bar in Pasadena, Texas, where part of *Urban Cowboy* was filmed), country dress fashions and crossover hits, most notably by Mickey Gilley, Juice Newton, Dolly Parton, Kenny Rogers, Ronnie Milsap, and Eddie Rabbitt.

1980. George Strait hits the Country Top Ten with "Unwound" (MCA 51104); his follow-up hits help provide the impetus—along with artists such as the Judds, Rick Skaggs, and Randy Travis—for the hard country revival. Based upon the musical values of honky tonk, bluegrass, and other classic retro styles, hard country was a reaction to the country pop sound then ascendant in Nashville.

September 1981. The rise of MTV provides the viability of music within a video context. The Nashville Network and Country Music Television appear in short order as cable TV alternatives for fans interested in C&W video clips, concerts, interviews, and news.

September 28, 1991. Garth Brooks's *Ropin' the Wind* (Capitol Nashville 96330) reaches number one on the pop album charts. Brooks would credit he implementation of the soundScan by *Billboard* for enabling country artists to compete with pop and R&B performers on a level playing field. During the 1990s, Billy Ray Cyrus, Lee Ann Rimes, and many other country stars would find mainstream success.

Early 1990s. "Black Hat Acts" such as Brooks, Clint Black, John Michael Montgomery, and Tim McGraw dominate the country charts. No Depression music—a combination of roots-oriented C&W, the folk mythology of Woody Guthrie, and alternative rock attitude—is widely recognized as a commercially viable genre. Notable artists include Son Volt, Wilco, and the Old '97s.

Late 1990s. Nashville discovers that sex sells. Photogenic stars—particularly youthful females such as Faith Hill and the Dixie Chicks—become hot commodities.

The drive within the country field for respectability in the eyes of the music business establishment as well as the population at large has been the overriding theme in the genre's development during the 20th century. The major record labels were content to allow the independents to dominate the field until after World War II. Radio was somewhat more responsive; however, the modest rise of barn dances and other live country music performances represented a relatively small dent in an overall picture dominated by big-time network programming. Much has been made of the appearance of WSM's *Grand Ole Opry* broadcasts in 1925. In reality the event's short-term impact was largely symbolic in nature; many other clear—channel radio stations (e.g., WLS, Chicago; WBAP, Ft. Worth; WWVA, Wheeling) had successful barn dance programs. In the long-term, though, the Opry acted as a magnet for the country music industry, providing a central focus for recording, promotional, recreational and archival activities (see "September 11, 1945" above). The "Nashville Sound," under the leadership of Chet Atkins, projected the aura of urban sophistication combined with a proper respect for stylistic roots needed to render country music a powerful commercial force within the entertainment business beginning in the mid-1960s. Despite recent challenges to its hegemony, Nashville remains the commercial center and artistic soul of country music, thereby endowing the field with a solidarity and unified posture missing in all other spheres of American popular music. Still, underneath this seemingly homogenous exterior can be found the diversified array of styles that have endowed country music with its present day character. An awareness of these styles is central to an understanding of the broader entity.

The leading subgenres (derived from music historians Hume, 1982; Malone, 1968; and Stambler, 1969) include:

1. *The Bakersfield Sound.* Music performed by musicians centered in Bakersfield, California, in the late 1950s and early 1960s; for example, Buck Owens, Merle Haggard, and Wynn Stewart. The style is rawer and more rhythmic than the Nashville Sound. The first time country music

produced in California achieved popularity on a national level, marking the beginning of the end of Nashville's domination of country music recording.

2. *Bluegrass.* A comparatively modern style; the chief difference between bluegrass and the string band music of the Appalachian region that preceded it is the emphasis the former places on rhythm and on instrumental virtuosity. Two major schools exist: the instrumental style, often compared to jazz, most frequently associated with Bill Monroe, the father of blue-grass music, and "the high lonesome sound" (vocal music), best exemplified by the Stanley Brothers' output. Flatt & Scruggs, via the *Beverly Hillbillies* and the college concert circuit, stimulated a revival of the style in the 1960s; many rock artists (e.g. the Grateful Dead, Gram Parsons) incorporated it into their work.

3. *Cajun.* Music made by French colonials who eventually settled in southern Louisiana. It incorporates many elements of the French culture of the region: (a) it is usually sung in the local patois, which is a corrupt form of the French language; (b) many bands include both an accordion player and a fiddler; and (c) most songs are played in three-quarter waltz time. No performer adhering to a pure Cajun style has ever been commercially successful in the country field; however, many Cajun-influenced musicians such as Moon Mullican, Jimmy C. Newman, and Doug and Rusty Kershaw have had country hits.

4. *Conjunto.* A style of music popular along the border between Mexico and the U.S., incorporating elements of both Cajun and German music. Conjunto bands usually employ an accordion player, while the music is played in either waltz or polka time. Doug Sahm, Augie Meyer, and Freddy Fender have all been heavily influenced by the sound.

5. *Country Blues.* Often used as a code phrase to refer to music made by white singers who have incorporated Black elements into their style; for example, Jimmie Rodgers, Hank Williams, Bill Monroe, and Ronnie Milsap.

6. *Country Rock.* Amorphous genre including anything from country songs sung with rock instrumentation to rock songs sung by country singers, to country songs sung by rock singers, to country music sung by anyone who is not from the country. Classic country is generally acknowledged to have been the creation of Gram Parsons; he brought country to the attention of many rock artists, helped stimulate the singer/songwriter movement beginning in the early 1970 and, in the South, encouraged country-based performers to fuse that genre with rock.

7. *Folk Music.* Refers to two major strains: (a) country folk, which includes songs that have been passed down orally from generation to generation, usually originating with European material. Noteworthy exponents have been Bradley Kincaid and the Carter Family. (b) Urban folk differs in that the music is generally employed to achieve a political end. Chief practitioners have included Woody Guthrie, Pete Seeger, Joan Baez, and Bob Dylan.

8. *Gospel Music.* Also divided into two styles: while Black gospel is the more energetic and rhythmic of the two, white gospel has exerted a greater influence on country music. Because the genre features a more emotional, exhortative singing style than is the case with country, gospel-influenced singers like Roy Acuff, Wilma Lee, and Stoney Cooper have changed country vocalizing completely and helped to place the solo singer in the foreground, thereby leading to the creation of a star system.

9. *Hard Country.* Generally means making no concessions to fad or fashion, using classic country instruments (usually amplified) and featuring the singer rather than the accompaniment or the song. Sometimes used as a synonym for "classic country"; that is, music not adulterated by rock or blues styles.

10. *Honky Tonk Music.* Originally referred to any music played in a honky tonk. Later, it meant music amplified to be heard over crowd noise and addressing the patrons' real concerns—adultery, divorce, rootlessness, and drinking. A subgenre of hard country; leading practitioners have included Ernest Tubb, Lefty Frizzell, Hank Williams, George Jones, Hank Thompson, and Gary Stewart.

11. *The Nashville Sound.* Technically the style played by a certain group of musicians working in Nashville in the late 1950s and early 1960s. Because record companies did not allow individual performers to use their own bands and producers while making a record, and because Chet Atkins, who headed the A & R division for RCA in Nashville, had such a large roster of talent to produce, the instrumental arrangements—which utilized the same group of session musicians—became both predictable and standardized. Compared to the country music that preceded it, the Nashville Sound is slick and sophisticated. Prime exponents include Jim Reeves, Webb Pierce, and Floyd Cramer.

12. *Old Time Music.* Refers to either precommercial country music or the work of modern musicians who play in the old styles. Sometimes used interchangeably with the term "country folk music."

13. *Outlaw Country.* Originally designated a loose-knit group of musicians—Waylon Jennings, Willie Nelson, Tompall Glaser, Billy Joe Shaver, Kris Kristofferson, for example—who objected to the common Nashville practice of awarding creative control of recording sessions to the record company's staff producers rather than to the artists themselves. These artists chose to work outside the existing system by pressuring the record labels to give them control over their own work. As a result, the outlaws produced some of the best work of their respective careers and sold equally well to the non-country market and the traditional country core audience. This success undermined the dominance of the Nashville Sound, rendering the movement passé.

14. *Progressive Country.* A term coined in Texas during the early 1970s, when young, rock-influenced musicians began mixing with mainstream country musicians at places like the Armadillo World Headquarters in Austin. Ironically, the genre is often traditional in approach;

for example, Asleep at the Wheel's revival of the classic western swing of the late 1930s. Frequently used interchangeably with "redneck rock."

15. *Rockabilly.* A hybrid formed out of the intermingling of rhythm & blues and country. The best-known practitioners began their careers with Sun Records in Memphis, including Elvis Presley, Jerry Lee Lewis, Carl Perkins, Johnny Cash, and Charlie Rich. Others such as the Everly Brothers, Eddie Cochran, Little Jimmy Dickens, and the Johnny Burnette Trio helped elevate rockabilly to a preeminent position in the 1950s.

16. *Singing Cowboy Music.* Refers to the film output of Gene Autry, Tex Ritter, the Sons of the Pioneers, and others in the 1930s and 1940s. Because many country performers adopted the dress of a movie cowboy, the "western" designation was added to "country" in the late 1940s.

17. *The Texas Sound.* This term is practically synonymous with progressive country and redneck rock. It has been used to mean any band from Texas; a futile categorization considering that the state has a variety of musical styles.

18. *Tex-Mex Country.* Nationally, the style is represented solely by Freddy Fender. On a local level, the sound thrives in cities like Austin and San Antonio, where bands employ accordions and six-string basses to produce a hybrid conjunto sound.

19. *Western Swing.* While the genre draws from country music for much of its instrumentation and lyrics, it differs with respect to its rhythms (derived mainly from New Orleans jazz of the 1920s and 1930s) and sophisticated dance orchestra arrangements. Chief exponents included Bob Wills and his Texas Playboys, Milton Brown and his Musical Brownies, and Spade Cooley. After a sharp decline in popularity in the 1950s and 1960s, western swing was revived by rock-influenced artists such as Asleep at the Wheel in the 1970s.

Although country music sales were not damaged in the industry declines of 1979, and indeed the category increased its market share to around 20 percent in the next few years, in 1985 country record sales began a dramatic fall, with star performers selling only near break-even points (about 80,000 sales). By the 1990s, however, the genre was hotter than ever, shrewdly positioning itself as the music of Middle America as alternative rock and rap artists came to be increasingly viewed as too radical for mainstream consumption. [Albert 1984; Hemphill 1970; Hume 1982; Malone 1968.]

Table 21

Brooks and Dunn

Filling the vacuum caused by dissolution of the Judds in 1991, Brooks and Dunn became the most popular country music duo of the 1990s. Although solidly within the

New Traditionist movement, their eclectic style—incorporating elements of folk, blues, Cajoun, jazz, and pop—is a product of differing musical backgrounds.

Born in Shreveport, Louisiana, Kix Brooks, first became interested in a music career as a result of his friendship with the daughter of legendary country-pop singer, Johnny Horton. In addition to performing in clubs and other venues throughout high school, he spent considerable time developing his songwriting skills. After school, he worked in a variety of jobs (e.g., the Alaskan pipeline, performing at Maine ski resorts) prior to taking a staff songwriting position with Don Gant's Tree Publishing in Nashville. During the 1980s, artists such as John Conlee, Highway 101, and the Nitty Gritty Dirt Band made the charts with his compositions. When time permitted, he attempted to launch a recording career. A single, "Baby, When Your Heart Breaks Down" (Avion 103; 1983) reached number seventy-three on the country charts. His debut LP, Kix Brooks (1989), failed to make much headway, due in part to lack of promotional support.

Born in Coleman, Texas, Ronnie Dunn was inspired to play music by his father, who played guitar in a traditional country string band. Learning bass, he played in honky-tonk bars while still in high school. After his family moved to Tulsa, he headed the Duke's County house band. Securing a recording contract with Churchill, he placed a couple of song—"It's Written All Over Your Face" (Churchill 94018; 1983) and "She Put the Sad in All His Songs" (Churchill 52383; 1984)—on the lower rungs of the country charts.

After deciding to move to Nashville, Dunn joined Tree Publishing, meeting Brooks in the process. They were soon writing and performing as a unit. Already familiar with Dunn's demo tapes, Arista's CEO Tim DuBois signed the duo to a contract. Their initial release, "Brand New Man" (Arista; 1990) rose to the top of the country charts. An album, Brand New Man (Arista 18658; 1991) followed; it went triple platinum by 1993, reaching the Top Ten on the pop charts, with the help of three more number one singles, "My Next Broken Heart" (Arista; 1991) and the double-sided hit, "Neon Moon"/"Boot Scootin' Boogie" (Arista; 1992). Due to their rock-inflected hard country approach, Brooks and Dunn's albums—Hard Workin' Man (Arista; 1993), Waitin' on Sundown (Arista; 1994), Borderline (Arista; 1996), If You See Her (Arista; 1998), Tight Rope (Arista; 1999), and Steers and Stripes (Arista; 2001)—have continued to sell well in the pop marketplace.

Table 22

Fiddlin' John Carson, March 23, 1868-Decemver 11, 1949

Fiddlin' John Carson was the first "hillbilly" recording artist to achieve nationwide popularity. Prior to his appearance on the scene, record companies had employed mainstream singers—the most example being light opera veteran Vernon Dalnart, whose rendition of "The Prisoner's Song," sold a reputed five million copies, while igniting a rage for country/folk recordings—and professional musicians sight-reading from sheet music arrangements.

Hailing from Fannin County, Georgia, Carson worked at a variety of jobs—horse racing jockey, foreman at a cotton mill, house painting, and moonshining—while winning his state's fiddling championship seven times. His regional reputation was further enhanced when he began performing on radio station WSB, Atlanta on September 9, 1922. Atlanta phonograph and record dealer Polk Brockman prevailed upon the General Phonograph Corporation to record Carson for its flagship label during one of its southern field trips. The first session, overseen on June 14, 1923 by the legendary producer, Ralph Peer, resulted in the release of "The Little Old Log Cabin in the Lane"/"The Old Hen Cackled and the Rooster's Going to Crow" (Okeh 4800). Brockman immediately placed an order for 500 copies, and the disc's success led Okeh to bring Carson to New York City to record twelve (some experts place the total at fourteen) tracks on November 7-8, 1923. In all, he would record approximately 150 discs for the company from 1923-1931, often backed by a string band, the Virginia Reelers. His material included square dances, British folk ballads, cowboy songs, minstrel tunes, Tin Pan Alley fare, and topical compositions celebrating the events of the day. Among his best-selling releases were "You Will Never Miss Your Mother Until She Is Gone" (Okeh 4994; 1924), "Fare You Well, Old Joe Clark" (Okeh 40038; 1924), "Arkansas Traveler" (Okeh 40108; 1924), "John Henry Blues" (Okeh 7004; 1924), and "Old Dan Tucker" (Okeh 40263; 1925).

Carson worked as an elevator operator in his later years. He would intermittently cut material for RCA, much of which updated his earlier recordings. There has been a revival of interest in Carson's work in recent decades, stimulated by Gene Wiggins' book, *Fiddlin' Georgia Crazy: Fiddlin' John Carson, His Real World and the World of His Songs* (University of Illinois Press, 1987) and Document Records' release of his complete recordings in the late 1990s.

Table 23

Dixie Chicks

The Dixie Chicks are part of the youth brigade in 1990s country music, a movement that has placed as much emphasis on sexy, good looks as on musical talent. The Chicks, however, are highly accomplished musicians—founding member Martie Seidel finished third in the 1989 National Fiddle Championships—capable of playing a wide range of styles, including folk, bluegrass, hard country, and adult contemporary pop.

Seidel and her sister, banjo player Emily Erwin, formed the group—named after the Little Feat recording, "Dixie Chicken"—in 1989 with bassist Laura Lynch and guitarist Robin Lynn Macy. Their debut album, *Thank Heavens for Dale Evans* (Crystal Clear; 1990), exuded a traditional country and western feel. The next two LPs—*Little Ol' Cowgirl* (Crystal Clear; 1992) and *Shouldn't a Told You That* (Crystal Clear; 1993)—were transitional in nature, as the group edged toward a more modern sound. Macy had departed before the third album, followed by Lynch shortly after the group signed with Sony's resurrected Monument label in 1995.

With youthful lead vocalist/guitarist Natalie Maines as a replacement, the trio's breakthrough album, *Wide Open Spaces* (Monument; 1998), had a look that was as contemporary as their hook-laden country-pop. *Wide Open Spaces* became the top-selling group LP in country music history, moving more than four million units within the first year of its release, due in part to three hit singles: "I Can Love You Better" (Monument; 1998), "There's Your Trouble" (Monument 78899; 1998; #1 C&W, #36 pop), and "Wide Open Spaces" (Monument; 1998; #1). It earned a Grammy for Best Country Album, while the Chicks were named Favorite New Country Artist at the American Music Awards in addition to capturing Best Vocal Group honors and the Horizon Award from the Country Music Association. *Fly* (Monument; 1999), fueled by the hit single, "You Were Mine" (Monument; 1999; #1 C&W, #34 pop), also dominated the country charts as well as winning two Grammys in 2000, Best Country Album and Best Vocal Performance by Country Duo or Group.

Table 24

Faith Hill, September 21, 1967-

Faith Hill typifies the 1990s wave of best-selling solo singers found in the pop-rock and country genres. Possessing cover girl good looks and a smooth, processed vocal style perfect for crossing over to the pop charts, she has become one of the top media stars of the new millennium, a familiar figure in magazine celebrity bios, posters, and television ads.

Born in Jackson, Mississippi, Hill began singing in a variety of settings at an early age. Interested in emulating Reba McEntire's career as a country artist, she moved to Nashville at age nineteen. After working in a number of temporary positions (e.g., selling T-shirts at Fan Fair), she made her performing debut with songwriter Gary Burr. Securing a recording contract with Warner Bros., her first single—"Wild One" (Warner Bros.; co-produced by Burr)—spent four weeks at number one on the country singles charts in the fall of 1993. Her debut album, *Take Me As I Am* (Warner Bros.; 1994) also did well, reaching the country Top Ten and earning a gold record for million dollar sales.

Follow-up albums—*It Matters to Me* (Warner Bros. 45872; 1995), *Faith* (Warner Bros. 47690, 1998; #7), and *Breathe* (Warner Bros. 47871; 1999; #1)—have maintained Hill's upward career trajectory, most notably, find increasingly greater success abroad (particularly Asia) and with a mainstream pop audience. Further media attention has been generated by her storybook marriage to dashing country star, Tim McGraw. She has also branched out into other projects, providing background vocals for the recordings of Matraca Berg, Vince Gill, McGraw, and others, in addition to appearing on film soundtracks—*Maverick* (1994), *Practical Magic* (1998), *Prince of Egypt* (1998), and *Grinch* (2000); the TV special, *King of the Hill* (1999); and the Carole King tribute album, *Tapestry Revisited* (1995).

Table 25

The Judds

The top selling country music duo in recording history, the Judds were a Nashville institution by the time mother Naomi (born Diana Judd, January 11, 1946, in Ashland Kentucky) retired from the entertainment business in 1991 due to chronic hepatitis. Their pure, unadorned harmonies, acoustic guitar-dominated arrangements, and old-fashioned song lyrics placed them in the vanguard of the New Traditionalists, a new wave of 1980s artists dedicated to reviving the aesthetic of post-World War II hard country music.

Naomi married at seventeen; on May 30, 1964 she gave birth to Christina Cininella, who would later change her name to Wynonna. Following her divorce, she moved to Los Angeles in 1968 with her two daughters, earning a living by modeling, secretarial work and various other positions. In 1976, they relocated to Morrill, Kentucky, a rural area where many nights were spent listening to country radio stations. Following the example of many local musicians, the family began singing to Wynonna's guitar. Naomi finished nursing studies during a brief interlude in Northern California before settling in Nashville in 1979 to attempt a music career.

Taking advantage of performing opportunities, most notably appearances on Ralph Emery's early morning radio program, the duo secured a contract with RCA in 1983. On the strength of Wynonna's distinctive lead vocals and Naomi's gentle harmonizing, the Judds placed one song after another into the upper reaches of the country charts during the 1980s, including the number one hits "Mama He's Crazy" (RCA 13772; 1984), "Why Not Me" (RCA 13923; 1984), "Girls Night Out" (RCA 13991; 1985), "Love Is Alive" (RCA 14093; 1985), "Have Mercy" (RCA 14193; 1985), "Grandpa" (RCA 14290; 1986), "Rockin' with the Rhythm of the Rain" (RCA 14362; 1986), "Cry Myself to Sleep" (RCA 5000; 1986), "I Know Where I'm Going" (RCA5164; 1987), "Maybe Your

Baby's Got the Blues" (RCA 5255; 1987), "Turn It Loose" (RCA 5329; 1988), and "Change of Heart" (RCA 8715; 1988). Albums such as *Why Not Me* (RCA 5319; 1984), *Rockin' with the Rhythm* (RCA 7042; 1985), *Heartland* (RCA 5916; 1987), and *Greatest Hits* (RCA 8318; 1988) proved even more successful, achieving platinum status on the pop album charts.

Although the act remained on top until disbanding in 1991, Wynonna initally had doubts about continuing as a solo artist. Encouraged by her mother, Wynonna went on to release five platinum LPs through 2000—*Wynonna* (Curb 10529; 1992; #4), *Tell Me Why* (Curb; 1993), *Revelations* (Curb; 1996), *The Other Side* (Curb; 1997), and *New Day Dawning* (Curb; 2000)—all of which have featured a wider range of styles (including folk, pop, and rock) than that characterizing the Judds. In the meantime, the duo reunited for a New Year's Eve, 1999 concert—released in spring 2000 as *The Judds Reunion: Live* (RCA)—and released a newly-recorded single, "Stuck in Love," available only on a bonus disc within the limited-edition version of *New Day Rising*.

Table 26

Loretta Lynn, April 13, 1935-

Thanks in part to the popular biopic, *Coal Miner's Daughter* (1980), Loretta Lynn is the best known female vocalist in country music history. This recognition, however, is also a byproduct of her lengthy run as a hit-making artist. Furthermore, she wrote many of her classic recordings despite little formal education.

Born Loretta Webb in rural Butcher's Hollow, Kentucky, at age thirteen she married nineteen-year-old Oliver "Moonshine" Lynn. The couple moved to Custer, Washington, where Loretta had four children by age seventeen. While help make a living by doing other people's laundry and sometimes picking strawberries with migrant workers, she began writing songs using a Sears Roebuck guitar. Her husband advised her to turn professional, arranging dates in local performing venues as her manager.
Lynn recorded her first song, "Honky Tonk Girl" (Zero 1011; 1960), for the California-based Zero label as an eighteen-year-old. They promoted the disc by visiting country radio stations across the nation; as a result, it reached number fourteen on the country charts. Shortly thereafter, in October 1960, she appeared on the Grand Ole Opry for the first time; she would be invited on as a full-time performer in 1962. In the meantime, she became a touring member of the Wilburn Brothers Show from 1960-1968 and secured a recording contract with Decca Records.

Following her first Top Ten country song, the Owen Bradley-produced "Success" (Decca 31384; 1962; #6), the hits came at sporadic intervals. However, she was rarely off the charts for the next two decades following the release of the classic "Don't Come

Home A'Drinkin' (With Lovin' On Your Mind) (Decca 32045; 1966: #1). Other number one singles included "Fist City" (Decca 32264; 1968), "Woman of the World (Leave My World Alone)" (Decca 32439; 1969), "Coal Miner's Daughter" (Decca 32749: 1970; #83 pop), "After the Fire In Gone" (Decca 32776; 1971; #56 pop; with Conway Twitty), "Lead Me On" (Decca 32873; 1971; with Conway Twitty), "One's On the Way" (Decca 32900; 1971), "Rated 'X'" (Decca 33039; 1972), "Love Is the Foundation" (MCA 40058; 1973), "Louisiana Woman, Mississippi Man" (MCA 40079; 1973; with Conway Twitty), "As Soon As I Hang Up the Phone" (MCA 40251; 1974; with Conway Twitty), "Trouble in Paradise" (MCA 40283; 1974), "Feelins'" (MCA 40420; 1975; with Conway Twitty), "Somebody Somewhere" (MCA 40607; 1976), "She's Got You" (MCA 40679; 1977), and "Out of My Head and Back in My Bed" (MCA 40832; 1977). Her down-home demeanor, uncompromising treatment of themes vitally important to her fans, and plaintive vocals earned her the title "Queen of Country Music."

Lynn became a pop culture phenomenon when her autobiography, written with the assistance of *New York Times* reported George Vecsey, *Coal Miner's Daughter*, was one of the Top Ten selling books of 1976. The 1980 film version starred Sissy Spacek, who earned an Oscar for Best Actress on the strength of her performance (which included singing the Lynn songs appearing on the soundtrack). Lynn's mainstream popularity was further cemented by a series of network TV appearances, including *Fantasy Island*, *The Dukes of Hazzard*, and *The Muppet Show*.

Lynn is now an institution within the Nashville Establishment. She was the first female artist to win the Country Music Association's Entertainer of the Year award (1972) as has won both the CMA Female Vocalist of the Year and Vocal Duo of the Year awards on three different occasions. She is also the owner of various successful business ventures, including the entire town of Hurricane Mills, Tennessee, her current place of residence.

Table 27

LeAnn Rimes, August 28, 1982-

Country singer LeAnn Rimes, whose powerful, evocative vocals invited comparisons with Patsy Cline in the mid-1990s, has gone on to set her own benchmarks for pop crossover success. Still a teenager at the outset of the twenty-first century, she is on course to become one of the most successful recording artists in country music history.

Born in Jackson, Mississippi but raised in Garland, Texas, Rimes cut her teeth singing in local talent contests. By age eleven she had recorded an album for the indie label, Nor Va Jak. She then caught the attention of Dallas deejay and record promoter Bill Mack, who took control of her career. On the strength of an active performing schedule and television appearances across Texas, Mack secured a record contract with the Curb label. The press release for her first single, "Blue" (Curb 76959; 1996; #26 pop), claimed that Mack had written it in the early 1960s for Cline; when the singer died in a plane crash, he'd waited thirty years to find the right vehicle for the song. (Although both Mack and Kenny Roberts had recorded "Blue" for Starday in the 1960s, and a rendition by Kathryn Pitt had been released in her native Australia in 1993, widespread dissemination of the story by music journalists fed the myth that Rimes was the anointed successor to Cline's tradition.

"Blue" entered the *Billboard Hot 100* at number three, selling more than 123,000 copies in its first week of release, the highest amount ever measured up that point by the SoundScan tracking system. She became the youngest singer in the history of the Country Music Association awards to receive a nomination, both for the Horizon Award and Best Country Singer. She also won the 1996 Grammy Award for Best New Artist.

Since this auspicious beginning, her albums—*Blue* (Curb; 1996), *Unchained Melody: The Early Years* (Curb; 1997), *You Light Up My Life: Inspirational Songs* (Curb; 1997), *Sittin' on Top of the World* (Curb; 1998), *LeAnn Rimes* (Curb; 1999) and *I Need You* (Curb; 2001)—and singles—"How Do I Live" (Curb 73022; 1997; #1 country, #2 pop), "You Light Up My Life" (Curb 73027; 1997; #34). "Looking Through Your Eyes" (Curb 73055; 1998; #18 pop), "Written in the Stars" (w/Elton John; Rocket/Curb 566918; 1999; #29 pop), and "Big Deal" (Curb 73086; 1999; #23 pop)—have sold well on both the pop and country charts. "How Do I Live" was intended as the theme for the film, *Con-Air*, but the producers ultimately selected Trisha Yearwood's version of the song, considering it a better fit. Nevertheless, the Rimes rendition held the record for *Billboard* pop chart longevity as of early 2002; sixty-nine weeks in 1997-1998. In addition to its strong performance on the pop and country charts, it topped both the Adult Contemporary and dance charts, selling more than three million copies. Only time will tell, however, whether Rimes goes on even greater success as an adult as did Stevie Wonder, or ultimately flames out like another youthful star, Brenda Lee.

Table 28

Hank Snow, May 9, 1914

Although relatively unknown in the United States until 1949, Canadian-born Hank Snow—initially referred to as the "Yodelling Ranger"—was a first-generation disciple of Jimmie Rodgers. Although his hard country singing style fell out of favor in the late 1950s, he enjoyed a number one hit, "Hello Love" (RCA 0215) as late as 1974. An elder statesman of the genre for last thirty years of his career, Snow enjoyed hit records in the U.S. for five decades (from the 1940s to the 1980s), ranking twenty-first in success on the country charts through 1988 (source: *Top Country Singles 1944-1988*).

After singing in Nova Scotia clubs during his teens, he was given his own radio show on CHNS-Halifax, in 1934. His popularity in that region led to a contract with RCA in 1936. He relocated to the U.S. in the mid-1940s, working on the WWVA-Wheeling Jamboree, in Hollywood with his performing horse, Shawnee, and KRLD-Dallas. Snow's first appearance on the Grand Ole Opry, January 7, 1949—although poorly received—helped break his first nationwide country hit, "Marriage Vows" (RCA; 1949; #10).

His next hit, the self-composed "I'm Movin' On" (RCA; 1950), became one of the most successful country recordings of all-time, remaining number one for twenty-one weeks (and on the charts for forty-four weeks), selling more than one million copies. Now an Opry regular, his rich baritone voice, crisp enunciation, and preoccupation with authentic Americana (e.g., trains, Old West bank robberies) made him one of the genre's top stars into the early 1960s. His best-selling recordings included "The Golden Rocket" (RCA 0400; 1950), "Rhumba Boogie" (RCA 0431; 1952), "I Don't Hurt Anymore" (RCA 5698; 1954; gold record, #1 twenty weeks), "Let Me Go, Lover" (RCA 5960; 1954), and "I've Been Everywhere" (RCA 8072; 1962).

A longtime ambassador for country music, the "Singing Ranger" continued touring intermittently after RCA terminated his recording contract in the early 1980s; Snow's forty-five years with the company is believed to be an industry record. He was elected to the Country Music Hall of Fame in 1979.

Table 29

Randy Travis

Randy Travis was an instrumental figure in country music's transition from crossover ambitions to hard country retrenchment. Along with George Strait, he was the genre's dominant male vocalist prior to the hegemony of neo-traditionalist "hat acts" in the early 1990s, whose style he'd played a major role in nurturing.

Born Randy Traywick in Marshville, North Carolina, his father—a farmer and construction company entrepreneur who greatly admired classic honky tonk singers like Hank Williams, George Jones, and Lefty Frizzell—encouraged him to learn guitar as an eight-year-old. By the end of the 1960s, he had teamed with brother Ricky to perform at area venues as the Traywick Brothers. Running away to nearby Charlotte at sixteen after his brother was incarcerated, he won a talent contest at Country City U.S.A. The bar's owner, Lib Hatcher, immediately hired him as a performer, cook, and dishwasher. She also became his legal guardian when a judge pronounced him one transgression short of a long jail term.

As his manager, Hatcher helped Travis sign with the Paula label in 1978. Two singles—including "She's My Woman" (Paula 431; #91 C&W—issued in 1979 flirted with the country charts. The couple (who would marry in May 1991) relocated to Nashville in 1982, where she managed the Nashville Palace. As the resident performer there, Travis made a recording, the independently released *Randy Ray Live*, sold largely at the nightclub.

The publicity ensuing from the album and his live shows lead to a record contract with Warner Bros. in 1985. His first release, "On the Other Hand" (Warner Bros. 28962; 1985), did not sell particularly well; however, when reissued following the Top Ten success of "1982" (Warner Bros. 28828; 1985), it rose to number one. His first LP for the label, *Storms of Life* (Warner Bros. 25435; 1986), achieved triple platinum sales. The follow-up, *Always & Forever* (Warner Bros. 25568; 1987), went quadruple platinum and helped earn Travis the Country Music Association's Male Vocalist of the Year award for 1987. It also contained "Forever and Ever, Amen" (Warner Bros. 28384; 1987) the first of seven straight number one country singles, followed by "I Won't Need You Anymore" (Warner Bros. 28246; 1987), "Too Gone Too Long" (Warner Bros. 28286; 1987), "I Told You So" (Warner Bros. 28256; 1987), "I Told You So" (Warner Bros. 27969; 1988), "Honky Tonk Moon" (Warner Bros. 27833; 1988), and "Deeper Than the Holler" (Warner 27689; 1988). Although his first nine Warner Bros. albums all achieved platinum or gold status, his aching vocals and bedrock country arrangements have not translated to a wider pop audience.

Although eclipsed commercially by rock-influenced artists such as Garth Brooks, Travis remained an important country artist in the 1990s. He switched labels, signing with the newly formed DreamWorks, in 1997. *Inspirational Journey* (DreamWorks, 2000), a collection of traditional and contemporary religious material, represented a stylistic change of pace typifying artists who have achieved institutional status.

Crooners & The Tin Pan Alley Pop Tradition

Crooning represented a singing style primarily identified with male performers that enhanced light voices. Stylistic features included pitch slides and turns on accented notes (short trills with the note immediately above). The genre originated in the mid-1920s, being particularly suited to radio and the electrical recording process which both encouraged a softer vocal delivery. The popularity of sweet bands in the 1930s (e.g., Leo Reisman, Eddy Duchin, Guy Lombardo, George Olsen) further cemented the commercial ascendancy of the style.

Crooners developed a symbiotic relationship with the swing bands which dominated the 1940s. The big band sound would alternate between hot, jazz-inflected instrumentals and pop ballads (which featured a lead singer utilizing a crooning style). The top bands in this mold were fronted by Glenn Miller, Tommy Dorsey, Jimmy Dorsey, Harry James, and Benny Goodman.

By the time of the genre's heydey in the 1940s, crooners had developed a cool, urbane delivery (singing was rarely overstated). The top male vocalists, in particular, were promoted as romantic vehicles to the listening audience, a device which was later copied by the teen idols of the rock 'n' roll era. These singers relied heavily on Tin Pan Alley songwriters for material. Most of the best known ballads composed in the twentieth century--e.g., Blue Moon," "Stardust," "Sentimental Journey," "I Only Have Eyes For You," Deep Purple," "Always," "I've Got You Under My Skin," "Smoke Gets in Your Eyes," "When or When"--were performed over and over again by crooners. As country, rhythm and blues, and rock 'n' roll became commercially established in the 1950s, crooners turned increasingly to the practice of "covering" recordings originating from these genres. Covers were geared to mainstream pop listeners who--in the opinion of the major record label executives--were unlikely to relate to the explicit lyrics, raw emotive singing, and crude arrangements of the originals. Pat Boone, Tony Bennett, Georgia Gibbs, and Gale Storm were particularly successful (at least from a commercial standpoint) in cutting cover renditions. As this practice became increasingly discredited, crooning receded to the outer margins of recording industry.

Top Artists and Their Recordings

Gene Austin--"When My Sugar Walks Down the Street" (w/Aileen Stanley) (1925); "Yearning (Just For You)" (1925); "The Fapper Wife" (1925); "Way Down Home" (w/Carson Robison) (1925); "Yes Sir! That's My Baby"/"Everything Is Hotsy Totsy Now" (1925); "Let It Rain, Let It Pour" (1925); "I Never Knew" (1926); "Five Foot Two, Eyes of Blue"/"Sleepy Time Gal" (1926); "Bye Bye, Blackbird"/"Ya Gotta Know How to Love" (1926); "Tonight You Belong to Me" (1927); "I've Got the Girl" (1927); "Someday, Sweetheart" (1927); "Ain't She Sweet?" (1927); "My Blue Heaven" (1927); "The Sweetheart of Sigma Chi" (1927/8); "My Melancholy Baby"/"There's a Cradle in Caroline" (1928); "The Lonesome Road" (1928); "Ramona"/"Girl of My Dreams" (1928); "Without You, Sweetheart" (128); "So Tired" (1928); "Just Like a Melody Out of the Sky" (1928); "Jeannine (I Dream of Lilac Time)" (1928); "Memories of France"/"Old Pals Are the Best Pals After All" (1928); "She's Funny That Way" (1929); "Carolina Moon" (1929); "Weary River" (1929); "Wedding Bells Are Breaking Up That Old Gang of Mine" (1929); "Little Pal" (1929); "I've Got a Feeling I'm Falling" (1929); "Ain't Misbehavin'" (1929); "Please Don't Talk About Me When I'm Gone"/"When Your Lover Has Gone" (1931)

Tony Bennett--"Because of You" (1951); "Cold, Cold Heart" (1951); "Rags to Riches" (1953); "Stranger in Paradise" (1953); "There'll Be No Teardrops Tonight" (1954); "Cinnamon Sinner" (1954)

Pat Boone--"Ain't That a Shame" (1955); "Tutti Frutti" (1955); "Friendly Persuasion" (1956); "Love Letters in the Sand" (1957)

Al Bowlly—"Goodnight Sweetheart" (1931); "Blue Moon" (1935)

Rosemary Clooney--"Come On-A My House" (1951); "Half As Much" (1952); "Botch-A-Me" (1952); "Hey There" (1954); "This Ole House" (1954); "Mambo Italiano" (1954)

Nat "King" Cole--"Nature Boy" (1948); "Mona Lisa" (1950); "Too Young" (1951); "Somewhere Along the Way" (1952); "Walkin' My Baby Back Home" (1952); "Pretend" (1953); "Answer Me, My Love" (1954); "Smile" (1954)

Russ Columbo--"You Call It Madness" (1931); "Good Night, Sweetheart" (1931); "As You Desire Me" (1932)

Perry Como--"Long Ago (And Far Away)" (944); "I Dream of You" (1945); "I'm Gonna Love That Gal"/If I Loved You" (1945); "Till the End of Time"/"(Did You Ever Get) That Feeling in the Moonlight" (1945); "Dig You Later (A Hubba-Hubba-Hubba)" (1945/6); "I'm Always Chasing Rainbows"/"You Won't Be Satisfied (Until You Break My Heart" (1946); "Prisoner of Love"/"All Through the Day" (1946); "They Say It's Wonderful" (1946); "Surrender" (1946); "Sonata" (1946/7); "Chi-Baba, Chi-Baba (My Bambino Go to Sleep)" (1947); "When You Were Sweet Sixteen" (1947); "I Wonder Who's Kissing Her Now" (1947); "Because" (1948); "Far Away Places" (1949); "Forever and Ever" (1949); "A - You're Adorable" (1949); "Some Enchanted Evening"/"Bali Ha'i" (1949); "A Dreamer's Holiday" (1949/50); Hoop-dee-Doo" (1950); "Patricia" (1950); "A Bushel and a Peck" (w/Betty Hutton) (1950); "You're Just in Love" (w/Fontane Sisters) (1950/1); "If" (1951); "Maybe" (1952); "Don't Let the Stars Get in Your Eyes" (1952/3); "Wild Horses" (1953); "Say You're Mine Again" (1953); "No Other Love" (1953); "You Alone" (1953); "Wanted" (1954); "Papa Loves Mabo" (1954); "Hot Diggity" (1956); "Round and Round" (1957); "Catch a Falling Star" (1958)

Bing Crosby--"Wrap Your Troubles in Dreams" (1931); "Out of Nowhere" (1931); "Just One More Chance" (1931); "Just One More Chance" (1931); "I Found a Million-Dollar Baby"/"I'm Through With Love" (1931); "At Your Command"/"Many Happy Returns of the Day" (1931); "Stardust"/"Dancing in the Dark" (1931); "I Apologize" (1931); "Good Night, Sweetheart" (1931); "Gems From 'George White's Scandals'" (1931); "Dinah" (1932); "Where the Blue of the Night (Meets the Gold of the Day)" (1932); "Lazy Day" (1932); "Sweet Georgia Brown" (1932); "Love Me Tonight" (1932); "Please" (1932); "Brother, Can You Spare a Dime?" (1932); "Just an Echo in the Valley"/"(I Don't Stand) A Ghost of a Chance With You" (1933); "You're Getting to Be a Habit With Me"/"Young and Healthy" (1933); "Shadow Waltz" (1933); "Learn to Croon" (1933); "My Love" (1933); "Thanks" (1933); "The Day You Came Along" (1933); "The Last Round-Up" (1933); "Temptation" (1933/4); "Did You Ever See a Dream Walking?" (1933); "Little Dutch Mill" (1934); "Good Night, Lovely Little Lady" (1934); "Love Thy Neighbor" (1934); "May I?" (1934); "Love in Bloom" (1934); "Two Cigarettes in the Dark" (1934); "June in January" (1934); "With Every Breath I Take" (1934/5); "Soon" (1935); "It's Easy to Remember" (1935); "I Wished on the Moon" (1935); "Without a Word of Warning" (1935); "Red Sails in the Sunset" (1935); "The Touch of Your Lips" (1936); "Robins and Roses" (1936); "I'm an Old Cowhand" (1936); "South Sea Island Magic" (1936); "Pennies From Heaven" (1936); "Sweet

Leilani" (1937); "Too Marvelous For Words" (1937); "Never in a Million Years" (1937); "The Moon Got in My Eyes" (1937); "It's the Natural Thing to Do" (1937); "Remember Me?" (1937); "Bob White" (1937); "When Mother Nature Sings Her Lullaby" (1938); "I've Got a Pocketful of Dreams" (1938); "Small Fry" (1938); "Alexander's Ragtime Band" (1938); "Mexicali Rose" (1938); "My Reverie" (1938); "You Must Have Been a Beautiful Baby" (1938); "You're a Sweet Little Headache" (1938); "Little Sir Echo" (1939); "An Apple For the Teacher" (w/Connee Boswell) (1939); "What's New?" (1939); "I'm Too Romantic" (1940); "The Singing Hills" (1940); "Sierra Sue" (1940); "Trade Winds" (1940); "Only Forever" (1940); "Dolores" (1941); "Deep in the Heart of Texas" (1942); "Be Careful, It's My Heart" (1942); "White Christmas" (1942); "Moonlight Becomes You" (1942); "Sunday, Monday, or Always" (1943); "People Will Say We're in Love" (1943); "San Fernando Valley" (1944); "I Love You" (1944); "Swinging on a Star" (1944); "Amor" (1944); "A Hot Time in the Town of Berlin" (w/Andrews Sisters) (1944); "Don't Fence Me In" (w/Andrews Sisters) (1944); "You Belong to My Heart" (1945); "On the Atchison, Topeka, and the Santa Fe" (1945); "It's Been a Long, Long Time" (1945); "I Can't Begin to Tell You" (1945); "Symphony" (1946); "Sioux City Sue" (1946); "Now Is the Hour" (1948); "Far Away Places" (1949); "Galway Bay" (1949); "Some Enchanted Evening" (1949); "Dear Hearts and Gentle People" (1949/50); "Play a Simple Melody" (1950); "Sam's Song" (1950/1)

Frank Crumit--"Oh! By Jingo! Oh! By Gee! (1920); "Sweet Lady" (1921); "A Gay Caballero" (1928)

Vic Damone--"You're Breaking My Heart" (1949); "My Heart Cries For You" (1950/1); "My Truly, Truly Fair" (1951); "On the Street Where You Live" (1956)

Doris Day--"Sentimental Journey" (w/Les Brown's Orchestra) (1945); "Love Somebody" (1948); "It's Magic" (1948); "Again" (1949); "A Guy Is a Guy" (1952); "Secret Love" (1954); "If I Give My Heart to You" (1954); "Que Sara, Sara (Whatever Will Be, Will Be)" (1955)

Cliff "Ukulele Ike" Edwards--"If You Knew Susie (Like I Know Susie)" (1925); "Paddlin' Madelin' Home" (1925); "Dinah" (1926); "Sunday" (1927); "Mary Ann" (1928); "I Can't Give You Anything But Love" (1928); "Singin' in the Rain" (1929); "When You Wish Upon a Star" (1940)

Tommy Edwards--"It's All in the Game" (1951; 1958)

Eddie Fisher--"Thinking of You" (1950); "Any Time" (1951/2); "Tell Me Why" (1952); "I'm Yours" (1952); "Maybe" (1952); "Wish You Were Here" (1952); "Downhearted" (1953); "I'm Walking Behind You" (1953); "Many Times" (1953); "Oh! My Pa-Pa" (1953/4); "I Need You Now" (1954); "Count Your Blessings" (1954/5)

Mary Ford, Les Paul and--"Tennessee Waltz" (1950/1); "Mockin' Bird Hill (1951); "How High the Moon" (1951); "The World Is Waiting For the Sunrise" (1951); "Tiger Rag" (1952); "My

Baby's Coming Home" (1952); "Lady of Spain" (1952); "Bye Bye Blues" (1953); "I'm Sitting On Top of the World" (1953); Vaya Con Dios" (1953)

Joni James--"Why Don't You Believe Me" (1952); "Have You Heard" (1953); "Your Cheatin' Heart" (1953); "Almost Always" (1953); "My Love, My Love" (1953)

Frankie Laine--"That's My Desire" (1947); "That Lucky Old Sun" (1949); "Mule Train" (1949); "The Cry of the Wild Goose" (1950); "Rose, Rose, I Love You" (1951); "Jealousy" (1951); "High Noon" (1952); "I Believe" (1953); "Tell Me a Story" (1953)

Peggy Lee--"Waitin' For the Train to Come In" (1945); "Golden Earrings" (1947/8); "Manana" (1948); "Riders in the Sky" (1949); "Lover" (1952); "Fever" (1958)

Dean Martin--"That's Amore" (1953); "Return to Me" (1956); "Memories Are Made of This" (1956)

Al Martino--"Here In My Heart" (1952)

Johnny Marvin--"Breezin' Along With the Breeze" (1926); "The Little White House" (1927); "'Deed I Do" (1927)

Patti Page--"All My Love" (1950); "The Tennessee Waltz" (1950); "Would I Love You (Love You, Love You)" (1951); "Mockin' Bird Hill" (1951); "Detour" (1951); "And So to Sleep Again" (1951); "I Went to Your Wedding"/"You Belong to Me" (1952); "Why Don't You Believe Me" (1952/3); "The Doggie in the Window" (1953); "Changing Partners" (1953); "Cross Over the Bridge" (1954)

Johnnie Ray--"Cry"/"The Little White Cloud That Cried" (1951); "Walkin' My Baby Back Home" (1952)

Dinah Shore--"Jim" (1941); "Blues in the Night" (1942); "Skylark" (1942); "Why Don't You Fall in Love With Me?" (1943); "You'd Be So Nice to Come Home To" (1943); "Murder, He Says" (1943); "I'll Walk Alone" (1944); "Candy" (1945); "Laughing on the Outside" (1946); "The Gypsy" (1946); "Doin' What Comes Natur'lly" (1946); "You Keep Coming Back Like a Song" (1946); "(I Love You) For Sentimental Reasons" (1947); "Anniversary Song" (1947); "I Wish I Didn't Love You So" (1947); "You Do" (1947); "Buttons and Bows" (1948); "Baby, It's Cold Outside" (w/Buddy Clark) (1949); "Dear Hearts and Gentle People" (1949/50); "My Heart Cries For You" (1950/1); "Sweet Violets" (1951)

Frank Sinatra--"All or Nothing at All" (1943); "You'll Never Know" (1943); "People Will Say We're in Love" (1943); "I Couldn't Sleep a Wink Last Night" (1944); "Saturday Night" (1945); "Dream" (1945); "Oh! What It Seemed to Be"/"Day By Day" (1946); "They Say It's Wonderful" (1946); "Five Minutes More" (1946); "I Believe" (1947); "Mam'selle" (1947); "Goodnight Irene"

(1950); "Young at Heart" (1954); "Three Coins in the Fountain" (1954); "Learnin' the Blues" (1955); "All the Way" (1957); "Witchcraft" (1957); "Strangers in the Night" (1966); "That's Life" (1966)

Rudy Vallee (and His Connecticut Yankees)--"Sweetheart of All My Dreams" (1929); "Marie" (1929); "Honey" (1929); "Weary River"/"Deep Night" (1929); "I'm Just a Vagabond Lover"; "Lonely Troubador" (1929); "A Little Kiss Each Morning" (1930); "Stein Song" (1930); "If I Had a Girl Like You" (1930; "Betty Co-Ed" (1930); "Confessin' (That I Love You)"; "You're Driving Me Crazy!" (1930/1); "Would You Like to Take a Walk?" (1931); "When Yuba Plays the Rhumba on the Tuba" (1931); "Life Is Just a Bowl of Cherries" (1931); "I Guess I'll Have to Change My Plan" (1932); "Let's Put Out the Lights" (1932); "Brother, Can You Spare a Dime?" (1932); "Just an Echo in the Valley" (1933); "Everything I Have Is Yours" (1934); "Orchids in the Moonlight" (1934); "You Oughta Be in Pictures" (1934); "Lost in a Fog" (1934); "On the Good Ship Lollipop" (1935); "Vieni, Vieni" (1937); "Oh, Ma, Ma" (1938); "As Time Goes By" (1943)

--Related Genre: Pop Singing Groups

Andrews Sisters--"Bei Mir Bist Du Schoen" (1938); "Hold Tight, Hold Tight" (1939); "Beer Barrel Polka" (1939); "Well All Right" (1939); "Say 'Si, Si'" (1940); "Ferryboat Serenade" (1940); "Beat Me, Daddy, Eight to the Bar" (1940/1); "(I'll Be With You) In Apple Blossom Time" (1941); "The Shrine of St. Cecilia" (1942/3); "Shoo-Shoo Baby" (1943/4); "Rum and Coca-Cola" (1945); "Rumors Are Flying" (w/Les Paul) (1946); "Near You" (1947); "Civilization" (w/ Danny Kaye) (1947/8); "Toolie Oolie Doolie" (1948); "Underneath the Arches" (1948); "I Can Dream, Can't I?" (1949/50); "I Wanna Be Loved" (1950)

The Crew Cuts--"Sh-Boom" (1954)

The Four Aces--"Sin" (1951); "Tell Me Why" (1951/2); "Stranger in Paradise" (1953/4); "Three Coins in the Fountain" (1954); "Mister Sandman" (1954/5)

The Four Lads--"Istanbul Not Constantinople)" (1953); "Skokiaan" (1954)

The Gaylords--"Tell Me You're Mine" (1952); "From the Vine Came the Grape" (1954); "The Little Shoemaker" (1954)

The Hilltoppers--"Trying" (1952); "I'd Rather Die Young" (1953); "P.S. I Love You" (1953); "To Be Loved"/"Love Walked In" (1953); "From the Vine Came the Grape" (1954); "Till Then" (1954)

Table 30

The Coming of the Crooners
By Ian Whitcomb

Certainly they've gone, like a murmur in the wind. Today in Australia shopping malls are cleared by the playing of crooner tunes. At least, that's what I caught the TV newsperson reporting in a comic-relief item at the end of the usual litany of worldwide death and destruction: "In Sydney, Australia the malls have solved the problem of teenage loitering after closing-time: Bing Crosby records are broadcast at maximum volume and the result is a mad kid stampede for the nearest exit."

How low has the once-mighty crooner fallen! Time was, in the early 1950s, when he seemed still secure as the staple of pop music—almost a quarter of a century since the start of sweet nothings murmured into a mike for mass public consumption. The year 1925 has seen both the triumph of pop song (as a way to sell product on commercial radio) and the advent of the intimate singer on record due to electrification. By 1955 the crooner was still at it: draped around the mike mooing a tried and tested balladry— the old tale of love gained or lost, of love unrequited or requited, romantically speaking. Offering up the same old thirty-two bars supported by the familiar wailing saxophones, squashed brass, and ever lightly tished and brushed percussion, crooning was the drooping tailgate of the Big Band era. It provided comfort to shop-girls and secretaries as they mooned around on the dance floor. It was also the bane of the old-time British songwriters, men who had written for big-chested Music Hall entertainers and trained vocalists who reeked of the great outdoors.

My great-uncle, Stanley Damerell, wrote such songs. He could never match the best of the American material, although in the early 1950s he did enjoy belated success when Perry Como revived a couple of his 1930s numbers, "Unless" and "If." Stanley's attitude towards the Yankee invaders was the same as the one expressed by his colleague Ralph Butler, a songwriter who specialized in stuff about farms and hiking. Butler would express himself earnestly to those who were near (and far) in his favourite London pubs: "This imported drivel is no more than the lugubrious lamentations of a disappointed lover! His tirade was delivered in a big and roast beefy voice, a stentorian instrument echoing his forebears in the days of Nelson or Drake. If my great-uncle was present he'd lift his beer mug in agreement and chime in with something like: "Exactly, old man, these crooners simply won't do! They're not real men. They're sapping the national virility!" Of course, he and butler and a host of other interested parties had been mouthing off this sort of sentiment for donkey's years—at least since the early 1930s when Crosby had almost boo-boo-booed them out of business.

A change was coming, however, which would wipe them all—crooners and disgruntled songwriters—off the face of pop: rock 'n' roll. It was heralded by Bill Haley, the one-time square dance caller who turned prophet with the success of "Rock Around the Clock." The arrival of genre's messiah, Elvis Presley, with all his wonderful, tingling fresh gargling and hiccuping, assured that things would never be the same again.

I remember it all so well. I brought Haley and Presley on 78 and LP. I withstood the jeers of the jazz fans at my school. I couldn't express what it was exactly that attracted me to the rock and rollers. They weren't saying anything that seemed important, but they shouted it with great excitement and managed to keep rolling along.

When Elvis released "Are You Lonesome Tonight?" following his hitch in the U.S. Army, I immediately fell for this stylistic shift: the sweetly descending melody, the solid supporting chords, and the sincerity of his voice, especially the narration. The King of rock 'n' roll had sold me on a 1920s ballad, the soft underbelly of the Jazz Age. I didn't realize the antiquity of the song at the time, not until I discovered—in the family collection of 78s that accompanied boating trips and picnics on summer days before World War II—the work of Gene Austin. A milestone in my life, his voice massaged me with the most glorious oil through those uneasy last years of adolescence when anything my elders said annoyed me. When I lashed out at them—accusing them of rampant capitalism and racism—I would be rightfully banished to my room. There, putting the needle on the battered old disc of "The Sweetheart of Sigma Chi," I knew I was in for what would later be called an "instant high."

While haunting the second hand shops for more Gene Austin discs, I came across the work of his brethren: "Whispering" Jack Smith and Ukulele Ike. This search continued when I arrived in America in the early 1960s and grew apace even as I passed through a swift life as a rock 'n' roll star. In fact, the rock that followed my era—replete with whining and finger pointing and the polemics of Bob Dylan and the other inheritors of the Woody Guthrie protest tradition—turned me even more towards the balladeers of the late 1920s, the pioneer crooners.

In my research for this book chapter, I made the surprising—yet reassuring—discovery that Gene Austin, the first million-selling crooner, had employed a Tom Parker as advance man (i.e., publicist) for his tent show tours of the South. This was the same Tom Parker who would become while known as the "Colonel" while managing Elvis. Maybe that was how Presley came to record "Are You Lonesome Tonight?" Undoubtedly, Parker knew the worth of the solid old songs and their low-breathing interpreters, thereby helping forge a continuum between rock and the crooners of yesteryear. Provided the right vehicle, Presley was able to transform the anguished ouch of rock, the rant and the roar to be heard above the crowd, into the still sweet voice of calm.

I hope, by now, I've established, for you the reader, my love of pioneer crooners. Like everything good and rare this ethereal music scene had a butterfly life; stagnation set in during the 1930s, followed by deterioration in the 1940s and, as already noted, decimation in the 1950s. By and large, the crooners of the 1920s were free spirits, splendid individualists who were generally permitted to go their idiosyncratic ways, Art Gillham and Little Jack Little being notable examples. And kinds of odd characters were allowed to record, including some who struggled to summon up wobbly notes, bolstered with ample injections of pizzazz (witness Gillham and Biff Hoffman).

The high tide of these early crooners came in 1929, just before the Stock Market Crash and the Great Depression that followed. In the deep night of the 1930s the big show-biz corporations took over, providing homogenized entertainment for the masses in something approaching assembly line fashion. But for that brief prior time the setting was ideal: the songs were still simple and peppy, the bands were jaunty, and the records sold in the millions. True, it was an ingenuous time in that the crooners had not yet become standardized and the bands not yet steamrollered into the flat chug of Swing. It was a time of plenty; a violent and corrupt world perhaps, but also one in which the crooners were able to play a pacifying role. This included restraining musicians who, given half a chance and a pint of hooch, might break out with nasty toots of boiling hot jazz and thus mutilate the melodies and rock the boat to death.

Musically speaking, the crooning era represented the first appearance of what would later become a pop formula; that is, the process of squeezing diversity through a strainer of familiarity. The giant produced by this tradition, Bing Crosby, effectively wiped out the eccentrics. By 1932, he was well on his way to becoming arguing the most successful entertainer of the twentieth century; lord of the airwaves, the top motion picture industry draw, and savior of the record industry. His astounding success begat a host of little Crosbies, all groaning and trilling and whistling. Although rhythm and blues and bebop jazz percolated through the sludge a bit in the 1940s, the crooner-clones held sway until the rise of the wild and unruly rockers. However, Presley's popularity gave rise to a host lookalike sound-alike teen idols, and the process had once again come full circle. This is how modern day popular culture works, aided and abetted by the mass media.

Thus far we've been traveling the high road overlooking the plain of sweeping statements; it's now time to descend into a lush valley of detail. The story begins in the nineteenth century, where the world of drawing rooms and minstrel shows propelled American vernacular singing into the twentieth century. Modern technology—most notably, the phonograph, radio, and the cinema—transformed pop music into a commodity which still retained the musical and lyrical sentiments of the Victorian romantic tradition. With the microphone becoming a totem pole of the early crooners, the crooning phenomenon would become international in scope. The natural American voice, conversational in tone with a touch of gentility, would become lingua franca of popular music.

This is a significant development. The American accent would, like Italian phrasing in opera, become the basis of a classic tradition. Even today, few will accept a love song sung in, say, a cut-glass British or Cockney accent. In nineteenth century America the problem was too much of the Italian operatic school and not even nativism in the local pop music scene. Society, imitative of the Old World on most fronts, urged singers to develop big and loud voices with lots of ornamentation—appogiature, mordents, portamenti, trills, etc.—and to exalt in virtuosity and exhibitionism, forgetting that early Italian opera had been plain and simple, a sort of speak-singing.

Not only was there no native American school of singing, but nineteenth century society tended to view natural, untrained singing as low culture, something associated with lower class laborers as well as saloons and drunken revelers. It is documented that Charles Dickens couldn't abide the street musicians who sometimes gathered below his window; it was fine if they followed their muse within the music hall, but in such close proximity they were undermining the bourgeoise refinement of his drawing room. Respectable Americans reflected European thought regarding pop singers; that saloon warblers, wandering minstrels, ballad mongers, and street singers were to be despised as barbarous and destructive.

The seeds of destruction, however, could be discerned beneath the surface of the American popular music scene. The experience of British entertainer Henry Russell, one of the more successful parlor singers of his age, helps shed light on this situation. Although he possessed a range of only five notes, they were pearly ones derived from years of formal training. From 1833 to 1841 he worked the genteel circuit, finding considerable success with songs such as "A Life on the Ocean Wave" and "Woodman, Spare That Tree." Like many of his European contemporaries he was shocked by instances of American barbarism such as comments by rustics that classical music performers spent the entire concert "jest tunin' up." In New Orleans he allegedly was shown up by a "nigger fiddler." Venturing into a Negro church service in New York, he was startled to hear an apparently leaderless choir swiftly garble an old-world psalm into a brand new melody ("The original tune simply ceased to exist!"). As for the Red

Indians he came into contact with, they were beyond the pale. He found their songs "hideous noises."

For Louis Frederic Ritter, the Alsatian author Music In America (1883), the defining question was: "Are the Americans up to European standards? Can they emulate us?" His investigations failed to turn up a national folk music. "The American landscape is silent; the American country people are not in possession of deep emotional power." And yet many later accounts would describe an extremely active folk scene. These observers would describe a bubbling crucible of ragtime, blues, and jazz. Country music was undergoing dynamic growth with string music in the hills and jews harps all over the place. There was a vogue for revivalist tent meeting songs. Then there were songs from mining camps, hobo campfires, sea shanties, railroad shouts, the call-and-response of the cotton fields, the cowboy ballads of the cattle trail, and songs of the anthricite and bituminous industries. And one mustn't forget the singing societies, the serenaders with their mandolins, the barbershop quartets, and the seven-note shape singers.

What of the singing styles? We read that the country people of hill, mountain, and range sang plainly without affectation. They stood straight and sang down the nose, often with their eyes shuts in modesty. (Saloon culture, of course, was another matter!) The Hutchinson family from New Hampshire, for example, were a popular touring folk group, singing together in simple harmony. The specialized in a morality ranging from the sanctimonious, through the sentimental, to the downright humorous. Their political agenda included temperance and Negro rights. As was pointed out at the time, they "vibrated to every popular breeze."

In the early years of the twentieth century the straightforward, unadorned singing style—the plain truth approach—was to be harnessed for the dissemination of revolutionary socialism. Joe Hill, the songster martyr of the Wobblies (Independent Workers of the World), appropriated the sing-along approach as an instrument for building a new world out of the ashes of the American political system. For Hill and his colleagues, songs were the weapons of change. His Little Red Song Book was full of tinder ("to fan the flames of discontent"), and he wasn't squeamish about seizing a current Tin Pan Alley (capitalist) hit and grafting on politicized words. In this fashion, Irving Berlin's 1910 ragtime composition, "Everybody's Doing It Now," was modified to become "Everybody's Joining It—One Big Union." Such songs reflected the power of song as polemic; Hill would note that "a song is learned by heart and repeated over and over, whereas a pamphlet is never read more than once." The Utah authorities executed Hill in 1915 and he soon became a folk legend, exerting a profound influence on Woody Guthrie, Pete Seeger, and other leaders of the urban folk movement.

At the outset of the twentieth century the voices described above were operating by and large in the underground, the music neither recorded nor in print. The story of American pop, however, has generally been focused on the urban arena. In the parlors and drawing rooms of the late nineteenth century one was likely to find a piano, its bench stuffed full of sheet music. This material was supplied by a burgeoning music publishing business, based in New York City, soon to be designated Tin Pan Alley.

These published songs included ballads peppered with "thees and "thous," and lines "When Aurora empurples the morn"; numbers advertised as "tender, elegant and chaste, and designed to produce a sob." Ladies—mostly younger women—bought the music and sang it at social gatherings. There were also raunchier items for the males, perhaps acquired as a souvenir of a recent night on Broadway; e.g., "If You Ain't Got No Money Then You Needn't Come Around," "All Coons Look Alike to Me," "Who Dat

Say Chicken in De Crowd?" What all of these songs had in common was the incorporation of the street vernacular—its colloquialisms, quaint phrases, and vulgarities. They reflected the vitality of urban centers, the throbbing, jostling mob babbling in countless unknown tongues. This was the real America, not a stilted copy of European high culture.

To meet the demand for this new type of song, the Tin Pan Alley writers created material which caricatured the immigrants comprising the new America; for example, "Marie From Sunny Italy," "Happy Heinie," and "The Yiddish Society Ball." The most widely depicted character in the American pop music, however, was the stereotypical African American. Since its origins in the 1840s, minstrelsy had depicted the black man as a social outsider. Because he was denied the main playing field, he could indulge in the sort of fun and games which resulted in ostracism by one's peers within mainstream white culture. A nation in search of instant mythic heroes (e.g., the frontiersman) and anti-heroes would rapidly assimilate such caricatures as Zip Coon, a black version of the man about town, and Old Black Joe, the folksy plantation hand.

The slang utilized in the minstrel song became the basis of the coon songs of the ragtime era beginning in the late 19th century. At the same time, the love ballad enjoyed comparable status with ragtime. Stephen Foster—composer of such classics as "Beautiful Dreamer" and "Jeannie With the Light Brown Hair"—was the spiritual father of this genre.

In the early years of the twentieth century evidence would suggest that the only crooning going on was that of mammy to child on the old plantation. The lyrics of many songs immortalized this picture; Al Jolson, the best known singer of his era, was still mining this vein in the World War I era with the hit recording "Rockabye Your Baby with a Dixie Melody." As to whether singers actually crooned—that is, sang softly in a person-to-person mode—scant documentation exists due to the abrupt intrusion of a mechanical device which converted most Americans into listeners, rather than performers, of music. The phonograph significantly altered the way music was presented to the public; the virtual indestructibility of recordings has also assured that historians receive a somewhat biased view of the past. We will never know first hand what the slight or tender of voice sounded like in those days. The recording horn of the pre-1925, acoustic era required leather-lunged belters accompanied by vibrant instrumentation (e.g., brass instead of violins in operatic arias).

Many recording executives had initially assumed that American consumers in the hinterlands would embrace recordings by opera singers and symphony orchestras. They soon learned, however, that the most bankable commodities were the shouters of coon songs and ragtime, including May Irwin, Len Spencer, Collins and Harlan, and Sophie Tucker.

Mention must be made here of Gene Greene, the self-styled "Ragtime King." His recording of "King of the Bungaloos" revealed little respect for the composer's ink, tearing the printed sheet into ragtime tatters and providing the example of scat singing on disc. In no way does he anticipate the smooth artiface of the crooner. Like the other horn blasters, he feels the impulse to bleat and bluster. His true originality lies in the asides; between the phrases he roars "zumm-zumm," like an exalted African ruler riding across the Nile on his very own crocodile, and "uh-huh!" with all the subtlety of a motorcycle engine. He indulges himself in an orgy of odd sounds made for their own sake, vocal flourishes that reel and rock us with delight, the very essence of what true jazz should be.

In the second chorus Greene proves he is far from finished, employing a sort of Pig Latin ("When I ri-ger-dide across the mighty Niger-dile") followed by a flurry of pure blather ("Im-bong-bung-bung zoodle-um-bo...") punctuated by what seems to be his own taxi horn impressions. He also mentions "eefin," the word later used by Cliff Edwards (a jazz-scatter-cum-crooner best known as "Ukelele Ike") to describe scat singing.

Greene was a vaudeville headliner during the heyday of the ragtime craze (the decade prior to America's entry into World War I). He was particularly popular in England where he starred in London music halls and recorded extensively for Pathe. Always energized, never sentimental, his easy—if eccentric—flow of language comes across as particularly modern; note the pronunciation of fire as "fie-yore" and desire as "dee-zi-yore" in a 1913 recording of "Oh, You Beautiful Doll," by the American Ragtime Octette. The Octette singers, like many of the theatrical ragtimers, seemed unable to shake the European conservatory style of the nineteenth century.

Greene is notable in that he sings squarely in the American vernacular, albeit within the hide-bound conventions of the minstrel show. He owes little to European influences. His gurgling hustle-bustle breaks through the grim castle walls of the recording machine, revealing that true personality could be registered on an acoustic record.

Greene continued to battle to be noticed into the late 1920s, when the jazz age was giving way to softer sounds. Although his approach had fallen out of fashion in the major urban centers, he could still find fans in the South who remembered "The Ragtime King." He toured the Dixie states in a large auto painted with a sign which read "The Human Singing Machine." By then an old vaude dog had to bark for attention and there was Greene, telling skeptical theater managers how he'd fill their houses to bursting point. On the stage he gave his all, laughing uproariously, strutting in a tried-and-true outfit of straw hat, blue blazer, and white trousers, testifying to the supremacy of anything below the Mason-Dixon, underscoring points with his cane.

One Billboard critic wrote that his act was "old and decrepit" and in need of updating.

This was the general consensus in the late 1920s when electronic entertainment media—radio, sound recordings, the talkies—were in the process of destroying vaudeville. In 1930 Greene was appearing at New York's Grand Opera House as "The Western Al Jolson"; however, there was only one Al Jolson, and he too would soon be having box-office troubles.

In the middle ground included crisp renditions of all manner of contemporary pop songs by expert mimics like Billy Murray, who combined the lyrical qualities of a nightingale with a machine gun vocal delivery in his comic specialties, and Henry Burr, who applied a trained, dulcet voice to sentimental ballads in the best drawing room tradition. They were both throw-backs to the post-Civil War stage tradition which tended to feature Irish-American tenors celebrating the Annie Rooneys and Sweet Rosie O'Gradys.

Twin pillars of the acoustic era, Murray and Burr interpreted everything Tin Pan Alley had to offer in workmanlike fashion, varying little from the composer's ink. The talking machine loved them, and they made thousands of recordings which reflected the many strains of the era's pop music.

If a little subtlety and variety was lost in the studio, then so be it. Theirs was a tough job, with lots of stamina needed for the vocal hurling. Murray was directed to make as many as forty versions of the same song. Accordingly, his characteristic "ping" and sharp accent on certain words, which cut nice thick grooves in the wax, was understandably subject to flagging and even ennui. This was mechanical work in the worst sense of the word. Singers would face a cold horn projecting from the black wall of the studio and try to inject some degree of excitement and conviction into the song material. A stiff band—jammed into the background space behind the soloist or vocal group—would attempt to coordinate its efforts with the general proceedings. When the number was finished, there would be neither clapping not any other form of encouragement, for fear of ruining the master. No wonder that very few personality quirks come through on the disc. Murray would tweak up the ends of phrases and every so often break into speech, as if to show that the recording process had a human dimension.

The American march king, John Philip Sousa, held views regarding the phonograph which ware shared by many of his contemporaries. In a journal article entitled "The Menace of Mechanical Music," he argued that talking machines were no substitute for the true-to-life sound of a nightingale's song. "It is the living, breathing example alone that is valuable to the student and can set in motion his creative and performing abilities." He added that these machines, while ingenious, "offer to reduce the expression of music to a mathematical system of megaphones, wheels, cogs, discs, cylinders and all manner of revolving things." Amateur music-making in the home will wither and die, "until there will be left only the mechanical device and the professional accountant." Working himself into a righteous frenzy, Sousa inquired, "Then what of the national throat? Will it not weaken? What of the national chest? Will it not shrink?" He even addressed our major topic of concern: "When a mother can turn on the phonograph, will she croon her baby to slumber with sweet lullabys, or will the infant be put to sleep by machinery?"

Women—at least those within the entertainment world—were not in the vanguard of the crooning movement. The leading female vocalists, most notably Irwin and Tucker, were to continue coon-shouting until it became known as jazz singing. They, not their male counterparts, best symbolized the energy of the Roaring Twenties. Miss Patricola would sing that she was ready for the "Hot Lips" of a dusky southern dude called "Lovin' Sam." Margaret Young countered with claims about the prowess of "Dancin' Dan" ans how "He May Be Your Good Man Friday (But He's Mine on Saturday Night)." Marion Harris, who often performed material written by African Americans, recorded "I Ain't Got Nobody" and "A Good Man Is Hard to Find."

Why were female vocalists, who had previously tended to follow the European art song model, now shrieking in such an indecorous manner? Leaving aside the limitations of acoustic recording (which required a stentorian approach), the answer resided outside of show business.

The aftermath of World War I saw the enfranchisement of women after nearly a century of political agitation. These gains provided a more liberal social arena within which women might express themselves. This new breed of females were symbolized by the flapper—so named from the way she flapped her elbows in jazz dances such as the Charleston—who sported knee-length skirts, taped-down breasts, and short hair. Flappers more directly assaulted public mores by smoking, swearing, and putting on lipstick in public. In 1922, when flappers, vamps, and shebas seemed to be on every movie screen, in every novel and newspaper, and the subject of countless songs and theatrical presentations, an editorial in The Pittsburgh Observer spoke of "a change for the worse, during the past year, in feminine dress, dancing, manners, and general moral attitudes." Clearly, after decades of reticence and the self-sacrifice demanded in the recent war effort, the gentler sex was ready to push for a change in social mores. Few women had forgotten that members of their sex had been arrested in the previous decade for turkey-trotting, smoking, and failing to wear a corset in public.

Outright rebellion, however, was not the force driving this new breed of American female. The flappers of the early 1920s would soon settle down, ready to become consumers in a nation that worshipped at the altar of Big Business. A New York Times article appearing in July 1922 prophesized this development:

> She'll don knickers and go skiing
> with you; she'll dive as well as you,
> perhaps better....Watch her five

> years from now and then be thankful
> that she will be the mother of the
> next generation, with the hypocrisy
> fluff and other "hokum" worn entirely
> off. You'll be surprised at what
> a comfort [she] will be in the days
> to come!

By 1927, the year that Gene Austin's "My Blue Heaven"—a hymn of praise ti the joys of domesticity—became one of the biggest selling records of all time, the flapper was consigned to the pages of history, replaced by the housewife presiding over a realm filled with creature comforts. In addition to marriage and children, her life now included beauty parlors, electric irons, washing machines, and hot water heaters. For entertainment her hand was on the radio dial and the electrically-recorded orthophonic discs she would play on the electric phonograph.

Women were now the major consumers of consumer goods, and nearly one quarter of the national income was being spent on leisure activities. Females were paying the piper and, by the late 1920s they were favoring high-voiced pipers with honeyed voices, men who gently persuaded from radio and record as if whispering mash words into your ear while dancing cheek to cheek.

These gentle souls reflected the growing urbanity of American life. The frontier had disappeared from the continental United States, and only one citizen in four lived in rural areas. Now that white collar professionals outnumbered manual workers, Americans looked for more sophisticated role models within the entertainment world. A Yale graduate with a sweet and sexy voice was one of the first to fill the bill. When Rudy Vallee opened at New York's Heigh Ho Club on January 8, 1928, he took his first step toward superstardom.

It's important to consider yet another element in the rise of the crooner—the technological dimension. This world—populated by transmitters, amplifiers, patch bays, line equalizers, modulators, and enunciators—would provide the vehicle for putting crooners across to the general public. Occupying the central place in this universe of gadgetry was the enunciator, the term for the microphone of radio's infancy. The microphone became the instrument by which crooners developed a revolutionary set of singing rules.

At radio's beginning, however, there were no mellow tones, only a storm of crackle and whistle and hum. Radio evolved out of the wireless, which functioned as a form of telephone for ship-to-shore communication and similar operations. In the World War I era a number of observers noted the potential of the wireless. For example, one broadcasting technician predicted that the airwaves were likely to become "the ultimate extension of personality in time and space." Three years earlier, in 1919, David Sarnoff, a Marconi employee who would later go on to build the Radio Corporation of America into an media empire, wrote a memo to his superiors describing a vision he had had about developing the radio into a "household utility" much like the piano or phonograph. In essence, he viewed the radio as an instrument for cultural advancement: "The idea is to bring music into the home by wireless. The receiver can be designed in the form of a simple radio music box…" He added that high culture would be brought to the masses everywhere with the result that "the oldest and newest civilizations will throb together at the same intellectual level and to the same artistic emotions."

While Sarnoff exhibited a firm grasp of the medium's potential for disseminating music programming, he missed the mark regarding the types of music that would ultimately dominate the airwaves. By 1922 there were a considerable number of radio sets with reasonably good speakers capable of pumping out sound which approximated the live concert environment. However, serious music based on European models such as the compositions of Johannes Brahms, Richard Strauss, and Gustav Mahler not only placed excessive technical demands on the emerging medium, but failed to resonate with the majority of American listeners.

The trial-and-error process of the early 1920s revealed that a natural type of voice—rather than a classically trained one—was best suited to radio microphones. An everyday, casual, off-the street and in-your-living room voice. So it was that all manner of folks were invited to step up to the radio mike.

Strolling singers—rank amateurs at best—were sometimes hauled in off the street. If the scheduled professional performers failed to show up, then the engineer might fill in by singing the latest pop hit to his own ukulele accompaniment. Radio, it was soon discovered, didn't require either the skills of the concert hall or the vaudeville stage. Rather, it preferred friendliness.

The carbon mike responded best when the voice was projected from about six inches away. Accordingly, talk programs and pop singers who employed a gentler mode of presentation soon became radio staples, along with the inevitable salesman. By 1925 radio sales and revenue exceeded that of the recording industry, and the programming framework had become standardized. At virtually every station one heard friendly announcers, promoting the benefits of goods that listeners hadn't realized they needed, before executing a smooth segue into a soft ballad.

While Vaughn De Leath could rightly claim to be "The Original Radio Girl' (she had participated in test broadcasts from inventor Lee DeForest's laboratory to an audience of wireless operators at sea as early as 1920), she did not initially reap the benefits of this medium. First to profit were song pluggers and demonstrators who took to the new medium like little boys to lollipops and, in doing so, fashioned a new kind of American vernacular singing which had little in common with the jazz, folk, and minstrel traditions then dominating the popular music scene.

The first singer fitting the crooner mold who enjoyed a notable degree of commercial success was Jack Smith, "The Whispering Baritone." Smith was a tall fellow with almost saturnine features, a dark hair slicked back from a well-defined widow's peak. He was known for his winning smile and full evening dress, but it was his deep-dish voice of quiet authority that impressed the New York area radio audience in 1925. Exuding an amiable unctuousness, he could sell a song or product like soap without leaving a trace of oil. He talked and sang with such an insinuating seductiveness that female listeners allegedly couldn't tell where the song ended and the sales pitch began.

Smith may have been born a baritone, but it was a German gas attack in World War I that made him a whisperer. His parents, ironically enough, were German immigrants; it wasn't until after the war, when he was an entertainer-at-the-piano in New York cafes and cabarets, that he had his name changed from Jacob Schmidt to Jack Smith. His widowed mother had worked hard as a laundress to pay for his piano lessons. It is not known from whence the perfect diction, clipped but rounded, originated. Undoubtedly, the absence of public address systems and mikes was a factor; as a result, singers possessing "small voices" found it necessary to project with a high degree of enunciation. It is said Smith's diction was so well developed that he could be heard clearly not only in intimate niteries but in large theaters as well.

To make ends meet Smith landed a job as a song demonstrator at a relatively new music publishing house owned by Irving Berlin. In a little booth, at a studio piano, he plugged songs in-house to selected members of the music trade. His presentations exuded a sly and subtle charm, a technique diametrically opposed to the hard, passionate selling of an Al Jolson. In order to keep the customer's attention trained on the words and melody—rather than the dance possibilities—of the song in question, Smith would limit his piano playing to the right hand, using the left hand to cup the cheek of his face, thereby presenting an image of good-humored nonchalance.

This simple performing style was deemed perfect for the simple type of song being developed for broadcasting needs. Radio executives informed Tin Pan Alley tunesmiths that a range of no more than five melody notes around the middle of the keyboard was most suitable for quality radio phonics.

Vaudevillians, a major source of pop singing talent, were either too loud or too expensive for radio. On the other hand, Jack Smith became a regular performer on New York's WMCA in the spring of 1925. Here, in a studio the size of an average drawing room (and decorated like one, too), he would start work by removing the mike from its normal place atop a raised flower-pot stand, then placing it on the closed lid of the baby grand. When the broadcast light came on, with right hand on the approved keyboard range and left hand on the mike, he'd lean in ever so close and start confiding his songs punctuated by references to other wares.

The popularity of "The Whispering Baritone," particularly among housewives and working girls, impressed Eddie King, manager of the Victor label's popular music division. Sensing the profit-making possibilities, King called Smith in for a recording session utilizing the recently developed electrical process. After almost a month of trial-and-error, the first Whispering Jack Smith sides were issued, beginning with "Cecilia." This song consisted of just a vocal and piano accompaniment along with a crisp sibilance that could be heard above the ubiquitous disc hiss.

At this point in time, with crooning still something of a specialty (and not yet referred to by name), Smith had a head start over song pluggers possessing similar stylistic deliveries in other cities. His dapper manner and polished urbanity also represented strengths; he was to become something of a celebrity, albeit short-lived, featured in radio and films. His stardom spread to Europe; his clipped accent and trim piano accompaniment struck a particularly responsive chord in London, where he regularly performed in addition to recording with the Bert Ambrose Orchestra.

Off the record Smith seemed haunted by demons of one sort or another. He found it necessary to seek solace in the bottle, becoming the despair of his manager. At one point, in the early 1930s, he threatened to leap from the top of a skyscraper. Saved in the nick of time by his manager and valet, he promptly disappeared, only to return drunk as a lord and behaving much worse. Was this behavior caused by the coming of Crosby & Co.? Or was it something far deeper, an insight into the ultimate chaos of life? The sly humor punctuating Smith's svelte and steady delivery offers only slight clues to the sinister undercurrent in his life.

Another song plugger had made his mark as a radio performer in the hinterlands even earlier than Smith. Art Gillham was a casual, rather eccentric presenter of song and patter. Although carrying on like a wandering minstrel of yore, he utilized the new technology in canny fashion. He was the first radio voice to carry the "Whispering" appellation, but his remoteness from New York City kept him from making an immediate jump to national celebrity.

Gillham had impressive musical roots. He was raised in St. Louis, then a hotbed of ragtime. By his late teens, he'd moved beyond his classical music training and was intent on mastering a gut-bucket piano style. In 1914, at the height of the ragtime dance craze, he joined a traveling band. The next year found him in Louisville where, years before, ragtime's first star entertainer, Ben Harney, had fashioned hit songs from scraps of old Negro refrains. He played a part in publishing a version of "Hesitation

Blues" in direct competition with W.C. Handy, the chief stenographer of the blues, an art form built around three flattened notes and three chords which was then bursting upon the public consciousness.

Dedicated to following commercial trends, Gillham tempered his blues with humor (e.g., "I had a sweet mama, so bashful and shy, when she mends her underwear she plugs the needle's eye") and image making. In 1919, while based in Los Angeles, he formed Art Gillham's Society Syncopators, and had them pose for publicity photos in crazy positions much like the Original Dixieland Jazz Band who were then enjoying huge record sales as trailblazers in New Orleans-styled jazz.

In 1922, he landed a position as song plugger and demonstrator for the Ted Browne Music Company of Chicago. One of his responsibilities consisted of dropping by radio station WDAP in the Drake Hotel and demonstrating the latest Ted Browne song sheets at the piano live on the air. In December 1922 the staff singer failed to show up at the station. Gillham, on a dare, took it on himself to fill this void. While aware of the fact that he couldn't really hold a note, Gillham nevertheless set the mike on the piano, got real close and effected an informal singing style. He seasoned his songs with humorous patter (e.g., "C'mon fingers—percolate!").

The listening audience responded positively and he became a regular broadcast fixture. Gillham would talk his way into each new plug as if the song he was performing had come to him on his way over to the station. His easygoing asides had the effect of creating an on-the-air persona; he would exclaim, "I'm a broken-down piano player jest tryin' to get by," or "I'm a fat and bald old fellow who wants his coffee." After a piano vamp redolent of of Midwestern prairie ragtime, he's launch into a piece like "I'm Drifting Back to Dreamland." Nostalgia for the old folks would be followed by something hot and saucy for the younger set; e.g., "The Deacon Told Me I Was Good" (told from the perspective of a young maiden after a closed session with her minister), with Gillham inserting a little scatting—"Doo-di-do-doo!—during the instrumental break.

At the time, the radio craze was peaking and it seemed that everyone was intent on establishing a broadcasting outlet. In 1923 individual stations were owned by newspapers, department stores, drug stores, hospitals, and dry cleaning concerns. With network hook-ups still in the future, Gillham—with Ted Browne's blessing—set off on a tour of independent stations, ranging from big beamers to one-lung operations. This heightened exposure helped him land a job with WSB, an Atlanta-based giant, in early 1924.

The WSB staff were taken aback by Gillham in the flesh. He was neither fat not bald, and was certainly no slave to coffee. In reality, he was thick-haired, trim, and well-dressed. Orange juice was his beverage of choice. And far from being a loser in affairs of the heart, he was a married man.

Gillham had further reason to be happy; he's recently been appointed Sales Manager of Ted Browne's company. As the head song plugger he was favorably situated to make hits. His biggest success from this period was "I Had Someone Else Before I Had You (And I'll Have Someone After You're Gone)."

Mr. Lambdin Kay, director and chief announcer at WSB, recognized a fellow operator in Gillham. Known to his listeners as "The Little Colonel," he was in actuality neither little nor a Colonel. He was, however, a shrewd promoter of anything falling within his range of self-interest which, in the mid-1920s included Gillham. While serving as radio editor for The Atlanta Journal, he published a piece on Art entitled "The Whispering Pianist." Gillham proudly adopted the appellation; while other "whisperers" would follow, he made a point of telling people that he was the first.

Although not adverse to a little outside help, Gillham possessed sufficient intelligence and ambition to further his own cause. After arriving in New York City in August 1924, Gillham and his wife sent telegrams to every recording manager with the news that a popular radio performer—whose resume included appearances on more than fifty U.S. stations and a listening audience as far away as New Zealand—could be heard on half hour programs starting at noon and 9 p.m. for a week on WJZ.

Pathe and Okeh made inquiries, but the best offer came from Frank Walker at Columbia. Gillham's acoustic were pleasing enough, but switch to the electric process enabled the Gillham intimacy to come through in all its quirky splendor. "Cecilia," a 1925 release, was particularly effective, featuring a Gillham lisp during the comic chorus.

Gillham's success was undercut to some extent by Victor's efforts to copy his style. Hot on the heels of Gillham's "Cecilia" came a version by Jack Smith, billed on the label as "The Whispering Baritone." When Smith went on to fame and fortune, Art was accused in some quarters of imitating the imitator. He would write a letter to The Music Trade Indicator protesting this state of affairs: "I have received word from good authority that this new artist was 'dug up' and promoted for the prime purpose of competing with me

and affecting the sales of my phonograph records." Obviously, there was big money to be made in the new "confidential" style. Art needn't have worried unduly; while Smith would achieve considerable success with the cocktail set and British audiences, he would remain dear to rural audiences, particularly in the Deep South.

A third member of this radiophonic band of ex-song pluggers was Little Jack Little. Born John Leonard in London, England, he spent most of his youth in Iowa. In Chicago at the same time as Gillham, he demonstrated for local publishers (as well as contributing many of his own compositions) before becoming a radio song salesman.

As previously noted, the carbon mike responded best when the singer got up close, and Leonard almost caressed it with his lips. A slow exhalation of breath would preface his interpretation of some standard ballad, the sort of stuff cut by the yard. The music and radio trade appreciated his tongue-in-cheek approach to the cliches of the genre. They were especially impressed by his economical piano playing punctuated by occasional bursts of agitated phrases and titillating cross-hand thumb melodies on the bass keys.

He was soon going by the moniker of "Little Jack Little, the Friendly Voice of the Cornfields," and established himself as a Midwestern radio staple. Like Gillham, he coined a number of signature catch phrases in order to distinguish himself from the clamoring voices already jamming the airwaves. One of his presentations always opened with "Here 'tis" and ended with "Yours very truly, Little Jack Little." He was best known, however, for composing and introducing a string of hits to the broadcast medium, beginning with "Jealous" in 1924. His recordings captured a rather hyper-accentuated personality, with a pronunciation so precise it seemed a breakdown was on the immediate horizon. His extraordinary reading of "Are You Lonesome Tonight?" revealed him at his most impish, leaning on his letters, tilting them just for fun, and displaying a pianistic split personality with a legato, lower register melody being attacked by cascades of chromatic notes. It was Jack who was lonesome to the bones. He eventually committed suicide in his Pal Springs home.

While the recordings of Gillham, Smith, Little, and other pioneer crooners revealed many quirky, often comic, delights, within a couple of years they were being directed to straight ballads in order to satisfy a demand created by Gene Austin's enormous record sales. The great tenor of the Southland may have started his recording career with scat singing, near-yodeling, and bird chirping effects (e.g., his duet with Aileen Stanley on "When My Sugar Walks Down the Street"), but following his massive success with "My Blue Heaven" in 1927, he was guided to romantic material like "Ramona" and "Girl Of My Dreams" and told to bridle his desire to be a white bluesman. Domesticity, love, and marriage were the primary themes for the recording industry in the midst of the economic boom of the 1920s.

Although these early crooners hailed from the street rather than the salon, in their efforts to bring a conversational style to American singing, they aimed at being model gentlemen. They eschewed the courser hillbilly, cowboy, and blues-shouter approaches, coming across instead as a kinder, gentler side of the Jazz Age, an antidote to the red-hot mamas. However, these pioneers—with their soothing voices, clear diction, and off-beat personalities—would be pushed aside by the lover-boy triumvirate of Vallee, Crosby, and Columbo.

The first wave of crooners were unceremoniously swept aside on the airwaves by the sudden rise of Rudy Vallee, a real-life Ivy League gent with a voice that exuded sex-appeal—something noticeably lacking in Gillham, Smith, et al. Although Vallee would later mature into a first-rate comic character actor, in his days as a crooning sensation he kept a poker face and let his wavy voice match his wavy hair. Off the record, he claimed his sex appeal consisted of a phallic quality in his singing. Be that as it may, it was obvious his voice—originating in his upper head and proceeding down his nose—projected through the mike with all the authority of lavender and lace. With his band starting as a radio "remote" from a New York club, he was being networked around the entire country by 1930. As a national institution, he elicited sighs from women and derisive snorts from their husbands and boyfriends. He was the first swooner-crooner; yes, the word "crooner" was at last in the everyday vernacular to describe this new radio sensation.

By 1932 a backlash had set in against crooners. Rudy Vallee was one thing—a civilized fellow you could invite to the club. Crosby and Columbo, however, came from more humble stock. Furthermore, a legion of copycat vocalists—indiscriminately modifying melody lines by means of scoops and swoops and adding silly little trills and boo-boos—dominated the airwaves. And Mr. and Mrs. America obviously considered radio to be an essential appliance; it seemed that most would sell their bathtub before doing without this trusted window to the world at large.

The press had a field day disseminating the attacks on the "crooning boom" by moral authorities. In January 1932 they quoted Cardinal O'Connell of Boston: "Crooning is a degenerate form of singing….No true American would practice this base art. I cannot turn the dial without getting these whiners and bleaters defiling the air and crying vapid words to impossible tunes." The New York Singing Teachers Association chimed in, "Crooning corrupts the minds and ideals of the younger generation." Lee DeForest, one of radio's inventors, regretted that his hopes for the medium as a dispenser of "golden argosies of tome" had become "a continual drivel of sickening crooning by 'sax' players interlaced with blatant sales talk." De Forrest could have been referring to our own Whispering Jack, who sonorously pitched a medicated cream for seniors afflicted in their private parts before sliding into a the question, "Can you remember back a few years when I sang this?"

The splendid RCA skyscraper—a "Cathedral of Commerce" situated in downtown Manhattan, still the show business capital of the world—housed the office of radio mogul David Sarnoff. Sarnoff could remember the old days when the medium was a crazy-quilt of too many stations and too few receivers with decent loudspeakers. Those vintage radio boxes had horns which made broadcasts sound no better than a phonograph. As for the murmurings, whisperings, groanings, moanings, etc., of the likes of Crosby and Company, Sarnoff didn't give a fig. In fact, he never listened to the invention he'd steered into the marketplace and, from there, into the homes of the masses. The fact that they hadn't taken to classical music was a pity, but one couldn't overlook the tendencies of the marketplace. Let them wallow in the soppy schlock peddled by crooners and their ilk. Although he'd played a major role in establishing the

NBC radio network and the purchase of Victor Records in 1929, Sarnoff was already looking ahead the commercial potentialities of television.

During the early years of the Depression, the crooners continued to be winnowed out until only those fitting the Crosby mold were left to provide the soft soap needed to ease the nation through the harsh everyday realities. The pioneers did, of course, soldier on.

Gillham's story represents a case in point. In 1932, a lucrative year for radio, record sales hit an all-time low. Gillham was still listed in the Columbia catalog, but only by a hair, with the aptly titled "Just a Minute More To Say Goodbye." Perhaps sensing his time had passed, he remarried and settled in Atlanta. There he went on to become head of a business college and owner of an office space rental firm, The Representative's Center.

Jim Walsh, music researcher and contributor (from the early 1940s through the 1980s) to *Hobbies—The Magazine For Collectors*, provided much of the information we have about Gillham. In 1957 he began corresponding with Gillham, who was now retired and residing in an Atlanta suburb with longtime wife Gertrude. This was the peak year for classic rock 'n' roll with notable releases by Elvis Presley, Little Richard, Chuck Berry , Jerry Lee Lewis, and other giants of the genre. But it was also a time for mellow balladeers like Pat Boone and Connie Francis (her hit, "Whose Sorry Now?" was originally a 1923 Tin Pan Alley hit). Austin himself managed to dent the Billboard charts after a two-decade absence with the self-penned "Too Late." Gillham or Smith—who'd died in 1951—would have been perfect as a narrator on "The Shifting Whispering Sands," one of the top smashes of 1957.

Gillham came across as hale and hearty in Walsh's Hobbies portrait. In his first letter to Walsh he expressed surprise that anybody would be interested in "my corny recordings." Noting the quality of 1957 releases, he added, "When I hear the beautiful jobs that are on the market now, I just don't tell anyone that I made records back in the dark ages." However, he did proudly point out that he was the artist—and composer—on the "first released electronically-recorded record, No. 328-D for Columbia," "You May Be Lonesome But You'll Be Lonesome Alone."

These phonograph records remain important as the only documentary evidence of the pioneer crooners. Somebody paid good money for each one at the time of release when the recording artists could have been heard for free on the radio. However these records were put to use, the crooners—an irritant to inventors and radio entrepreneurs, denounced in the press and pulpit—were viewed as a passing fancy, a mere fad. In 1932 the New York Times reassured its readers: "They sing like that because they can't help it. Their style is begging to go out of fashion….Crooners will soon goo the way of tandem bicycles, mah jongg and midget golf."

So much for ephemeral radio. But those black shellac 78 r.p.m. discs, with their appetizing graphics, can live forever. It handled with loving care, these material objects mature, displaying wise old facial lines in their grooves. You can't see the sound of a CD so how can you be sure it isn't just magic? Grooved discs testify, and not only when revealed by a needle; many are worn and scarred by years of giving pleasure—joy, comfort, laughter, tears—so that they now present the listener with a monster bacon-and-egg fry-up. Clearly, somebody loved them. I do so wonder who.

Walsh, in the September 1957 issue of Hobbies, gives us a glimpse of one such record lover. He recalled a conversation with a "veteran record dealer" about how silly girls were getting over Elvis the Pelvis. "Did I ever tell you," smiled the dealer, "about the girl who had a crush on 'The Whispering Pianist,' Art Gillham?" It was a summer morning in 1929 when she came into his store, asking to audition "a syrupy thing," a new Gillham release. In the stifling air-tight booth she played that record over and over, from nine o'clock until two-thirty in the afternoon, coming out one or twice for water. "I thought I'd go nuts!" said the dealer. The title was "I Love You—I Love You—I Love You, Sweetheart Of All My Dreams."

Now I happen to particularly like this version of the song. There are several recorded versions of this straight-forward, no-conditions-attached declaration of utter and complete love. Rudy Vallee's interpretation enjoyed the greatest commercial success, while Johnny Marvin did a workmanlike job, applying his light, lyrical tenor voice to a bouncy rhythm accompaniment. Gillham's approach, however, is most captivating because, in his usual manner, he winsomely pleads for your attention. He clearly got one girl's attention on that summer day in 1929, and he gets at the entrance of the new millenium.

The song is an impressive example of how Gillham works his art. With the violin taking care of the melody, Art is free to mold the rather mundane verses into an inspired monologue—a plea that only the most hard-hearted of listeners can refuse. The personal touches render his entreaties more believable: "Listen sweetheart, why are you sad and blue? Please come over here dear....Sit down real close to me....Let me tell you how I feel...." He then moves on to the chorus, his trademark quavering notes made acceptable due to the sincerity of his delivery. A supple guitar line supplies Gillham with all the sweet harmony that is needed. Then suddenly, in the last chorus, he shifts into a special patter lyric, doubling the word flow, pledging to love her morning, noon, and night, promising to let her do anything she likes and, what's even more important, to say anything she likes. Note that Art keeps his love talk down to earth (e.g., he employs the phrase "real close" rather than the more grammatically correct "really close") in keeping with his disc persona as a friendly down-home Mid-westerner of the old school who, though full of pre-war pathos, can nevertheless play some pretty peppy barrelhouse jazz piano. In such a manner, the Jazz Age was made to embrace the old verities.

Gillham's claim to the contrary, apparently nobody knows for certain when the first electrics appeared; I'm not about to risk a surmise only to be raspberried at a later date by some dedicated sleuth armed with facts and figures to prove me wrong. Somehow I want to trust Art; perhaps it's the cracker barrel honesty he exhibits within the shellac grooves.

A number of facts, however, can be ascertained regarding the evolution of "ortho" recordings. (To me, "ortho" means sound that shoots like an arrow straight to the heart; it is "right" in the ethical sense of "faithfulness" and "honesty." The Victor label, which coined the phrase "orthophonic" sound, may have inferred a different meaning, but to me it is synonymous with the well-recorded electrical 78s of the late 1920s. They provided a warmth often missing in later recordings, no matter how high the fi is reckoned to be. But then, perhaps the secret of the warmth lies in the human sound box rather than through the science of mankind.)

It appears that the first electric recording was made in Great Britain in 1920 for Columbia under the supervision of two engineers, the Honorable Lionel Guest and Captain H.O. Merriman. Their offering was "Abide With Me," performed by a choir, congregation, and the band of His Majesty's Grenadier Guards, at Westminster Abbey. I have no idea how the record sounded; I only know what it looks like and that they used a telephone mouthpiece rather than a microphone. That may have been a fatal mistake. Suffice it to say that the British effort led to no further progress along these lines. (This was perhaps due in part to the fact that, as upper-class Englishmen, they were amateur explorers rather than professional enntrepreneurs.)

In the United States, however, at the Western Electric research division of Bell Telephone Laboratories, part of the mighty A.T. & T. combine, scientists took note of the British experiment. The trick was to convert real sounds into electrical impulses via the medium of the microphone, and thence, through an amplifying vacuum tube (like radio), and finally back to real life auditory information. Sometime in 1924, with the sales of both records and sound reproduction equipment plunging to unprecedented lows, the scientists demonstrated their electric test discs to Victor executives. The latter were undoubtedly astounded; for the first time you could hear the high end of the sound spectrum (a little shrill, it is true) and gut-shaking bass (a little boomy, for sure). Above all, the sound was amazingly loud, and brimming with energy; the scientists noted that their electric discs reproduced 5 ½ octaves as opposed to the mere three of the then-current acoustics.

At the time Victor had tons of acoustic hardware and software sitting in warehouses (not to mention stock in retail outlets), so they hummed and hawed. While Victor procrastinated the scientists took their formula to Columbia Records. A licensing deal was struck and Columbia was recording with the new process by the fall of 1924 (presumably Gillham was one of the first artists brought into the studio). Victor was forced to come aboard. The other record industry giant, Edison, gamely stuck to its trusted acoustic process. Owner Thomas A. Edison operated with a hands-on policy, preferring the phonograph to all his other inventions.

Edison loved music more than the money-making process associated with the record industry. Even as electronics and corporate-sponsored research were engulfing his less complicated Victorian world, Edison would state: "Of all the various forms of entertainment in the home, I know of nothing that compares with music. It is safe and sane; appeals to all the finer emotions; tends to bind family influences with a wholesomeness that links old and young together. If you will consider for a moment how universally the old 'heart songs' are loved in the homes, you will realize what a deep hold music has in the affections of the people."

Edison professed to know what the people ought to like—the very same parlor songs he'd known and cherished going back as far as the Civil War, including "Beautiful Dreamer," "Silver Threads Among the Gold," and "I'll Take You Home Again, Kathleen" (he'd requested this one for his own funeral). These were songs of nostalgia for a better time and place, far from the 1920s madcap cash chase to a syncopated rhythm.

Edison's decision to stay with the acoustic process—as well as cylinders—brought pleas from his employees to reconsider. A Mr. Miller wrote him in Memo #749, "Don't you think we could make some royalty arrangement with A.T. & T. for the use of this system?" The old gent scribbled his reply onto the note, "I could have taken this up without paying anybody....They cannot record without distortion." He chose instead to concentrate on marketing beautifully-crafted cabinets such as the Louis XVI model in Circassian Walnut and the development of long-playing Diamond Discs.

Edison would eventually surrender to the blessed vacuum tube, but shortly thereafter his company went broke, the fatal blow issued by the October 1929 stock market crash. The electric process, perfect for hot dance bands and the intimate crooners, represented a trend that couldn't be bucked; nevertheless, I admire the old man for his tenacity and moral stance. I'm sure that if he had worked closely with a Gillham, Smith, Little, or Austin, he would have succumbed to their mother's milk music. After all, they—like his nineteenth century favorites—were offering simple, clear melodies, with the added dimension (thanks to electricity) of a deep bedding of harmony, accented by a prominent bass line.

Electrical recording couldn't have come at a better time. The record industry, which had enjoyed peak sales of 100 million discs during 1921, was mired in a frightful slump by 1925. Why buy a tinny sounding record when you got better fidelity on the radio, and for free? By spring 1925 the first electric releases from Victor and Columbia were on the market, but existing phonographs made them sound harsh, strident, and muddy. New hardware was the order of the day. Victor led the recovery, proclaiming November 2 as "Victor Day." Long lines formed early outside stores for the heavily-advertised demonstrations of the Orthophonic Victrola. Record sales started rising once more, continuing an upward swing through 1929, albeit below the 1921 high-water mark. Radio was the mass medium of preference, with the Talkies coming on strong.

The recording managers and their assembled vocal talent immediately recognized that it was a whole new ballgame. The embryonic crooners began developing a new array of hitherto hidden talents. Once of the veterans of acoustic recording, Frankly Baur—enjoying considerable success as first tenor of the mellifluous close harmony group, The Revelers, by the mid-1920s—expressed his relief over the turn of events: "The strain on the singer is immeaburably eased. A record can be made in exactly one-third the time it used to take, and no longer is it necessary for us to nearly crack out throats singing into that hated horn." Nor would there be any more of the physical humiliation of the old days, when singers had to duck down during an instrumental passage or by pushed by the recording director so as to be close to the horn for low notes (and then pulled back for the high ones).

Veterans of the recording horn, who had served the labels well, didn't deserve such rough treatment. The recording studio managers—never known for gentleness and consideration in their handling of artists—now had a new reason to goad and intimidate their charges. Victor's Eddie King exerted such pressure on the venerable Billy Murray during the "Roll 'Em Girls" session that the latter had remonstrated, "Heck, I'm no crooner." Unfortunately, the results proved him right; Murray was obviously holding back, a self-bridling horse used to being frisky, and the result sounded unnatural.

The failure of Murray, the most successful acoustic era singer, revealed with grim finality that the heyday of the leather-lunged Irish-American tenors—booming out sentimental ballads as well comic songs of the ethnic and minstrel variety—had passed. Industry insiders tended to downplay the impact of the electrical recording process. Victor bandleader Nat Shilkret noted, "Tenors gave us plenty of grief for a while. At first they sounded rather thick, like baritones; at times they were hollow. But all voices were finally conquered. However, the conquest by condenser, vacuum, and amplifier revealed in stark fashion that certain veteran voices were married for life to the horn; no amount of play-acting could endow them with the geniality of a Gillham, Smith, or Little. An electric Murray sounded like an acoustic Murray; the only difference was that the band provided a fuller ambience, while Billy appeared to be a rail-thin pixie trapped in a box.

Musically speaking, it must have been galling for Henry Burr—with his perfect intonation—to be outsold by Gillham with his trail of wounded notes. The Whispering Pianist's small voice and limited melodic range, however, were assets as far as the all-important female customers were concerned; here was humanity, here was vulnerability, here was a fellow clearly suffering (e.g., the 1928 Columbia release, "Nobody's Lonesome But Me") and in need of succoring. In contrast, Burr—with his concert platform manner and publicity photos in a wing collar—did not sound convincing singing "I Found A Million Dollar Baby (In a Five and Ten Cent Store)" (Victor; 1926).

While some acoustic era artists seemed ill-equipped to make the transition to electrical recording, others were liberated by the new conditions. Frank Crumit was a case in point; he began recording in 1919, belting out songs with the best of them. With the advent of the microphone, he underwent a metamorphosis, exuding a suave, silky charm. His subtle phrasing and pleasing timbre spanned the sentimental ballads of Stephen Foster and the sophisticated Tin Pan Alley fare produced by the likes of George and Ira Gershwin. Crumit went to become a major radio personality, co-starring with his wife, singer Julia Sanderson.

Although he enjoyed only modest success on the airwaves, Gene Austin also made a smooth transition to electrical recording. Although exhibiting an affinity for the blues, ragtime, and country and western music as a youth, his voice—perhaps the most lyrical of any of the crooners—was best suited for caressing the microphone. Austin's considerable success as a recording artist—he probably sold more records than any other performer during the latter half of the 1920s—underscored the universal appeal of his relaxed and gently articulated mode of delivery.

Cliff Edwards also negotiated this stylistic shift with the greatest of ease. Unlike the other early crooners, he possessed strong jazz inclinations. His improvisational bent consisted of breaking into nonsense syllables, a technique he referred to as "eefing," which probably dated back at least as far as the 1890s when Ben Harney was introducing ragtime songs onstage at Tony Pastor's vaudeville theater in New York City. His eefing effectively complements a portrait of domestic bliss in "Halfway to Heaven" (Columbia; 1928). He sings about a cottage, surrounded by flirting butterflies, which includes a little lady, cooking behind a kitchen curtain, and peering out the window for his return, which is signaled by his guttural moaning, or eefin. Unfortunately, the lovely

landscape Edwards depicted on record was not reflected in his own life; like Austin, he had a string of unsuccessful marriages and a lifelong fight with alcoholism.

None of the early microphone masters seemed to pay more than passing attention to the sex appeal factor. It was apparent that the masculine ideal had changed considerably since the turn of the century when the muscular type held sway over women's hearts. By the 1920s the male star prototype had softened, melting from He-Man into Dream Boy, from the George O'Brien look into pretty Buddy Rogers. Variety, which made a point of keeping abreast of such trends, attributed the rise of the softer image as an effort to "compensate for the hard sexiness of females, on-screen and off."

Pop songwriters began poking fun at the androgynous American landscape; i.e., girls with boy's short hair, boys in billowing bags falling just short of skirt-dom. Edgar Leslie defined the situation in succinct terms with his 1925 hit, "Masculine Women! Feminine Men!" He noted that Sister Susie is learning to shave, while her brother absolutely adores his permanent wave: "Once you used to kiss your little sweetie in the hall—Now you'll find that you are kissing her brother Paul." Leslie's Alley associate Con Conrad—composer of "Margie" and "Ma! He's Making Eyes At Me"—enjoyed considerable popularity as a provider of saucy songs for the proliferating "drag" and "pansy" entertainment circuit of New York and other major cities.

There had been a general open-mindedness in urban centers with respect to the more outlandish aspects of homosexuality going back at least as far as the Victorian era. "Fairies" and "sissies" were acceptable—and even "worthy of mercy"—so long as they were openly visible. In the New York of the 1900s drag halls had even operated at Madison Square Garden, attended by high society, including the Astors and Vanderbilts. In the 1920s a vogue existed for "pansy" clubs and revues, highlighted in 1927 by Mae West's theatrical extravaganza, The Drag, which featured forty chorus boys tossing off such one-liners as "When I walk up 10th Avenue, you can smell the meat sizzling in Hell's Kitchen," and describing a gown as "trimmed with excitement in front." In mainstream vaudeville Frank Fay and Jack Benny used the limp-wrist and undulating walk effect for laughs and, in Benny's case, for character creation.

This is not to imply that America as a whole was turning gay (in fact, a backlash was imminent during the 1930s); rather, I am simply setting the scene for the social acceptance of high-pitched male singers even as the microphone rendered deeper and wider tones more pleasing. This might help explain this golden age of upper register tenors; the heaven-stroking sound of a Nick Lucas or a Morton Downey. But then the high voice had long been the hallmark of both the Italian bel canto (Lucas) and Irish vernacular (Downey) styles.

These factors, however, do not completely explain the grip that Rudy Vallee had on millions of American females, as 1929 sank from an everybody-happy high through the stock market crash and into the Great Depression. His success caused newspapers to warn of the "Vallee Peril" caused by this "punk from Maine" with the "dripping voice; mounted police to be called in to beat back crowds of screaming, swooning females at his vaudeville shows; the theatrical trailer for his first film, The Vagabond Lover, to exclaim, "Men Hate Him! Women Love Him!"; and entertainer Jimmy Durante to complain, "He became an epidemic or national calamity or something, because your girl friends were always wondering why you don't croon the way he does."

Martha Gellhorn—who later married Ernest Hemingway, that paradigm of macho—argued, in a 1929 magazine article entitled, "Rudy Vallee, God's Gift To Us Girls," that the gift was inherently non-threatening. In his popular radio program, which began with his floating greeting, "Heigh ho, everybody," beamed in from a New York City night club, he stood like a statue, surrounded by clean-cut collegiate band musicians and cradling a saxophone in his arms. He would then commence crooning—almost keening—with eyes closed and head up at the sky. He was, he liked to tell reporters, "pouring out his soul" in the process of delivering a song to his audience.

Wholesome in appearance, there was nothing sexy in his face, hair, or body. The allure lay exclusively in that supremely radiophonic voice, a perfect match for the mikes, amps, and speakers of the time. So Rudy happened to be in the right place at the right time. This point was underscored by a 1929 Literary Digest article entitled, "New Rudy Vallee Voice Is Catnip." In the piece William Bolitho effectively described how the catnip worked its magic:

> By the divine accident or miracle,
> that is what makes arts nearer
> religion than science, the voice
> that starts its strange journey at
> the microphone hardly more than
> banal fills the air at its destination
> with some sort of beauty, and
> with that rarest charm of beauty—
> uniqueness, novelty.

The sweeping success of the Vallee novelty voice inevitably leveled the popular singing field. The quirky Gillhams and Smiths fell back to the sidelines. The void was filled by a host of soft modulators, all following the lead set by Vallee and his well-bred, almost bland, vocalizing. They included Chester Gaylord, "The Whispering Serenader"; Eddie Walters, who insinuated a somewhat campy aura; Les Backer, a singer capable of convincingly updating old chestnuts like "You Tell Me Your Dream"; and Bostonian Jack Miller, whose "From Sunrise To Sunset" was creamy croon perfection. Veterans were also made over to fit the new mold; Nick Lucas, for instance, was now billed as "The Crooning Troubador." There were also songwriters with little of no vocal training now being billed as crooners, including Fats Waller's writing partner, Andy Razaf; Freddy Rose, later a partner in the pioneer Nashville publishing firm, Acuff-Rose; Sam Coslow, who had demonstrated for Edison and would go on write Crosby anthems; and Sammy Fain, composer of sentimental ballads like "Wedding Bells (Are Breaking Up That Old Gang of Mine)."

Women were far less likely to be heard by the late 1920s. Of all those brash babies of the early Jazz Age, Sophie Tucker was one of the few still standing. She had been around since the "coon shouting" vogue. Her 1929 hit, "I'm the Last of the Red Hot Mamas," showed her unwillingness to bend to the then-currently crooning craze. Her aggressive style took no prisoners. Her collaborations with males required that the latter take a submissive role. Tucker's accompanist Ted Shapiro, for instance, would sometimes hum and murmur along to her solos, like a little sailboat bobbing beside a battleship.

Another ragtime-cum-jazz-baby veteran, Blossom Seeley, also employed a male vocalist as a back-up. A Vitaphone short shows them at work; Seeley is demonstrative and brassy while husband Benny Fields fans her admiringly, singing his answers in a crooning manner. His husky, easy-going delivery had much in common with Crosby's signature sound; both operated in a deeper register than that characterizing the 1920s tenors. However, his manner--both live and on film—was emasculated in tone, much in keeping with the early crooners.

The hits of the day continued to speak of male submission; for instance, "I'm Confessin'," "Guilty," "Just One More Chance," and "Prisoner of Love." Furthermore, one Ellen O'Grady, in a letter to The New York Times responding to the news that President Hoover had invited Vallee to "sing a song to chase depression," claimed crooners were creating a "depression of spirit." In her opinion, this was not surprising in that Webster's Dictionary defined crooning as "a continuous hollow sound, as cattle in pain; to bellow."

The effete male image subsided with the advent of the 1930s. The transition was most obvious in Hollywood; the gangster genre depicted James Cagney squashing a grapefruit in his girl's face because she talked too much and countless close-ups of the Humphrey Bogart sneer.

Leaving the bigger picture to social historians, it is time to focus on the next wave of crooners, tracing how and why the public preference shifted from high tenors to baritone huskies. By early 1932 a crooning triumvirate was generally acknowledged to dominate popular music. Dick Robertson's recording, "Crosby, Columbo & Vallee" (Romeo, 1931) satirized this state of affairs, noting that bachelors and married men must "stick together" and fight these "public enemies" who, in dominating the airwaves and "singing of "couples beneath stars above" and such "nonsense," are "stealing all our blondes" and "breaking up our happy homes." In the days before radio ruled the home, according to Robertson, you threw a gigolo out into the alley, but "now you can't say a word."

By this time it was evident that Vallee was not the man to spearhead this shift in public taste. The picture of a soulful youth with golden hair and blue eyes mewing in a garden stage setting with classic columns and a splashing fountain represented a hangover from the late 1920s. In contrast, Crosby and Columbo looked and sounded like they might have the right tools for plumbing the depression. They did not pretend to possess a Park Avenue background. They didn't sport fancy French names complete with accent grave, nor claim Ivy League credentials.

Columbo hailed from a working class Italian Catholic background. His violin playing could be excused in view of his manly physique. As a sideman with Gus Arnheim's Orchestra in the late 1920s he had obediently played his assigned role in a vocal trio—a then fashionable adjunct to a nightclub band—warbling like a trained canary. When Crosby struck big in the early 1930s, however, he'd lowered his voice to sound husky and hunky.

Crosby, of course, never seemed to bother about changing anything. Training was not in his line. Unlike Gillham. Austin, Smith, Little, Vallee, or Columbo, he played no instrument—unless you count the kazoo and sock cymbal. He never bothered to learn to read a note of music. He never rehearsed a song all the way through. He was truly natural in manner and, as such, he appeared to be an average all-round good guy. The men could identify with him, whereas Vallee was just too high on that damned Greek pedestal.

Bing (what a sensibly low-falutin' name!) was Irish Catholic and, like Columbo, possessed common origins. Yes, he'd been to college, but unlike Vallee, who'd obsessed over the classical meanderings and ragtimey novelties of saxist Rudy Weidoft (even taking the man's first name), Bing had followed the more masculine pursuit of hot jazz. He and his pal Al Rinker (later his partner in Paul Whiteman's Rhythm Boys) had bought every eefing Cliff Edwards record immediately upon release. In their vaudeville act Bing scatted the "bop-bop-de-do-do" like a wild and crazy jazz boy should do. Off-stage he behaved likewise, boozing it up and running into cop trouble. The avant-garde crowd at Berkeley—where Crosby regularly performed with Rinker—loved his music and stage manner. He belonged to the vanguard of "cool" and "laid back."

In late 1927, Rudy Vallee—then gigging as a Ben Bernie sideman—noticed Crosby's special insouciance. It was a debutante party at a Baltimore gym and the Bernie band was taking a break, letting the Rhythm Boys entertain off on the side. Nobody was paying much attention until Bing stepped into the center of the gym and sang a solo ballad. There was no mike, no megaphone. Vallee would later write: "When he had finished, there was a deafening roar of applause which would have called for at least one or two encores. Instead, he walked off the floor past where we sat, his classic features expressionless, his patrician nose just a bit up in the air. You might have thought him deaf, so unaware he seemed of the sensation he had created."

Crosby's walk may have seemed snooty, but clearly he had the common touch. After a stint with Gus Arnheim at the Cocoanut Grove in Hollywood (which he lived up to his nickname of "Binge" with hoarse readings of ballads spiced with ribald interpolations, most notably on "What Is It"), he went on to radio network fame, movie stardom, and most importantly, a pivotal role as one of the saviors of the record industry. By the late 1930s, Crosby had established his image as a family entertainer. Gone were the late-night melodramatic cries for "Just One More Chance"; now, the world was presented with a carefully packaged, happy-go-lucky fellow who liked sports and wore sloppy clothes. Everything he approached—be it Christmas, Irish, Hawaiian, Dixie, or Western songs—emerged with his distinctive touch. He would become the king of World Music, tourist-style. And whatever the lyrics, "Der Bingle" placed them in the easy listening category—with a touch of jazz phrasing, a relic of his crazy days. Much like eating at McDonald's in Moscow, with Bing you could be sure of receiving the normal standard fare.

Crosby's greatest accomplishment was to transcend the confines of the crooning school, something none of his contemporaries had been able to do. In later years, comfortably established as a musical institution, he would poke fun at his crooner-sensation years; e.g., the "hot mush" in his throat often contained too many frogs due to late night carousing, insisting he was nothing special because "most people who've ever sung in a kitchen quarter or in a showerbath sing like me." At the time, though, he was shrewd and tough enough behind the scenes. His Rhythm Boy pals were discarded when not needed and reporters were treated with kid gloves. When asked for advice on breath control and intonation by a neophyte singer, "The Groaner" answered, "Sing from the belly—that's where the money." This relaxed public manner took its toll; private rooms where Crosby had stayed awhile were littered with broken or chewed pencils.

As a vocal heavyweight and acceptable Average Joe in the Depression, Crosby was saved the humiliations suffered by Vallee. The press could imagine Crosby and Columbo as working stiffs—hell, they never took singing seriously, did they? But Valle and the high tenors exhibited all the earmarks of drones. Could they mend a fuse or change a tire?

On January 23, 1931, The New York Times reported, with considerable zest, that Vallee had been a "target for two large grapefruit that had seen better days" during a concert at a Boston theater. The perpetrators, the reporter was happy to state, "got off with a police lecture." The number that had triggered the incident was "Oh, Give Me Something To Remember You By." Had the guilty parties, allegedly Ivy League undergraduates, been offended by the dangling preposition, of by the preposterous figure of Vallee, limp of bearing and singing like a contented nanny goat, performing piffle while the world whirled into an abyss?

Vallee would later reflect on this event in his memoir, *My Time Is Your Time*, "I was pretty damn shaken I can tell you." He ordered the show to go on, noting, "I launched into an all-out impression of Al Jolson, theorizing that my previous vocalizing perhaps had been lacking in virility and masculinity." He appeared intent on demonstrating that, if unconvincing as just one of the guys (in the manner of Crosby), he was at least a real guy." But what the hell, there were other ways to make a living, and Vallee was to prove it through a subsequent career as radio host and character comedian. A listen to some Crosby recordings later in 1931 evidently convinced him that "this young man was going to push Pappy Vallee right off his throne."

Vallee would go on to stake a place in real world by contributing a recording of "Brother, Can You Spare a Dime?" Crosby would compete with his own version in 1932, the year when, along with breadlines and bank failures, the sale of records hit an all-time low. On the whole, however, the crooners left social commentary to comedians; it was a crooner's job to take people's minds off bad times by singing of romance amidst moonlight and roses rather than drumming up a polemical People's Music a la Woody Guthrie. The crooners were undoubtedly comfortable operating within their assigned framework. They were part of a powerful show business industry which, in the 1930s, had the moral and market imperative to help its audience forget its real-life troubles.

When Columbo died suddenly in 1934 the field was wide open for Bing. The subsequent swing era would be littered with crooners, virtually all of whom paid homage in the media and on the bandstand. One notable exception was the South African-born singer, Al Bowlly, who recorded over 1,000 sides between 1927 and 1941 before dying from an air raid bomb which hit his London flat. His material ranged from standard Tin Pan Alley fare to the comparative exoticism of Africaan and Jewish numbers (and even a couple of Shakespeare sonnets). His voice had a steady quality all its own, and women in particular seemed quite susceptible to its charms. A simple soul who loved to box and always wore a gold crucifix, Bowlly reportedly was so moved by some of the ballads he was assigned to record that he'd dissolve into tears during the recording session.

My stated goal of imparting the essence of the crooning tradition to you, the reader, would not be complete without a reference or two to the passionate friendship I had with these frozen voices of long ago. It started shortly after World War II, when the vice-headmaster of my prep school allowed me to (carefully) place the tone arm of his radio-gram (a beautiful piece of polished walnut furniture, flowing in front with names like Hilversum and Moscow, and from the back, should you crawl there, from a humming yellow ochre forest of vacuum tubes that we knew as "valves") onto a fragile 78 r.p.m. disc which revolved placidly on the turntable.

The magic would begin as you sat back and wallowed in the warmth of the tubby sound. More often than not the singer would be Frank Crumit (pronounced "Croom-it" in England, and beloved by all classes there) accompanied by his guitar; the romantic tale in "Riding Down To Bangor" pulled the listener in, but not half as much as the singular, silky lure of that voice. Outside the weather was typically "inclement" (to use the preferred word of vice-headmaster Captain T.D. Manning), but the dinning of the rain on the corrugated iron of the study only reinforced the siren call of the recording, calling me far away from the bitter, sighing coast of Seaford, Sussex, in 1949.

On a summer afternoon some years later, I am lying at the bottom of a punt on a little man-made lake near a holiday village by the Suffolk coast. The lake water laps arounds me, but I'm not paying attention. A portable windup HMV gramophone plays Bing Crosby; "Galway Bay" backed by "Home on the Range." Both places sound appetizing and a lot more comfortable than being an overweight teenage schoolboy enjoying none of the perks associated with a growing sexual awareness. Where did Crosby and Crumit live? Inside the gramophone, of course, behind the curtain.

At the outset of the 1960s, confronting the question of what on earth to do in life after compulsory schooling. Go back to school, I decide, to Trinity College, Dublin. Gene Austin inspired the move, singing from a snappy electric Dansette portable located in our thick-walled, thickly-carpeted family flat on Putney Heath, London: "Each sweet co-ed like a rainbow trail…" ("The Sweetheart of Sigma Chi").

The crooners even accompanied me in the midst of a rock 'n' roll career as a "One Hit Wonder," singing the same old story of love under the moon and the stars, in the still of the night, in a shady nook, by a waterfall, in a gypsy tea room, in a little hula heaven, in a shelter from a shower, on a little dream ranch, by the seaside where the waves are whispering goodnight so sweetly I'll forget that they've changed my name to a number…

Encounters in the 1970s with real-life crooners, combined with random personal experiences, helped temper my dangerously mawkish attachment to this music. On one occasion, a girl friend, Vicki, and I were walking along a beach and, as was usual for me when there was nothing pressing to say, I softly murmured the words to an old song—in this case, the chorus of "You Were Meant For Me." I had reached "You were all the sweet things rolled into one" when Vicki stopped dead in her tracks, looked me straight in the eyes and said, "You really meant that! How sweet!" I was stunned and embarrassed, all the while wondering if the next move expected of me was an engagement proposal. This episode warned me of the danger inherent in unrestrained crooning.

Around that time I also had the opportunity to spend a day with Rudy Vallee in the course of researching my book, After the Ball—Pop Music From Rag to Rock. While staying in Hollywood with friends in the music business, they suggested I simply ring him up; his number, after all, was listed in the phone book. He'd been in the papers as a result of his campaign to get the name of his street changed from Pyramid Drive to Rue de Vallee. My friends laughingly remarked that when the authorities refused his request Vallee threatened to change his name to Rudy Pyramid.

When I rang him up, he responded in hearty fashion, inviting me up to his house for tennis and dinner. Arriving at the wild and wooded estate located on top of one of

Hollywood's hills, I saw no sign of The Vagabond Lover. I figured he must be out and about, living up to his name. I wandered around, under the watch of Latino servants, admiring the garage's revolving driveway and the tennis court perched on the edge of the hilltop, over the Rudy Vallee museum. I also noted the public pay telephone kiosks and the metal signs stuck in the flower telling smokers to mind their manners.

Eventually the crooner, accompanied by his glamorous blonde wife, made his entrance. He was fresh from ocean cruising and ready for champagne and caviar. Following this snack we knuckled down to some tennis. Vallee made his own rules, generally in his favor. He did, however, gracefully offer me a few points. Afterwards, he took me on a tour of the archives under the court where he lectured me on the collection of megaphones and saxophones and stacks of scrapbooks documenting every known reference to the Vallee name in print.

Inside the house there was more champagne, followed by a one-man show starring my host, telling how he'd made love to some great silent screen siren on this floor, tooting a saxophone, singing a bawdy verse about bedding Dolores Del Rio, reciting "How Fights Start in Bars," and ending with a virtuoso performance of "The Old Sow" accompanied by realistic pig noises. Rudy, his wife, and I finally had dinner at a table that seemed a mile long. Rudy and I were situated at opposite ends of the table; I knew he was there because his red plaid jacket shone brightly and I could make out assorted bits of gossip. When I heard snoring I knew it was time to leave, negotiating my way through a pack of dogs on the way out.

Many years, and a number of dogs later, I inherited a delightful mixed breed from Vallee's widow. Inspector had been Rudy's favorite, I was told, and had been at his master's side, licking his face, when he died watching his old friend, Ronald Reagan, delivering a presidential speech on television. Inspector came with meager belongings: a red leather leash and collar, a packet of frankfurters, a megaphone, and a portfolio of pictures showing him munching tapes of Vallee's radio shows, observing the star slumped in an armchair, and attempting to terrorize a pants-suited Dorothy Lamour. He showed no interest at all when I screened *The Vagabond Lover*.

My relationship with vintage crooner Nick Lucas was warmer, albeit much less grand. We met in professional circumstances at the Mayfair Music Hall in Santa Monica where we were both appearing as performers. He always struck me as sprucely dressed, clear-spoken and chipper in spirit.

In 1975 I arranged for Nick to be filmed as part of a television series on which I was working, a British-made history of popular music entitled, *All You Need Is Love*. It went so well that I was able to get him into an Irish documentary on Hollywood; we filmed him in the garden of his apartment house, a suitable spot for tiptoeing through the tulips. In addition to his signature song, "Tiptoe," he sang "Baby Face," inviting me to join him with my ukulele on the second chorus. "Remember to play the right chords in the sequence," he whispered as the clapper was posed to come down on its board.

A few years later we were on the same bill at the Variety Arts Roof Garden in downtown Los Angeles. Again, he invited me to play along with him; again, he admonished me to play the right chords, especially tonight as we'd be doing "Tiptoe." "Lots of folks don't play the right chords, you know." But I did okay in his show and he gave me the wink. I was touched by his on-stage reference to not minding Tiny Tim's version because "I smile every time I go to the bank." You see, as a songwriter I knew that he hadn't received any royalties because his name wasn't on the sheet music. Nor had he taken a cut-in, a common practice in the Tin Pan Alley heydays (Rudy Vallee and Gene Austin were known to accept cut-ins in exchange for exposing a new number).

Compared to the splendor of the Vallee lifestyle, Lucas lived quite modestly and apparently had to continue working in order to make ends meet. I believe he had a lady admirer who lived out in Hemet; I know he used to go there quite often. Every now and then we'd meet for lunch at the place of his choice, a cafeteria patronized by senior citizens on limited budgets. Over chicken pot pie or Salisbury steak I'd pepper Nick with questions relating to his glory days. But he never seemed particularly interested—he wasn't forthcoming and couldn't remember dates (I had to supply them)—and expressed only mild surprise when I informed him that his guest slot during the early days of Nashville's Grand Ole Opry had helped make him tremendously influential with later generations of country and western performers. Nick turned the table talk to more pressing things like how much I was currently being paid for gigs at the Mayfair or Roof Garden. The last time I sang with him was outdoors at a Republican rally of some kind or other on the lot of a Ford auto dealership in a rather unsalubrious part of Hollywood.

I glancingly ran across Sam Coslow (a side-of-the-mouth quintessential crooner in his day), but by this time—the early 1970s—he was a wealthy retired music executive and multi-hit songwriter living in Florida and traveling regularly to London. We were having cocktails and canapes when I congratulated him on having written one of the first druggie songs, "Marahuana," for the 1930s Paramount picture, Murder at the Vanities." He looked dumbfounded. What was I talking about? And then he changed the subject. But he was very kind to me later when, back in Hollywood, I got on the wrong side of the editor of an expose news rag and was threatened with a sharp sleaze attack. I called Sam in Florida and he arranged for some heavies to pay a visit to the muckraker. Nothing more was heard, nor did I ever see or hear from Caslow again. I wish I'd asked him more questions about those crooning years.

I wish I'd known that Cliff Edwards was located just down the street from me, living in virtual poverty. He died in July 1971, a charity case, at the Virgil Convalescent Hospital, in Hollywood. Likewise, I wish I'd known that Gene Austin lived in nearby Palm Springs, entertaining at the electric organ of his mobile home. He would die in January 1972;

Nick Lucas was one of his pall bearers. These artists and others of their generation could have helped put me straight, wised me up, and dressed me down. I could have learned something.

Now I'm something of a lone contender in a silent ring. Of course, the recordings of the deceased masters lie waiting and ready to prove their point while I battle on as a live performer, singing in a similar, conversational, confidential manner. I try to avoid slavish copying, rather expressing myself in a manner best accommodating my own limited skills.

Is crooning an art in the aesthetic sense? Is it a thing of beauty and universal appeal, possessing an extraordinary significance? Without presuming to have the definitive answer, I can say that I do keep coming back to the singers and songs of this tradition whenever I'm brimming over with happiness or sadness. Fortunately, sadness rhymes with gladness, and jolly with melancholy, and so on. This quaint little self-contained world—archaic, no doubt, and far from the rant and the cant and the bland and the brown of today—continues to hold me, for better or worse, in peaceful captivity.

When I try—in repose—to conjure up the essence of that world, I start with a memory from years past: It is a muggy summer night North London, just after a quick storm, streets slippery with grease and lined by rows of nondescript attached houses, and I'm hurrying to a tube train to take me home. Weighed down with old records just purchased from local dealer buffs, I pass by men of uncertain age wearing stained clothes and meal remains on their faces and beards.

Glancing quickly to my left, through an open door and into a parlor, I spy an old woman sitting in profile on a sofa. She's leaning forward, hands clasped in front, listening intently while nodding and smiling, to music from a wind-up gramophone facing her. I recognize the voice of Al Bowlly but I don't know the song. From the shadows I watch her behavior in what appears to be a moment of time recaptured. The lyrics have something to do with a past longing at a dance. When the waltz tune comes to an end she turns around and stares out the front door, into the wet and steamy street, straight through me. She is silently crying. I hurry on, moved and not a little embarrassed over this scene. I make a mental note to check up on this recording.

I later determine the identity of the song: "I'm Saving the Last Waltz For You," written by Joseph George Gilbert and Horatio Nicholle (the pen-name of publisher Lawrence Wright). The piece was recorded in London on July 1, 1938 by Felix Mendelssohn & His Orchestra with a vocal refrain by Al Bowlly. It's a catchy tune in a time-honored pattern, with warhorse words like "arms" and "forsake" as well as two redundant uses of "just" and a pseudo-poetic line construction ("In your arms I'm just longing to be"). So says the critical self.

But the emotional self—the one that unabashedly accepts love, pity, and nostalgia—knocks aside the critical self and takes in the sincerity of Bowlly and the poignancy of the song's scenario: he's been looking at her all evening through as she dances with everyone but him. Even so, he's saved the last waltz especially for her. Yes, the critical self gets up off the floor and asks why Al didn't simply go over and ask her for a dance much earlier in the evening. However, that is beside the point in the world of the sentimental song. When you're enraptured you don't reason why, you go simply go with your emotions to that ineffable place from which you hope never to return.

Notes

(1) Art seems to have been in Louisville at this point in time. However, the 1915 version of "Hesitation Blues," published by Gillham's pal, Billy Smythe, credits only Smythe and a certain Scott Middleton. Reputedly, Smythe and Middleton later accompanied Gillham to California, but there the trio's trail disappears. Smythe turns up playing piano on Gillham's last commercial release, a Bluebird record made at a hotel in San Antonio, Texas in 1934. In the meantime, Gillham's name was added to the writer credits of "Hesitation Blues" when it was republished by the Jack Mills Company of New York in 1924. (Mills, whose brother Irving co-wrote "Lovesick Blues" and went on to manage Duke Ellington, specialized in the blues and black music in general.) Gillham first recorded "Hesitation Blues" via the acoustic process for Gennett, a Richmond, Indiana-based label best known for recording jazz, gospel, hillbilly music, and Klan anthems. Since no copies have even been found, it would appear that this recording was never released. In February 1925 he recorded the song again, this time as an electric for Columbia. The release—a rollicking version full of amusing couplets backed by a cracking good piano—reveals that Gillham modified the approach called for in the 1915 Billy Smythe score. The fact that it also differed from W.C. Handy's rendition would seem to indicate that "Hesitation Blues" ("Hesitating" according to the Handy version), like so much early, roots-oriented pop, was a "floating" folk song of no known authorship. Performers, amateur and professional alike, contributed their own lines and melody switches to the tried-and-true blues, a form which evidence suggests surfaced at the turn of the century as a ribald "slow drag" dance-song accompaniment to staged movements of sporting house ladies.

Variations of "Hesitation Blues" can be found in collections of black folk songs published in the middle 1920s; these songbooks state that the material was found in the American South between 1915 and 1917. Did these southerners learned "Hesitation Blues" from the published versions, or were they re-creating by polishing, and then presenting their creation to the world in the time-honored folk process—a process devoid of copyright and royalty considerations? My guess is that Gillham and Smythe picked up a version of the song while they were living in St. Louis in 1914. "Hesitation" waltzes were the rage and, therefore, their composition appears to have been a commentary on the dance fad. Evidence indicates that Gillham met Smythe shortly before 1914; at the time, Art was enrolled at St. Louis University and Billy worked as a local music publisher (he enjoy modest success with the release of his "Ten Penny Rag" in 1911). It is possible that Smythe, the older and more experienced of the two, taught Gillham how to rag at the piano. Billy was an active in the St. Louis scene as a pianist; the city was at the forefront of ragtime innovation. Early pioneers included composer and performer Tom Turpin, who ran a popular saloon in the 1890s, and John Stark, a publisher whose clients included Scott Joplin, moved his business there in the early 1900s.

(2) Ted Brown's real name was Fred Fred Brownold. He'd been a ragtime composed in turn-of-the-century St. Louis when John Stark published his "Manhattan Rag" (1905). Two years later he wrote "That Rag," a collection of melodies that had been floating around the ragtime world of saloons and sporting houses. Later, he moved to Chicago and started his own publishing company. The trail of Browne, Smythe, and Gillham shows the connection between Victorian ragtime and Jazz Age electronics, from sheet music to radio airwaves.

(3) Mrs. Louisa Canada Gillham had won fame as a coloratura soprano with the San Carlo Opera Company.

(4) This surmise is compromised somewhat by the fact that Edison had no ear for harmony. Sam Coslow, later to become an arch-crooner (with a way mooing out of the side of his mouth) and composer of the Crosby hit, "Learn to Croon," said as much based upon his stint as Edison's song-scout in the early 1920s. He related that the great man judged a new song by its tune alone; harmonies were forbidden. The pop standard, "Carolina in the Morning," for instance, sounded so see-saw monotonous as a naked melody that Edison rejected it, just as he'd rejected Rachmaninoff for playing too loudly and Al Jolson's brother Harry as a "Jew trying to sound like a Negro."

(5) Victor soon replaced Murray—both as a premier solo artist and Aileen Stanley's singing partner—with crooning pioneer Johnny Marvin.

(6) Crumit's delivery on "My Honey's Lovin' Arms" (Columbia; 1922) reflected a self-conscious effort to mimic the big-voiced acoustic era singers. He is dead on the beat, military style, rolling his r's, and exhibiting a pronounced nasal tone.

(7) A Paramount musical short from that period featured Frances Williams gaily singing of problems with her current boy friend who keeps demanding, "Let's don't and say we did." John Gilbert, then a handsome screen idol, is her delight, but "It seems my boy friend likes him, too."

(8) In the 1933 movie, Broadway Through a Keyhole, a young woman intently

appraised Columbo during a nightclub scene as he led the band, fiddle tucked underneath his arm. Approvingly, she delivered her verdict: "He doesn't look like a crooner."

Table 31

Gene Austin

Lemuel Eugene Lucas, better known as Gene Austin, was born June 24, 1900 in Gainesville, located in the Red River Valley of north Texas. He was the only child of Nova and Belle Lucas, both Missouri natives. Nova, the son of George Washington and Kate Lucas, would die in 1943, long after he and Belle were divorced. Belle, the daughter of Alva and Elmansa Hearrel, was a descendent of a famous Shoshone maiden, Sacajawea, her great, great grandmother. Sacajawea - known as the "Bird Woman" and celebrated for her courage, resourcefulness, and good humor - accompanied Lewis and Clark in their expedition from North Dakota to the Pacific Coast, 1800-1806. Belle would die August 3, 1956 and be buried alongside Nova in Gainesville.

In his autobiography, Gene would recall those early developmental years with considerable fondness.

> My Texas childhood...was rich in the stuff that mattered most to a small boy
> at the start of the twentieth century. Plenty of room to grow in, fresh air
> and sunshine, nourishing simple food, friendly neighbors, pleasant
> climate horses, cattle, rabbits, chickens; and most of all, first-hand contact
> with the singing cowboys. It was a typical Mark Twain childhood.

Gainesville was located in cattle country crossed by the Chisholm Trail, the fabled thoroughfare traveled by cowboys and steers on the way to the stockyards of the Upper Midwest. While still a toddler, Gene would wander off to the Trail while his mother was engaged in chores, drawn to the western trail songs sung by the cowboys during the cattle drives. His access to this music, however, was cut short by Belle - who upon hearing these songs re-enacted at home by Gene - denied him access to "at dreadful trail where any bolting steer could trample my child to death, or gore him!"

Restricted from enjoying one form of forbidden fruit, Gene substituted another in short order, gravitating to the parlour houses located on a few side streets of the town which presided over a thriving prostitution trade. Hearing the exotic improvisations of the piano-playing "professors," he inched his way up to the stoop, eventually being invited inside by the friendly occupants. This district became the new center of Gene's life, and he curried favor by running errands for the professors and attractive ladies of the night. His mother's suspicions were again aroused when he echoed this new music at home; despite his evasive responses to her inquiries, she soon discovered the source of his new material, and once again he was denied access to what he perceived to be an innocent pleasure.

Gene, however, had greater distractions to deal with at this time. His parents didn't get along. The headstrong Belle, who longed for adventure and travel, had tired of life with Nova, a gentle soul who was unwilling to assert his preordained authority. Acquiring a divorce, Belle took Gene off for a prolonged visit with her relatives, an unruly lot given to extended bouts of arguing and fighting.

She eventually returned to Gainesville and, in short order, decided to marry a blacksmith named Jim Austin. Jim insisted soon after the marriage that his young stepson adopt the Austin family name.

Although a county seat, Gainesville was small enough to afford daily encounters between Belle, Jim, and Nova. It appears that this circumstance played a large role in Jim's decision to move his family to Louisiana and open his own "smithy." Gene would later relate that he instantly disliked his new home in the swampy village of Yellow Pine.

> The air was heavy, the shadows thick and plentiful, the sky visible only
> in patches, the rains frequent, the insects, heat and humidity unbearable;
> this could never replace what I had left behind. What a change! Then
> and there whatever feeling I could have had for Big Jim vanished.
> To me it seemed my adventurous days were over, because the area
> was infested with snakes and alligators, creatures I didn't like; and
> there were bogs, quagmires and quicksand. Also, I couldn't understand
> the people, who spoke unlike us Texans; and worst of all, I couldn't
> hear any of my favorite music…All I heard was Mother nagging me to
> go to school; and after school, Big Jim ordering me to make myself
> useful around the shop.

To make matters worse, Jim began drinking heavily and "nice" families shunned the Austins due their humble working class background. As a result, Gene instinctively withdrew into a shell.

While loitering after my school in order to delay the inevitability of chores in the forge, Gene discovered the songs of cotton pickers working the nearby plantations. One of the workers, a kindly old black man named Esau, befriended Gene after hearing him singing along to the music. Over his parent's protestations, Gene regularly visited Esau's shanty in "The Quarter" for the next ten years. "Uncle Esau" provided the human dignity and understanding Gene required in the face of a steady stream of beatings and verbal abuse at home.

By his early teens, Gene had because big and strong enough to stand up to his stepfather. When Jim came at him one day, threatening to beat the music out of him, his rebellious spirit surged to the fore. "You an' that ol' smithy can go to the devil! I've taken my last punishment from you," Gene snarled back. After an evening stopover with Uncle Esau, Gene went to the local railroad yard in order to catch the first freight train passing through Yellow Pine. His brief adventure as a runaway took him back to Gainesville where he became reacquainted with his natural father, Nova Lucas. A fracas with one of the town's leading businessmen, a Colonel Mills, however, resulted in his father advising him to return to Jim and Belle.

But Gene's inability to submit to his stepfather's enforced regimen of physical labor without the pleasures of Uncle Esau's company and plantation music caused him to leave home again shortly after his return. Hopping a train which carried him deep into the heart of Texas, he began fraternizing with the professors with the hope of adding to his repertoire of songs. He moved on to wide array of jobs, including selling balloons for a circus and playing a calliope for a traveling carnival. Gene would later provide the following assessment of this period of his life:

> In my wildest imagination, I had never thought that the wanderlust of my mother had rubbed off on me. But I soon developed a restlessness that kept me on the go; fortunately for me I was always able to hustle some grub and a place to sleep. I became good at my job, but not wanting to limit myself as a parlor-house professor, I decided to try my luck in cabarets, which today would be considered honky tonks, singing the songs of Uncle Esau's people, as well as songs I had picked up from the cowboys on the trail, and the parlour-house "blues." I became an itinerant entertainer, and my wanderings took me all over the country.

Gene eventually matriculated to New Orleans. Associates always seemed to be touting that city, arguing that if you could make it there as a singer, then you could succeed anywhere. He soon located the parlour-house district and, shortly thereafter, joined the army as one of General Pershing's recruits for the ill-starred Mexican expedition. In pursuit of the elusive Pancho Villa, Gene's army service—which largely consisted of inclement weather, treachery from civilians, and ambush from guerrillas—was abruptly terminated when fellow soldier Tom Mix, the future film cowboy star, instigated a check on his date of birth.

Discharged from the military and back in New Orleans, Gene picked up where he'd left off. Becoming a top entertainer in parlour houses, he moved on the cabaret circuit. On the eve of his seventeenth birthday, he received a special delivery letter from his mother indicating that she and Jim were coming to take him back home. In the face of this dilemma, Gene again enlisted in the army and was assigned to the 156th Infantry of the 39th Division. After four months of guard duty on the New Orleans docks, with most of his off-duty time spent performing in the parlour-houses, he was transferred to Camp Merritt, New Jersey, where he did stevedore work in the depot detail.

Wishing for more adventure, Gene—responsible for getting a company onto a troopship headed for France--absent-mindedly-on-purpose remained aboard until the boat had sailed out well beyond docking area. Following an obligatory reprimand by the commanding officer, he was rewarded with immediate assignment to a company scheduled to leave for the front. Surviving a year of battle in the trenches, Gene became a victim of the 1918 Spanish flu epidemic. During his convalescence, he met a Medical Corps dentist, Lieutenant Knapp, who had admired his singing at the military "Y" hut. Knapp convinced him that becoming a dental assistant would be a good trade to learn, not only while in the army but as a civilian.

He stayed in Paris for a year after the signing of the Armistice, working as Lieutenant Knapp's assistant. On the way home, Knapp offered to take Gene on as an associate if he would go to dental school. Following a stint in a preparatory school, Gene enrolled in the University of Maryland dental program. In addition to working in Knapp's office, he continued performing in obscure night clubs, which helped in financing his education. By now familiar with the problems in getting some patients to pay their bills, Gene switched to law school, convinced he'd be of greater use if he could help Dr. Knapp collect outstanding accounts.

One night another performer, Roy Bergere, who'd been impressed by Gene's singing during a night club engagement, suggested that they work together in vaudeville. It didn't take much persuasion for Gene to begin rehearsals for a piano-and-song act with his new partner after apologizing to Knapp that the entertainment business would always be his first love. A break-in date at a Philadelphia theatre, however, was so poorly received that the manager felt impelled to cancel the balance of the engagement. Undeterred, the duo headed to New York City, spending several lean months in an attempt to secure vaudeville bookings.

During his free hours, Gene began developing another dimension of his musical talent, that of songwriting. He relates that the inspiration behind his first successful song composition came about while sitting on a city park bench, watching people walk by as sparrows in the trees engaged in morning singing.

> Before long, I became bothered by a tune in my subconscious mind
> that seemed to be crying to be written. The unknown tune soon found
> its way to the surface. The rhythmic sound of high heels fell into place
> with the "tweet-tweets" of the sparrows. Without much knowledge of
> what I was doing, I pulled out a pencil and some paper and wrote these

words, "When my sugar walks down the street, all the birdies go tweet-tweet-tweet." I continued to write until I had completed the entire chorus and a verse.

Several days later, Gene came up with the idea for another song while riding the elevator up to his hotel room. When Gene absent-mindedly dropped the shells of the peanuts he was eating on the floor, the elevator operator groaned, "Mistuh Gene, how come you do me like you do?" Feeling that these words succinctly expressed his misgivings about the recent months of futility in New York, Gene quickly improvised a melody to complete the song.

"How Come You Do Me Like You Do" was not only accepted by the song publisher, Mills Music, Inc., but Austin and Bergere were engaged to help promote it. This work enabled the duo to make valuable contacts with both performers and cabaret owners. After the song became a big hit, they began a successful run playing at Lou Clayton's Mahjong Club. When Bergere started working professionally with his new wife, Gene continued there as a single until prohibition agents found sufficient liquor on the premises to have it shut down.

Hoping to eventually break into the vaudeville circuit, Gene began working for the song publishers, Stark & Cowan, as a general demonstrator. (The firm would publish the Austin and Bergere composition, "Tell Me If You Want Somebody Else," in 1924.) During one appointment in April 1924, he met his future wife, a vaudeville dancer still in her teens named Kathryn Arnold. Despite the awkward arrangement of having to include her mother as a chaperone on all of their dates, the courtship proceeded smoothly and, on June 16, 1924, they were married.

The August 16, 1924 issue of *Billboard* would report that Austin was employed as a songwriter and contact man with the recording companies by Jack Mills, Inc., an up and coming music publisher. The first week on the job proved unproductive; Gene, who'd always subscribed to the conventional wisdom that "songs write themselves," found himself pressing in trying to come up with a decent song. He was rescued from his immediate dilemma when directed to demonstrate the Mills catalog to the Vocalion label. After listening to a few songs, the executive—recognizing Gene's regional dialect--confided to him about a "southern problem" facing the company.

> There's a chain of music stores in Nashville that sent up a blind
> man to record some hill-billy songs. They happen to be one of
> our largest accounts and we can't afford to offend them. But
> this George Reneau's voice sounds absolutely impossible.

Sympathetic about the plight of both Vocalion and the blind musician, who wanted nothing more than to return home, Gene agreed to try lending his voice to some recording sessions. The approach clicked, and Austin cut a series of records to Reneau's guitar and harmonica accompaniment between April 1924 and February 1925, including "The Wreck on the Southern 97"/"Lonesome Road Blues" (#14809), "You Will Never Miss Your Mother Until She Is Gone"/"Life's Railway To Heaven" (#14811), and "Turkey in the Straw"/"Little Brown Jug" (#14812). The label on these releases read as follows: "Sung & Played by George Reneau – The Blind Musician of the Smoky Mountains – Guitar and Mouth Harp." Although Austin professed no great affinity for country music, the credibility of his singing and yodeling reflected its close proximity during his youth combined with his natural skills for mimicry. The success of these releases spurred Edison to bring the duo into the studio to record many of the same songs during September 1924.

In the meantime, Reneau confided that he was on the "Oregon Short Line" (out of money). Gene suggested that Reneau play his guitar and harmonica on New York street corners while he kept a lookout for the cops. This ploy proved so successful that the blind musician had second thoughts about returning home; only Gene's warnings that they would inevitably be apprehended by the law convinced Reneau to board a train headed back to Nashville.

Austin's big break as a recording artist came when Mills asked him select some songs and demonstrate them to Victor's star singer, Aileen Stanley. After being introduced to Miss Stanley and musical director Nat Shilkret at the Victor Company studios, he ran through his first selection, the self-penned "When My Sugar Walks Down the Street." He couldn't believe his ears when Stanley responded, "Don't bother with the others, this is just what I wanted. Thank you, young man." After listening to the song one more time, Shilkret then took him aside and said, "you're going to sing on [Miss Stanley's] record. You know, young man, I have a hunch if you cut some recordings alone, we may be able to start a new style of singing in popular records, I'm going to take a chance on you. I'll give you a hundred dollars a record. If they sell, we can talk about a contact."

When asked what gave him the idea for his type of singing, Austin replied, "Well, Mister Shilkret, when I came to New York, all the singers were tryin' to follow the great Al Jolson. I knew I could never sing as loud or perhaps as good as Mister Jolson, so since he was always talkin' about how his mammy used to croon to him, I just croon like his mammy." This conversation would appear to have Austin placing himself in the vanguard of the crooning tradition.

While crooning didn't become a full-fledged movement within the record industry until the introduction of electronic microphones by the major labels in mid-1925, Austin's soft, laid-back style translated well using the acoustic process. However, he was not the only singer to achieve success employing this type of understated vocal technique prior to the advent of electronic recording. In 1924 Cliff Edwards, popularly known as

"Ukelele Ike," enjoyed success with "It Had to Be You," "All Alone," and other releases for Pathe and the American Records conglomerate, as did Nick Lucas, "the Crooning Troubador," with the Brunswick label. Furthermore, Whispering Jack Smith, Johnny Marvin, and others possessing a crooning delivery were extremely popular with record buyers shortly after the electronic process became widely used. Nevertheless, Austin's immense success--among singers, he was only rivaled in popularity by Al Jolson during the 1920s—made it inevitable that he would be viewed as the figurehead, if not the actual originator, of the crooning genre.

Austin accompanied Stanley on "When My Sugar Walks Down the Street" in Victor's New York City studio, January 30, 1925. On the strength of this performance, more sessions followed over the next three months, including a duet with country performer Carson Robison, comic sketches accompanied by Billy "Yuke" Carpenter, and "tenor with orchestra" fare. His first hit release of note, "Yearning," backed by "No Wonder" (Victor 19625), was recorded March 12, 1925.

Austin felt confident enough about his prospects to quit his job with Mills Music. While waiting for the public's verdict on his first group of releases, he and his wife put together an act and hit the road. By the time they hit Columbus, Ohio, however, Nat Shilkret was on the phone, exclaiming, "For heaven's sake, Gene, why did you run off without letting us know where you were going? I spent over a week trying to locate you. I have good news for you. All I've heard for the last month is, 'More Gene Austin records!' I want you to leave immediately and get back to New York as fast as you can."

One hit record seemed to follow another during Austin's early years as a Victor recording artist. He claims that royalties during the first three months for his first four records under the Victor contract totaled ninety-six thousand dollars; he carried the uncashed check around for a considerable period of time in order to impress skeptics. Nurtured by his wife, and—in view of the uniqueness of his singing style—given free rein by his label to select song material, Austin would look back on this period as the happiest of his life. He prided himself in his ability to find first-rate material that had often been ignored or rejected by established singers. Notable choices from that first year included "Yes Sir, That's My Baby" (composed by Gus Kahn and Walter Donaldson), "The Flapper Wife" (Beatrice Burton-Carl Rupp), "Five Foot Two, Eyes of Blue" (Young-Lewis-Henderson), "Sleepy Time Gal" (Alden-Egan-Lorenzo-Whiting), and "Sweet Child" (Whiting-Lewis-Simon). However, he remained uneasy over his inability to convince Victor officials of his need to interpret the soulful music he'd learned from Uncle Esau. But for the time being, he and Kathryn focused on adjusting to a significantly more lavish lifestyle punctuated by a beautiful new home, a large car, expensive clothes, and access to the best that New York night life could offer.

Eventually the pressures that are a natural by-product of success began to undercut his peace of mind. He became defensive when told that the Tin Pan Alley denizens were convinced he could turn any song into gold. Decades later, he would comment, "They were so wrong. I'd always told them hit songs don't care who sings them. They wouldn't take no for an answer; and when I refused to be pushed into a song I didn't think suited me, I got the reputation of being high hat and hard to get along with."

Austin decided that automobile tour back to his hometown of Yellow Pine would be just the ticket for regaining a fresh perspective on a career that seemed to be rapidly spinning out of control. On the way down to Louisiana, he pointed out the milestones of his life to Kathryn. The visit with Jim and Belle, who had relocated to the nearby town of Minden, went smoothly; they both seemed to be deeply impressed by Gene's newfound celebrity. As soon as he had finished an informal performance for houseguests on the first evening home with his parents, he slipped off the visit his beloved mentor, Uncle Esau. Esau, refusing Gene's offer to buy him a new home, proved as kindly and helpful with his counsel as he had in the past. Austin's chief regret was that he still hadn't shared the secret of this special relationship with his wife.

The next morning, Austin was awoken from a deep sleep by a phone call from Nat Shilkret in New York. He exclaimed, "We are flooded with so many orders for new Gene Austin records, I want you to come back as fast as you can make it. Can you leave immediately?" Austin hastily made preparations to return back East, but not before arranging the purchase of a large farm house for his parents as well as providing funds for Esau's immediate needs.

After meeting his recording obligations, Austin formed his own music publishing company with the aim of placing African American songs in a position to be recorded by Victor and the other major labels. He also began booking personal appearances as a means of funding his new venture as well as to popularize this music. Caught up in a whirlwind of conferences with songwriters, booking agents, theatrical managers, bankers, and record company executives, Austin agonized that Kathryn always seemed stuck with either "a moody husband or an absent one." He justified the situation to her by noting that in the uncertain world of show business, it was best to "get it while the getting's good."

One day not long after Austin's return from Louisiana, the latest batch of records he'd sent Esau was returned with the word "deceased" stamped crosswise across the package. Despite his outward success, Austin relates that his personal life fell into complete disarray.

> For months to come, I tried to cling onto a form of communication with Esau's spirit. The practice of spiritualism left me shaken and lost in a solitariness of forsaken gloom. This was the beginning of such gnawing doubts and fears that I turned to another spirit, alcohol, to

> bolster my imagination into believing that I was a complete individual and did have the power and initiative to carry on without the help of the one I believed had supreme authority and held the key or controlling influence over my voice, deeds and person.

He added that heavy drinking, rather than numbing the pain, made him temperamental, arrogant, and belligerent. In the process, he disappointed, even hurt, those closest to him. Realization of the impact of his behavior led to further self-recrimination.

By mid-1925, his records were so popular in England that London's prestigious Princess Club made Austin an offer to perform there. He eagerly accepted, in part to escape the stifling atmosphere of New York, but also to hopefully make contact with British scientists then investigating survival after death. The English reserve, combined with his own extreme shyness, dictated against Austin's wishes to gain entry to a scientific séance. In his words, "The net result of my three months in London was that the supply of Gene Austin records was sold out in England as well as in America; and 'Nipper' was yelping for his star to hurry back; and I picked up some English songs for my music company's catalog, which turned out to be hits."

Upon his return to the States, Austin, thirsting for the blues music of his youth, began frequenting the Harlem club scene. One of his new associates was pianist Fats Waller, who had first approached Austin with songs to publish while he was employed at Mills Music. He also was attracted by Harlem's reputation for "conjur" activity, believing that it accounted for his career. Looking only for proof of the continuation of the bond between Esau and himself, he gave any "prince" or "princess" a fair trial, stipulating only that he be treated as any other client from downtown.

One of his recordings from this period, "Me Too" (Victor 20143)—coupled with "For My Sweetheart," has baffled more than one fan of early sound recording history. Recorded in New York on August 12, 1926, the song exhibits a considerable amount of rumbling noise, a feature one wouldn't expect of a release from a major artist on the label then known for the highest quality sound reproduction. One researcher, Don Peak, consulted the August 13, 1926 issue of *The New York Times* for clues. The front page headlines read, "STORM TIES UP CITY TRAFFIC, FLOODS SUBWAYS, KILLS BOY" and "LIGHTNING STARTS 15 FIRES."

Other records recorded on that day do not display similar background noise. However, Austin's cut included a spare accompaniment (violin and piano, only), whereas some of the other releases featured a fuller band arrangement. Furthermore, the full impact of the storm may have been limited to the Austin session. Regarding the aesthetic judgment of the Victor brass in deciding to release the track, *The New Amberola Graphic* (Number 47, Winter 1984) observed that "most [sound reproduction] machines in use in 1926 were not sensitive enough to reproduce the low frequency of rumbling thunder, so it is safe to assume that the customers never even noticed it."

Following another stage tour, while his wife remained back home with her family in St. Louis expecting their first child, Austin entered the Victor studios resolved to record a song which had been in the files of a leading publishing for several years. As noted by David Ewen, in *All the Years of American Popular Music*,

> "My Blue Heaven"...was written in 1924, three years before its publication; (Walter) Donaldson wrote it one afternoon at the Friars Club in New York while waiting for his turn at the billiard table. George Whiting, then appearing in vaudeville, adapted the lyrics to the melody and used it in his act, but the song failed to attract much attention. For three years it lay in discard until Tommy Lyman, a radio singer, picked it up for use as his theme song.

By now, Austin's arrangement with Victor regarding the choice of material to record had soured. He was convinced that the best material which he brought to the company's attention was going to other artists. In view of his own family situation, he felt this was one song he had to commit to disc. He pleaded, and finally gave Nat Shilkret an ultimatum that he wouldn't do another session unless his interpretation was commercially released. According to Austin, an agreement was reached for "My Blue Heaven" to be coupled with "Are You Thinking of Me Tonight?", the most highly regarded song among those he was planning to record at that time.

Austin relates that it was scheduled last on the September 14, 1927 recording agenda in order minimize potential conflicts with the Victor brass. However, as soon as satisfactory takes had been achieved for the other songs, the orchestra members put away their instruments and filed out of the studio. When Austin complained, Shilkret replied, "I'm sorry Gene. I didn't know at the time I made you that promise that the musicians had another date and would have to leave. We can make it another day." H. Allen Smith, in *A Short History of Fingers*, documents the singer's refusal to back down:

> I grabbed an old guy with a cello and talked him into standing by. Then I grabbed a song plugger who could play pretty fair piano. And the third fellow I got was an agent who could whistle – bird calls and that sort of thing. I made the record with those three.

When Austin proved intractable, Shilkret resigned himself to the possibility of Austin's first major flop. To the contrary, however, it immediately struck a chord with the American public. Austin would later claim, in an interview published by the *Los Angeles*

Times (March 8, 1959, Part V) that the record sold over eight million copies. The song would also have an unhappy postscript; ready to leave for St. Louis with a freshly pressed copy of "My Blue Heaven" to be united with his family, he received a telegram notifying him of the death of his newborn son.

Following an interlude of healing, which consisted primarily of "soaking up the blues and booze" with Waller and other musicians in Harlem, Austin was able to return to his apartment and once again deal with responsibilities of both his career and everyday life. Kathryn finally agreed to return from St. Louis provided he maintained certain standards of sober behavior. Gratified at his improvement, she agreed accompany him to activities involving New York's social elite. Since Kathryn seemed to particularly enjoy weekend excursions on their stockbroker's yacht, Gene suggested they purchase one of their own. The process of gathering information on boats and navigation helped bring the couple closer together. They submitted blueprints to a custom boat builder in Maryland who'd come highly recommended. The yacht, paid in full by a certified check for seventy-five thousand dollars, was delivered to a Hudson Rover mooring directly alongside the couple's apartment. Christened My Blue Heaven, Austin convinced his wife that a whopping party was needed to launch it in style. He would recall,

> What people came to see us off! Songwriters and music
> publishers, vaudeville and night club headliners, agents,
> stockbrokers, newspaper columnists. Walter Donaldson,
> Benny Davis, composer of my first big hit record, "Yearning,"
> Harry Warren and I took turns at the little piano rolled out on
> the deck. Aileen Stanley and I re-created our duet of "All the
> birdies go tweet-tweet-tweet." The fun was endless, there was
> A spirit of friendship; and even Jimmy Walker, popular mayor
> of New York, dropped in for a couple of choruses of his famous
> song, "Will You Love Me in December as You Do in May"!

The Austin's planned itinerary - sailing to New Orleans and then up the Mississippi, across the Great Lakes and the St. Laurence, and completing the voyage down the North Atlantic back to New York – was widely covered by the media. With the boat setting sail in a southerly direction, the first few days were spent touring the Atlantic coast. Night were spent in ports along the way.

Upon reaching Southport, North Carolina, Captain Ott told Austin that a storm warning had been issued on the receiving radio; the Coast Guard was advising those in the vicinity that the winds could reach hurricane force. Due to the danger of floundering in shallow waters if they stuck to the inland route, Ott recommended that they head out to sea and ride out the bad weather. The storm hit with intense fury almost immediately after the boat had left the harbor. With no sending equipment on their radio, the captain focused his efforts on locating one of the small islands in the area in order to beach the vessel. With Kathryn in virtual hysterics, Austin retreated to his liquor cabinet and poured out his troubles to the steward inside the galley.

When calm weather finally appeared, it came with astonishing suddenness. Surrounded by heavy blankets of fog and unsure of their location, the crew retreated to the cabinet radio set. Out of the static they heard a voice say,

> Those were three more songs introduced and made famous
> by Gene Austin. Once again, we repeat, the Coast Guard
> had abandoned the search for the famous crooner's boat, My
> Blue Heaven, and all the hands aboard must be presumed to
> be drowned….

Captain Ott turned off the radio in disgust. Austin, however, was probably not as surprised over hearing his own obituary. Earlier in the year, *Variety* (February 22, 1928) had included a news note stating, "Austin was last week reported killed in a Milwaukee automobile smash-up, the Boston "Transcript" carrying a report to that effect. It is merely one of the recurring popular pastimes of killing off recording artists." Perhaps this is why Austin turned the radio back on. The voice was now telling listeners that a storm-battered cruiser – its crew evidently washed overboard – had been found on a Carolina beach. It went on,

> The wrecked boat is believed to be the Blue Heaven. Coast Guard
> headquarters give little hope that the man who sang his way into
> America's heart could have survived the terrible hurricane.
> Will each of you just tuning in, join me as we continue our
> memorial program for Gene Austin. The beloved singing
> star lives in our hearts as we take a musical tour back through
> the years, back over the career that brought fame, success and
> wealth. Only five short years ago, Austin came out of the
> relative obscurity of vaudeville and music publishing to become
> the brightest tar of the new phonograph record business
> Here is one of his most recent hits and the song his yacht was
> named for, "My Blue Heaven."

The crew's reverie was interrupted by the captain's announcement that the fog had lifted. A Coast Guard cutter was spotted on the way back to the mainland. The Austins were given a lift ashore, wishing to return to New York as soon as possible, they had obtained a ride to the railroad station before their identity was public knowledge.

Back in New York, Austin had to contend "questions, wisecracks and comments" from the public, the fear of losing his voice (perhaps not unwarranted considering the abuse – heavy drinking, irregular hours, and inclement weather – it had taken), and Kathryn's worries over their expected child. Nevertheless, he had much to be thankful about. The February 22, 1928 issue of *Variety* had reported, "The biggest selling popular vocal artist on all records now is Gene Austin, exclusive Victor artist whose 'Forgive Me' recording went over 500,000 disks and 'My Blue Heaven' will exceed that. Austin's records sell 100,000 blind to the dealers without [being] previously heard." The September 14-16, 1927 recording sessions for Victor had yielded a bumper crop of hits; besides "My Blue Heaven," "There's a Cradle in Carolina" (#21015-A), "My Melancholy Baby" (#21015-B), "The Sweetheart of Sigma Chi" (#20977-B), and "The Lonesome Road" (#21098-A) all qualified as bestsellers. (The latter song would be the only composition not written by Hammerstein and Kern to be included in the 1929 Universal Pictures production of the immensely successful musical, *Show Boat*.)

Furthermore, the latest series of Victor releases – culled from sessions spread over the March-May 1928 period – seemed likely to keep Austin at the forefront of contemporary popular music. "Ramona," backed by "Girl of My Dreams" (#21334), would prove to be his strongest coupling ever. "Ramona," the theme song of a successful motion picture bearing the same name, would eventually sell nearly as many copies as "My Blue Heaven." Around this time, Austin's accountant allegedly informed him that Victor had thus far paid him royalties representing the sale of more than seventy-five million records. While he may have been tormented by feelings that his success was undeserved, there seemed little doubt that his popularity would continue undiminished for some time into the future.

Victor's willingness to allow Austin to selectively record blues-flavored material represented yet another positive development in his life. He was particularly attracted to Fats Waller's compositions; in 1929 alone he recorded his old friend's "I've Got a Feeling I'm Falling" (Victor 22033-B), "Ain't Misbehavin'" (Victor 22068-A), and "My Fate Is in Your Hands" (Victor 22223-A). The recording of the latter song, which included Waller on piano, has been the subject of a number of widely told anecdotes. Shortly after his harrowing experience on the high seas, Austin received a special delivery letter with the news that Waller had been incarcerated for failing to pay his back alimony. As related by Ed Kirkeby, in his Waller biography, *Ain't Misbehavin'*, Austin rushed to court with the necessary bail money. The judge, pointing to Waller in the dock, noted sternly, "This man has been before this court too many times for failure to pay his alimony dues – this cannot go on any longer. Is there any special reason why I should release this man on bail?" Austin, seemingly taken aback by the question, nimbly responded, "Well, your honor, I do have a record session this afternoon, and if this man is not there to play the piano for me, it will put quite a few other musicians out of a job – and jobs are hard to come by these days." According to Austin's own biography, the judge replied, "Gene, I doubt your incredible story. However, I've give Waller a reprieve on these conditions, that you be responsible to see he pays up his alimony...and I want those records as soon as they are available and YOU are to be the presenter." Waller and his benefactor then stopped off at a nearby speakeasy where he demonstrated two songs he claimed to have just written in the "Hotel Alimony," "My Fate Is in Your Hands" and "Ain't Misbehavin'." Upon hearing them, Austin exclaimed, "You've got yourself a couple of hits there, boy. I knew some day you would do it. I'm glad you forgot to pay that back alimony. You just keep runnin' outa dough so you get thrown back in the pokey, if that's where you can write these kind of songs. I'm recordin' tomorrow, so let's go to my boat where we won't be disturbed." There, with the help of a bottle, Waller spent most of the night orchestrating the songs.

Although in close agreement with Kirkeby regarding the events in this episode, Austin's recollection of he matter is flawed in at least one respect. According to Victor session ledgers, Waller's signature work, "Ain't Misbehavin'," was recorded in three takes by Austin on July 30, 1929. "My Fate Is In Your Hands" was the next Waller song to be recorded by Austin, on November 25, 1929. According to the ledger, the session consisted of only this song because a fuse blowing in the studio switch box; Austin had to leave before the electrician could correct the problem. In that Austin did not record another Waller song until June 9, 1930 (i.e., "Rollin' Down the River"), it appears his friend had nothing else of sufficient merit to interest him in late November 1929. During the November 25 session, an argument started when the musicians learned that Austin planned to have Waller play the piano part. Austin recalled,

> When they found out that Fats didn't belong to the musicians'
> union, there was an uproar. I assured the musicians that
> before the day out out, he'd become a member. More
> and more objections were fired at me, till I finally insisted,
> "Dammit! He's gonna play! These are his songs, an' he's
> the only one who can improvise on the piano like I want them
> played."

Kirkeby states that racial considerations were behind the initial refusal of the session musicians to work with Waller. He adds, "The record was eventually made with with the accompanying orchestra grouped around one microphone, while Fats was placed at the opposite end of the studio by himself." Austin's account of the session portrayed both himself and the studio accompanists in a more favorable light.

> All else failing, I announced I refused to go through with the
> date. Fats seemed to be embarrassed by all this, and
> suggested for me to go ahead without him, that he would sit
> down and show the piano player what he had in mind.
> After the musicians heard his first run-through, each one
> stood up and applauded, and I could see their heads nodding
> to the leader that they would take a chance and play with a
> non-union musician, making me the guarantor that it would be
> taken care of.

Whatever actually took place, Austin could rightly take credit for having helped Waller join the Victor family of recording artists. The two would remain close friends for the rest of their lives.

In the meantime, Austin's voice did not improve sufficiently during the several months beginning in December 1928 to enable him to go back into the studio. He became heavily involved in the stock market as a means of keeping his mind occupied. When his daughter, Anne, was born in December, he used this happy event to justify a new round of heavy drinking. Thoroughly disgusted by his behavior, Kathryn took Anne to St. Louis to live with her parents. Austin engaged a nose, ear and throat specialist, who told him, "Gene, it could be...cancer. We in the medical field know so little about this dread disease. Your throat looks very angry. I suggest you give it a long rest. Quit smoking and drinking. Stay out of the night air for awhile. I can only recommend just what I told you."

With both his life and career at risk, Austin traveled back to Louisiana to visit his mother. His mother's eccentricities, however, ruined whatever hopes he might have had about finding a haven for relaxation. Annoyed at what she perceived to be price gouging by the utilities, Belle had adopted tactics that left her without oil and gas service. Austin later recalled his frustration this situation:

> I never felt so da'gone weary in my entire twenty-nine years.
> "Why can't things be easy an' nice once in a while?" I moaned
> to myself. The money I sent and the bills I paid each month
> could keep them in luxury. I was so disgusted over her not
> paying the measly light bill. Why, those dozen [oil] lanterns
> cost more than three times the amount of the bill! I had always
> hoped that some day my little mother would conquer her wild
> spirit so she could acquire the normalcy of average intelligence
> and pride that could rule out forever her gift of creating scenes
> and the crafty scheming that brought trouble to her and those
> around her.

After sorting out what problems he could, Austin paid his respects at Esau's grave and pointed his automobile back to New York. Upon his return, he found a letter from his wife's attorney finalizing their divorce. Unable to live in the apartment which held so many memories of better days with his family, Austin moved to a suite in a mid-Manhattan hotel. He adopted a routine of drinking and listening to music on the radio alone in these new surroundings.

One morning in October 1929 Austin awoke to the sound of loud rapping at his door. Four unidentified men entered his suite, begging for a drink. As they downed a bottle of whiskey, Gene was informed of the recent stock market crash. Although his losses were great, he was far from destitute. He would later reflect,

> I had certain assets, thanks to the foresight of Victor Herbert, Gene Buck and that wonderful attorney, Nathan Burkan, along with Silvio MacDonough, George Maxwell and Jay Witmark, who had organized the American Society of Composers, Authors and Publishers, to assure that no member need ever meet the fate of unfortunate Stephen Foster.

Although his recording and music publishing activities proved far less lucrative in the 1930s, Austin found some measure of success through radio and film work as well as concert performing. In 1934 alone he performed in film short, *Ferry-Go-Round* (RKO) as well as the features *Sadie McKee* (Metro-Goldwyn-Mayer) and *Gift of Gab* (Universal). While Austin performed on many of the leading radio shows—including *Hollywood on the Air* and *The Magic Key Show*—he professed not to have cared much for the medium during its infancy. However, he took credit for pioneering the use microphones in concert venues.

> I had heard presidential candidate Warren G. Harding speak over an apparatus in an auditorium, which gave me the idea of using a sound amplifying system in my personal appearances. I had the Victor engineers develop a portable compact model for me to take along on tours, thus becoming, I think, the first performer to use such a set-up. Rudy Vallee, who had become very popular, asked me about it, and I made him a present of the duplicate emergency set I always had taken with me on tour.

One of Austin's more interesting live appearances resulted from a Long Island socialite's offer relayed through a prominent society orchestra leader, Meyer Davis. According to the terms, he was to receive one thousand dollars for a brief fifteen-minute performance at a party in the man's mansion. After a brief altercation with a male heckler, Austin was led back to the music room by an apologetic host, who stated, "The hell with them. I've been a great admirer of yours, Gene, and I invited you here for my own entertainment." Austin was happy to perform in that setting solely for his host.

One of Austin's chief activities during tours consisted of making appearances at local stores to autograph records. During one such session, he smugly told the clerk, "Looks like they still come out for me, eh, ol' buddy." He received his comeuppance when the young man hesitantly replied, "I play your records all the time, Mistuh Austin, and love them, and recommend them to my customers. But when Saturday comes, people crowd in here from farms miles around to get the latest Vernon Dalhart records. They say that's the kind of music they understand."

At the height of the Depression, Austin decided to settle in Chicago. The Windy City, then famous as a haven for gangsters such as Al Capone and Jack Dillinger, featured a diversified night scene which attracted musicians of every stripe. He was able to rent a large home, lavishly furnished and located in the fashionable part of town, for a very reasonable price. In addition to performing in Syndicate-controlled clubs, he again opened his house to "wine, women and jam sessions." During this period, Gene met his second wife, Agnes Antelline, as part of a blind date.

Wishing to share his Southern homeland with Agnes, Austin combined their honeymoon with a concert tour. While on tour, he learned that the Surburban Gardens in New Orleans was available for leasing. He asked his manager at the time, Bob Kerr, to make arrangements for taking over the club. He then hired jazz musician, Wingy Manone, a New Orleans native then active in Chicago, to organize a house band. One of these musicians, bass player Johnny Candido, caught Austin's fancy and they began performing together live. After a few weeks at the club, Candido coaxed Gene out into the streets to audition a talented, but bashful, guitarist. Austin later recalled,

> I knew guitar players were a dime a dozen, and at the same time had enough respect for Johnny, who wouldn't waste time with ordinary musicians, so we went outside. I watched Otto Heimel pick up his guitar and, holding it in his left hand, set off at a run across the strings with an art and knowledge of this instrument denied any other man at that time. It was this man from whom, in my opinion, all the great guitar players of today learned. I hired him that night, and formed an act, Gene Austin and his Candy and Coco.

The group proved extremely successful with Candy and Coco developing a unique sense of comedy that audiences loved. Their popularity, which led to many tempting offers for out-of-town live performances, helped re-ignite Austin's wanderlust. Receiving a good offer for the club, Gene sold out and relocated to Charlotte, North Carolina, which was closely situated to many of the venues interested in securing his services. Shortly thereafter, Agnes gave birth to daughter who was named Charlotte after their place of residence. Charlotte would later make a name for herself as an actress under contract with 20th Century-Fox.

Austin's luck soured a few months later when he collapsed from exhaustion while performing onstage. The theatre owner, undoubtedly aware of Austin's past reputation for carousing and noting the bottle of booze standing on the singer's dressing table (which Austin claims to have kept around as a gesture of hospitality to guests), immediately fired him and issued the edict, "I'm goin' to blast you to every theatre owner all over the country. You'll never play another date! I'll see to that! You're through!"

With a potential blacklist by clubs facing him, Austin took his wife's advice and moved to Hollywood in hopes of finding steady work in motion pictures. Considering the area a perfect place to raise a family, Gene succeeded in getting his mother—by then married a third time and possessing a daughter, Irene—to settle nearby. He offered the owner of the failing Clover Club on Sunset Strip his services along with those of Candy and Coco free of charge for a couple of weeks, banking on the likelihood that the act would prove good for business. His hunch proved correct, with the clientele including many movie stars, directors, writers and producers, some of whom made offers for the act to appear in films.

When Austin refused to accede to the club owner's demand that his group perform in a smaller area in order to accommodate more customers, he was fired. The act was immediately signed by the renown Coconut Grove in the Ambassador Hotel and went on to even greater success. Wishing to keep both his career and second marriage together, Austin abandoned his former drinking habits, earning that sobriquet "the Sarsaparilla Kid" in the process.

Although the money associated with film offers proved hard to resist, Austin soon decided that this medium was not his "cup of tea." Lacking the dark handsome looks in the Valentino mold required of matinee idols as well as the patience and discipline to become a good dramatic actor, he focused on the songwriting and performing side of movie production.

A major break came Austin's way in the summer of 1935 when close friend Mae West—aware that he had composed songs tailored to performers with a diversified array of styles, from Broadway belter Sophie Tucker to dance-oriented bandleader Ted Lewis—asked him to provide a sexy Oriental blues number for her upcoming film, *Klondike Annie*. Having been told that it was needed by the following afternoon, he immediately sat down and wrote "I'm an Occidental Woman in an Oriental Mood for Love." When West and producer William LeBaron heard the piece, Austin was given the assignment of writing the rest of the songs for the picture. By the time the film went into production on September 16, 1935, he was also penciled in as a performer, playing the organ and singing in a scene depicting a Nome, Alaska settlement house. The role seemed tailor-made in that it reminded him of his early days as a parlor-house professor.

Despite numerous offers to tour with Candy and Coco, Austin took over a defunct night club on Vine Street in order to have the semblance of a normal family life. Named My Blue Heaven, the club became a popular hangout for both tourists and Hollywood stars.

This success led to a series of guest appearances on the *Joe Penner Show* beginning in the fall of 1936. The radio program was broadcast on WABC at 6 p.m. each Sunday for network distribution. The popularity of these spots resulted in his being billed as a regular artist for two full seasons beginning January 17, 1937. Each program usually featured Austin for one song along with Candy (now Russell Hall on string bass) & Coco. The duo was now billed as "Coco & Malt" because show sponsor, Coco-Malt, didn't want to give listeners the impression that they were marketing a candy product.

Dividing his time and energy between the club and radio program (which alone entailed three or four days of rehearsals) soon proved overtaxing to Austin in addition to severely disrupting life at home. This dilemma was solved when jazz singer Louis Prima, an old friend who—like Austin—had spent much of his early career in New Orleans, agreed to take over the club. This venue, renamed The Famous Door, would play a significant part in launching Prima's successful career as a live performer and recording artist.

When the second season with the Penner show proved less taxing (one day for rehearsal and one for the broadcast), Austin purchased another defunct night club, this one located on Beverly Boulevard in Hollywood. The second My Blue Heaven was also a commercial success, attracting many patrons who fondly recalled their courtship rituals in the parlor with his classic recordings playing in the background.

The film vogue for singing cowboys provided Austin with his next challenge. Given his background—listening to authentic western songs and observing the range riders as they passed by on the Chisolm Trail combined with his years as an assistant to Big Jim at the forge—Gene was captivated when offered a chance to star in this type of picture. Selling his club for a solid profit, he went on a crash diet in order to properly fit the seat of a saddle and immersed himself in the technical details of shooting westerns. The resulting film, *Songs and Saddles*, was made by Road Show Pictures as an independent venture, with Austin contracted to receive a portion of the profits.

Austin's deep involvement with the project assured his receptiveness to producer requests that he stimulate business by making personal appearances at theaters showing the picture. The tour was continually on the go, some days taking in as many as three or four cities. Despite its commercial viability, the stress and exhaustion ensuing from these appearances caused Agnes to return to Hollywood with Charlotte.

During the tour Austin met Billy Wehle, the owner of a traveling tent show. Wehle tried to talk Austin into joining him in this enterprise, promising to deliver vast audiences for his performances. Austin would later recall, "With my gullible nature, Waley's [sic] con hit me in my vulnerable spot, memories of Uncle Esau's prophecy that people would come from far and near to hear me. I told him to let me think it over, and if he'd come back the next day I'd give him my answer."

Austin's manager, Bob Kerr, was not in the least bit intrigued by Wehle's proposition, preferring to quit rather than get involved with a tent show. Austin, however, decided to become a part of the venture, promising to meet up with Wehle in Albany, Georgia after finishing his film tour commitments. The March 4, 1939 issue of *Billboard*, which carried the dateline February 25, Valdista, Georgia, reported that Wehle had signed Austin and Candy & Coco to appear in his show. The April 15, 1939 issue of *Billboard* (dateline April 8) indicated that the show, entitled "Star-0-Rama of 1939" and featuring Gene Austin, had opened in Moultrie, Georgia. Further news briefs from the publication between May 6-June 17 noted Austin's involvement with the show at stops in Chattanooga, Tennessee, Staunton, Virginia, and Jacksonville, Florida.

After several months on the road with the tent show, Wehle asked Austin to consider taking over the enterprise. The July 8, 1939 issue of *Billboard* reported that the singer would be taking over on July 10; three weeks later, the publication referred to the show, then playing in Raleigh, North Carolina, as the "Ball of Fire Revue." The show's continual name changes—the September 9, 1939 issue of *Billboard* referred to it as "Models and Melodies"—would seem to indicate that Austin was struggling with marketing considerations. Remembering his positive impressions of a young press agent and manager in Tampa, Florida he'd met while plugging *Songs and Saddles*, Austin now asked Tom Parker to come aboard as manager of the show. He remembered, "It was obvious Tom knew his business by the way he went about things. In a short while he had the show going full blast, attendance was great, and it looked like we would never know anything but success and money. Bookings poured in."

Despite the generally good turnouts, the tent show was embroiled in controversy by the end of the season. According to Austin, most of the ample profits were attached for back taxes owed by Wehle. While Austin hadn't been aware of this liability, the federal government insisted that he was responsible for the bill. *Billboard*'s pages, however, told a different story; the September 23, 1939 issue indicated that Wehle had filed an attachment suit against the enterprise for alleged back payments due. The trial was scheduled to begin in Mobile, Alabama on February 1, 1940.

As a result, Austin found it necessary to head back to Hollywood with Candy and Coco to earn the money needed both for his trial defense and to reopen the show following season, while Parker and a skeleton crew managed to scrape by in winter quarters in Gainesville, Texas. The act headlined at Sardi's while also participating in the film, *My Little Chickadee*, beginning November 12. He began assembling a company of performers early in 1940 for the upcoming tent show season. In the meantime, the performers warmed up for the tour with engagements at Spokane, Portland, Denver, and elsewhere. The bad luck returned once Austin reunited with Parker in his old hometown in early May 1940. He recalled,

> The second season barely started before the threats of war began to
> slow down attendance. We were saddled with the obligation of
> paying back taxes, which had to be met on time; this caused me

to fall behind in meeting the weekly payroll. When some of the hands became unmanageable and insisted on their money to satisfy their imbibing habits, hell broke loose. It was only Tom's knack of handling people that kept them from coming after me, by telling them I was an open-handed guy and they' all get bonuses when the money started rolling in. Other shattering misfortunes like storms, tornadoes and hurricanes contributed to out hard times.

Austin's troubles were compounded when Wehle won a judgment against the show in early July. Matters became so desperate that Austin found it necessary to close the show July 30 in Newport News, Virginia. Wehle appears to have gained little satisfaction from these developments. The August 17, 1940 issue of *Billboard* reported that he had been unable thus far to collect any judgment money from Austin. On September 7, 1940, the periodical noted that the U.S. Bureau of Internal Revenue planned to auction the physical property associated with the Models and Melodies show. This decision was necessitated by non-payment of assessed taxes due from both Wehle and Austin.

Before heading for New York City, where he planned to renew his professional contacts, Austin's wife informed him of her plans to obtain a divorce in Las Vegas on grounds of non-support. The split became official October 12, 1940 with Agnes being awarded custody of their seven-year-old daughter.

Taking a train back East, he became more closely acquainted with Doris Sherrell, a sixteen-year-old who had performed the second season with his tent show. Before disembarking, he offered to provide her with singing lessons free of charge. While making the rounds in New York, Austin made a point of visiting the Sherrell home in New Jersey. After providing Doris with some vocal pointers, the family issued him a standing invitation. Although there was a twenty-four year difference in age, the two were shortly head over heels in love. However, two obstacles—the likelihood that her parents would be against marriage at such a tender age, and the opposition of her church to such a relationship with a divorced man—kept the couple apart for the time being.

While co-headlining with vaudevillian showman Ken Murray at the Earle Theatre in Washington, D.C., the two developed the concept for a show to be entitled "Blackouts." At the close of the Washington engagement, Murray left for Hollywood to secure financial backing and Austin returned to New York with a double proposition for Doris: a secret marriage and a spot in the show teamed with her sister Grace.

They worked with the show until Austin again felt the urge to take on new challenges. He assembled a troupe consisting of the Whippoorwills—four musicians he'd first hired for the 1940 tent show tour when Candy and Coco left after a dispute over wages—and the Sherrells, and toured the country. He also found time in the early 1940s to perform in a series of three-minute music clips for the Soundies Distributing Corporation of America and Murray Hollywood Productions; several of these featured Doris.

Following a year of secrecy, Austin informed the Sherrells that he was their son-in-law. Thus liberated, the couple headed for a brief vacation in Las Vegas prior to returning to Hollywood. After winning a considerable sum of money at the gaming tables, however, Austin decided to open a new Blue Heaven club on the strip. This time, however, his venture was compromised by the war effort, which had created many problems in acquiring food, liquor, and other necessities associated with running a successful club and gaming facility. Furthermore, on one particular night a patron won big at the dice tables; Austin suspected foul play, but couldn't substantiate his suspicions. As a result, he was forced to accept concert bookings in order to keep the club afloat. Bad publicity proved to be last straw leading to the closing of the club. While en route to one of his performance venues, Austin noticed the following headline on a newspaper resting on a train seat: "GAMBLER'S WIFE SHOT AT HIM OUTSIDE GENE AUSTIN'S BLUE HEAVEN CLUB IN LAS VEGAS."

Due to her own career aspirations, Austin saw little of his wife for the next couple of years. He spent the time touring and carousing in much the same fashion as before. While performing in St. Louis, he met the woman who would eventually become his fourth wife. Austin had always made it a point to wander around a club where he was playing, asking guests if they had any special requests. An extremely attractive woman wearing a pink outfit asked to hear one of his early recordings, "I Wish I Had Died in My Cradle." After the show, the woman—by now he'd learned her name was LouCeil Hudson—explained to him why the song had a special meaning:

> My dearest girl friend was working in a record shop and I used to drop
> in after school and listen to your records. As I had used up most of
> my allowance, she promised to buy this one. We would visit each other
> many a night and have us a Gene Austin concert. I never dreamed I'd
> have the experience of the artist in person singing the song for me.

The couple were married in 1949 following a whirlwind three-month courtship. The record LouCeil's girl friend had saved many years before was presented to them as a memento. Regarding the marriage, Austin would later reflect, "Perhaps it was because I was more mature or I had a constant companion; or rather because I had a feeling of being understood. Whatever the secret, it built a solid relationship between us that formed a strong foundation to our marriage as the years went by."

Since both of them found Las Vegas to their liking when Austin played there, they decided to settle there in the early 1950s. Gene continued to tour on a regular basis. His only recording activity between 1948 and 1957 took place in New York City on

November 23-24, 1953. During the sessions, he re-cut twelve of his vintage hits for RCA Victor. Austin was featured on vocals and piano; further accompaniment was provided by George Barnes, electric guitar, and Frank Carroll, string bass.

Austin's career underwent a significant revival when NBC-TV broadcast "The Gene Austin Story" on *The Goodyear Television Playhouse*, Sunday, April 21, 1957. The program featured George Grizzard in the title role with Austin dubbing the vocals. At the end of the hour show Austin made an appearance singing his latest composition, "Too Late." The RCA release of the song (#20-6880) became his first hit—reaching number 75 on the *Billboard* pop singles chart in early June 1957—since "Ridin' Around in the Rain" (Victor 24663) in July 1934. He was also in demand on network television, appearing on *The Ed Sullivan Show* (NBC), *The Jimmy Dean Show* (CBS), *The Red Skelton Show* (CBS), *The Today Show* (with Dave Garroway; NBC), *The Jack Payne Show* (BBC), *The Woolworth Hour*, and Patti Page's *The Big Record* (CBS).

Austin continued performing around in clubs, hotels, and other venues throughout the 1960s. He also purchased another club, The Chalet, located in a Dallas shopping center, in December 1961. According to longtime friend, John Dunagan, an Anheuser-Busch distributor based in the Missouri area, the royalties from songs he wrote and recorded proved to be his main source of income during this period. He began taking a special interest in the careers of two successful country singers, godson David Houston and cousin Tommy Overstreet.

Austin entered politics briefly in 1962, opposing incumbent Nevada Governor Grant Sawyer in the Democratic primary. An article appearing in the May 17, 1962 issue of the *New York Post*, offering the following take from the singer regarding his campaign prospects: "Campaigning is nothing new to me. After all, it's just like show business." The ticket, which included Eddie Jackson (of Clayton-Jackson-Durante fame), lost to Sawyer and his running mate, former film star Rex Bell.

Austin and LouCeil were divorced in June 1966. Shortly thereafter, in early 1967, he married Gigi Theodora, a woman decades his junior who reportedly was born in Greece and attended Cambridge University in Great Britain. By this time, Austin had relocated to the Miami area. Florida Governor Haydon Burns proclaimed June 24, 1966, the date of his sixty-sixth birthday, to be "Gene Austin Day" in recognition of his "distinguished career."

Other honors followed. In February 1971 he appeared on Merv Griffin's CBS-TV tribute to popular music composers and later in the year he stated in an published interview that he'd assisted in establishing the Museum of Jazz, based in New Orleans, sometime around 1956. His final live performance took place at the Jack London Club in Palm Springs, California, where he ushered in 1972 singing his old hits.

Austin died on January 24, 1972, at the age of seventy-one, in Palm Springs' Desert Hospital. He had been suffering from cancer for ten months. Five of his recordings comprised the music at the funeral, including "My Blue Heaven" and a song written by him especially for this event and recorded two years earlier, "There's a New Blue Heaven in the Sky." The pallbearers included Dunagan, Bill Putnam, Rick Adams, Jon Antelline, Dave Covey, Harry Segal, Phillip Moody, Jack Pepper, Hartley Cassidy, and fellow recording artist Nick Lucas.

Gene Austin Compositions

How Come You Do Me Like You Do (1924)
Tell Me If You Want Somebody Else, 'Cause Somebody Else Wants Me (1924)
A Thousand Miles From Here (1924)
Just About Sundown (1924)
I Had A Good Gal But The Fool Laid Down And Died (1924)
I'm Going Where The Climate Fits My Clothes (1924)
Wanted, Someone To Love (1924)
Charleston Charley (1924)
When My Sugar Walks Down The Street (1924)
What Makes Me Love You Like I Do (1925)
I Had A Sweet Mama, But She's Turned Sour Now (1925)
Abie's Irish Nose (1925)
I Wonder Why I Love You (1925)
What Makes Me Love You Like I Do (1925)
The Gambler's Sweetheart (1926)
When The Moon Shines Down Upon The Mountain (1926)
All That You Left Me Were Two Empty Arms (1926)
Why Do You Tell Me, You Love Me (1927)
The Voice Of The Southland (1927)
'Til I Found You (1928)
Old Pals Are The Best Pals After All (1928)
I've Changed My Mind (1928)
The Lonesome Road (1928)
Please Come Back To Me (1929)
Trying, To Love You (1930)
Whipporwill, Go Tell My Honey That I Love Her (1931)
My Success (1931)
When The Roll Is Called By The Fireside (1931)
Git Along (1933)
When A St. Louis Woman Comes Down To New Orleans (1934)
Ridin' Around In The Rain (1934)
Out Of The Blue (1935)

Mister Deep Blue Sea (1935)
It's Never Too Late To Say No (1935)
That May Not Be Love, But It's Wonderful (1935)
I Hear You Knockin' But You Can't Come In (1935)
Open Up Your Heart And Let The Sunshine In (1935)
I'm An Occidental Woman In An Oriental Mood For Love (1935)
It's Better To Give Than To Receive (1935)
Little Bar-Butterfly (1935)
Cheer Up Little Sister (1935)
Occidental Woman (1936)
Under The Spell Of A Voodoo Drum (1936)
I'm In A Mellow Mood (1938)
Take Your Shoes Off, Baby, And Start Runnin' Through My Mind (1942)
Oh, What A Mess I'm In (1943)
I've Given My Life To The Business (1944)
I'm A Rootin', Shootin', Tootin' Man From Texas (1944)   First recorded in 1936 as
        "Rootin', Shootin', Tootin' Man From Texas."
Nothin' Doin' (1944)
Crazy Song (1944)   Also known as "But I'm Alright."
Keep A-Knockin', But You Can't Come In (1948)
(Bad Boy) Dream On, Little Plowboy (1949)
Oh, These Lonely Nights (1953)
Too Late (1957)
Please (1957)
The More I See Of Somebody Else (1957)
Sounds In The Night (1957)
Wise Guy (1957)
My Restless Heart (1957)
I'm Not The Braggin' Kind (1957)
My Rosita, My Own (1957)
If You Only Had A Heart For Me (1957)
Wonder (1957)
There's A New Blue Heaven (1957)
Goofin' (1958)
Sweetheart Of Demolay (1958)
The Jass Story; an original musical play by Gene Austin [text only] (1958)
Lovely Lou'siana Moon (1963)
Here's To You (1964)
This Life Of Mine (1965)
I Don't Want Nobody (1965)
Miami In The Morning (1968)
Let Me Lean Against Your Shoulder (1968)
The Trip (1968)

Dora (1968)
Golden Wedding Waltz (1968)
Texas (1968)
That Fatal Day In Dallas (1968)
What Happens To My Friends On Sunday? (1968)
Somebody Lied (1968)
I'm All In, Out, And Down (1968)
On A Rainy Afternoon (1968)
Back Street (1968)
I Know Why (1968)
The Moment I Found You (1968)
Lonesome Train (1968)
Springtime, Ringtime, And You (1968)

Songs Published By Gene Austin, Inc.

Someday You'll Pass This Way Again (1928)
Then Came The Down (1928)
Down By The Old Front Gate (1928)
Divine Lady (1928)
Wear A Hat With A Silver Lining (1928)
Anyone Can See With Half-An-Eye, I'm Crazy Over You (1928)
Blowing Kisses Over The Moon (1928)
On Riverside Drive (1928)
She's Got A Great Big Army Of Friends (1928)
Long, Long Ago (1928)
Daddy O'Mine (1929)
A Garden In The Rain (1929)
Peace Of Mind (1929)
I Gotta Have You (1929)
At Twilight (1929)
I Knew We Two Were One (1929)
Blue Morning (1929)
Keep Your Overcoat Open (1929)
Who's The Who (1929)
Maybe I'm Wrong (1929)
What Do I Care (1929)
Please Come Back To Me (1929)
Dreary Night (1929)
Trying (1929)
When You Dance With An Old Sweetheart (1929)
With Love And Kisses (1930)

You're Flying High - But You'll Do A Tail-Spin For Me (1930)
Be Careful With Those Eyes (1930)
Would You Care (1930)
Lonely Stowaway (1930)
To-Night Or Never (1931)
I Wish I Knew A Bigger Word Than Love (1931)
My Success (1931)

Sheet Music With Austin Cover

Carolina Mammy (Leo. Feist Inc., 1922)
It's Not The First Time You Left Me (But It's The Last Time You'll Come Back) (Waterson, Berlin & Snyder Co., 1923)
Montmartre Rose (Edw. B. Marks Music Co., 1925)
I Wish I Had Died In My Cradle (Before I Grew Up To Love You) (Shapiro, Bernstein & Co., 1926)
Since I Found You (Shapiro, Bernstein & Co., 1926)
Yesterday (Ted Browne Music Co., 1926)
I'm Still In Love With You (Austin, Bloom & Koelher, Inc., 1927)
My Melancholy Baby (Joe Morris Music Co., 1927)
My Blue Heaven (Leo. Feist Inc., 1927)
So Tired (Harold Rossiter Music Co., 1927)
Tomorrow (Forster Music Pub. Inc., 1927)
The Voice Of The Southland Keeps Callin' Me Home (Austin, Bloom & Koelher, Inc., 1927)
Why Do You Tell Me, You Love Me (When You Don't Mean A Word You Say) (Ted Browne Music Co., 1927)
After My Laughter Came Tears (Shapiro, Bernstein & Co., 1928)
Ashes Of Love (M. Whitmark & Sons, 1928)
Bluebird Why Don't You Call On Me? (J.W. Jenkins Son's Music Co., 1928)
Carolina Moon (Joe Morris Music Co., 1928)
Dream River (Joe Morris Music Co., 1928)
Old Pals Are The Best Pals After All (Irving Berlin, Inc., 1928)
The Saint Louis Blues (Revised Edition) (Handy Bros. Music Co., Inc., 1928)
I Got A Woman, Crazy For Me: She's Funny That Way (Villa Moret Inc., 1928)
Then Came The Dawn (Gene Austin, Inc., 1928)
You Wanted Someone To Play With (I Wanted Someone To Love) (Empire Music Co., 1928)
All That I'm Asking Is Sympathy (Joe Morris Music Co., 1929)
Dream Mother (Joe Morris Music Co., 1929)
I Ain't Got Nothin' For Nobody But You (Empire Music Co., 1929)
My Fate Is In Your Hands (Santly Bros., Inc., 1929)

On Riverside Drive (Gene Austin Inc., 1929)
Please Come Back To Me (Gene Austin Inc., 1929)
Wedding Bells (Are Breaking Up That Old Gang Of Mine) (Watterson, Berlin & Snyder Co., 1929)
I Have A Sweetheart (And Mother Is Her Name) (Red Star Music Co., Inc., 1930)
Moonlight (Frank Capano & Co., Inc., 1930)
You Cried Your Way Into My Heart (But Laughed Yourself Right Out Again) (Frank Capano & Co., Inc., 1930)
Building A Home For You (Santly Bros., Inc., 1931)
Me Minus You (Leo. Feist, Inc., 1932)
The Night When Love Was Born (Leo. Feist, Inc., 1932)
To-ward Morning (Dancing With You) (Bibo-Lang, Inc., 1933)
Blue Sky Avenue (Harms Inc., 1934)
Talkin' To Myself (Harms, Inc., 1934)

Discography

--Singles: 78s and 45s

1924

Edison 51422-L   Arkansas Traveler (credited to The Blue Ridge Duo) Also Blue Amberol Cylinder 4936
 51422-R   Little Brown Jug (credited to The Blue Ridge Duo)   Also Blue Amberol Cylnder 4973
 51498-L   Life's Railway To Heaven (credited to The Blue Ridge Duo)   Also Blue Amberol Cylinder 4968
 51498-R   You Will Never Miss Your Mother Until She Is Gone (credited to The Blue Ridge Duo)   Also Blue Amberol Cylinder 4961
 51502-L   Susie Ann (credited to The Blue Ridge Duo)   Also Blue Amberol Cylinder 4978
 51502-R   Turkey In The Straw (credited to The Blue Ridge Duo)   Also Blue Amberol Cylinder 4977
 51515-L (matrix 9728)   Blue Ridge Blues (credited to Blue Ridge Duo)   Also Blue Amberol Cylinder 4976
 51515-R (matrix 9727)   Lonesome Road Blues (credited to The Blue Ridge Duo) Also Blue Amberol Cylinder 4975
 51611-L   Got The Railroad Blues   Also Blue Amberol Cylinder 5058
Vocalion A 14809   The Wreck on the Southern 97 (credited to George Reneau)   Also Vocalion A 5029
 B 14809   Lonesome Road Blues (credited to George Reneau)   Also Vocalion B 5029

A 14811   You Will Never Miss Your Mother Until She Is Gone (credited to George Reneau)   Also Vocalion A 5030
B 14811   Life's Railway To Heaven (credited to George Reneau)   Also Vocalion B 5030
A 14812   Turkey In The Straw (credited to George Reneau)   Also Vocalion A 5031
B 14812   Little Brown Jug (credited to George Reneau)   Also Vocalion B 5031
A 14813   Casey Jones (credited to George Reneau)   Also Vocalion A 5032
B 14813   Arkansaw Traveler (instrumental; credited to George Reneau)   Also Vocalion B 5032
A 14814   Here, Rattler, Here (Calling the Dog) (credited to George Reneau who takes the vocal)   Also Vocalion A 5033
B 14814   When You And I Were Young, Maggie (credited to George Reneau)   Also Vocalion B 5033
A 14815   Blue Ridge Blues (credited to George Reneau)   Also Vocalion A 5034
B 14815   Susie Ann (credited to George Reneau)   Also Vocalion B 5034
A 14821   A Thousand Miles From Here (w. Roy Bergere)   Also Guardsman 7004
B 14821   All Day Long (w. Roy Bergere)   Also Guardsman 7004
A 14841   Sally Gooden (w. Uncle "Am" Stuart)   Also Brunswick 1002, Vocalion A 5037
A 14846   Old Liza Jane (w. Uncle "Am" Stuart)   Also Brunswick 1004
A 14896   Smoky Mountain Blues (credited to George Reneau)   Also Vocalion A 5049
B 14896   Red Wing (credited to George Reneau)   Also Vocalion B 5049
A 14897   The C & O Wreck (credited to George Reneau)   also Vocalion A 5050
B 14897   Jesse James (credited to George Reneau)   Also Vocalion B 5050
B 14916   Choo Choo (I Gotta Hurry Home) (w. The Ambassadors)   Also Vocalion X 9523
A 14918   The Baggage Coach Ahead (credited to George Reneau; vocal by Reneau)   Also Vocalion A 5052 and Silvertone 3047 (credited to George Hobson)
B 14918   Softly and Tenderly (credited to George Reneau)   Also Vocalion B 5052 and Silvertone 3047 (credited to George Hobson)
A 14930   The New Market Wreck (credited to George Reneau)   Also Vocalion B 5054 and Silvertone 3052 (credited to George Hobson)
B 14930   The Bald-Headed End Of The Broom (credited to George Reneau)   Also Vocalion B 5054 and Silvertone 3052 (credited to George Hobson)

A 14946   I've Got The Railroad Blues (credited to George Reneau) Also Vocalion A 5055
B 14946   Birmingham (credited to George Reneau)   Also Vocalion B 5055
A 15046   My Redeemer (credited to George Reneau; vocal by Reneau) Also Vocalion A 5064
B 15046   We're Floating Down The Stream Of Time (credited to George Reneau; vocal by Reneau)   Also Vocalion B 5064

1925

Victor 19585-A   When My Sugar Walks Down The Street (w. Aileen Stanley and Nat Shilkret & His Orchestra)
19599-A   The Only, Only One For Me (w. Nat Shilkret & His Orchestra)
19599-B   I Never Knew How Much I Love You (w. Nat Shilkret & His Orchestra)
19625-A   Yearning (Just For You)   Also Zonophone 3880
19625-B   No Wonder (That I Love You)   Also Zonophone 3880
19637-A   Way Down Home (w. Carson Robison)
19638-A   The Flapper Wife (w. Nat Shilkret & His Orchestra aka International Novelty Orchestra)
19649-A   Joanna (w. International Novelty Orchestra)
19649-B   Nora Lee (w. Inernational Novelty Orchestra)
19656-A   Everything Is Hotsy Totsy Now (w. Billy "Yuke" Carpenter)
19656-B   Yes Sir, That's My Baby (w. Billy "Yuke" Carpenter)
19677-A   Let It Rain, Let It Pour   Also Zonophone 3901
19677-B   What A Life (When No One Loves You)   Also Zonophone 3901
19857-A   Save Your Sorrow (w. Nat Shilkret)
19864-B   I Never Knew
19899-A   Sleepy Time Gal (w. Dave Franklin and May Singhi Breen) Also His Master's Voice EA 32
19899-B   Five Foot Two, Eyes Of Blue (Has Anybody Seen My Girl) (w. Dave Franklin and May Singhi Breen)   Also His Master's Voice EA 32
19928-B   Sweet Child (I'm Wild About You) (w. Dave Franklin)   Also His Master's Voice B 2293 and EA 30
19950-B   How I Love Her And She Loves Me Is Nobody's Business (w. Dave Franklin) Also Canadian Victor 19953-B and His Master's Voice B 2350
20030-B   My Bundle Of Love   Also His Master's Voice B 2359
Vocalion A 14991   The Prisoner's Song (credited to George Reneau; vocal by Reneau) Also Vocalion A 5056 and Silvertone 3045 (credited to George Hobson)
B 14991   The Lightning Express (credited to George Reneau)   Also Vocalion B 5056 and Silvertone 3045 (credited to George

          Hobson)
- A 14997 Rock All Our Babies To Sleep (credited to George Reneau)   Also Vocalion A 5057 and Silvertone 3044 (credited to George Hobson)
- B 14997 Little Rosewood Casket (credited to George Reneau)   Also Vocalion B 5057 and Silvertone 3044 (credited to George Hobson)
- A 14998 Wild Bill Jones (credited to George Reneau; vocal by Reneau)   Also Vocalion A 5058 and Silvertone 3046 A (credited to George Hobson)
- B 14998 The Letter Edged In Black (credited to George Reneau; vocal by Reneau)   Also Vocalion B 5058 and Silvertone 3046 B (credited to George Hobson)
- A 14999 Wild And Reckless Hoboes (credited to George Reneau; vocal by Reneau)   Also Vocalion A 5059
- B 14999 Woman's Suffrage (credited to George Reneau; vocal by Reneau)   Also Vocalion B 5059

1926

Victor 19968-B Behind The Clouds   Also His Master's Voice B 2345
- 20044-A Ya Gotta Know How To Love   Also His Master's Voice B 2350
- 20044-B Bye Bye, Blackbird   Also His Master's Voice B 2345 and Sunbeam P-507 (LP)
- 20084-A Tamiami Trail (w. Frank Banta)   Also His Master's Voice B 2349
- 20084-B But I Do - You Know I Do (w. Frank Banta)   Also His Master's Voice B 2349
- 20107-B Here I Am (w. Frank Banta)   Also His Master's Voice EA 142
- 20143-A For My Sweetheart   Also His Master's Voice EA 127
- 20143-B Me Too   Also His Master's Voice B 2359
- 20336-B Some Day (w. Nat Shilkret and the Victor Orchestra)
- 20371-A To-night You Belong To Me   Also His Master's Voice B 2442 and EA 142
- 20371-B It Made You Happy When You Made Me Cry   Also His Master's Voice B 2442
- 20397-A I've Got The Girl (w. Abel Baer)   Also His Master's Voice B 2422
- 20411-A (I've Grown So Lonesome) Thinking Of You (w. Abel Baer)   Also His Master's Voice AM 743 and B 2441
- 20411-B Sunday (W. Abel Baer)   Also His Master's Voice B 2432
- 20478-A Everything's Made For Move (w. Art Fowler)   Also His Master's Voice B 2455
- 20673-A When The Moon Shines Down Upon The Mountain (credited to pseudonym Bill Collins)

1927

Bluebird B-6815-B   Yesterday
      B-7751-A   Ain't She Sweet (w. Nat Shilkret & His Orchestra)   Also Montgomery Ward M-7061-B
Victor 20561-A   Forgive Me (w. Nat Shilkret & His Orchestra)   Also His Master's Voice EA 208
    20561-B   Someday Sweetheart (w. Abel Baer)   Also His Master's Voice EA 208 and Sunbeam P-507 (LP)
    20568-A   Ain't She Sweet? (w. Nat Shilkret & His Orchestra)   Also His Master's Voice B 2488 and EA 185
    20568-B   What Do I Care What Somebody Said   Also His Master's Voice B 2488 and EA 275
    20569-A   Muddy Water   Also His Master's Voice B 2529
    20569-B   My Idea Of Heaven (Is To Be In Love With You)   Also His Master's Voice B 2515 and EA 185
    20673-B   Cindy (credited to pseudonym Bill Collins)
    20716-A   C'est Vous (It's You) (w. Jacques Renard and His Orchestra)   Also His Master's Voice B 5349
    20730-A   One Sweet Letter From You (w. Abel Baer)
    20730-B   Yesterday   Also Bluebird B-7751-A, Electrola E.G. 723, His Master's Voice B 2564 and AM 919
    20964-A   My Blue Heaven (w. Herb Borodkin, Milton Rettenberg, and Bob McGimsey)   Also Electrola E.G. 753, Victor 24573-A, His Master's Voice B 2644 and EA 262, and RCA Victor 47-1510 (45 r.p.m.)
    20964-B   Are You Thinking Of Me To-night?   Also His Master's Voice B 2644 and EA 262
    20977-A   Are You Happy? (w. Nat Shilkret & His Orhcestra)   Also His Master's Voice B 2642 and EA 261
    20977-B   The Sweetheart Of Sigma Chi   Also Bluebird B-6815-A, Montgomery Ward M-7061-A, His Master's Voice B 2642 and EA 261
    21015-A   There's A Cradle In Carolina (w. Nat Shilkret & His Orchestra)   Also His Master's Voice EA 275
    21015-B   My Melancholy Baby (w. Nat Shilkret & His Orchestra)   Also Victor 24640-B
    21080-B   Nothin' (w. Nat Shilkret and the Victor Orchestra)   Also His Master's Voice B 5429 and EA 344
    21098-A   The Lonesome Road   Also His Master's Voice B 3018 and EA 550

1928

Bluebird B-7751-B   The Dream Girl Of Pi K.A. (w. orchestra)

Victor 21329-A Tomorrow   Also His Master's Voice EA 350
 21329-B So Tired   Also His Master's Voice EA 350
 21334-A Ramona (w. Viola Klaiss and orchestra) Also Victor 24573-B, RCA Victor WPT-6, 599-9114, and EPA 5132 (all RCA releases are 45 r.p.m.; the latter two are promotional)
 21334-B Girl Of My Dreams (w. Bob McGimsey, Nat Shilkret & Orchestra Also His Master's Voice B 2852 and EA 341
 21374-A Without You, Sweetheart   Also His Master's Voice EA 360
 21374-B In My Bouquet Of Memories (w. Nat Shilkret & His Orchestra) Also His Master's Voice B 2789 and EA 360
 21454-A Just Like A Melody Out Of The Sky (w. Nat Shilkret & His Orchestra) Also His Master's Voice B 2803 and EA 394
 21454-B I Can't Do Without You (w. Nat Shilkret and band) Also His Master's Voice B 2803
 21545-A Memories Of France (w. Nat Shilkret and His Orchestra) Also His Master's Voice EA 413
 21545-B Old Pals Are The Best Pals After All (w. Nat Shilkret & His Orchestra) Also His Master's Voice EA 413
 21564-A Jeannine (I Dream Of Lilac Time) (w. Nat Shilkret & His Orchestra) Also His Master's Voice B 2854 and EA 400
 21564-B Then Came The Dawn (w. orchestra) Also His Master's Voice B 2854 and EA 427
 21714-A St. Louis Blues (w. orchestra, including Glenn Miller, Benny Goodman and Del Staigers) Also Bluebird B-6863-A
 21714-B The Voice Of The Southland Also Electrola E.G. 1149, His Master's Master's Voice B 2904 and EA 482
 21779-A Sonny Boy (w. orchestra) Also His Master's Voice EA 451
 21779-B (I Got A Woman, Crazy For Me) She's Funny That Way (w. orchestra) Also His Master's Voice EA 451
 21798-A I Can't Give You Anything But Love (w. Nat Shilkret & His Orchestra) Also His Master's Voice EA 470
 21798-B I Wonder If You Miss Me Tonight (w. Nat Shilkret & His Orchestra) Also His Master's Voice B 2953 and EA 470
 21827-A Sentimental Baby (w. Ben Pollack and His Park Central Orchestra) Also La Voce del Padrone R 14070 and Zonophone EE 144
 21833-A Carolina Moon (w. Andy Sannella and orchestra) Also His Master's Voice B 2995, RCA Victor WPT-6 and 27-0015 (45 r.p.m.)
 21833-B I Wish I Had Died In My Cradle (Before I Grew Up To Love You) Also His Master's Voice B 3294
 21916-A The Dream Girl Of Pi K.A. (w. orchestra)
 21916-B My Sorority Sweetheart (w. orchestra)

1929

Bluebird B-7557-A A Garden In The Rain (w. Nat Shilkret & His Orchestra)
Victor 21856-A Weary River (w. Nat Shilkret & His Orchestra)   Also Special Exploitation Record, His Master's Voice B 2995 and EA 512
       21856-B The Song I Love (w. Nat Shilkret & His Orchestra)   Also His Master's Voice EA 512
       21893-A Wedding Bells Are Breaking Up That Old Gang Of Mine (w. Ed Smalle, Dick Robertson and Leonard Joy & His Orchestra)   Also His Master's Voice B 3063 and EA 527
       21893-B That's What I Call Heaven (w. Leonard Joy & His Orchestra)   Also His Master's Voice B 3063
       21915-A Dream Mother (w. Nat Shilkret & His Orchestra)   Also His Master's Voice B 3077 and EA 547
       21915-B A Garden In The Rain (w. Nat Shilkret & His Orchestra)   Also His Master's Voice EA 547
       21952-A Little Pal (w. Nat Shilkret & His Orchestra)   Also His Master's Voice B 3113 and EA 590
       21952-B Why Can't You? (w. Nat Shilkret & His Orchestra)   Also His Master's Voice B 3113 and EA 590
       22033-A Maybe! - Who Knows? (w. Leonard Joy & His Orchestra)   Also His Master's Voice B 3117 and EA 593
       22033-B I've Got A Feeling I'm Falling (w. Leonard Joy & His Orchestra)   Also His Master's Voice B 3117 and EA 593
       22068-A Ain't Misbehavin' (w. Leonard Joy & His Orchestra)   Also His Master's Voice B 3185
       22068-B Peace Of Mind (w. Leonard Joy & His Orchestra)   Also His Master's Voice B 3201
       22128-A How Am I To Know? (w. Nat Shilkret & His Orchestra)   Also His Master's Voice B 3255 and EA 698
       22128-B Please Come Back To Me (w. Nat Shilkret & His Orchestra)   Also His Master's Voice B 3255 and EA 645
       22223-A My Fate Is In Your Hands (w. Fats Waller and Leonard Joy & His Orchestra)   Also His Master's Voice B 3297
       22223-B All That I'm Asking Is Sympathy (w. Leonard Joy & His Orchestra)   Also His Master's Voice B 3297 and EA 698

1930

Victor 22299-A St. James' Infirmary (w. Leonard Joy & His Orchestra)   Also Bluebird B-6863-B
       22299-B After You've Gone (w. Leonard Joy & His Orchestra)   Also Alberti Special Record L.24635, His Master's Voice EA 1376, and Victor 24640-A

22341-A To My Mammy (w. Leonard Joy & His Orchestra) Also His Master's Voice B 3502 and EA 804
22341-B Let Me Sing And I'm Happy (w. Leonard Joy & His Orchestra) Also His Master's Voice B 3502 and EA 803
22416-A Under A Texas Moon (w. Leonard Joy & His Orchestra) Also His Master's Voice EA 764
22416-B Telling It To The Daisies (w. Leonard Joy & His Orchestra)
22451-A Absence Makes The Heart Grow Fonder For Somebody Else (w. Leonard Joy & His Orchestra)
22451-B Rollin' Down The River (w. Leonard Joy & His Orchestra) Also His Master's Voice B 3572
22490-A When They Changed My Name To A Number (w. Leonard Joy & His Orchestra)
22490-B For Sweethearts Only (w. Leonard Joy & His Orchestra)
22518-A Nobody Cares If I'm Blue (w. Leonard Joy & His Orchestra) Also His Master's Voice B 3690
22527-A If I Could Be With You (One Hour To-Night) (w. Nat Shilkret & His Orchestra)
22527-B This Side Of Paradise (w. Nat Shilkret & His Orchestra)
22539-A A Vision Of Virginia (w. Andy Sannella) Also His Master's Voice EA 832
22539-B Alabama Lullaby (w. Andy Sannella) Also His Master's Voice EA 832
22601-A You're Driving Me Crazy (What Did I Do?) (w. Leonard Joy & His Orchestra) Also His Master's Voice B 3762
22601-B Crying Myself To Sleep (w. Leonard Joy & His Orchestra) Also His Master's Voice B 3762

1931

Bluebird B-7557-B Please Don't Talk About Me When I'm Gone
Hit Of The Week L3 Now That You're Gone (Ahora que ya te fuiste) (w. Hit Of The Week Orchestra)
Perfect 12760 A Faded Summer Love/Goodnight Sweetheart (w. orchestra) Also Banner 32291, Conquerer 7903, Oriole 2355, and Romeo 1729; a different version of each song was released on Apex 41441, Royal 91227, Sterling 91227, Domino 51017, and Ace 51017
12790 The Lonesome Road (w. orchestra) Also Banner 32385, Oriole 2418, Romeo 1805
15513 What Is It?/Who Am I (w. orchestra) Also Banner 32259, Conquerer 7820, Oriole 2333, Romeo 1703, Apex 41399, Crown 91197, Sterling 291197, Domino 51001, Ace 351001, Decca F-2619/F-2686, and Imperial 2627 ("Who Am I" only)

15514 Maybe It's The Moon/How's Your Uncle? (w. orchestra) Also Banner 32256, Conquerer 7853, Oriole 2335, Apex 41400, Crown 91198, Sterling 291198, Royal 391198, Domino 51001, Ace 351001, and Decca F-2686/F-2619

15521 If I Didn't Have You/In A Dream (w. orchestra) Also Banner 32281, Oriole 2345, Romeo 1716, Apex 41419, Sterling 291205, Domino 51012, Ace 351012, and Imperial ("If I Didn't Have You" only)

15526 Guilty/Blue Kentucky Moon (w. orchestra; actually Ed Kirkeby's orchestra) Also Banner 32285, Oriole 2352, Romeo 1721, Apex 41425, Crown 91211, Sterling 291211, Royal 391211, Domino 51014, Sun 251014, and Ace 351014; "Guilty" coupled with releases by other artists on Imperial 2617 and Melotone 12245 (Canadian)

15542 Lies/I'm Sorry Dear (w. orchestra) Also on Banner 32325, Oriole 2380, Rome 1752, Sterling 91235, Royal 91235, Domino 51024, and Ace 51024

Victor 22635-A When Your Lover Has Gone (w. Leonard Joy & His Orchestra) Also His Master's Voice B 3903

22635-B Please Don't Talk About Me When I'm Gone Also His Master's Voice B 3936

22687-A Now You're In My Arms (w. Leonard Joy & His Orchestra)

22687-B If You Should Ever Need Me (w. Leonard Joy & His Orchestra)

22739-A Without That Gal (w. Nat Shilkret & His Orchestra) Also His Master's Voice B 3922

22739-B I'm Thru With Love (w. Nat Shilkret & His Orchestra) Also His Master's Voice B 3922

22806-A Blue Kentucky Moon   Also HMV EA 969

22806-B Love Letters In The Sand   Also HMV B 3997 and EA 969

22891-B Mood Indigo (w. Nat Shilkret & His Orchestra) Also His Master's Voice N 4251

1932

Perfect 12862 Just A Little Home For The Old Folks (A Token From Me)/A Little Street Where Old Friends Meet (w. members of Dorsey Brothers Orchestra) Also Banner 32614, Conquerer 8081, Melotone M 12529, Oriole 2595, Melotone 91450, Crown 91450, and Decca F-3332/F-3392

12901 A Ghost Of A Chance/When I Was A Boy From The Mountains (And You Were A Girl From The Hills) (w. members of Dorsey Brothers Orchestra) Also Banner 32729, Melotone M 12658, Oriole 2673, Romeo 2046, and Decca F-3332/F-3392

1933

Perfect 12963 Did You Ever See A Dream Walking?/Build A Little Home (w. Candy Candido and Otto "Coco" Heimel)   Also Banner 32920, Conquerer 8260, Melotone M 12864, Oriole 2808, Romeo 2181, Melotone 91687, and F-3861/F-3933

12968 Easter Parade/Everything I Have Is Yours (w. orchestra, including Jimmy Dorsey, Joe Venuti, Candy and Coco)   Also Banner 32935, 2816, Romeo 2189, Melotone M 12878 and 91685; "Everything I Have Is Yours" also available on Conquerer 8263, Rex 8110, and Decca F-3861

13044 Dear Old Southland/Jam House Blues (w. Candy and Coco)   Also Banner 33172, Melotone M 13139, Oriole 2974, Romeo 2384, and Melotone 91845; "Dear Old Southland" also available on Decca F-3933

1934

Victor 24663-A Ridin' Around In The Rain (w. Candy Candido and Otto "Coco" Heimel)   Also His Master's Voice N 4337

24663-B All I Do Is Dream Of You (w. Otto "Coco" Heimel and Arthur "Monk" Hazel)   Also His Master's Voice EA 1376

24725-A Blue Sky Avenue (w. Otto "Coco" Heimel and Leo Dunham)

24725-B When The Roll Is Called By The Fireside (w. Otto "Coco" Heimel and Leo Dunham)

Vocalion 2833-A Kingfish Blues/New Orleans (w. Candy and Coco; Austin plays piano only)   Also Brunswick 500506 ("New Orleans" coupled with "Bugle Call Rag") "Candy" is Leo Dunham

2833-B China Boy/Bugle Call Rag (w. Candy and Coco; Austin plays piano only)   Also Brunswick 500506 ("Bugle Call Rag" coupled with "New Orleans") "Candy" is Leo Dunham

1936

Decca 904 A Until Today (w. Victor Young and His Orchestra)

904 B When I'm With You (w. Victor Young and His Orchestra)   Also Decca F-6091

926 A If I Had My Way (w. Victor Young and His Orchestra)

926 B I Cried For You (w. Victor Young and His Orchestra)   Also Decca F-6091

1937

Decca 1578 A Thrill Of A Lifetime (w. Bob Mitchell)   Also Panachord 26031

1578 B   Marie (w. Bob Mitchell)   Also Panachord 25997
1656 A   Dear Old Southland (w. Candy and Coco)   Also Panachord 26027
1656 B   China Boy (w. Candy and Coco)   Takes A and C both issued under
  This number
3102 A   Paradise Isle (w. Sam Koki and His Islanders)   Also Decca 3102
  (Canadian)
3102 B   Down Where The Trade Winds Blow (w. Sam Koki and His Islanders)
  Also Decca 3102 (Canadian)
Panachord 26027   China Boy (w. Candy and Coco)   Take C only

1938

Bluebird B-7557-A   A Garden In The Rain   remastering of March 13, 1929 recording
  B-7557-B   Please Don't Talk About Me   remastering of February 5, 1931
    Recording
Decca 1832 A   Music, Maestro, Please! (w. orchestra)   Also Panachord 25997
  1832 B   I'm In A Mellow Mood (w. orchestra)   Also Panachord 26031

1941

Decca 3939 A   Tonight You Belong To Me (w. instrumental accompaniment)
  4175 A   If I Could Be With You (One Hour Tonight) (w. instrumental
    accompaniment)   Also Coral 60050 A
  4175 B   Forgive Me (w. instrumental accompaniment)

1942

Decca 3939 B   Carolina Moon (w. instrumental accompaniment)
  4333 A   My Blue Heaven (w. instrumental accompaniment)
  4333 B   Yesterday (w. instrumental accompaniment)
  4354 A   Ramona (w. instrumental accompaniment)   Also Coral 60050 B
  4354 B   Jeannine (I Dream Of Lilac Time) (w. instrumental accompaniment)

1945

4 Star 1010   Frankie And Johnny/Gene Austin Blues
  My Blue Heaven/But I'm Alright
  Melancholy Baby/Wrong Kind Of Man
  Someday Sweetheart/Here It Is Springtime

1947

Austin GA 501/GA 502   Keep A Knocking/Sweetheart Of Sigma Chi (w. Otto Heimel

GA 503/GA 504 You're Gonna Cause Me Trouble/My Blue Heaven (w. Otto Heimel and Red Wootten) A copy has never been located; Its existence is purely speculative.

GA 505/GA 506 Melancholy Baby/Lonesome Road (w. Otto Heimel and Red Wootten)

GA 507/GA 508 Under The Spell Of The Voodoo Drum/Ain't Misbehavin' (w. Otto Heimel and Red Wootten)

GA 501/GA 505 Keep A Knocking/My Melancholy Baby (w. Les Paul) "Keep A Knocking" also on Universal U-100 and Musicana 7012

GA 502/GA 504 Sweetheart Of Sigma Chi/My Blue Heaven (w. Les Paul) "My Blue Heaven" also on Universal U-100 and Musicana 7012

GA 503/GA 506 You're Gonna Cause Me Trouble/Lonesome Road (w. Les Paul

GA 509/GA 510 Broken Dreams/Ace In The Hole (w. Les Paul) "Ace In The Hole" (edited version) also on Universal DF-1007, London 567 and L.567

London 566 Hush Little Darling/Git Along (w. The Medolarks)

London 567 Ace In The Hole/I'm Crying Just For You (w. Les Paul Trio) Also London L.567 "Ace In The Hole" an edited version of GA 510

Universal U-100 My Blue Heaven/Keep A Knockin' (w. Les Paul and rhythm accompaniment) Also Musicana 7012, Austin GA 504 ("My Blue Heaven") and GA 501 (Keep A Knockin') All issues other than Austin label have electronic reverberation added.

U-122 Cala-California/Yearning (w. Les Paul and The Honeydreamers) Also Musicana 7016

U-130 T-E-X-A-S Spells Texas/Dream On Little Plowboy (w. rhythm accompaniment) Also Universal Double Feature DF 2009

U-131 Give Me A Home In Oklahoma/I'm Coming Home (w. rhythm accompaniment)

U-141 Don't Hang Around/Dream On Little Plowboy (B-side same as U-130)

Universal Double Feature DF 1006 My Blue Heaven/Lonesome Road (w. Sammy Porfirio's Orchestra) Also Fraternity F-779 (45 rpm release)

DF 1007 Ace In The Hole/Frankie And Johnnie (w. Les Paul) "Ace In The Hole" an edited version of Austin GA 510

DF 2008 Sunflower/Careless Hands (w. Sammy Porfirio's Orchestra)

1953

RCA EPA-4057   Ramona/She's Funny That Way/I'm In The Mood For Love/The Sweetheart Of Sigma Chi/Sleepy Time Gal/My Blue Heaven (EP) (w. George Barnes and Frank Carroll)   Also RCA EPB-3200, RCA RCX-113, RCA 547-0346 (selections 1-3) and RCA 547-0347 (selections 4-6)

EPB-3200   Lonesome Road/Someday Sweetheart/Who/How Come You Do Me Like You Do/One Sweet Letter From You/I Can't Give You Anything But Love (EP) (w. George Barnes and Frank Carroll)   Also RCA 547-0346 (selections 4-6) and RCA 547-0347 (selections 1-3)

1957

RCA 20-6880   Too Late/That's Love (w. orchestra directed by Charles Grean)   Also RCA 47-6880 (45 rpm release)

A Porter's Love Song To A Chamber Maid/I Could Write A Book (w. orchestra directed by Charles Grean)   Also RCA 47-6969 (45 r.p.m. release)

Wonder/I'm Not The Braggin' Kind (w. orchestra directed by Charles Grean)   Also RCA 47-7117 (45 r.p.m. release); "I'm Not The Braggin' Kind" also on RCA EPA-1-1547 (45 r.p.m.)

RCA EPA-1-1547   Memories Of You/Where The Shy Little Violets Grows/Take Your Shoes Off Baby (45 r.p.m. release)

1958

RCA 20-7237   Sweetheart Of De Molay/The Sunshine Of Your Smile (w. orchestra And chorus directed by Charles Grean)   Also RCA 47-7237 (45 rpm release)

1960

Dot 160   My Blue Heaven/Ramona (w. Billy Vaughn Orchestra)   Also Goldies P-2699 (45 r.p.m. releases)

1967

Professional recording session producing stereo master tape; not issued on disc (w. vocal and instrumental accompaniment)
St. Louis Blues (3:04 min.)
Evergreen Lady Of Spring (1:43 min.)

You're Gonna Cause Me Trouble (2:33 min.)   Duet with Mona Clark
Lazy Lou'siana Moon (2:10 min.)
Chopsticks (2:08 min.)
Moanin' Low (2:31 min.)
Can't Help Lovin' That Man Of Mine (1:44 min.)   Vocal by Mona Clark
How Come You Do Me Like You Do? (2:23 min.)   Duet with Mona Clark
See You When Your Troubles Get Like Mine (2:45 min.)
Nobody's Sweetheart Now (1:30 min.)
After You've Gone (1:47 min.)

--Long Playing Records

Decca DL 8433   My Blue Heaven (195?)   Reissue of Decca material
Dot DLP-3300   Gene Austin's Great Hits (w. orchestra directed by Billy Vaughn)
        Also Dot DLP-25300 (stereo)
Fraternity F-1006   Gene Austin And His Lonesome Road (1957)   Reissue of Universal
        material.
RCA LPM-1547   Restless Heart (w. orchestra directed by Charles Grean) (1957)
   LPM-2490   My Blue Heaven (1962)   Reissue of Victor material
   LPM-3200   My Blue Heaven (w. George Barnes and Frank Carroll) (1953)
       10-inch disc
   VPM-6056   This Is Gene Austin (1972)   Recorded May 9, 1961 at Western
       Recorders, Hollywood)
Sunbeam P-507   Old Pals Are The Best Pals (1978)   Reissue of Victor material
Vik LVA-1007   All-Time Favorites By Gene Austin (1955?)   Same as "X"
       LVA-1007
   LX-998   All-Time Favorites By Gene Austin (1957)   Same as "X" LVA-1007
"X" LVA-1007   Gene Austin Sings All-Time Favorites (1955)   Reissue of Victor
       material

--Radio Transcriptions

Standard Program Library R109   (w. Candy and Coco)   recorded August 1935
   A 498   Why Do I Love You ("Show Boat")
   A 499   Stormy Weather ("Cotton Club Parade")
   A 500   Sometimes I'm Happy ("Hit The Deck")
   A 501   Sally ("Sally")
   A 502   Lonesome Road
   A 503   Solitude
   A 504   Old Rocking Chair
   A 505   Don't Leave Me Daddy
Standard Program Library R110   (w. Candy and Coco)   recorded July 1935, nos. 1-4;
  August 1935, nos. 5-9)

    A-476 Honeysuckle Rose
    A-477 I Kiss Your Hand Madame
    A-478 I'm Coming Virginia
    A 479 My Blue Heaven
    A 506 Riverside Drive
    A 507 Yearning
    A 508 Remember
    A 509 New Orleans
    A 510 You're More Than Love

Standard Program Library R111 (w. Candy and Coco) recorded October 1935
    A 543 Smoke Rings
    A-544 Fair Weather Mama
    A 545 Who ("Sunny")
    A-546 The Two Of Us
    A-551 Smoke Gets In Your Eyes ("Roberta")
    A 552 Someday Sweetheart
    A 553 Pretty Is As Pretty Does
    A 554 Git Along

Standard Program Library R112 (w. Candy and Coco) recorded October 1935
    A-555 Sleepy Time Gal
    A-556 Voodoo Drums
    A-557 Sweetheart Of Sigma Chi
    A-558 Some Of These Days

Thesaurus Record 377 (Nathaniel Shilkret Orchestra/vocals by Felix Knight and Gene Austin) recorded c. May 1937
    Red Mill Valley Medley (vocal by Knight)
    Spanish Serenade
    I'm A Rockin' In The Saddle (vocal by Austin)
    Indian Summer

Thesaurus Record 408 (Nathaniel Shilkret Orchestra/vocals by Yvonne Doran, Gene Austin and Felix Knight) recorded c. May 1937
    Sweet Adeline Medley (vocals by Doran and Austin)
    Blue Danube
    Then You'll Remember Me (vocal by Knight)
    Zigeuner

Thesaurus Record 414 (Nathaniel Shilkret Orchestra/vocals by Gene Austin and Felix Knight) recorded c. May 1937; reissued as Thesaurus Record 414-775
    Somebody Loves Me (vocal by Austin)
    If I Should Send A Rose (vocal by Knight)
    Fleurette
    Cuban Serenade

Standard Program Library R121 (w. Candy and Coco) recorded August 11, 1938
    I'm Coming Home

    I Fell Down And Broke My Heart
    Rootin' Tootin' Shootin' Man From Texas
    Song Of The Saddle
    Why Can't I Be Yours Tonight (nos. 1-5 from "Songs And Saddles")
    I'm In A Mellow Mood
    One Sweet Letter From You
    Forgive Me
Standard Program Library R-122 (w. Candy and Coco)   recorded August 11, 1938
    Dear Old Southland
    Stardust
    I Cried For You
    Tomorrow
    Muddy Water
    If I Had My Way
    The Meanest Gal In Town
    The Last Round Up (from "Ziegfeld Follies")
Thesaurus Record 636 (w. Candy and Coco)   allegedly recorded February 27, 1939
    Sleepytime Gal
    I Wonder Who's Kissing Her Now
    I'm Getting Sentimental Over You
    Blue Sky Avenue
Thesaurus Record 651 (w. Candy and Coco)   allegedly recorded February 27, 1939
    I'm Coming Home
    I Fell Down And Broke My Heart
    Why Can't I Be Your Sweetheart Tonight
    Song Of The Saddle
Thesaurus Record 683 (w. Candy and Coco)   allegedly recorded February 27, 1939
    Smoke Rings
    Sweetheart Of Sigma Chi
    Tomorrow
    I Cried For You
Thesaurus Record 704 (w. Candy and Coco)   allegedly recorded February 27, 1939
    My Blue Heaven
    Melancholy Baby
    Girl Of My Dreams
    Then Came The Dawn
Thesaurus Record 709 (w. Candy and Coco)   allegedly recorded February 27, 1939
    Marie
    Old Fashioned Love
    Lonesome Road
    Yearning
Naval Air Reserve Show #19 (w. George Barnes and His Octet) c. 1948
    I Can't Give You Anything But Love (vocal by the Five Singing Honeydreamers)

    My Blue Heaven (vocal by Austin)
    Surrender Dear (vocal by the Five Singing Honeydramers)
    Goose Pimples (instrumental)
Treasury Department "Guest Star" No. 563 (w. Del Sharbutt and Harry Sosnik and His
  Orchestra) c. 1957
    Exactly Like You (w. Harry Sosnik and His Orchestra)
    Medley: I Thought About You/How Come You Do Me Like You Do/Bye Bye
    Blackbird (w. guitar, string bass and drums accompaniment)
    Medley: I'm Not The Braggin' Kind/Lonesome Road/My Blue Heaven (w. guitar,
      string bass and drums accompaniment)
    Lullaby Of Broadway (w. Harry Sosnik and His Orchestra)

--Compact Discs

Living Era CD AJA5217   Gene Austin: The Voice Of The Southland (1996)
                Recordings date from the 1925-1936 period.
Take Two TT 414CD   Gene Austin: A Time To Relax (1995) 20 of Austin's
                best known hits recorded between 1925-1936; includes
                "Album Notes" by Randy Skretvedt.

Filmography

Sadie McKee (Metro-Goldwyn-Mayer; released May 11, 1934) 88 min.
Ferry-Go-Round (RKO Radio Pictures; copyright September 14, 1934) 22 min.
Gift Of Gab (Universal Pictures; released September 24, 1934) 70 min.
Night Life (RKO Radio Pictures; copyright September 13, 1935) 22 min.
Klondike Annie (Paramount Prouctions; released February 21, 1936) 77 min.
Bad Medicine (RKO Radio Pictures; copyright May 4, 1936) 15 min.
Trailing Along (RKO Radio Pictures; copyright September 20, 1937) 18 min.
Songs And Saddles (Road Show Pictures; released 1938) 65 min.
My Little Chickadee (Universal Pictures; released February 9, 1940) 83 min.
One Dozen Roses (Soundies Distributing Corp. of America; copyright June 22, 1942)
      3 min.
That Rootin' Tootin' Shootin' Man From Texas (Soundies Distributing Corp. of America;
      copyright July 13, 1942) 3 min.
I Hear Ya Knockin' But Ya Can't Come In (Soundies Distributing Corp. of America;
      copyright August 3, 1942) 3 min.
Take Your Shoes Off Daddy (Murray Hollywood Productions; released c. 1943) 3 min.
      Doris Sherrell sings with Austin playing piano.
I Hear Ya Knockin' But Ya Can't Come In (Murray Hollywood Productions; released
      c. 1943) 3 min. Doris Sherrell sings with Austin playing piano.
You're Marvellous (Martin Murray Productions; released c. 1943) 3 min.

Boogie Woogie Wedding (Martin Murray Productions; released c. 1943) 3 min.
  Doris Sherrell sings with Austin playing piano.
(My) Melancholy Baby (Marti Murray Productions; released c. 1943) 3 min.
Keep A Knockin' (Martin Murray Productions; released c. 1943) 3 min. Doris
  Sherrell sings with Austin playing piano.
My Blue Heaven (Martin Murray Productions; released c. 1943) 3 min.
I Want To Be Bad (Soundies Distributing Corp. of America; copyright March 13, 1944)
  3 min.
I Want To Lead A Band (Soundies Distributing Corp. of America; copyright March 27,
  3 min.
Moon Over Las Vegas (Universal Pictures; released April 28, 1944) 69 min.
Imagine (Soundies Distributing Corp. of America; copyright April 10, 1944) 3 min.
Follow The Leader (Monogram Pictures; released June 3, 1944) 65 min.
Pagliacci Swings It (Universal Pictures; released June 14, 1944) 15 min.
My Blue Heaven (Soundies Distributing Corp. of America; copyright March 19, 1945)
  3 min.
Fried Green Tomatoes (Universal Pictures & Act III Communications; copyright 1991)
  Austin heard singing "My Blue Heaven" approximately 12 minutes into the film;
  despite the reference to Victor, RCA and BMG in the closing credits, the
  recording here was made for Decca in 1942.

Bibliography

Agan, John A. "The Voice of the Southland: Louisiana's Gene Austin," *North Louisiana
  Historical Association Journal*. XXVIII:4 (Fall 1997) 123-137.
Cohen, Norm, and Tor Magnusson. "George Reneau: A Discographical Survey,"
  JEMF Quarterly. (XV:56 (Winter 1979) 208-214. Covers the impact Austin had
  On Reneau's recording career.
Kay, George W. "Gene Austin—Balladeer from the Bayou," *The Second Line*. XXI
  (January-February 1969) 149-153.
Lamparski, Richard. *Whatever Became of...? Second Series*. New York: Crown,
  1968. Also published in Canada by General Publishing Company Limited.
Magnusson, Tor. "Fats Waller: Some Considerations on Two Recording Dates,"
  Annual Review of Jazz Studies I (1982) 79-84.
Magnusson, Tor. "Fats Waller with Gene Austin on the Record," *Journal of Jazz
  Studies*. 4:1 (Fall 1974) 75-83.
Magnusson, Tor. "The Gene Austin Recordings," *Matrix* (Hayes, Middlesex, Great
  Britain). n91 (February 1971) 1-2; n92 (April 1971) 1-4; n93 (July 1971) 5-6; n94
  [no date] 7-8; n95 (December 1971) 9-10; n96 (April 1972) 11-12; n97
  (September 1972) 13-16; n98 (November 1972) 17-18; n99/100 (April 1973) 19-
  22; n101 (August 1973) 23-24; n102/103 (May 1974) 25-28; n104 (August 1974)
  1:I-2:I; n107/108 (December 1975) 29-32.

Magnusson, Tor. "The Gene Austin Recordings," *Skivsamlaren* (Goteborg, Sweden). n15 (February 1983) 1-82. Survey of Austin's sound recordings, films, radio and television appearances, sheet music, and song compositions (both those written by Austin and those published by Gene Austin, Inc.).

Magnusson, Tor, and Don Peak. "Gene Austin's 'Candy and Coco': the Identity of the Second 'Candy' Disclosed," *Storyville*. n145 (March 1991) 4-7.

McAndrew, John. "Star Studded Shellac," *The Record Changer*. 14:3 (1955) 16.

Pabst, Ralph M. *Gene Austin's Ol' Buddy*. Phoenix, AZ: Augury Press, 1984. Allegedly edited transcripts of tape recordings made by Austin; in effect, his autobiography.

Parish, James R., and Michael R. Pitts. "Gene Austin," In: *Hollywood Songsters – A Biographical Dictionary*. New York: Garland, 1991. pp. 47-51.

Peak, Don, and Tor Magnusson. "Les Paul with Gene Austin: the '40 Masters'," *Record Research*. 231/232 (October 1987) 1, 4-5.

Pitts, Michael R. "Pop Singers on the Screen," *Film Fan Monthly*. n112 (October 1970) 15-18.

Scott, John L. "Gene Austin's Star Overcomes Eclipse," *Los Angeles Times*. (March 8, 1959) part V, p. 2.

Smith, H. Allen. "A Crooner Comes Back," *The Saturday Evening Post*. 230:9 (August 31, 1957) 25, 66-68.

Smith, H. Allen. "A Friend in Las Vegas," In: *A Short History of Fingers and Other State Papers*. Boston: Little, Brown and Company, 1964? pp. 44-57. Also published in Canada by Little, Brown & Company Limited.

Smith, H. Allen. "Gene Austin's Phone Call," In: *The Best of H. Allen Smith*. New York: Trident, 1972. p. 211ff.

Taylor, Erma. "Presenting Gene Austin – America's Favorite Recording Artist of Ten Years Ago Is Still a Big Seller, But Now He Has His Own Orchestra and Crashes the Movies," *The Metronome*. (October 1934) 35-36, 41.

Walsh, Jim. "Favorite Recording Artists – Gene Austin," *Hobbies*. (February 1957) 34-36, 55, 64; (March 1957) 30-32.

Walsh, Jim. "Singer and Record 'Fiend' Find Much to Talk About," *Johnson City Press* (Tennessee). (April 27, 1939) 10.

Williams, Ned E. "Gene Austin Began on a Calliope," *Metronome Magazine*. (September 1928) 51, 63.

Table 32

Bing Crosby

Considerable confusion exists regarding Bing Crosby's birth date; the singer himself, in his autobiography, *Call Me Lucky*, would state, "I've seen several dates listed for my birth in various publications, among them, 1901, 1903, and 1906. I'd like to take 1906, but 1904 is the one I was stuck with." Baptismal entries at St. Patrick's Church, combined with sister Catherine's Tacoma birth certificate (October 3, 1904) indicate that he was born Harry Lillis Crosby on May 2, 1903 at the family's home on 1112 North J Street.

He was fourth child of Harry Lowe and Catherine Helen Crosby (maiden name Harrigan). Besides Catherine and Bing, other offspring included Laurence Earl (Larry), January 3, 1895; Everett Nathaniel, April 5, 1896; Henry Edward (Ted), July 30, 1900; Mary Rose, May 3, 1906; and George Robert (Bob), August 25, 1913.

The Harrigan family had Irish-Catholic roots; Catherine, known as Kate, was born February 7, 1873, in Stillwater, Minnesota. Her family would later migrate to Tacoma, where she met her future husband. The Crosby family appears to have been of Danish origin; their forebears were allegedly Vikings who settled the British Isles during the eighth through tenth centuries. Bing's brother Larry found that the *Mayflower* had included a Crosby, a damsel said to have married Thomas Brewster, one of the Pilgrim Fathers. Bing's paternal great-grandfather, Nathaniel, a sea captain hailing from Worcester, Massachusetts, traded in the Far East and helped found Portland prior to helping settle Olympia, Washington.

Harry, born in Olympia on November 28, 1870, attended a year or so of college before becoming a bookkeeper. A charming, easygoing man from a good family and engaged in a good profession, he was undoubtedly a solid catch for the pretty, level-headed Kate. His conversion to Catholicism cleared any barriers to their union, and the marriage took place in the early 1890s.

Harry was a bookkeeper for the country treasurer during Bing's early years, but a change in political administration caused him to lose his job. Like many other inhabitants along the Coast with limited prospects, he found Spokane enticing. Located two hundred miles eastward near the Idaho border, Spokane was located in a fertile wheat belt and, as a railroad center, it was becoming the logging and mining center of the region. Harry found work there as a bookkeeper for the Inland Brewery and sent for the family in July 1906.

The family residence, a two-story, four-bedroom rented house on Sinto Avenue, was located on the northeast side of the city, across the Spokane River from the business and manufacturing districts. The home—comfortably equipped with indoor plumbing and electricity, and located near stores and trolley lines which ran to the downtown sector—would become the hub of Bing's childhood years. A number of the more formative institutions of his life—Webster, a grade school, a Jesuit-administered high school-college complex named Gonzaga, and the adjoining church, St. Aloysius—were located within three blocks of his home.

Bing received his famous nickname around 1910. At this time he became a fan of the "Bingville Bugle," which occupied a full page of the Spokane *Spokesman Review*'s Sunday edition. Taking the appearance of the front page of a newspaper published in the mythical Bingville, the humor feature included short country-bumpkin stories about town citizens sometimes illustrated by cartoon spots. A next-door-neighbor friend, Valentine Hobart, noticed that caricatures of the cartoon residents had stocky, pear shapes and protruding ears exactly like those possessed by young Harry. Valentine began calling him Bingo from Bingville. Other school peers picked up the phrase, which soon was shortened simply to Bingo; eventually the *o* was dropped and the youngster was known to all thenceforth as Bing.

Music was always seemed a key ingredient of life within the Crosby household. One memorable payday evening Bing's father returned home toting two large packages containing a phonograph complete with a large speaker horn in addition to several records featuring baritone Denis O'Sullivan, marches by John Philip Sousa and other bandleaders, and a collection of songs from Gilbert and Sullivan's operetta, *The Mikado*. On another occasion, Dad Crosby went without a new suit he had been saving for in order to purchase a piano. Kate made sure that her daughters received lessons on the instrument; however, none of the boys displayed an interest. Every Sunday evening the Crosbys would engage in a family songfest. Dad Crosby would bring out his mandolin and four-string guitar, and everyone would gather round their favorite pop standards. Kate possessed a rich contralto voice—she'd been a member of the church choir in Tacoma prior to responsibilities of motherhood—and the children (except for Everett, who reputedly couldn't carry a tune in a bucket) did a creditable job of contributing the harmony parts.

It is perhaps not surprising that Bing's involvement in music typified his easygoing, albeit self-assured, approach to life in general. Shepherd and Slatzer have noted,

> Even in grade school, Bing…was…what is called a quick
> study in show business; he had something akin to total recall.
> This was true for people's names and faces, which ingratiated
> him with the adults in his early years and with the relatively
> unknown technicians or bit-part actors he met during his
> professional life. But at Webster and at Gonzaga High
> School and at college, his extraordinary ability was used
> to get ordinary grades with as little time and effort as he could
> get away with.

Barry Ulanov, in *The Incredible Crosby*, has succinctly addressed the forces behind Crosby's increasing realization that music had the potential to become more than a mere hobby in his life.

> It was "life-worship" that impelled his musical career, organized it, carried it along. At no point in the early years, years of whistling and singing and beating almost aimlessly on doors and pots and pans and rude drum equipment, did Bing consciously imagine himself a singer or a musician. He was fascinated with music, as many of his school friends were. He was sufficiently interested to convert his whistling and singing and drumming, as he had his abilities to sweep up floors and push buttons and pick berries, into a job of work. When, during the school years, he and his friends…knocked together a band, it was easy for him to make the band his major interest. The impulse was there; all that was needed was the organization of a vehicle to transport the impulse from whistling at work to working at whistling.

Bing entered Gonzaga College in September 1920. In addition to the baseball team and cheerleading, his extracurricular activities included joining the college band. The latter activity gave him access to a bass drum and six like-minded musicians; in short order they formed a dance combo known as The Juicy Seven. Bing's contributions included both drumming and periodic vocal turns. While they apparently weren't very good—employing stock arrangements which were not only dated but called for instrumentation the outfit lacked—they managed to obtain gigs at school dances and occasional off-campus parties.

After a couple years with The Juicy Seven, Bing received a telephone call that was to prove a watershed development in his music career. Al Rinker, whose group, The Musicaladers, needed a competent drummer, asked him to come by for a tryout. Rinker would later recall the group's first practice session with Bing.

> We went over a couple of tunes and we knew right away that this guy had a beat. Not only that, but he picked up his megaphone, and he could *sing*! So this was *great*, a real surprise to us.

For his part, Bing was impressed that The Musicaladers performed the latest hits, utilizing the harmonies, phrasings, and voicings of the hot, avant-garde bands of the day. While not yet accomplished musicians, The Musicaladers became extremely popular in the Spokane area, most notably with the younger generation, who tended to dislike the "old-fashioned" music of their elders.

By September 1925, however, three of the band members had left for college and another attempted to break into the Los Angeles music scene, leaving only Al and Bing. During the course of hanging out, playing golf and going to parties, they began experimenting as a singing duo.

Hearing that the Clemmer Theater was looking for a quartet to perform between motion pictures, they acquired three singers, utilizing Al as an accompanist. They were hired, but following a week of lackluster results, the management fired all of the singers but Bing.

After performing solo for a few shows, Bing convinced them to let him sing with Rinker. Al would remember, "The audience loved us. So we stayed there about five weeks, making about thirty dollars a week each, and this was big money for us. That's how we began singing together professionally."

With Bing now earning more money on the side as a musician than beginning attorneys typically were paid for full-time work, he cast aside his earlier ambition of studying law. When the Clemmer Theater decided to revert back to showing films without a stage show, however, Al and Bing were suddenly unemployed in a town which appeared to be a dead-end for anyone harboring show business aspirations. Accordingly, they decided to try their luck in Los Angeles, where Al's sister, Mildred Bailey, was just beginning her career singing in speakeasies, and Bing's brother Everett was selling trucks.

Arriving on Los Angeles in their 1916 topless Model-T Ford, the boys sought out Mildred Bailey, who used her show-business contacts to help them find work. In short order, they were hired at $75 a week each to perform in the Fanchon and Marco traveling variety show called *The Syncopation Idea*. The show included jugglers, comedians, dancing girls, and other vaudevillians, starting out in small cities like Glendale and Long Beach, and moving north to San Francisco and Sacramento, where the tour ended thirteen weeks later. The experience enable them to polish their act and, by tour's end, they were doing encores.

Back in Los Angeles, Al and Bing caught on with a musical show called *Will Morrissey's Music Hall Revue* for $150 a week. Billed as "Two Boys and a Piano," they proved adept at stopping the show, with audiences demanding encores. Morrissey helped booked the duo for a notable one-night engagement at the Olympic Auditorium, where they shared the stage with such established stars as Eddie Cantor, Fannie Brice, George Jessel, Jackie Coogan, Pola Negri, and Charlie Chaplin, and took them to exclusive Hollywood parties. After the Los Angeles run, the Morrisey Revue played in San Diego's Spreckels Theater, the Capital Theater in San Francisco, and the Lobero Theater in Santa Barbara for an additional eight weeks.

While the revue was still playing in Los Angeles, the Paramount Publix chain signed the duo to perform in stage shows which complemented film showings at two theaters, The Grenada in San Francisco and the Metropolitan in Los Angeles. The contact, which paid the act $300 a week, took effect as soon as the Morrisey Revue closed or when Al and Bing's affiliation with the show terminated, whichever came first. Billed as Crosby and Rinker, they played—along with the rest of the troupe—four shows a day, five on weekends. Although now playing in far more prestigious venues, they continued to be show stoppers. Shepherd and Slatzer stated,

> The word that best describes audience reaction to Al and Bing at this stage of their careers is *delight*. Their zest and energy and enthusiasm were contagious. Their musical ability knew no bounds, and they continually nudged at— and often broke through—the very limits of contemporary music of the day, with a good measure of jazz worked into the fabric of their presentation....As a duo, their voices complemented one another, and with Al's arrangement, they'd break from the melody line, exploring the subtleties of minor chords or the augmented and diminished facets of major chords before modulating ingeniously back on track, the throbbing, relentlessly hypnotic rhythm driving them along. And their audiences followed the, Pied Piper-like, joyous and astonished at the new avenues of musical exploration. Technically, the audience didn't know what the boys were doing, but they liked it. And the boys were probably not technically analytical about what they were doing, either; it was gut level, and it worked.

While Crosby and Rinker were playing their second engagement at the Metropolitan, Paul Whiteman, leader of the most popular band in the world, arrived in Los Angeles to perform at Sid Grauman's Million Dollar Theater. According to Crosby biographer, Charles Thompson, Jimmy Gillespie, Whiteman's manager, saw the duo and recommended them to his boss. Whiteman then sent viola player Matty Malneck and pianist Ray Turner to see the act. They brought back highly favorable reports; Malneck indicated the duo had an infectious style, "like hearing a great jazz player for the first time." Whiteman sent word for Crosby and Rinker to come back for a visit, and immediately offered them a job with his organization. He went on, "I'll start you at $150 a week each, and you can make extra money from recordings and from a couple of Broadway plays we're going to be in; we're signed to do a how called *Lucky* and one called *Whoopee*. Eleven months from the day they'd left Spokane to seek fame and fortune, they signed a contract to sing with Whiteman's band.

How did Crosby and Rinker achieve so much in such a comparatively short period of time? Shepherd and Slatzer offered the following explanation:

> There was no shortage in the twenties of duos who could sing and play piano—and with pleasing voices, too. Every small city in the country could turn out a dozen of them to

form the lines outside vaudeville producers' audition halls—fresh kids with good voices, pleasing personalities, and talent. But for any such duo to crack vaudeville—which was just a hard to break into as television or motion pictures is today—to steal shows from seasoned, professional headliners, and then to rocket straight to the top as a featured act with the most famous popular orchestra in the world at the time—all in less than a year—is the stuff of Hollywood movies. It couldn't happen in the real world. But it did. The explanation of their incredible feat boils down to one rock-hard fact: the act rested and rose on Al Rinker's arrangements; without them, as good as their voices and show-business instincts were, they would have been just another singing duo and piano act with pleasing voices.

While Crosby and Rinker were completing their contractual arrangement with Paramount Publix, Don Clark, a former Whiteman sideman whose orchestra was playing at the Biltmore Hotel in Los Angeles, asked them to cut a record with his musicians. Music historians have speculated that news of duo's agreement with Whiteman may have been the primary reason Clark sought out their services. As a result, Al and Bing sang on two songs recorded October 18, 1926 in the grant ballroom of the Biltmore. One selection, "Don't Somebody Need Somebody?" was never released. The other, "I've Got the Girl," composed by Walter Donaldson, perhaps best known for pop standards such as "My Blue Heaven" and "Carolina in the Morning," was issued by Columbia backed by the instrumental, "Idolizing."

The release proved to be something of an embarrassment. According to Bob Osborn and Vernon Wessley Taylor, whose comments appeared along with a limited-edition, 7-inch LP issued by the Bing Crosby Historical Society of Tacoma in 1980, Columbia apparently thought that the master cut of the record was slow. In an effort to achieve a jazzier sound, the recording was speeded up when duplicated were cut for release. Both Al and Bing would later admit that they sounded like a pair of chipmunks chattering in the background.

After a one-week engagement at Spokane's Liberty Theater, from November 21 through November 27, accented by visits with family and friends, Crosby and Rinker headed to Chicago to meet up with Whiteman. Despite at least one awkward moment—a piano they were pushing offstage following their segment in one particular concert tipped over, requiring the combined efforts of Al, Bing, and Whiteman himself to get it back on its wheels as the audience roared with laughter—the duo continued to elicit a favorable response. During the three-theater run in Chicago, they had the opportunity to cut another record, "Wistful and Blue," recorded December 22, 1926 at the Concert Hall on Michigan Avenue. Whiteman also went out of his way to take them around town, introducing them to important people. Rinker would later recall, "Whiteman seemed to be quite proud of us. We were young and eager, and I think it was because we were fresh and very enthusiastic that he took more than a casual interest in us."

Crosby and Rinker's success continued in the cities where Whiteman played enroute to the East Coast. Their New York City debut at the Paramount Theatre on Times Square in January 1927, however, brought them face-to-face with failure for the first time since they'd turned professional. By the time Whiteman opened his own club at 48th and Broadway in February 18, they had been reduced to performing during intermission; for most of the run they worked as stagehands. In 1980, Rinker offered the following explanation for their poor reception in the Big Apple:

> People didn't seem to understand what we were doing! We'd go: bop-bop-de-do-do / de-doodle-eeaaaa [snapping his fingers while singing scat] and stuff like that. And they didn't know what the hell we were doing! And now that I think about it, I don't blame them. The New York audience was mostly Jewish—provincial in its own way—staid; you know what I mean. They were used to great entertainers of a certain tradition like Jolson, Cantor, and Sophie Tucker, who were *belting* out songs. [Imitating Jolson here] Mammmeee! Mammmeee! They *really* let you have it! But we were *intimate*. That wasn't what they expected, and they didn't like it.

In February 1927, with Al and Bing's career in jeopardy, violinist Matty Malneck suggested they get together with Harry Barris, a singer and piano player who was in danger of being let go because Whiteman can't find a place for him in the organization. Having to lose, all three were receptive to the idea. Rinker recalled the meeting arranged by Malneck,

> We talked, then Barris played a couple of his songs. One of them was "Mississippi Mud," which he had composed—James Cavanaugh had done the lyrics—and we liked it. We talked some more, fooled around at the piano a bit, then we said "Let's learn it." So we started harmonizing and arranging it, all four of us chipping in ideas, and then we finished, it sounded great to Bing and me because we had another voice there. And Barris could *really* swing, you know. So we learned "Mississippi Mud" and another number, "Ain't She Sweet," We thought that was great, too, because it was another song for us, and we were anything but intimate in our delivery.

Malneck then herded the trio over to Whiteman's club for an audition, where they performed the two numbers; they sang in three-part harmony with Barris and Rinker playing pianos accented by Bing's filigrees on a hand-held cymbal. The bandleader was delighted and immediately put them on at the club, billed as Paul Whiteman's Rhythm Boys. They were enthusiastically received, and were on their way to becoming one of the hottest trios ever to perform.

Back in Whiteman's good graces for the time being, Bing cut his first disc as a solo artist on March 7, 1927. The song, "Muddy Water," was recorded by Victor at Leiderkranz Hall in Manhattan with accompaniment by the Whiteman Orchestra. Shortly thereafter, on April 29, 1927, The Rhythm Boys made their first record with Whiteman, "Side By Side" (Victor). The Rhythm Boys also contributed a number, "Sam, the Accordion Man," to the musical *Lucky*, which ran for seventy-one performances at the New Amsterdam Theater beginning March 22.

After *Lucky* closed, the Whiteman orchestra toured the United States. Rather than taking the trio with him, Whiteman booked them as headliners on the vaudeville circuit for forty-five weeks. His rationale for this decision remains a topic for conjecture. Rinker believed it was because Whiteman didn't consider their act suitable for concerts. Crosby biographers such as Thompson and Ulanov, however, repeated the Crosby organization's take on the issue, that the trio was relegated to the vaudeville tour in disgrace. Numerous people associated with Crosby at the time, including some of Whiteman's musicians, have argued that Whiteman—while fond of Bing and impressed with his talent—would get incensed at his irresponsible behavior, particularly his drinking binges and tendency for missing engagements.

It could easily be argued that headlining the Keith-Albee-Orpheum circuit—the top vaudeville venue at the time—was not a completely depressing experience. They were earning a $1000 per week for just two twelve- to fifteen-minute shows a day. There was plenty of left to play golf, attend college football games as they toured the Midwest, and enjoy the company of star-struck young women. Despite these distractions, the trio was on its best behavior, not missing engagements, and earning uniformly positive reviews. The Rhythm Boys also participated in more than a dozen recording sessions independent of Whiteman; the first, on June 20, 1927, resulted in two records, "Mississippi Mud"/"I Left My Sugar Standing in the Rain" and "Sweet Li'l"/"Ain't She Sweet."

When the tour ended during the summer of 1928, The Whiteman office apparently continued to book the act into New York area venues for the next few months, occasionally with the orchestra itself. In the meantime, Whiteman was planning new challenges for his organization with The Rhythm Boys as a featured attraction.

Whiteman had been one of last big-name holdouts with the radio medium, believing it would undercut record sales and personal appearances. The grind of producing a weekly show acted as another deterrent to such a move. However, when Old Gold cigarettes made him a lucrative offer, he approached NBC about doing a show. Much to his surprise, the network turned him down, explaining "We already have a cigarette account."

Whiteman immediately took his package over to CBS. *The Old Gold-Paul Whiteman Hour* was broadcast from New York City at 9 p.m., Tuesday, to an estimated fourteen million radio sets. Part of the arrangement had Whiteman and his various ensembles, including The Rhythm Boys, jump from the Victor label to Columbia. Old Gold also agreed to sponsor a radio tie-in for a projected motion picture featuring Whiteman, *King of Jazz*. An entire train was leased for the trip out to the West Coast, the Old Gold-Paul Whiteman Special, with stops at sixteen cities along the way.

Prior to the Western trip, Whiteman and The Rhythm Boys played in another Broadway musical, *Whoopee*, which opened December 4, 1928 at the New Amsterdam Theater. The Whiteman orchestra replaced George Olsen's orchestra in the show and was then itself replaced when Whiteman headed for Hollywood. The Rhythm Boys also recorded the hit song from the work, "Makin' Whoopee," for Columbia on December 11, 1928.

Bing's first solo recording for Columbia, "My Kinda Love"/"Till We Meet"—cut March 14, 1929 and featuring a piano, violin, and guitar accompaniment—represented yet another pivotal development in his career. In a May 1929 letter to his mother, he wrote that "my name is being prominently featured in the newspapers and in the broadcasts, and considerable invaluable publicity thus redounds to me." Shepherd and Slatzer have interpreted this to mean that Crosby was already thinking in terms of a solo career, citing information provided by family biographers.

> Bing was approached by a well-known agent who made him an attractive
> offer to stay in New York, under the agent's personal management. It's
> said that the agent offered to pay Bing's expenses until he got work for
> Bing in radio and possibly musical comedy. Bing is said to have been
> tempted but to have turned the agent down because he had a good
> thing going with The Rhythm Boys and doubted his ability as a single,
> and because the agent's offer was just too speculative.

When the Whiteman entourage reached Los Angeles on June 6, 1929 they were caught up in a swirl of preparatory activities: lighting tests, film tests, sound tests, and so forth. Whiteman's doubts about the project were compounded by the fact that Universal Pictures had yet to create a script. With the movie company picking up the tab for the Whiteman orchestra—close to $10,000 a week in all—individual members were left to pursue their own interests.

In addition to hosting parties in a large lease home on Fairfax and playing golf, Crosby made the rounds of the movie studios. According to Whiteman biographer Glenhall

Taylor, the studios spent, collectively, more than seventy thousand dollars in screen tests on Bing, and none offered a contract. One casting director allegedly turned him down because of his protruding ears.

At some point during their West Coast residency, The Rhythm Boys played the Montmartre Café—an exclusive dining and dancing spot on Hollywood Boulevard where film celebrities went to be seen—for several weeks. During this engagement, they became the "discovery" of the movie colony and the talk of the town. This popularity appears to have been a key factor in the trio's decision to part with Whiteman shortly after the completion of *King of Jazz* in March 1930. Furthermore, Bing—the spokeman for the groung—seems to have harbored some resentment that a feature solo for the film, "Song of the Dawn," originally promised to him was shot with John Boles while Bing was locked up in the county jail for public intoxication. Shepherd and Slatzer's assessment of the forces behind the breakup, however, appears to have been closest to actual fact.

> The boys had never really been enthusiastic about going back with
> Whiteman after they finished their vaudeville tour. They had had more
> freedom as an individual act; they weren't subject to the discipline
> that Whiteman insisted upon; they didn't have to sit through hours of
> performance holding dummy instruments on the bandstand; they had
> had star billing, rather than being an appendage of a famous orchestra;
> and finally, they wanted to stay on the West Coast, where they felt
> assured of starring as a trio and of getting movie work as well.

Whiteman had scheduled a tour up the West Coast which would continue into Canada and back to the East. In Seattle, The Rhythm Boys left the band for good. From all reports, the departure for amicable on both sides.

The trio returned to Los Angeles, signing on with booking agent Leonard Goldstein. A chance meeting with an oil company executive that sponsored a local radio variety show emceed by Walter O'Keefe resulted in a thirteen week booking. This was followed by a stint at the prestigious Cocoanut Grove nightclub. Although their salary was no more than Al and Bing had made when they first signed with Whiteman, the club offered other advantages. The owner, Abe Frank, had installed a radio studio and his shows were broadcast nightly from ten to twelve along a Pacific Coast network reaching as far north as Seattle and east to Denver. Entertainment was diversified, featuring two full orchestras, conducted by Gus Arnheim and Carlos Molina, respectively, and a trio called The Three Cheers.

At the Cocoanut Grove, The Rhythm Boys became the hottest act in town. Besides the Montmartre fans who followed them there, they became very popular with the college crowd. The crowd response to Crosby singing led to solo stints—both live and in the recording studio—with the Arnheim orchestra. Shepherd and Slatzer have noted that Bing's success was largely due to his development of innovative singing style.

> Prior to this time, Bing was delivering songs in a smooth manner not unlike the lyrical style used by Irish tenors of the day, concentrating on producing "pretty" pear-shaped tones and adhering to the melody, which resulted in his sounding much like the voicing of a technically correct but uninspired alto saxophone solo. But at the Grove, Bing seems to have brought all of his musical experience to bear on his delivery, and the result was the first stage of a totally new style of singing, different from that of any singer before him and much copied by all who followed.

Vernon Wesley Taylor elicited the following insights from Kenny Allen, a vocalist with The Three Cheers Trio who had the opportunity to observe the Crosby phenomena firsthand during this period:

> I've given a lot of thought to the phenomenon of the popular singer. After all, I tried to be one myself. Well, Bing, besides that intonation of his, had a very nice sense of swing; that's hard to manage even once in a while. Most of us were not only afraid to do it, we hoped the whole idea of it would go away. But Crosby did it all the time—fast songs, slow songs, silly songs, sad songs. It didn't seem to matter with him. He didn't look like he gave a damn, and yet he still managed to make you think he did.

With the premiere of *King of Jazz* at New York City's Roxy Theatre in June 1930, The Rhythm Boys received more film offers. Pathe engaged them in a couple of "two-reeler" musical shorts, *Ripstitch the Tailor* (never released) and *Two Plus Fours* (1930). They next appeared in the features *Check and Double Check*, a 1930 RKO release starring radio comedians Amos and Andy, and *Confessions of a Co-Ed* (Paramount, 1931). *Reaching For the Moon* (United Artists, 1931), starring Douglas Fairbanks, was notable for two Crosby firsts; a solo ("When Folks Up North Do the Mean Lowdown") and a spoken part (two words: "Hi, gang").

At this time, Bing had begun focusing on his solo work at the Cocoanut Grove to the detriment of The Rhythm Boys spots. His partners didn't seem particularly concerned about this state of affairs. Barris was able to put more energy into composing, supplying Crosby with some of the best material during his early career, including "I Surrender, Dear" and "It Must Be True." Rinker would reflect, "I had less and less to do at the Grove, but I had my own interests apart from work, and I really didn't give it much thought at the time." He went on to success as a radio, then television, producer.

During the Grove residency, Bing met and wooed Dixie Lee (aka Wilma Winnifred Wyatt), a young actress felt by many film insiders to possess the potential to become the next blonde bombshell. Their marriage on September 29, 1930 at the Blessed Sacrament Church on Sunset Boulevard brought such newspaper headlines as: "20th Century Fox Star Married Obscure Crooner." Crosby's relative obscurity, however, was soon to become a thing of the past.

Clashes with Frank over missed engagements at the Grove had usually ended with Crosby's salary being docked. When he walked out on one occasion—followed by Rinker and Barris—Frank retaliated by getting the Musicians' Union to blacklist the trio. The impossibility of finding work, combined with the members' outside interests, led to the breakup of The Rhythm Boys. Going on alone seemed like the only logical move for Crosby. "I Surrender, Dear," recorded for Victor on January 19, 1931 with accompaniment by the Arnheim band, had became Bing's first notable solo hit.

Bing's first step as a solo act was to have personal manager brother Everett play a more active role in his career. His wife brought John O'Melveny, a lawyer she had met at Fox, into the organization. O'Melveny effectively sorted out the ban, thereby enabling Crosby to find work. Bing was impressed enough to retain O'Melveny as his lawyer for forty-five years.

No longer hindered by the ban, Everett secured a contract from Mack Sennett for Bing to appear in six film shorts, each one to be based on songs with which he was associated. The films—all shot in 1931—included *I Surrender Dear*, *Just One More Chance*, *Billboard Girl*, *Dream House*, *Sing Bing Sing*, and *Where the Blue of the Night*.

Everett's next goal was to obtain a national radio show for Bing. William Paley, president of CBS, quickly signed him for $600 a week in the fall of 1931. Despite a three-day postponement due to throat problems, Bing was an immediate hit with radio listeners. As the broadcast grew in stature, Cremo Cigars came aboard as the show's sponsor.

If any doubt remained that Crosby was smashing success as a solo artist, Everett got him ten-week contract to headline at New York City's Paramount Theatre, where he had flopped along with Al Rinker during the Whiteman period. The stint, which began November 1931 and paid $2500 a week, broke all house records and was extended to twenty-nine weeks, another venue first. Paramount manager Bot Weitman also contributed to Crosby's rise in popularity. Thompson notes,

> The so-called Battle of the Baritones was another of Weitman's gimmicks
> to pull the crowds in. He put the handsome Russ Columbo with his
> Valentino looks into the Brooklyn Paramount a few miles from the
> Manhattan one. Russ, a former colleague of Bing's in the Gus

> Arnheim days at the Cocoanut Grove, was now making something of a
> name as a crooner. And an artificial rivalry was being whipped up purely
> for publicity. Bing and Columbo were really the best of friends—although
> the public were not led to think so.

Some entertainment business observers, including fellow crooner Rudy Vallee, have argued that Crosby might never have achieved the success he did if Columbo had lived. Lyricist Johnny Mercer felt otherwise, stating,

> Columbo would have done very well, but I don't think he had what Bing had.
> He didn't have Bing's original talent. He copied Bing. He didn't have Bing's
> line of talk and he didn't have Bing's personality. He was a different kind of
> man.

With his popularity reaching new heights, Crosby returned to Hollywood to appear in the film, *The Big Broadcast of 1932*. In contrast to the days when his ears had scared away many movie moguls, he was now considered money in the bank. In the midst of production, Paramount signed him to make five films over a period of three years for a fee of $300,000. Bing would end up making fifty-eight pictures with the studio, including some of the biggest box-office successes of all time. Paramount head Adolph Zukor, later recalling that Crosby had expressed reservations about his acting abilities, offered the following assessment:

> He doesn't have to act; he can just be himself and that's enough. That's
> what he was and that's why he was different to anybody else, and yet he
> reached stardom and popularity not only in this country but all over the
> world.

Crosby also found time to tour in 1932, hiring pianist-conductor Lennie Hayton and former Whiteman guitarist Eddie Lang. In New York, he met a young comic named Bob Hope who was sharing the bill with him at the Capitol Theatre. Although they wouldn't formally team up for another seven years, Thompson notes that they immediately recognized the potential for working together professionally.

> It was there, between shows, that Hope and Crosby displayed their natural
> but competitive good humour. Many of the patrons thought they were
> indulging in plain old bar talk, but as Bob was to reveal more than forty
> years later, they knew it was the start of something big: "The chemistry
> was so good and it was a great piece of electricity, because things were
> happening all the time—new, fresh things and that's always great for anything."

By 1934 Crosby was a major star on three fronts—radio, film, and sound recordings. He was receiving ten thousand letters per months and there were close to 100 fan clubs established worldwide. Rudy Vallee himself allegedly saw the writing on the wall after hearing Bing singing "Beside a Shady Nook." Vallee provided his own interpretation of the song on his radio program and then announced to his eighteen million listeners: "This man Bing Crosby, who has recorded this number for Gus Arnheim, is going to push me off my throne."

Despite Crosby's regular appearances in motion pictures and broadcasts (by the mid-1930s he was averaging three movies a year along with the weekly radio show), his recordings were probably most responsible for the vast size of his audience. At the time of his death, he was estimated to have waxed some 4000 songs with combined sales of 400,000,000. (Furthermore, new recordings—in the latest electronic configurations—seem to appear almost daily.) Up to 1934, Bing had recorded extensively with both of the major U.S. labels—Victor and Columbia. On August 8, 1934, however, he became the first artist to sign with the newly founded Decca, headed by visionary Jack Kapp. While Crosby virtually carried the fledging label on his shoulders during the mid-1930s, his career in turn owed much to Kapp's sound policies. Bing would later comment,

> He was tremendously competent. I was impressed with what he'd done and had great faith in him. He developed a recording programme for me that involved every kind of music. I sang with every kind of band and every kind of vocal group—religious songs, patriotic songs and even light opera songs. I thought he was crazy, but I had confidence and went along with his suggestions!

In 1935, the Kraft Music Hall, then radio's best known program, invited Crosby to participate in an experimental broadcast. The December 5 show had host Paul Whiteman performing in New York, while Crosby, backed by Jimmy Dorsey's orchestra, sang from Hollywood. It was an immense success, and before the end of the year Bing was signed as the new host. The program, now based in Hollywood, quickly became the medium's number one offering, attracting a listening audience of roughly 50,000,000.

When Jimmy Dorsey—concerned that only one radio program per week was undercutting his identity as a major big band leader—expressed his wish to leave the Kraft organization after two years, John Scott Trotter was brought in as the orchestra leader. Trotter, who'd made a name as the arranger for the Hal Kemp band, became a major architect of the Crosby sound, staying with the Kraft show for more than 300 broadcasts. Bing took an immediate liking to the musical director and let him significantly modify the style of the orchestra. In essence, Trotter shifted the melody line from the band over to Crosby, making sure that the saxophones didn't interfere with his voice. He offered the following justification for this policy: "If you listen to some of his early records, they've got saxophones practically in exactly the same range as Bing—and that is lethal."

During the 1930s, it could be argued that Crosby film accomplishments lacked far behind his stature in radio, performing venues, and the recording industry. The "Road" series would change that perception in dramatic fashion. Beginning with *Road to Singapore*, the series—which encompassed seven films made over a twenty year period—ultimately broke all existing box office records as well as creating a new style of cinema. With Hollywood in the midst of a South Sea Island fad calculated to provide escapist fare for a world facing the harsh realties of economic depression and global warfare, Paramount decided to team Bing and Bob Hope, a pairing which had already produced inspired comedy on the airwaves. The films were notable for enabling the two stars to ad-lib almost at will. Co-star Dorothy Lamour would later recall,

> That's the way it was, the whole way through; you never knew
> what they were going to say. You kind of had that feeling
> that maybe they stayed home the night before and read their
> scripts to see who could out-do the other.

Shortly after the second film of the series, *Road to Zanzibar*, was released the U.S. became a direct participant in World War II. Cutting back on his radio and film activities, Crosby shifted the bulk of energies to raising money for the Armed Forces. One tour, which teamed him with Jimmy Van Heusen, covered more than 5,000 miles stateside as they performed for servicemen and visited hundreds of hospital wards. The trips, which lasted throughout the war years, were extremely taxing, averaging three show a day in camps across the nation.

In late summer 1944 Crosby travelled to Europe to help boost morale among American military personnel and the Allied citizenry. In addition to live performances and personal appearances, he was persuaded to broadcast to Germany from London. He talked and sang in phonetic German, expressing the hope that soon the German nation would know the freedoms enjoyed by Americans and Britons. From that time on, the enemy fondly referred to him as "Der Bingle."

While Crosby was less visible in the mass media during the war years, his work reached new heights for both commercial success and artistic achievement. *Holiday Inn*, released in 1942, became the top grossing musical up to that time. Its Irving Berlin score included "Easter Parade" and "White Christmas"; Crosby's rendition of the latter song is probably the biggest-selling record of all time, estimated to sold more than 30,000,000 units at the time of his death.

The following year, Bing began work on *Going My Way*; cast as a Catholic priest, his performance earned him an Oscar from the Academy of Motion Picture Arts and

Sciences for best actor in 1944. The film also won the New York critics' Golden Globe award as best motion picture and propelled Bing to the top of the box-office draw chart for the fifth consecutive year. In addition, the soundtrack included two of his most popular records ever, "Swinging on a Star" (which received an Oscar as song of the year) and an updated rendition of "Silent Night.

Bing's role as Father O'Malley was reprised in *The Bells of St. Mary's*; it went on to become the biggest money-maker of 1945. He also made brief film appearances in support of the war effort. He sang "Buy Bonds" in Twentieth Century-Fox's *All Star Bond Rally* and "We've Got Another Bond to Buy" in *Hollywood Victory Caravan*. During the war he is estimated to have sold Victory Bonds worth over $14,500,000.

Crosby was now at the pinnacle of his popularity. Evidence of his popularity seemd to be everywhere:
- The National Father's Day Committee named him the "Number One Screen Father of 1945."
- G.I.s, in a poll sponsored by *Yank* magazine, voted him the person doing the most for their morale overseas.
- At a time when gold records were rare, three more of his releases reach that plateau (bringing the total to twelve): "Too-ra-loo-ra-loo-ral," "Don't Fence Me In," and "I Can't Begin to Tell You."
- At least two entertainment trade publications— *The Motion Picture Herald* and *Radio Daily*— voted him the most profitable star for the second consecutive year.
- *Box-Office Magazine* named him "the year's Top All-American Male Star."
- "The International British Poll" voted him 'the Top International Star."
- *The Motion Picture Daily Fame Poll* designated him the "Top Radio Master of Ceremonies" for the fourth consecutive years and "Top Male Vocalist" for the ninth straight year.
- *Billboard*'s poll of army camps had him receiving far more votes than the combined tallies of his chief singing rivals, Frank Sinatra, Perry Como, and Dick Haymes.

Despite these successes, the rise of Sinatra—particularly after his boffo appearances at New York's Paramount around Christmastime 1942, when girls allegedly screamed and swooned for the first time in show business annals—was viewed by some as a threat to

Bing's hegemony within the entertainment field. Sinatra himself admitted that he had been inspired by Crosby, stating, "I don't believe that any singer has enjoyed the unanimous acclaim of the American public, as well as performers and musicians, as much as Bing." Rather than slavishly copying the latter's style, however, he made it clear he was seeking fame and fortune on his own terms. Likewise, Bing paid his respects to Sinatra's talent, even inviting the young singer to appear on the November 16, 1944 broadcast of the *Kraft Music Hall*.

Much in the same manner as the "Battle of the Baritones" in the early 1930s, the clash between "the Swooner versus the Crooner" was hype as a result of its box office appeal. Sinatra soon acquired his own radio show and his chief gag writer, Carroll Carroll, continued to function in this capacity for Crosby as well. Carroll would later outline the characterizations supplied to each star: "Bing was the avuncular elder man who wanted to see a young man come along and make it; Frank was the impatient newcomer who wanted to push everything aside and get in there."

In the summer of 1946 Crosby negotiated a break with Kraft and signed on with the Philco Radio Corporation. The program was carried by ABC which agreed to pay Bing $25,000 a week and stock. In addition, approximately 400 independent stations each provided him $100 per broadcast, thereby supplementing his pay with another $40,000. Wednesday was promoted as "Bingsday" by the network. Philco went along with Bing's wish to transcribe *The Crosby Show* as long as it maintained high ratings. This enabled him to stockpile shows, leaving relatively long periods of time free to pursue other professional and recreational interests. In short order, other radio stars began following his example.

During this period Crosby became directly involved in a wide variety of activities outside of performing. His first notable investment of this type had been the Del Mar Turf Club, located north of San Diego, in 1937. He sold his one-third interest in the racetrack in April 1946 to avoid a conflict of interest relating to his part ownership of the Pittsburgh Pirates major league baseball franchise. His interest in professional sports continued with the purchase of a ten percent interest in the Los Angeles Rams National Football League franchise on December 13, 1949. In 1948 Bing joined forces with Jock Whitney, at one time the U.S. Ambassador to England, to market Minute Maid orange juice concentrate. He worked out an arrangement with Philco to tout the product on the radio, taking advantage on preferential options to purchase stocks and shares in the venture. Other investments included Bing's Things, Inc., which marketed toys, clothing, and other products; oil drilling in Louisiana and Oklahoma; banking in California and Arizona; livestock in both the U.S. and South America; ice-cream distribution; and the acquisition of real estate.

Crosby was no longer merely an entertainment giant, but an American institution as well. *The Music Digest* estimated that his recordings filled more than half of the 80,000 weekly hours allotted to recorded radio music at the time, that his radio show was heard by 25 million listeners weekly, and that each film was seen by 250 million viewers. *Women's Home Companion* voted Bing the leading film star, an honor repeated for the next four years. The proliferation of Crosby references in films and other mass media attests to the fact that his name was a household word (e.g., in *Billy Rose's Diamond Horseshoe*, a 20th Century-Fox motion picture released in 1945, Betty Grable sings "I'd love a double order of Bing").

Musicologists, journalists, and other cultural observers continued to devote considerable newsprint space and broadcast time to the dissection of Crosby's singing style. J.T.H. Mize discussed how he might melt a tone away, scoop it "flat and sliding up to the eventual pitch" as a "glissando," sometimes "sting a note right on the button," and take diphthongs for "long musical rides." He argued that "some of his prettiest tones are heard on *ng*'s" and inventoried the Crosby arsenal of vocal effects, including "interpolating pianissimo whistling variations," sometimes arpeggic, at other times trilling. Osterholm would state,

> Prior to 1934 he sometimes displayed the brassiness of Jolson, Cantor, and Ted Lewis...and by 1946 these old-fashioned "plagues" still occasionally crept in. Henry Pleasants thinks Bing's best range was G to G or even lower and that only about this time was he able "slowly to sort out what worked on the microphone and to eliminate what was superficial or incompatible." Still, Bing's voice was incomparable, which Charles Henderson called "phonogenic" and Pleasants "microgenic." His early upper mordents, light and fast, produced a "slight catch, or choke, or sob which was to remain one of the most attractive of his vocal devices," according to Pleasants.

By 1949, as the cultural changes were gathering momentum in postwar America, cracks began appearing in the firmament of Crosby the institution. He slipped the second place in the film star poll; the first time since 1943 that he hadn't been voted most popular. The Philco show was losing its mass appeal; the last broadcast would take place on June 1. *A Connecticut Yankee in King Arthur's Court*, which cost more than three million dollars to produce, earned only three million in America during its first year of release.

Nevertheless, many signs of outward success could still be found. British distributors named Bing the most popular international star in 1948. In November he made eight appearance in London's Empress Hall for $400,000. In Communist Czechoslovakia, an overflow crowd reportedly assembled in October 1949 in a Prague theater to hear—and applaud—Crosby records. In 1950 *Women's Home Companion* announced that Bing was voted the most popular male star for the fifth consecutive year. Between 1946 and 1950 he had nine more recordings achieve gold status—"McNamara's Band," "South America, Take It Away," the *Merry Christmas* album, "Alexander's Ragtime Band," The

Whiffenpoof Song," "Now Is the Hour," Galway Bay," "Dear Hearts and Gentle People," and "Sam's Song," a duet with son Gary—making it twenty-one million sellers in his career overall.

During the early 1950s, Crosby's impeccable public image was tarnished somewhat by domestic problems. The May 9, 1950 issue of the *Los Angeles Times* reported O'Melvany and brother Larry had substantiated rumors that Bing and Dixie had "strained relations." Larry went on to say he hoped for a separation and knew nothing about supposed divorce plans. While vacationing in Europe at the time—without Dixie—Crosby narrowly avoided a fifth stay in jail, on this occasion for violating the grass near the Champs Elysees while awaiting a luncheon appointment. In the spring of 1951 a Vancouver hotel clerk insultingly refused Bing and companion Bill Morrow a room because they were unshaven. In addition, son Gary was drawing attention for boorish behavior of his own, which included chaffing at his father's attempts to impose discipline.

Meanwhile, Bing Crosby Productions committed wholeheartedly to television. In early 1950, the organization produced the first ten 26-minute films at Hal Roach Studios for a weekly series sponsored by Proctor & Gamble called *The Fireside Theater*. Another 24 shows would soon follow. Bing himself had first appeared on TV December 19, 1948, when he sang in "A Christmas Carol" for NBC. Beginning with his second appearance on February 27, 1951, when he sang several songs on *The Red Cross Program* (NBC), he became increasingly visible in the new medium. His third appearance took place on June 21, 1952, as he joined Bob Hope and Dorothy Lamour in a telethon concerning with financing the American Olympic team. Nevertheless, he stated his preference for radio and other projects, while allowing, "Sure, I'll get into television eventually, when I find the right format. I don't think radio is dead—nor ever will be."

In 1952 Crosby signed with General Electric to host a radio program for $16,000 a week; the contract included a clause that he would receive about $50,000 as a package for a television show. In the meantime, his film schedule remain heavy as work commenced on *Road to Bali* along with brief appearance in *The Greatest Show on Earth* and the Dean Martin-Jerry Lewis vehicle, *Scared Stiff*. In September he set sail for Europe to film *Little Boy Lost*.

While abroad Bing received word that Dixie was dying of ovarian cancer. He returned home October 4, Dixie meeting him at Union Station with the aid of daily blood transfusions. She had a relapse the following morning , as Bing prepared for the General Electric program, which premiered on October 9. Dixie died October 31, one day before she was to have turned 41.

Crosby went into private mourning with Judy Garland and Jimmy Stewart serving as guest hosts on the radio show for two weeks. By early 1953 he had returned to work on a full-time basis. When he began dating Mary Murphy, a Paramount starlet, and divorcee Mona Freeman rumors began circulating in the mass media.

Crosby justified an April 1, 1953 appearance on a Bob Hope television show by stating, "I want to keep in touch with the public and if you're not on TV it appears you're out of touch." Motion pictures occupied the bulk of his attention in the latter months of the year; he began filming *White Christmas* in August and *The Country Girl* in October. George Seaton, director of *The Country Girl*, touted Bing's performance as a drunken singer, asserting that it was more remarkable than the standard excellence expected of a Marlon Brando. He would be nominated for Best Actor at the March 30, 1955 Academy Awards; however, Brando won for his unforgettable performance in *On the Waterfront*.

The Bing Crosby Show, his first TV special, was broadcast January 3, 1954 on CBS. The reviews for the program, which featured Bing singing several songs and guests Jack Benny and Sheree North, were decidedly cool. Jack Gould of the *New York Times* stated, "Bing would be a natural for TV and will be when he takes a great interest in this medium's requirements." Crosby seemed unconvinced regarding television's potential. After filming his second special, which aired in April 1954, he announced that "it's my last. Why do I do it? I don't need it. I won't do TV again, not unless I lose my job in the movies." Crosby's final radio show for General Electric occured May 30, 1954, with his son Gary taking over the show for the summer. In the fall Bing hosted daily fifteen-minute programs with the Buddy Cole Trio and Ken Carpenter, which ran on CBS until 1962.

Decca decided to honor Crosby by assembling a special album of 89 songs, many re-recorded and all complemented by an audio commentary. The musical biography included the bulk of Bing's most popular—and most critically acclaimed—songs as well as a 24-page illustrated biography and discography. In the meantime, his opinions regarding the rhythm and blues-inflected sounds then becoming popular were published in the November 2, 1954 issue of *Look*. In his essay, entitled "I Never Had to Scream," he noted popular music had changed, "but not all for the better, by any fair means or foul."

Despite his reservations about the state of pop music at the time, Crosby remained a commercially viable recording artist. According to Osterholm, "each jukebox in America offered at least four Crosby songs." In early 1956, while Elvis Presley was becoming a national obsession, Bing earned two more gold records—his twenty-second and twenty-third—for the single, "True Love," a duet with actress Grace Kelly, and the album in which it was featured. Nevertheless, during a brief trip to England in the summer of 1956, the *London Express* ran the following headline: "Is Bing Crosby Going Out—Or Has He Gone?"

Undoubtedly bowing to pressure to update his style, Crosby recorded a rock 'n' roll-inflected song, "Seven Nights a Week," in January 1957. However, he continued to champion the old guard. When music publishers and disc jockeys were being investigated regarding possible payola violations in the late 1950s, he made the following point in a letter to the Senate Commerce Committee: "It galls me exceedingly to see so much trash on our airlines and TV screens while the work of the talented and dedicated songwriters is crowded out of the picture."

Crosby remained busy making films in 1956. In February he began work on *High Society*, which featured a Cole Porter score. After a brief recuperation following surgery for kidney stones and a minor eye problem, he returned to the Paramount lot to finish filming *Anything Goes*. The TV film, *High Tor*, was aired March 10; despite generally high marks for the music, the overall production received cool reviews. He also learned that he'd been nominated once more for Best Actor, this time for *The Country Girl*.

After several postponements over a two-year period, Crosby secretly married actress Kathryn Grant in Las Vegas October 24, 1957. Despite some adjustment problems—Kathryn would later relate that on returning to their Hollywood home she had been shocked to find a portrait of Dixie in the bathroom and a blanket cover on their double bed bearing the initials D.L.C.—the marriage lasted up to Bing's death two decades later. Their union would produce three children: Harris Lillis Junior, born August 8, 1958; Mary Frances, September 14, 1959; and Nathaniel Patrick, October 29, 1961.

The second marriage and subsequent family appears to have spurred a marked change in Crosby. According to Army Archerd, an entertainment journalist who knew Bing for twenty-five years,

> I think it was the rebirth of his life and a new impetus for
> him to continue in show business. I doubt whether he
> would really have gone on—as successfully as he had
> in this second-half of his life—had he not married again
> and had this wonderful second family. I think he got the
> urge to be Bing Crosby again.

Crosby finally committed himself to television in a big way when he signed a five-year contract with ABC in June 1958. Its terms included a two-million-dollar payment to star in two one-hour shows per year in addition to producing another ten on film. His first special per the agreement was aired in October 1958. Including Dean Martin, Mahalia Jackson, and Patti Page among the guests, it received uniformly high marks. The October 13 issue of *Time* noted, "Bing Crosby's topnotch ABC special last week swayed along with rocking-chair ease; its spare (but expensive) sets and casual tone made the usual frenetic TV variety shows look sick by comparison."

Throughout the 1950s the media seemed to carry stories about the misadventures of the four sons from Crosby's first marriage with alarming regularity. Furthermore, his marriage to Kathryn seemed to exacerbate the problems he had in communicating with them. Evidently feeling the public deserved an explanation, Bing granted an interview to Joe Hyams of the Associated Press in late March 1959. In the two-part series, entitled "How Bing Crosby 'Failed' His Four Sons," he observed, "I guess I didn't do very well bringing my boys up. I think I failed them by giving them too much work and discipline, too much money, and too little time and attention." Other periodicals published their own take on the situation. All of the sons except Gary—who had been stunned at the public disclosure, which he chose to interpret as an apology—immediately came to their father's defense in the mass media. In the end, Bing's public reputation emerged largely unscathed by the episode.

By the 1960s Crosby was widely perceived as one of the entertainment industry's elder statesman. While still capable of boffo box office feats, his best days were considered to be long past. Like other Hollywood titans such as Bob Hope and Jerry Lewis, Bing lent his time and public persona to variety of charitable causes. His Crosby Clambake, now a major international event, garnered further attention in January 1960 when Bing, prompted by a newspaper column written by baseball legend Jackie Robinson, forced the Professional Golfers Association to rescind certain racial discrimination practices. Honors from outside the show business community included having President John F. Kennedy as a house guest in his Palm Springs home.

On June 9, 1960 Crosby received a platinum record for "White Christmas" from the Hollywood Chamber of Commerce. The inscription noted that he had sold more than 200 million records and led the whole recording industry into prominence and profitability. *Variety* noted at the time that royalty figures seemed to indicate that Bing's rendition of "Silent Night" had outsold "White Christmas"; sales were so high that it was evidently hard to ascertain actual facts on a conclusive basis. The following week, on June 15, Crosby was responsible for an interesting footnote in mtion picture history, finishing three films in one day. The movies included *High Time*, in which he starred as jaunty old college student, as well as cameo spots in *Let's Make Love* and *Pepe*.

Crosby's extra curricular activities—all of which typically combined work with pleasure—included travel, golf, and a charter membership in the Clan, better known in the mass media as the Rat Pack. Although the best known members were Dean Martin, Sammy Davis, Tony Curtis, Peter Lawford, and nominal leader Frank Sinatra, there were evidently a number of other stars in the set-up when it began. Davis would later reflect,

> Bing was a member based upon the fact that the Clan really started with Bogart and Betty Bacall. Crosby, though he wasn't at every party, would be there at certain times; he'd leave early if he had to go fishing or somewhere but he'd

> have dinner….he made no bones about how much fun he was
> having. He used to day, "Do you guys live like this all the time?"

This association would lead to Crosby's involvement in the film, *Robin and the Seven Hoods* (1964), a tongue-in-cheek depiction of Chicago's gangster era during the Roaring Twenties, which co-starred Sinatra, Martin, Davis, and Falk.

While Crosby now lived a life of, in Thompson's words, "less work and more play," his professional life would remain the envy of many a younger entertainer. In late December 1960, for instance, he recorded 101 songs in eight marathon sessions. He also continued making films, commenced a daily radio program co-starring Rosemary Clooney for CBS in February 1960, and maintained his string of appearances in TV specials, including those starring show business colleagues (e.g., Perry Como's *Kraft Music Hall* aired on NBC March 16, 1960).

Crosby was asked to host the filmed premiere of *The Hollywood Palace*, a television variety show, which took place January 4, 1964, three days before his mother's death at the age of 90. He continued to host the program every few weeks until the final production in February 1970. In late summer 1964 he began filming his only TV series, *The Bing Crosby Show*, which would air on ABC during the 1964-65 season. Co-stars of the sitcom included Beverly Garland as his wife, Carol Faylen and Diane Sherry as the children, and Frank McHugh as the live-in handyman. Critics gave positive reviews at the outset; however, their impressions became less enthusiastic as the season progressed. His television work also included hosting *The Grand Award of Sports* live from the New York City Theater in Flushing Meadow during the 1964-65 World's Fair.

In 1965 Crosby was cast in a non-singing role as the drunken doctor in a Cinemascope remake of the classic John Ford western *Stagecoach*. Considering the fact that the 1939 original had garnered three Oscars, including a Supporting Actor award by Thomas Mitchell as the character now being played by Crosby, many might have questioned the prudence as taking on such a challenge. Bing, however, had no reservations about signing aboard:

> It was a chance to do a character and I wanted to try it. They had a
> big cast and I knew it had been a success before. There were
> some people who thought we were foolish to make the picture,
> because the original one was such a legend. I went to see it
> and great as it was it really isn't much of a film to look at any more.
> It's more dated than any picture I can recall ever seeing.

The 20th Century-Fox production would be the last film for Crosby. In 1972 he would claim he never officially retired from movie making. After turning down yet another script, he would explain,

> If one came along, and it wasn't dirty or pornographic, or lascivious, or full of smut and was a good role, I'd do it. But I don't think there are many of those films around, unless you get one with Disney.

Crosby occasionally went public during the last decade of his life regarding what he perceived to be the low standards of the entertainment media. The following comments, directed largely against the film industry in early 1972, were typical of his stance:

> I really think its disgraceful what they're doing on the screen now, and they're starting to do it on television too. I think the entertainment media has got a lot of things to be responsible for....I'm sure it's that no other medium in the history of the world had had such a profound influence on manners, dress, coiffure, speech or behavior as the motion picture. And now they are selling, furiously, moral irresponsibility. I think it's wicked.

Crosby's work output was indeed scaled back in the latter half of the 1960s. Aside from his regular stints in *The Hollywood Palace*, he appeared in only two or three television shows a year. He recorded a mere two songs in 1966, and was limited to one session in 1967, on October 31, which resulted in "Step to the Rear" and "What Do We Do with the World?" After waxing forty-one songs during seven sessions in 1968, he would record only three songs in 1969. His studio works would continue to be sporadic from 1970 through 1974 as well.

While Crosby's professional load became increasingly lighter in the early 1970s, he maintained a high level of involvement with charitable activities. He appeared on *The Bob Hope Show* on January 27, 1970 as part of a benefit for the Eisenhower Medical Center then under construction at Palm Springs. In 1971 he teamed with Hall of Fame baseball player Ted Williams in a banquet dedicated to saving the Atlantic salmon. The following year Bing served as the national chairman of the fund drive for the Arthritis Foundation.

His successful December 9, 1973 TV special, *Bing Crosby's Sun Valley Christmas Show*, provided evidence that he remained a show business institution. The NBC broadcast attracted a then record audience of 49,270,000 viewers.

Crosby's public activities were halted for a time when a rapidly growing cyst was found in his left lung on New Year's Day, 1974. Nearly half of his left lung was removed on January 13; it was determined to have been caused by a rare fungal infection contracted during a recent African safari. Back home on January 26, he resigned himself to a long recovery pottering around his half-million-dollar estate.

In the spring Bing began to cautiously test his voice. To his relief, he found that it remained strong and possessed of the familiar mellow tone long considered a Crosby trademark. His renewed vigor, combined with, in Thompson's words, "the special awareness that comes with a close brush with death," inspired him to embrace a new series of ambitious projects. These activities included British Decca's planned release of a series of his classic radio shows; the scheduled August 1975 issue of a seven-disc set of the hundred best Crosby songs by MCA, through the World Record Club; a jazz recording session accompanied only by piano; and six three-hour recording sessions in London aimed at producing twenty-six songs for two fiftieth-anniversary albums to be released by the U.K. arm of United Artists.

In mid-1975 Bing assembled a road show, "Bing Crosby and Friends," which included wife Kathryn, Rosemary Clooney, and the Joe Bushkin Trio. The troupe would tour for the next two years, gaining additional performers along the way. In addition, he made a large number of TV appearances during the balance of 1975 and the following year, including co-hosting *The Bell Telephone Jubilee* with Liza Minnelli on March 21, 1976.

Crosby's only live album to be officially released during his lifetime was produced from a successful two-week engagement in June 1976 at the London Palladium. His British stay also included many taped TV shows and public appearances.

On the heels further concerts and charitable activities, "Bing Crosby on Broadway" opened for a two-week run at the Uris Theater beginning December 7, 1976. Osterholm provided the following assessment of the stint for the December 15 issue of the *Worcester (Mass.) Evening Gazette*:

> Bing Crosby proves with little apparent effort that his baritone voice
> has gained far more in richness than the little steadiness it has lost
> in the highest register....Bing's voice is still very strong, and he can
> turn up a lot of volume when he wishes. He still has a respectably
> high range, stopping at one high note to state that he had just
> invaded the territory of Andy Williams.

Crosby returned to world headlines when he fell into a twenty-foot-deep orchestra pit while taping a CBS special commemorating his fiftieth anniversary in the entertainment business at the Ambassador Auditorium in Pasadena, California March 3, 1977. Although grabbing for a piece of scenery helped to break his fall, it was found that he had ruptured a disc at the base of his spine. He underwent a prolonged recuperation. At his age, it was hard to determine how he would be affected. Eleven weeks after the accident, however, he appeared on the *Barbara Walters Special*, doing a little dance step with Barbara as they walked arm-in-arm and, because it was drizzling, singing a few bars of "Singing in the Rain."

He returned to the gold course in short order and his "Bing Crosby and Friends" did a concert at Concord, California in mid-August as a tune-up for a planned tour of Norway, Sweden, and England. The troupe performed at Momarkedet August 25 in a benefit for the Norwegian Red Cross. In September Bing taped his last Christmas special, his forty-second (going back to radio), in London for CBS. The program, titled *Bing Crosby's Merrie Olde Christmas* and featuring guest star David Bowie, was aired on November 30. He also found time to record his last album, *Seasons*, with British producer Ken Barnes; it would become his twenty-fourth gold record.

"Bing Crosby and Friends" opened September 26 at the London Palladium, playing to sell-out crowds through October 10. *Variety* published the following review of the show:

> Undoubtedly, the highlight of this two and a half hour show, in for Two weeks at this vaud flagship, is a stint when Bing Crosby and the Joe Bushkin Quartet glide smoothly through a medley of chestnuts including "White Christmas" and an up-beat arrangement of "Old Man River".... [Crosby] always looked relaxed and confident, whether gagging with the capacity audience, duetting with wife, Kathryn, or son, Harry, or singing along with Rosemary Clooney....The audience was predominantly middle-aged to elderly, and much of Crosby's show is designed to take advantage of the singer's tremendous nostalgia appeal.

On October 13 Crosby flew to Spain for golf and game shooting. His wife and family employee Alan Fisher remained behind to help Harry, Jr. get settled in the London Academy of Music and Dramatic Arts, where he would be a student for the next three years. At the La Moraleja Golf Club the next day, he challenged Valentin Barrios, the former Spanish champion, and Cesar de Zulueta, president of the club. Teamed with Manuel Pinero, then Spanish champion, Bing was reportedly in the best of humor, joking and singing throughout the match, which they won by one stroke. He collapsed from a massive heart attack while walking away from the eighteenth hole. He passed away without regaining consciousness as an ambulance was taking him to the Red Cross Hospital in Madrid.

Television stations in Spain interrupted their programs with the news, and word quickly spread across the globe. Tributes immediately began pouring in from a vast number of friends and admirers. President Jimmy Carter offered the following eulogy:

> all the roads he traveled in his memorable career, Bing Crosby remained a gentleman, proof that a great talent can be a good man despite the pressures of show business. He lived a life his fans around the world felt was typically American: successful, yet modest; casual, but elegant.

His crooning rival, Frank Sinatra, would comment,

> Bing's death is almost more than I can take. He was the father
> Of my career, the idol of my youth, and a dear friend of my
> maturity. His passing leaves a gaping hole in our music and
> in the lives of everybody who ever loved him. And that's just
> about everybody. Thank god we have his films and his records
> providing us with his warmth and talent forever.

Harry, Jr. and Alan Fisher accompanied the casket containing Bing's body back to Los Angeles on October 17. Funeral services were held, unannounced, on October 19, at Paul's Church, near the UCLA campus in Westwood. Crosby had wanted only his wife and seven children to be in attendance; however, Kathryn modified the request to include Bing's living brother and sister, Bob and Mary Rose, as well as a small number close friends and associates. The body was then taken some five miles to Holy Cross Cemetery with his six sons serving as pallbearers. His oak casket was placed alongside that of first wife, Dixie. With all adjacent plots taken, Bing had himself buried at a depth of eight to nine feet, thereby giving Kathryn the option of being buried in his plot, above him, if she wishes.

The Crosby Legacy

Ample evidence exists to suggest that Crosby was the most popular entertainer on the twentieth century. From 1926, the date of his first commercial record release, until his death in 1977, he was constantly in demand as a recording artist, film actor, radio—and later, television—personality, and concert performer. Jose Ferrer offered the following assessment of his talent: "Bing Crosby is like Mr. Everything of all time."

His singing, of course, was central to understanding his appeal. In addition to virtually defining the crooning tradition, he was widely held to be a premier jazz interpreter. Earl Orkin would write,

> Bing Crosby was one of the greatest of all jazz singers. Although
> he could and often did sing just about anything, he grew up in the
> world of Bix Beiderbecke and Hoagy Carmichael, and jazz was
> always what he loved best. (Unlike Sinatra, for instance, he always
> phrased the music, not the words.) Short of Louis Armstrong or
> Billie Holiday perhaps, there is no better role-model for an aspiring
> jazz singer that Bing.

Osterholm attempted to ascertain Crosby's importance as a singer in commercial terms. Conceding for a moment that Elvis Presley, who died two months before Bing, sold 500 million records since 1954, and that Bing sold only 400 million since 1926, we could, for a simple method, compare relative sales in relation to population by comparing the nation's population at the mid-points of their careers. Adjusting Presley's sales by the audience in Crosby's time, it would be about 365 million, Crosby's sales would be 508 million in Presley's time. Moreover, in the 1930s, when Bing was first popular, record sales were very low because of the Depression, and many people also maintain that Bing has actually sold more than 500 million records.

This success was instrumental in enabling Crosby to assume a larger than life persona. According to Thompson,

> Bing Crosby is probably the most-loved character in the world apart from the creations of Walt Disney. For a half century he has dispensed much joy and much entertainment for the benefit of millions who were never ever to meet him but felt that they knew him and in him had a friend. A colossal, enveloping warmth of affection has justly come his way through the years. Even if the image of the casual, lazy pipe-smoking crooner was not completely true it would not matter. He was Bing, Mr. Family Man, Mr. Clean.

The Crosby image was, in fact, the crooner image personified. The relaxed, gentle touch first defined by 1920s trailblazers such as Gene Austin and Rudy Vallee ultimately became identified with Crosby alone. The evolutionary process was largely completed by the mid-1930s, with Vallee's popularity on the wane and Columbo, who was widely acknowledged to be a Crosby clone, coming to a tragic end. From this point onward, the vitality of the crooning tradition was sapped by the Spokane supernova. Faced with a stylistic dead-end, the genre was easily pushed aside by the rhythm and blues-based sounds of the 1950s.

Discography

According to Crosby's leading discographer, J. Roger Osterholm, the singer recorded more than 2200 songs (many as duplicates; over 1600 individual songs in all) spanning a period of 52 years. In contrast, Elvis Presley—Crosby's closest rival in total record sales (both were reputed to have about 500 million disks as of 1994), and one of his many stylistic imitators (31 Crosby songs were reinterpreted by the King of rock 'n' roll)—cut 500-odd songs through 24 years. Countless anthologies including one or more Crosby tracks have been issued in every disk format. Only those releases with contents substantially given over to Crosby material have been considered for inclusion in this listing.

1926

Columbia 142785   I've Got The Girl   (w. Don Clarke Biltmore Hotel Orchestra)
Victor   37285   Wistful And Blue   (w. Paul Whiteman & His Orchestra)

1927

Victor 20418   Lonely Eyes   (w. Paul Whiteman Chorus)/Wistful And Blue   (featuring
        Paul Whiteman & His Orchestra; w. Al Rinker)
    20508   Muddy Water   (featuring Paul Whiteman & His Orchestra)
    20513   That Saxophone Waltz   (featuring Paul Whiteman & His Orchestra;
        w. Al Rinker, Charles Gaylord, Jack Fulton, And Austin Young)
    20627   Side By Side   (featuring Paul Whiteman & His Orchestra; w. The
        Rhythm Boys)/Pretty Lips   (featuring Paul Whiteman & His Orchestra;
        w. Al Rinker)
    20646   I'm In Love Again   (featuring Paul Whiteman & His Orchestra; w. Al
        Rinker, Charles Gaylord, Jack Fulton, and Austin Young)
    20679   Magnolia   (w. The Rhythm Boys)
    20683   Shanghai Dream Man   (featuring Paul Whiteman & His Orchestra; w. Al
        Rinker, Charles Gaylord, Jack Fulton, and Austin Young)
    20751   I'm Coming, Virginia   (featuring Paul Whiteman & His Orchestra; w. The
        Rhythm Boys)
    20783   Ain't She Sweet - Sweet Lil/I Left My Sugar Standing In The Rain -
        Mississippi Mud   (w. The Rhythm Boys)   Also Victor 24240
    20828   My Blue Heaven   (featuring Paul Whiteman & His Orchestra; w. Jack
        Fulton, Charles Gaylord, Austin Young, and Al Rinker)
    20882   The Calinda (Boo-Joom, Boo-Joom, Boo!)   (featuring Paul Whiteman &
        His Orchestra; w. Jack Fulton, Charles Gaylord, and Austin Young)
    20883   Five Step/It Won't Be Long Now   (w. The Rhythm Boys)
    20973   Missouri Waltz   (featuring Paul Whiteman & His Orchestra: w. Al Rinker,
        Charles Gaylord, Jack Fulton, and Austin Young)

1928

Columbia 1401   Evening Star   (featuring Paul Whiteman & His Orchestra)
        Constantinople/Get Out And Get Under The Moon   (w. Paul
        Whiteman Chorus)
    1441   Because My Baby Don't Men Maybe Now   (featuring Paul Whiteman
        & His Orchestra)
        'Tain't So, Honey, 'Tain't So   (featuring Paul Whiteman & His
        Orchestra)/That's My Weakness Now   (w. The Rhythm Boys)
        Chiquita/Lonesome In The Moonlight   (w. Paul Whiteman Chorus)

1455 That's Grandma/Wa Da Da (w. The Rhythm Boys)
1465 I'm On The Crest Of A Wave (featuring Paul Whiteman & His Orchestra; w. Jack Fulton, Charles Gaylord, and Austin Young)/ Georgie Porgie (w. Paul Whiteman Chorus)
1496 I'd Rather Cry Over You (featuring Paul Whiteman & His Orchestra)
1505 Out Of Town Gal (featuring Paul Whiteman & His Orchestra; w. The Rhythm Boys)
50070 La Paloma (w. Paul Whiteman Chorus)
50098 Silent Night, Holy Night/Christmas Melodies (featuring Paul Whiteman & His Orchestra)

Okeh 40979 Mississippi Mud (w. Frank Trumbauer)

Victor 21103-A Changes (featuring Paul Whiteman & His Orchestra; w. Al Rinker, Harry Barris, Jack Fulton, Charles Gaylord, and Austin Young) Also Victor 25370
21103-B Mary (featuring Paul Whiteman & His Orchestra) Also Victor 26415
21104 Miss Annabelle Lee (w. The Rhythm Boys)
21218 Ol' Man River/Make Believe (featuring Paul Whiteman & His Orchestra) Also Victor 25249
21240 Sunshine (featuring Paul Whiteman & His Orchestra; Al Rinker, Jack Fulton, Charles Gaylord, and Austin Young)
21274 Mississippi Mud/From Monday On (featuring Paul Whiteman & His Orchestra; w. Al Rinker, Jack Fulton, Charles Gaylord, and Austin Young; Irene Taylor and Harry Barris also on "Mississippi Mud") Also Victor 25366 (Mississippi Mud), 25368 and 27688 (From Monday On)
21302 What Price Lyrics? (w. The Rhythm Boys) Also Victor 24349
21315 March Of The Musketeers (featuring Paul Whiteman & His Orchestra; w. Al Rinker, Charles Gaylord, Jack Fulton, Austin Young, and Cullen)
21365 I'm Wingin' Home (featuring Paul Whiteman & His Orchestra; w. Al Rinker, Charles Gaylord, Jack Fulton, and Austin Young)
21389-A I'm Afraid Of You (featuring Paul Whiteman & His Orchestra)

Also Victor 27685

21389-B My Pet (featuring Paul Whiteman & His Orchestra; w. Al Rinker, Charles Gaylord, and Jack Fulton)
21398 You Took Advantage Of Me (featuring Paul Whiteman & His Orchestra; w. Jack Fulton, Charles Gaylord, and Austin Young)/Do I Hear You Saying? (featuring Paul Whiteman & His Orchestra; w. Al Rinker and Charles Gaylord) Also Victor 25369 (You Took Advantage Of Me)
21431 Dancing Shadows (featuring Paul Whiteman & His Orchestra; w. Al Rinker, Charles Gaylord, and Jack Fulton)
21438 Louisiana (featuring Paul Whiteman & His Orchestra; w. Jack Fulton, Charles Gaylord, and Austin Young) Also Victor 25369

21453 It Was The Dawn Of Love (featuring Paul Whiteman & His Orchestra; w. Al Rinker, Charles Gaylord, and Austin Young)
21464 There Ain't No Sweet Man (featuring Paul Whiteman & His Orchestra) Also Victor 25675)
21678 Grieving (featuring Paul Whiteman & His Orchestra; w. Al Rinker, Charles Gaylord, and Jack Fulton)
35934 Metropolis, Part Three (w. Paul Whiteman Chorus)
35992 High Water (featuring Paul Whiteman & His Orchestra) Also Victor 36186
36199 Mississippi Mud (featuring Paul Whiteman & His Orchestra; w. The Rhythm Boys) Also Victor 39000 and 67200
39003 Let 'Em Eat Cake (w. Paul Whiteman Chorus)

1929

Columbia 1629 My Suppressed Desire/Rhythm King (featuring Paul Whiteman & His Orchestra; w. The Rhythm Boys)
1683 Makin' Whoopee (featuring Paul Whiteman & His Orchestra; w. Jack Fulton, Charles Gaylord, and Austin Young)
1694 I'll Get By/Rose Of Mandalay (w. Ipana Troubadors)
1755 Coquette/My Angeline (w. Paul Whiteman & His Orchestra)
Louise (featuring Paul Whiteman & His Orchestra)
1773 Till We Meet Again/My Kinda Love
Louise/So The Bluebirds And The Blackbirds Got Together (w. The Rhythm Boys)
1822 Reaching For Someone (featuring Paul Whiteman & His Orchestra)
Your Mother And Mine (featuring Paul Whiteman & His Orchestra; w. Al Rinker and Harry Barris)
Orange Blossom Time/Your Mother And Mine (featuring Paul Whiteman & His Orchestra)
Baby, Oh Where Can You Be?/I Kiss Your Hand, Madame
1862 S'posin' (featuring Paul Whiteman & His Orchestra)
Little Pal/I'm In Seventh Heaven (featuring Paul Whiteman & His Orchestra)
1945 Oh Miss Hannah (featuring Paul Whiteman & His Orchestra)
Waiting At The End Of The Road (featuring Paul Whiteman & His Orchestra)
At Twilight (featuring Paul Whiteman & His Orchestra)
2001-A Gay Love Also Velvetone 2536, Clarion 5476, Harmony 1428, and Diva 3428
2001-B Can't We Be Friends?
(I'm A Dreamer) Aren't We All?/If I Had A Talking Picture Of You (featuring Paul Whiteman & His Orchestra; Jack Fulton, Al Rinker,

and Harry Barris also on "(I'm A Dreamer) Aren't We All?")
2023 Great Day (featuring Paul Whiteman & His Orchestra)
Great Day/Without A Song (featuring Paul Whiteman & His Orchestra)
Okeh 41181 Let's Do It/The Spell Of The Blues (w. Dorsey Brothers)
41188 If I Had You (w. Sam Lanin's Orchestra)/My Kinda Love (w. Dorsey Brothers)
41228 I'm Crazy Over You/Susianna (w. Sam Lanin's Orchestra)

1930

Columbia 2047 A Bundle Of Old Love Letters (featuring Paul Whiteman & His Orchestra)
After You've Gone (featuring Paul Whiteman & His Orchestra)
2163 Song Of The Dawn
A Bench In The Park/Happy Feet (featuring Paul Whiteman & His Orchestra)
2170 I Like To Do Things For You (featuring Paul Whiteman & His Orchestra; w. The Rhythm Boys)
You Brought A New Kind Of Love To Me/Living In The Sunlight, Loving In The Moonlight (featuring Paul Whiteman & His Orchestra)
A Bench In The Park (w. The Rhythm Boys)
2224 Sittin' On A Rainbow (w. Paul Whiteman Chorus)
50070 La Golondrina (w. Paul Whiteman Chorus)
Victor 22528 Three Little Words (w. Duke Ellington and The Rhythm Boys) Also Victor 25076
22561 It Must Be True/Fool Me Some More (featuring Gus Arnheim and His Orchestra) Also Victor 25280 (It Must Be True)
22580 Them There Eyes/The Little Things In Life (featuring Gus Arnheim & His Orchestra; w. The Rhythm Boys) Also Bluebird 7102 (The Little Things In Life)

1931

Brunswick 6090 Out of Nowhere/It You Should Ever Need Me Also Brunswick 80043
Just One More Chance/Were You Sincere? (w. Victor Young's Orchestra) Also Brunswick 80044 (Just One More Chance)
I'm Through With Love/I Found A Million-Dollar Baby Also Brunswick 80045 At Your Command/Many Happy Returns Of The Day Also Brunswick 80058 Star Dust/Dancing In The Dark
6169 Dancing In The Dark/Star Dust Also Brunswick 80056
I Apologize/Sweet And Lovely Also Brunswick 80057 (1944)

6200-A   Now That You're Gone   Also Brunswick 80044
6200-B   A Faded Summer Love   Also Brunswick 80055
   Too Late/Good Night, Sweetheart (w. Victor Young's Orchestra)
   Also Brunswick 80046
20102   Gems From "George White's Scandals" (w. Mills Brothers,
   Boswell Sisters, & The Victor Young Orchestra)
20105   St. Louis Blues (w. Duke Ellington)   Also Columbia 55003)
20106   Face The Music Medley, Part One
20109   Lawd, You Made The Night Too Long (w. Don Redman)
Victor 22618   I Surrender, Dear (featuring Gus Arnheim & His Orchestra)   Also
   Victor 25280
22691   Ho Hum!/I'm Gonna Get You (featuring Gus Arnheim & His Orchestra;
   w. Loyce Whiteman)
22700   One More Time/Thanks To You (featuring Gus Arnheim & His
   Orchestra)
22701-A   Just A Gigolo (w. Harry Barris and members of Gus Arnheim's
   Orchestra)   Also Bluebird 7118
22701-B   Wrap Your Troubles In Dreams (w. Harry Barris and members of Gus
   Arnheim's Orchestra)   Also Bluebird 7102
24078   Poor Butterfly (featuring Paul Whiteman & His Orchestra; w. Al Rinker,
   Charles Gaylord, Jack Fulton, and Austin Young)

1932

Brunswick 6226   Where The Blue Of The Night (Meets The Gold Of The Day)/I'm
   Sotty, Dear
6240   Dinah/Can't We Talk It over? (w. Mills Brothers)   Also Brunswick
   6485 Snuggled On Your Shoulder (Cuddled In Your Arms)/I Found
   You
6259   Starlight/How Long Will It Last
6268   Love, You Funny Thing!/My Woman
6276   Shadows On The Window/Shine (w. Mills Brothers)   Also Brunswick
   6485 and Columbia 4305-M (Shine) Paradise/You're Still In My
   Heart
   Happy-Go-Lucky You And Broken Hearted Me/Lazy Day (w. Isham
   Jones' Orchestra)
6320-A   Sweet Georgia Brown (w. Isham Jones' Orchestra)   Also
   Brunswick 6635, Vocalion 2867, Melotone 13127, Romeo 2336,
   Conqueror 8363 and 9551, Okeh 2867, Banner 33160, Perfect
   13034, Oriole 2962, and Lucky 60010
6320-B   Let's Try Again (w. Isham Jones' Orchestra)
   Cabin In The Cotton/With Summer Coming On (w. Lennie
   Hayton's Orchestra)

6351-A Love Me Tonight
6351-B Some Of These Days (w. Lennie Hayton's Orchestra) Also Vocalion 2869, Melotone 13130, Okeh 2869, Conqueror 8366 and 9551, Brunswick 635, Lucky 60010, Banner 33163, Perfect 13037, Oriole 2965, Columbia 4305-M, and Romeo 2339
Please/Waltzing In A Dream (w. Anson Weeks' Orchestra)
6406 How Deep Is The Ocean/Here Lies Love Also Columbia 4301 (How Deep Is The Ocean)
Brother, Can You Spare A Dime?/Let's Put Out The Lights (w. Lennie Hayton's Orchestra)
6427 I'll Follow You/Some Day We'll Meet Again

1933

Brunswick 6454 Just An Echo In The Valley/ (I Don't Stand) A Ghost Of A Chance With You
Street Of Dreams/It's Within Your Power
You're Getting To Be A Habit With Me/Young And Healthy (w. Guy Lombardo & His Royal Canadians)
You're Beautiful Tonight, My Dear (w. Guy Lombardo & His Royal Canadians)
6480-B Try A Little Tenderness
I've Got The World On A String/Linger A Little Longer In The Twilight Also Columbia 4301-M (I've Got The World On String)
You've Got Me Crying Again/What Do I Care, It's Home
6525-B My Honey's Lovin' Arms (w. Mills Brothers) Also Columbia 4304-M
6533-A Someone Stole Gabriel's Horn (w. Dorsey Brothers) Also Melotone 13170, Perfect 13055, Banner 33203, Vocalion 2879 and 4522, Oriole 2998, Okeh 2879 and 4522, Conqueror 8417, and Romeo 2372
6533-B Stay On The Right Side Of The Road (w. Dorsey Brothers) Also Melotone 13169, Banner 33202, Vocalion 4522, Romeo 2371, Conqueror 8416 and 9557, Perfect 13054, Oriole 2997, and Okeh 4522
6594 Learn To Croon/Moonstruck (w. Jimmie Grier's Orchestra)
6599-A I've Got To Sing A Torch Song (w. Jimmie Grier's Orchestra)
6599-B Shadow Waltz (w. Jimmie Grier's Orchestra) Also Melotone 13136, Conqueror 8372 and 9553, Okeh 2877, Banner 33169, Romeo 2345, Vocalion 2877, Perfect 13043, and Oriole 2971-A
Down The Old Ox Road (w. Jimmie Grier's Orchestra) Also Melotone 13135, Columbia 4303, Romeo 2344, Conqueror 8371, Banner 33168, Perfect 13042, and Oriole 2970

6601-B Blue Prelude (w. Jimmie Grier's Orchestra)   Also Vocalion 2868, Melotone 13128, Conqueror 8364 and 9553, Romeo 2337, Okeh 2868, Banner 33161, Perfect 13035, and Oriole 2963
There's A Cabin In The Pines/I've Got To Pass Your House To Get To My House
My Love/I Would If I Could, But I Can't (w. Jimmie Grier's Orchestra)
6643-A Thanks (w. Jimmie Grier's Orchestra)   Also Columbia 4303-M, Vocalion 2870, Melotone 13131, Okeh 2870 and 33164, Conqueror 8367, Perfect 13038, Oriole 2966, Banner 33164, Romeo 2340, and Silvertone 8367
6643-B Black Moonlight (w. Jimmie Grier's Orchestra)   Also Melotone 13127, Vocalion 2867, Conqueror 8364 and 9553, Romeo 2336, Okeh 2867, Banner 33160, Perfect 13034, and Oriole 2962-A
The Day You Came Along (w. Jimmie Grier's Orchestra)   Also Vocalion 2830, Melotone 13132, Columbia 8368, Romeo 2341, Okeh 2830, Banner 33165, Perfect 13039, and Oriole 2967
6644-B I Guess It Had To Be That Way   Also Melotone 13165, Banner 33198, Perfect 13050, Oriole 2993, Okeh 2878, Conqueror 8412, and Romeo 2367
6663-A The Last Round-Up (w. Lennie Hayton's Orchestra)   Also Columbia 4302-M, Vocalion 2879, Okeh 2879, Banner 33203, Perfect 13055, Oriole 2998 Melotone 13170, Conqueror 8417, and Romeo 2372
6663-B Home On The Range (w. Lennie Hayton's Orchestra)   Also Columbia 4302-M, Melotone 13131, Vocalion 2870, Lucky 60003, Romeo 2340, Okeh 2870, Conqueror 8367, Banner 33164, Perfect 13038, and Oriole 2966
6694-A Beautiful Girl (w. Lennie Hayton's Orchestra)   Also Melotone 3132, Conqueror 8368, Romeo 2341, Okeh 2830, Banner 33165, Perfect 13039, Oriole 2967, and Vocalion 2830
6694-B After Sundown   Also Melotone 13135, Conqueror 8371, Romeo 2344, Banner 33168, Perfect 13042, and Oriole 2970-A
Temptation (w. Lennie Hayton's Orchestra)   Also Melotone 13136, Okeh 2877, Banner 33169, Romeo 2345, Perfect 13043, Oriole 2971, Conqueror 8372, and Vocalion 2877
6695-B We'll Make Hay While The Sun Shines (w. Lennie Hayton's Orchestra)   Also Vocalion 2868, Melotone 13128, Romeo 2337, Conqueror 9557 and 8364, Okeh 2868, Banner 33161, Perfect 13035, and Oriole 2963
6696-A Our Big Love Scene   Also Melotone 13133, Banner 33166, Romeo 2342, Conqueror 8369, Perfect 13040, and Oriole 2968
6696-B We're A Couple Of Soldiers My Baby And Me   Also Melotone

                13129, Banner 33162, Romeo 2338, Conquror 8365, Perfect 13036, and Oriole 2964
- 6724-A Did You Ever See A Dream Walking? (w. The King's Men)
- 6724-B Let's Spend An Evening At Home   Also Vocalion 2869, Melotone 13130, Conqueror 8366, Okeh 2869, Banner 33163, Perfect 13037, Oriole 2965 and Romeo 2339

1934

Brunswick 6794-A Little Dutch Mill (w. Jimmie Grier's Orchestra)   Also Melotone 13133, Conueror 8369, Romeo 2342, Banner 33166, Perfect 13040, and Oriole 2968
- 6794-B Shadows Of Love   Also Melotone 13134, Conqueror 8370, Okeh 2834, Banner 33167, Romeo 2343, Perfect 13041, Oriole 2969, and Vocalion 2834
- 6852-A Love Thy Neighbor (w. Nat Finston's Orchestra)   Also Okeh 2845, Banner 33201, Perfect 13053, Oriole 2996, Melotone 13168, Vocalion 2845,, Conqueror 8415, and Romeo 2370
- 6852-B Ridin' Around In The Rain (w. Jimmie Grier's Orchestra)   Also Melotone 13167, Okeh 2835, Banner 33200, Romeo 2369, Perfect 13052, Oriole 2995, Vocalion 2835, and Conqueror 8414
- 6853-A May I? (w. Nat Finston's Orchestra)   Also Melotone 13167, Okeh 2835, Banner 33200, Perfect 13052, Conqueror 8414, Romeo 2369, Oriole 2995, and Vocalion 2835
- 6853-B She Reminds Me Of You (w. Jimmie Grier's Orchestra)   Also Melotone 13168, Okeh 2845, Banner 33201, Romeo 2370, Perfect 13053, Oriole 299, Vocalion 2845, and Conqueror 8415
- 6854-A Good Night, Lovely Little Lady   Also Melotone 13134, Okeh 2834, Romeo 2343, Banner 33167, Perfect 13041, Oriole 2969, Vocalion 2834, and Conqueror 8370
- 6854-B Once In A Blue Moon (w. Nat Finston's Orchestra)   Also Melotone 13129, Conqueror 8365, Banner 33162, Perfect 13036, Romeo 2338, and Oriole 2964
- 6936-A Love In Bloom (w. Irving Aaronson's Orchestra)   Also Melotone 13165, Romeo 2367, Okeh 2878, Vocalion 2878, Banner 33198, Perfect 13050, Conqueror 8412, and Oriole 2993
- 6936-B Straight From The Shoulder (w. Irving Aaronson's Orchestra)   Also Melotone 13169, Banner 33202, Perfect 13054, Oriole 2997, Conqueror 8416, and Romeo 2371
-       I'm Hummin' - I'm Whistlin' - I'm Singin'/Give Me A Heart To Sing To (w. Irving Aaronson's Orchestra) Also Melotone 13166, Banner 33199, Perfect 13051, Oriole 2994, and Romeo 2368

Decca 100 I Love You Truly/Just A Wearyin' For You

101 Let Me Call You Sweetheart/Someday Sweetheart
    The Moon Was Yellow (And The Night Was Young)/The Very Thought Of You (w. George Stoll Orchestra)
    Two Cigarettes In The Dark/The Sweetheart Waltz
      With Every Breath I Take/Maybe I'm Wrong Again (w. George Stoll Orchestra)
    June In January/Love Is Just Around The Corner (w. George Stoll Orchestra)

1935

Decca 391-A (Swanee River) Old Folks At Home   Also Decca 18804
   391-B It's Easy To Remember (w. The Rhythmettes & Three Shades of Blue/ George Stoll Orchestra)   Also Decca 3731-B
     Soon/Down By The River (w. George Stoll Orchestra)
   543 I Wished On The Moon/Two For Tonight (w. Dorsey Brothers Orchestra)
     I Wish I Were Aladdin/From The Top Of Your Head (w. Dorsey Brothers Orchestra)
     Without A Word Of Warning/Takes Two To Make A Bargain (w. Dorsey Brothers Orchestra)
     Red Sails In The Sunset/Boots And Saddle (w. Victor Young's Orchestra)   Also Decca 2677-A (Boots And Saddle)
     On Treasure Island/Moonburn (w. Joe Sullivan and Victor Young's Orchestra)
     Silent Night, Holy Night (w. Guardsmen Quartette and Victor Young's Orchestra)
   631 My Heart And I/Sailor Beware

1936

Decca 756 Lovely Lady/Would You? (w. Victor Young's Orchestra)
     The Touch Of Your Lips/Twilight On The Trail (w. Victor Young's Orchestra)   Also Decca 2677-B
     We'll Rest At The End Of The Trail/Robins And Roses (w. Victor Young's Orchestra)   Also Decca 2678-A
     It Ain't Necessarily So/I Got Plenty Of Nuttin' (w. Victor Young's Orchestra)
   870 Empty Saddles/Roundup Lullaby (w. The Guardsmen and Victor Young's Orchestra)
   871 I'm An Old Cowhand/I Can't Escape From You (w. Jimmy Dorsey & His Orchestra)   Also Decca 2679 (I'm An Old Cowhand)
     Song Of The Islands/Aloha Oe (Farewell To Thee) (w. Dick McIntyre & His Harmony Hawaiians)

　　　　　Hawaiian Paradise/South Sea Island Magic (w. Dick McIntyre & His
　　　　　　Harmony Hawaiians)
　　　905　Shoe Shine Boy/The House Jack Built For Jill   Also Decca 3601-A (Shoe
　　　　　　Shine Boy)
　　　　　A Fine Romance/The Way You Look Tonight (w. Dixie Lee Crosby)   Also
　　　　　　Decca 23681
　　　　　Me And The Moon/Beyond Compare (w. Victor Young & His Orchestra)
　　　　　Pennies From Heaven/Let's Call A Heart A Heart (w. George Stolle & His
　　　　　　Orchestra) Also Decca 25230
　　　　　So Do I/One, Two, Button Your Shoe (w. George Stolle & His Orchestra)
　　　　　　Also Decca 25232
　　　1044　Just One World Of Consolation/Dear Old Girl (w. The Three Cheers)

1937

Decca 1175　Sweet Leilani/Blue Hawaii (w. Lani McIntyre & His Hawaiians)
　　　　　Sweet Is The Word For You/I Have So Little To Give You (For Love
　　　　　　Alone) (w. Victor Young's Orchestra)
　　　　　Too Marvelous For Words/What Will I Tell My Heart? (w. Jimmy Dorsey
　　　　　　& His Orchestra) Also Decca 25193 (Too Marvelous For Words)
　　　　　Moonlight And Shadows/I Never Realized (w. Victor Young's Orchestra)
　　　　　The One Rose (That's Left In My Heart)/Sentimental and Melancholy
　　　　　　(w. Victor Young's Orchestra) Also Decca 3541-A (The One Rose)
　　　　　Never In A Million Years/In A Little Hula Heaven (w. Jimmy Dorsey &
　　　　　　His Orchestra)
　　　1234　My Little Buckaroo/What Is Love? (w. Victor Young's Orchestra) Also
　　　　　　Decca 2679-B (My Little Buckaroo)
　　　1301-A Peckin' (w. Jimmy Dorsey & His Orchestra)
　　　　　The Moon Got In My Eyes/(You Know It All) Smarty (w. John Scott
　　　　　　Trotter's Orchestra)
　　　　　It's The Natural Thing To Do/All You Want To Do Is Dance (w. John
　　　　　　Scott Trotter's Orchestra)
　　　　　Remember Me?/I Still Love To Kiss You Goodnight (w. John Scott
　　　　　　Trotter's Orchestra) Also Decca 18866 (Remember Me?)
　　　　　Can I Forget You?/The Folks Who Live On The Hill (w. John Scott
　　　　　　Trotter's Orchestra)
　　　1483-B Bob White (Whatcha Gonna Swing Tonight?)/Basin Street Blues
　　　　　　(w. Connee Boswell and John Scott Trotter's Orchestra)
　　　　　Sail Along, Silvery Moon/When You Dream About Hawaii (w. Lani
　　　　　　McIntyre & His Hawaiians)

1938

Decca 1554   When The Organ Played "Oh Promise Me"/Let's Waltz For Old Time's Sake (w. Eddie Dunstedter)
There's A Gold Mine In The Sky/In The Mission By The Sea (w. Eddie Dunstedter)   Also Decca 2678-B (There's A Gold Mine In The Sky)
1616   Dancing Under The Stars/Palace In Paradise
On The Sentimental Side/My Heart Is Taking Lessons (w. John Scott Trotter's Orchestra)   Also Decca 25233
Moon Of Manakoora/This Is My Night TO Dream (w. John Scott Trotter's Orchestra)
1794   Don't Be That Way/Little Lady Make-Believe   Also Decca 3603-B
Let Me Whisper I Love You (w. John Scott Trotter's Orchestra)/Sing Low, Sweet Chariot (w. Paul Taylor Choristers)   Also Decca 3540-A
1845   Sweet Hawaiian Chimes/Little Angel
When Mother Nature Sings Her Lullaby (w. Eddie Dunstedter)/Darling Nellie Gray (w. Paul Taylor Choristers)   Also Decca 3540-B (Darling Nellie Gray
1887-A   Alexander's Ragtime Band (w. Connee Boswell, Eddie Cantor, and John Scott Trotter's Orchestra)
1887-B   Home On The Range - True Confession (w. Connee Boswell and John Scott Trotter's Orchestra)
Now It Can Be Told/It's The Dreamer In Me (w. John Scott Trotter's Orchestra)
I've Got A Pocketful Of Dreams/A Blues Serenade (w. John Scott Trotter's Orchestra)   Also Decca 3543-A (A Blues Serenade)
Don't Let That Moon Get Away/Laugh And Call It Love (w. John Scott Trotter's Orchestra)
Mr. Crosby And Mr. Mercer/Small Fry (w. Johnny Mercer and Victor Young's Small Fryers)   Also Decca 3600-A (Small Fry)
Mexicali Rose/Silver On The Sage (w. John Scott Trotter's Orchestra)
2023   Without A Song (w. Paul Whiteman)
2123   My Reverie/Old Folks (w. Bob Crosby's Orchestra)
You Must Have Been A Beautiful Baby/Summertime (w. Bob Crosby's Orchestra)

1939

Brunswick 6533   Someone Stole Gabriel's Horn (recorded March 14, 1933; w. Dorsey Brothers Orchestra)
Decca 2200   You're A Sweet Little Headache/Joobalai (w. John Scott Trotter's Orchestra)
I Have Eyes/The Funny Old Hills (w. John Scott Trotter's Orchestra)
It's A Lonely Trail (When You're Travelin' All Alone)/When The Bloom Is On The Sage (w. John Scott Trotter's Orchestra)

2257-A   Just A Kid Named Joe (w. John Scott Trotter's Orchestra) Also Decca 3601-B
2257-B   The Lonesome Road (w. John Scott Trotter's Orchestra) Also Decca 3541-B
    I Cried For You/Let's Tie The Old For-Get-Me-Nots (w. John Scott Trotter's Orchestra) Also Decca 3542-A (I Cried For You)
    My Melancholy Baby/Between A Kiss And A Sigh (w. John Scott Trotter's Orchestra) Also Decca 3542-B
2315   Ah! Sweet Mystery Of Life//Sweethearts (w. Victor Young's Orchestra)
    I'm Falling In Love With Someone/Gypsy Love Song (w. Frances Langford)
    East Side Of Heaven/Sing A Song Of Sunbeams (w. John Scott Trotter's Orchestra)
    That Sly Old Gentleman (From Featherbed Lane)/Hang Your Heart On A Hickory Limb Also Decca 3600-B (That Sly Old Gentleman)
    Deep Purple/Star Dust (w. Matty Malneck & His Orchestra) Also Decca 25285
2385   Poor Old Rover (w. The Foursome)/Little Sir Echo (w. The Music Maids)
    God Bless America/The Star-Spangled Banner (w. Max Terr's Mixed Chorus and John Scott Trotter's Orchestra) Also Decca 23579
    And The Angels Sing/S'posin' (w. The Music Maids and John Scott Trotter's Orchestra) Also Decca 3543-
2447   I'm Building A Sailboat Of Dreams/Down By The Old Mill Stream
    Whistling In The Wildwood (w. John Scott Trotter's Orchestra)
    Alla En El Rancho Grande/Ida, Sweet As Apple Cider (w. The Foursome and John Scott Trotter's Orchestra)
2535   I Surrender, Dear/It Must Be True Also Decca 25229
    (Ho-Die-Ay) Start The Day Right/Neighbors In The Sky (w. Connee Boswell and John Scott Trotter's Orchestra)
2640   An Apple For The Teacher (w. Connee Boswell and John Scott Trotter's Orchestra)/Still The Bluebird Sings Also Decca 3602-A (An Apple For The Teacher)
    Go Fly A Kite/A Man And His Dream (w. John Scott Trotter's Orchestra)
    What's New?/Girl Of My Dreams (w. John Scott Trotter's Orchestra) Also Victor 18866 (Girl Of My Dreams)
    Home On The Range/Missouri Waltz
2680   When You're Away/Thine Alone
    Gus Edwards Medley/In My Merry Oldsmobile (w. The Music Maids) Also Decca 3602 (Gus Edwards Medley)
    My Isle Of Golden Dreams/To You Sweetheart, Aloha (w. Dick McIntyre & His Harmony Hawaiians)
    Ciribiribin (They're So In Love)/Yodelin' Jive (w. Andrews Sisters and Joe Ventuti's Orchestra)

2874 Somebody Loves Me/Maybe

1940

Decca 2948-A Wrap Your Troubles In Dreams (w. Jimmy Dorsey and His Orchestra)
         Also Decca 25193
     2948-B Between 18th & 19th On Chestnut Street (w. Connee Boswell and John
          Scott Trotter's Orchestra)
          I'm Too Romantic/The Moon And The Willow Tree (w. John Scott
            Trotter's Orchestra)
          Sweet Potato Piper (w. The Foursome and John Scott Trotter's
            Orchestra)/Just One More Chance (w. John Scott Trotter's
            Orchestra)
          Tumbling Tumbleweeds/If I Knew Then (What I Know Now) (w. John
            Scott Trotter's Orchestra)   Also Decca 4200-B
          The Singing Hills/Devil May Care (w. John Scott Trotter's Orchestra)
            Also Decca 4200-A
     3098-A I Dream Of Jeanie With The Light Brown Hair   Also Decca 18801
     3098-B The Girl With The Pigtails In Her Hair   Also Decca 3603
     3118-A Yours Is My Heart Alone   Also Decca 23716
     3118-B Beautiful Dreamer   Also Decca 18802
          Sierra Sue/Marcheta (w. John Scott Trotter's Orchestra)
          I Haven't Time To Be A Millionaire/April Played The Fiddle (w. John
            Scott Trotter's Orchestra)
          The Pessimistic Character/Meet The Sun Half-Way (w. John Scott
            Trotter's Orchestra)
          On Behalf Of The Visiting Firemen/Mister Meadowlark (w. Johnny
            Mercer and Victor Young's Orchestra)
     3257 I'm Waiting For Ships That Never Come In/Cynthia
     3297/3298 Ballad For Americans (Four Parts)   Also Decca DA 3554/3555
          A Song Of Old Hawaii/Trade Winds (w. Dick McIntyre's Orchestra)
     3300 Only Forever/When The Moon Comes Over Madison Square
          That's For Me/Rhythm On The River
     3321 Can't Get Indiana Off My Mind/I Found A Million-Dollar Baby
          Where The Blue Of The Night (Meets The Gold Of The Day) (w.
            Paradise Island Trio)/The Waltz You Saved For Me
     3388 Legend Of Old California/Prairieland Lullaby
          Do You Ever Think Of Me?/You Made Me Love You (w. Merry Macs and
            Victor Young's Orchestra)

1941

Decca 3450 Please/You Are The One (w. John Scott Trotter's Orchestra)

3477   When I Lost You/When You're A Long Long Way From Home
       Along The Santa Fe Trail/I'd Know You Anywhere (w. John Scott Trotter's Orchestra) Also Decca 4201 (Along The Santa Fe Trail)
       A Nightingale Sang In Berkeley Square/Lone Star Trail (w. John Scott Trotter's Orchestra)   Also Decca 4201-B
      New San Antonio Rose/It Makes No Difference Now (w. Bob Crosby's Orchestra) Also Decca 18766
      Did Your Mother Come From Ireland?/Where The River Shannon Flows (w. The King's Men & Victor Young's Orchestra)

3614   Chapel In The Valley/When Day Is Done
3636   It's Always You/You Lucky People You
3637   You're Dangerous/Birds Of A Feather
      Dolores (w. Merry Macs and Bob Crosby's Bob Cats)/De Camptown Races (w. The King's Men)

3689-B   Yes Indeed/Tea For Two (w. Connee Boswell)
3731   With Every Breath I Take (w. The Rhythmettes and Three Shades Of Blue)
      My Buddy/I Only Want A Buddy - Not A Sweetheart
      Paradise Isle/Aloha Kuu Ipo Aloha (w. Paradise Island Trio)
      You And I/Brahms' Lullaby (Cradle Song) (w. John Scott Trotter's Orchestra)
      Be Honest With Me/Goodbye, Little Darlin', Goodbye (w. John Scott Trotter's Orchestra)   Also Decca 18767 and 25231
      'Til Reveille/My Old Kentucky Home (w. John Scott Trotter's Orchestra) Also Decca 18803

3887   Pale Moon (w. Merry Macs)/Who Calls?
      You Are My Sunshine/Ridin' Down The Canyon (w. Victor Young's Orchestra)   Also Decca 18768
      You're The Moment Of A Lifetime (w. Floras Negras)/No Te Importe Saber (Let Me Love You Tonight)
      The Waiter And The Porter And The Upstairs Maid/Birth Of The Blues (w. Mary Martin and Jack Teagarden's Orchestra)
      The Whistler's Mother-In-Law/I Ain't Got Nobody (w. Muriel Lane and Woody Herman's Woodchoppers)

4000   Sweetheart Of Sigma Chi/Dream Girl of Pi Kappa Alpha   Also Decca 25228
      Day Dreaming/Clementine (w. The Music Maids and Hal Hopper)

4064   Do You Care?/Humpty Dumpty Heart
      Shepherd Serenade (w. W. Harry Sosnik's Orchestra)/The Anniversary Waltz (w. Victor Young's Orchestra)   Also Decca 23716 (Anniversary Waltz)

1942

Decca 4152 Oh! How I Miss You Tonight/Dear Little Boy Of Mine
Deep In The Heart Of Texas (w. Woody Herman's Woodchoppers)/Let's All Meet At My House (w. Muriel Lane and Woody Herman's Woodchopper's
4163-B Blue Shadows And White Gardenias
Sing Me A Song Of The Islands/Remember Hawaii (w. Dick McIntyre & His Harmony Hawaiians)
4183 Blues In The Night/Miss You (w. John Scott Trotter's Orchestra)
I Don't Want To Walk Without You/Moonlight Cocktail (w. John Scott Trotter's Orchestra)
4193-A Skylark (w. John Scott Trotter's Orchestra)
The Lamplighter's Serenade/Mandy Is Two (w. Victor Young's Orchestra)
4339 The Singing Sands Of Alamosa/I'm Drifting Back To Dreamland
Conchita, Marquita, Lolita, Pepita, Rosita, Juanita Lopez/The Old Oaken Bucket
4367 Hello, Mom/A Boy In Khaki - A Girl In Love
18278 Lily Of Laguna (w. Mary Martin)/Wait Till The Sun Shines, Nellie (w. Mary Martin, Jack Teagarden, and Bob Crosby's Bob Cats)
18316 I'm Thinking Tonight Of My Blue Eyes/I Want My Mama   Also Decca 18769 (I'm Thnking Tonight Of My Blue Eyes)
18354 Just Plain Lonesome/Got The Moon In My Pocket
18360 Mary's A Grand Old Name/The Waltz Of Memory (w. John Scott Trotter's Orchestra)
18371 When My Dreamboat Comes Home (w. John Scott Trotter's Orchestra)
18391 When The White Azaleas Start Blooming/Nobody's Darlin' But Mine (w. Victor Young's Orchestra)   Also Decca 18770
18424 Happy Holiday (w. The Music Maids)/Be Careful, It's My Heart (w. John Scott Trotter's Orchestra)
18425 Abraham/Easter Parade (w. Ken Darby Singers)
18426 I've Got Plenty To Be Thankful For/Song Of Freedom (w. Ken Darby Singers
18427 I'll Capture Your Heart (w. Fred Astaire and Margaret Lenhart)/Lazy
18429 White Christmas (w. The Ken Darby Singers and John Scott Trotter's Orchestra)/Let's Start The New Year Right (w. Bob Crosby's Orchestra)
18432-A My Great, Great Grandfather
18510-A Silent Night, Holy Night (w. Max Terr's Mixed Chorus)
18513-A Moonlight Becomes You
18531-B Darling, Je Vous Aime Beaucoup
18432-B The Bombadier Song (w. The Music Maids and Hal Hopper)

18510 Silent Night (w. Max Terr's Chorus and John Scott Trotter's Orchestra) reissued as #23777 in 1946)
18511 Faith Of Our Fathers/God Rest Ye Merry Gentlemen (w. Max Terr's Mixed Chorus)
18513 Moonlight Becomes You/Constantly (w. John Scott Trotter's Orchestra)
18514 The Road To Morocco/Ain't Got A Dime To My Name
18531-A I Wonder What's Become Of Sally

1943

Decca 18561 Sunday, Monday, Or Always/If You Please (w. Ken Darby Singers)
18564 People Will Say We're In Love/Oh, What A Beautiful Mornin' (w. Trudy Erwin and The Sportsmen Glee Club)
18570 I'll Be Home For Christmas/Danny Boy (w. John Scott Trotter's Orchestra)
18580-A The Day After Forever   Also Decca 18704-B
18580-B It Could Happen To You   Also Decca 23686
23277 Pistol Packin' Mama/Victory Polka (w. Andrews Sisters and Vic Schoen & His Orchestra)
23281 Jingle Bells/Santa Claus Is Comin' To Town (w. Andrews Sisters and Vic Schoen's Orchestra)

1944

Decca 18586 Poinciana (Song Of The Tree)/San Fernando Valley (w. John Scott Trotter's Orchestra)
18595 I Love You/I'll Be Seeing You (w. John Scott Trotter's Orchestra)
18597 Swinging On A Star/Going My Way (w. Williams Brothers Quartet and John Scott Trotter's Orchestra)
18608 Amor/Long Ago (And Far Away) (w. John Scott Trotter's Orchestra)   Also Decca 23680
18621 Too-Ra-Loo-Ra-Loo-Ra/I'll Remember April (w. John Scott Trotter's Orchestra)   Also Decca 18704 (Too-Ra-Loo-Ra-Loo-Ra)
23350 Is You Is Or Is You Ain't (Ma' Baby)/A Hot Time In The Town Of Berlin (w. Andrews Sisters and Vic Schoen & His Orchestra)
23364 Don't Fence Me In/The Three Caballeros (w. Andrews Sisters and Vic Schoen & His Orchestra)   Also Decca 23484 (Don't Fence Me In)
Victor 27685 Lovable (featuring Paul Whiteman and His Orchestra)
27688 That's Grandma (w. The Rhythm Boys)

1945

Decca 18635 Evelina/The Eagle And Me (w. Camerata's Orchestra)

18640 Sleigh Ride In July/Like Someone In Love (w. John Scott Trotter's Orchestra)
18644 Let's Take The Long Way Home/I Promise You
18649 More And More/Strange Music
18658 All Of My Life/A Friend Of Yours (w. John Scott Trotter's Orchestra)
18675 June Comes Around Every Year/Out Of This World
18686 If I Loved You/Close As Pages In A Book (w. John Scott Trotter's Orchestra)
18690 On The Atchison, Topeka, And The Santa Fe/I'd Rather Be Me (w. Six Hits & A Miss and John Scott Trotter's Orchestra)
18705 Ave Maria/Home Sweet Home (w. Victor Young Choir)
18708 It's Been A Long, Long Time (w. The Les Paul Trio)/Whose Dream Are You?
18720 Aren't You Glad You're You?/In The Land Of Beginning Again (w. John Scott Trotter's Orchestra)
18721 The Bells Of St. Mary's/I'll Take You Home Again, Kathleen
18731-A Walking The Floor Over You   Also Decca 18770
18735 Symphony
18743 It's Anybody's Spring/Welcome To My Dream
18746 Day By Day/Prove It By The Things You Do (w. Mel Torme and His Mel-Tones)
18790 Personality/Would You?
18801 Nell And I
18802 Sweetly She Sleeps, My Alice Fair
18804 Old Black Joe
18829 These Foolish Things/They Say It's Wonderful
18860 You May Not Love Me
18887 Just One Of Those Things
18898 Begin The Beguine/September Song   Also Decca 23754 (September Song)
23379 Ac-Cent-Tchu-Ate- The Positive/There's A Fellow Waiting In Poughkeepsie (w. Andrews Sisters and Vic Schoen & His Orchestra)
23392 Just A Prayer Away/My Mother's Waltz (w. Ken Darby Singers and Victor Young's Orchestra)
23410 Yah-Ta-Ta, Yah-Ta-Ta (Talk, Talk, Talk)/You've Got Me Where You Want Me (w. Judy Garland and Joseph Lilley's Orchestra)
23413 You Belong To My Heart/Baia (w. Xavier Cugat's Orchestra)
23417 My Baby Said Yes/Your Socks Don't Match (w. Louis Jordan & His Tympany Five)
23437 Good, Good, Good/Along The Navajo Trail (w. Andrews Sisters and Vic Schoen & His Orchestra)
23457 I Can't Begin To Tell You/I Can't Believe That You're In Love With Me (w. Carmen Cavallaro's Orchestra)

      40000   Put It There, Pal/The Road To Morocco (w. Bob Hope)

1946

Decca 18735   Symphony/Beautiful Love (w. Victor Young's Orchestra)
- 18746 Day By Day (w. Mel Torme & His Mel-Tones and instrumental trio; recorded 1945)
- 18790 Personality (w. Eddie Condon's Orchestra)
- 18860 Just My Luck
- 18829 They Say It's Wonderful (w. Jay Blackton's Orchestra)
- 18887 Night And Day
- 18912 Early American/Iowa
- 23469 Give Me The Simple Life/It's The Talk Of The Town (w. Jimmy Dorsey's Orchestra)
- 23482 Mighty Lak' A Rose/The Sweetest Story Ever Told (w. The Song Spinners)
- 23495 McNamara's Band/Daer Ol Donegal (w. The Jesters and Bob Haggart & His Orchestra)
- 23508 Sioux City Sue/You Sang My Love Song To Somebody Else (w. The Jesters and Bob Haggart & His Orchestra)
- 23510 I'll Be Yours (J'Attendrai)/We'll Gather Lilacs
- 23530 I've Found A New Baby/Who's Sorry Now
- 23547 Haste Manana/Siboney
- 23569 South America, Take It Away/Get Your Kicks On Route 66 (w. Andrews Sisters and Vic Schoen & His Orchestra)
- 23636 Baby, Won't You Please Come Home/That Little Dream Got Nowhere
- 23646 Cuba (w. Trudy Erwin)
- 23647 You Keep Coming Back Like A Song/Getting Nowhere (w. John Scott Trotter's Orchestra)
- 23648 Everybody Step/Serenade To An Old-Fashioned Girl
- 23649 All By Myself/I've Got My Captain Working For Me Now
- 23650 A Couple Of Song And Dance Men (w. Fred Astaire)
- 23655 Sweet Lorraine/The Things We Did Last Summer
- 23661 Gotta Get Me Somebody To Love/Pretending
- 23678 Till The Clouds Roll By
- 23679 Dearly Beloved/I've Told Every Little Star
- 23680 All Through The Day
- 23686 When You Make Love To Me

1947

Decca 23739   A Gal In Calico/Oh But I Do (w. The Calico Kids)
- 23745 Among My Souvenirs/Does Your Heart Beat For Me?

23754 Temptation
23784 So Would I
23804 Connecticut/Mine (w. Judy Garland)
23819 Easter Parade (w. Victor Young's Orchestra)
23840 That's How Much I Love You/Rose Of Santa Rosa (w. Bob Crosby's Orchestra)
23843 On The Sunny Side Of The Street (w. LionelHampton)
23848 As Long As I'm Dreaming/Smile Right Back At The Sun
23849 Country Style/My Heart Is A Hobo
23850 Gotta Get Me Somebody To Love/What Am I Gonna Do About You? (w. Les Paul Trio)
23885 Tallahassee/Go West Young Man (w. Andrews Sisters and Vic Schoen & His Orchestra)
23954 I Do, Do, Do Like You/The Old Chaperone (w. The Skylarks)
23975 Feudin' and Fightin' (w. Bob Haggart & His Orchestra)
23990 Wiffenpoof Song/Kentucky Babe (w. Fred Waring's Glee Club)
23999 The Freedom Train (w. Andrews Sisters and Vic Schoen & His Orchestra)/The Star Spangled Banner (recitation)
24100 I Still Suits Me (w. Lee Wiley)/Kokomo, Indiana (w. The Skylarks)
24101 You Do/How Soon (Will I Be Seeing You) (w. Carmen Cavallaro's Orchestra)
24114 After You've Gone/Blue (w. Eddie Condon)
24170 I Kiss Your Hand, Madame
40012 Lullaby (From "Jocelyn")/Where My Caravan Has Rested (w. Jascha Heifetz)
40038 Alexander's Ragtime Band (EP; w. Al Jolson and Morris Stoloff's Orchestra)
40039 There's No Business Like Show Business (EP; w. Andrews Sisters, Dick Haymes, and Vic Schoen & His Orchestra) Includes Anything You Can Do

1948

Decca 24269 Pass The Peace Pipe/Suspense
24273 Happy Birthday - Auld Lang Syne (w. Ken Darby Singers)
24278 Ballerina/Golden Earrings (w. John Scott Trotter's Orchestra)
24279 Now Is The Hour/Silver Threads Among The Gold (w. Ken Darby Choir)
24282 You Don't Have To Know The Language/Apalachicola, Fla (w. Andrews Sisters and Vic Schoen & His Orchestra)
24283 But Beautiful/The One I Love
24295 Galway Bay/My Girl's And Irish GIrl (w. Victor Young's Orchestra)
24433 Blue Shadows On The Trail (w. Ken Darby Choir and Victor Young's Orchestra)/A Fella With An Umbrella

24481   160 Acres (w. Andrews Sisters and Vic Schoen & His Orchestra)

1949

Decca 24524   If You Stub Your Toe On The Moon (w. The Rhythmaires)
24532   Far Away Places (w. Ken Darby Choir)
24609   Some Enchanted Evening/Bali Ha'i
24616   Careless Hands (w. Ken Darby Singers and Perry Botkin's Orchestra)
24618   Riders In The Sky (w. Ken Darby Singers and Perry Botkin's Orchestra)
24798   Dear Hearts And Gentle People (w. Jud Conlon's Rhythmaires and Perry Botkin's Orchestra)/ Mule Train (w. Perry Botkin's Orchestra)
24800   Way Back Home (w. Fred Waring's Pennsylvanians)

1950

Decca 24820   Have I Told Ou Lately That I Love You? (w. Andrews Sisters and Vic Schoen & His Orchestra)
24827   Quicksilver (w. Andrews Sisters and Vic Schoen & His Orchestra)
24863   Chattanoogie Shoe Shine Boy (w. Vic Shoen's Orchestra
27018   I Didn't Slip - I Wasn't Pushed - I Fell (w. Sy Oliver's Orchestra & Aristokats)
27111   La Vie En Rose/I Cross My Fingers (w. Axel Stordahl's Orchestra)
27112   Play A Simply Melody/Sam's Song (credited to "Gary Crosby & Friend"; w. Matty Matlock's Orchestra)
27117   All My Love (w. Victor Young & His Orchestra)
27159   Rudolph, The Red-Nosed Reindeer (w. John Scott Trotter's Orchestra)
27219   Beyond The Reef/Harbor Lights (w. Lynn Murray's Orchestra)
27229   Silver Bells (w. Carol Richards)
40181   A Crosby Christmas (EP; w. Gary, Phillip, Dennis, and Lindsay Crosby)

1951

Decca 27239   A Marshmellow World (w. Sonny Burke's Orchestra)
27477   Sparrow In The Tree Top (w. Andrews Sisters and Vic Schoen & His Orchestra)
27577   When You And I Were Young, Maggie, Blues/Moonlight Bay (w. Gary Crosby)
27623   Gone Fishin' (w. Louis Armstrong)
27653   Shanghai
27830   Domino (w. John Scott Trotter's Orchestra)
40839   There's No Business Like Show Business (w. Dick Haymes and Andrews Sisters)

1952

Decca 28255 Zing A Little Zong (w. Jane Wyman)
      28265 Till The End Of The World (w. Grady Martin & His Slew Foot Five)
      28419 Cool Water/South Rampart St. Parade
      28470 You Don't Know What Lonesome Is/Open Up Your Heart
      28511 Keep It A Secret/Sleighbell Serenade (w. Jud Conlon's Rhyhmaires)

1953

Decca 28581 Hush-A-Bye/Mother Darlin'
      28733 Tenderfoot/Walk Me By The River
      28743 Granada/It Had To Be You
      28814 Madenoiselle De Paree/Embrasse Moi Ben-De

1954

Decca 28955 Down By The Riverside (w. Gary Crosby)/What A Little Moonlight Can Do
      28969 Changing Partners (w. Jud Conlon's Rhythmaires)/Y'all Come
      29024 Secret Love/My Love, My Love
      29054 Young At Heart/I Get So Lonely (w. Guy Lombardo & His Royal Canadians)
      29147 Call Of The South/Cornbelt Symphony (w. Gary Crosby)
      29251 Count Your Blessings (Instead Of Sheep)/What Can You Do With A General (w. Joseph Lilley's Orchestra)
      29357 Song From Desire/Who Gave You The Rose (w. Alfred Newman & His Orchestra)

1955

Decca 29410 The Search Is Through/The Land Around Us
      29483 Farewell/Jim, Johnny & Jonas
      29568 All She Said Was "Unh Huh"/She's The Sunshine Of Virginia
      29636 Angel Bells/Let's Harmonize

1956

Capitol 3506 Now You Has Jazz (w. Louis Armstrong)
      3507 True Love (w. Grace Kelly)/Well Dad You Evah? (w. Frank Sinatra)
Decca 29817 When You're In Love/John Barleycorn
      29850 In A Little Spanish Town (w. The Buddy Cole Trio)
      29981 Swanee/Honeysuckle Rose (w. The Buddy Cole Trio)

1957

Decca 30262   Around The World (In Eighty Days)
Kapp 196   How Lovely Is Christmas

1969

Amos 111   Hey Jude/Lonely Street
          It's All In The Game/More & More

1970

Daybreak 1001   And The Bells Rang/Time To Be Jolly

--78 R.P.M. Album Sets

Brunswick B-1012   Bing Crosby, Volume 1
        B-1015   Bing Crosby, Volume 2
Columbia M-555   Crosby Classics
Decca A-10   Music Of Hawaii   Crosby heard on two sides: "Song Of The Islands" and
        "Aloha Oe"
   A-50   Patroitic Songs For Children   Crosby heard on two sides: "God Bless
        America" and "The Star-Spangle Banner"
   A-69   Cowboy Songs
   A-96   George Gershwin Popular Songs   Crosby heard on two sides: "Maybe"
        And "Somebody Loves Me"
   A-134   Ballad For Americans: In Four Parts
   A-140   Favorite Hawaiian Songs
   A-159   Christmas Music   Crosby heard on two sides: "Silent Night, Holy Night"
        And "Adeste Fideles"
   A-181   Star Dust
   A-193   Hawaii Calls   Crosby heard on two sides: "A Song Of Old Hawaii" and
        "Trade Winds"
   A-202   Small Fry
   A-221   Crosbyana
   A-250   Under Western Skies
   A-396   Holiday Inn
   A-403   Merry Christmas
   A-405   Going My Way   Includes a song not in picture, "Home Sweet Home"
   A-410   Bells Of St. Mary's   Includes a song not in picture, "I'll Take You
        Home Again, Kathleen"
   A-417   Don't Fence Me In   Also Decca A-559
   A-420   The Happy Prince (Plays the Prince in Oscar Wilde's fairy tale)

A-423 Road To Utopia
A-440 Stephen Foster Songs   Also Decca A-482
A-453 What So Proudly We Hail (4 sides)
A-460 Favorite Hawaiian Songs, Volume 1
A-461 Favorite Hawaiian Songs, Volume 2
A-481 Blue Skies
A-485 Bing Crosby - Jerome Kern
A-505 Victor Herbert Melodies
A-547 El Bingo
A-553 The Small One (Narrates Charles Tazewell's Christmas story)
A-578 Bing Crosby - Drifting And Dreaming
A-621 St. Valentine's Day - Bing Crosby
U3 The Man Without A Country (Narrates the Edward Everett Hale story)
Victor P-4 Bix Beiderbecke Memorial Album (w. Paul Whiteman & His
        Orchestra; Crosby heard on ten of twelve sides)
    P-100 A Souvenir Program (w. Paul Whiteman & His Orchestra; Crosby heard
        on nine of ten sides)

--Long-Playing Albums

Amos 7001 Hey Jude/Hey Bing! (1969)
Brunswick BL-54005 Bing In The 1930's
    BL-58000-1 Bing Crosby
Columbia CL-2502 Der Bongle
    CL-6027 Crosby Classics Vol. 1
    CL-6105 Crosby Classics Vol. 2
Decca DL-4086 My Golden Favorites
  DL-4250 Easy To Remember
  DL-4251 Pennies From Heaven
  DL-4252 Pocket Full Of Dreams
  DL-4253 East Side Of Heaven
  DL-4254 The Road Begins
  DL-4255 Only Forever
  DL-4256 Holiday Inn
  DL-4257 Swinging On A Star
  DL-4258 Accentuate The Positive
  DL-4259 Blue Skies
  DL-4260 But Beautiful
  DL-4261 Sunshine Cake
  DL-4262 Cool Of The Evening
  DL-4263 Zing A Little Zong
  DL-4264 Anything Goes
  DL-5010 Foster

DL-5011	El Bingo
DL-5020	Christmas Greetings (w. Andrews Sisters)
DL-5037	St. Patrick's Day
DL-5039	St. Valentine's Day
DL-5052	Bells Of St. Mary's
DL-5063	Don't Fence Me In
DL-5064	Porter
DL-5081	Gershwin
DL-5092	Holiday Inn Selections
DL-5105	Blue Of The Night
DL-5107	Cowboy Songs Vol. 1
DL-5119	Drifting & Dreaming
DL-5122	Hawaiian Favorites Vol. 1
DL-5126	Stardust
DL-5129	Cowboy Songs Vol. 2
DL-5272	Emperor Waltz
DL-5284	Mr. Music
DL-5298	Hits From Broadway Songs
DL-5299	Favorite Hawaiian Songs
DL-5302	Go West Young Man
DL-5310	Way Back Home
DL-5323	Bing With Dixieland Bands
DL-5326	Yours Is My Heart Alone
DL-5331	Country Style
DL-5340	Down Memory Lane
DL-5343	Down Memory Lane Vol. 2
DL-5403	When Irish Eyes Are Smiling
DL-5499	Song Hits Of Paris
DL-5508	Some Fine Old Chestnuts
DL-5520	Bing Sings Hits
DL-5556	Country Girl (w. Andrews Sisters)
DL-6000	Small One
DL-8083	White Christmas
DL-8110	Lullaby Time
DL-8128	Merry Christmas (1955)
DL-8207	Shillelaghs And Shamrocks (1958)
DL-8210	Home On The Range
DL-8365	Twilight On The Trail
DL-8419	A Christmas Sing With Bing Around The World (1956)
DL-8687	Around The World With Bing Crosby
DL-8780	Bing In Paris
DL-8781	That Christmas Feeling
DL-9054	Bing - Musical Autobiography, 1927-1934

    DLP-5001 Jerry Kern Songs
    DLP-6001 Ichabod Crane
Golden Age 5023 Crosby's Radio Shows (1978) (w. original radio cast)
MCA 3031 Bing Crosby's Greatest Hits (1977; 1939-1947 recordings)
Reprise 2020 America, I HearYou Singing (1964) (w. Frank Sinatra and Fred Waring)
United Artists/K-Tel NE-951 Bing Crosby On Broadway (Bing Crosby At The London Palladium) (1976) (w. Rosemary Clooney and the Crosby Family)

--Compact Discs

Affinity CD AFS 1021-2 The Jazzin' Bing Crosby, 1927-1940 2-CD set with 24-page Booklet; 48 cuts. (EEC release)
Ariola Express 295040 Bing Crosby—Dream a Little Dream of Me Includes material originally cut by Brunswick and Okeh (U.K. release)
Ariola Express 295040-201 Bing Crosby 16 tracks; 14 with Gus Arnheim's Orchestra, 1 with Paul Whiteman, 1 with Duke Ellington (German release; also released as BPCD-5092 in Australia)
ASV AJA-5043 Here Lies Love 18 songs. (U.K. release)
AJA-5072 On The Sentimental Side 20 tracks. (U.K. release)
Axis CDAX-701592 The Stars In Song Crosby duets with several other stars. (Australian release)
BBC CD-648 Bing Crosby: 1927-1934 Culled from the LP, *The Golden Years in Digital Stereo* (U.K. release); also issued as ABC 836172-2 in Australia
BBC CD-766 Classic Crosby 1931-1938 18 tracks. (U.K. release; also issued in Australia as ABC-838985)
Bar One BC-012 Bing's Hollywood - Alternate Takes
    BC-013 Bing - Beyond Compare
    BCT-001 Bing Crosby's Treasury
Bella Musica BMCD-89921 Bing Crosby 18 tracks; monaural mix
Bluebird CD-6845-2 Bix Beiderbecke – Bix Lives Includes eight Crosby songs.
BNR CD 211 The Quintessential Bing Crosby 2-CD set; 50 tracks culled from *The Complete Bing Crosby*.
Castle Communications CCSCD-275 The Collection 24 songs accompanied by Buddy Cole; augmented by Pete Moore's Orchestra. (U.K. release)
CBS Special Products A2-201 The Bing Crosby Story 2-CD set; 16 songs per disc. Collection OR-0084 Bing Crosby [Classics] 18 tracks (U.K. release)
Columbia C3K-44229 Bing Crosby The Crooner: The Columbia Years 1928-1934 3-CD set; released in the U.K. as CBS 465596.
Columbia CK 48974 16 Most Requested Songs
Companion 6187152 Twenty Golden Memories (Danish release)

Conifer CDHD-123   Remembering 1927-1934 (U.K. release)
Conquistador CONQ-004)   Bing Crosby—Eleven Historic Recordings   11 tracks
Curb D2-77340   All-Time Best Of Bing Crosby
  D2-77617   Best Of Bing Crosby And Fred Astaire
Daybreak 824705-2   Bing And Basie
Decca Jazz GRD 603   Bing Crosby And Some Jazz Friends   Early recordings; many are duets; also released as MCA GRP-16032
Dejavu DVCD-2078   Bing Crosby Christmas Collection   12 tracks
  DVLP-2124   The Bob Hope Collection   Includes 9 Crosby songs. (U.K. release)
  DVRECD-16)   The Bing Crosby Story (U.K. release)
Double Play GRF-016   Everything I Have Is Yours   29 tracks.
Echo Jazz EJCD-12   Bing Crosby   16 tracks (U.K. release); alternate title: *Big Band Days*
EMI 72438575472   50th Anniversary Concert – Palladium
Entertainers CD-0248   The Best of Bing Crosby. 23 tracks; Volume 2 of 3-part set entitled *The Crooners* (with Frank Sinatra and Dean Martin)
Evasound EMD-002   Bing Crosby—Please   (Australian release)
Flapper Past CD-9739   Bing Crosby – That's Jazz (U.K. release)
  CD-9784   The Movie Hits   22 songs culled from Crosby's early films.
GNP Crescendo GNPD-9044   The Radio Years, Vol. 1   12 tracks; includes solos and duets with Judy Garland, Connee Boswell and George Burns.
  GNPD-9046   The Radio Years, Vol. 2   12 solos and duets.
  GNPD-9051   The Radio Years – 1931-1943
  GNPD-9052   The Radio Years – 1944-1953
Golden Olden GOR CD101   A Little Bit Of Irish: Bing Crosby
Hallmark 306722   Bing Sings Country
Harmony HARCD-120   Portrait Of A Song Stylist   14 tracks accompanied by Buddy Cole; augmented by Pete Moore's Orchestra. (U.K. release)
Intertape 500-027   Bing Crosby   (U.K. release)
JSD JSPCE-701   Bing Crosby And Jimmy Durante—Start Off Each Day With a Song (U.K. release)
  JSPCE-702   Bing Crosby And Judy Garland (U.K. release)
Laserlight 5411   A Visit To The Movies
  12732   American Legends
  15-411   A Visit To The Movies   A reissue of the February 1968 LP, *Thoroughly Modern Bing*, minus 1 track.
  15-444   White Christmas   17 tracks; source appears to have been the Kraft Music Hall radio programs. (U.K. release)
Lasertech 944D   The Bing Crosby Collection
Living Era AJA 5005-R   Bix 'n' Bing (U.K. release)
  AJA 5147   Bing Crosby And Friends

London 820-552-2   Where The Blue Of The Night (U.K. release)
       820-553-2   Out Of Nowhere (U.K. release)
       820 586-2   Bing: Feels Good, Feels Right (U.K. release)
MCA 33XD-511   Merry Christmas   14 tracks. (Japanese release)
     255-199-2   White Christmas   4-track EP.
     256 137-2   Sixteen Original World Hits – Golden Gate Collection (Australian release)
     D2-11503   B.C. And The Andrews Sisters
     DMCAT-111   Bing Crosby – White Christmas   3 songs. (U.K. release)
     DMCL-1607   The Best of Bing Crosby (U.K. release)
     DMCL-1777   White Christmas   Film soundtrack; 10 songs, 9 with Crosby. (U.K. release)
     DMCTV 3   Twenty Golden Greats (U.K. release)
     JVC-499   Bing Crosby Sings Again
     JVC-500   Bing Crosby Sings Christmas Songs
     MCAD-1620   Bing Crosby's Greatest Hits
     MCAD-5764   Bing Crosby Sings Again   Also released as JVC-499
     MCAD-5765   Bing Crosby Sings Christmas Songs   Also released as JVC-500
     MCAD-11719   Bing's Gold Records
     MCAD-25205   Bing Crosby - Holiday Inn
     MCAD-25989   Bing Crosby - Blue Skies
     MCAD-31367   Swinging On A Star   12 tracks.
     MCD 18348   My Greatest Songs – Bing Crosby   14 tracks. (Australian release)
     MSD-35082   Bing Crosby's Hawaii
     MSD3-37079   36 All-Time Greatest Hits
Magic Dawe 3   Bing Crosby And Friends   15 radio duets with Ethel Merman, Judy Garland, the Andrews Sisters, Bob Crosby, Patti Page, Al Jolson, etc. (U.K. release)
Magic Dawe 48   Bing Swings   19 songs featuring many accompanists and duets from The Philco and Chesterfield radio shows. (U.K. release)
Parade PAR 2021   Bing Crosby – The Most Welcome Groaner (U.K. release; also issued as part of a 3-CD set entitled *We Must Never Say Goodbye*. Parade PAK-904)
Parrot PARCD-001   Peggy Lee With Bing Crosby   Features duets with Peggy Lee and Fred Astaire. (U.K. release)
Pickwick PWK-065   Bing Crosby Sings The Great Songs (U.K. release)
     PWK-088   Bing Crosby Sings More Great Songs (U.K. release)
     PWKS-561   Christmas With Bing (U.K. release)
Pilz CD 44-5445-2   Crosby Family Christmas   10 cuts with 5 including his sons; appear to be taken from radio programs.
Pilz CD 44-5446-2   Christmas With Bing And Frank   Culled from a 1957 Sinatra TV program.
Pro-Arte CDD-432   Pennies From Heaven

CDD-437   Paper Moon – Paul Whiteman   Includes 9 tracks with Crosby as a vocalist.
CDD-457   Pocketful Of Dreams   18 tracks.
RCA 9678-2-R   Paul Whiteman And His Orchestra: The Victor Masters   Includes 8 Cuts with Crosby as a vocalist.
BVCJ-2029   Bing With A Beat   (Japanese release)
R25J-1003   Fancy Meeting You Here   13 duets with Rosemary Clooney. (Japanese release)
Readers Digest RDCD-121-6   The Bing Crosby Years   6-CD set; 112 tracks, 45 featuring Crosby. (U.K. release)
Regal 1572742   Classic Performances   Includes 16 standards. (Australian release)
Sandy Hook SH-2095   Blues Skies Soundtrack
Saville CDSVL 219   Sing A Song Of Sunbeams   18 cuts. (U.K. release)
Silver Eagle SED-10633, Disc 1   Bing Sings: All About Love   (part of 3-CD set entitled *The Complete Bing Crosby*)
Silver Eagle SED-10633, Disc 2   Bing Swings: Straight Down The Middle   (part of 3-CD set entitled *The Complete Bing Crosby*)
Silver Eagle SED-10633. Disc 3   From Broadway To Hollywood   (part of 3-CD set entitled *The Complete Bing Crosby*)
Sony/Collectors Series   The Bing Crosby Story
Spectrum U-4016)   Bing and Louis Live   (U.K. release)
Stagedoor SDC-8087   Bing Crosby   (U.K. release)
Starlite CDS-51058   Bing Crosby With Gary Crosby And The Andrews Sisters
Telstar TCD-2469   Christmas With Bing Crosby   20 songs; 2 are duets with David Bowie. (U.K. release)
Timeless Jazz Nostalgia CBC 1-004   Bing Crosby: 1926-1932   24 tracks (U.K. release)
Verve UDCD 670   Bing Sings Whilst Bregman Swings
Warwick 1005   10th Anniversary Collection   U.K. release of the 3-CD set *The Complete Bing Crosby*.
World Star WSC-99055   White Christmas (Australian release; also issued in Italy by Lotus with number CD-5001)
WSC-99056   High Society (Australian release; also issued in Japan as CAP TOCP-6587)

Filmography

King Of Jazz (Universal, 1930)
Two Plus Fours (1930) (short)
Ripstitch The Tailor (1930) (short)
Confessions Of A Co-Ed (1931)
Reaching For The Moon (1931)

Billboard Girl (1931) (short)
Dreamhouse (1931) (short)
Sing, Bing, Sing (1931) (short)
Bring On Bing (1931) (short)
The Big Broadcast Of 1932 (Paramount Publix, 1932)
Hollywood On Parade (1932) (short)
Just One More Chance (1932) (short)
College Humor (Paramount, 1933)
Going Hollywood (Cosmopolitan Pictures Production, 1933)
Too Much Harmony (Paramount, 1933)
Please (1933) (short)
Blue Of The Night (1933) (short)
We're Not Dressing (Paramount, 1934)
She Loves Me Not (Paramount, 1934)
Just An Echo (1934) (short)
I Surrender Dear (1934) (short)
Here Is My Heart (Paramount, 1934)
Mississippi (Paramount, 1935)
Two For Tonight (Paramount, 1935)
The Big Broadcast Of 1936 (Paramount, 1935) (guest appearance)
Star Night At The Coconut Grove (1935) (short)
Rhythm On The Range (Paramount, 1936)
Pennies From Heaven (Paramount, 1936)
Waikiki Wedding (Paramount, 1937)
Double Or Nothing (Paramount, 1937)
Swing With Bing (1937) (short)
Doctor Rhythm (Paramount,1938)
Sing You Sinners (Paramount, 1938)
Don't Hook Now (1938) (short)
East Side Of Heaven (Universal, 1939)
Paris Honeymoon (Paramount, 1939)
The Star Maker (Paramount, 1939)
If I Had My Way (Universal, 1940)
Rhythm On The River (Paramount, 1940)
Road To Singapore (Paramount, 1940)
Road To Zanzibar (Paramount, 1941)
Birth Of The Blues (Paramount, 1941)
Angels Of Mercy (1941) (short)
The Road To Victory (1941) (short)
Road To Morocco (Paramount, 1942)
Holiday Inn (Paramount, 1942)
My Favorite Blonde (1942) (Crosby unbilled)
Star Spangled Rhythm (Paramount, 1942)

Dixie (Paramount, 1943)
Going My Way (Paramount, 1944)
Princess And The Pirate (1944) (Crosby unbilled)
Here Comes The Waves (Paramount, 1944)
Out Of This World (1945) (voice only)
The Bells Of St. Mary's (RKO, 1945)
Duffy's Tavern (Paramount, 1945)
Road To Utopia (Paramount, 1945)
All-Star Bond Rally (1945) (short)
Hollywood Victory Caravan (1945) (short)
Blue Skies (Paramount, 1946)
Welcome Stranger (Paramount, 1947)
Road To Rio (Paramount, 1947)
Variety Girl (Paramount, 1947)
My Favorite Brunette (1947) (Crosby unbilled)
The Emperor Waltz (Paramount, 1948)
A Connecticut Yankee In King Arthur's Court (Paramount, 1948)
Top O' The Morning (Paramount, 1948)
The Adventures Of Ichabod And Mr. Toad (Paramount, 1948) (voice only)
Mr. Music (Paramount, 1950)
Riding High (Paramount, 1950)
Here Comes The Groom (Paramount, 1951)
Just For You (Paramount, 1952)
Road To Bali (Paramount, 1952)
The Greatest Show On Earth (1952) (Crosby unbilled)
Son Of Paleface (1952) (Crosby unbilled)
Little Boy Lost (Paramount, 1953)
Scared Stiff (1953) (Crosby unbilled)
White Christmas (Paramount, 1954)
The Country Girl (Paramount, 1954)
High Society (MGM, 1956)
Anything Goes (Paramount, 1956)
Bing Presents Oreste (1956) (short)
Man On Fire (MGM, 1957)
Showdown At Ulcer Gulch (1958) (short)
Alias Jesse James (1959) (Crosby unbilled)
Say One For Me (Twentieth Century Fox, 1959)
High Time (Twentieth Century Fox, 1960)
Let's Make Love (1960)
Pepe (1960) (Crosby plays himself)
The Road To Hong Kong (United Artists, 1962)
The Sound Of Laughter (1963) (documentary)
Robin And The Seven Hoods (Warner Brothers, 1964)

Stagecoach (Twentieth Century Fox, 1966)
Cinerama's Russian Adventure (1966) (Crosby provides narration)
Bing Crosby's Washington State (1968) (short)
That's Entertainment (1974)

Sources

Barnes, Ken. *The Crosby Years*. New York: St. Martin's, 1980. Includes chronological discography and filmography.
Bassett, John, and others. *The Bing Crosby LP-ography*. 1977. Rev. ed.; originally published in 1973.
Bauer, Barbara. *Bing Crosby*. New York: Pyramid, 1977. Focuses on Crosby's film career.
Bing Crosby: A Pictorial Tribute. New York: Dell, 1977.
Bing Crosby on Broadway [64-page Uris Theatre playbill]. New York: Dell, 1977.
Bishop, Bert, and John Bassett. *Bing: Just for the Record*. [private publication] 1980. Discography of Crosby's commercial recordings.
Bookbinder, Robert. *The Films Of Bing Crosby*. Secaucus, NJ: Citadel, 1977. Covers 55 feature film roles, 17 cameo appearances, one TV movie, two narrative contributions, and an anthology.
Carpozi, George, Jr. *The Fabulous Life Of Bing Crosby*. New York: Manor, 1977. pap.
Crosby, Bing. *Bing Crosby*. 1991.
Crosby, Bing, and Pete Martin. *Call Me Lucky*. Introduction by Gary Giddins. Da Capo Press, 1993. Reprint of Crosby's 1953 autobiography published by Simon Schuster. Also serialized in *The Saturday Evening Post* (February 14, 21, 28, March 7, 14, 21, 28, and April 4, 1953) and a *Reader's Digest Condensed Book*.
Crosby, Gary, and Ross Firestone. *Going My Own Way*. 1983. Garden City, NY: Doubleday, 1983. Centers on Crosby's harsh treatment of his eldest son.
Crosby, Kathryn. *Bing and Other Things*. New York: Meredith, 1967. Covers her life in general with a particular emphasis on her marriage to Crosby.
Crosby, Kathryn. *My Life With Bing*. Wheeling, IL: Collage, 1983. Covers the period up to 1965. While candid in tone, some stories vary from Bing and other things.
Crosby, Ted, and Larry Crosby. *Bing*. New York: World, 1937. Revised by Ted Crosby as *The Story of Bing Crosby* in 1946; includes a Foreword by Bob Hope.
Friedland, Michael. *Bing Crosby: An Illustrated Biography*. Andre Deutsch Ltd., 1999.
A Guy Called Bing. Manchester, U.K.: World Distributors, 1977.
Koenig, Joseph L. *Bing*. New York: Dell, 1977. pap.
Martin, George V. *The Bells of St. Mary's*. New York: Grosset & Dunlap, 1946.
Mello, Edward J., and Tom McBride. *Bing Crosby Discography*. San Francisco, January 31, 1947.

Mielke, Randall G. *The Road To Box Office: The Seven Film Comedies Of Bing Crosby, Bob Hope And Dorothy Lamour, 1940-1962*. McFarland & Company, 1997.

Mize, J.T.H. *Bing Crosby and the Bing Crosby Style: Crosbyana Thru Biography-Photography-Discography*. Chicago: Whi Is Who in Music, Inc., 1946. Revised in An alphabetized discography through 1947; includes listings of album sets and Brunswick masters released on other labels.

Morgereth, Timothy A. *Bing Crosby: A Discography, Radio Program List And Filmography*. Jefferson, NC: McFarland, 1987. A chronological listing of recordings To 1957, radio shows to 1954, and motion pictures.

Netland, Dwayne. *The Crosby: Greatest Show in Golf*. New York: Doubleday, 1975.

O'Connell, Sheldon, with Gordon Atkinson. *Bing: A Voice for All Seasons*. [private publication] 1984.

Osterholm, J. Roger. *Bing Crosby: A Bio-Bibliography*. Greenwood Publishing Group, 1994.

Paradissis, A.G. *The Bing Book of Verse*. Melbourne, Australia: Globe, 1983.

Pleasants, Henry. *The Great American Popular Singers*. New York: Simon and Schuster, 1974. Each chapter focuses on an important popular music vocalist; Crosby's significant legacy is discussed at length.

Pugh, Colin. *Alternate Bing Crosby*. Bristol, U.K., 1988. A listing of alternate recording takes by Crosby.

Reynolds, Fred. *The Crosby Collection: Part One, 1926-34*. Gateshead, Tyne & Wear, U.K.: John Joyce and Son, 1991.

Reynolds, Fred. *Road to Hollywood: The Bing Crosby Films*. Rev. ed. Gateshead, Tyne & Wear, U.K.: John Joyce and Son, 1986. The first edition includes a Foreword by Crosby.

Rosenbaum, Linda. *Bing Crosby Album*. Lorelei, 1977.

Shepherd, Donald, and Robert F. Slatzer. *Bing Crosby: The Hollow Man*. New York: St. Martin's, 1981. Reprinted by Pinnacle (New York, 1982).

Thomas, Bob. *The One and Only Bing*. New York: Grosset & Dunlap, 1977. Includes "A Special Tribute to Bing Crosby," by Bob Hope.

Thompson, Charles. *Bing: The Authorized Biography*. London: W.H. Allen & Co., 1976. Also published by David McKay (New York, 1976) and Magna Print Books (Litton, Yorkshire, 1976). Revised as *The Complete Crosby*.

Ulanov, Barry. *The Incredible Crosby*. New York: Whittlesey House/McGraw-Hill, 1948.

Zwisohn, Laurance J. *Bing Crosby: A Lifetime of Music*. Los Angeles: Palm Tree Library, 1978. Includes a Foreword by song composer James Van Heusen. While biographical in tone, the bulk of the work lists Crosby's recordings in alphabetical order.

Table 33

Russ Columbo

Russ Columbo's career reads as a metaphor of unfulfilled promise; for what might have been. By the time of his tragic death at the age of twenty-six, he was generally conceded to reside at the pinnacle of the crooning genre, the chief rival to the hegemony enjoyed by Rudy Vallee and Bing Crosby. Like these stars, his popularity cut across fan publications, sound recordings, radio, and the cinema. Yet Columbo's legacy - a body of recorded work intermittently spread over a mere five years - provides slim evidence in support of such a lofty assessment. As a result, he has received only passing mention from the vast majority of sources concerned with chronicling the popular music of that era.

Born January 14, 1908, Ruggerio de Rodolfo Columbo came from a large Catholic family. His parents, Nicholas and Julia Columbo (died, May 1942 and August 1944, respectively), gave birth to numerous children, including Albert (d. August 1946), Anthony (d. February 1965), John (d. August 1967), Alonzo (death date unknown), Fiore (d. 1929), Florence Columbo LoDuca (d. 1919), Anna Columbo (d. September 1940), and Carmela Columbo Tempest (d. January 1986), and an unidentified number who died as infants.

Evidence differs as to whether the place of birth was in San Francisco or Camden, New Jersey; at any rate, he seems to have spent portions of his early childhood in both locations. As his Italian-born father was a theater musician, Russ grew up in an atmosphere permeated by music. He was provided guitar and violin lessons beginning as a young boy.

While a teenager, his family moved from the Napa Valley, California town of Calistoga to Los Angeles. There, Russ joined his high school's orchestra as a violinist. In addition, he was able to secure additional experience playing "mood music" in small combos on silent movie sets. Film companies of that day utilized musicians as a means of helping actors achieve the proper frame of mind for interpreting their respective roles. One of these gigs resulted in actress Pola Negri taking an interest in Columbo. Negri, one of the leading film stars of the 1920s, had been romantically involved with the famed Rudolph Valentino. Noting a physical resemblance between the two, she assisted Russ in landing small roles in a number of late 1920s movies.

At the same, Columbo regularly found work as a violinist in hotel and theater orchestras around Los Angeles. When a band singer became ill immediately prior to a CBS radio program being broadcast from the Hollywood Roosevelt, Russ was quickly recruited to go on as his replacement. As a result, he able to secure a position with Gus Arnheim and His Cocoanut Grove Orchestra. The Arnheim association elevated Columbo to the big leagues. Arnheim - a widely known pianist, composer, and bandleader who'd played with Abe Lyman during 1921-1923 - toured the U.S. and Europe heading his own ensemble in the mid-1920s. Notable musicians under his baton over the years would include Jimmie Grier, Woody Herman, Earl Hines, Stan Kenton, Bing Crosby, Shirley Ross, and actor Fred MacMurray. He began recording in 1928 (his first release was "I Can't Do Without You"; Okeh 41057) and his 1931 release, "Sweet and Lovely," would be one of the biggest hit recordings of all-time. Russ would be regularly featured on records as his lead vocalist between 1929-1931 prior to making it big on his own.

While officially signed as a violinist, Arnheim considered Columbo a standby vocalist because his featured singer, Bing Crosby, had exhibited erratic behavior brought on largely by bouts of heavy drinking. When Grove's manager, Abe Frank, attempted to levy a fine on Crosby for missing a show, the talented singer left for good. Tabbed to fill the void, Columbo immediately flourished as Arnhaim's featured vocalist. Building on the bit movie parts filmed during the day to supplement his band work by night, Russ attracted considerable public attention for his scenes with the Arnheim band in the 1929 musical, *Street Girl*.

After touring the East Coast with Arnheim, Columbo attempted to strike out on his own, forming a band and opening a nightclub with two of his brothers in Los Angeles. The Depression-era economy, however, greatly limited his success on both fronts. But his fortunes resumed an upward trajectory when Con Conrad - best known as the composer of "Ma, He's Making Eyes at Me" and the first song to win an Academy Award, "The Continental" - offered to manage him. Allegedly aggressive to a fault, Conrad used all of his persuasive powers to convince Columbo that he was, in the words of Crosby biographer Barry Ulanov, "the great singer of the time and would have no trouble with his career." Conrad took Russ out of his nightclub and band, in which he had been playing violin and guitar and singing a little in the Crosby style, bought him a top hat and resplendent dress suit, and had him photographed to best advantage. These efforts enabled Columbo land a contract for an NBC radio program airing weekdays at 11 p.m..

When Bing Crosby was signed to head a comparable program for CBS in the same time slot, network executives saw the potential for a publicity bonanza. The rivalry - which was further fueled by Crosby's defection from RCA to record for Brunswick, followed by RCA's signing of Columbo - was billed as the "Battle of the Baritones" and some of the resulting coverage strained the boundaries of good taste. Ulanov notes,

> Columnists, taking advantage of a good story, began to quote the two men about each other in a manner and a parlance that neither of them would employ about anybody, much less about his chief rival. And then one very amusing story started going the rounds. "A lot of people seem to think Russ Columbo is Bing Crosby under another name," wrote one critic.

> Another asked, "Are Bing Crosby and Russ Columbo one and the same person?"

The rivalry seemed convincing in that their renditions of many songs—e.g., "Stardust," "Goodnight Sweetheart," "Sweet and Lovely," "Street of Dreams," "Paradise"—were only days apart. Columbo actually recorded Crosby's signature tune, "Where the Blue of the Night (Meets the Gold of the Day)," five days before Crosby did. Furthermore, Bob Weitman, manager of Paramount Theatres, booked Columbo into the Brooklyn Paramount and then Crosby into the Manhattan Paramount, just a few miles away.

In reality, the singers remained on friendly terms. Crosby, in a newspaper column that appeared over his signature, praised a Columbo record. He also had played a part in the composition of Russ's theme song, "You Call It Madness, But I Call It Love," which was, nevertheless, paraphrased by wags as "You Call It Crosby, But I Call It Russ." Columbo, undoubtedly sensitive to claims that he was a Crosby clone, attempted to focus on the differences between their vocal deliveries. The NEA Service carried the following self-appraisal in 1931:

> I'm not a crooner - or a blues singer or a straight baritone.
> I've tried to make my phrasing different, and I take a lot of
> liberty with the music. One of the things [audiences] seem to
> like best is the voice obbligato on repeat choruses - very much
> as I used to do them on the violin.

The contrasting qualities of their voices was even more pronounced than this comment would suggest. Despite, certain stylistic similarities, the timbres differed to a striking degree. Columbo possessed soft, sweet, creamy voice which had a tendency to border on blandness. Crosby, on the other hand, had a rougher, stronger, more vigorous instrument, typically informed by jazz phrasing. Even his ballads were vehicles for the expression of greater rhythmic bite and a richer palette of tonal coloring. Hemming and Hajdu have noted further differences between two singers:

> [Columbo] almost always sounded deadly serious, sometimes even
> pretentious, about the romantic lyrics he sang - in contrast to Crosby's
> way of distancing himself from them with a degree of self-irony and
> occasional kidding. Yet there is no denying the gently nonthreatening
> appeal of Columbo's voice and approach – and the soothing effect his
> voice had on millions of listeners in the depths of the Depression. It's
> a style that also clearly influenced the most romantic of the big-band
> singers of the mid-1930s, such as Art Jarrett and Jack Leonard.

In the meantime, extramusical qualities were a key ingredient in Columbo's success. His striking good looks - black hair, dark eyes, a smooth olive complexion, and athletic physique - graced a multitude of posters, sheet music covers, fan magazines, and trade publications. NBC billed him as "The Romeo of the Airwaves," while his amorous image was augmented by a series of well-publicized romances, including singer Dorothy Dell, actress Sally Blane (Loretta Young's sister), and Hannah Williams.

Columbo's considerable songwriting skills helped further his career as well. A number of his hit recordings were self-penned, including "Prisoner of Love," "You Call It Madness (But I Call It Love)," and "My Love." Professing to enjoy composing almost as much as performing, he told one interviewer, "I write late at night mostly - and get some of my best ideas after I've gone to bed" (a statement likely to have had additional layers of meaning to his legion of female fans).

Columbo's popularity on the radio made it possible to surround himself with first-rate talent. In the spring of 1932, for instance, a rapidly maturing Benny Goodman was hired to front his dance band. The offer proved sufficiently attractive to inspire Goodman to fill his ensemble with excellent jazz musicians like Gene Krupa, Babe Russin, and Joe Sullivan. He functioned as musical director when the band was booked for the summer into the Woodmansten Inn, a roadhouse located close to Manhattan, enabling Columbo to mix with customers when he wasn't singing. Reviews of the engagement appear to have been decidedly favorable - the *Variety* review of the May 5 opening called the band's music "dance inspiring" - but Con Conrad was not happy with the results. According to Goodman,

> It was a good little band, but Conrad wound up getting me at me because whenever we played for dancing people seemed to really like it. I mean, we'd play "Between the Devil and the Deep Blue Sea" or some song like that, and all of a sudden the joint was rocking. He'd say, "Hey, wait a minute – you guys aren't supposed to be the attraction here," and he meant it.

As a result, Goodman - temporarily stymied in his efforts at leading his own band - was left no recourse but to retreat to the anonymity of radio studios, while Columbo would be mated with a succession of sweet orchestras which served merely to accentuate the romantic qualities of his crooning style.

By 1933, during a lull in his recording activities, Columbo became more actively involved in film acting. He was signed to his first starring role that year in a two-reeler titled *That Goes Double*, which had him playing a dual role - as himself and as a look-alike office worker - in addition to singing three songs, "Prisoner of Love," "You Call It Madness (But I Call It Love)," and "My Love." Although his acting in this short was widely considered to be more self-conscious and less "natural" than Crosby's comparable efforts from the same period with Paramount, Columbo's rising celebrity -

combined with his suave good looks and robust masculinity - assured him of further opportunities in Hollywood productions.

Broadway Thru a Keyhole (1933) provided Columbo his first romantic lead in a feature-length film. One of Darryle F. Zanuck's earliest productions for his recently formed Twentieth Century Pictures, it also starred Constance Cummings and included spot appearances by a host of Broadway and vaudeville veterans, most notably Blossom Seeley, Frances Williams, Texas Guinan, Eddie Foy, Jr., and Abe Lyman and His Band. While Columbo received mixed reviews as an actor - he appeared wooden in contrast with the vitality displayed by many of the bit players - one of the songs he introduced in the picture, "You're My Past, Present, and Future," became a major hit. The film's box office performance was also helped by a windfall of unexpected publicity; Al Jolson, convinced that the Walter Winchell-based script depicted a situation in his romance with Ruby Keeler too faithfully for his liking, instigated a public altercation by punching the gossip columnist.

Perhaps due to his less-than-rave notices for his work in *Broadway Thru a Keyhole*, Columbo was reduced to a cameo role in his next film, *Moulin Rouge* (Twentieth Century Pictures). Even during his brief segment onscreen, he was forced to share the spotlight with the Boswell Sisters and headliner Constance Bennett, performing the Harry Warren and Al Dubin-penned standard, "Coffee in the Morning and Kisses at Night."

While Columbo's fledging movie career temporarily stalled, new opportunities arose in other venues. He was offered a new NBC prime-time radio series early in 1934. Emanating "deep in the heart of Hollywood," in the words of presenter Cecil Underwood, the program aired every Sunday night. Introduced as "the Romeo of songs, here with songs to delight your ears and heart," Columbo would open with the greeting "Good evening, my friends," followed by his theme, "You Call It Madness," which would also return as his closing number. His song selection featured a blend of hit recordings and plugs for material from current films, including "With My Eyes Wide Open I'm Dreaming" from *Shoot the Works*, "I've Had My Moments" from *Hollywood Party*, and "Rolling In Love" from *The Old Fashioned Way*.

At the same time, Columbo signed a new recording contract with Brunswick (once again filling the void left by the departure of Crosby to another label, in this case, Decca). Despite the absence of precise sales figures, his releases from that period reputedly sold exceedingly well. According to Robert Deal, he was reportedly earning more than $500,000 a year from all sources—a vast sum at the time.

These developments appear to have spurred Universal Pictures to select him for a major part (as Gaylord Ravenal) in the heavily-publicized film version of the Kern-Hammerstein musical, *Showboat*. When that project was temporarily put on hold due to production problems, Columbo was assigned an interim lead in *Wake Up and Dream*, a low-budget, standard backstage musical also starring June Knight, Wini Shaw, and Roger Pryor.

Titled *Castles in the Air* in Great Britain and initially referred to in press releases as *The Love Life of a Crooner*, this film - which would be released a month after Columbo's untimely death - might well have proved a springboard to better roles in the future. Despite the inherent banalities of a run-of-the-mill script, his part seemed designed to reveal a darker side and wider acting range than that demonstrated by chief rival Crosby up until then. In contrast to the "good guy" roles characterizing Crosby's output at Paramount, Columbo played an egotistical singer who attempted to steal away his best friend's girl. The movie also showed his singing in good light, as exemplified by the posthumously released hit, "When You're In Love" (Brunswick 6972), with an accompaniment by Jimmie Grier & His Orchestra.

Universal's announcement in press releases while Columbo was still alive that his next film role would be as a toreador in *Men Without Fear*, gives some credence to the scenario that he was on the verge of challenging Crosby's hegemony as the leading crooner of the 1930s. Furthermore, he was rumored to be in line for choice roles in two other motion picture projects, Universal's *Glamour* (which would have reunited him with former co-star Constance Cummings who, in personal correspondence in the late 1990s, fondly recalled her professional relationship with Columbo) and *Sweet Music*, which eventually was released in 1935 by Warner Bros., starring Rudy Vallee. The latter film included the song, "I See Two Lovers," which initially appeared in *Wake Up and Dream*.

Public interest in Columbo was further hyped by his romance with actress Carole Lombard. In the fall of 1933, a short time after her divorce from actor William Powell, Lombard fell in love with the singer. For his part, Columbo responded favorably to her zany behavior as well as accepting her salty language, something which had offended a number of her male friends in the past. Although marriage seemed a distinct possibility, Lombard's close associates doubted that the affair would come to that. According to gossip columnist Hedda Hopper, "the couple's relationship was based on many things – but not sex." Hopper cited a number of traits which caused her to question Columbo's masculinity, including the considerable trouble he spent on his hair and sun-tanning treatments as well as his habit of carrying around a pocket-mirror produced on occasion to gaze at himself in public. It is indisputable, however, that Lombard was devoted to him and made every effort to help further his film career. She invited Columbo onto film sets to observe the filmmaking process and to pick up pointers on acting. He repaid this favor by coaching her in the two songs she was designated to sing in the movie *White Woman*.

By September 1934 it was clear that Crosby's career had thus far been more successful than his own. Columbo had appeared in only four films during 1933-1934, two of which he did not star in. Crosby on the other hand had starred in six features during the same time span. Furthermore, the material he had been given to sing in films trailed far behind that provided Crosby with regard to both quality and sheer quantity. While Crosby's film music played a significant role in propelling him to stardom, Columbo's song hits were for-the-most-part limited to recordings and radio broadcasts. Deal states "he had the greater romantic appeal but very little chance to demonstrate any versatility and it seems likely that there were more sides of him to be seen on film than his presenters had up to that time revealed to the cinema audiences."

Columbo and Lombard continued to date up to his death; they could be seen dining and dancing at the Cocoanut Grove most Wednesday nights. His last recording session took place on August 31, 1934; he concluded with the Allie Wrubel and Mort Dixon composition, "I See Two Lovers."

On September 2, just hours before his regular Sunday evening radio program, Columbo stopped by to see his life-long friend, Lansing V. Brown, Jr., who lived with his parents at 584 Lillian Way in Beverly Hills. He was going to have some publicity shots taken by Brown, who was highly respected as still camera man, and much in demand as a portrait photographer. After the photos had been taken, they talked about a common interest, antique pistol collecting. Brown then produced a pair of duelling pistols which dated from the Civil War, part of his own collection of curios. He placed the head of a match under the rusty hammer of one of the pistols with a flourish, then pulled the trigger to ignite the match in order to light a cigarette. The pistol, which evidently hadn't been used for over sixty-five years, still housed a charge of powder and an old bullet. The chick of the hammer caused the charge to explode and the corroded bullet struck the top of a table located between the two friends, ricocheted, striking Columbo in the left eye, then entering his brain.

Rushed to the Good Samaritan Hospital, it was discovered that the bullet, after piercing the center of the brain, had fractured the rear wall of the skull. A brain specialist summoned to the scene, Dr. George Paterson, counseled against the delicate operation being considered unless Columbo's rapidly waning strength could be restored. The singer lingered in agony for six hours before dying; the doctors were amazed that he hadn't been killed instantly. Bedside mourners included members of his family and former girlfriend, Sally Blane. Those outside in the hospital corridor included Lombard, who had heard of the tragedy by telephone at Lake Arrowhead where Columbo was to have joined her to vacation the following week, film producer Carl Laemmle, and other film celebrities.

Brown would collapse following police interrogation; their suspicions had been aroused by a statement from a servant who alleged that he'd heard Columbo and the photographer arguing violently in the den. However, Brown was released following a court inquest. The verdict: "This jury finds that Russ Columbo came to his death by a gun wound accidentally inflicted by Lansing Brown. Brown is absolved of all blame...." The singer's relatives and friends agreed with this ruling. A number of professional "dirt" diggers, an inevitable consequence of the Hollywood scene, spread stories of suicide due to an unrequited romance. Brown would grieve until his own passing decades later.

A crowd of 3000 persons attended funeral services at the Sunset Boulevard Catholic Church in Hollywood. The pallbearers were Bing Crosby, Gilbert Roland, Walter Lang, Stuart Peters, Lowell Sherman, and Sheldon Keate Callaway.

Columbo's seven surviving brothers and sisters conspired to keep news about the death from their mother. Having suffered a heart attack two days prior to Columbo's accident, they were concerned that the shock of hearing about his death would kill her. A story was concocted about Columbo agreeing to a five-year tour abroad. While money from his life insurance policy was used to support her, the deception was maintained for a decade until she died. The family employed a variety of stratagems during this period including sending letters, allegedly written by the singer, which contained newsy accounts, tender sentiments, and reports of his many successes. Warren Hall noted, in the October 8, 1944 issue of *The American Weekly* (a Sunday supplement distributed in the Hearst syndicated newspapers), that they took the further precaution of imprinting each envelope with a rubber stamp to simulate a London postmark. The same stamp was conspicuous on the wrappings of the Christmas and birthday gifts which arrived "from your loving son."

The family also played records in order to simulate his radio program. The only radio shows actually heard in the Columbo household were those that made no mention of bandleaders. Even though his mother was almost totally blind, all newspapers coming into the house were carefully censored. Lombard assisted by corresponding with Mrs. Columbo, explaining that her son was unable to visit because he was performing in the major cities of Europe. All visitors were warned to speak as though Russ were still alive and more popular than ever. According to Hall, when Mrs. Columbo died in 1944 at the age of 78, her last words were: "Tell Russ…I am so proud…and happy."

Many music historians have openly questioned whether the "Battle of the Baritones" would have turned out differently if Columbo's life hadn't been tragically ended. According to Deal,

> Rudy Vallee was one man in the business who thought so, on account of Crosby's drinking habits in the early thirties, believing that Bing may have lost some popularity if Columbo's career had continued. Johnny Mercer disagreed for he took the view that Columbo did not possess

Crosby's original talent and did not have the type of personality that gave Crosby such a universal appeal. By 1934, if not before, Russ Columbo was the finest singer of love songs in the United States and the one who had the greatest attraction for women, although the timbre of his voice also appealed to men – as did Bing Crosby's and Al Bowlly's. Columbo phrased rather like Crosby, in a voice more silkily textured than that of his "rival" but it is doubtful if he could have handled the more rhythmic sort of number which Crosby excelled at or, indeed, the country and western type of song, such as "Home On The Range," "The Last Round-Up" or "Empty Saddles" that Bing featured so successfully. Russ Columbo did represent the most serious challenge to Crosby and at only twenty-six years of age – he was five years younger than Bing – it is reasonable to assume that his best years were still to come. It says something for the talent and popularity of the man that it was to be almost six years before another serious challenger – in the person of Frank Sinatra – forced his way into the reckoning.

Despite the relatively limited number of recordings made by Columbo during his lifetime, Crosby is probably the only crooner predating the Sinatra era to had been honored by more reissues. Over the years there have been a notable number of tribute albums to Columbo, including those of Paul Bruno, Gordon Lewis, Steve Mason, and Jerry Vale. Although not yet a reality, many singers—including Perry Como, Don Cornell, Johnny Desmond, and Tony Martin—have been considered for the leading role in a film biography of Columbo. In the 1950s a television drama featuring Tony Curtis as the crooner got as far as the planning stage.

Discography

1930

Victor 22546   A Peach Of A Pair (credited to Gus Arnheim and His Orchestra)   Also His Master's Voice B 5953

1931

Victor 22801   Guilty/I Don't Know Why (I Just Do) (w. orchestra)   Also His Master's Voice B 3997/B 4042
   22802   You Call It Madness (But I Call It Love) (w. orchestra)/Sweet And Lovely (w. Nat Shilkret and His Orchestra)   Also Bluebird B 6503 and His Master's Voice B 3984/His Master's Voice B 3984 and Victor 27635
   22826   Good Night, Sweetheart/Time On My Hands (w. Nat Shilkret & His

     Orchestra) Also Victor 27636/Bluebird B 6503
  22861 You Try Somebody Else/Call Me Darling (Call Me Sweetheart, Call Me Dear) (w. Leonard Joy and His Orchestra) Also Victor 27634
  22867 Where The Blue Of The Night (Meets The Gold Of The Day) (w. Leonard Joy and His Orchestra)//Prisoner Of Love (w. Nat Shilkret and His Orchestra) Also His Master's Voice B 4079 and Victor 27637/His Master's Voice B 4079 and Victor 27635
  22903 Save The Last Dance For Me/All Of Me (w. Leonard Joy and His Orchestra) Also Victor 27634 (Save The Last Dance For Me)

1932

Victor 22909 You're My Everything/Just Friends (w. Leonard Joy and His Orchestra)
  22976 Paradise/Auf Wiedersehen, My Dear (w. Leonard Joy and His Orchestra) Also Victor 27636/Victor 27637
  24045 Just Another Dream Of You/Living In Dreams (w. orchestra)
  24076 As You Desire Me/The Lady I Love (w. orchestra) Also His Master's Voice B 6265 (As You Desire Me)
  24077 My Love/Lonesome Me (w. orchestra)
  24194 Street Of Dreams/Lost In A Crowd (w. orchestra)
  24195 Make Love The Thing/I Called To Say Goodnight (w. orchestra)

1934

Brunswick 6972 When You're In Love/Let's Pretend There's A Moon (w. Jimmie Grier and His Orchestra) Also Decca F-5405/Decca F-5596
Decca F-5405 When You're In Love/Too Beautiful For Words (w. Jimmie Grier and and His Orchestra)
  5001S Too Beautiful For Words/I See Two Lovers (w. Jimmie Grier and His Orchestra) Also released on Special Editions label

1941

RCA Songs Made Famous By The Golden Voice Of Russ Columbo (78 album set culled from the October 1931-April 1932 sessions)

--45 RPM Recordings

RCA/Collector's Record #3 You Call It Madness/My Time Is Your Time (Rudy Vallee) (a mail-in promotion with the purchase of Halo Shampoo, dating from the late 1950s/early 1960s)

--Long Playing Albums/Cassettes

Bluebird CPL1-1756(e)   Russ Columbo – A Legendary Performer (1977)   Includes: Just Friends; Where the Blue of the Night; All of Me; Time On My Hands; Save the Last Dance for Me; Auf Wiedersehen, My Dear; Paradise; I Don't Know Why; You Call It Madness; Prisoner of Love; Just Another Dream of You; My Love

Bronco Gegund   [Russ Columbo air checks] (variation of Totem 1031 LP)

Golden Legends 2000/1   The Films Of Russ Columbo (consists of songs from Columbo's last three films as well as the complete transcription of his short, *That Goes Double*

Pelican LP 141   Russ Columbo - Prisoner Of Love (from the June-November 1932 Victor sessions)

RCA LPL1-1798   Russ Columbo; A Legendary Performer (1976)

   LPT-5   Columbo, Crosby And Sinatra (196?)

   LSA 3066   Love Songs By Russ Columbo (1972)   Includes: Call Me Darling; Sweet and Lovely; Just Friends; Where the Blue of the Night; You Try Somebody Else; You're My Everything; All of Me; Time On My Hands; Save the Last Dance For Me; Auf Wiedersehen, My Dear; Paradise

   LVA-1002   Love Songs By Russ Columbo (195?)   Also released in the 1950s (with different cover artwork) as LX-996 and LPM-2072

Russ Columbo Archives   Gone But Not Forgotten; 51 Great Songs By The Romantic Voice Of Russ Columbo   (4 album set)

Sandy Hook 2006   Russ Columbo (1978)   Includes: Peach of a Pair; Street of Dreams; The Lady I Love; I Call To Say Goodnight; I Don't Know Why; I See Two Lovers; You Call It Madness; Lonesome Me; My Love; Lost in a Crowd; Make Love the King; Guilty; Prisoner of Love; Goodnight Sweetheart

Russ Columbo On The Air—1933-34 (1980)   Air checks similar to Totem 1031 LP; includes: More Than You Know; Time on My Hands; You're My Past, My Present and My Future; Coffee in the Morning; Lover; You Call It Madness; The House Is Haunted; Time On My Hands; Easy Come, Easy Go; With My Eyes Wide Open I'm Dreaming; Stardust; True; Rolling In Love; I've Had My Moments; I'm Not Lazy, I'm Dreaming

Totem 1031   Russ Columbo On The Air (consists of air checks from Columbo's 1934 radio program)

Zodiac ZR3003   Russ Columbo – Broadcasts & Movies, 1932-34 (cassette) (1980) Broadcasts: You Call It Madness; Who; Time on My Hands; I've Got To Pass Your House; You're My Past, My Present and My Future; Coffee in the Morning; Lover; Poor Folks; I've Had My

Moments; I'm Not Lazy, I'm Dreaming. Movies: Broadway Thru a
Keyhold; Wake Up and Dream (excerpts)

--Compact Discs

Living Era (Great Britain)   Prisoner Of Love (1997)
Take Two   Russ Columbo: Save The Last Dance For Me (1994)

Filmography

Gus Arnheim And His Ambassadors (Vitaphone/Warner Bros., ca. 1929) (10 min.)
Wolf Song (Paramount, 1929)
The Street Girl (Radio Pictures, 1929)
Dynamite (Metro-Goldwyn-Mayer, 1929)
The Wonders Of Women (Metro-Goldwyn-Mayer, 1929)
Hello, Sister (Sono Art-Worldwide, 1930)
The Texan (Paramount, 1930)
Hellbound (Tiffany, 1931)
That Goes Double (Vitaphone/Warner Bros., 1933) (short)
Broadway Thru A Keyhole (Twentieth Century/United Artists, 1933)
Moulin Rouge (Twentieth Century/United Artists, 1934)
Wake Up And Dream (Universal, 1934)   British title: Castles In The Air; referred to
   In early press releases as The Love Life Of A Crooner

Sources

Coslow, Sam. *Cocktails For Two: The Many Lives OF Giant Songwriter Sam
   Coslow*. Arlington House Publishers, 1977.
Deal, Robert T. *The Story of Russ Columbo*. Middlesex, England: Hampton/Memory
   Lane, 1988.
Hall, Warren. "Kept Alive By Conspirators," *The American Weekly*. (October 8,
   1944) 19.
"He's Thrilling, Girls, This Russ Columbo!" *Anderson (Indiana) Bulletin*. (November
   28, 1931) 5.
Hemming, Roy, and David Hajdu. "Russ Columbo," In: *Discovering Great Singers of
   Classic Pop*. New York: Newmarket Press, 1991. pp. 54-58.
Lamparski, Richard. *Lamparski's Hidden Hollywood*. New York: Fireside Books,
   1981.
Parish, James Robert. *The Hollywood Celebrity Death Book*. Pioneer Books, 1993.
Parish, James Robert, and Michael R. Pitts. "Russ Columbo," In: *Hollywood Songsters
   - A Biographical Dictionary*. New York: Garland Publishing, 1991.

Ramsey, Walter. "The Tragic Death of Russ Columbo," *Radio Stars*. (December 1934) 34-36, 83, 85, 87, 89, 91.

"Russ Columbo Proves Latest Sensation of Broadway," *Anderson (Indiana) Daily Bulletin*. (September 12, 1931) 5.

THE CLASSIC ROCK 'N' ROLL ERA

Rockabilly

Definition

A blend of country & western and rhythm & blues, rockabilly arose in mid-1950s. The genre's stylistic legacy--it pointed the way to classic rock 'n' roll--far outweighed its commercial impact. By the late 1950s, virtually all rockabilly practitioners had been subsumed by either pop-rock or country music.

Elvis Presley: the Genre's Seminal Figure

Elvis Presley is a supreme figure in American life, one whose presence, no matter how banal or predictable, discourages any comparisons. He is honored equally by long-haired rock critics, middle-aged women, the city of Memphis (it named a major road after him), and even a president (Richard Nixon had him over to the White House, and made him an honorary narcotics agent). While other music stars define different versions of America, Presley's career almost has the scope to take in the whole of America: poor boy makes good, the rebel without a cause, the denizen of respectability who joined the army (when he really wouldn't have had to) and made clean movies, the comeback kid (after a decade of mediocre musicmaking, he reinvented himself as a leatherclad rocker), the glitter king reigning over the gambling casinos, and mysterious recluse. His music encompasses not only the hits of the period, but patriotic recitals, country gospel, dirty blues, and Vegas pop schlock.

Numerous journalists and music historians have attempted to recount Presley's watershed moment in the evolution of rock 'n' roll. Most accounts go something like this: There are four men in the cramped Sun Records studio: bassist Bill Black, guitarist Scotty Moore, producer Sam Phillips in the back, and the sexy young kid thumping his guitar as he sings, nineteen-year-old Elvis Presley. It's 1954. Sam Phillips is doing all right for himself. He has been among the first to record men who will be giants in the world of postwar blues: B.B. King, Junior Parker, and Howlin' Wolf. There are many others ready to follow in their footsteps, but he has deeper aspirations. In Presley, he sees the new world order: a white boy, culturally influenced by country and gospel, who can sing the blues.

The four of them, having reached a momentary musical impasse, take a break. They all seem to realize that they're on the brink of something big; however, they can't quite seem to put it all together. Their conservation--about music, naturally--comes around to the blues, interpreters like Arthur Crudup. You know that one song he did? It goes like this! Presley picks up his guitar and starts riffing. In a second he is singing, "That's all right, mama, that's all right with me..." Black and Moore pick up the groove behind him.

Their hijinks get Phillips' attention. Liking what he hears, he encourages the musicians to try it one more time without any changes--this time with the tape machine running. The song is cut in rapid order. They all listen to the playback, make a few comments, and then leave the studio.

Phillips further ponders the implications of what he has captured on tape. Would he be able to get any radio stations to play such a record? White disc jockeys probably would avoid it because it sounded like black music, whereas blacks were likely to consider it too hillbilly. Still, it sounded great!

Phillips went ahead and released a run of records. In doing so he ushered in the heyday of Sun Records and the rockabilly sound. The music had a fast, aggressive feel: simple, crisp drumming, vibrant guitar licks, wild country boogie piano. The music spurred a generation of young Southern musicians to search out Phillips and his imitators in hopes of building their own legacy.

As a creative force, rockabilly faded almost as soon as the general public became aware of its existence. The total output was slim; even with Presley's Sun singles included, the genre sold less records than releases of Fat Domino alone. Nevertheless, it fixed, in the words of Greil Marcus (*Mystery Train*), "the crucial image of rock 'n' roll: the sexy, half-crazed fool standing on stage singing his guts out." Marcus furthur elaborates,

> Most significantly, the image was white. Rockabilly was the only style of early rock 'n' roll that proved white boys could do it all--that they could be as strange, as exciting, as scary, and as free as the black men who were suddenly dominating America's airwaves. These were two kinds of white counterattack on the black invasion of white popular music that constituted rock 'n' roll: the attempt to soften black music or freeze it out, and the rockabilly lust to beat the black man at his own game.

Top Artists and Their Recordings

Johnny Bond--"Hot Rod Lincoln" (1960)

Jimmy Bowen--"I'm Stickin' With You" (1957)

Sonny Burgess—"We Wanna Boogie" (1956)

Johnny Burnette Trio--"Tear It Up" (1956); "Midnight Rain" (1956); "Honey Hush" (1956); "Lonesome Train" (1956); "Rock Billy Boogie" (1957)

Ray Campi –"Catapillar" (1956)

Johnny Cash--"I Walk the Line" (1956)

Sanford Clark--"The Fool" (1956)

Ral Donner--"Girl of My Best Friend" (1961); "You Don't Know What You've Got" (1961); "Please Don't Go" (1961); "She's Everything" (1961/2)

Charlie Feathers—"Defrost Your Heart" (1956)

Wanda Jackson--Let's Have a Party" (1960); "Right or Wrong" (1961); "In the Middle of a Heartache" (1961)

Buddy Knox--"Party Doll" (1957); "Rock Your Little Baby to Sleep" (1957); "Hula Love" (1957); "Somebody Touched Me" (1958); "Lovey Dovey" (1960/1)

Jerry Lee Lewis--"Whole Lot of Shakin' Going On" (1957); "Great Balls of Fire" (1957/8); "Breathless" (1958); "High School Confidential" (1958); "What's I Say" (1961)

Bob Luman--"Let's Think About Living" (1960)

Carl Mann--"Mona Lisa" (1959); "Pretend" (1959)

Janis Martin--"Will You, Willyum" (1956)

Guy Mitchell--Ninety-Nine Years" (1956); "Singing the Blues" (1956); "Crazy With Love" (1956); "Knee Deep in the Blues"/"Take Me Back Baby" (1957); "Rock-A-Billy" (1957)

Roy Orbison--"Ooby Dooby" (1956)

Carl Perkins--"Blue Suede Shoes" (1956); "Boppin' the Blues" (1956); "Honey Don't" (1956); "Dixie Fried" (1956); "Your True Love" (1957); "Pink Pedal Pushers" (1958); "Pointed Toe Shoes" (1959)

Elvis Presley--"That's All Right, Mama"/"Blue Moon of Kentucky" (1954); "I Don't Care If the Sun Don't Shine" (1954); "Baby, Let's Play House" (1954); "Heartbreak Hotel"/"I Was the One" (1956); "Blue Suede Shoes" (1956); "I Want You, I Need You, I Love You"/"My Baby Left Me" (1956); "Don't Be Cruel"/"Hound Dog" (1956); "Love Me Tender"/"Anyway You Want Me" (1956); "Love Me"/"When My Blue Moon Turns to Gold Again" (1956/7); "Too Much"/"Playing For Keeps" (1957); "All Shook Up" (1957); "Teddy Bear"/"Loving You" (1957); "Jailhouse Rock"/"Treat Me Nice" (1957); "Don't/"I Beg of You" (1958); "Wear My Ring Around Your Neck"/"Doncha Think It's Time" (1958); "Hard Headed Woman"/"Don't Ask Me Why" (1958); "One Night"/"I Got Stung" (1958); "A Fool Such As I"/"I Need Your Love Tonght" (1959); "A Big Hunk of Love"/"My Wish Came True" (1959); "Stuck on You" (1960)

Johnny Preston--"Running Bear" (1959/60); "Cradle of Love" (1960); "Feel So Fine" (1960)

Charlie Rich--"Lonely Weekends" (1960)

Billy Lee Riley--"Flying Saucers Rock 'N' Roll" (1957)

Charlie Ryan--"Hot Rod Lincoln" (1960)

Jack Scott--"Leroy"/"My True Love" (1958); "With Your Love" (1958); "Goodbye Baby" (1958/9); "The Way I Walk" (1959); "What in the World's Come Over You" (1960); "Burning Bridges"/"Oh, Little One" (1960); "It Only Happened Yesterday" (1960)

Warren Smith--"So Long I'm Gone" (1957); "Ubangi Stomp" (1957)

Conway Twitty--"It's Only Make Believe" (1958); "The Story of My Love" (1959); "Mona Lisa" (1959); "Danny Boy" (1959); "Lonely Blue Boy" (1959/60); "What Am I Living For" (1960)

Malcolm Yelvington—Drinkin' Wine Spodee-O-Dee" (1955)

Table 34

DORSEY BURNETTE, December 28, 1932-August 19, 1979
JOHNNY BURNETTE, March 25, 1934-August 1, 1964

The Burnette brothers, Dorsey and Johnny, are best remembered for their seminal rockabilly recordings for Coral in the mid-1950s. Although sales fell far short of the standard set by their friend, Elvis Presley, the sheer verve and energy communicated by the trio's records influenced the aesthetics of British and American rock stars in the 1960s and 1970s. Aerosmith, Foghat, and the Yardbirds are just a few of the acts who have recorded the trio's songs.

Born in Memphis, Dorsey and Johnny Burnette grew up listening to country music, particularly on the Grand Ole Opry radio broadcasts. Learning to play string instruments at an early age, they began performing at local functions while still in school. By the early 1950s, their country band was a popular draw at dances and clubs throughout the Mississippi delta region. Initially, the brothers were not sure that music represented a viable career option; Dorsey, for one, tried pro boxing and spent six years studying for an electrician's license. They began to reconsider after winning the "Ted Mack Amateur Hour" competition four straight times; they then toured with the show, playing such venues as Madison Square Garden and the White House.

While working at the Crown Electric Company in Memphis during 1954, Dorsey and Johnny decided to form a rockabilly trio with fellow employee, guitarist Paul Burlison. Word about their dynamic live act led to a contract with Coral Records. Although some of the Johnny Burnette Trio's early releases went on to become rock 'n' roll classics—most notably, "Honey Hush"/"Train Kept A-Rollin'" (Coral 61759; 1956) and "Tear It Up" (Coral 61852; 1956)—none entered the national charts.

Feeling constricted on their home turf, the Burnettes relocated to the Los Angeles area. Concentrating on their songwriting skills, they were soon supplying teen idol Ricky Nelson with a steady stream of hits: "Waitin' in School" (Imperial 5483; 1957; #18), "Believe What You Say" (Imperial 5503; 1958; #4), "It's Late" (Imperial 5565; 1959; #9), and "Just a Little Too Much" (Imperial 5595; 1959; #9). Encouraged, the brothers decided to return to performing, but as solo acts. Dorsey was the first to have a hit record with "Tall Oak Tree" (Era 3012; 1960; #23), followed by "Hey Little One" (Era 3019; 1960; #48). The darkly handsome Johnny was groomed as a teen idol, scoring soon thereafter with the lushly romantic confections, "Dreamin' (Liberty 55258; 1960; #11), "You're Sixteen" (Liberty 55285; 1960; #8), "Little Boy Sad" (Liberty 55298; 1961; #17), and "God, Country and My Baby" (Liberty 55379; 1961; #18). The younger brother's career was prematurely ended, however, by a boating accident.

After failing to achieve any more pop hits through the mid-1960s, Dorsey turned to country material. He found success on the country charts in the 1970s with self-penned songs such as "In the Spring (The Roses Always Turn Red)" (Capitol 3307; 1972; #21), "I Just Couldn't Let Her Walk Away" (Capitol 3404; 1972; #40), "Darlin'" (Capitol 3678; 1973; #26), "Molly (I Ain't Getting' Any Younger)" (Melodyland 6007; 1975; #28), and "Thing I Treasure" (Calliope 8004; 1977; #31). In addition, his gospel compositions—most notably, "The Magnificent Sanctuary Band"—were widely recorded by other artists. Newly signed with Elektra/Asylum Records, his career was still in high gear when he died on heart attack at his Woodland Hills, California home.

The Burnette's legacy has remained prominent with the re-release of both their trio work and solo pop recordings. Furthermore, their sons also went on to enjoy hit recordings; Dorsey's son, Billy, scored with "Don't Say No" (Columbia 11380; 1980; #68) as well as creasing the country charts with several songs, and Johnny's son, Rocky, with "Tired of Toein' the Line" (EMI America 8043; 1980; #8).

Table 35

Roy Orbison, April 23, 1936-December 6, 1988

Although Roy Orbison's musical roots were in country and rockabilly, he is remembered as perhaps the greatest rock ballad singer of all-time. During his induction to the Rock and Roll Hall of Fame in January 1987, Bruce Springsteen provided the following tribute: "When I went in to the studio to make *Born to Run*, I wanted to write words like Bob Dylan that sounded like Phil Spector, but with singing like Roy Orbison. But nobody sings like Roy Orbison."

Born in Vernon, Texas, Orbison began learning how to play guitar from his father at age six. He headed his own country band, the Wink Westerners, and had a radio show on Vernon's KVWC while still attending high school. While attending North Texas State College in Denton, he organized a new group and began performing on television and at local venues. One of the new rockabilly artists passing through the area, Johnny Cash, recommended that Orbison send a demo tape of his material to Sun Records owner, Sam Phillips. He included the song, "Oooby Dooby," realizing that it was similar to what Sun was releasing in the mid-1950s. The single (Sun 242; 1956) would reach number fifty-nine on the pop charts.

Although now typecast as a rock 'n' roll artist, Orbison still aspired to sing country-flavored ballads. As a result, he jumped at the opportunity to become a staff songwriter with Nashville-based music publisher, Acuff-Rose, in 1957. Among his earliest compositions with the company was "Claudette" (Cadence 1348; 1958; #30), recorded by the Everly Brothers. Firm co-owner, Wesley Rose, became his manager, securing a recording contract with Monument Records in 1959. One of earliest exponents of orchestrated country-pop—his success would have considerable impact on Chet Atkins' Nashville Sound—Orbison placed twenty Monument singles on the charts during the early 1960s, including "Only the Lonely" (#412; 1960; #2), "Blue Angel" (#421; 1960; #9), "Running Scared' (#438; 1961; #1), "Crying" (#447; 1961; #2), "Dream Baby" (#456; 1962; #4), "In Dreams" (#806; 1963; #7), "Mean Woman Blues" (#824; 1963; #5), "It's Over" (#837; 1964; #9), and "Pretty Woman" (#851; 1964; #1).

In 1965, he signed with MGM Records in order to have greater access to film and television work. Although record sales declined noticeably, he got to act and sing in his first movie, *Fastest Guitar Alive* (1966). Before he could recover his hit-making touch, however, he suffered two personal tragedies—the death of his wife in a 1966 motorcycle accident, followed by the loss of two children when his Nashville home caught fire in 1967. Because his recording success had involved his input at all levels of the process—including songwriting, arranging, and recording—he retreated into the routine of live performing. Administrative turmoil within the MGM hierarchy further complicated efforts to resurrect his recording career.

Orbison's popularity in Europe, Australia, and other parts of the world led him to concentrate on international tours during the 1970s. While his records sold well abroad, stateside releases—including Mercury recordings in the mid-1970s after departing MGM—met with public indifference. Other artists, however, began enjoying success with new renditions of his classics by the end of the decade, most notably

Orbison's own recording career also showed signs of revival by the late 1970s. Signing with Elektra in 1978, his debut album, *Laminar Flow* (Asylum 198; 1979), was widely praised by the rock press. A duet with Emmylou Harris, "That Lovin' You Feelin' Again" (Warner Bros. 49262; 1980), which appeared on the soundtrack of the film *Roadie*, won a Grammy for Best Country Performance by a Duo or Group with Vocal, his first such award.

Orbison's career was provided an additional boost when director David Lynch included "In Dreams" in his film, *Blue Velvet* (1986). The following year his new label, Virgin, released *In Dreams: The Greatest Hits* (Virgin 90604), which consisted of new interpretations of his 1960s hits. Shortly thereafter, a September 1987 Coconut Grove tribute concert, A Black and White Night," featuring stars such as Springsteen, Elvis Costello, Jackson Browne, and Bonnie Raitt in backup roles, was widely broadcast on PBS-TV. In 1988, a chance meeting with Dylan, George Harrison, Jeff Lynne, and Tom Petty led to the formation of laid-back supergroup, the Traveling Wilburys; the resulting LP, *Traveling Wilburys, Volume One* (Wilbury 25796; 1988), achieved double-platinum sales. In the meantime, he finished work on *Mystery Girl* (Virgin 91058; 1989; #5), which became his highest-charting album, due in part to the success of the single, "You Got It" (Virgin 99245; 1989; #9), his first Top Ten hit in twenty-five years. Although his artistic rebirth was disrupted by a fatal heart attack, the 1990s saw the release of most of his recorded legacy on compact disc, including hitherto unavailable live and studio material. *King of Hearts* (Virgin 86520), a compilation of unissued and posthumously completed tracks, charted in late 1992.

Table 36

Carl Perkins, April 9, 1932-January 19, 1998

Although he had comparatively few hit recordings, Carl Perkins is regarded to be one of the trailblazers of rock 'n' roll. Perkins' reputation is built largely on his songwriting skills; however, it is also a product of a lengthy career as a performer and recording artist.

Born to a sharecropping family in Tiptonville, Tennessee, Perkins was one of the many young rockabilly performers (others included Johnny Cash, Roy Orbison, Jerry Lee Lewis, Billy Lee Riley, and Charlie Rich) drawn to Sam Phillips' Sun Records studio following Elvis Presley's early success there. Playing a dance one night, Perkins was inspired by the sight of a young man's pride in his footwear to write the song, "Blue Suede Shoes" (Sun 234). Recorded December, 19, 1955, the song rose high on the pop (#2), country (#1), and R&B (#2) charts early the following year. However, a serious car crash en route to appear on TV's "Perry Como Show" in late March 1956 sidelined him for many months, significantly dampening his career momentum. When recovered, Perkins creased the charts a few more times with "Boppin' the Blues" (Sun 243; 1956; #7 C&W, #60 pop), "Dixie Fried" (Sun 249; 1956; #10 C&W), "Your True Love" (Sun 261; 195; #13 C&W, #67 pop), "Pink Pedal Pushers" (Columbia 41131; 1958; #17 C&W, #91 pop), and "Pointed Toe Shoes" (Columbia; 1959).

When the hits stopped, he continued performing live; an English tour in 1963 spurred the Beatles to record three songs from his repertoire: "Everybody's Trying to Be My Baby," "Honey Don't," and "Matchbox." After overcoming chronic drug and alcohol abuse, he played with Johnny Cash's road show ten years beginning in the mid-1960s. His solo spots on Cash's 1969-1971 network television run led to another Columbia recording contract. Two album release—*On Top* (Columbia 9931; 1969) and *Boppin' the Blues* (with NRBQ; Columbia 9981; 1970) were modest sellers in the rock market, while nine of his singles made the country charts between 1966-1987 (for the Dollie, Columbia, Mercury, and America labels).

In 1976, Perkins formed his own band, the C.P. Express, featuring sons Stan on drums and Greg on bass guitar. By the late 1980s, they were calling themselves the "Imarocker" band (augmented by sax great Ace Cannon). Although he would record new material on occasion, much of it tended to be imbued with nostalgia, including *Ol' Blue Suede's Back* (Jet 208; 1978)—comprised of updated country-rock versions of classic 1950s songs, it sold more than 100,000 copies in England—and *The Class of '55* (1985), which also featured Cash, Lewis, and Orbison augmented by admirers such as John Fogerty and Rick Nelson. These releases, however, were overwhelmed by the glut of reissues devoted to his Sun tracks, including *Lil' Bit Of Gold* (Rhino 373015; 1988), *The Carl Perkins CD Box Set* (Charly 2; 1990), and *The Classic Carl Perkins* (Bear Family 15494; 1990).

Perkins received many tributes during the latter years of his life, most notably induction into the Rock and Roll Hall of Fame in 1987. An authorized biography, David McGee's *Go, Cat, Go! The Life and Times of Carl Perkins, the King of Rockabilly*, appeared in 1994.

The Rise of Rock 'n' Roll

<u>The Aesthetic Perspective</u>

Rock 'n' roll, in the popular mind, was born fully realized in the mid-1950s, a product of the fusion of equal parts of rhythm and blues, country, and Tin Pan Alley pop music. In reality, the evolution of these styles into rock 'n' roll was the product of a long-term process of experimentation characterized by countless hybrid mutations. Robert Palmer, *in The Rolling Stone Illustrated History of Rock & Roll* (1980), notes,

> In a very real sense, rock was implicit in the music of the first Africans brought to North America. This transplanted African music wasn't exactly boogie-woogie or jazz, but it did have several characteristics which survive in American music today. It was participatory; often a song leader would be pitted against an answering chorus, or a solo instrument against an ensemble, in call-and-response fashion. It sometimes attained remarkable polyrhythmic complexity, and always had a kind of percussive directionality or rhythmic drive. Vocal quality tended to be hoarse or grainy by European standards, though there was also considerable use of falsetto. Melodies fell within a relatively narrow range and often incorporated flexible pitch treatment around certain "blue notes." There was some improvisation, but always within the limits of more or less traditional structures.

All these characteristics are evident in quite a few rock 'n' roll records. For example, in "What'd I Say," Ray Charles calls out a lead melody while a chorus responds, and riffing horns answer his piano figures. His band's rhythm section drives relentlessly, and superimposes fancy accent patterns over the basic beat. His voice has a hoarse, straining quality, with occasional leaps into falsetto. His melody is narrow in range and blueslike, and the improvisation which occurs never threatens the continuity of the song's gospel-derived metric and harmonic structure.

One shouldn't conclude from these similarities that pure African music was somehow transformed into rock 'n' roll. Music in Africa was always flexible, ready to accommodate new influences from the next village or from foreign cultures, and in America plantation owners and preachers tried to stamp it out entirely. Accordingly, it adapted. The traits that survived without much alteration tended to be of two kinds. Some were musical imponderables like vocal quality or rhythmic drive, aspects of style so basic to the culture they were rarely considered consciously and were therefore immune to conscious change. Others--blues scales, call-and-response forms--were close enough to some varieties of European folk music to be assimilated and perpetuated by whites.

The Man-Centered Perspective

Arnold Shaw, in *The Rockin' 50s* (1974), has attempted to pin down the birth of rock 'n' roll to a specific date: If one had to pick the recording session at which rock 'n' roll was born, it would be the date on April 12, 1954 at the Pythian Temple on Manhattan's West Side at which Bill Haley and the Comets cut "Rock Around the Clock."

It is certain, however, that rock 'n' roll songs existed before Haley's record topped the charts in 1955. Some historians have singled out the Crows whose uptempo r & b recording, "Gee," scored heavily on the pop charts in early 1954. As early as 1951 Jackie Brenston—nominally fronting Ike Turner's band--hit number one with "Rocket 88," which featured a wild saxophone solo, a boogie-woogie beat carried by a fuzzed-out, overamplified electric guitar, and lyrics celebrating the automobile. Haley himself covered the song and by 1952 was recording full-fledged rockers like "Rock the Joint."

Still, the fact that remains that these, and other, rock 'n' roll prototypes appear in retrospect as oddities which made a dent upon the public consciousness and then disappeared. In contrast to these hits, "Rock Around the Clock" inspired a movement. The fact that the song framed a popular movie was no small factor in its favor; *Blackboard Jungle* caused riots among youth worldwide while the Haley recording inspired countless imitations.

Haley represented a temporary phenomenon, though; he accumulated only three Top Ten hits during his lengthy career. It wasn't until Elvis Presley achieved superstar status--first via television appearances in 1956 (on the Steve Allen, Tommy Dorsey, and Ed Sullivan shows), followed by radio, jukebox, and cinema saturation--that the commercial preminence of rock 'n' roll was assured.

Peter Guralnick, in *The Rolling Stone Illustrated History of Rock & Roll* (1980), argues that it would be easy to underestimate Presley's role in the development of the genre.

> In some ways the reaction may seem to have been out of proportion, for Elvis Presley was in retrospect merely one more link in a chain of historical inevitability. His ducktail was already familiar from Tony Curtis, the movie star whose pictures Elvis haunted at the Suzore No. 2 in Memphis; the hurt, truculent expression we had seen before in Marlon Brando's motorcycle epic, *The Wild One*. His vulnerability was mirrored by James Dean, whose first movie, *East of Eden*, was released in April 1955, just as Elvis's own career was getting under way. His eponymous sneer and the whole attitude it exemplified—not derision exactly but a kind of scornful pity, indifference, a pained acceptance of all the dreary details of square reality—was foreshadowed by Brando, John Garfield, the famous picture of Robert Mitchum after his 1948 pot bust. Even his music had its historical parallels, not just in the honky-tonk clatter of Bill Haley and his Comets but in the genuine popular success that singers like Frankie Laine and Johnnie Ray--and Al Jolson, Mildred Bailey, even Bing Crosby in an earlier era—had enjoyed in bringing back black vocal Stylings to the white marketplace.

The fact remains that Presley's astounding commercial success (fourteen consecutive million-sellers simultaneously topping the pop, country, and r & b charts following his signing with RCA) has been duplicated only by the Beatles in the post-World War II era. And this success assured rock 'n' roll of mainstream acceptance. As noted by Guralnick,

> Today, like every trend and tidal wave that comes along in our consumer oriented society, with its voracious appetite for novelty and its pitiless need to reduce what it does not understand, [Presley's] achievement has been subsumed, his art has been converted to product, and rock and roll itself has become part of the fabric of corporate America.

The truly revolutionary nature of Presley's career cannot be fully appreciated until one considers the legions of disciples that followed in his stead. Their names--Jerry Lee Lewis, Buddy Holly, Eddie Cochran, Rick Nelson, Conway Twitty, Gene Vincent, Johnny Cash, Jack Scott, Roy Orbison, Bob Luman, Frankie Avalon, Bobby Rydell, Fabian, Bobby Darin, and many others--read like a roll call of rock 'n' roll's early years. The first generation of rock 'n' roll stars unleashed a movement which Charlie Gillett, in *Making Tracks* (1974), has termed "the only revolution in the 80-year-old history of the American record industry."

The entire structure of the industry was to be overhauled in the latter half of the 1950s. Segregated audiences became a thing of the past and the artist-and-repertoire men who had dominated the first fifty years of the twentieth century gradually gave way to freelance songwriters who were close to their audience both in age and outlook. Often the artists themselves wrote and produced their own songs. Despite continued attacks by groups having a vested interest in rock 'n' roll's demise, including the older record labels (whose control of the industry had been broken by the independent companies), the American Society of Composers, Authors and Publishers (whose sales of sheet music, piano rolls, and recordings of Tin Pan Alley songs had been seriously eroded by Broadcast Music Incorporated's virtual monopoly of c & w, r & b, and rock 'n' roll material); and various defenders of the status quo (ministers, educators, parents, lunatic fringe groups, etc.), which climaxed with the congressional payola hearings in 1959-1960, the genre emerged intact if in a somewhat chastened and watered-down form. While the hits during 1959-1963 were in a decidedly softer vein than the representative output of the Beat Era (1956-1958), the ascendancy of the Brill Building brand of pop (comprised of songwriters--e.g., Carole King and Gerry Goffin, Neil Sedaka and Howard Greenfield, Barry Mann and Cynthia Weil--and artists usually still in their teens) reaffirmed that the new order was there to stay. Within a short time, even the majority of record company executives, talent managers, and concert promoters were young people.

The Socio-Economic Perspective

The prevailing mythology of rock 'n' roll's origins employs the following scenario. The recording industry was expanding in the early 1950s due to improving materials (vinyl was displacing shellac) and technology (e.g., high fidelity, the transistorization of radios). Popular music, already a major portion of that industry, encompassed a wide array of traditions already familiar to most Americans.

During the years immediately following World War II, certain pop styles (e.g., r & b, the blues, gospel) remained regional in nature. However, the ongoing migration of southern blacks to the northern urban centers in significant number since the World War I era assured the presence of radio stations and record stores across the nation catering to regional music styles. Since neither radio-dial-twiddling nor shopping around were easily censored, increasing numbers of white youth began listening to r & b, and then rock 'n' roll. Local disc jockeys, jukebox operators, record retailers, and independent record label owners noted this trend and began to promote r & b music for white listeners. The bland state of pop music in the early 1950s helped facilitate the defection of young listeners.

The post-World War II boom engendered a hitherto unequaled scale of working class and middle class affluence. Both pocket money and widely available part-time work swelled the disposable income of high schoolers and college kids. The overall effect was to create a large group of independent-minded youth, possessing relatively high spending power and increased leisure time (much higher numbers of them were now remaining in school).

The search for "novelty" sounds, a result of the competitive economic environment characterizing the record industry (most notably the attempts of independent record companies to outflank the majors), led to "cover versions" of dance blues and vocal group successes within the "race" market which were directed at the white pop audience. This practice also had its parallels regarding jazz and country material; however, the r & b market received the greatest attention due to pressure from teen listeners and the predisposition of adventurous deejays and studio producers to take artistic and economic risks. These cover versions were normally produced by "acceptable" white artists, and involved changes in musical style and the occasional cleaning up of song lyrics. While the early wave of covers invariably outsold the originals, they helped arouse interest in the latter and had the long-term effect of familiarizing white pop audiences with some of the conventions of black music styles. Ultimately, some white musicians began to specialize in a "half-way" style perhaps best exemplified by Bill Haley and the Comets' "Rock Around the Clock."

A cluster of media events coalesced at this time to shoot the Haley style--and that of smoother black r & b artists such as Chuck Berry and Fats Domino--into national prominence: (1) the popularity of the soundtrack to *Blackboard Jungle* (1954), which facilitated the rise of its opening number, "Rock Around the Clock," to the top of the pop music charts; (2) the appearances of Elvis Presley on *The Grand Ole Opry* and several high visibility TV variety programs, including *The Ed Sullivan Show*; and (3) the rise of more teen films featuring rock 'n' roll music such as *Rock, Rock, Rock* (1956), *Rock Around the Clock* (1956), and *The Girl Can't Help It* (1957).

The competitive logic of the record industry again kicked in, producing a race to imitate the initial successes and to promote the music with all the resources at hand. The independents saw their chance to compete on more equal terms with the majors since both were relatively new to the style. As no one was very sure as to how to predict who or what would be successful, many young artists were signed up to produce rock 'n' roll. Others were converted overnight, from aspiring crooners or country singers into imitation Elvises.

The resulting over-production and financial chaos ensured that this situation would not go on indefinitely. By 1958, the initial explosion of production of rock 'n' roll was over. The revolution, however, had left a lasting impression: (1) a number of indies were able to establish themselves as small majors; (2) a new generation of producers, artists, and songwriters gained a foothold within the industry; and (3) some r & b artists shared in the breakthrough, performing their own music as they would be doing anyway, but now reaching young white listeners.

Top Artists and Their Recordings

--Major White Artists

Eddie Cochran--"Sittin' in the Balcony" (1957); "Summertime Blues" (1958); "C'mon Everybody" (1958/9)

Bill Haley and the Comets--"Shake, Rattle and Roll" (1954); "Dim, Dim the Lights" (1954/5); "Mambo Rock"/"Birth of the Boogie" (1955); "Rock Around the Clock" (1955); "Razzle-Dazzle" (1955); "Burn That Candle" (1955); "See You Later, Alligator" (1956); "R-O-C-K"/ "The Saints Rock 'N Roll" (1956); "Rip It Up" (1956); "Rudy's Rock" (1956); "Skinny Minnie" (1958)

Dale Hawkins--"Susie-Q" (1957); "La-Do-Dada" (1958)

Ronnie Hawkins--"Mary Lou" (1959)

Buddy Holly (and the Crickets)--"That'll Be the Day" (1957); "Peggy Sue" (1957); "Rave On" (1958); "Early in the Morning" (1958); "It Doesn't Matter Anymore" 91959)

Brenda Lee--"One Step at a Time" (1957); "Sweet Nothin's" (1959/60); "I'm Sorry"/"That's All You Gotta Do" (1960); "I Want to Be Wanted" (1960)

Ritchie Valens--"Come On, Let's Go" (1958); "Donna"/"La Bamba" (1958/9)

Gene Vincent--"Be-Bop-A-Lula" (1956); "Lotta Lovin'"/"Wear My Ring" (1957); "Dance to the Bop" (1957/8)

--Major Black Artists

Chuck Berry--"Maybelline" (1955); "Roll Over Beethoven" (1956); "School Day" (1957); "Rock and Roll Music" (1957); "Sweet Little Sixteen" (1958); "Johnny B. Goode" (1958); "Carol" (1958); "Almost Grown" (1959); "Back in the U.S.A." (1959); "Nadine" (1964); "No Particular Place to Go" (1964); "You Never Can Tell" (1964); "My Ding-A-Ling" (1972); "Reelin' and Rockin' (1972/3)

Fats Domino--"Ain't That a Shame" (1955); I'm in Love Again" (1956); "Blueberry Hill" (1956); "Blue Monday" (1957); "I'm Walkin'" (1957)

Screamin' Jay Hawkins--"I Put a Spell on You" (1957)

Little Richard--"Tutti-Frutti" (1956); "Long Tall Sally"/"Slippin' and Slidin'" (1956); "Rip It Up" (1956); "Lucille" (1957); "Jenny, Jenny" (1957); "Keep a Knockin' (1957); "Good Golly, Miss Molly" (1958); "Ooh! My Soul" (1958)

Lloyd Price--"Just Because" (1957); "Stagger Lee" (1958/9); "Where Were You (On Our Wedding Day)?" (1959); "Personality" (1959); "I'm Gonna Get Married" (1959)

Larry Williams--"Short Fat Fannie" (1957); "Bony Maronie" (1957)

Jackie Wilson--"Reet Petite" (1957); "To Be Loved" (1958); "Lonely Teardrops" (1958/9); "That's Why" (1959); "I'll Be Satisfied" (1959); "You Better Know It" (1959); "Talk That Talk" (1959/60); "Night"/"Doggin Around" (1960); "All My Love"/"A Woman, A Lover, A Friend" (1960); "Alone at Last"/"Am I the Man" (1960); "My Empty Arms" (1961)

Table 37

Everly Brothers

The Everly Brothers were responsible for revealing the possibilities for close, two-part harmonizing as the primary focus in rock music, thereby greatly influencing later acts such as the Beatles, the Hollies, Simon and Garfunkel, the Byrds, the Turtles, and Crosby, Stills and Nash. They also pioneered the use of country influences—not only the high-lonesome vocals, but the emphasis on melody and Appalachian-styled acoustic guitar work—within a pop-rock context. Their sound remains timeless, as evidenced by the chart-topping success of Extreme's Everlys knock-off, "More Than Words" (A&M 1552) in 1991.

Don and Phil Everly—born February 1, 1937 and January 19, 1939, respectively, in Brownie, Kentucky—began singing with their parents, well-known country performers Ike and Margaret Everly, on KMA-radio, Shenandoah, Iowa, beginning in 1945. Shortly after forming as a straight country duo in 1954, the brothers signed with Columbia. Failing to achieve success, they eventually were taken on by Cadence in part due to their photogenic good looks; label owner/producer Archie Bleyer was interested at the time in breaking into the newly emerging teen market.

The debut single, "Bye Bye Love" (Cadence 1315; 1957; #2), featuring their aching vocals augmented by electric guitar flourishes and a lilting rock 'n' roll beat, was a smash hit, providing the direction for a long string of chart successes with the label, including "Wake Up Little Susie" (Cadence 1337; 1957; #1), "All I Have to Do Is Dream" (Cadence 1348; 1958; #1), "Bird Dog"/"Devoted to You" (Cadence 1350; #1/#10), "Problems" (Cadence 1355; 1958; #2), "('Til) I Kissed You" (Cadence 1369; 1959; #4), "Let It Be Me" (Cadence 1376; 1960; #7), and "When Will I Be Loved" (Cadence 1380; 1960; #8). In addition to the extraordinary musicality of the Everlys, the popularity of these discs owed much to high quality material (often composed by the husband-and-wife team of Boudleaux and Felice Bryant) and peerless Nashville studio musicians. The lovely echoed guitar work by Chet Atkins in the Bryants' "All I Have to Do Is Dream," for instance, all but guaranteed the song's success.

The duo switched labels when offered a lucrative contract by the fledging Warner Bros. in 1960. A number of the Warner releases—including the singles "Cathy's Clown" (Warner Bros. 5151; 1960; #1), "So Sad" (Warner Bros. 5163; 1960; #7), and "Walk Right Back" (Warner Bros. 5199; 1961; #7), and the albums *It's Everly Time!* (Warner Bros. 1381; 1960; #9) and *A Date with the Everly Brothers* (Warner Bros. 1395; 1960; #9)—represented their creative apex, thanks in part to more thorough, polished production work. However, the Everlys also exhibited a greater inclination to record middle-of-the-road, maudlin material during this period, most notably, "Ebony Eyes" (Warner Bros. 5199; 1961; #8), "Crying in the Rain" (Warner Bros. 5501; 1962; #6), and "That's Old Fashioned" (Warner Bros. 5273; 1962; #9).

By 1963, the Everly Brothers were finding it hard to crack the Top Forty, despite the release of many excellent recordings. Shifting their artistic focus to albums did little to help matters; the pioneering country-rock concept LP, *Roots* (Warner Bros. 1752; 1968), considered by many to be the duo's most sophisticated effort up to that time, attracted little attention. A string of further commercial failures culminated in an acrimonious split in 1973.

A decade of futile solo projects, however, spurred a reunion in 1983. A moderately successful live album, *The Everly Brothers Reunion Concert* (Passport 11001; 1984; #162), recorded September 1983 at London's Albert Hall led to several well-crafted country-pop releases with PolyGram: *EB 84* (Mercury 822431; 1984; #8)—fueled largely by the Paul McCartney-penned single, "On the Wings of a Nightingale" (Mercury; 1984; #50) and a nostalgic video which received heavy MTV rotation, *"Born Yesterday"* (Mercury 826142; 1986; #83), and *Some Hearts* (Mercury 832520; 1989). Due to increasingly marginal sales, virtually no recordings have been released by the Everlys from 1990 onward. Nevertheless, they continue to perform, regularly receive accolades as elder statesmen of rock—including induction into the Rock and Roll Hall of Fame (1986) and treatment in musicals such as *Bye Bye Love:The Everly Brothers Musical* (1998) and *Dream, Dream, Dream* (2000)—and are well represented on compact disc by a host of album reissues and anthologies, most notably on Charly in England and Rhino in the U.S.

Table 38

Little Richard, December 5, 1932-

One of the leading pioneers of early rock 'n' roll, Little Richard's frenetic singing style helped bring down the covering phenomenon, whereby the major labels assigned mainstream singers to record smoothed-over versions (often with sanitized lyrics) of original R&B hits geared to the pop charts. Although teen crooner Pat Boone garnered comparable sales with his awkward covers of two early Little Richard songs—"Tutti Frutti" (Dot 15443; 1956) and "Long Tall Sally" (Dot 15457; 1956)—his remaining hits faced no competition in crossing over to a mainstream audience.

Born Richard Wayne Penniman in Macon, Georgia, his primary musical influences as a youth were singing in the church choir and playing saxophone in his high school band. When bluesman Buster Brown's singer failed to show up at a local concert, Richard—then age fourteen—filled in. While touring with the band, he began wearing his trademark pompadour and was billed as "Little Richard" for the first time. He was working variety shows when Zenas Sears—a WGST, Atlanta, deejay—helped him get a contract with RCA. His first session on October 16, 1951 resulted in four recordings: "Every Hour" (a hit in the Georgia area due to on-the-air plugs by Sears), "Goin' to Get Rich Quick," "Taxi Blues," and "Why Did You Leave Me." He would cut four more tracks on January 12, 1952, but they failed to catch on with the public. He then recorded eight songs (with his group the Tempo Toppers) on February 25 and October 5, 1953 for the Houston-based Peacock label, again with negligible results.

Little Richard spent the next couple of years touring the southeast with his new backup band, the Upsetters. A tip from R&B singer Lloyd Price led him to send a demo tape to Specialty records in February 1955. Producer Bumps Blackwell sensed his potential for communicating the same kind of gospel-blues blend that had made Ray Charles a star. The first session produced "Tutti Frutti" (Specialty 561; 1955), which reached number two on the R&B chart (and number seventeen on the pop listing despite the Boone cover). Over the next three years, Little Richard recorded a prodigious number of hits (mostly his own compositions), including "Long Tall Sally"/ "Slippin' and Slidin' (Specialty 572; 1956; #1 R&B, #6 pop/#2 R&B), "Rip It Up"/"Reddy Teddy" (Specialty 579; 1956; #1 R&B/#8 R&B), "She's Got It"/"Heebie Jeebies" (Specialty 584; 1956; #9 R&B/#7 R&B), "The Girl Can't Help It" (Specialty 591; 1956; #7 R&B), "Lucille"/"Send Me Some Lovin'" (Specialty 598; 1957; #1 R&B/#3 R&B), "Jenny, Jenny"/"Miss Ann" (Specialty 606; 1957; #2 R&B, #10 pop/#6 R&B), "Keep A Knockin' (Specialty 611; 1957; #2 R&B, #8 pop), and "Good Golly, Miss Molly" (Specialty 624; 1958; #4 R&B, #10 pop). His popularity was reinforced by appearances in three early rock 'n' roll films: *Don't Knock the Rock*, *The Girl Can't Help It*, and *Mister Rock 'n' Roll*.

Despite his wild performing antics and gender-bending lifestyle, Little Richard felt a calling to become a preacher. By the late 1950s he was only performing religious music; however, he decided to return to rock music in 1963. Subsequent recordings for a variety of labels—including Vee-Jay, Okeh, Reprise, and Green Mountain—failed to generate more than moderate sales. By the early 1970s he was appearing in rock 'n' roll revival shows and expanding into non-musical endeavors. His critically acclaimed acting role in the 1986 motion picture, *Down & Out in Beverly Hills*, represented his most notable post-1950s artistic achievement. [White. 1984.]

Table 39

Ritchie Valens, May 13, 1941-February 3, 1959

The importance of Valens' short-lived career is largely symbolic in nature; he was the Latin recording artist to have an impact on the rock era charts. In his wake, would follow Dave "Baby" Cortez, Chris Montex, Sunny and the Sunglows, the Premiers, Cannibal and the Headhunters, and many others.

Born Richard Stephen Valenzuela in Pacoima (outside Los Angeles), California, Valens learned to play guitar guitar as a youth and formed a band, the Silhouettes, while in high school. He signed a contract with Del-Fi Records in spring 1958, and just missed the Top Forty that fall with "Come On, Let's Go" (Del-Fi 4106). He followed with a double-sided hit, "Donna"/"La Bamba" (Del-Fi 4110; 1958-1959), reaching numbers two and twenty-two, respectively, on the *Billboard Hot 100* chart. Ironically, the latter track, based on a traditional Mexican wedding song, has proven to be his most popular recording (a 1987 biopic based on his life, and featuring the music of Los Lobos, was entitled *La Bamba*).

At this point in time, Valens was in great demand as a performer, appearing on national television programs and package tours. On February 3, 1959, a small plane carrying Valens, Buddy Holly, and the Big Bopper (aka J.P. Richardson) crashed near Clear Lake, Iowa immediately following a concert. His studio recordings, which essentially fit on one compact disc, have been released in many editions since his death.

THE BRILL BUILDING ERA

Overview

Rock historians tend to view the 1959-1963 period as an interregnum linking the classic rock 'n' roll of the mid-1950s, a genre—according to popular legend—that was dominated by the likes of Elvis Presley, Little Richard, Jerry Lee Lewis, Chuck Berry, and Buddy Holly, and the vibrant British Invasion, which was to spur the American Renaissance and ultimately, the voyage of discovery that was progressive rock. The material served up by Tin Pan Alley-styled songwriters (largely based in Manhattan), combined with the controlling instincts of major label executives, cast a pall of orthodoxy on the made-to-order product lines—most notably, teen idols, novelty songs, a kaleidoscopic array of dances, girl groups, and instrumentals—geared to teen consumption. Calculated image and artiface—all wrapped in a safely bland package—was substituted for the spontaneity and edgy rebelliousness of the pioneering rockers who—at the onset of the 1960s—were either dead or out of the picture, whether pursuing other vocations (Presley, the U.S. Army; Little Richard, preaching) or in disgrace (Lewis banned from the mass media after marrying his thirteen-year-old second cousin, Berry in jail for violating the Mann Act).

In truth, however, this period as considerably more than the so-called Dark Ages of rock history. Some genuinely excellent music was produced, both nationally by the majors and regionally by smaller record companies. Although often embracing indescribably bad performers such as Fabian and Annette Funicello (hyped by *American Bandstand*, Hollywood beach flicks, and robotic DJs), teens continued by confound the cultural taste-makers by embracing unheralded gems-in-the-rough (e.g., the Hollywood Argyles' "Alley-Oop") and works of uncompromising genius (e.g., Phil Spector's Wall-of-Sound productions). A rapid succession of dynamic new styles arose—commercial folk, surf music, and soul—with important implications for the future evolution of pop music.

Furthermore, the eras serving as chronological bookends were not as musically scintillating as sometimes portrayed by revisionist historians and the media. Much of the best rockabilly, R&B, and doo-wop music of the 1950s was rarely heard on the radio or covered by the mass media, much less available in record stores. In contrast with the politically correct oldies programs of the present day—dedicated to playing the original versions of seminal hits—1950s broadcasts were dominated by the pallid covers served up by the powerful majors, particularly RCA, Columbia, Decca, Mercury, and Capitol. And many of British acts popular stateside in 1964-1965 were offering up lame rehashes of early rock 'n' roll classics. Likewise, the passage of time has obscured the proliferation of instantly disposable fluff released by the Bachelors, the Hullabaloos, and Billy J. Kramer and the Dakotas.

The Teen Idols

The teen idol phenomenon cut across the entire American popular culture spectrum, embracing the music business, television, radio, Hollywood films, comic books, fan magazines, and general merchandising tie-ins. In all of these media, the formula consisted of selling products associated with photogenic, well-mannered young people (generally ranging in age from early teens to the mid-twenties) to teenage consumers. The process had the implicit blessing of parents and other authority figures given the alternative; that American youth would fall under the influence of more rebellious cultural icons, including juvenile delinquents feared to inhabit the street corners of every 1950s town and, of course, rock 'n' roll stars.

The first wave of rock 'n' rollers had put both parents and record industry executives on the defensive. The wild performing antics of black and white musicians alike seemed to hint at a wide array of antisocial behaviors. While Elvis Presley—hep cat clothes and surly looks, notwithstanding--was soon being portrayed by the media as a likeable mama's boy, the extra-musical escapades of many rock 'n' roll artists soon confirmed the worst fears of adult moralists. Jerry Lee Lewis defiantly defended his marriage to a thirteen-year-old second cousin, and Chuck Berry was convicted of a violation of the Mann Act for transporting an under-aged girl across a state line. Even the Platters, smooth ballad interpreters, were involved in a sex and drugs scandal.

The major record companies, outflanked by smaller independent labels in signing early rock 'n' roll stars, saw an opportunity to create and promote a new musical trend in which they controlled the talent. This strategy had initially failed when calypso failed to catch on beyond a brief flurry of hits in early 1957. However, with the loss of many early rock stars due to legal problems, military service, religious convictions (Little Richard entered the seminary in 1958), fatal accidents (e.g., Buddy Holly, Ritchie Valens, the Big Bopper, Eddie Cochran), mishaps which disrupted career momentum (e.g., Gene Vincent, Carl Perkins), and the failure to find quality song material for follow-up recordings, the industry-wide push of teen idol surrogates caught on in a big way.

The ingredients of a teen idol recording included an attractive (usually white, conservatively attired, and well groomed) young media star singing simple lyrics about typically middle-class teen concerns. Given the fact that many idols couldn't really sing, the sugary pop arrangements—exhibiting a mere trace of the big beat—took on even greater importance. Many of the singers were already stars in another medium (usually TV or movies), thereby virtually assuring the success of promotional efforts on the part of the record labels. Nevertheless, stories of teen idols literally discovered on their front porches (Fabian Forte) abounded in fan publications. If the combined forces of the industry (label promotion, trade ads, and exposure on both radio playlists and *American Bandstand*) were marshalled on behalf of a young performer (no matter how lame), anything was possible. The formula consistently worked from the late 1950s up to the mid-1960s. By then, the onslaught of British Invasion artists (many of whom were cleverly market in teen idol fashion), followed by changing cultural mores, rendered the image anachronistic.

Top Artists and Their Recordings

Paul Anka--"Diana" (1957); "You Are My Destiny" (1958); "Crazy Love"/"Let the Bells Keep Ringing" (1958); "My Heart Sings" (1958/9); "Lonely Boy" (1959); "Put Your Head on My Shoulder" (1959); "It's Time to Cry" (1959/60); "Puppy Love" (1960); "My Home Town" (1960); "Summer's Gone" (1960); "The Story of My Love" (1961); "Tonight My Love, Tonight" (1961); "Dance On, Little Girl" (1961); "Love Me Warm and Tender" (1962); "A Steel Guitar and a Glass of Wine" (1962); "Eso Beso (That Kiss)" (1962)

Annette--"Tall Paul" (1959); "First Name Initial" (!959/60); "O Dio Mio" (1960); "Pineapple Princess" (1960)

Frankie Avalon--"Dede Dinah" (1958); "Ginger Bread" (1958); "I'll Wait For You" (1958); "Venus" (1959); "Bobby Sox to Stockings"/"A Boy Without a Girl" (1959); "Just Ask Your Heart" (1959); "Why" (1959/60)

Donnie Brooks--"Mission Bell" (1960)

Johnny Burnette--"Dreamin'" (1960); "You're Sixteen" (1960); "Little Boy Sad" (1961); "God, Country and My Baby" (1961)

Buzz Clifford--"Baby Sittin' Boogie" (1961)

Mike Clifford--"Close to Cathy" (1962)

Johnny Crawford--"Cindy's Birthday" (1962); "Your Nose Is Gonna Grow" (1962); "Rumors" (1962); "Proud" (1963)

James Darren--"Goodbye Cruel World" (1961); "Her Royal Majesty" (1962); "Conscience" (1962)

Shelley Fabares--"Johnny Angel" (1962)

Fabian--"Turn Me Loose" (1959); "Tiger" (1959); "Hound Dog Man"/"This Friendly World" (1959)

Hayley Mills--"Let's Get Together" (1961)

Rick Nelson--"I'm Walking"/"A Teenager's Romance" (1957); "You're My One and Only Love" (1957); "Be-Bop Baby" (1957); "Stood Up"/"Waitin' in School" (1957/8); "Believe What You Say"/"My Bucket's Got a Hole in It" (1958); "Poor Little Fool" (1958); "Lonesome Town"/"I Got a Feeling" (1958); "Never Be Anyone Else But You"/"It's Late" (1959); "Just a Little Too

Much"/"Sweeter Than You" (1959); "I Wanna Be Loved" (1959); "Young Emotions" (1960); "Travelin' Man"/"Hello Mary Lou" (1961); "A Wonder Like You"/"Everlovin'" (1961); "Young World" (1962); "Teen Age Idol" (1962); "It's Up to You" (1962/3); "Fools Rush In" (1963); "For You" (1963/4)

Paul Petersen--"She Can't Find Her Keys" (1962); "My Dad" (1962/3)

Ray Peterson--"Tell Laura I Love Her" (1960); "Corinna, Corinna" (1960/1)

Gene Pitney--"Town Without Pity" (1961/2); "(The Man Who Shot) Liberty Valence" (1962); "Only Love Can Break a Heart" (1962); "Half Heaven--Half Heartache" (1962/3); "Mecca" (1963); "Twenty-Four Hours From Tulsa" (1963); "It Hurts to Be in Love" (1964); "I'm Gonna Be Strong" (1964); "Last Chance to Turn Around" (1965); "She's a Heartbreaker" (1968)

Bobby Rydell--"Kissin' Time" (1959); "We Got Love" (1959); "Wild One"/"Little Bitty Girl" (1960); "Swingin' School"/"Ding-A-Ling" (1960); "Volare" (1960); "Sway" (1960); "Good Time Baby" (1961); "I've Got Bonnie" (1962); "I'll Never Dance Again" (1962); "The Cha-Cha-Cha" (1962); "Wildwood Days" (1963); "Forget Him" (1963/4)

Linda Scott--"I've Told Every Little Star" (1961); "Don't Bet Money Honey" (1961); "I Don't Know Why" (1961)

Bobby Vee--"Devil or Angel" (1960); Rubber Ball" (1960/1); "Take Good Care of My Baby" (1961); Run to Him (1961); "Please Don't Ask About Barbara" (1962); "Sharing You" (1962); "Punish Her" (1962); "The Night Has a Thousand Eyes" (1962/3); "Charm" (1963); "Come Back When You Grow Up" (1967)

Table 40

Christina Aguilera, December 18, 1980-

Christina Aguilera came along at the perfect time in pop music history; with pre-teens possessing more disposable income than ever before, teen idol recording stars became a hot commodity in the 1990s. Furthermore, Hispanic performers captured an increasing share of music industry revenue during this decade. Add Aguilera's striking good looks, exuberant singing style, accomplished stage skills, and a major label promotional budget, and chart success would seem to have been a foregone conclusion.

Due largely to her father's military career, Aguilera traveled widely as a youth until the family settled in Wexford, Pennsylvania. After starting out in Pittsburgh area talent shows, she appeared on the TV series *Star Search* at age eight and garnered a cast slot on *The New Mickey Mouse Club* four years later. Her recording career commenced with a hit single in Japan, "All I Wanna Do," a duet with Keizo Nakanishi. She next recorded "Reflection" for inclusion on the soundtrack of the animated feature, *Mulan* (1998).

Signing a recording contract with RCA in 1998, her debut album—*Christina Aguilera* (RCA 67690; 1999; #1)—would sell more than ten million copies over the next year, assisted by two number one singles, "Genie in a Bottle" (RCA 65692; 1999) and "What a Girl Wants" (RCA 65960; 1999). Aguilera's superstar status was affirmed by an invitation to perform at the Super Bowl XXXIII Halftime Show and a 1999 Grammy award for Best New Artist.

With import singles and albums flooding the market, two more albums were issued domestically in 2000, *Mi Reflejo* (RCA), a Spanish-language collection geared to her huge Hispanic following, and *My Kind of Christmas* (RCA). The following year she would collaborate with Lil' Kim, Mya, and Pink in the chart-topping single, "Lady Marmalade" (Twentieth Century-Fox 497 561-2; 2001; from the film soundtrack to *Moulin Rouge*), formerly a number one hit for Labelle in 1975. With her popularity remaining at a peak level through 2001, Aguilera appears likely sustain her storybook career well into adulthood.

Table 41

Frankie Avalon, 1938-

A child prodigy of the trumpet, Frankie Avalon starred on Paul Whiteman's radio and TV programs, both of which were based in the Philadelphia area in the early 1950s. By 1957, he signed with Chancellor Records as a vocalist. The label's owners, Bob Marcucci and Peter de Angelis, also took on the management of his career.

Avalon's scored his first national hit in early 1958 with a Marcucci-de Angelis composition, "Dede Dinah" (Chancellor 1011). A prime exponent of the teen idol school, he enjoyed five Top Ten hits the following year, including three million sellers—"Venus" (Chancellor 1031), "Just Ask Your Heart" (Chancellor 1040), and "Why" (Chancellor 1045).

Although his recordings were less successful in the early 1960s, Avalon became a major Hollywood film star. His acting credits included *Guns of the Timberland* (1960), *The Carpetbaggers* (1962), and a string of beach party movies produced by American International Pictures. From the 1960s to the 1990s, he divided his time between television and film acting—most notably, *Grease* (1978) and *Back to the Beach* (1987), club appearances, and occasional recording sessions. A disco version of his number one hit, "Venus" (De-Lite 1578), was his last charting single. By the late 1970s, he became increasingly active performing on the rock and roll revival circuit. [Stambler, 1989]

Table 42

Pat Boone, June 1, 1934-

Pat Boone was the most successful of the teen idols; only Rick Nelson came close to his thirty-eight Top Forty hits. His accomplishments are tainted, however, because many of his early hits were cleaned-up cover versions that outsold the aesthetically superior originals, including Fats Domino's "Ain't That a Shame, the El Dorados' "At My Front Door," Little Richard's "Tutti Frutti" and Long Tall Sally," Ivory Joe Hunter's "I Almost Lost My Mind," Joe Turner's "Chains of Love," and the Five Keys' "Gee Whittakers!"

Allegedly a direct descendant of frontier legend Daniel Boone, he lettered a three sports and served as student body president while attending high school in Nashville. Marrying country & western star Red Foley's daughter, Shirley, he attended David Lipscomb College in Nashville before transferring to North Texas State. While there he won a local talent show, which led to an appearance on Ted Mack's program and then a one-year stint on Arthur Godfrey's amateur hour.

In the mid-1950s Boone recorded a number of modestly successful singles for Nashville's Republic Records. He recording of "Two Hearts" (Dot 15338; 1955) was the first of fifty-nine charting singles (through late 1966) for that label. His number one hits included "Ain't That a Shame" (Dot 15377; 1955), "I Almost Lost My Mind" (Dot 15472; 1956), "Don't Forbid Me" (15521; 1956-1957), "Love Letters in the Sand" (Dot 15570; 1957), "April Love" (Dot 15660; 1957), and "Moody River" (Dot 16209; 1961). During the late 1950s, he was arguably surpassed only by Elvis Presley as a pop culture hero. He starred in fifteen films, most notably *Bernadine* (1957), *April Love* (1957), and *State Fair* (1962). In addition, he had his own television series, *The Pat Boone-Chevy Showroom* (ABC) from 1957-1960.

When the hits stopped coming, Boone continued recording for various labels, including Tetragrammaton and Curb. He continued to write books dispensing advice, including *Pray to Win* (1981) and the teen-oriented *Twixt Twelve and Twenty*, *Between You, Me and the Gatepost*, and *The Care and Feeding of Parents*. Since 1983 he has hosted a contemporary Christian radio show heard nationwide on approximately 200 stations. In addition to appearing on many TV programs, he has starred in a number of stage productions (e.g., *The Will Rogers Follies* in Branson, Missouri). [Romanowski and George-Warren. 1995]

Table 43

Brenda Lee, December 11, 1944-

Known as "Little Miss Dynamite," Brenda Lee—along with the more middle-of-the-road oriented Connie Francis—was the dominant female star during the early rock 'n' roll era. Her powerful, worldly-wise voice, capable of negotiating rave-up rockers as well as tender voice, seemed incongruous with her youth.

Born Brenda Mae Tarpley in Atlanta, she began singing by age seven on local radio and television programs. When her father died a year later, her income helped support the family. Her big break came when she met Red Foley's manager, Dub Albritten, in 1956. He booked her on Foley's shows, which led to national TV appearances. On July 30 of that year she recorded "Rockin' Around the Christmas Tree" (Decca 30776) with producer Owen Bradley in Nashville; it became her first hit. Tours of both the U.S. and Europe followed; to satisfy French promoters, who's thought she was an adult, Albritten started the rumor that she was a thirty-two-year-old midget.

With the release of "Sweet Nothin's" (Decca 30967; 1959; #4), Lee enjoyed a string of hits that ran through the 1960s, including "I'm Sorry"/"That's All You Gotta Do" (Decca 31093; 1960; #s 1/6), ""I Want To Be Wanted" (Decca 31149; 1960; #1), "Emotions" (Decca 31195; 1960-1961; #7), "You Can Depend On Me" (Decca 31195; 1961; #6), "Dum Dum" (Decca 31272; 1961; #4), "Fool #1" (Decca 31309; 1961; #3), "Break It To Me Gently" (Decca 31348; 1962; #4), ""Everybody Loves Me But You" (Decca 31379; 1962; #6), "All Alone Am I" (Decca 31424; 1962; #3), and "Losing You" (Decca 31478; 1963; #6). By the time she was twenty-one she had recorded 256 tracks for Decca. Recognizing that her style ran counter to pop tastes at the time, she shifted her emphasis to the country music business in the early 1970s. In addition to chart success—Top Ten recordings included "Nobody Wins" (MCA 40003; 1973), "Sunday Sunrise" (MCA 40107; 1973), "Wrong Ideas" (MCA 40171; 1974), "Big Four Poster Bed" (MCA 40262; 1974), "Rock On Baby" (MCA 40318; 1974), "He's My Rock" (MCA 40385; 1975), "Tell Me What It's Like" (MCA 41130; 1979), "The Cowgirl and the Dandy" (MCA 41187; 1980), and "Broken Trust" (MCA 41322; 1980)—she did a syndicated interview program based in Nashville and had occasional acting roles (e.g., Smokey and the Bandit 2).

With lifetime record sales estimated to have exceeded 100 million, Lee has won many honors including the National Academy of Recording Arts and Sciences Governors Award.

Table 44

The Monkees

The Monkees were a manufactured group—a revolutionary concept at the time—created by Columbia Pictures producers. Their concept consisted of a television sitcom based on the adventures of a rock band. While the extraordinary success enjoyed by both the NBC-TV show between 1966-1969 and Monkees' recordings validated the prefab notion (and laid the groundwork for the bubblegum genre), the later problems ensuing from the independent thinking of band members led to the creation of cartoon rock stars and recordings cut by anonymous studio musicians for imaginary acts.

Despite the fact that the foursome comprising the Monkees had a reasonable amount of experience as musicians—although Mickey Dolenz had been a child actor, Peter Tork had been part of the 1960s Greenwich Village folk scene, Mike Nesmith was performing in Los Angeles folk clubs, and David Jones had sung in London musicals and television programs—their label insisted that session players provide the instrumental backing on the first couple of albums, *The Monkees* (Colgems 101; 1966; #1) and *More of the Monkees* (Colgems 102; 1967; #1). When the band, with Nesmith as spokesperson, rebelled against this policy, Colgems ceded them full musical control. Although lacking the polish of its predecessors, the first LP under the new arrangement, *Headquarters* (Colgems 103; 1967; #1), enjoyable a comparable chart run.

The later albums—*Pisces, Aquarius, Capriosrn & Jones Ltd.* (Colgems 104; 1967; #1), *The Birds, the Bees & the Monkees* (Colgems 109; 1968; #3), the movie soundtrack, *Head* (Colgems 5008; 1968; #45), *Instant Replay* (Colgems 113; 1969; #32), *The Monkees Present* (Colgems 117; 1969; #100), and *Changes* (Colgems 119; 1970)—featured musical experimentation and songwriting contributions by band members. Tork departed in 1968 due to musical differences, and when NBC dropped the show and record sales slowed to a trickle the following year, the Monkees disbanded. While the Nesmith found success both a solo recording artist and in the production of conceptual videos (*Michael Nesmith in Elephant Parts* won the 1981 Grammy for video of the year), Dolenz and Jones—whose acting careers had lost momentum—formed a marginally popular Monkees revival band in the mid-1970s called (for legal reasons) Dolenz, Jones, Boyce and Hart.

In the mid-1980s, a resurgence of interest in the band due to cable TV reruns of the NBC episodes inpired Dolenz, Jones, and Tork to re-form the Monkees. In addition to issuing CD editions of the original albums (six of which made the charts in 1986), Rhino began releasing new material by the band, including *Pool It!* (Rhino 70706; 1987; #72) and *20th Anniversary Concert Tour 1986* (Rhino; 1987). The revival gained momentum in the new decade, with Nesmith coming aboard for the LP, *Justus* (Rhino; 1996), which coincided with Rhino's release of the TV show episodes in a twenty-one volume video anthology. In 2000, VH1 broadcast a made-for-TV film of their career, *Daydream Believer*.

Table 45

'N Sync

"N Sync represents the late 1990s variant of the bubblegum supergroup. Like their antecedents—the Monkees, the Partridge Family, the New Kids on the Block, the Spice Girls, and the Backstreet Boys—'N Sync has combined slick record production values with intensive multi-media marketing and promotion.

Two members of the group—JC Chasez and Justin Timberlake—worked together on the Disney Channel's *The Mickey Mouse Club*. Both temporarily relocated to Nashville, where they pursued solo careers while sharing the same vocal coach and songwriters. When things failed to click, Timberlake hooked up with Joey Fatone and Chris Kirkpatrick back in Orlando; they contacted Chasez, who agreed to join the proposed band in 1996. James Lance Bass was recruited later to fill out the lineup.

Their debut album, *'N Sync*, originally released in Germany on BMG Ariola Munich, became hugely popular across Europe, largely on the strength of two hit singles, "I Want You Back: (RCA 65348; 1997) and "Tearing Up My Heart" (RCA; 1997). Released in the U.S. on RCA (#67613) in spring 1998, and promoted by a nationwide tour of roller rinks, the LP duplicated its overseas success. Intended to capitalize on their career momentum, *Home for Christmas* (RCA; 1998) was issued later that same year. The third album, *No Strings Attached* (Jive 41702), parlayed a buoyant pop sound to exceed even the most optimistic expectations, selling almost two-and-a-half million copies during its first week of release in spring 2000 and lingering for months in the Top Ten pop charts. A DVD concert (also available in the videotape configuration), *Live at Madison Square Garden* (Jive 41739), was issued in December 2000. The next LP, *Celebrity* (Jive 41758; 2001) reinforce their hold on Adult Contemporary, dance, and Top Forty playlists.

Dance Crazes

Rock 'n' roll originated as a populist form of dance music. And while its elastic framework encompasses many genres which place little emphasis on a pronounced dance beat (e.g., ambient, avant garde), various dance forms have always figured prominently in rock history. With the possible exception of the disco era, greater attention was paid to this component in the early 1960s than at any time since the ascendancy of Elvis Presley.

Media coverage of the initial wave of rockabilly, r & b, and classic rock 'n' roll in the mid-1950s tended to focus on the musical and live performing attributes of major stars such as Presley, Little Richard, Chuck Berry, Bill Haley, Jerry Lee Lewis, and Buddy Holly. The sheer theatrical virtuousity of these artists rendered discussion of other rock industry phenomena to a secondary level. Nevertheless, these years were marked by a number of important dance-related developments. The lindy hop, a 1950s variation of popular swing era steps, was popularized by the TV program, *American Bandstand*, which shifted from a Philadelphia- based market to national syndication in 1957. Elevating a number of talented local teen dancers to the status of regular cast members, host Dick Clark also provided an outlet for exposing new dances to young viewers across the nation. With Bobby Freeman ("Do You Wanna Dance"; a Beach Boy cover version also made the Top Ten charts) Danny and the Juniors ("At the Hop"), and other artists extolling the virtues of dancing in general, individual steps such as the stroll were able to achieve maximum saturation through this venue.

Motivated by a desire to maintain higher viewer ratings and exploit his other music business interests, Clark was constantly on the lookout for new trends. When an obscure b-side of a Hank Ballard single, "The Twist," became associated with an emerging new dance, Clark encouraged local Philadelphia label, Cameo/Parkway, to issue their own version of the song. A new singer, Chubby Checker, with only one minor hit to his credit up to that time ("The Class"; 1959), was tapped to cut the song. Released in the summer of 1960, "The Twist" zoomed up to the top of the singles chart. The dance's simplicity--almost anyone not possessing a lower back ailment could do it in convincing fashion--caused it to catch on not only with teens but adults as well. By late 1961, the jet set crowds were photographed dancing the twist at New York's famed Peppermint Lounge. Countless twist songs were recorded, many of them entering the bestselling charts.

Even before the fad had run its course, record companies began issuing recordings featuring new (or revived) dances. *American Bandstand* and other media outlets rush to promote these releases, thereby ensuing a steady succession of fresh dance sensations. Cameo/Parkway--led by Checker himself, Bobby Rydell, Dee Dee Sharp, the Orlons, and the Dovells--was most directly associated with the dance craze movement. However, the phenomenon cut across the entire pop music industry. Across the Atlantic, British beat bands such as the Beatles ("Twist and Shout") and the Swinging Blue Jeans ("Hippy Hippy Shake") found it expedient to cut dance material. Although new dances continued to appear in pop recordings throughout the 1960s, the movement's momentum was severely disrupted by the British Invasion, followed by American Renaissance counter-trends, including soul, folk rock, and assorted West Coast styles. By the mid-1960s dance music had gone underground, predominantly to the discotheques. When it re-entered the American popular music mainstream as disco in the early 1970s (the rise of the hustle, the bump, and the freak, notwithstanding), dancing tended be more of a generic, free-form affair.

Top Artists and Their Recordings

Steve Alaimo--"Mashed Potatoes" (1962)

The Applejacks--"Mexican Hat Rock" (1958); "Rocka-Conga" (1958/59); "Bunny Hop" (1959)

Hank Ballard and the Midnighters--"The Twist" (1959; 1960); "Finger Poppin' Time" (1960); "The Hoochi Coochi Coo" (1960/1); "The Continental Walk" (1961); "The Switch-A-Roo"/"The Float" (1961); "Do You Know How to Twist" (1962)

Ray Barretto--"El Watusi" (1963)

The Beatles--"Twist and Shout" (1964)

Archie Bell and the Drells--"Do the Choo Choo" (1968)

Bill Black's Combo--"Twist-Her" (1962); "Twistin'-White Silver Sands" (1962); "Monkey-Shine" (1963)

Gary "U.S." Bonds--"Dear Lady Twist" (1962); "Twist, Twist Senora" (1962)

Al Brown's Tunetoppers--"The Madison" (1960)

James Brown--"Mashed Potatoes U.S.A." (1962); "The Popcorn" (1969)

Dave Brubeck Quartet--"Bossa Nova U.S.A." (1963)

Ray Bryant Combo--"Madison Time" (1960)

Cannibal and the Headhunters--"Land of 1000 Dances" (1965)

The Capitols--"Cool Jerk" (1966)

Chubby Checker--"The Twist" (1960; 1961/62); "The Hucklebuck" (1960); "Pony Time" (1961); "Dance the Mess Around" (1961); "Let's Twist Again" (1961); "The Fly" (1961); "Twistin' U.S.A." (1961); ""Slow Twistin'" (1962); "La Paloma Twist" (1962); "Dancin' Party" (1962); "Limbo Rock" (1962); "Popeye the Hitchhiker" (1962); "Let's Limbo Some More" (1963); 'Birdland" (1963); "Twist It Up" (1963); "She Wants T' Swim" (1964); "Let's Do the Freddie" (1965); "Hey You! Little Boo-Ga-Loo" (1966)

The Contours--"Can You Jerk Like Me" (1964/5)

Sam Cooke--"Twistin' the Night Away" (1962)

Don Covay--"The Popeye Waddle" (1962/3)

Danny and the Juniors--"Twistin' U.S.A." (1960); "Twistin' All Night Long" (1962)

The Dells--"(Bossa Nova) Bird" (1962)

The Diamonds--"The Stroll" (1958)

The Dovells--"Bristol Stomp" (1961); "Do the New Continental" (1962); "Bristol Twistin' Annie" (1962); "Hully Gully Baby" (1962); "The Jitterbug" (1962); "Stop Monkeyin' Aroun'" (1963)

Fantastic Johnny C--"Boogaloo Down Broadway" (1967)

Freddie and the Dreamers--"Do the Freddie" (1965)

Bobby Freeman--"(I Do the) Shimmy Shimmy" (1960); "The Mess Around" (!961); "C'mon and Swim" (1964); "S-W-I-M" (1964)

Ernie Freeman--"The Twist" (1962)

The Goodtimers--"Pony Time" (1961)

The Isley Brothers--"Twist and Shout" (1962); "Twistin' With Linda" (1962)

Ernie K-Doe--"Popeye Joe" (1962)

Nat Kendrick and the Swans--"(Do the) Mashed Potatoes (Part 1)" (1960)

Chris Kenner--"Land of 1000 Dances" (1963)

King Curtis--"Do the Monkey" (1963)

Major Lance--"The Monkey Time" (1963)

The Larks--"The Jerk" (1964/5)

Little Eva--"The Loco-Motion" (1962); "Let's Turkey Trot" (1963); "Old Smokey Locomotion" (1963)

Herbie Mann--"Philly Dog" (1966)

The Mar-Keys--"Pop-Eye Stroll" (1962); "Philly Dog" (1966)

The Marvelettes--"Twistin' Postman" (1962)

The Miracles--"Mickey's Monkey" (1963); "Come On Do the Jerk" (1964/5)

The Olympics--"(Baby) Hully Gully" (1960); "Shimmy Like Kate" (1960); "The Bounce" (1963); "Baby, Do the Philly Dog" (1966)

The Orlons--"The Wah Watusi" (1962); "Shimmy Shimmy" (1964)

The Pastel Six--"Cinnamin Cinder (It's a Very Nice Dance)" (1963)

Bobby "Boris" Pickett--"Monster Mash" (1962)

Wilson Pickett--"Land of 1000 Dances" (1966); "Funky Broadway" (1967)

Elvis Presley--"Bossa Nova Baby" (1963); "Do the Clam" (1965)

The Rollers--"The Continental Walk" (1961)

Bobby Rydell--"The Cha-Cha-Cha" (1962)

Santo and Johnny--"Twistin' Bells" (1960)

Dee Dee Sharp--"Mashed Potato Time" (1962); "Gravy (For My Mashed Potatoes)" (1962); "Ride!" (1962); "Do the Bird" (1963)

The Sherrys--"Pop Pop Pop-Pie" (1962)

Huey "Piano" Smith and the Clowns--"Pop-Eye" (1962)

Jimmy Soul--"Twistin' Matilda" (1962)

Rufus Thomas--"The Dog" (1963); "Walking the Dog" (1963); "Can Your Monkey Do the Dog" (1964); "Somebody Stole My Dog (1964); "Do the Funky Chicken" (1970); "(Do the) Push and Pull, Part 1" (1970); "Do the Funky Penguin" (1971)

The Vibrations--"The Watusi" (1961)

Junior Walker and the All Stars--"Do the Boomerang" (1965)

Table 46

Chubby Checker, 1941-

A native of South Carolina, Ernest Evans grew up in Philadelphia performing for classmates along with friends such as future teen idol Fabian Forte. The owner of the meat market, where Evans worked after school, arranged a private recording session with *American Bandstand* host, Dick Clark. As Evans completed a Fats Domino imitation, Clark's wife asked him his name. When he indcated "my friends call me Chubby," she playfully responded, "Like in Checker?" That episode of humorous word play inspired Evans' professional name.

The resulting Christmas novelty, "The Class" (which featured impressions of popular singers by Checker), attracted the attention of the Cameo-Parkway label, which decided to release the record commercially (Parkway 804; 1959). His breakthrough came when Clark advised Cameo-Parkway to record "The Twist," a dance number written by r & b singer Hank Ballard and released as the B-side of "Teardrops on Your Letter" (King 5171; 1959), by Ballard and his group, The Midnighters. Checker sang his parts over an already-recorded instrumental track; released June 1959 (Parkway 811; 1960), the record took nearly fourteen months to reach the charts. Checker's nonstop itinerary of interviews, TV dates, and live appearances (he is said to have lost thirty pounds during one three-week stretch of demonstrating the Twist) ultimately paid off, however, when the single reached top of the *Billboard Hot 100* in September 1960.

The Twist phenomenon inspired a rapid succession of additional dance fads. Due to his close relationship with Clark and a savvy record label, Checker was well positioned to continue as the King of Dance King. His dance hits included "The Hucklebuck" (Parkway 813; 1960), "Pony Time" (Parkway 818; 1961), ""Dance the Mess Around" (Parkway 822; 1961), "Let's Twist Again" (Parkway 824; 1961), "The Fly" (Parkway 830; 1961), "Slow Twistin'" (Parkway 835; 1962), "Limbo Rock"/"Popeye the Hitchhiker" (Parkway 849; 1962), "Let's Limbo Some More" (Parkway 862; 1963), "Birdland" (Parkway 873; 1963), and "Twist It Up" (Parkway 879; 1963).

When the dance craze subsided, Checker managed to record additional hits, most notably "Loddy Lo"/"Hooka Tooka" (Parkway 890; 1963) and "Hey, Bobba Needle" (Parkway 907). However, his popularity was ultimately eclipsed by the British Invasion and American Renaissance styles such as surf music, soul, and folk-rock. Checker has continued to perform extensively, occasionally attempting large-scale comebacks. [Gilbert and Theroux. 1982.]

Rock Instrumentals

Rock instrumentals--as opposed to pop instrumentals such as Percy Faith's number one hit, "A Summer Place," Bert Kaempfert's "Wonderland By Night," Mr. Acker Bilk's "Stranger on the Shore," and Bent Fabric's "Alley Cat"--employ rock-based styles built around one or more of the following features: a simple riff, a catchy melody, some form of electronic gimmickry. (The Surfaris' 1963 surf classic, "Wipe Out," utilized all of the above; i.e., the driving rhythmic motif on the tom-toms, the lead guitar line, and manic song title announcement at the outset of the record.) While instrumentals have generally been viewed by rock critics as a category of novelty material which has had little impact on rock history, the genre did enjoy a brief run as a seminal style in the early 1960s. Rock instrumentals were originally performed by r & b dance outfits in vogue throughout the 1950s. Usually featuring either organists (e.g., Dave "Baby" Cortez), honky-tonk pianists (e.g., Bill Doggett), or saxophonists (e.g., Lee Allen, King Curtis), these bands enjoyed a regional reputation, trying out new dances and musical ideas in front of intensely loyal audiences. The lack of a vocalizing frontman arose out of the desire of most bands to engage in uninhibited jams combined with their audiences' preoccupation with drinking and dancing.

By the late 1950s instrumental combos were entering the national singles chart with increasing regularity. The Champs' five-week stay at number one with "Tequila" in the spring of 1958 was particularly hard to ignore. And while that group was unable to sustain a run of hit recordings, Duane Eddy, who pioneered a twangy, bass-heavy guitar style, and Elvis Presley's original bassist, Bill Black, were able to achieve a measure of chart longevity. Other rock instrumentalists scoring high on the charts included Link Wray, easily the most technically proficient guitarist of that era; Johnny and the Hurricanes, known for rock arrangements of old standards (e.g., "Red River Rock" was an adaptation of "Red River Valley"); Cozy Cole, a veteran drummer possessing a swing style; Sandy Nelson, a young percussionist who employ a straightforward rock 'n' roll style; Santo and Johnny, a Canadian duo whose sound was built around an Hawaiian steel guitar; and Lonnie Mack, most famous for his reinterpretation of Chuck Berry's "Memphis" sans lyrics.

These--and other--instrumentalists found success because they offered an exciting alternative to the watered down material provided by teen idols and middle-of-the-road pop stylists. Due to the preponderance of local bands playing instrumental music devoid of any impulse to imitate national fads, record companies could tap an unlimited reservoir of fresh talent in their efforts to market this genre. Demand was further enhanced by the radio deejays' practice of using instrumentals to lead into news segments; this meant that at least two of these songs were likely to be played each hour.

The release of the Ventures' "Walk--Don't Run" in the summer of 1960 proved to be a watershed event in rock instrumental annals. The Seattle-based quartet became the most successful instrumental act during the rock era. Featuring polished arrangements and technically precise playing, the band inspired an entire generation of young guitarists. The Ventures' albums outsold their singles, finding a market in Europe and Japan as well. The group even released songbooks with play-along discs to assist budding musicians.

The surfing craze infused new energy into the genre during the 1962-1964 period, supplying a succession of classic songs (e.g., "Pipeline," "Penetration," "Let's Go Trippin'") and new groups, including Dick Dale and the Deltones, The Chantays, the Pyramids, and the Marketts. However, by this time the glory days of rock instrumentals were already numbered due to competition from newly emerging styles such as soul music, the girl groups, and the dance crazes. The British Invasion provided the final blow in largely displacing American recordings on radio playlists.

Top Artists and Their Recordings

Bill Black's Combo--"Smokie--Part 2," (1959/60); "White Silver Sands" (1960); "Josephine" (1960); "Don't Be Cruel" (1960); "Blue Tango" (1960); "Hearts of Stone" (1961); "Ole Buttermilk Sky" (1961); "Movin'"/"Honky Train" (1961); "Twist-Her" (1961/2); "Twistin'-White Silver Sands" (1962); "So What" (1962; 1965); "Do It--Rat Now" (1963); "Monkey-Shine" (1963); "Comin' On" (1964); "Tequila" (1964); "Little Queenie" (1964); "Turn on Your Love Light" (1968)

Booker T. and the M.G.'s--"Green Onions" (1962); "Jellybread" (1962/3); "Chinese Checkers" (1963); "Mo-Onions" (1964); "Soul Dressing" (1964); "Boot-Leg" (1965); "My Sweet Potato" (1966); "Hip Hug-Her" (1967); "Groovin'"/"Slim Jenkin's Place" (1967); "Soul-Limbo" (1968); "Hang 'Em High" (1968/9); "Time Is Tight" (1969); "Mrs. Robinson" (1969); "Slum Baby" (1969); "Something" (1970); "Melting Pot" (1971)

James Brown (and the JBs)--"Night Train" (1962); "Every Beat of My Heart" (1963); "Try Me" (1965)

Ace Cannon--"Tuff" (1961/2); "Blues (Stay Away From Me)" (1962); "Sugar Blues" (1962); "Cottonfields" (1963); "Searchin'" (1963)

The Champs--"Tequila" (1958); "El Rancho Rock"/"Midnighter" (1958); "Chariot Rock" (1958); "Too Much Tequila" (1960); "Tequila Twist"/"Limbo Rock" (1962); "Limbo Dance" (1962)

Cozy Cole--"Topsy, Part II" (1958); "Topsy, Part I" (1958); "Turvy, Part II" (1958)

Duane Eddy--"Movin' N' Groovin'" (1958); "Rebel-'Rouser" (1958); "Ramrod" (1958); "Cannonball" (1958); "The Lonely One" (1959); "Yep!" (1959); "Forty Miles of Bad Road" (1959); "The Quiet Three" (1959); "Some Kind-A Earthquake" (1959); "First Love, First Tears" (1959); Bonnie Came Back" (1959/60); "Shazam!" (1960); "Because They're Young" (1960); "Kommotion" (1960); "Peter Gunn" (1960); "Pepe" (1960/1); "Theme From Dixie" (1961); "Ring of Fire" (1961); "Drivin' Home" (1961); "My Blue Heaven" (1961); "Deep in the Heart of Texas" (1962); "The Ballad of Paladin" (1962); "(Dance With the) Guitar Man" (1962); "Boss Guitar" (1963); "Lonely Boy, Lonely Guitar" (1963); "Your Baby's Gone Surfin'" (1963); "The Son of Rebel Rouser" (1964)

Jorgen Ingmann--"Apache" (1961); "Anna" (1961)

Johnny and the Hurricanes--"Crossfire" (1959); "Red River Rock" (1959); "Reveille Rock" (1959); "Beatnik Fly" (1960); "Down Yonder" (1960); "Rocking Goose" (1960); "Revival" (1960); "You Are My Sunshine" (1960); "Ja-Da" (1961)

Lonnie Mack--"Memphis" (1963); "Wham!" (1963); *The Wham of That Memphis Man!* (1964); "Honky Tonky '65" (1965)

The Marketts—"Balboa Blue" (1962); "Surfer's Stom[" (1962); "Out of Limits" (1963/4); "Vanishing Point" (1964); "Batman Theme" (1966)

The Mar-Keys--"Last Night" (1961); "Morning After" (1961); "Pop-Eye Stroll" (1962); "Philly Dog" (1966)

Sandy Nelson--"Teen Beat" (1959); "Let There Be Drums" (1961); "Drums Are My Beat"/"The Birth of the Beat" (1962); "Drummin' Up a Storm"/"Drum Stomp" (1962); "All Night Long" (1962); "And Then There Were Drums" (1962); "Teen Beat '65" (1964)

Rock-A-Teens--"Woo-Hoo" (1959)

Santo and Johnny--"Sleep Walk" (1959); "Tear Drop" (1959); "Caravan" (1960); "Twistin' Bells" (1960); "Hop Scotch" (1961); "I'll Remember (In the Still of the Night)" (1964)

The Ventures--"Walk--Don't Run" (1960); "Perfidia" (1960); "Ram-Bunk-Shush (1961); "Lullaby of the Leaves" (1961); "(Theme From) Silver City" (1961); "Blue Moon" (1961); "Lolita Ya-Ya" (1962); "The 2,000 Pound Bee, Part 2" (1962/3); "Walk--Don't Run '64" (1964); "Slaughter on Tenth Avenue" (1964); "Diamond Head" (1965); "Secret Agent Man" (1966); "Hawaii Five-O" (1969); "Theme From "A Summer Place" (1969)

The Village Stompers--"Washington Squarc" (1963); "From Russia With Love" (1964); "Fiddler on the Roof" (1964)

The Virtues--"Guitar Boogie Shuffle" (1959); Guitar Boogie Shuffle Twist" (1962)

The Viscounts--"Harlem Nocturne" (1959/60; 1965); "Night Train" (1960); "Wabash Blues" (1960/1)

Link Wray, and His Ray Men--"Rumble" (1958); "Raw-Hide" (1959); "Jack the Ripper" (1963); "Red Hot" (1977)

Table 47

The Ventures

The most successful American instrumental group during the rock era, the Ventures led the way in establishing the guitar-based sound dominating popular music from 1960 onwards. Their distinctive sound—pulsing drums and metallic, twanging guitars—spanned a wide range of material (e.g., calypso, blues, Latin, psychedelia, folk rock, Merseybeat), surviving many changes in public taste. Many genres—most notably, surf music, the British Invasion, power pop, and alternative rock—have been influenced by the band.

Based in Seattle, the Ventures' first release, "Walk Don't Run" (Dolton 25), reached number two on the pop charts in August 1960. They had fourteen hits in all during the 1960s, including the Top Ten recordings "Walk Don't Run '64" (Dolton 96; 1964) and "Hawaii Five-O" (Liberty 56068; 1969). In 1965, the band issued one of the most popular instructional records ever, *Play Guitar with the Ventures* (Dolton 16501). The Ventures—which included founding members Bob Bogle (guitar, bass) and Don Wilson (guitar)—continued to tour extensively into the 21st century, long after the hits stopped coming. [Romanowski and George-Warren. 1995]

Novelty Songs

Novelty songs have always been a fixture on the popular music charts--and they probably always will be. Acoustic era recording artists such as monologist Cal Stewart and singer Billy Murray built lasting careers around the release of a steady stream of comedy material. Spike Jones raised musical cacaphony to new heights in the 1940s while helping the nation to cope with the tensions brought on by World War II. Weird Al Yankovic's satirical parodies of hit records from the 1980s and 1990s have kept the genre fresh up to the present day.

Novelty material, however, seems have been released with much greater frequency, and gone to achieve much greater commercial success, during the interregnum spanning the decline of classic rock 'n' roll in the late 1950s up through the eve of the British Invasion. The popularity of the genre during this period probably owes much to the dearth of first-rate mainstream pop material being issued. Nevertheless, the "genius factor" cannot be entirely discounted here; that is, certain individuals, by means of sheer talent, imposed their own stamp upon the era, irrespective of other existing trends or market conditions.

Bill Buchanan and Dickie Goodman were two such geniuses, albeit with a predisposition towards artistic dementia. In late summer of 1956, the duo hit upon the idea of splicing brief snippets of then current pop hits into a rather formless narrative which simulated onsite reporting of an alien visitation along the lines of Orson Welles' 1938 radio broadcast of H.G. Wells' *The War of the*

Worlds. "The Flying Saucer (Parts 1 & 2)"--accented by recognizable cameos by the likes of Fats Domino, Little Richard, the Platters, and many others--was immediately beseiged by a host of lawsuits relating to copyright infringement as it raced up the charts, eventually peaking at number three. It quickly became apparent to the music business, however, that "The Flying Saucer" had stimulated a renewed interest in the songs it had appropriated as sound bites, prompting *Billboard* to note, "Several publishers are [now] piqued at not being included on the disk." Thus exonerated, the twosome proceeded to satirize their predicament in "Buchanan and Goodman on Trial" (1956). By the following year, however, with the release of "Flying Saucer the 2nd" and "Santa & the Satellite (Parts 1 & 2)"--as well as the appearance of copycats (e.g., George and Louis' "The Return of Jerry Lee"; 1958)--the formula had worn thin. Buchanan worked briefly with Bob Ancell, achieving modest success with a spoof of B-grade horror/fantasy flicks, "The Creature (Parts 1 & 2)," in late 1957. Goodman continued to mine the musical "cut-in" subgenre throughout the 1960s and 1970s, although only enjoying one major hit, the million-selling "Mr. Jaws" (#4; 1975).

The speeded-up voice technique and sci-fi thematic material continued to provide inspiration in 1958, most notably in John Zacherle's "Dinner with Drac," David Seville's "The Witch Doctor," and Sheb Wooley's "The Purple People Eater." The latter songs spent many weeks in the number one position, inspiring a lifelong commitment to the novelty genre on the part of Seville and Wooley (the former, whose real name was Ross Bagdasarian, enjoyed a long string of hits as creator of the Chipmunks, while Wooley, employing the nom d'plume Ben Colder, satirized a steady succession of 1960s pop hits a la Weird Al Yankovic).

Answer songs--that is, the practice of recording a tune which either directly answered a question posed by an earlier hit or acted as a sequel (thereby capitalizing on the popularity of the original)--almost rivaled the balance of the novelty genre's output. Two rock music scholars, Dr. B. Lee Cooper and Fred Haney, have thus far produced two substantial monographs devoted entirely to this phenomenon. Two of the more popular examples of the genre have been Jeanne Black's "He'll Have to Stay" (a response to Jim Reeves' big 1959 hit, "He'll Have to Go") and Shep and the Limelites' "Daddy's Home" (1961). The latter song took the formula far beyond the follow-up stage in that it represented an ongoing installment of a series of love songs composed by James Sheppard, first as the leader of the doo-wop group, The Heartbeats (who started the cycle with "A Thousand Miles Away" in 1956), and then later as the ad of the Limelites.

By the dawn of the 1960s, song parodies had become the leading form of novelty recording. Three different versions of the song immortalizing the comic strip character, Alley Oop, reached the Top 40 in the summer of 1960; the Hollywood Argyles rendition went all the way to number one. Jimmy Dean's huge hit, "Big Bad John" (#1; 1961), inspired at least five send-ups, including Phil McLean's "Small Sad Sam" (1962). Ron Dante, later the voices of the Archies ("Sugar Sugar"; #1, 1969) and the Cuff Links, reached the top twenty with the Detergents' "Leader of the Laundromat," which applied black humor to the Shangri-Las' morbid girl-group classic, "Leader of the Pack" (#1; 1954).

Well established as a music style by this time, rock 'n' roll found soon found that it was potentially lucrative to satirize itself. The Marcels' exaggeration of doo-wop conventions in "Blue Moon" (a 1934 Rodgers and Hart composition) reached number one in 1961. The rhythm and blues vocal group genre had been lampooned as early as 1957 by a Canadian pop aggregate, the Diamonds (pictured below). When the group's rather vicious send-up, "Little Darlin'" (number 2 for eight weeks in 1957) achieved success of unforseen proportions, they were consigned to mining the style well into the 1960s. Other notable doo-wop novelties included the Edsels' "Rama Lama Ding Dong" (1958; reissued in 1961), Barry Mann's "Who Put the Bomp (In the Bomp, Bomp, Bomp)" (1961), and Johnny Cymbal's "Mr. Bass Man" (1963).

Intermittant revivals of horror/science fiction themes also continued well into the sixties as exemplified by the Ran-Dells' "Martian Hop" (1963) and Bobby "Boris" Pickett's "Monster Mash," a Karloffian exploitation of the dance craze, the Mashed Potato. The latter recording not only spent five weeks perched atop the singles charts in fall 1962, but enjoyed a second top ten run in 1973. Novelty songs found countless other topics to address from a humorous perspective as well, including fashion--e.g., Edd Byrnes' "Kookie, Kookie (Lend Me Your Comb)"; Brian Hyland's "Itsy Bitsy Teenie Weenie Yellow Polka Dot Bikini" (#1; 1960)--and self-deprecation (e.g., Larry Verne's "Mr. Custer" and Murry Kellum's "Long Tall Texan").

The significant drop-off in novelty tunes by 1964 appears to been a direct result of the upsurge in creative output enjoyed by rock music with the onslaught of British beat imports and the   ensuing American renaissance encompassing surf music, folk rock, soul, garage/punk, and an array of additional indigenous styles. Furthermore, the rise of social relevance in rock lyrics appears to have deflated rock's sense of humor. Songs like the Barbarians' "Are You a Boy or Are You a Girl" (1965) and the Fraternity of Man's "Don't Bogart Me" (1968) were undeniably funny, but possessed a hard edge (the underlying message portion) which lifted them out of the novelty category.

Top Artists and Their Hit Recordings

Big Bopper--"Chantilly Lace" (1958); "Big Bopper's Wedding" (1958)

Black, Jeanne--"He'll Have to Stay" (1960); "Oh, How I Miss You Tonight" (1961)

Buchanan and Ancell--"The Creature (Parts 1 & 2)" (1957)

Buchanan and Goodman--"The Flying Saucer (Parts 1 & 2)" (1956); "Buchanan and Goodman on Trial" (1956); "Flying Saucer the 2nd" (1957); "Santa & the Satellite (Parts 1 & 2)" (1957)

The Cheers--"Black Denim Trousers" (1955)

The Chipmunks--"The Chipmunk Song" (#1; 1958); "Alvin's Harmonica"   (1959); "Ragtime Cowboy Joe" (1959)

The Chips--"Rubber Biscuit" (1958)

The Coasters--"Charlie Brown" (1959); "Along Came Jones" (1959); "Little Egypt" (1961)

Ben Colder--"Don't Go Near the Eskimos" (1962); "Still No. 2" (1963); "Detroit City No. 2" (1963)
See also: Sheb Wooley

Cymbal, Johnny--"Mr. Bass Man" (1963)

Skeeter Davis--"(I Can't Help You) I'm Falling Too" (1960); "My Last Date (With You)" (1960/1)

The Detergents--"Leader of the Laundromat" (1964)

The Diamonds-"Little Darlin'" (1957)

Dicky Doo and the Don'ts--"Nee Nee Na Na Na Na Nu Nu" (1958)

Charlie Drake--"My Boomerang Won't Come Back" (1962)

The Edsels--"Rama Lama Ding Dong" (1958; 1961)

The Five Blobs--"The Blob" (1958)

George and Louis--"The Return of Jerry Lee" (1958)

Rolf Harris--"Tie Me Kangaroo Down, Sport" (1963)

The Hollywood Argyles--"Alley-Oop" (1960)

Hyland, Brain--"Itsy Bitsy Teenie Weenie Yellow Polkadot Bikini"   (1960)

The Ivy 3--"Yogi" (1960)

Kellum, Murry--"Long Tall Texan" (1963)

Barry Mann--"Who Put the Bomp (In the Bomp, Bomp, Bomp)" (1961)

Nervous Norvus--"Transfusion" (1956); "Ape Call" (1956)

Bill Parsons--"The All American Boy" (1959)

Bobby "Boris" Pickett--"Monster Mash" (1962)

The Playmates--"Beep Beep" (1958)

The Ran-Dells--"Martian Hop" (1963)

The Royal Teens--"Short Shorts" (1957)

David Seville--"Witch Doctor" (1958)

Dodie Stevens--"Yes, I'm Lonesome Tonight" (1960)

Ray Stevens--"Ahab, the Arab" (1962); "Harry the Hairy Ape" (1963)

Verne, Larry--"Mr. Custer" (1960)

Sheb Wooley--"The Purple People Eater" (1958) See also: Ben Colder

The Payola Scandal

John Morthland provided a succinct description of the payola phenomenon and the situation prior to 1959 deejay scandal in *The Rolling Stone Illustrated History of Rock & Roll* (revised edition):

> Payola--the narrow definition: pay (cash or gifts) for radio airplay—has been a factor in radio since the medium's inception. In the Fifties, the practice flourished among rock 'n' roll disc jockeys. Payola padded their frequently paltry salaries, and it helped the new music reach its intended audience, no matter how small the label on which it appeared. By the late Fifties, in fact, a swarm of independent labels recording rock had broken the stranglehold of the majors--in particular, Columbia, RCA and Decca--on the sales and airplay of popular records.

As Morthland further noted, the American Society of Composers, Authors and Publishers (ASCAP) also had reason to be unhappy with the state of affairs at that time. The publishing house had become a dominant force in the music business through its licensing agreements regarding the sales of sheet music, piano rolls, and the recordings of Tin Pan Alley songs. A battle between ASCAP and the radio stations--whose programming had become increasingly committed to airing recorded music during the latter 1930s and early 1940s--spurred the latter to boycott ASCAP material and establish their own publishing firm, Broadcast Music Incorporated (BMI). ASCAP's history of ignoring black and country music compositions, combined with the tendency of many radio stations to target regional tastes overlooked by the major networks (ABC, NBC, and CBS) enabled BMI to secure a near monopoly on the material in these genres.

The advent of rock 'n' roll, itself largely a product of the marriage of rhythm and blues and country, assured the continued dominance of BMI within the youth music market.

Therefore, it appeared to be a case of protecting vested interests when ASCAP pushed for the House Legislative Oversight subcommittee to broaden its inquiry into corrupt broadcasting practices--centered up to 1959 on television quiz programs--to cover payola practices within radio. According to the perspective held by many within the record industry, the payola investigation would assist in stamping out rock 'n' roll--already reeling from the loss of many of its top stars and faced with an onslaught of media friendly teen idols--altogether.

The music business quickly closed ranks in the face of outside political interference. ABC-TV forced *American Bandstand* host Dick Clark to unload his holdings in other music-related activities, ranging from record companies to publishing houses. In response to Federal Trade Commission directives, a number of independent record labels and distributors filed consent orders agreeing to eliminate payola. Such moves enabled the industry to withstand formal House hearings in early 1960. Clark, whose deportment under interrogation was that of a model citizen, was not found guilty of directly engaging in payola practices.

On the other hand, Alan Freed, the deejay most clearly identified with the rise of rock 'n' roll, refused to testify despite an offer of immunity. A pariah within the field he'd helped so much to nurture, he was ultimately found guilty on two counts of commercial bribery.

In the end, the committee recommended anti-payola amendments to the Federal Communications Acts which prohibited the payment of cash or gifts in exchange for airplay, and required radio stations to police such activities. These amendments formally became law on September 13, 1960.

While the overall impact of the hearings remains unclear, it is clear that the general media circus surrounding them far over- shadowed whatever concrete results might have taken place. The smaller independent labels had been forced to compete on more equal terms the majors and their superior publicity and distribution networks. As a result, many of the former went of business during the early 1960s. Nevertheless, new labels continued to surface--and sometimes achieve great success--in the upcoming years. Payola itself continued to be employed within the industry, giving rise to yet another scandal in the early 1970s centered around Columbia Records president Clive Davis and allegations of bribes involving money, sex, and drugs.

Table 48

Alan Freed, December 15, 1922-January 20, 1965

Perhaps best known for coining the phrase "rock 'n' roll," deejay/show promoter Alan Freed played an important role in the development an aesthetic for the newly emerging genre. For example, he steadfastly refused to play cover versions of rhythm and blues originals on his radio programs in the 1950s. Although his large broadcast audience constituted a major source of power within the record industry, it paled next the near-monopoly enjoyed on television by Dick Clark's *American Bandstand* or the king-making positions of a select group of record label executives and producers.

Born in Johnstown, Pennsylvania, Freed first attracted attention in 1951 as a WJW, Cleveland, disc jockey specializing in the latest R&B recordings. He used his popularity as a springboard to organize live shows throughout the Midwest featuring R&B and rock 'n' roll artists. The words "rock" and "roll" had appeared, individually and collectively, in a number of R&B songs prior to the early 1950s when he began using the phrase to denote the new youth-oriented music appearing on the airwaves with increasing frequency. His identification with the genre led WINS, New York, to hire him as its feature deejay following the decision to adopt a rock format in 1954. His Brooklyn Paramount shows on the Easter and Labor Day weekends in 1955, which featured an interracial mix of rock and R&B stars, drew such large crowds that pop music's industry-wide color bar was soon lifted.

The 1960 "payola" hearings conducted by the House Subcommittee on Legislative Oversight, chaired by Arkansas Democrat Oren Harris, effectively destroyed his career. Indicted for accepting $30,000 from six labels in return for radio plugs, Freed—whose uncompromising support of rock 'n' roll and black performers offended the record industry's old guard—took the fall for a practice that pervaded all levels of the music business. Under investigation by the I.R.S. for tax evasion and in poor health during the early 1960s, he died of uremia at the comparatively young age of forty-two.

With the rise of serious rock journalism beginning in the late 1960s, Freed has received widespread credit for his contributions to rock's early stages of development. His legacy also lives on in his 1950s film appearances and Paramount Pictures' *American Hot Wax* (1978), which depicted the events surrounding the 1959 "First Anniversary of Rock 'n' Roll" concert held at the Brooklyn Paramount.

Commercial Folk Music

Folk music in recorded form almost could be said to represent a contradiction in terms. True folk culture, including folk art forms, arose out of the shared activities and traditions of essentially rural communities. Cultural anthropologists came to define folk music as music created by the people (not by one composer) as a communal experience. From this perspective, real folk music belonged to the public domain, its origins forever lost in the hazy, undocumented past. Furthermore, it could not be disseminated by means of the mass media--published notation books, phonograph recordings, films, etc.--in an urbanized, industrial society. Urban musicians attempting to perform this orally transmitted genre came to be termed "folk interpreters." To everyday Americans, however, anyone playing traditional folk material or topical songs composed in a similar style constituted a folk music artist.

Whatever category to which they belonged, folk-based practitioners have achieved commercial success in various guises throughout American history. The rise of the minstrel tradition in the 1830s enabled audiences in the nation's northern urban centers to hear the indigenous music of southern blacks. The suffering caused by the Great Depression and an array of social inequities during the 1930s spurred the development of a more radicalized folk music. The activist stance espoused by performers such as Woody Guthrie and Pete Seeger found a large following during the 1930s and early 1940s. Many of the leading artists of the 1960s folk revival would trace their roots back to the social imperatives of this earlier generation.

The conservative wave sweeping America in the 1950s--a product of economic prosperity and the political paranoia ensuing from the outset of the Cold War--forced the more socially conscious folk music artists (e.g., the Weavers) underground. The triumphant return of the Weavers to the stage and the desire in some quarters for an adult alternative to the teen-oriented rock 'n' roll fad then sweeping the nation, helped push folk music back into the cultural mainstream. The decidedly non-controversial Kingston Trio illustrated the commercial potential of the genre by means of a string of best-selling album releases and equally lucrative tours of college campuses. Folk performers like Joan Baez and Peter, Paul and Mary also achieved immediate success in the album market, thereby filling the void left by the calypso's inability to remain commercially viable beyond 1957-1958.

The social activism engendered by the Kennedy Administration further stimulated the folk market. By early 1963 television was saturated by the hootenanny craze, providing a promotional vehicle for the influx of photogenic artists sporting collegiate clothes and hairstyles and singing about a better society for all. John F. Kennedy's assassination on November 22, 1963 tempered this communal optimism to a considerable degree, and disrupted the momentum of the folk music movement. The rise of the British Invasion in early 1964 swept aside all competition, pushing folk performers back down to the lower reaches of the singles and album charts. Many of the young folk musicians, intrigued by the progressive musicality displayed by the leading British bands, began experimenting with a hybrid of folk lyrics and rock's rhythmic drive; within another year folk rock would be the next big trend. The aesthetics of commercial folk music, however, have continued to be nurtured by artists such as the Nitty Gritty Dirt Band, Tracy Chapman, and the Indigo Girls.

Top Artists and Their Recordings

Joan Baez--*Joan Baez* (1960); *Joan Baez 2* (1961); *In Concert/Part One* (1963); *In Concert/Part Two (1963); Joan Baez 5 (1964)*; *Farewell Angelina* (1965); *Portrait* (1966)

The Brothers Four--"Greenfields" (1960)

Woody Guthrie--*Columbia River Collection* (1941; reissued 1987); *Dust Dowl Ballads* (reissued 1988); *Cowboy Songs/Southern Mountain Hoedowns* (194?; reissued 1995); *Struggle* (194?; reissued 1990); *Nursery Days* (reissued 1992)

The Highwaymen--"Michael" (1961)

Ian and Sylvia--"Four Strong Winds" (1964); "You Were on My Mind"   (1965)

Burl Ives--*The Wayfaring Stranger* (1947); *Burl Ives Sings* (1981)

The Kingston Trio--*The Kingston Trio* (1958); *The Kingston Trio At Large* (1959); *Here We Go Again!* (1959); *Sold Out* (1960); *String Along* (1960); *The Kingston Trio: The Guard Trio* (10-CD box set covering 1957-1961; released 1997)

Leadbelly--*Midnight Special* (reissued 1991); *Gwine Dig a Hole to Put the Devil In* (reissued 1991); *Let It Shine on Me* (reissued 1991); *Go Down Old Hannah* (reissued 1994); *Nobody Knows the Trouble I've Seen* (reissued 1994); *The Titanic* (ressued 1994)

Chad Mitchell Trio--*Mighty Day on Campus* (1962); *At the Bitter End* (1962); *Blowin' in the Wind* (1963)

The New Lost City Ramblers--The Early Years, 1958-1962 (1991)

Phil Ochs--*Farewells and Fantasies* (3-CD box set; released 1997)

Peter, Paul and Mary--*Peter, Paul and Mary* (1962); *Movin'* (1963); *In the Wind* (1963)

The Rooftop Singers--"Walk Right In" (1963); "Tom Cat" (1963)

Tom Rush--*Tom Rush* (1965)

Mike Seeger--*Music From the True Vine* (1972); *Fresh Oldtime String Band Music* (1988)

Pete Seeger--*Darling Corey* (1950); *Goofing Off Suite* (1955); *American Industrial Ballads* (1957); *The Bitter and the Sweet* (1962); *Live at Newport* (1963); *Children's Concert at Town Hall* (1963); *Waist Deep in the Big Muddy and Other Love Songs* (1967); *The Essential Pete Seeger* (Folkways collection 1950-1774; released 1978)

Dave Van Ronk--*Dave Van Ronk/Folksinger* (1962); *Inside Dave Van Ronk* (1962)

Doc Watson--*Treasures Untold* (1964); *Old Timey Concert* (1967); *Ballads From Deep Gap* (1967); *The Essential Doc Watson* (1973); *Doc Watson on Stage* (1982)

The Weavers--"Goodnight Irene" (1950); "On Top of Old Smokey" (1950); "Tzena, Tzena, Tzena" (1950); *The Weavers on Tour* (1955); *The Weavers at Carnegie Hall* (1955); *The Weavers at Carnegie Hall, Vol. 2* (1963); *The Weavers Reunion at Carnegie Hall, 1963* (reissued 1987); *Almanac* (1963); *Classics* (reissued 1987); *Wasn't That a Time* (4-CD box set, 1992)

Table 49

Phil Ochs, December 19, 1940-April 9, 1976

In many ways, Phil Ochs was a victim of Bob Dylan's critical and commercial success in the 1960s. He gained little solace from the fact that many considered him second only to Dylan as a writer of political polemics within the New York City folk scene. After all, Dylan had applied his prodigious composing skills to virtually the entire spectrum of American popular song—including love laments, talking blues, protest anthems, surrealistic free verse, country ballads, and straight-ahead rockers, whereas he had chosen to specialize in anti-establishment diatribes framed within an urban folk vernacular. Furthermore, as Dylan reached far beyond his localized counterculture roots to achieve the status of a popular culture icon, Ochs would become increasingly marginalized by the new musical trends he seemed unable to adapt to.

Ochs attended military school in Virginia and pursued a journalism degree at Ohio State University before deciding to pursue a career as a singer/songwriter. After a brief stint with the Singing Socialists (later known as the Sundowners), he ended up in New York City as a solo performer. His first album, *All the News That's Fit to Sing* (Elektra 7/269; 1964), caused a sensation within the East Coast folk scene. His strident commentaries on topical issues, most notably his criticism of the Vietnam War effort (e.g., "Draft Dodger Rag"), in the next LP, *I Ain't a' Marchin' Anymore* (Elektra 7/287; 1965), further advanced his celebrity.

The failure to produce a mass anthem with universally appealing imagery such as Dylan's "Blowin' in the Wind," considerably slowed the upward trajectory of Ochs' career. Following a couple of uneven albums—*Phil Ochs in Concert* (Elektra 7/310; 1966) and *Pleasures of the Harbor* (A&M 4133; 1967)—he shifted his base of operations to Los Angeles. The recordings produced there—*Tape from California* (A&M 4148; 1968), *Rehearsals for Retirement* (A&M 4181; 1969), *Greatest Hits* (all new recordings; A&M 4253; 1970), and *Gunfight at Carnegie Hall* (A&M 9010; recorded April 1970; released 1975 only in Canada)—featured session musicians in order to achieve a slicker, more rock-oriented sound (including orchestral arrangements).

Living in Africa and London during the early 1970s, Ochs returned to New York in 1974 to record the protest song, "Here's to the State of Richard Nixon" (A&M) and organize a concert protesting the U.S.-instigated military junta in Chile. Following his suicide by hanging, brother Michael Ochs compiled an anthology release, *Chords of Fame* (A&M 4599; 1976). Now remembered primarily for his seminal mid-1960s protest recordings, he is well represented by CD compilations (many featuring previously unavailable material) and reissues of his original albums.

Table 50

Tom Rush, February 8, 1941-

Born in Portsmouth, New Hampshire, Rush began working the Cambridge, Massachusetts, coffeehouse circuit in the early 1960s while earning his B.A. from Harvard. Although immediately categorized as a folksinger, his early albums—two with Prestige in 1963 and a 1965 Transatlantic release—reflected his career-long eclectic leanings, which included experimentation with the blues, jazz, classical arrangements, and rock instrumentation. His recorded material was divided between self-penned songs, traditionals, and astutely chosen compositions by other singer-songwriters (e.g., Joni Mitchell, James Taylor).

After signing with Elektra Records at the height of the folk-rock boom, Rush's albums—*Take A Little Walk With Me* (Elektra 7308; 1966), *The Circle Game* (Elektra 74018; 1968), and *Classic Rush* (Elektra 74062; 1971)—began appearing on the pop charts. Although never achieving true stardom, his albums with Columbia—*Tom Rush* (Columbia 9972; 1970). *Wrong End of the Rainbow* (Columbia 30402; 1970), *Merimack County* (Columbia 31306; 1972), and *Ladies Love Outlaws* (Columbia 33054; 1974)—continued to sell moderately well in the early 1970s. Never comfortable as a mainstream label artist, he founded Maple Hill Productions in 1980. He began arranged a series of concerts under the Club 47 name (in tribute to the 1960s Cambridge coffeehouse) in order to nurture modern folk artists. He also established his own mail-order record label, Night Light Recordings. In addition to composing, recording, and touring over the years, he has remained deeply committed to a wildlife protection organization, the Wolf Fund. [Romanowski and George-Warren. 1995.]

The Specter Sound

Perhaps the only notable popular music genre to have originated with, solely maintained by, and finally terminated at the whim of one individual, the Spector Sound (or "wall of sound," the name by which it was more widely known) referred to the productions of Phil Spector. Born in New York on December 26, 1940, Spector's love of popular music--particularly rhythm and blues and the rapidly emerging rock 'n' roll--inspired him to form a group, the Teddy Bears, in his Los Angeles high schoo, and to record one of his compositions, "To Know Him Is To Love Him" (according to legend, inspired by the inscription on his father's tombstone). The record, released by the Dore label in August 1958, raced up the national singles charts, remaining in the Top Ten for eleven weeks, including three weeks in the number one position.

This unprecedented debut netted the group only three thousand dollars, convincing Spector of the need for a new set of guidelines to assist in navigating the music industry jungle. Alan Betrock listed these rules in his book, *Girl Groups: The Story of a Sound*:

(1) Music must be emotional and honest.
(2) Create a sound on record that no one can copy or "cover."
(3) Make sure you get your money.
(4) There's never a contract without a loophole.

Rule number four provided an escape from his Dore contract on the grounds that group members were minors and their arrangement had not been sanctioned by either their parents or court of law. Finding that his hit had opened other doors to the industry, Spector became a studio apprentice for a succession of publishing houses and record companies, including Jamie/Trey and Atlantic/Atco.

Following a string of production successes in the early 1960s--including Ray Peterson's "Corrina, Corinna" (1960), Curtis Lee's "Pretty Little Angel Eyes" (1961), Gene Pitney's "Every Breath I Take" (1961), and the Paris Sisters' "I Love How You Love Me" (1961)--he formed a record company (Philles) with Lester Sill in which artistic control would rest entirely in his hands. In short order, Spector was acquiring material from leading Brill Building firms such as Aldon and producing records for a growing stable of recording acts.

The first notable chart successes for Philles were by the Crystals, a black female quartet. However, Spector refused to be bound by the normal conventions of record making, often employing musicians on a per session basis to match the sounds he had within his head. In this manner, his first number one hit, the Crystals' rendition of the Gene Pitney composition, "He's a Rebel," was actually recorded by Darlene Love, backed by the Blossoms.

By early 1963 it was evident that Spector had found the system he wanted for making truly creative recordings which, due to their intelligent lyrics and preponderance of musical hooks, also possessed huge sales potential. Betrock describes the elements of this formula, which was, in actuality, a *style* of recording rather than a specific *sound* (the sound tended to vary significantly from record to record):

> For starters, Spector would take as long as necessary to get what he
> wanted. It may have taken hours for the drum sound, or hours for the
> blend of guitars, but Phil would stick at it. Sometimes it would come
> quickly, but often the sessions went on for sixteen hours straight or until
> everyone just couldn't play or listen back anymore. Sometimes he would
> record the same song with different arrangements or at different tempos,

or use the same track and try out different vocalists until just the right combination was found. Often, finished or close-to-finished recordings would never be issued--despite the fact that everyone close to Phil said they were hits--because they just didn't meet Phil's standards....All of Spector's records during this time were made on 3-track machine, and then mixed down to mono for singles releases. Spector did not like stereo, and his recording style was not geared to make stereo masters. He wanted everything to blend together, to rise and fall together without the prominence of any one sound or instrument; others would try to get a clean sound on all their instruments, to try and isolate those individual sounds--Spector wanted just the opposite....Most of the time was not spent in actual recording, but in getting sounds, balances, microphone placements, and so on, all blended just the right way....When it was time to record, all the music would be recorded on one track. The guitars, basses, pianos, horns, percussion, and drums would be blended together on that track incorporating the amp sounds, room leakage sounds, and [the studio's] echo chambers. If Phil could get one musical track recorded in one lengthy session, he was satisfied. Another day and a second track would be used for the vocals, and another day and the final track would be used for strings. Then the mixing would begin. One would think that with only three tracks to mix together, it would be a simple process, but mixes took hours, and sometimes days....When it was all over, everyone waited to see when, and if, the record would come out.

While the Crystals' classic hit recordings may have been instrumental in laying the foundation of the Spector legend, the group's unhappiness over their royalty earnings and the management of their career caused a breakdown of the working relationship between the two parties. Spector soon focused his attention on other acts, most notably the Ronettes and the Righteous Brothers.

By 1966, however, he found it increasingly harder, in the face of changing musical tastes combined with the realignment of working relationships between artists and record company personnel (i.e., the most successful performers were demanding complete control of the creative process, from songwriting to studio recording and production), to retain his hitmaking edge. The failure of perhaps his most ballyhooed release, Ike and Tina Turner's "River Deep, Mountain High," to penetrate beyond the lower reaches of the charts, drove him into a self-imposed retirement. He would occasionally return to studio production if a particular project suited him (e.g., rescuing the Beatles' *Let It Be* sessions from oblivion). However, with his greatest work well behind him, the Spector touch appeared to be all too mortal.

Top Artists and Their Hit Recordings

Alley Cats--"Puddin N' Tain (1963)

The Beatles--*Let It Be* (1970)

Bob B. Soxx & the Blue Jeans--"Zip-A-Dee Doo-Dah" (1963)

Checkmates, Ltd. (featuring Sonny Charles)--"Black Pearl" (1969)

The Crystals--"There's No Other (Like My Baby)" (1961); "Uptown" (1962); "He's a Rebel" (#1; 1962); "He's Sure the Boy I Love" (1963); "Da Doo Ron Ron" (1963); "Then He Kissed Me" (1963)

Curtis Lee--"Pretty Little Angel Eyes" (1961)

Darlene Love--"(Today I Met) The Boy I'm Gonna Marry" (1963); "Wait Til' My Bobby Gets Home" (1963)

The Paris Sisters--"I Love How You Love Me" (1961)

Ray Peterson--"Corinna, Corinna" (1960)

Gene Pitney--"Every Breathe I Take" (1961)

The Righteous Brothers--"You've Lost That Lovin' Feelin'" (#1; 1964); "Unchained Melody" (1965); "Ebb Tide" (1965)

The Ronettes--"Be My Baby" (1963); "Baby, I Love You" (1963); "(The Best Part of) Breakin' Up" (1964); "Do I Love You" (1964); "Walking in the Rain" (1964)

The Teddy Bears--"To Know Him Is to Love Him" (#1; 1958)

Ike and Tina Turner--"River Deep-Mountain High" (1966)

Table 51

Ellie Greenwich, October 23, 1940-August 26, 2009

Although best known as the composer of many early 1960s classic rock songs, the multi-talented Ellie Greenwich also excelled as a singer, studio arranger and producer, and music business entrepreneur. Her songs—recorded by stars such as Lesley Gore, the Dixie Cups, the Shangri-Las, Jay and the Americans, the Exciters, and Phil Spector's Philles roster—were unsurpassed in reflecting the teen experience of that era.

Born within the suburban confines of Long Island, Greenwich sang at school functions and first tried her hand at songwriting while majoring in education at Hofstra University. Her only recording—released by RCA in 1958—was a failure commercially. After graduating in 1961, she briefly tried teaching English at nearby General Douglas MacArthur High School. Realizing she was more interested in popular music than literature, she began working for the songwriting/production team of Jerry Lieber and Mike Stoller. She also sought an outlet for her singing, making demonstration tapes of other writers' songs—in the early 1960s she was referred to as the "Demo Queen of New York"—and supplying all of the voices in the studio for a vocal group, the Raindrops, which also included her husband and songwriting collaborator, Jeff Barry. The act's biggest hits—"What a Guy" (Jubilee 5444; 1963; #41) and "He's the Kind of Boy You Can't Forget" (Jubilee 5455; 1963; #17)—featuring tight production values and nonsensical vocal flourishes, represented prime examples of the neo-doo-wop tradition.

Some of Greenwich's finest compositions were supplied to Spector, including the Ronettes' "Be My Baby" (Philles 116; 1963; #2) and "Baby, I Love You" (Philles 118; 1963; #24), the Crystals' "Da Doo Run Run" (Philles 112; 1963; #3) and "Then He Kissed Me" (Philles 115; 1963; #6), and Darlene Love's "(Today I Met) The Boy I'm Going To Marry" (Philles 111; 1963; #39). She also worked closely with the Red Bird label, owned by Leiber, Stoller, and George Goldner, providing such hits as the Dixie Cups' "Chapel of Love" (Red Bird 001; 1964; #1) and "People Say" (Red Bird 006; 1964; #12), the Jelly Beans' "I Wanna Love Him So Bad" (Red Bird 10003; 1964; #9), and the Shangri-Las' "Leader of the Pack" (Red Bird 008; 1964; #5).

Taking a cue from the Red Bird operation, she and her husband turned increasingly to publishing and production work in the mid-1960s, most notably with Neil Diamond. Among the singles ensuing from the collaboration were "Solitary Man" (Bang 519; 1966; #55), "Cherry, Cherry" (Bang 528; 1966; #6), "I Got the Feelin'" (Bang 536; 1966; #16), "I Thank the Lord for the Night Time" (Bang 547; 1967; #13), "Kentucky Woman" (Bang 551; 1967; #22), and "Shilo" (Bang 575; 1970; #24).

Various personal problems, including the breakup of her marriage and substance abuse—and changing popular music fashions led to a drop-off in productivity by the late 1960s. She revived her career, however, by focusing on radio and television commercials through her firm, Pineywood Productions. In the early 1970s, Greenwich wrote ad material for Ford, Cheerios, Prince Albert Tobacco, and other companies. She also contributed vocals to jingles for the likes of Beechnut, Clairol, Coca-Cola, Noxzema, and Helena Rubenstein.

At the height of the rock 'n' roll revival, she recorded an album of her classic hits, *Let It Be Written, Let It Be Sung* (Verve 5091; 1973). Deemed by critics to be even better than her 1968 release, *Ellie Greenwich Composes, Produces, and Sings* (United Artists 6648), she spent much of the 1970s and early 1980s performing live. This success led to support for a Broadway musical based on her songs; *Leader of the Pack* opened in early 1985 to mixed reviews and modest box-office success. The income derived from reissues of recordings of her compositions, though, has continued to pay high dividends.

The Girl Groups

With the exception of the teen idols, girl groups were the only genuinely distinctive genre to peak in the early 1960s. The genre owed its success largely to the 1959 payola investigations, combined with increased attacks on rock 'n' roll's alleged bad influence on teenagers. These factors stimulated a change in image and musical focus among record companies and radio disc jockeys. Radio's efforts to clean house led to the concentration of power in the hands of the program director who, in turn, adopted national playlists and a tightened Top Forty format. There was a resulting decline in regional hits produced by small record labels; the pop music industry was driven by the ongoing search for the next big trend. Heavy reliance on proven formulas became the modus operandi as the balance of power shifted to a select group of record executives, studio producers, staff songwriters, and media personalities.

Girl groups proved to be one of the more successful formulas to be mined again and again by those labels committed to the youth market. Music historians have sometimes fallen prey to a revisionist perspective of that era which interprets the rise of girl groups--and female performers in general (e.g., Connie Francis, Brenda Lee, Lesley Gore)--as early evidence of the increasing assertiveness of women in the workplace and within Society in general. In point of fact, however, girl groups were strongly manipulated by powerful men who were well-connected within the record industry. Successful girl groups were prized in large because they were easily pliable, generally submitting to outside control with a minimal display of rebellious attitude. The younger the performers, the more likely they were to accept the strict order of the system. This at least in part explains why few groups were able to sustain a successful recording career beyond a hit recording or two.

The Chantels were the first girl group to rise above the one-hit wonder status which limited the impact of acts such as the Paris Sisters ("I Love How You Love Me"; 1956), the Teen Queens ("Eddie My Love"; 1955), and the Poni-Tails ("Born Too Late"; 1957). The group--originally a quintet whose members were all classmates at Saint Anthony of Padua School in the Bronx--were discovered backstage at an Alan Freed rock 'n' roll revue by Rama/Gee/Gone record producer Richard Barrett while waiting to meet their idol, Frankie Lymon (of the Teenagers). The Chantels' second release, "Maybe" (1958), proved to be a seminal event in the girl group genre. Its importance is noted by Alan Betrock, in his book, *Girl Groups: The Story of a Sound*:

> Upon its release, the record literally exploded—its impact and appeal were
> simply undeniable. Barrett kicks off the record with a series of piano triplets,
> a wailing vocal chorus jumps in, and then [lead singer] Arlene [Smith] tears
> your heart out with one of the most searing and honest vocal performances

ever. It all came together here; the churchy-gospel influences meshed with a commercial rhythm & blues sensibility. Utterly convincing and profoundly moving, "Maybe" packs even more of a wallop when one realizes that Arlene Smith was only sixteen at the time of the recording session, and the record Still captivated both teenagers and adults. The Chantels records were not polished—their rough edges and even occasional wrong notes are there to hear if you search hard enough--but it was their utter intensity and atmospheric realism that carried them into a class all their own. "Maybe" entered the national charts at #55, and the next week had reached #32. Yet this incredible burst of popularity caused problems for...End Records, because they simply could not meet demand fast enough. In many cities bootleggers moved in, selling thousands of records before [End] could fill the orders....Because of these sales and order discrepancies, the record only reached #15 nationally, but it stayed on the charts for over a third of a year. Not only was "Maybe" one of the biggest selling records of its time, but its sound greatly influenced musicians and producers for years to come.

The Shirelles were the first girl group to realize any notable degree of commercial and artistic success following in the stylistic path established by the Chantels. When the Shirelles' first few releases achieved only modest success, producer Luther Dixon decided to sweeten up their heavily r & b sound through the use of strings. He struck paydirt with the West Indian-inflected "Tonight's the Night" (1960), followed by the Carole King/Gerry Goffin composition, "Will You Love Me Tomorrow." The latter song was a hit around the world, remaining number one for five weeks on the U.S. singles charts. The arrangement--featuring swirling strings accented by a snare drum figure which inverted the traditional rock beat and added on a slight rhythmic shuffle--spurred record industry movers and shakers to try to incorporate and enlarge upon its techniques. In addition, its success drove home the idea that the right song, combined with the right singer and right arranger and right producer, represented the best blueprint for making a pop record.

While the Shirelles went on to enjoy many other hit singles, most notably the chart topper, "Soldier Boy" (1962), many other competitors were attempting to interpret the formula in their own ways. Producer Phil Spector was building his own roster of girl groups on the Philles label (see: The Spector Sound) and many of Berry Gordy's biggest hits for the Motown-Tamla-Gordy (aka the Motown Sound) combine were recorded by all-female aggregates. Don Kirshner and his Aldon publishing company, located in the heart of the Brill Building complex in Manhattan, supplied songs to many record companies who, in turn, matched them up with contracted girl groups. By 1962, his firm had eighteen writers on staff, between the ages of 19 and 26, including the Barry Mann-Cynthia Weil, Gerry Goffin-Carole King, and Neil Sedaka-Howard Greenfield teams. In addition, number of record companies achieved success in large part due to girl group recordings. These included Red Bird-Blue Cat, Cameo-Parkway, Chancellor, Jamie-Guyden, and Swan.

The decline of the girl group sound was a product of a complex chain of events. Betrock, the genre's leading historian, described this process in the following manner:

The British Invasion is often cited as the main reason that the girl-group sound was washed off the airwaves. This is a broad oversimplification, and for the most part, not accurate. During 1964...girl-group records did tremendously well on the U.S. charts. Number One records were scored by Mary Wells, The Dixie Cups, The Supremes, and The Shangri-Las; the Number One spot was held by girl groups for 25 percent of the entire year (about the same percentage as the previous year), and other major hits were recorded by The Ronettes, Martha & The Vandellas, Lesley Gore, The Jelly Beans, and numerous others. But the British Invasion did herald the era of new sounds and of self-contained groups that wrote and played their own material. Most popular trends or genres in music run their course within three years, partly because they capture the tenor of their times so well, and partly because dozens of second-rate imitations flood the market and the public soon overdoses on the particular sound. If the girl groups were beaten away by a sound, it was not only the British sound, but also surf, Motown, folk-rock, and blue-eyed soul. More importantly, it was the writers and producers who voluntarily dropped out of the scene, fearing that they could not compete with the new sounds.

Despite the relatively short duration of the girl group sound, its legacy continues to shine brightly. The classic songs of the genre (e.g., "The Locomotion," "Will You Love Me Tomorrow," "Da Doo Ron Ron") have regularly been revived by contemporary stars, while its stylistic features have been recreated by countless other performers. New Wave girl groups (e.g., the Go-Gos, the Bangles), the riot grrrl movement, and pop confections like the Spice Girls all represent variations of the original mold.

Top Artists and Their Hit Recordings

The Ad Libs--"The Boy From New York City" (1965)

The Angels--"My Boyfriend's Back" (1963)

The Blue-Belles(, Patti LaBelle and)--"I Sold My Heart to the Junkman" (1961)

The Caravelles--"You Don't Have to Be a Baby to Cry" (1963)

The Chantels--"Maybe" (1958); "Look in My Eyes" (1961)

The Chiffons--"He's So Fine" (1963); "One Fine Day" (1963); "Sweet Talkin' Guy" (1966)

Claudine Clark--"Party Lights" (1962)

The Cookies--"Chains" (1962); "Don't Say Nothing Bad About My Baby" (1963)

The Crystals--"He's A Rebel" (1962); "Da Doo Ron Ron" (1963); "Then He Kissed Me" (1963)

The Dixie Cups--"Chapel Of Love" (1964); "People Say" (1965)

The Exciters--"Tell Him" (1963)

The Girlfriends--"My One and Only Jimmy Boy" (1963)

The Jaynetts--"Sally Go Round the Roses" (1963)

The Jelly Beans--"I Wanna Love Him So Bad" (1964)

Little Eva--"The Locomotion" (1962); "Keep Your Hands Off My Baby"   (1963)

Martha & the Vandellas--"Come and Get Those Memories" (1962); Heatwave" (1963); "Dancing in the Streets" (1964); "Nowhere to Run" (1965); "Jimmy Mack" (1967)

The Marvelettes--"Please Mr. Postman" (1961); "Playboy" (1962); "Don't Mess With Bill" (1964)

The Murmaids--"Popsicles and Icicles" (1963)

The Orlons--"Wah-Watusi" (1962); "Don't Hang Up" (1962); "South Street" (1963)

The Paris Sisters--"I Love How You Love Me" (1956)

The Pixies Three--"442 Glenwood Avenue" (1963)

The Raindrops--"What a Guy" (1963); "The Kind of Boy You Can't Forget" (1963)

Reparata and the Delrons--"Whenever a Teenager Cries" (1963)

The Ronettes--"Be My Baby" (1963); "Baby I Love You" (1964); (Best Part of) Breaking Up" (1964)

The Shangri-Las--"Remember (Walking in the Sand)" (1964); "Leader of the Pack" (1964); "Give Him a Great Big Kiss" (1965); "I Can Never Go Home Anymore" (1965)

Dee Dee Sharp--"Mashed Potato Time" (1962); "Ride" (1962)

The Shirelles--"Tonight's the Night" (1959); "Dedicated to the One I Love" (1960); "Will You Love Me Tomorrow" (1960); "Mama Said" (1961); "Baby It's You" (1961); "Soldier Boy" (1962); "Foolish Little Girl" (1963); "Don't Say Goodnight and Mean Goodbye" (1963)

The Supremes(, Diana Ross and)--"Where Did Our Love Go" (1964); "Baby Love" (1964); "Come See About Me" (1964); "I Hear a Symphony" (1965); "My World Is Empty Without You" (1966); "You Can't Hurry Love" (1966); "You Keep Me Hangin' On" (1966); "Love Is Here and Now You're Gone" (1967); "Love Child" (1967)

The Toys--"Lover's Concerto" (1965); "Attack" (1965)

Mary Wells--"Two Lovers" (1962); "You Beat Me to the Punch" (1963); "My Guy" (1964)

THE BRITISH INVASION

The British Invasion was, quite simply, one of the watershed developments in American popular music history. The phenomenon involved the virtual domination of AM radio and the record industry in the United States by British artists, particularly the beat groups who had proved adept at recycling the American rhythm and blues and rockabilly songs of the 1950s.

The convergence of a number of events set provided the appropriate setting for this onslaught. Perhaps of greatest importance, American rock 'n' roll had been undergoing a steady decline in quality since the major record companies--aided and abetted by other media outlets, most notably Top 40 radio and Dick Clark's "American Bandstand"--had harnessed it and begun releasing a tamer product. The pop hegemony enjoyed by teen idols such as Frankie Avalon and Fabian had driven many youth to commercial folk and jazz, while a seemingly endless stream of novelty songs (e.g., Sheb Wooley's "Purple People Eater," David Seville's "Witch Doctor," Larry Verne's "Mr. Custer," and Brian Hyland's "Itsy Bitsy Teeny Weeny Yellow Polka Dot Bikini") and dance crazes proved unsuccessful in cultivating a substantial core following for rock 'n' roll.

In the meantime, the British music scene appeared incapable of producing much more than pale Elvis Presley imitators (e.g., Cliff Richard, Billy Fury, and Marty Wilde) and bland pop along the lines of Mr. Acker Bilk, whose "Stranger on the Shore" (1962) was one of the few British imports to make a substantial dent in the stateside charts prior to 1964. However, the pop underground in Great Britain was quietly brewing something far more potent starting in the mid-1950s. The skiffle music craze (a uniquely English form of folk revival music drawing heavily on American material) led by Lonnie Donegan spurred the baby boomer generation to form their own bands. The most notable of these aggregates--then known by names such as the Quarrymen and the Silver Beatles--would go on to spearhead the British Invasion.

It's hard to imagine the invasion taking place without the Beatles. Many of the bands swept along on the Fab Four's coattails to the top of the American charts possessed no more talent than the bland teen idols they had displaced. The Beatles, however, were another matter. Three of members--the songwriting team of John Lennon and Paul McCartney, and, to a lesser extent, lead guitarist George Harrison--were capable of producing first-rate material. After a brief period of covering American r & b, pop, and country standards, the group went on to compose a long string of rock classics, many of which are likely to be performed for generations to come. The band members were also all excellent musicians, thanks in large part to years spent performing in small clubs in England and Germany. Lennon and McCartney both were superb vocalists, capable of putting across rave-up rockers and introspective ballads in an equally convincing manner.

Despite the band's ability--so easy to assess in retrospect-- success in the U.S. might easily have eluded them had not conditions proved ripe for receptiveness on the part of the American public. The Beatles, under the skilled management of Brian Epstein, had attempted a number of times in 1963 to secure a hit record on the American charts. Songs like "Love Me Do," "From Me to You," "Please Please Me," and "She Loves You"--all hits in the U.K.--had gone nowhere when released by various labels in the states. By late 1963, however, the nation was caught up in communal sense of mourning, brought on by the assassinaton of popular President John F. Kennedy. The Beatles--with their cheeky wit (as evidenced in countless news interviews punctuating the whirlwind visits to the U.S. during the early months of 1964) and catchy, upbeat pop songs--proved to be the perfect anecdote America's collective depression. In addition, the mop-top hairstyle exhibited by the band members garnered considerable attention. As had been the case with Elvis Presley's heavily greased DA hairstyle of the mid-1950s, the Beatles look engendered considered controversy on the part of the adult establishment when it first assaulted the public consciousness. It provided instant credibility with America's youth, who were always in search of culture symbols to both collectively identify with and flaunt in the face of authority figures as an act of rebellion.

Within a matter of weeks in January 1964, catapulted by round-the-clock radio play and appearances on the "Ed Sullivan Show," the Beatles went from complete unknowns to household names in the U.S. With "I Want to Hold Your Hand" perched in the number one position on the *Billboard* "Hot 100," record companies owning the distribution rights to earlier Beatles hits rushed them back out into the marketplace. At one point in the spring, the band held down all top five positions on the national singles chart.

These developments made a substantial impression on the British music scene. British artists of every stripe--from beat groups to purveyors of easy listening fare--were hurriedly signed up by American labels and promoted through the mass media with a vengeance. In the weeks immediately following the appearance of the Beatles, countless other U.K. recording acts--some of whom had realized very little success in their own country--enjoyed heavy radio play and print coverage stateside. The first onslaught of British performers to achieve success on the American charts included Dusty Springfield, the Dave Clark Five, the Searchers, Billy J. Kramer, and Peter and Gordon. Perhaps of even greater importance, countless other British youths were inspired to become musicians, resulting in a steady stream of talent which, many would argue, has remain undiminished to the present day.

By early summer the floodgates had burst open; there seemed to be more British artists than American on the airwaves. Indeed, a considerable number of established U.S. acts--to say nothing of the more marginal recording artists--virtually disappeared from the charts in 1964 (some never to return). Stars suddenly thrust into the periphery of record industry included Dion, Fats Domino, Rick Nelson, Neil Sedaka, Connie Francis, Brenda Lee, Roy Orbison, the Everly Brothers, and Chubby Checker. Even Presley's career was sent into a tailspin. After eight years of uninterrupted success, he enjoyed only one top ten hit ("Crying in the Chapel"; which charted in 1965 but was recorded in 1960) prior to his revival in 1969 with "In the Ghetto" and "Suspicious Minds." Only a handful of American artists continued to thrive in 1964 and beyond, most notably the Beach Boys and the Four Seasons. New homegrown talent found it necessary to incorporate elements of the merseybeat sound such as the trademark jangly guitars and seamless three-part vocal harmonies. The garage punk and folk rock movements were particularly influenced by English rock bands. Some American groups--for example, Beau Brummels and the Sir Douglas Quintet in 1965--found it expedient to ape the British Invasion look to the extent of carefully covering up their native origins.

Probably the most positive result of the British Invasion was its role in clearing away the musical deadwood which had found a home on the American charts. With many of the long established American acts--as well as countless lesser luminaries--unable to compete with the host of often lackluster British stars, fresh stateside talent was more readily able to garner the attention of record company executive. Within a year or two of the initial British onslaught, a new wave of American musicians had already laid the groundwork for the creative renaissance in popular music during the latter half of the 1960s.

Top Artists and Their Hit Recordings

--The First Wave

The Animals(, Eric Burdon and the)--"The House of the Rising Sun" (1964); "See See Rider" (1966); "San Franciscan Nights" (1967)

The Beatles--"I Want to Hold Your Hand" (#1; 1964); "She Loves You" (#1; 1964); "Please Please Me" (1964); "Twist and Shout" (1964); "Can't Buy Me Love" (#1; 1964); "Do You Want to Know a Secret" (1964); "Love Me Do" (#1; 1964); "P.S. I Love You" (1964); "A Hard Day's Night" (#1; 1964); "I Feel Fine" (#1; 1964); "She's a Woman" (1964); "Eight Days a Week" (#1; 1965); "Ticket to Ride" #1; (1965); "Help!" (#1; 1965); "Yesterday" (#1; 1965); *Rubber Soul* (1965); "We Can Work It Out" (#1; 1966); "Day Tripper" (1966); "Nowhere Man" (1966); "Paperback Writer" (#1; 1966); *Revolver* (1966); "Yellow Submarine" (1966); "Penny Lane" (#1; 1967); "Strawberry Fields Forever" (1967); *Sgt. Pepper's Lonely Hearts Club Band* (1967); "All You Need Is Love" (#1; 1967); "Hello Goodbye" (#1; 1967); "Lady Madonna" (1968); *The White Album* (1968); "Hey Jude" (#1; 1968); "Get Back" (#1; 1969); *Abbey Road* (1969); "The Ballad of John and Yoko" (1969); "Come Together" (#1; 1969); "Something" (1969); "Let It Be" (#1; 1970); "The Long and Winding Road" (#1; 1970)

Chad and Jeremy--"A Summer Song" (1964)

The Dave Clark Five--"Glad All Over" (1964); "Bits and Pieces" (1964); "Can't You See That She's Mine" (1964); "Because" (1964); "I Like It Like That" (1965); "Catch Us If You Can" (1965); "Over and Over" (#1; 1965); "You Got What It Takes" (1967)

Petula Clark--"Downtown" (#1; 1965); "I Know a Place" (1965); "My Love" (1966); "I Couldn't Live Without Your Love" (1966); "This Is My Song" (1967); "Don't Sleep in the Subway" (1967)

Freddie and the Dreamers--"I'm Telling You Now" (1965); "Do the Freddie" (1965)

Gerry & the Pacemakers--"Don't Let the Sun Catch You Crying" (1964); "How Do You Do It?" (1964); "Ferry Cross the Mersey" (1965)

Herman's Hermits--"Can't You Hear My Heartbeat" (1965); "Silhouettes" (1965); "Mrs. Brown You've Got a Lovely Daughter" (1965); "Wonderful World" (1965); "I'm Henry III, I Am" (1965); "Just a Little Bit Better" (1965); "A Must to Avoid" (1966); "Listen People" (1966); "Leaning on the Lamp Post" (1966); "Dandy" (1966); "There's a Kind of a Hush" (1967)

The Hollies--"Look Through Any Window" (1965); "Bus Stop" (1966); "Stop Stop Stop" (1966); "Carrie-Anne" (1967); He Ain't Heavy, He's My Brother" (1969); "Long Cool Woman" (1972); "The Air That I Breathe" (1974)

The Honeycombs--"Have I the Right?" (1964)

The Kinks--"You Really Got Me" (1964); "All Day and All of the Night" (1965); "Tired of Waiting For You" (1965); "Lola" (1970)

Billy J. Kramer with the Dakotas--"Little Children" (1964); "Bad to Me" (1964)

Lulu (& the Lovers)--"Shout" (1964); "To Sir With Love" (1967)

Manfred Mann--"Do Wah Diddy Diddy" (#1; 1964); "Mighty Quinn" (1968)

The Mindbenders(, Wayne Fontana and the)--"Game of Love" (1965); "A Groovy Kind of Love" (1966)

The Moody Blues--"Go Now!" (1965); *Days of Future Passed* (1967); *In Search of the Lost Chord* (1968); *On the Threshold of a Dream* (1969); *To Our Children's Children's Children* (1970); *A Question of Balance* (1970); *Every Good Boy Deserves Favour* (1971); *Seventh Sojourn* (1972)

The Nashville Teens--"Tobacco Road" (1964)

Peter and Gordon--"A World Without Love" (1964); "I Go To Pieces" (1965); "Lady Godiva" (1966)

The Rolling Stones--"Time Is On My Side" (1964); "The Last Time" (1965); "(I Can't Get No) Satisfaction" (#1; 1965); "Get Off Of My Cloud" (#1; 1965); "As Tears Go By" (1965); "19th Nervous Breakdown" (1966); "Paint It, Black" (#1; 1966); "Mother's Little Helper" (1966); "Have You Seen Your Mother, Baby, Standing in the Shadow?" (1966); "Ruby Tuesday" (#1; 1967); "Jumpin' Jack Flash" (1968); "Honky Tonk Women" (#1; 1969); "Brown Sugar" (#1;

1971); "Tumbling Dice" (1972); "Angie" (#1; 1973); "Miss You" (#1; 1978); "Start Me Up" (1981)

The Searchers--"Needles and Pins" (1964); "Love Potion Number Nine" (1965)

Dusty Springfield--"Wishin' and Hopin'" (1964); "You Don't Have to Say You Love Me" (1966); "Son of a Preacher Man" (1969)

The Swingin' Bluejeans--"Hippy Hippy Shake" (1964)

Them--"Here Comes the Night" (1965); "Gloria" (1966)

Whitcomb, Ian--"You Turn Me On" (1965)

The Who--"My Generation" (1965); "I Can See For Miles" (1967); *Tommy* (1969), *Live at Leeds* (1970); *Who's Next* (1971); *Quadrophenia* (1973)

The Yardbirds--"For Your Love" (1965); "Heart Full of Soul" (1965); "I'm a Man" (1965); "Shapes of Things" (1966); "Over Under Sideways Down" (1966)

The Zombies--"She's Not There" (1964); "Tell Her No" (1965); "Time of the Season" (1969)

--The Second Wave

Bee Gees--"New York Mining Disaster 1941" (1967); "To Love Somebody" (1967); "Holiday" (1967); "Massachusetts" (1967); "I've Gotta Get a Message to You" (1968); "I Started a Joke" (1968); "Lonely Days" (1970); "How Can You Mend a Broken Heart" (#1; 1971); "Jive Talkin'" (#1; 1975); "Nights on Broadway" (1975); "You Should Be Dancing" (#1; 1976); "Love So Right" (1976); "How Deep Is Your Love" (#1; 1977); "Stayin' Alive" (#1; 1978); "Night Fever" (#1; 1978); "Too Much Heaven" (#1; 1978); "Tragedy" (#1; 1979); "Love You Inside Out" (#1; 1979)

Blind Faith--*Blind Faith* (1969)

Joe Cocker--*With a Little Help From My Friends* (1969); *Joe Cocker* (1969); *Mad Dogs & Englishmen* (1970)

Cream--*Fresh Cream* (1967); *Disraeli Gears* (1967); *Wheels of Fire* (1968); *Goodbye* (1969)

Deep Purple--"Hush" (1968); "Kentucky Woman" (1968); "Smoke on the Water" (1973)

Free--"All Right Now" (1970); *Fire and Water* (1970); *Highway* (1971)

Jethro Tull--*Stand Up* (1969); *Benefit* (1970); *Aqualung* (1971); *Thick as a Brick* (1972); *Living in the Past* (1972); *A Passion Play* (1973); *War Child* (1974)

John, Elton--*Elton John* (1970); *Tumbleweed Connection* (1971); *Madman Across the Water* (1971); *Honky Chateau* (1972); *Don't Shoot Me I'm Only the Piano Player* (1973); *Goodbye Yellow Brick Road* (1973); *Caribou* (1974); *Captain Fantastic and the Brown Dirt Cowboy* (1975); *Rock of the Westies* (1975)

Van Morrison--"Brown-Eyed Girl" (1967); *Astral Weeks* (1969); *Moondance* (1970); *His Band and the Street Choir* (1971); *Tupelo Honey* (1971); *Saint Dominic's Preview* (1972)

Mott the Hoople--*Mott the Hoople* (1970); *All the Young Dudes* (1972); *Mott* (1973); *The Hoople* (1974)

The Move--*Shazam!* (1969); *Message From the Country* (1971)

Pink Floyd--*Piper at the Gates of Dawn* (1967); *Ummagumma* (1969); *Atom Heart Mother* (1970); The Dark Side of the Moon (1973); *Wish You Were Here* (1975); *Animals* (1977); *The Wall* (1979); *The Final Cut* (1983); *A Momentary Lapse of Reason* (1987)

Procol Harum--"A Whiter Shade of Pale" (1967); *Shine on Brightly* (1968); *A Salty Dog* (1969); *Home* (1970); *Broken Barricades* (1971); *Live in Concert with the Edmonton Symphony Orchestra* (1972)

Spooky Tooth--*Spooky Two* (1969); *The Last Puff* (1970)

The Status Quo--"Pictures of Matchstick Men" (1968)

Traffic--*Mr. Fantasy* (1968); *Traffic* (1968); *Last Exit* (1969); *John Barleycorn Must Die* (1970); *The Low Spark of High Heeled Boys* (1971); *Shoot Out at the Fantasy Factory* (1973)

The Troggs--"Wild Thing" (#1; 1966); "Love Is All Around" (1968)

--The Third Wave

Bad Company--"Can't Get Enough" (1974); "Feel Like Makin' Love" (1975)

Electric Light Orchestra--*Electric Light Orchestra II* (1973); *On the Third Day* (1973); *Eldorado* (1974); *Face the Music* (1975); *A New World Record* (1976); *Out of the Blue* (1977); *Discovery* (1979); *Xanadu* (with Olivia Newton-John; 1980)

Emerson, Lake & Palmer--*Emerson, Lake & Palmer* (1971); *Tarkus* (1971); *Pictures at an Exhibition* (1972); *Trilogy* (1972)

Stealers Wheel--"Stuck in the Middle with You" (1973)

10cc--"I'm Not in Love" (1975); "The Things We Do For Love" (1977)

Thin Lizzy--*Jailbreak* (1976)

Wings(, Paul McCartney and)--"Another Day" (1971); "Uncle Albert/Admiral Halsey" (1971); "My Love" (1973); "Live and Let Die" (1973); "Jet" (1974); "Band on the Run" (1974); "Junior's Farm" (1975); "Listen to What the Man Said" (1975); "Silly Love Songs" (1976); "Let 'Em In" (1976); "With a Little Luck" (1978)

Yes--*Fragile* (1972); *Close to the Edge* (1972); *Tales From Topographic Oceans* (1973); *Relayer* (1974)

Table 52

Animals

The Animals, thanks in large part to Eric Burdon's powerful, gritty vocals, were one of the most authentic-sounding rhythm and blues revival groups of the British Invasion. The band was also one of the few First Wave acts to make a successful transition from mainstream pop to progressive rock in the late 1960s.

All members of the Animals' original lineup—Burdon, organist Alan Price, lead guitarist Hilton Valentine, bass guitarist Bryan "Chas" Chandler, and drummer John Steel—came from working class families in the Newcastle, England area. After becoming the top pop band in their home town in 1962-1963, the group—feeling that a more dramatic name would increase their chances for a commercial breakthrough—dropped the Alan Price Combo moniker in favor of "the Animals" (taken from audience remarks that they played like a bunch of wild animals). The Animals relocated to London in late 1963, where club dates and television appearances (beginning with BBC's "Saturday Club," December 27, 1963) led to a record contract with British Columbia.

The band's second single, "House of the Rising Sun" (MGM 13264; 1964), a Price arrangement of an African American folk song, reached number one in both England and the United States. Although Price's fear of flying and loss of the spotlight to Burdon led to his departure (he was replaced by the classical-trained organist, Dave Rowberry), the Animals remained a top-selling singles act throughout the mid-1960s with hits such as "I'm Crying" (MGM 13274; 1964; #19), "Don't Let Me Be Misunderstood" (MGM 13311; 1965; #15), "We Gotta Get Out of This Place" (MGM 13382; 1965; #13), "It's My Lfe" (MGM 13414; 1965; #23), and "Don't Bring Me Down" (MGM 13514; 1966; #12).

By mid-1966, with competing artists such as the Beatles and the Beach Boys releasing increasingly sophisticated material, Burdon opted to reorganize the band around most talented musicians such as guitarist/violinist John Weider, guitarist Vic Briggs, bass guitarist Danny McCulloch and drummer Barry Jenkins. Although now focusing on album releases—including *Winds of Change* (MGM 4484; 1967; #42), *The Twain Shall Meet* (MGM 4537; 1968; #79), *Every One of Us* (MGM 4553; 1968; #152), and *Love Is* (MGM 4591; 1969; #123)—complete with socially-relevant lyrics and extended instrumental jams, Eric Burdon and the Animals (as they were now billed) continued to produce best-selling singles, most notably "See See Rider" (MGM 13582; 1966; #10), "When I Was Young" (MGM 13721; 1967; #15), "San Franciscan Nights" (MGM 13769; #9), "Monterey" (MGM 13868; 1967; #15), and "Sky Pilot" (MGM 13939; 1968; #14).

Ever conscious of prevailing trends, Burdon broke-up the group with psychedelia on the wane and formed the funk-oriented War. After the top-selling recording, "Spill the Wine" (MGM 14118; 1970; #3), War left Burdon to pursue mainstream funk success. The original members of the Animals would reform in 1976 to record *Before We Were So Rudely Interrupted* (United Artists 790; 1977). A later reunification would result in *Ark* (I.R.S.70037; 1983) and the live *Rip It to Shreds* (I.R.S.70043; 1984). From the mid-1980s onward, the group performed largely in various rock revival tours. In 1994 the Animals were inducted into the Rock and Roll Hall of Fame.

Table 53

Bee Gees

Many pop music artists have parlayed an eclectic blend of musical styles to achieve commercial success, but the Bee Gees are one of the few to remain on top despite a complete image makeover. Whatever genre assayed by the group, be it British Invasion pop, Baroque ballads, rhythm and blues, disco, or adult contemporary—their recorded output has been distinguished by immaculate three-part vocal harmonies, flawless arrangements and production work, and songwriting of the highest order.

Although the group (particularly in the late 1960s) has sometimes included added personnel, the primary members have always been the three Gibb brothers, Barry (born September 1, 1947) and the twins, Robin and Maurice (born December 22, 1949). They first performed in public at an amateur talent show in Manchester's Gaumont British Theatre in 1955 as "The Blue Cats.". After the family emigrated to Brisbane, Australia in 1958, the trio began performing live as well as appearing on radio and television. Within two years the brothers have been awarded a weekly TV series and secured an eighteen-month residency at Beachcomber Nightclub in Surfers Paradise. Their popularity with Australian youth led to a contract with Festival Records in late

1962. The group's first single, "Three Kisses of Love" (available on: *Bee Gees: The Early Years, Vol. 2*; Excelsior 4402; 1980), was released in January 1963, making Australia's Top Twenty. A string of hits followed, climaxed by three number one hits in 1966: "Wine and Women," "I Was a Lover, a Leader of Men" (both on: *Bee Gees: The Early Years, Vol. 1*; Excelsior 4401; 1980), and "Spicks and Specks" (*Rare Precious & Beautiful*; Atco 33-264; 1968).

Primed to achieve international popularity, the family relocated to England in February 1967. The early months there were spent recording *The Bee Gees' First* (Atco 223; 1967), which included three U.S. Top Twenty singles: "New York Mining Disaster" (Atco 6487; 1967), "To Love Somebody" (Atco 6503; 1967), and "Holiday" (Atco 6521; 1967). The album also earned them the "Beatles imitators" label; their father, Hugh Gibb, refuted the charge, noting, "In actual fact we began recording before the Beatles...we came from Manchester, which is only 30 miles from Liverpool. It is rubbish to say we copied the Beatles' sound, it wasn't their sound, it was an English sound that began with Tommy Steele and skiffle." (liner notes to: *Bee Gees: The Early Years, Vol. 2*)

Despite such criticisms, the group enjoyed a long run of hit singles—including "I Gotta Get a Message to You" (Atco 6603; 1968), "I Started a Joke" (Atco 6639; 1968), "Lonely Days" (Atco 6795; 1970), and "How Can You Mend a Broken Heart" (Atco 6824; 1971)—and moderate-selling LPs—most notably, *Horizontal* (Atco 233; 1968), *Idea* (Atco 253; 1968), *Odessa* (Atco 702; 1969), *Best of Bee Gees* (Atco 292; 1969), *2 Years On* (Atco 353; 1971), *Trafalgar* (Atco 7003; 1971), and *To Whom It May Concern* (Atco 7012; 1972)—interrupted only by Robin's brief departure in 1969 to pursue a solo career. By 1974, however, sales of their increasingly over-produced recordings had dropped off to the point where Atco demanded a stylistic change more in tune with the contemporary music scene. The resulting release, the R&B-disco flavored *Main Course* (RSO 4807; 1975), placed the Bee Gees squarely into the pop mainstream with the help of three Top Twenty singles (including the chart-topper, "Jive Talkin'," RSO 510). During the latter half of the 1970s, no act enjoyed greater chart success. Three of the group's contributions to the *Saturday Night Fever* soundtrack (RSO 4001; 1977)—"How Deep Is You Love" (RSO 882; 1977), "Stayin' Alive" (RSO 885; 1977), and "Night Fever" (RSO 889; 1978)—spent a total of fifteen weeks at the top of the *Billboard Hot 100*. At one point the Bee Gees had five of their compositions in the Top Ten (including songs recorded by Samantha Sang and brother Andy Gibb). The soundtrack remained number one on the album charts for twenty-four weeks; it was estimated at the time to be the best-selling LP in history. They also earned five Grammies for their work on the film soundtrack project in 1978.

Faced with the unenviable task of trying to top their hitherto unprecedented success, the Bee Gees moved away from disco with *Spirits Having Flown* (RSO 3041; 1979), which included three number one singles: "Too Much Heaven" (RSO 913; 1978), "Tragedy" (RSO 918; 1979), and "Love You Inside Out" (RSO 925; 1979). However, album releases comprised of new material from that point onward exhibited a marked decline in sales. While the group's songs continued to exhibit beautiful melodies, lush harmonizing, and polished production work, they appeared predictable compared with earlier cutting-edge releases. Furthermore, Top Forty radio stations seemed less inclined to place new Bee Gees records in rotation. On the other hand, they would remain a fixture within the adult contemporary format until the deaths of Maurice and Robin early in the 21st century anded the band's career.

Table 54

Dave Clark Five

The Dave Clark Five were on offshoot of the Tottenham Hotspurs (suburban London) soccer team; the band was started in order to raise money for a match in Holland. The drummer, Dave Clark, soon took on the main songwriting, producing, and managing responsibilities.

The DC5, as they were frequently called, were one of the first British Invasion groups to achieve hit status in the United States. Between 1964-1967, they placed twenty-four singles and thirteen albums on the charts. Among their notable successes were "Glad All Over" (Epic 9656; 1964), "Bits and Pieces" (Epic 9671; 1964), "Can't You See That She's Mine" (Epic 9692; 1964), "Because" (Epic 9704; 1964), "Catch Us If You Can" (Epic 9833; 1965), and the number one hit "Over and Over" (Epic 9863; 1965).

Unlike many of their British compatriots, who favored softer romantic or novelty styles, the DC5 featured a loud, dynamic sound punctuated by Denis Payton's blaring sex and Clark's taut snare drum figures. Mike Smith's gruff vocals and the densely-textured production work added to the overall sense of excitement. However, the group lacked the ability—or inclination—to develop beyond the simple formulas that had initially resulted in fame and fortune. With poor record sales and new popular music trends such as psychedelia and progressive rock, the band split up in 1970. Smith has continued to record in various projects, while Clark found success in business, including television production and releasing a double-CD retrospective of original DC5 masters in 1993. [Schaffner. 1983]

Table 55

Herman's Hermits

Although considered to be a lightweight novelty act by many rock music critics, Herman's Hermits were one of the most successful British Invasion acts, selling more than forty million records between 1964-1967. The group was formed in 1963 when Peter Noone, a Manchester School of Music student with limited stage and BBC-TV experience, hooked up with an area rock band, the Heartbeats.

Famed record producer Mickie Most began working with them in 1964; their debut single, a remake of the Earl-Jean song, "I'm Into Something Good" (MGM 13280), topped the British charts and sold over a million copies worldwide. The following year, the Hermits placed more songs in the U.S. Top Ten (seven) than the Beatles: "Can't You Hear My Heartbeat" (MGM 13310), "Silhouettes" (MGM 13332), "Mrs. Brown You've Got A Lovely Daughter" (MGM 13341), "Wonderful World" (MGM 13354), "I'm Henry VIII, I Am" (MGM 13367), "Just A Little Bit Better" (MGM 13398), and "A Must To Avoid" (MGM 13437).

The hit recordings had disappeared by early 1968 due to public interest in heavier rock styles. The group dissolved in 1971 during heated legal disputes over royalties payments. Noone tried to launch a solo career and hosted a BBC-TV series for three years in the 1970s. During the 1980s, he recorded both solo and with the Tremblers; he also appeared in the Broadway production of *The Pirates of Penzance* and hosted the VH-1 show, *My Generation*. By the 1990s, Noone had reformed the Hermits to perform in various oldies tours. [Romanowski and George-Warren. 1995.]

Table 56

Searchers

Although overshadowed by fellow Liverpudlians, the Beatles, the Searchers were one of the most accomplished British Invasion bands. Their close, four-part harmonies and rich, jangling guitar lines presaged the commercial ascendancy of folk-rock bands such as the Byrds.

The Searchers, named after John Ford's classic 1956 film, starring John Wayne, were formed in 1961 to play behind British vocalist Johnny Sandon. The group—originally comprised of guitarist John McNally, guitarist Mike Pender, bassist Tony Jackson, and drummer Chris Curtis—later struck out on their own, playing the Star Club (Hamburg, Germany) in the wake of the successful run there by the Beatles. A residency at Liverpool's Iron Door club led A&R man Tony Hatch to offer them a record contract. After charting in the U.K. with the Drifters' "Sweets for My Sweet" (Pye; released in U.S> as Mercury 72172) in 1963, the band achieved success on both sides of the Atlantic—number one in England, number thirteen in the U.S.—with the million-selling "Needles and Pins" (Kapp 577; 1964). More hits—including "Don't Throw Your Love Away" (Kapp 593; 1964), "Love Potion Number Nine" (Kapp 27; 1964), "What Have

They Done to the Rain" (Kapp 644; 1965), and "Bumble Bee" (Kapp 49; 1965)—and international tours followed.

When their recordings stopped charting, the Searchers continued to earn a living playing British clubs and cabarets. Signing with Sire Records, the band returned briefly to the public eye with two album releases, *The Searchers* (Sire 6082; 1980) and *Love's Melodies* (Sire 3523; 1981). Always hampered by the absence of a talented composer within the group, the inclusion of high quality material by Tom Petty, John Fogerty, Moon Martin, Alex Chilton, and other contemporary songwriters on the Sire LPs elicited critical raves. Nevertheless, both discs sold poorly and the band returned to the touring circuit.

Table 57

Shadows

The Shadows have often been described, somewhat erroneously, as the "British Ventures." While each band established a standard within its own nation for producing consistently high quality guitar-dominated, instrumental recordings, the Shadows actually began producing hit singles one year before the Ventures. Furthermore, they doubled as a backing band for England's premier rock star of the day, Cliff Richard, and released a considerable number of their own recordings with vocals.

The two musicians with the Shadows from start to finish, guitarists Hank Marvin and Bruce Welch, met in school at Newcastle and formed a skiffle group, the Railroaders. In April 1958, they began playing in a Soho (London) coffee bar, the Two I's. By summer, they'd met Richard, who invited them to join his backup band, along with Jet Harris and Tony Meehan (who would remain members until the mid-1960s). While playing in London area clubs, Richard and his group, then known as the Drifters, submitted a demo disc to EMI. Securing a contract, they quickly became the most successful recording act in Great Britain on the strength of such hits as "Living Doll" (ABC-Paramount 10042; 1959; #1 UK, #30 US) and "Travellin' Light" (ABC-Paramount 10066; 1959; #1 UK). Marvin's dazzling technique would inspire a generation of British rock guitarists, including Eric Clapton, Jeff Beck, and Pete Townsend.

By 1960, the band—now called the Shadows—was releasing its own records including "Kon-Tiki" (Atlantic 2135; 1961; #1 UK), "Wonderful Land (Atlantic 2146; 1962; #1 UK), and "Dance On" (Atlantic 2177; 1962; #1 UK). Unlike other British instrumental acts (e.g., Mr. Acker Bilk, the Tornadoes), the group was never able to make chart headway stateside. Their signature hit, "Apache" (Columbia; 1960; #1 UK), was successfully covered by Danish guitarist Jorgen Ingmann in the U.S. market (Atco 6184; 1961; #2). They also composed the music for a series of London Palladium pantomime shows—

Aladdin (1964), *Babes in the Wood* (1965), and *Cinderella* (1965)—in addition to scoring and performing in the 1964 film, *Rhythm & Greens*. The group also continued to collaborate with Richard on stage, television, and the movies.

After the departure of bassist John Henry Rostill and drummer Brian Bennett in 1968, the band was officially dissolved. Marvin and Welch continued to work to Richard for a time, but joined forces with Australian guitarist John Farrar to form the Crosby, Stills and Nash-styled band, Marvin, Welch and Farrar. The trio released two commercial unsuccessful LPs, *Marvin, Welch and Farrar* (Capitol 760; 1971) and *Second Opinion* (Sire 7403; 1972), that nevertheless featured an exquisite blend of accomplished songwriting, close-harmony singing and acoustic guitar textures. A final project, *Marvin & Farrar* (EMI 11403; 1973), appeared while the group was in the process of disintegrating. Farrar would gain immediate fame for his production work with Olivia Newton-John in the early 1970s.

All ex-Shadows have remained active in the music business, with various members re-forming many times over the years. Despite efforts to succeed with newly recorded material, fans both in England and abroad have shown a distinct preference for the classic 1960s tracks. Numerous anthologies have been released since the 1970s, the most comprehensive being the six-CD set, *The Early Years, 1959-1966* (EMI 7971712; 1991).

Table 58

10cc

The Manchester-based 10cc were rivaled only by singer/songwriter Randy Newman as multi-level humorists—spanning satire, black comedy, word play, and nonsense verse—within the rock music scene. 10cc also excelled within the realm of pure music—all members were consummate songwriters and studio producers both inside and outside of the band.

10cc was a spin-off of the novelty group, the Hotlegs, famous for the hit, "Neanderthal Man" (Capitol 2886; 1970; #2 UK, #23 US). Hotlegs personnel—vocalist/guitarist/bassist Eric Stewart, formerly with the Mindbenders; vocalist/ guitarist/keyboardist Lol Crème; and vocalist/drummer Kevin Godley—joined forces with ex-Mindbenders vocalist/bassist Graham Gouldman (who'd penned hit songs for the Yardbirds, the Hollies and Herman's Hermits) in mid-1972. Following several singles—including the British hits, "Donna" (UK/Decca 6; 1972; #2 UK) and "Rubber Bullets" (UK/Decca 36; 1973; #1 UK)—a debut LP, *10cc* (UK 53105; 1973; #36 UK), was released, attracting little attention stateside.

By the time a second album, *Sheet Music* (UK 53207; 1974; #9 UK, #81 US), appeared, favorable reviews and word-of-mouth regarding the band's rich vocal textures, strong melodic hooks, polished arrangements, and witty song lyrics ensured greater sales. 10cc peaked commercially with *The Original Soundtrack* (Mercury 1029; 1975; #4 UK, #15 US), driven by the lush ballad, "I'm Not in Love" (Mercury 73678; 1975; #1 UK, #2 US), which featured hundreds of overdubbed voices intoning wry verses such as "I keep your picture upon the wall/It hides the messy stain that's lying there." The next LP, *How Dare You* (Mercury 1061; 1976; #5 UK), sold marginally in the U.S. without the presence of a catchy single.

Godley and Crème—widely acknowledged to be the experimental half of the band—departed to work as a duo, releasing the three-disc set, *Consequences* (Mercury 1700; 1977; #52 UK), which promoted their new "gizmo" guitar device. They would gain recognition as topflight video producers in the 1980s, working with the likes of Herbie Hancock and Frankie Goes to Hollywood. Gouldman and Stewart continued at the helm of a less barbed edition of 10cc, releasing *Deceptive Bends* (Mercury 3702; 1977; #3 UK, #31 US)—which included the hit "The Things We Do for Love" (Mercury 73875; 1976; #6 UK, #5 US), *Live and Let Live* (Mercury 28600; 1977; #14 UK), *Bloody Tourists* (Mercury 6160; 1978; #3 UK, #69 US), *Look Hear!* (Warner Bros. 3442; 1980; #35), *Ten Out of 10* (Warner Bros. 7150 048; 1981), and *Window in the Jungle* (Warner Bros. 28; 1983; #70 UK) prior to dissolving the band in late 1983.

The four original members would reunite in 1991, releasing *Meanwhile* (Polydor 513279; 1992). Despite limited audience interest, Gouldman and Stewart recorded another LP, *Mirror Mirror* (Avex 6; 1995), with distribution limited to Great Britain.

Table 59

Yardbirds

The Yardbirds are generally considered to be one of the most influential bands in rock history. They anticipated progressive rock by experimenting with an eclectic array of musical styles and helped usher in a new virtuosity, particularly for the electric guitar. They were at the forefront of virtually every notable technical innovation for that instrument during the mid-1960s, including feedback, fuzztone, and modal playing. Nevertheless, the Yardbirds remain best known for extra-musical developments: the presence of three of England's greatest rock guitarists—Eric Clapton, Jeff Beck, and Jimmy Page—within the band at one time or another, and the evolution of Page's New Yardbirds into the leading heavy metal act of the 1970s, Led Zeppelin.

Formed in 1963, the London-based Yardbirds—whose original members included lead singer/harmonica player Keith Relf, drummer Jim McCarty, bassist Paul Samwell-Smith, rhythm guitarist Chris Dreja, and lead guitarist Eric Clapton—built a reputation as a blues revival band before recording the albums *Five Live Yardbirds* (British Columbia 1677; 1964; reissued in U.S. as bootleg and as CD on Charly 182; 1989) and *Sonny Boy Williamson and the Yardbirds* (Fontana; 1965; reissued as CD by Repertoire 4776; 1999). Clapton departed after the session that produced "For Your Love" (Epic 9790; 1965; #6)—notable for its innovative harpsichord and bongos arrangement—convinced that the band was becoming too commercial. With Beck on lead guitar, the Yardbirds reached their creative and commercial peak on *For Your Love* (Epic 26167; 1965; #96), *Having a Rave Up with The Yardbirds* (Epic 26177; 1965; #53), and *Over Under Sideways Down* (Epic 26210; 1966; #52).

In mid-1966, Samwell-Smith left the band; his replacement, the session veteran Page, sometimes would play second lead guitar, the most notably example being "Happenings Ten Years Time Ago" (Epic 10094; 1966; #30), which featured one of the most dynamic double guitar solos in rock history. However, Beck departed for a solo career in October 1966; the sole album produced by the remaining quartet, *Little Games* (Epic 26313; 1967; #80), featured bland material and stilted arrangements in an attempt to move into the commercial mainstream.

The band dissolved in mid-1968 with Page and Dreja then forming the New Yardbirds, the precursor to Led Zeppelin. Beck, McCarty, Dreja, and Samwell-Smith joined with guitarist Rory Gallagher and keyboardist Max Middleton to record two LPs in the mid-1980s. The Yardbirds' classic recordings, as well as previously unreleased live material and studio outtakes, have continued to be issued in countless retrospectives over the years.

AMERICAN RENAISSANCE

Surf Music

Surfing, which became popular with Hawaiian nobility centuries ago, caught on as a popular recreational activity along the California coast during the post-World War II period. By the early 1960s, surfing had developed into a youth subculture. The surfing lifestyle was widely disseminated by publications such as John Severson's *Surfer Magazine* and series of excellent film documentaries produced by Bruce Brown, including *Slippery When Wet* (1959), *Barefoot Adventure* (1961), and *Endless Summer*, which documented the mythological worldwide search for the ultimate wave. This way of life was described by Rob Burt and Patsy North, in *West Coast Story*:

> The surfer was not only different in the way he mastered his board at Malibu, but in the way he dressed. He wore pendletons, white levis, baggies; his hair was sun-bleached (or helped a little by peroxide), and he used slang surfing terms: "woodie" described his souped-up old wooden-sided station wagon, which he used to haul his boards; a "goofy foot" was a surfer who rode with his right foot forward on the board. He would most likely have a "hobie" surf-board, built of Clark Foam, and would use a special wax to prevent him from a having a "wipe-out." Schools were divided into the "Surfers" and the "Ho-Dads," who kept up a friendly rivalry.

Although he failed to achieve national stardom, guitarist Dick Dale is generally credited with introducing surf music. Backed by the Del-Tones, he developed a strong following in the Southern California area as the "Pied Piper of Balboa," most notably via weekend dances at the Rendezvous Ballroom. The essentially instrumental sound--a visceral stew of wailing saxophones and atmospheric guitar accented by a pounding twelve-bar bass beat--attempted to evoke tremendous sense of power felt through bonding with the forces of nature while surfing.

The Beach Boys almost single-handedly made the surf sound a national sensation through the addition of evocative song lyrics. Brian Wilson's compositional gifts were so fertile that he was able to give a number one hit to the comedy rock duo, Jan and Dean, while keeping his own band supplied with a steady succession of Top Ten material. That gift, "Surf City," catapulted Jan and Dean past second echelon surf interpreters such as the Surfaris, the Chantays, the Astronauts, the Challengers, the El Caminos, the Fantastic Baggys (featuring P.F. Sloan and Steve Barrie, later to make a name in protest music), and the Marketts. Like the Beach Boys, however, Jan and Dean were savvy enough to avoid too close an identification with the surf sound, mining the car songs genre ("Drag City"), new fads such as skateboarding ("Sidewalk Surfin'"), and assorted novelty material ("Batman").

At its peak, between 1963 and 1965, surf music was as popular with eastern and midwestern youth as in its native Pacific Coast environment. Bands like the Minneapolis-based Trashmen, Chicago's Rivieras, and New York's Trade Winds all climbed the upper reaches of the singles charts with surf songs. In addition, Hollywood supplied a steady stream of beach movies, most notably American International Pictures. The studio's highly successful titles--including *Beach Party*, *Muscle Beach Party*, *Beach Blanket Bingo*, *How to Stuff a Wild Bikini*, *Bikini Beach*, and *Ski Party*--helped expose many surf acts to a mainstream audience. Other popular surf films included *Surf Party*, *Girls on the Beach*, and *Ride the Wild Surf*.

Surf music gradually lost its momentum in the mid-1960s in the face of changing fashions. The pressing social imperatives of the period (e.g., civil rights, the Vietnam War) rendered the genre irrelevant. It retreated back to its former subculture status; however, a small core of cult bands (e.g., Man or Astro-Man, Agent Orange) have continued to produce new music utilizing surf sound conventions into the new millenium.

Top Artists and Their Recordings

The Astronauts--"Baja (Ba-Ha)" (1963)

The Beach Boys--"Surfin'" (1962); "Surfin' Safari" (1962); "Surfin' U.S.A." (1963); "Surfer Girl" (1963); "Do It Again" (1968)

The Chantays--"Pipeline" (1963)

Dick Dale and His Del-Tones--"Let's Go Trippin' (1961/2); "The Scavenger (1963)

Jan and Dean--*Jan and Jean Take Linda Surfin'* (1963); "Surf City" (1963); "Honolulu Lulu" (1963); "Ride the Wild Surf" (1964)

The Marketts--"Surfer's Stomp" (1962); "Balboa Blue" (1962)

The Pyraminds--"Penetration" (1964)

The Rivieras--"California Sun" (1963/4)

The Sunrays--"I Live For the Sun" (1965)

The Surfaris--"Wipe Out"/"Surfer Joe" (1963); "Point Panic" (1963)

The Trade Winds--"New York's a Lonely Town" (1965)

The Trashmen--"Surfin' Bird" (1963/4)

Car Songs/Hot Rod Music

Car songs, like surf music, were largely a Southern California phenomenon. They were a byproduct of the region's active hot rod scene, which had evolved from the illegal street races of the 1940s to the Bonneville Salt Flats speed weeks and drag strips of the 1960s. Hot rodding included its own crew of culture heroes, including customizer George Barris and drivers "Big Daddy" Garlits and Craig Breedlove, who set a series of land speed records in his "Spirit of America." In addition to musical tributes, the hot rod scene was lionized by Hollywood films, plastic car models available in hobby shops, and Bob Peterson's mass circulation periodical, *Hot Rod*.

Recognizing the presence of the subculture of potential consumers (not to mention the vicarious interest of middle American youth as a whole), a nucleus of talented Los Angeles-based songwriters and arrangers/producers began fueling the craze in the early 1960s, most notably Brian Wilson of the Beach Boys, Jan Berry of Jan and Dean, Roger Christian (a deejay at KFWB), Gary Usher, Terry Melcher, and Bruce Johnston. Usher--who contributed to the success of the Hondells' hits, "Little Honda" and "My Buddy Seat," and many the Surfaris' recordings--teamed with Christian to produce hit recordings and film soundtracks. Johnston and Melcher masterminded the success of the Ripchords (e.g., "Hey Little Cobra) and had their own hits as Bruce and Terry: "Custom Machine" and "Summer Means Fun."

As with surf music, the rise of folk rock and protest music in essence submerged the car song genre. The Beach Boys began experimenting with more progressive styles, augmented by the addition of Johnston to enable Wilson to avoid touring, thereby concentrating on songwriting and studio production. Jan Berry, on the brink of creating increasingly sophisticated sounds of his own, nearly died when his Corvette Stingray crashed at the fabled Dead Man's Curve. Melcher and Usher teamed up to produce the latest West Coast sensation, the Byrds.

Top Artists and Their Recordings

The Beach Boys--"409" (1962); "Shut Down" (1963); "Little Deuce Coupe" (1963); "Fun, Fun, Fun" (1964); ""Little Honda" (1964)

Bruce and Terry--"Custom Machine" (1964)

Dale, Dick, and the Del-tones—"Mr. Eliminator" (1964); "Wild, Wild Mustang" (1964)

The Duals--"Stick Shift" (1961)

The Hondells--"Little Honda" (1964); "My Buddy Seat" (1964/5)

Jan and Dean--"Drag City" (1963/4); "Dead Man's Curve" (1964); "The Little Old Lady From Pasadena" (1964)

The Rip Chords--"Hey Little Cobra" (1963/4); "Three Window Coupe" (1964)

Ronny and the Daytonas--"G.T.O." (1964); "Bucket 'T'" (1964/5)

The Routers--"Let's Go" (1962); "Sting Ray" (1963)

Folk Rock

Folk rock fused the commercial folk tradition of the early 1960s with the rock songcraft best exemplified by the Beatles. Its most notable features included the eclectic blending of electric and acoustic instruments, group harmonies, and poetic--often political with a pronounced anti-establishment mesage--song lyrics. The genre, which reached its commercial and artistic zenith for a brief period during 1965-1966, was a product of experiments by young urban folk interpreters such as Bob Dylan, Jim (later Roger) McGuinn, and Barry McGuire. These, other performers, also incorporated the work of topical/protest singer/songwriters including Phil Ochs, Tom Paxton, Eric Andersen, Buffy Saint-Marie, Tim Hardin, Janis Ian, Leonard Cohen, Joni Mitchell, and Jackson Browne. The keynote of the movement was rebellion--rebellion against a wide range of social mores, the anti-commercial snobbery of the urban folk movement (e.g., the organizers of the Newport Folk Festival who were scandalized by Dylan's use of an electric support band in 1965), and their own pretentions regarding the moral and aesthetic values of traditional music.

Folk rock became a national obsession when the Byrds' cover of a Dylan composition, "Mr. Tambourine Man," reached number one on the pop singles charts in the early summer of 1965. This was followed by Sonny and Cher's "I Got You Babe" and Dylan's own "Like a Rolling Stone." During this era, however, artists were disinclined to stay in one place. For a brief moment, pop stars found they could pursue art while also cultivating monetary success and a large following. As a result, the studio experiments of the Beatles and like-minded artists pulled folk rockers toward the progressive rock vanguard. By mid-1966, folk rock was little more than a lingering memory. Nevertheless, it left a substantial imprint upon the pop world, influencing country rock, the singer/songwriter movement, the softer side of psychedelia, and various regional sounds such as San Francisco rock and Tex-Mex.

Folk rock continued to thrive abroad, in England and the Commonwealth countries. Beginning with Donovan's blend of Dylanesque lyrics and exotic instrumentation, British folk rock evolved back to an emphasis on home-grown song material. This folk material was typically framed by electric instruments and a rock steady beat. Spurred by the virtuostic talents of bands like Fairport Convention, Pentangle, and Steeleye Span, British folk rock thrived for more than a decade beginning in the late 1960s; many of the musicians originally part of the movement remain active today.

Top Artists and Their Recordings

Buffalo Springfield—*Buffalo Springfield* (1966); *Again* (1967); *Last Time Around* (1968)

The Byrds--*Mr. Tambourine Man* (1965); *Turn! Turn! Turn!* (1965); *Fifth Dimension* (1966); *Younger Than Yesterday* (1967); *Notorious Byrd Brothers* (1967)

Bob Dylan--*Bringing It All Back Home* (1965); *Highway 61 Revisited* (1965); *Blonde on Blonde* (1966); *John Wesley Harding* (1967)

The Fugs--*First Album* (1965); *The Fugs* (1966); *Tenderness Junction* (1968); *It Crawled Into My Hand, Honest* (1968)

The Holy Modal Rounders--*Indian War Whoop* (1967); *Holy Modal Rounders, Vol. 1* (1968); *Holy Modal Rounders, Vol. 2* (1968); *Moray Eels Eat the Holy Modal Rounders* (1969)

Jim Kweskin Jug Band--*Best of the Jim Kweskin Jug Band* (1968)

Lovin' Spoonful--*Do You Believe in Magic* (1965); *Daydream* (1966); *Hums of the Lovin' Spoonful* (1966); *Everything Playing* (1967)

The Mamas and the Papas--*If You Can Believe Your Eyes and Ears* (1966); *The Mamas and the Papas* (1966); *Deliver* (1967)

Barry McGuire--*Eve of Destruction* (1965); *This Precious Time* (1966)

Simon and Garfunkel--*Sounds of Silence* (1966); *Parsley, Sage, Rosemary and Thyme* (1966); *Bookends* (1968)

Sonny and Cher--*Look at Us* (1965); *The Wondrous World of Sonny and Cher* (1966); *In Case You're in Love* (1967)

The Turtles--*It Ain't Me Babe* (1965); *You Baby* (1966); *Happy Together* (1967)

--British Folk Rock

Sandy Denny--*Fotheringay* (1970); *Sandy Denny* (1970); *The Northstar Grassman and the Ravens* (1971); *Sandy* (1972); *Rock On* (1972); *Like an Old Fashioned Waltz* (1973)

Donovan--*Catch the Wind* (1965); *Fairytale* (1965); *Sunshine Superman* (1966); *Mellow Yellow* (1966); *For Little Ones* (1967); *Wear Your Love Like Heaven* (1967); *Donovan in Concert* (1968); *The Hurdy Gurdy Man* (1968)

Fairport Convention--*Fairport Convention* (1968); *What We Did on Our Holidays* (1968); *Heyday* (1968); *Unhalfbricking* (1969); *Liege and Lief* (1969); *Full House* (1970); *Angel Delight* (1971); *Babbacombe Lee* (1972)

The Incredible String Band--*The Incredible String Band* (1966); *The 5000 Spirits or the Layers of the Onion* (1967); *The Hangman's Beautiful Daughter* (1967); *Wee Tam* (1968); *The Big Huge* (1968); *Changing Horses* (1969); *I Looked Up* (1970); *U* (1970); *Be Glad for the Song Has No Ending* (1970)

Ian Matthews--*Matthews Southern Comfort* (1970); *Second Spring* (1970); *Later That Same Year* (1971); *If You Saw Thro' My Eyes* (1972); *Tigers Will Survive* (1972); *Valley Hi* (1973); *Some Days You Eat the Bear...and Some Days the Bear Eats You* (1974)

Pentangle--*The Pentangle* (1968); *Sweet Child* (1969); *Basket of Light* (1970); *Cruel Sister* (1971); *Reflection* (1971); *Solomon's Seal* (1972); *Pentangling* (1973)

Steeleye Span--*Hark! The Village Wait* (1970); *Please to See the King* (1971); *Ten Man Mop* (1971); *Below the Salt* (1972); *Parcel of Rogues* (1973); *Now We Are Six* (1974); *Commoner's Crown* (1975); *All Around My Hat* (1975)

The Strawbs--*Strawbs* (1969); *Dragonfly* (1970); *Just a Collection of Antiques and Curios* (1970); *From the Witchwood* (1971); *Grave New World* (1972)

--Australian Folk Rock

The Seekers--*Georgy Girl* (1967); *The Seekers' Greatest Hits* (1967)

Table 60

Byrds

The Byrds were the first recording act to popularize folk rock, a blend of British Invasion-influenced rock—with its chiming guitars and seamless harmonies—and the socio-political poetry typifying the best folk music song lyrics. Not content to be known as a Bob Dylan cover band, they pioneered extended raga-rock jams, studio electronic effects and are generally credited with producing the first true country rock album, *Sweetheart of the Rodeo*.

The group's original members—lead guitarist/vocalist Roger McGuinn, guitarist/vocalist Gene Clark, Rhythm guitarist/vocal David Crosby, bassist Chris Hillman, and drummer Michael Clarke—were all folk and bluegrass performers based in the Los Angeles area who'd become fascinated by the songcraft and fashion sense exhibited by the Beatles. Manager Jim Dickson helped secure a recording contract with Columbia, and the band's first release, the Dylan-penned "Mr. Tambourine Man" (Columbia 43271; 1965) topped the charts, driven by McGuinn's trademark twelve-string guitar and tight three-part harmonies reminiscent of the Everly Brothers as filtered through the Beatles. The Byrds' first three albums—*Mr. Tambourine Man* (Columbia 9172; 1965), *Turn! Turn! Turn!* (Columbia 9254; 1965), and *Fifth Dimension* (Columbia 9349; 1966)—further refined the formula, which became the template for a host of imitators, including the Turtles, Simon and Garfunkel, Barry McGuire, We Five, and soft rock pioneers, the Mamas and the Papas.

By the 1966, rock's superstars—the Beatles (particularly on *Revolver*, Captitol 2576) the Rolling Stones, and the Beach Boys, among others—were pushing the boundaries of sonic possibilities in the recording studio, integrating hitherto exotic instruments such as sitars and harpsichords, electronics (e.g., feedback, phasing), and multi-tracking into the framework of the pop song. The Byrds remained on the cutting edge with two adventurous LPs, *Younger Than Yesterday* (Columbia 9442; 1967) and *The Notorious Byrd Brothers* (Columbia 9575; 1968), but the lack of major hit singles limited commercial success.

Internal differences led to fragmentation of the group; Crosby helped found Crosby, Stills and Nash and Gene Clark pursued a solo career (as well as collaborating with the Gosdin Brothers). With McGuinn now in charge—augmented by the only remaining charter member, bluegrass veteran Hillman—they released the landmark country rock LP, *Sweetheart of the Rodeo* (Columbia 9670; 1968), featuring the material and lead vocals of Gram Parsons. Although Hillman and Parsons left to form the Flying Burrito Brothers, McGuinn continued to explore a country-inflected rock style in later album releases: *Dr. Byrds & Mr. Hyde* (Columbia 9755; 1969), *Ballad of Easy Rider* (Columbia 9942; 1969), *The Byrds [Untitled]* (Columbia 30127; 1970), *Byrdmaniax* (Columbia 30640; 1971), and *Farther Along* (Columbia 31050; 1971).

McGuinn elected to pursue a solo career; his recorded work was stylistically similar to the 1970s Byrds LPs. Short-term reunions of various group members have occurred over the years, resulting in the following releases: *Byrds* (Asylum 5058; 1973), *McGuinn, Clark and Hillman* (Capitol 11910; 1979), McGuinn, Clark and Hillman's *City* (Capitol 12043; 1980), *McGuinn and Hillman* (Capitol 12108; 1980), and *The Byrds* (Columbia 46773; 1990; a retrospective box set including two tracks from a 1990 Roy Orbison tribute and four new compositions recorded by Crosby, Hillman, and McGuinn). The band was inducted into the Rock and Roll Hall of Fame in 1991.

Table 61

Donovan (Leitch)), May 10, 1946-

Donovan was a highly derivative artist. He always appeared to be jumping on the latest stylistic bandwagon, be it commercial folk, folk rock, protest music, pop-psychedelia, the singer-songwriter vogue, or even heavy metal. Nevertheless, his popularity was not unwarranted; he was an extremely gifted composer and projected considerable sincerity and warmth both live and on record.

Born in Glasgow, Scotland, he relocated to London with his family at age ten. Following a year of college, he attempted to break into the music business by recording demos of his material. These recordings would enable him to land a regular slot on the British rock TV variety show, *Ready Steady Go*, in early 1965. The program provided a springboard to the U.K. pop charts.

Donovan's British recordings, combined with an appearance at the 1965 Newport Folk Festival, laid the groundwork for commercial success in America. Following the acoustic-flavored hits, "Catch the Wind" (Hickory 1309; 1965; #23), "Colours" (Hickory 1324; 1965; #61), and "Universal Soldier" (Hickory 1338; 1965; #53), Donovan—under the sure hand of producer Mickie Most—began recording more rock-oriented songs. His chart singles—most notably, "Sunshine Superman" (Epic 10045; 1966; #1), "Mellow Yellow" (Epic 10098; 1966; #2), "Hurdy Gurdy Man" (Epic 10345; 1967; #5), and "Atlantis" (Epic 10434; 1969; #7)—and albums—*Sunshine Superman* (Epic 26217; 1966; #11), *Mellow Yellow* (Epic 26239; 1967; #14), *A Gift From a Flower to a Garden* (Epic 171; 1968; #19), *Donovan in Concert* (Epic 26386; 1968; #18), *The Hurdy Gurdy Man* (Epic 26420; 1968; #20), *Donovan's Greatest Hits* (Epic 26439; 1969; #4), *Barabajagal* (Epic 26481; 1969; #23), *Open Road* (Epic 30125; 1970; #16), and *Cosmic Wheels* (Epic 32156; 1973; #25)—featured a diversified palette of instrumental colors and mystical lyrics. Much of his flower-power aura derived from his conversion in 1967 to Maharishi Mahesh Yogi's brand of meditation—as opposed to drug use—as a means of mind expansion.

When the hits stopped coming, Donovan shifted his attention to scoring films, including *If It's Tuesday This Must Be Belgium* (1969), *The Pied Piper* (German, 1972), *Tangled Details* (animation feature, 1973), and *Brother Sun, Sister Moon* (1973). He also composed a theatrical revue, *7-Tease* (1975; a hard-rock soundtrack was issued in 1974) and published a volume of poetry, *Dry Songs and Scribbles*, while touring and recording sporadically. In the early 1990s, the Manchester band, Happy Mondays, helped revive interest in his work; however, real commercial success has continued to elude him. To many of today's youth, he is best known as the father of actress Ione Skye (*Say Anything*, *River's Edge*) and actor Donovan Leitch, Jr.

Table 62

Pentangle

Pentangle was widely perceived as past of the British folk rock movement which arose in the latter half of the 1960s. However, the group was far more eclectic than the leading exponents of the genre—most notably, Fairport Convention, Steeleye Span, and Lindisfarne—with a recorded repertoire that spanned jazz, blues, Indian ragas, traditional English folk music, and self-penned pop-rock material.

This eclecticism was largely the result of the diversified backgrounds of the group members. Pentangle's music featured the interplay of two acoustic guitar virtuosos, Bert Jansch and John Renbourne. Jacqui McShee's unadorned vocals possessed a crystalline purity which effectively conveyed the emotional depth of traditional folk ballads; the fact that Jansch and Renbourne were also very capable singers made possible the inclusion of additional colors and textures. Bassist Danny Thompson and drummer Terry Cox provided a jazz-inflected underbelly to the overall group synergy. The dynamic blend of these sometimes disparate elements in *The Pentangle* (Reprise 6315; 1968; #21 UK, #192 US) opened a new direction for the British folk scene.

Although later releases failed to measure up to the promise of the debut LP, Pentangle's sheer musicality and inherent good taste ultimately redeem them all. The double album, *Sweet Child* (Reprise 6334; 1969), employs a half-studio/half-live format. The solo segments provide much insight as to the respective contributions of each member. The jazzy, improvisational feel of these early works is largely absent from *Basket of Light* (Reprise 6372; 1970; #5 UK, #200 US); a more standardized folk-rock approach tends to dominate most the tracks.

The group's best-known recording, *Cruel Sister* (Reprise 6430; 1970; #51 UK, #193 US), revealed the encroachment of progressive rock values. Side two of the original disc consisted of an extended suite-like treatment of the traditional ballad, Jack Orion. Despite fine musicianship and the use of varied instrumentation (including wind instruments and muted electric guitars), the critical consensus held that the piece failed to sustain interest. Later albums—*Reflection* (Reprise 6463; 1971; #183), *Solomon's Seal* (Reprise 2100; 1972; #184), and *Pentangling* (Transatlantic 29; 1973; compilation of earlier material; not issued in U.S. until 1977)—saw the group revert back to a more predictable song set format. Although more original material began to appear, most of it lacked the distinctiveness of the classic folk material.

Since Pentangle's breakup in 1973, individual members remained active in the music business. Jansch and Renbourne, in particular, issued a considerable number of critically acclaimed solo albums. The original group members got back together to record *Open the Door* (Varrick 017; 1985). Jansch and McShee—along with a shifting lineup of supporting players—kept Pentangle going until the mid-1990s. McShee has continued to use the name within the context of what is essentially a solo career.

Table 63

Turtles

The Turtles illustrated the dilemma facing most rock acts at a time when commercial viability was tied to maintaining an ongoing string of hit singles. Despite a strong melodic sense and two of the finest pop singers of that era, Mark Volman and Howard Kaylan (born Kaplan), the band felt compelled to continually shift stylistic gears in order to retain an audience. The pressures generated by such compromises appears to have played as much of a role as the widely known legal disputes with the White Whale label over finances in the group's demise.

The nucleus of the Turtles—Volman, Kaylan, Al Nichol, and Chuck Portz—began performing together while still attending high school in southern Los Angeles. While attending local colleges, they added drummer Don Murray to the lineup. Known as the Crossfires in 1964-1965, the band's sound was modeled after their idols, the Beatles. A series of weekend engagements with Manhattan Beach's Rebellaire Club resulted in owner Reb Foster's offer to manage them. One of his first moves was to secure a recording contract with the newly formed White Whale. The debut album, *It Ain't Me Babe* (White Whale 7111; 1965), had a pronounced folk-rock feel, with two protest numbers—"It Ain't Me Babe" (White Whale 222; 1965; #8) and "Let Me Be" (White Whale 224; 1965; #29)—doing well on the singles charts.

As folk-rock faded, the Turtles turned increasingly to pop-rock featuring non-controversial lyrics. Hit songs included one of the most perfectly constructed rock recordings ever, "Happy Together" (White Whale 244; 1967; #1), "She's Rather Be With Me" (White Whale 249; 1967; #3), "You Know What I Mean" (White Whale 254; 1967; #12), "She's My Girl" (White Whale 260; 1967; #14), "Elenore" (White Whale 276; 1968; #6), and "You Showed Me" (White Whale 292; 1969). "Eleanore" represented the high point of the band's aesthetic disillusionment. Written from a sarcastic point-of-view, with overly sentimental, stilted Tin Pan Alley-styled verses, its commercial success confounded group members. Their albums—most notably, *Happy Together* (White Whale 7114; 1967), *The Turtles! Golden Hits* (White Whale 7115; 1967), *The Turtles Present the Battle of the Bands* (White Whale 7118; 1968), *Turtle Soup* (White Whale 7124; 1969), *The Trutle! More Golden Hits* (White Whale 7127; 1970)—also sold well throughout the latter half of the 1960s.

Unhappy with the direction their music had taken and hopelessly entangled in litigation over financial issues with White Whale, the group disbanded in 1970. Interested in exploring a more satirical bent, Volman and Kaylan joined Frank Zappa's Mothers of Invention. Their vocals rendered Zappa's work more musically accessible than any other phase of his career. They then formed Phlorescent Leech and Eddie (later Flo and Eddie), releasing a long string of albums that expanded the boundaries of humor within a progressive rock format. The duo's creative energies spanned a wide range of activities, including live performing, journalism, and radio work. They also took an increased interest in the Turtles' legacy, working with Rhino Records to release anthologies of both classic tracks and rare materials—*The Turtles – 1968* (Rhino 901; 1978), *20 Greatest Hits* (Rhino 5160; 1984), *Chalon Road* (Rhino 70155; 1987), *Shell Shock* (Rhino 70158; 1987), and *Turtle Wax; The Best of the Turtles, Volume 2* (Rhino 70159; 1988)—as well as the original LPs. The company also produced video documentary of the band's career, *Happy Together* (#976000; 2000), in the DVD format.

Protest Music

Although, the protest music movement of the mid-1960s represented a stylistic spinoff of the folk-rock genre, its ancestry can be clearly discerned as far back as the colonial era in American history; the revered "Yankee Doodle" falls within this category. The output of seminal commercial folk artists such as Woody Guthrie, Leadbelly, and Peter Seeger in the pre-World War II period, the Weavers in the 1950s, and Bob Dylan, Joan Baez, Phil Ochs, and Peter, Paul and Mary in the early 1960s laid the foundation for later protest material.

Other than concern regarding the sudden escalation of the Vietnam conflict, topical matter in mid-1960s protest songs differed little from its immediate antecedents; e.g., civil rights, nuclear disarmament, international peace. The music, however, had evolved from acoustic-oriented folk stylings to rock-based rhythms. Softer material--generally performed by commercial folk artists or singer-songwriters--continued to be released, but it now comprised a comparatively small portion of the total protest output.

Barry McGuire's "Eve of Destruction," which entered the singles charts in August 1965, represented a symbolic milestone in the protest song movement. Although far from being an early example of the genre, it was the first such recording to reach number one and, in the process attracted a considerable degree of controversy. Criticized for its extreme pessimism, the song was ultimately banned by many radio station program directors.

Despite efforts to suppress the song--or perhaps largely because of them--McGuire's hit inspired a rash of similar releases. But whereas "Eve of Destruction" focused on a condemnation of war in general, much protest material which followed directly criticized America's involvement in Vietnam. By 1966, rising troop commitments, casualty figures, and draft quotas all contributed to an increasing anti-war sentiment on the part of American youth. For the next couple of years, the growth and popularity of protest songs roughly paralleled the escalation of America's war effort in Southeast Asia.

By 1968, however, the number of anti-war songs released sharply declined and these seemed to lack immediacy and forcefulness of earlier material. H. Ben Auslander, in a 1981 *Journal of American Culture* article, offered the following explanation for this decline: "...performers and audiences alike were physically and spiritually exhausted by the war against the war and simply did not want to be reminded of the conflict any more than was necessary. Another possible reason may be that many shared the sense of manic resignation expressed by Phil Ochs in his last anti-Vietnam song, "The War is Over." The fervor with which the Nixon administration suppressed subversive behavior in general may well have also contributed to the protest song movement's loss of vitality.

Top Artists and Their Recordings

--Commentary on Social Conformity

Janis Ian--"Society's Child" (1967)

The Searchers--"Take Me For What I'm Worth" (1966)

Pete Seeger--"Little Boxes" (1964)

Neil Young--"Here We Are in the Years" (1969)

--Condemnation of Police Brutality

Buffalo Springfield--"For What It's Worth" (1966)

--Condemnation of the U.S. Selective Service

Donovan--"To Susan on the West Coast Waiting" (1968)

Arlo Guthrie--"The Alice's Restaurant Massacree" (1967)

Phil Ochs--"The Draft Dodger Rag" (1965); "I Ain't Marchin' Anymore" (1965)

Peter, Paul and Mary--"The Great Mandala" (1967)

--Condemnation of the Vietnam War

The Association--"Requiem for the Masses" (1967)

Joan Baez--"Saigon Bride" (1967)

Country Joe and the Fish--"I-Feel-Like-I'm-Fixin'-To-Die Rag" (1967)

Crosby, Stills, Nash and Young--"Ohio" (1970)

Donovan--"The War Drags On" (1965)

Earth Opera--"American Eagle Tragedy" (1969)

Jefferson Airplane--"Volunteers" (1969)

Phil Ochs--"Talkin' Vietnam Blues" (1964); "White Boots Marching in a Yellow Land" (1968)

Tom Paxton--Lyndon Johnson Told the Nation" (1965)

The Plastic Ono Band--"Give Peace a Chance" (1969)

Pete Seeger--"Waist Deep in Big Muddy" (1967)

--Criticism of the Justice System

Moby Grape--"Murder in My Heart For the Judge" (1968)

--General Condemnation of War

Eric Burden and the Animals--"Sky Pilot" (1968)

Glen Campbell--"The Universal Soldier" (1965)

Donovan--"The Universal Soldier"(1965)

The Doors--"The Unknown Soldier" (1968)

Bob Dylan--"Masters of War" (1963)

The Fugs--"Kill For Peace" (1965)

Barry McGuire--"Eve of Destruction" (1965)

Peter, Paul and Mary--"Cruel War" (1962)

Kenny Rankin--"The Dolphin" (1969)

Malvina Reynolds--"What Have They Done to the Rain?" (1963)

The Searchers--"What Have They Done to the Rain?" (1964)

Simon and Garfunkel--"Seven O'Clock News/Silent Night" (1966)

--Inhumanity of Mankind/Hypocrisy

Henson Gargill--"Skip a Rope" (1967/8)

Jeannie C. Riley--"Harper Valley P.T.A." (1968)

Spanky and Our Gang--"Give a Damn" (1968)

Soul Music

Whereas rhythm and blues had always been largely secular in its concerns, soul music's tone and message possessed a decidedly apocalyptic cast. The genre appropriated both the gospel stylings Ray Charles had grafted onto rhythm and blues and elements of religious imagery. Sam Cooke perhaps best exemplified the latter contribution, utilizing the smooth approach of sophisticated pop music as well as the ethereal harmonies reminiscent of the Soul Stirrers, the gospel quartet with whom he'd former sang. In the words of one of the genre's chief exponents, Atlantic Records artist, Solomon Burke, "The business of soul music was salvation."

Its ascendancy in the early 1960s owed much, however, to an opportune confluence of developments. *Rolling Stone* journalist Peter Guralnick has described soul as "a peculiarly good-hearted and optimistic sort of music," a reflection of a period when black pride was largely manifested in civil rights activism. More specifically, soul represented a kind of conscious anachronism; a prideful exploration of cultural roots in the face of a century-long movement toward assimilation into white mainstream society.

This explains the appeal of soul to the black community. However, it was also more popular with mainstream white society than had been the case with any predominantly African American music style up to that time. Crossover success was made possible by the record industry's broad-minded attitude regarding racial interaction combined with the efforts of British rock bands to champion the cause of American r & b musicians (a practice later adopted by many stateside rock performers as well).

The success of soul music, however, was most indebted to the availability of large roster of genuinely talented artists. Some, such as James Brown and Ray Charles, had spent the 1950s at the vanguard of the r & b cross-fertilization which led to the emergence of soul. Others--most notably Solomon Burke, Wilson Pickett, Otis Redding, and Aretha Franklin--were seminal in establishing the style's vocabulary. Burke, a vastly underrated artist who never was able to crack the top twenty pop singles chart, possessed a smooth, lush voice, which hinted at barely contained power, and exhibited a mastery of gospel techniques, including heartfelt sermonizing, caressing melodic interludes, and rumbling bass notes.

During its commercial heyday, soul split off into a number of regional styles. The most successful of these included:

(1) the Chicago Sound, a softer, ballad-oriented variant whose most distinctive feature consisted of male falsetto leads;

(2) the Memphis Sound, a loose, gritty blend of country and r & b, best exemplified by the Stax/Volt label releases;

(3) the Motown Sound, which employed gospel-like vocal work within a pop framework featuring a "hot" mix of shrill, hissing cymbals, booming bass, and a sweet overlay of strings;

(4) the Muscle Shoals Sound, a funky, countrified hybrid developed at Rick Hall's Fame Studios in Florence, Alabama;

(5) the Sound of Philadelphia, a direct descendant of the Chicago Sound featuring lush arrangements (masterminded by two production teams headed by Thom Bell and Kenny Gamble/Leon Huff) within which each instrument is clearly identifiable; and

(6) blue-eyed soul, a label embracing a wide stylistic array of white interpreters of the genre.

Each of these offshoots was built around a stable cast of producers and session musicians who were responsible for placing a recognizable stamp on all recordings. Nevertheless, most of the studios (and labels) involved had the collective insight--and flexibility--required to enable the particular strengths of individual acts to come through. For example, the rougher styles characterizing Jr. Walker's instrumental work and the singing of Martha and the Vandellas flourished amidst the slick professionalism of the Motown recording process.

By the early 1970s, despite the continued success of selective recordings (particularly the then peaking Philly Soul), the genre was beginning to succumb to its essentially conservative instincts: its insistence on a unified tradition, stylistic purity, and simplified mode of communication. Many of the record companies committed to soul were either undergoing growing pains in the process of reaching out for major label status (e.g., Atlantic, Motown) or on the threshold of going out of business (e.g., Stax, the Chicago-based Vee-Jay). Furthermore, newly emerging black musical styles were now vying for a larger share of the commercial marketplace, most notably funk and disco. In the face of constantly changing fashions, soul--already seen by industry taste-makers and record consumers as hopelessly old-fashioned--would be forced to assume a greatly diminished profile within popular music world.

Top Artists and Their Recordings

--Chicago Soul

Jerry Butler--"For Your Precious Love" (1958; 1966); "He Will Break Your Heart" (1960); "Find Another Girl" (1961); "I'm Telling You" (1961); "Moon River" (1961); "Make It Easy on Yourself" (1962); "Need to Belong" (1963); "Mr. Dream Merchant" (1967); "Never Give You Up" (1968); "Hey, Western Union Man" (1968); "Are You Happy" (1968/9); "Only the Strong Survive" (1969); "Moody Woman" (1969); "What's the Use of Breaking Up" (1969)

Jerry Butler, and Betty Everett--Let It Be Me" (1964)

Gene Chandler--"Duke of Earl" (1962); "Just Be True" (1964); "Bless Our Love" (1964); "What Now" (1964/5); "Nothing Can Stop Me" (1965); "Groovy Situation" (1970)

Dee Clark--"Nobody But You" (1958/59); "Just Keep It Up" (1959); "Hey Little Girl" (1959); "How About That" (1959/60); "Your Friends" (1961); "Raindrops" (1961)

The Impressions--"Gypsy Woman" (1961); "It's All Right" (1963); "Talking About My Baby" (1964); "I'm So Proud" (1964); "Keep on Pushing" (1964); "You Must Believe Me" (1964); "Amen" (1964); "People Get Ready" (1965); "Woman's Got Soul" (1965); "You've Been Cheatin'" (1965); "We're a Winner" (1967/8); "Fool For You" (1969); "This is My Country" (1968); "Choice of Colors" (1969); "Check Out Your Mind" (1970); "Finally Got Myself Together (I'm a Changed Man)" (1974)

Curtis Mayfield--"(Don't Worry) If There's a Hell Below We're All Going to Go: (1970); "Freddie's Dead" (1972); "Superfly" (1972); "Future Shock" (1973); "Kung Fu" (1974)

--Motown Sound

The Contours--"Do You Love Me" (1962)

The Four Tops--"Baby I Need Your Loving" (1964); "Ask the Lonely" (1965); "I Can't Help Myself" (1965); "It's the Same Old Song" (1965); "Something About You" (1965); "Shake Me, Wake Me (When It's Over)"; "Reach Out I'll Be There" (1966); "Standing in the Shadows of Love" (1966/7); "Bernadette" (1967); "7 Rooms of Gloom" (1967); "You Keep Running Away" (1967); "Walk Away Renee" (1968); "If I Were a Carpenter" (1968); "It's All in the Game" (1970); "Still Water (Love)" (1970); "Just Seven Numbers" (1970); "MacArthur Park" (1971)

Marvin Gaye--"Stubborn Kind of Fellow" (1962); "Hitch Hike" (1963); "Pride and Joy" (1963); "Can I Get a Witness" (1963); "You're a Wonderful One" (1964); "Try It Baby" (1964); "Baby Don't You Do It" (1964); "How Sweet It Is to Be Loved By You" (1964); "I'll Be Doggone" (1965); "Pretty Little Baby" (1965); "Ain't That Peculiar" (1965); "One More Heartache" (1966); "Your Unchanging Love" (1967); "You" (1968); "Chained" (1968); "I Heard It Through the Grapevine" (1968); "Too Busy Thinking About My Baby" (1969); "That's the Way Love Is" (1969); "The End of Our Road" (1970); "What's Going On" (1971); "Mercy Mercy Me (The Ecology)" (1971); "Inner City Blues" (1971); "Trouble Man" (!972/3); "Let's Get It On" (1973); "Come Get to This" (1973); "Distant Lover" (1974); "I Want You"(1976); "Got to Give It Up--Pt. 1" (1977)

Marvin Gaye and Diana Ross--"You're a Special Part of Me" (1973); "My Mistake" (1974)

Marvin Gaye and Tammi Terrell--"Ain't No Mountain High Enough" (1967); "Your Precious Love" (1967); "If I Could Build My Whole World Around You" (1967); "Ain't Nothing Like the Real Thing" (1968); "You're All I Need to Get By" (1968); "Keep on Lovin' Me Honey" (1968); "Good Lovin' Ain't Easy to Come By" ((1969)

Marvin Gaye and Mary Wells--"Once Upon a Time"/"What's the Matter With You Baby" (1964)

Marvin Gaye and Kim Weston--"It Takes Two" (1967)

Gladys Knight and the Pips--"Everybody Needs Love" (1967); "I Heard It Through the Grapevine" (1967); "The End of Our Road" (1968); "It Should Have Been Me" (1968); "The Nitty Gritty" (1969); "The Friendship Train" (1969); "You Need Love Like I Do" (1970); "If I Were Your Woman" (1970); "I Don't Want to Do Wrong" (1971); "Make Me the Woman That You Go Home To" (1971/2); "Help Me Make It Through the Night" (1972); "Neither One of Us (Wants to Be the First to Say Goodbye)" (1973); "Daddy Could Swear, I Declare" (1973)

Martha and the Vandellas--"Coma and Get These Memories" (1963); "Heat Wave" (1963); "Quicksand" (1963/4); "Dancing in the Street" (1964); "Wild One" (1964/5); "Nowhere to Run" (1965); "You've Been in Love Too Long" (1965); "My Baby Loves Me" (1966); "I'm Ready For Love" (1966); "Jimmy Mack" (1967); "Love Bug Leave My Heart Alone" (1967); "Honey Chile" (1967);

The Marvelettes--"Please Mr. Postman" (1961); "Twistin' Postman" (1962); "Playboy" (1962); "Beechwood 4-5789" (1962); "Too Many Fish in the Sea" (1964); "I'll Keep Holding On" (1965); "Don't Mess With Bill" (1966); "The Hunter Gets Captured By the Game" (1967); "When You're Young and in Love" (1967); "My Baby Must Be a Magician" (1967/8)

The Miracles(, Smokey Robinson and)--"Shop Around" (1960/1); "What's So Good About Good-By" (1962); "I'll Try Something New" (1962); "You've Really Got a Hold On Me" (1962/3); "A

Love She Can Count On" (1963); "Mickey's Monkey" (1963); "I Gotta Dance to Keep From Crying" (1963/4); "I Like It Like That" (1964); "That's What Love Is Made Of" (1964); "Ooh Baby Baby" (1965); "The Tracks of My Tears" (1965); "My Girl Has Gone" (1965); "Going to a Go-Go" (1965/6); (Come 'Round Here) I'm the One You Need" (1966); "The Love I Saw in You Was Just a Mirage" (1967); "More Love" (1967); "I Second That Emotion" (1967); "If You Can Wait" (1968); "Yester Love" (1968); "Special Occasion" (1968); "Baby, Baby Don't Cry" (1969); "Doggone Right"/"Here I Go Again" (1969); "Abraham, Martin and John" (1969); "Point It Out" (1969/70); "The Tears of a Clown" (1970); "I Don't Blame You at All" (1971); "Do It Baby" (1974); "Love Machine (Part 1)" (1975)

Diana Ross--"Reach Out and Touch (Somebody's Hand)" (1970); "Ain't No Mountain High Enough" (1970); "Remember Me" (1970/1); "Reach Out I'll Be There" (1971); "Surrender" (1971); "Good Morning Heartache" (1973); "Touch Me in the Morning" (1973); "Last Time I Saw Him" (1974); "Theme From Mahogany" (1975/6); "Love Hangover" (1976); "One Love in My Lifetime" (1976); "Gettin' Ready For Love" (1977/8); "The Boss" (1979); "Upside Down" (1980); "I'm Coming Out" (1980); "It's My Turn" (1980/1)

Diana Ross and Lionel Richie--"Endless Love" (1981)

The Supremes--"When the Lovelight Starts Shining Through His Eyes" (1963/4); "Where Did Our Love Go" (1964); "Baby Love" (1964); "Come See About Me" (1964); "Stop! In the Name of Love" (1965); "Back in My Arms Again" (1965); "Nothing But Heartaches" (1965); "I Hear a Symphony" (1965); "My World Is Empty Without You" (1966); "Love Is Like an Itching in My Heart" (1966); You Can't Hurry Love" (1966); "You Keep Me Hangin' On" (1966); "Love Is Here and Now You're Gone" (1967); "The Happening" (1967); "Reflections" (1967); "In and Out of Love" (1967); "Forever Came Today" (1968); "Some Things You Never Get Used To" (1968); "Love Child" (1968); "I'm Livin' in Shame" (1969); "The Composer" (1969); "No Matter What Sign You Are" (1969) ; "Someday We'll Be Together" (1969); "Up the Ladder to the Roof" (1970); "Everybody's Got the Right to Love" (1970); "Stoned Love" (1970); "Nathan Jones" (1971); "Floy Joy" (1072); "Automatically Sunshine" (1972); "I'm Gonna Let My Heat Do the Walking" (1976)

The Supremes/Four Tops--"River Deep--Mountain High" (1970/1)

The Supremes/The Temptations--"I'm Gonna Make You Love Me" (1968/9); "I'll Try Something New" (1969)

The Temptations--"The Way You Do the Things You Do" (1964); "I'll Be in Trouble" (1964); "Girl (Why You Wanna Make Me Blue)" (1964); "My Girl" (1965); "It's Growing" (1965); "Since I Lost My Baby" (1965); "My Baby" (1965); "Get Ready" (1966); "Ain't Too Proud to Beg" (1966); "Beauty Is Only Skin Deep" (1966); "(I Know) I'm Losing You" (1966); "All I Need" (1967); "You're My Everything" (1967); "It's You That I Need" (1967); "I Wish It Would Rain" (1968); "I Could Never Love Another" (1968); "Please Return Your Love to Me" (1968);

"Cloud Nine" (1968/9); "Run Away Child, Running Wild" (1969); "Don't Let the Joneses Get You Down" (1969); "I Can't Get Next to You" (1969); "Psychedelic Shack" (1970); "Ball of Confusion" (1970); "Unena Za Ulimwengu (Unite the World)" (1970); "Just My Imagination" (1971); "Superstar" (1971); "Take a Look Around" (1972); "Papa Was a Rollin' Stone" (1972); "Masterpiece" (1973); "The Plastic Man" (1973); "Hey Girl" (1973); "Let Your Hair Down" (1973/4); "Happy People" (1974/5); "Shakey Ground" (1975); "Glasshouse" (1975)

Jr. Walker and the All Stars--"Shotgun" (1965); "Do the Boomerang" (1965); "Shake and Fingerpop" (1965); "(I'm a) Road Runner" (1966); "How Sweet It Is" (1966); "Pucker Up Buttercup" (1967); "Come See About Me" (1967/8); "Hip City--Pt. 2 (1968); "What Does It Take" (1969); "These Eyes" (1969); "Gotta Hold On to This Feeling" (1970); "Do You See My Love" (1970)

Mary Wells--"I Don't Want to Take a Chance" (1961); "The One Who Really Loves You" (1962); "You Beat Me to the Punch" (1962); "Two Loves" (1962/3); "Laughing Boy" (1963); "Your Old Stand By" (1963); "You Lost the Sweetest Boy"/"What's Easy for Two Is So Hard for One" (1963); "My Guy" (1964)

(Little) Stevie Wonder--"Fingertips" (1963); "Workout Stevie, Workout" (1963); "Hey Harmonica Man" (1964); "Uptight" (1965); "Nothing's Too Good for My Baby" (1966); "Blowin' in the Wind" (1966); "A Place in the Sun" (1966); "Travlin' Man" (1967); "I Was Made to Love Her" (1967); "I'm Wondering" (1967); "Shoo-Be-Doo-Be-Doo-Da-Day" (1968); "You Met Your Match" (1967); "For Once in My Life" (1968); "I Don't Know Why"/"My Cherie Amour" (1969); "Yester-Me, Yester-You, Yesterday" (1969); "Never Had a Dream Come True" (1970); "Signed, Sealed, Delivered I'm Yours" (1970); "Heaven Help Us All" (1970); "We Can Work It Out" (1971); "If You Really Love Me' (1971); "Superwoman" (1972); "Superstition" (1972/3); "You Are the Sunshine of My Life" (1973); "Higher Ground" (1973); "Living For the City" (1973/4); "Don't You Worry 'Bout a Thing" (1974); "You Haven't Done Nothin'" (1974); "Boogie on Reggae Woman" (1974/5); "I Wish" (1976/7); "Sir Duke" (1977); "Another Star" (1977); "As" (1977/8); "Send One Your Love" (1979); "Master Blaster (Jammin')" (1980); "I Ain't Gonna Stand For It" (1980); "That Girl" (1982); "Do I Do" (1982)

--Memphis (Stax) Sound

William Bell--"I Forgot to Be Your Lover" (1969)

Booker T. and the M.G.'s--"Green Onions" (1962); "Jellybread" (1963); "Chinese Checkers" (1963); "Book-Leg" (1965); "Hip Hug-Her" (1967); "Groovin'" (1967); "Soul Limbo" (1968); "Hang 'Em High" (1968/9); "Time Is Tight" (1969); "Mrs. Robinson" (1969)

James Carr--"You've Got My Mind Messed Up" (1966); "The Dark End of the Street" (1967); "A Man Needs a Woman" (1968)

Arthur Conley--"Sweet Soul Music" (1967); "Shake, Rattle and Roll" (1967); "Funky Street" (1968); "Ob-La-Di, Ob-La-Da" (1969)

Eddie Floyd--"Knock on Wood" (1966); "I've Never Found a Girl" (1968); "Bring It on Home to Me" (1968)

Isaac Hayes--"Walk on By"/"By the Time I Get to Phoenix" (1969); "Never Can Say Goodbye" (1971); "Theme From Shaft" (1971); "Do Your Thing" (1972); "Theme From the Men" (1972); "Joy--Pt. 1" (1973/4)

Mar-Keys--"Last Night" (1961)

Otis Redding--"Mr. Pitiful" (1965); "I've Been Loving You Too Long" (1965); "Respect" (1965); "Satisfaction" (1966); "Fa-Fa-Fa-Fa-Fa" (1966); "Try a Little Tenderness" (1966/7); "(Sittin' On) The Dock of the Bay" (1968); "The Happy Song" (1968); "Amen" (1968); "Papa's Got a Brand New Bag" (1968/9)

Sam and Dave--"Hold On! I'm a Comin'" (1966); "Soul Man" (1967); "I Thank You" (1968)

Johnnie Taylor--"Who's Making Love" (1968); "Take Care of Your Homework" (1969); "Testify (I Wonna)" (1969); "Steal Away" (1970); "I Am Somebody, Part II" (1970); "Jody's Got Your Girl and Gone" (1971); "I Believe in You" (1973); "Cheaper to Keep Her" (1973); "We're Getting Careless With Our Love" (1974); "Disco Lady" (1976); "Somebody's Gettin' It" (1976)

Carla Thomas--"Gee Whiz" (1961); "B-A-B-Y" (1966)

Rufus Thomas--"Walking the Dog" (1963); "Do the Funky Chicken" (1970); "(Do the) Push and Pull, Part I" (1970/1); "The Breakdown (Part I)" (1971)

--Muscle Shoals Sound

Arthur Alexander--"You Better Move On" (1962); "Anna" (1962)

Aretha Franklin--"I Never Loved a Man" (1967); "Respect" (1967); "Baby I Love You" (1967); "A Natural Woman" (1967); "Chain of Fools" (1967/8); "(Sweet Sweet Baby) Since You've Been Gone"/"Ain't No Way" (1968); "Think" (1968); "The House That Jack Built"/"I Say a Little Prayer" (1968); "See Saw"/"My Song" (1968); "The Weight" (1969); "I Can't See Myself Leaving You" (1969); "Share Your Love With Me" (1969); "Eleanor Rigby" (1969)

Jimmy Hughes--"Steal Away" (1964)

Percy Sledge--"When a Man Loves a Woman" (1966); "Warm and Tender Love" (1966); "It Tears Me Up" (1966); "Love Me Tender" (1967); "Take Time to Know Her" (1968)

Joe Tex--"Hold What You've Got" (1964/5); "I Want to (Do Everything For You)" (1965); "A Sweet Woman Like You" (1965/6); "S.Y.S.L.J.F.M. (The Letter Song)" (1966); "Show Me" (1967); "Skinny Legs and All" (1967); "Men Are Gettin' Scarce (1968); "I Gotcha" (1972)

--Sound of Philadelphia

Blue Magic--"Sideshow" (1974); "Three Ring Circus" (1974)

The Delfonics--"La-La Means I Love You" (1968); "Break Your Promise" (1968); "Ready or Not Here I Come" (1968/9); "You Got Yours and I'll Get Mine" (1969); "Didn't I (Blow Your Mind This Time)" (1970); "Trying to Make a Fool of Me" (1970)

The Intruders--"Cowboys to Girls" (1968); "(Love Is Like A) Baseball Game" (1968); "I'll Always Love My Mama (Part 1)" (1973)

MFSB--"TSOP" (1974)

The Manhattans--"Don't Take Your Love" (1975); "Kiss and Say Goodbye" (1976); "Shining Star" (1980)

Harold Melvin and the Bluenotes--"If You Don't Know Me By Now" (1972); "The Love I Lost (Part 1)" (1973); "Bad Luck (Part 1)" (1975); "Wake Up Everybody (Part 1)" (1975/6)

The O'Jays--"Back Stabbers" (1972); "Love Train" (1973); "Time to Get Down" (1973); "Put Your Hands Together" (1973/4)' "For the Love of Money" (1974); "I Love Music (Part 1)" (1975/6); "Livin' For the Weekend" (1976); "Use Ta Be My Girl" (1978); "Forever Mine" (1979/80)

Billy Paul--"Me and Mrs. Jones" (1972); "Thanks For Saving My Life" (1974)

The Spinners--"I'll Be Around" (1972); "Could It Be I'm Falling in Love" (1972/3); "One of a Kind (Love Affair)" (1973); "Ghetto Child" (1973); "Mighty Love--Part 1" (1974); I'm Coming Home" (1974); "Love Don't Love Nobody--Part 1" (1974); "Living a Little, Laughing a Little" (1975); "They Just Can't Stop It the (Games People Play)" (1975); "Love or Leave" (1975/6); "The Rubberband Man" (1976); "Working My Way Back to You/Forgive Me, Girl" (1979/80); "Cupid/I've Loved You For a Long Time" (1980)

The Stylistics--"Stop, Look, Listen" (1971); "You Are Everything" (1971/2); "Betcha By Golly, Wow" (1972); "People Make the World Go Round" (1972); "I'm Stone in Love With You" (1972); "Break Up to Make Up" (1973); "You'll Never Get to Heaven" (1973); "Rockin' Roll Baby" (1973); "You Made Me Feel Brand New" (1974); "Let's Put It All Together" (1974)

The Three Degrees--"When Will I See You Again" (1974)

--Blue-Eyed Soul

Hall(, Daryl) and (John) Oates--"She's Gone" (1974; 1976); "Sara Smile" (1976); "Do What You Want, Be What You Are" (1976); "Rich Girl" (1977); Back Together Again" (1977); "It's a Laugh" (1978); "Wait For Me" (1979); "How Does It Feel to Be Back" (1980); "You've Lost That Lovin' Feeling" (1980); "Kiss On My List" (1981); "You Make My Dreams" (1981); "Private Eyes" (1981); "I Can't Go For That (No Can Do)"; "Did It in a Minute" (1982); "Your Imagination": (1982); "Maneater" (1982)

The (Young) Rascals--"I Ain't Gonna Eat Out My Heart Anymore" (1965/6); "Good Lovin'" (1966); "You Better Run" (1966); "Come On Up" (1966); "I've Been Lonely Too Long" (1967); "Groovin' (1967); "A Girl Like You" (1967); "How Can I Be Sure" (1967); "It's Wonderful" (1967); "A Beautiful Morning" (1968); "People Got to Be Free" (1968); "A Ray of Hope" (1968/9); "Heaven" (1969); "See" (1969); "Carry Me Back" (1969)

The Righteous Brothers--"Little Latin Lupe Lu" (1963); "You've Lost That Lovin' Feelin' (1964/5); "Just Once in My Life" (1965); "Unchained Melody" (1965); "Ebb Tide" (1965); "(You're My) Soul and Inspiration" (1966); "He" (1966); "Go Ahead and Cry" (1966); "Rock and Roll Heaven" (1974); "Give It to the People" (1974); "Dream On" (1974)

Mitch Ryder (and the Detroit Wheels)--"Jenny Take a Ride!" (1965/6); "Little Latin Lupe Lu" (1966); "Devil With a Blue Dress On & Good Golly Miss Molly" (medley; 1966); "Sock It to Me-Baby!" (1967); "Too Many Fish in the Sea & Three Little Fishes" (medley; 1967); "What Now My Love" (1967)

Table 64

Booker T. & the MGs

Although best known for a series of tight, funky instrumental hits released in the 1960s, Booker T. & the MGs exerted a far greater influence as the house band for all Stax/Volt recording artists. In addition, two members—keyboardist Booker T. Jones and lead guitarist Steve Cropper—handled key songwriting (Cropper wrote such hits as Otis Redding's "Dock of the Bay," Wilson Pickett's "In the Midnight Hour," and Aretha Franklin's "See Saw"), arranging, and production duties for the label.

The band's core members—which included, in addition to Jones and Cropper—drummer-guitarist Al Jackson, Jr. and bassist Donald "Duck" Dunn—coalesced around the Stax studios in Memphis as backup musicians during the early 1960s. One of the informal jam sessions led to a decision to record "Green Onions," jointly composed by

Booker, Cropper, Jackson, and drummer Lewis Steinberg. The single (Stax 127; 1963) would reach number one on the R&B charts, then crossing over to pop (#3). Booker T. & the MGs continued to produce best-selling singles, including the Top Forty hits ""Hip Hug-Her" (Stax 211; 1967), "Groovin'" (Stax 224; 1967), "Soul-Limbo" (Stax 0001; 1968), "Hang 'Em High" (Stax 0013; 1968), "Time Is Tight" (Stax 0028; 1969), and "Mrs. Robinson" (Stax 0037; 1969). The group's LPs were also commercially successful, eleven of them—including *Green Onions* (Stax 701; 1962), *Hip Hug-Her* (Stax 717; 1967), *Back To Back* (Stax 720; 1967), *Uptight* (Stax 2006; 1969), *The Booker T. Set* (Stax 2009; 1969), and *Melting Pot* (Stax 2035; 1971)—making the pop album charts.

The Booker T. & the MGs' first phase ended with Jones' decision to relocate to Los Angeles in 1970 following a dispute with Stax. He would record albums in the 1970s with his wife, Priscilla Coolidge, and do production work for Rita Coolidge, Earl Klugh, Willie Nelson, and Bill Withers. In the meantime, Cropper became in-house producer at TMI Studios. The band reorganized as the MGs in 1973 around Jackson and Dunn; new members included Bobby Manuel and Carson Whitsett. When Stax went out of business in 1975, plans were made to reconstitute the original quartet. Eight days later, however, Jackson was killed in a shooting incident. The others decided to go ahead with the reunion, bringing in drummer Willie Hall, a Stax alumnus who'd worked with the Bar-kays and Isaac Hayes. Over the years, the band has continued in a low-key mode, combining recording and performing as a group with separate activities by individual members. [Stambler. 1989]

Table 65

Otis Redding, September 9, 1941-December 10, 1967

A one-of-a-kind soul stylist equally adept at rave-up houserockers and soft, caressing ballads, Otis Redding is remembered as much for his potential as for what he actually accomplished. Toiling for years on the R&B circuit before a breakthrough performance at the 1967 Monterey Pop Festival positioned him on the verge of mainstream stardom, he would die tragically in a small plane crash at age twenty-six.

The Macon, Georgia-native did not seemed destined for a recording career until given an audition at Stax Records while serving as a chauffeur for an aspiring band headed by Johnny Jenkins. Redding's first release, "These Arms of Mine" (Volt 103; 1963), reached the Top Twenty on the national R&B charts. Stax immediately signed him to a long-term contract, and with Booker T and the M.G.s guitarist Steve Cropper serving as arranger/producer, Redding recorded a long string of R&B hits—many self-composed—including "Mr. Pitiful" (Volt 124; 1965; #41 pop, #10 R&B), "I've Been Loving You Too Long" (Volt 126; 1965; #21 pop, #2 R&B), "Respect" (Volt 128; 1965; #35 pop, #4 R&B), "Satisfaction" (Volt 132; 1966; #31 pop, #4 R&B), "My Lover's Prayer" (Volt 136;

1966; #61 pop, #10 R&B), ""Try a Little Tenderness" (Volt 141; 1966; #4), "Tramp" (Stax 216; 1967; #26 pop, #2 R&B), and "Knock On Wood" (Stax 228; 1967; #30 pop, #8 R&B).

By the summer of 1967, when his Monterey appearance captured the imagination of white rock fans, Redding's singles were beginning to become fixtures on the pop charts. The widely acclaimed Queen of Soul, Aretha Franklin, would take one of his compositions, "Respect" (Atlantic 2403; 1967), to the top of the pop charts. Furthermore, a mere two-and-a-half weeks before his death, he recorded a song that close associates felt would propel him to mainstream success, "(Sittin' on the) Dock of the Bay" (Volt 157; 1968; #1 pop, #1 R&B).

Although only modest sellers during his lifetime, Redding's albums—all of which have been reissued as compact discs—have remained in demand up to the present day. The material from his original LP releases—*Pain In My Heart* (Atco 161; 1964; #103), *The Great Otis Redding Sings Soul Ballads* (Volt 411; 1965; #147), *Otis Blue/Otis Redding Sings Soul* (Volt 412; 1965; #75), *The Soul Album* (Volt 413; 1966; #54), *Complete & Unbelievable...The Otis Redding Dictionary of Soul* (Volt 415; 1966; #73), *King & Queen* (Stax 716; 1967; #36), *Otis Redding Live In Europe* (Volt 416; 1967; #32), *The Dock of the Bay* (Volt 419; 1968; #4), *The Immortal Otis Redding* (Atco 252; 1968; #59), and *Otis Redding In Person At the Whiskey A Go Go* (Atco 265; 1968; #52)—is also available through countless retrospective compilations.

Table 66

Righteous Brothers

The Righteous Brothers were the best known—and most commercially successful—exponents of blue-eyed soul (i.e., whites displaying black gospel/blues/R&B influences in their singing style). However, during their peak period of success, between 1963-1967, they were able to transcend stylistic categorization, appealing to teenage music consumers, an older mainstream pop audience, and blacks alike. The duo's biggest hits—"You've Lost That Lovin' Feelin'" (Philles 124; 1964; #1), "Unchained Melody" (Philles 127; 1965; #4), and "Soul and Inspiration" (Verve 10383; 1966; #1)—continue to top polls tabulating all-time favorite recordings.

Tenor Bill Medley and bass singer Bobby Hatfield—both of whom had sung in rock bands while attending high school in Southern California—met at an area club in 1962. Finding that their voices—and personalities—meshed, they decided to work together. Moonglow Records signed them to a contract shortly thereafter, releasing the albums *Righteous Brothers Right Now!* (Moonglow 1001; 1964; #11), *Some Blue-Eyed Soul* (Moonglow 1002; 1964; #14), *This Is New* (Moonglow 1003; 1965; #39), and *Best of the*

Righteous Brothers (Moonglow 1004; 1966; #130) as well as the charting singles "Little Latin Lupe Lu" (1963) and "My Babe" (1963).

While with Moonglow, the duo's work displayed a loose, funky edge highlighted by the call-and-response vocal interplay between Medley and Hatfield. One of the leading record producers of the day, Phil Spector, was sufficiently impressed to bring them over to his Philles label. The singles featuring Spector's production work—"You've Lost That Lovin' Feelin'," "Just Once In My Life" (Philles 127; 1965; #9), "Unchained Melody," and "Ebb Tide" (Philles 130; 1965; #5)—instantly elevated the Righteous Brothers to the top of the music business (even their Moonglow albums charted for the first time). Although Spector considered singles to be the most important art form, their albums—*You've Lost That Lovin' Feelin'* (Philles 4007; 1965; #4), *Just Once In My Life* (Philles 4008; 1965; #9), and *Back To Back* (Philles 4009; 1965; #16)—also sold well.

Aware of Spector's reputation for valuing the song over the artist, the Righteous Brothers signed with Verve Records. Their first hit for the label, "Soul and Inspiration'," revealed a strong Spector influence. However, later album releases—most notably, *Soul & Inspiration* (Verve 5001; 1966; #7), *Go Ahead and Cry* (Verve 5004; 1966; #32), *Sayin' Somethin'* (Verve 5010; 1967; #155), *Souled Out* (Verve 5031; 1967; #198), and the live *One For the Road* (Verve 5058; 1968; #187)—attempted to showcase the duo's dynamic stage presence and affinity for pop standards.

Despite these efforts at creative growth, Medley felt the need to explore his options as a songwriter and solo performer. The decision to terminate the partnership was made public in early 1968, although Hatfield expressed a desire to continue the act with a new partner. When both floundered in their new career paths, they decided to get back together, allowing the official announcement to be made on a February 1974 broadcast of the "Sonny and Cher Comedy Hour." The Righteous Brothers would enjoy another major hit, "Rock and Roll Heaven" (Haven 7002; 1974; #3), but Medley retired for five years following the murder of his wife in 1976.

Medley and Hatfield would perform together intermittently over the years after appearing on an *American Bandstand* anniversary TV special in 1981. Medley's top priority, however, continued to be his solo career. He signed with Planet Records in 1982, and would later have a number one hit, "(I've Had) The Time of My Life" (RCA 5224; 1987), a duet with Jennifer Warnes (the song also earned a Grammy Award for Best Pop Performance by a Duo or Group with Vocal). "Unchained Melody" returned to the charts (#13 pop, #1 adult contemporary) in 1990 as a result of its inclusion of the *Ghost* soundtrack. A newly recorded version of the song (Curb 76842; 1990; #19/#4 sales) achieved platinum status. The continued success of various compilations of the classic singles over the years—*Anthology (1962-1974)* (Rhino 71488; 1990) earned a gold record, while *Best of the Righteous Brothers* (Curb 77381; 1990) went platinum—have added further luster to the Righteous Brothers' legacy.

Table 67

Sam and Dave

Sam Moore, born October 12, 1935, in Miami, and David Prater, born May 9, 1937, in Ocilla, Georgia, were the most popular black duo of the 1960s. Both grew up singing in church, and were veterans of the southern club circuit prior to meeting at Miami's King of Hearts club in 1961. When Prater forgot the lyrics to Jackie Wilson's "Doggin' Around," at an amateur night show, Moore—who was acting as MC—coached him through the song. They went on to become a fixture in the Miami club scene, eventually singing with Roulette Records.

They switched to Atlantic in 1965, where executive Jerry Wexler loaned them out to the Stax label. Their gospel fervor was effectively captured on recordings by the Stax production/songwriting team of Isaac Hayes and David Porter. While most readily identified with the rhythm and blues market, the team known as "Double Dynamite" nevertheless crossed over to the pop charts with hits such as "Hold On, I'm Comin'" (Stax 189; 1966), "Soul Man" (Stax 231; 1967), and "I Thank You" (Stax 242; 1968).

At the peak of their success, Moore and Prater were barely speaking to one another. Although they broke up in 1970, there were several efforts at reunification. Following the Blues Brothers' hit remake of "Soul Man" (Atlantic 3545; 1978), the duo was besieged with bookings from clubs across the country. Their last show together took place New Year's Eve, at San Francisco's Old Waldorf; Prater then began touring with Sam Daniels. In 1983 Moore would tell the *Los Angeles Herald Examiner* that the instigating factor in their feud was that he'd "lost respect" for his ex-partner when Prater shot his own wife during a 1968 domestic dispute. Prater would die April 9, 1988 in a Georgia automobile accident. Moore continued his career, singing on Bruce Springsteen's *Human Touch* (Columbia 53000; 1992). Later in 1992, Sam and Dave were inducted into the Rock and Roll Hall of Fame. [Romanowski and George-Warren. 1995.]

Table 68

Percy Sledge, November 25, 1941-

Sledge will be forever identified with the classic soul ballad, "When a Man Loves a Woman" (Atlantic 2326; 1966), which blended his intense, gospel-inflected vocal with an ethereal organ accompaniment. Success did not come overnight for the singer; he spent the first half of the 1960s performing in the region surrounding his native

Alabama. He was a member of the Esquires Combo when he decided to go solo in 1966. Following the release of "When a Man Loves a Woman," which reached number one on both the pop and R&B charts, he scored Top Twenty hits with "Warm and Tender Love" (Atlantic 2342; 1966), "It Tears Me Up" (Atlantic 2358; 1966), and "Take Time to Know Her" (Atlantic 2490; 1968).

Sledge's recording career stalled by the late 1960s, but he has continued to tour the U.S., Japan, and Great Britain through the 1990s. The appearance of "When a Man Loves a Woman" in the popular film, *Platoon* (1987), spurred a revival of interest in Sledge. That same year the song was re-released in the U.K., where it reached number two on the pop charts. In 1989 he won the Rhythm and Blues Foundation's Career Achievement Award.

Table 69

Sly and the Family Stone

Sly and the Family Stone helped pioneer one of dominant styles of the 1970s, funk music. Their variant fused the psychedelic rock of the late 1960s with classic soul; in that sense, it differed considerably from the bass-heavy grooves of mainstream funk. As popular on the pop charts as with urban black youth, the group greatly influenced the careers of later crossover giants such as George Clinton, mastermind of the Parliament/ Funkadelic collective, Rick James, and Prince.

The creative core of Sly and the Family Stone, Texas-native Sylvester Stewart, developed an impressive music business resume in Sam Francisco during the mid-1960s, excelling as a disc jockey (KSOL, KDIA), songwriter, and record producer for the likes of Beau Brummels, Bobby Freeman, and the Mojo Men with Autumn Records. His first attempt at heading a group, the Stoners, failed in 1966; however, Sly and the Family Stone—including his brother, guitarist Freddie Stone, sister Rosie Stone, who played sang and played keyboards and harmonica, and a cousin, bassist Larry Graham, who would form Graham Central Station in the early 1970s—attracted sufficient local attention in 1967 to garner a contract with Epic Records.

The group's debut LP, *A Whole New Thing* (Epic 30333; 1967) failed to attract much attention. However, the follow-up album, *Dance to the Music* (Epic 26371; 1968; #142), and the exuberant title song (Epic 10256; 1968; #8) elevated them to the forefront of the rock scene. The group maintained its momentum with a steady stream of hit singles—most notably, "Everyday People" (Epic 10407; 1968; #1), "Hot Fun in the Summertime" (Epic 10497; 1969; #2), "Thank You (Falettinme Be Mice Elf Agin)" (Epic 10555; 1970; #1), and "Family Affair" (Epic 10805; 1971; #1)—and albums: *Life* (Epic 26397; 1968; #195), *Stand!* (Epic 26456; 1969; #13), *Greatest Hits* (Epic 30325; 1970;

#2), *There's A Riot Goin' On* (Epic 30986; 1971; #1), and *Fresh* (Epic 32134; 1973; #7). The uplifting, anthem-like quality of Sly and the Family Stone's early work gave way to a decidedly more negative, militant tone in *There's A Riot Goin' On*; however, the uniformly high quality of Sly's musical ideas and production work made it the most successful—artistically and commercially—of his albums.

Sly's drug problems in the 1970s led to an increasing inability to meet concert commitments and lackluster studio work. He ceased to perform or record for several prior to attempting a comeback with the October 1979 release of *Back on the Right Track* (Warner Bros. 3303) Unfortunately, the album lacked strong material and Stone spent much of the 1980s fighting drug convictions. Sly and the Family Stone were inducted into the Rock and Roll Hall of Fame in 1993. Rumors have periodically surfaced since then that the group would soon be releasing new material. In the meantime, their classic recordings have appeared in a host of compilation releases, including *The Collection* (Castle Communications 307; 1991) and *Takin' You Higher – The Best of Sly & the Family Stone* (Sony 471758; 1992; reissued on Epic 477506; 1994).

Table 70

Wilson Pickett, March 18, 1941-January 16, 2006

Although Wilson Pickett spent a comparatively brief amount of time as a hit-making force, for many, he was considered to be the classic soul singer. His rough, gritty voice was perfectly suited for uptempo material, melding a gospel fervor to a funky backbeat.

Pickett started out singing gospel music in church, first in his hometown of Prattville, Alabama, and then in Detroit between 1955-1959. In 1959, Willie Schofield invited him to join his R&B vocal group, the Falcons, best known for the recording, "You're So Fine" (Unart 2013; 1959; #2 R&B, #17 pop). He would go on to contribute many compositions to their repertoire, most notably "I Found a Love" (LuPine 1003; 1962; #6 R&B).

Pickett's dual talents as a singer-songwriter made a solo career inevitable. His departure from the Falcons followed a successful audition with Double-L Records, headed by R&B legend Lloyd Price, in 1963. He immediately scored two successive R&B hits with the self-composed "If You Need Me" (Double-L 713; 1963; #30) and "It's Too Late" (Double-L 717; 1963; #7).

His breakthrough to a larger pop audience came shortly after his contract was purchased by Atlantic Records in 1964. Assisted by the label's marketing muscle and the decision to have him record with Stax—then affiliated with Atlantic in order to gain a wider market for its own artists—Pickett found immediate success with such hits as "In the Midnight Hour" (Atlantic 2289; 1965; #1 R&B, #21 pop), "634-5789" (Atlantic 2320; 1966; #1 R&B, #13 pop), "Land of 1,000 Dances" (Atlantic 2348; 1966; #1 R&B, #6 pop), "Mustang Sally" (Atlantic 2365; 1966; #6 R&B, #23 pop), "Funky Broadway" (Atlantic 2430; 1967; #1 R&B, #8 pop), "Sugar Sugar" (Atlantic 2722; 1970; #4 R&B, #25 pop), "Engine Number 9" (Atlantic 2765; 1970; #3 R&B, #14 pop), "Don't Let the Green Grass Fool You" (Atlantic 2781; 1971; #2 R&B, #17 pop), "Don't Knock My Love – Pt. 1" (Atlantic 2797; 1971; #1 R&B, #13 pop), and "Fire and Water" (Atlantic 2852; 1972; #2 R&B, #24 pop). The tight, stripped-down rhythm accompaniment provided by members of the Stax house band, Booker T. and the MGs (with production by Steve Cropper), proved to be the ideal foil for the dynamic tension communicated by Pickett's vocals. His albums also sold well in the latter half of the 1960s, including *The Exciting Wilson Pickett* (Atlantic 8129; 1966; #21), *The Wicked Pickett* (Atlantic 8138; 1967; #42), *The Sound of Wilson Pickett* (Atlantic 8145; 1967; #54), *The Best of Wilson Pickett* (Atlantic 8151; 1967; #35), *I'm In Love* (Atlantic 8175; 1968; #70), *The Midnight Mover* (Atlantic 8183; 1968; #91), *Hey Jude* (Atlantic 8215; 1969; #97), *Wilson Pickett in Philadelphia* (Atlantic 8270; 1970; #64), and *The Best of Wilson Pickett, Vol. II* (Atlantic 8290; 1971).

Pickett's sales dropped off considerably in the early 1970s as soul was superseded by new black urban styles such as funk, disco, and reggae. He continued to tour extensively both stateside and abroad, although his new recordings—for RCA (1973-1975), Wicked (1975-1977), Big Tree (1977-1979), EMI America (1979-mid-1980s), and Motown (late 1980s)—had trouble competing with reissues of his vintage soul material. He attracted considerable publicity in the early 1980s by uniting with Joe Tex, Don Covay, and other 1960s black singers as the Soul Clan. His legend receive added luster when the highly acclaimed film, *The Commitments* (1991), portrayed him as soul music's Holy Grail. Further recognition came with his induction into the Rock and Roll Hall of Fame in 1991.

REGIONAL STYLES

Defining Statements

Arriving at a clear-cut definition as to exactly what constitutes a regional style of popular music. Major recording centers such as New York City and Los Angeles encompass far too many genres and different studios to enable one particular musical form or approach too predominate. Locales featuring a significant number of live performing venues—most notably, Las Vegas and Branson, Missouri—also tend to attract a stylistically diversified array of artists.

Other cities have become the focal point for a given genre; this can mean that stylistically-related artists establish a common home base or simply hang out within a particular scene on a regular basis. Denver (early 1970s country rock), Miami (late 1970s Caribbean-inflected funk), and Portland (late 1990s alternative rock) have functioned as a magnet for certain like-minded musicians and their fans; however, they all failed to leave a discernable recorded music legacy.

Nevertheless, many cities in the U.S. alone have become identified with the origin—or development—of a certain style. This identity is generally the result of a fortuitous blend of cultural elements, including high-profile recording studios (featuring producers and session players whose services are in high demand), commercially successful record companies, sufficient live concert options to keep musicians close to home as well as facilitating the exchange of musical ideas, an abundance of mass media outlets, and a local populace possessing the resources and aptitude required to support a viable scene. Twentieth-century urban centers possessing all or most of these preconditions (with the entrenched genre and time frame of peak popularity noted in parentheses) have included:

- Memphis (blues; 1900-1915)
- New Orleans (traditional jazz/dixieland; 1910-1920)
- Kansas City (small combo jazz; 1930s)
- Nashville (mainstream country/Nashville Sound; 1940s-present)
- Memphis (rockabilly; 1950s)
- New Orleans (R&B; 1950s)
- Chicago (soul; 1958-early 1970s)
- Greenwich Village, New York (commercial folk; early 1960s)
- Detroit (Motown soul; 1960-early 1970s)
- Memphis (Stax soul; 1961-early 1970s)
- Los Angeles/Southern California (surf sound/car songs/soft rock/country rock; early 1960s-mid-1970s)
- San Francisco (psychedelia/progressive rock; mid-1960s-early 1970s)
- Muscle Shoals, Alabama (soul; mid-1960s-early 1970s)
- San Antonio (Tex-Mex/conjunto; mid-1960s-present)
- Philadelphia (Philly soul; late 1960s-late 1970s)

- Boston (Bosstown Sound; 1968-1969)
- Macon/Atlanta, Georgia (southern rock; late 1960s-mid-1970s)
- Austin, Texas (outlaw country; 1970s)
- Minneapolis (funk-punk; 1980s)
- Athens, Georgia (indie rock; early 1980s)
- Washington, D.C. (go-go; mid-1980s)
- Seattle (grunge; late 1980s-early 1990s)

New Orleans Sound

The New Orleans Sound is built upon the cultural diversity of this cosmopolitan seaport. Since its inception, rock 'n' roll has drawn upon the city's musical sources; i.e., the ensemble playing of black funeral bands, the syncopated "second line" rhythms of Mardi Gras parades, the country blues from the nearby Mississippi delta, barrelhouse piano stylings, and various forms of jazz improvisation, most notably the Dixieland genre.

The godfather of the modern scene may well have been the postwar r & b piano man, Professor Longhair. Born Henry Byrd in 1918, Longhair adapted the raucous chords of barrelhouse playing into a more refined mode of delivery to which he added Latin rhythms and gently sung blues lyrics. His music contained the core substratum of all New Orleans rock 'n' roll: a rugged, rolling bass riff constructed around the carefree interplay of piano, string bass, guitar, and saxophone. As noted by Langdon Winner, in *The Rolling Stone Illustrated History of Rock & Roll* (rev. ed.), "Weaned on blues and boogie, Crescent City musicians have never been afraid to load up the lower end of the scale with more instrumentation than seems reasonable. On top of that foggy rumble it becomes possible to contrast the higher range of a fine tenor sax or the voice of a good r & b shouter and generate a marvelous tension in the music."

The individuals most responsible for harnessing this style were Dave Bartholomew--trumpeter and leader of the finest New Orleans r & b band during the post-World War II era, who wrote, arranged, and played for Fats Domino and most other key recording artists of the 1950s--and Cosimo Matassa, owner and chief engineer of J & M Studio, where all of the New Orleans acts recorded. The superior acoustics and laid-back "live" feel in Matassa's work attracted notable performers from across the nation, including Little Richard and Ray Charles.

When the original r & b-inflected sound grew somewhat stale in the late 1950s, a young pianist, writer, and producer, Allen Toussaint, spearheaded a revitalization of the city's musical conventions. He produced a series of successful records for small labels in the area such as Minit, Instant, A.F.O., and Fury. They all included his trademark--a lively but light-handed background riff--and the use of ingenious hook lines, often delivered at a pause in the music at the end of a chorus. Two of his biggest hits, Ernie K-Doe's "Mother-In-Law" and Chris Kenner's "I Like It Like That," provided textbook examples of these features.

When Toussaint entered the army in 1963, New Orleans music lost much of its creative momentum. His return to the scene a couple of years helped stimulate yet another rebirth of the sound. However, changes in national tastes consigned much of the city's output to regional popularity. Nevertheless, the music continued to play a vital role in the development of other notable rock styles, including Motown, the Stax Sound, British beat groups, and reggae.

Top Artists and Their Recordings

Jimmy Clanton--"Just a Dream" (1958); "Venus in Blue Jeans (1962)

The Dixie-Cups--"Chapel of Love" (1964)' "People Say" (1964); "Iko Iko" (1965); "Little Bell" (1966)

Fats Domino--"Ain't That a Shame" (1955); "I'm in Love Again" (1956); "Blueberry Hill" (1956); "Blue Monday" (1957); "I'm Walkin'" (1957); "Valley of Tears" (1957); "Whole Lotta Loving" (1958/9); "I Want to Walk You Home" (1959); "Be My Guest" (1959); "Walking to New Orleans" (1960)

Lee Dorsey--"Ya Ya" (1961); "Working in the Coal Mine" (1966); "Holy Cow" (1966)

Frankie Ford--"Sea Cruise" (1959)

Barbara George--"I Know" (1962)

Clarence "Frog Man" Henry--"Ain't Got No Home" (1956/7); "But I Do" (1961)

Jesse Hill--"Ooh Poo Pah Doo--Part II" (1960)

Joe Jones--"You Talk Too Much" (1960)

Ernie K-Doe--"Mother-In-Law" (1961)

Chris Kenner--"I Like It Like That, Part 1" (1961)

Smiley Lewis--"I Hear Your Knocking" (1955)

Bobby Marchan--"There's Something on Your Mind, Part 2" (1960)

The Meters--"Cissy Strut" (1969)

Aaron Neville--"Tell It Like It Is" (1966/7)

Lloyd Price--"Lawdy Miss Clawdy" (1952); "Stagger Lee" (1958/9);   "Personality" (1959); "I'm Gonna Get Married" (1959)

Shirley and Lee--"Let the Good Times Roll" (1956; 1960)

Huey "Piano" Smith and the Clowns--"Don't You Just Know It" (1958)

Table 71

Fats Domino, February 26, 1928-

Fats Domino was one of the most consistent rhythm and blues hit-makers of all-time. He wrote and recorded rock standards years before "rock 'n' roll" became a household phrase. His engaging, inimitable style helped facilitate the transition of popular R&B artists to the pop charts at the outset of the rock era.

A lifetime New Orleans resident, Domino taught himself the popular piano techniques of his day, including the blues, boogie-woogie, and ragtime. In the mid-1940s, local band leader Dave Bartholomew hired him as his regular pianist. This job led to his 1949 recording contract with the Los Angeles-based Imperial label, and the Domino-Bartholomew songwriting partnership.

His debut single, "The Fat Man" (Imperial 5058; 1950), was a Top Ten R&B hit. For a dozen years, Domino would release at least one Top Ten single every year; his number one R&B releases included "Goin' Home (Imperial 5180; 1952; #30 pop), "Ain't That a Shame" (Imperial 5348; 1955; #10 pop), "All By Myself" (Imperial 5357; 1955), "Poor Me" (Imperial 5369; 1955), "I'm In Love Again" (Imperial 5386; 1956; #3 pop), "Blueberry Hill" (Imperial 5407; 1956; #2 pop), "Blue Monday" (Imperial 5417; 1956; #5 pop), "I'm Walkin'" (Imperial 5428; 1957; #4 pop), and "I Want to Walk You Home" (Imperial 5606; 1959; #8 pop). Despite the drop-off in chart singles by the early 1960s, he remained in demand as a theater and nightclub attraction. Furthermore, his albums continued to sell well. When he moved to ABC-Paramount in 1963, Imperial retained many of them in the catalog, most notably *Rock and Rollin' With Fats* Domino (Imperial 9004; 1956), Fats *Domino – Rock and Rollin'* (Imperial 9009; 1956), *This Is Fats Domino!* (Imperial 9028; 1957), and *Million Sellers By Fats* (Imperial 9195; 1962). He recorded for a number of other labels as well in the 1960s, including Mercury, Sunset, and Liberty/United Artists.

By the 1970s, Domino had cut back sharply on his concert tours, limiting his out-of-town work largely to Las Vegas and Lake Tahoe. His recordings were more widely available in England and Europe than at home; American fans often found it necessary to seek out import anthologies. He has continued to record and perform intermittently in the recent years. His first major-label LP release in twenty-five years, *Christmas Is a Special Day* (1993), received critical acclaim but had limited sales.

The Calypso Craze

Calypso, a gentle Caribbean-based folk style, enjoyed a brief vogue in the United States which far outweighed its ultimate impact on the overall development of popular music. The national sensation created by Elvis Presley's music in early 1956 created both a commercial and cultural backlash. This reaction was spear- headed by both the major American record companies and the nation's intelligentsia, who found the crude beat and raw sexuality exuded by Presley and his legion of imitators to be morally as well as aesthetically offensive. Calypso, a marginal branch of third world music at the time, was in essence seized upon by these forces as an anecdote to the obnoxious teen music that threatened to overwhelm the established cultural--and economic--order of things.

Harry Belafonte, a handsome, articulate young singer of West Indian extraction, was annointed the leader of the counter-insurgence. He had first entered the U.S. singles charts with a lovely folk ballad, "Jamaica Farewell," in late October 1956. The record remained very popular for over a half year, and was followed up by the top five hit, "Banana Boat (Day-O)," and a steady succession of bestselling album releases.

Belafonte's success inspired a slew of imitators in the calypso mold, including the Tarriers and Terry Gilkyson and the Easy Riders, who would both reach the number four position with "The Banana Boat Song" and "Marianne," respectively. Many mainstream pop singers began recording calypso material as well. The Fontana Sisters, Steve Lawrence, and Sarah Vaughan all reached the top twenty with their own renditions of "The Banana Boat Song." The record industry, most notably trade publications such as *Billboard* expended a considerable amount of attention to the fad, even going so far as to hype it as a successor in popularity to rock 'n' roll.

The craze soon lost its momentum, however, and the hit recordings stopped coming. Calypso was quickly absorbed back into the commercial folk music movement. In Jamaica itself, the style soon was eclipsed by the rise of a succession of new pop amalgams in the 1960s: ska, rock steady, and reggae. By this time, calypso was largely marketed through festivals in the Caribbean islands to attract nostalgic middle American tourists.

Top Artists and Their Recordings

Harry Belafonte--*Belafonte* (1956); *Calypso* (1956); "Jamaica Farewell" (1956/7); "Mary Boy Child" (1956/7); "Banana Boat (Day-O)" (1957); *An Evening With Belafonte* (1957); "Hold 'Em Joe" (1957); "Mama Look at Bubu" (1957); "Island in the Sun"/"Cocoanut Woman" (1957); *Belafonte Sings of the Caribbean* (1957); *Jump Up Calypso* (1961); *Calypso in Brass* (1967)

Terry Gilkyson and the Easy Riders--"Marianne" (1957)

The Tarriers--"The Banana Boat Song" (1956/7)

Reggae

Reggae is a collective term for a number of successive forms of Jamaican popular music, isolated examples of which have dented the U.S. Top Forty since the early 1960s. It is characterized by a loping beat, a strong dose of rhythm and blues, and recording techniques which have been simultaneously original in concept and primitive in execution. It has had an impact on 1970s rock that was far greater than its moderate commercial success.

The genre was a product of a diverse array of influences, including African-derived children's games, the ecstatic Christian Pocomania cult, Garveyite Rastafarians, and New Orleans rhythm and blues, which was broadcast all over the Caribbean via clear-channel radio stations in the late 1950s. These forces did not converge until the appearance of transistor radios revived Jamaican interest in popular music recordings. Out of this state of affairs emerged the "sound system man," who operated a generator-powered hi-fi rig mounted on the back of a flatbed truck which would be driven to rural areas for dances. These operators, utilizing catchy handles such as "Duke Reid," generated large audiences of fans.

In the early 1960s, the dearth of New Orleans talent (and corresponding drop-off of available imports) forced sound system men to make their own records. Primitive studios sprang up around Jamaica. The first recordings were bad copies of New Orleans music; the Jamaican musicians couldn't seem to get the New Orleans rhythm right. This "wrong" rhythm became standardized, and ska was born with its strict, mechanical emphasis on the offbeat (mm-*cha!* mm-*cha!*). One notable example of the ska style, Millie Small's "My Boy Lollipop," became a Top Ten hit in the United States.

By 1965, ska had ben superceded by the slow, even more rhythmic "rock steady" genre. Sound system men began employing deejays, who would "toast" or talk over the instrumental B-side of a record. The DJ--prime exponents included Prince Buster, Sir Collins, King Stitt, and U Roy--would improvise rhymes about his sexual prowess and the greatness of the sound system operator. This practice also became known as "dubbing"; some of it was "rude" (i.e., dirty; in Jamaican slang "dub" is equivalent to sexual intercourse.

Poppa-top was the next link in the evolutionary chain; bubblier than rock steady, it loosened up the beat to the point where greater rhythmic division was possible. The leading exponent of the style, Desmond Dekker, became a one-hit wonder in the U.S. with his 1969 Top Ten release, "Israelites."

The release of the Maytals' "Do the Reggay," in 1968, served notice that a new form had entered the marketplace. Jamiacan music had been expanding the role of the bass for much of the 1960s; reggae brought the bass to the forefront, emphasizing the complex interrelationship between it, the trap drums, and the percussion instruments. The beat was interspersed with silences, the pulse divided as finely as sixty-four times, and cross-rhythms abound. The bass appeared to be the lead instrument, with the guitar reduced to playing "change," mere scratching at a chord. Keyboard and horns were utilized to thicken the texture.

Despite the success of some reggae-styled material in the U.S. (e.g., Johnny Nash's "I Can See Clearly Now" and "Stir It Up," Eric Clapton's "I Shot the Sheriff"), the genre remained relatively unknown to most Americans until the U.S. release of the film, *The Harder They Come*, starring Jimmy Cliff, in 1973. It became a cult favorite and opened the door to the American market for other reggae artists.

Its widespread acceptance in the states was hampered by the scarcity of live reggae music. This was because (1) most of the records used the same pool of studio talent, and (2) most Jamaicans couldn't afford night clubs or stage show performances. The most famous reggae performer was Bob Marley, whose recordings featured protest lyrics, first-rate melodies, high quality production values, and seamless blend Jamaican roots and rock conventions (which enabled him please both his original followers and U.S. fans).

Marley's promising career was abruptly cut short by his death from lung cancer in 1981. Nevertheless, reggae has left a substantial musical legacy, including hip hop, disco dubs with a DJ rapping over the track, and an expansion of the rhythmic possibilities in rock (as realized by artists as diverse as Jimmy Buffett, the Grateful Dead, the Clash, Police, the Flying Lizards, the Selector, Generation X, the Slits, the English Beat, Public Image Ltd., and UB40. The genre has also long served the cultural and information needs of its people and supports the world's most successful self-contained Third World record business.

Top Artists and Their Recordings

Big Youth--"Pass the Dutchie" (1984)

Black Uhuru--*Chill Out* (1982); **Now** (1990)

Burning Spear--*Marcus Garvey* (1975)

Jimmy Cliff--*The Harder They Come* (1975); *Follow My Mind* (1975); *Special* (1982)

Culture--*International Herb* (1979)

The Heptones--*Night Food* (1976)

The Inner Circle--*Everything Is Great* (1979)

Bob Marley and the Wailers/The Wailers--*Catch a Fire* (1973); *Burnin'* (1974); *Natty Dread* (1975); *Rastaman Vibration* (1976); *Live!* (1976); *Exodus* (1977); *Kaya* (1978); *Babylon By Bus* (1978); *Survival* (1979); *Uprising* (1980); *Chances Are* (1981)

Ziggy Marley and the Melody Makers--*Conscious Party* (1988); *One Bright Day* (1989); *Jahmekya* (1991)

The Mighty Diamonds--*Right Time* (1976)

Steel Pulse--*True Democracy* (1982); *Earth Crisis* (1984); *State of...Emergency* (1988)

Third World--*Journey to Addis* (1978); *The Story's Been Told* (1979); *Third World, Prisoner in the Street* (1980); *Rock the World* (1981); *You've Got the Power* (1982); *All the Way Strong* (1983); *Sense of Purpose* (1985); *Serious Business* (1989)

Toots and the Maytals--*Funky Kingston* (1975); *Reggae Got Soul* (1976)

Peter Tosh--*Legalize It* (1976); *Bush Doctor* (1978); *Mystic Man* (1979); *Wanted Dread and Alive* (1981); *Mama Africa* (1983); *Captured Live* (1984)

San Francisco Sound

Generally speaking, the San Francisco Sound embraced the rock-related music being produced in the Bay Area during the latter half of the 1960s. Some music historians have insisted upon a more narrow description of the genre, focusing on the free-form, jam-oriented rock played byseminal bands such as the Jefferson Airplane and the Grateful Dead. Others have chosen to emphasize extra-musical trappings such as the communal hippie lifestyle--accented by heavy usage of psychedelic drugs, free love, and the spiritual quest for one's self identity--espoused by many of the popular performers and their audience.

Both interpretations fall somewhat short of the mark in evoking the true character of the San Francisco Sound. From a strictly musical standpoint, the performers using the Bay Area as a home base defied stylistic categorization, ranging from the Beatlesque pop of Beau Brummels to the jug band nostalgia of Dan Hicks to the Latin rock of Santana. Furthermore, the cultural dimensions of this scene not only came to symbolize the changing mores of a nation at large, but forever modified the basic configuration of the popular music industry. Gene Sculatti and Davin Seay, in *San Francisco Nights*, note that the events associated with this sound,

> ...freed pop musicians from 40 years of showbiz orthodoxies, providing the first real alternative to Tin Pan Alley tradition. In the process it set

the music industry on its ear, grating unprecedented artistic control, and a shot at undreamt of fame and fortune, for those who would follow. Grace Slick and Janis Joplin pioneered two bold new models for women in pop, while Country Joe McDonald, Jerry Garcia and others helped to elevate the mere musician to the status of political firebrand and cosmic pundit.

These points, however, merely scratch the surface. Jack McDonough, author of *San Francisco Rock*, offers a more detailed list of the groundbreaking music culture developments which emanated from the Bay Area:

(1) What became accepted at the time as a breakthrough in recording contracts--giving the artist such amenities as a higher royalty rate and control over production and artwork of his albums-- was originated by Steve Miller while in San Francisco in the late 1960s.

(2) The Grateful Dead negotiated a contract under which a rock band, like jazz musicians, could collect royalties based on minutes-per-side rather than songs-per-side.

(3) Progressive FM radio was founded in San Francisco during this period, and K101 became the first FM stereo station west of the Mississippi.

(4) Rock concerts as events warranting full stage production values and theatrical props were pioneered there.

(5) The notion of booking a nightclub as if it were a small concert hall was first introduced in the area.

(6) Rock-and-roll poster art was perfected there, as were the visual techniques of the modern light show.

(7) Rock journalism was brought to full international respectability by *Rolling Stone*.

The Haight-Ashbury scene collapsed less than two years after the excitement engendered by Kesey's acid tests, Golden Gate Park be-ins, and related activities caused a mass exodus of young people to the Bay Area. The musical and cultural legacy of the scene, however, can be traced up to the present day.

Top Artists and Their Recordings

Big Brother and the Holding Company--"Down on Me" (1968); "Piece of My Heart" (1968); *Cheap Thrills* (1968)

The Charlatans--*The Charlatans* (1967)

Country Joe and the Fish--*Electric Music for the Mind and Body* (1967); *I-Feel-Like-I'm-Fixin'-To-Die* (1967); *Together* (1968); *Here We Go Again* (1969); *C.J. Fish* (1970)

The Grateful Dead--*The Grateful Dead* (1967); *Anthem of the Sun* (1968); *Aoxomoxoa* (1969); *Live Dead* (1970); *Workingman's Dead* (1970); *American Beauty* (1970); *The Grateful Dead* (1971); *Europe '72* (1972)

Great Society--*Conspicuous Only In Its Absence* (1968); *How It Was* (1968)

Hot Tuna--*Hot Tuna* (1970); *First Pull Up, Then Pull Down* (1971); *Burgers* (1972); *The Phosphorescent Rat* (1973); *America's Choice* (1973); *Yellow Fever* (1975); *Hoppkorv* (1976); *Double Dose* (1977); *Final Vinyl* (1979)

It's a Beautiful Day--*It's a Beautiful Day* (1969); *Marrying Maiden* (1970); *Choice Quality Stiff/Anytime...* (1971)

The Jefferson Airplane--*The Jefferson Airplane Takes Off* (1966); *Surrealistic Pillow* (1967); "Somebody to Love" (1967); "White Rabbit" (1967); *After Bathing at Baxter's* (1967); *Crown of Creation* (1968); *Bless Its Pointed Little Head* (1969); *Volunteers* (1969)

The Loading Zone--*The Loading Zone* (1968); *One For All* (1970)

The Steve Miller Band--*Children of the Future* (1968); *Sailor* (1968); *Brave New World* (1969); *Your Saving Grace* (1969); *Number Five* (1970); *Rock Love* (1971); *Recall the Beginning...A Journey From Eden* (1972)

Moby Grape--*Moby Grape* (1967); *Wow!/Grape Jam* (1968); *'69* (1969); *Truly Fine Citizen* (1969); *Twenty Granite Creek* (1971)

Mother Earth--*Living With the Animals* (1969); *Make a Joyful Noise* (1969); *Bring Me Home* (1971)

Quicksilver Messenger Service--*Quicksilver Messenger Service* (1968); *Happy Trails* (1969); *Shady Grove* (1970); *Just For Love* (1970); *What About Me* (1971); *Quicksilver* (1971); *Comin' Thru* (1972)

Sons of Champlin--*Loosen Up Naturally* (1969); *The Sons* (1969)

The Sopwith Camel--*The Sopwith Camel* (1967)

Table 72

Country Joe and the Fish

Country Joe and the Fish were the most overtly political band identified with the San Francisco Sound of the late 1960s. The band also blended the populist folk music tradition (band leader Country Joe McDonald would release a Woody Guthrie memorial LP in the 1970s) with pronounced dada leanings.

Allegedly named after Joseph Stalin by his leftist parents, McDonald began recording in the mid-1960s, most notably three "Rag Baby" EPs which were sold on the streets in Berkeley. He then formed a folk duo with Barry Melton (aka "the Fish") in 1965. The act soon expanded into an electric band, including Bruce Barthol, David Cohen, and Chicken Hirsh. Their debut release, *Electric Music for the Mind and Body* (Vanguard 79244; 1967), was immediately hailed as a rock classic, featuring satirical lyrics and acid rock dominated by Melton's swirling organ lines. Amidst continued personnel changes, the band released four more studio albums before disbanding: *I-Feel-Like-I'm-Fixin'-To-Die* (Vanguard 79266; 1967), *Together* (Vanguard 79277; 1968), *Here We Are Again* (Vanguard 79299; 1969), and *C.J. Fish* (Vanguard 6555; 1970).

McDonald decided to embark on a solo career at the outset of the 1970s. He would go on to release over twenty LPs and contribute music to several Hollywood films. Signing with Fantasy Records in the mid-1970s, he briefly reunited with the original Fish to produce an album. Much of his best recordings in the 1980s were distributed primarily in Europe, where he had toured regularly since 1967. Melton was also active for many years as a performer and recording artist. After participating in a succession of club dates with the Dinosaurs in 1982, he completed a law degree the following year. Cohen went on to produce an instruction album for Kicking Mule that demonstrated the playing techniques of Carlos Santana, Duane Allman, Chuck Berry, Bo Diddley, B.B. King, Jerry Garcia, and other seminal guitarists. [McDonough. 1985.]

Table 73

Janis Joplin, January 19, 1943-October 4, 1970

Just as she had defied social conformity while growing up in Port Arthur, Texas, Janis Joplin paid little to musical conventions. The agonizingly insecure young white women, having grown up in a seemingly normal middle class environment, sang the blues with an emotional intensity and straightforward honesty rarely equaled before or after her brief, meteoric career. While few female singers can hope to match the depth of feeling communicated in her comparatively small body of work, many have been influenced by the sheer exuberance she brought to every song she sang—both live and in the studio.

Leaving home at seventeen, Joplin first tried singing professionally at country and western venues in the Houston area. Within a few years she had moved out to California, alternating between various colleges and folk singing gigs around San Francisco. Making little headway there in 1965 and early 1966, she opted for a job singing with a Texas country act. Shortly thereafter, however she was induced to return to the Bay Area by Chet Helm, who told of a promising new group that needed a female vocalist, Big Brother and the Holding Company. Almost immediately upon joining the band in June 1966, word of her extraordinary talent spread through the local music scene. Big Brother's electrifying performance at the Monterey Pop Festival in the summer of 1967 captured the attention of the entire record industry, The band was signed by Mainstream Records, and an album, *Big Brother and the Holding Company* (Mainstream 6099; 1967), was released in late 1967.

The group's first appearance on the East Coast, at New York's Anderson Theater in February 1968, led to a contract with Columbia Records. The ensuing LP, *Cheap Thrills* (Columbia 9700; 1968) was both an artistic and commercial tour de force, reaching number one on the pop album charts. As the dominant force within Big Brother, it was inevitable that Joplin would strike out on her own, citing the band members' limitations as musicians. Her first solo release, *I Got Dem Ol' Kozmic Blues Again Mama!* (Columbia 9913; 1969) was indeed more accomplished, the wide range of material all tied together by Joplin's raw delivery. She was at work on her next album, the country-inflected *Pearl* (Columbia 30322; 1970), when she was discovered dead of a heroin overdose at Hollywood's Landmark Hotel. A single from the posthumously released LP, "Me and Bobby McGee" (Columbia 45314; 1971), would top the *Billboard Hot 100*.

Much like her deceased peers, Jimi Hendrix and Jim Morrison, Joplin has remained an important force within the rock scene. A seemingly endless flood of magazine articles, books, and films (both documentaries and fictionalized accounts) discussing her life and music have appeared on the marketplace. Columbia has continued to issue recordings culled from studio outtakes, live performances, and previously released material, most notably *Joplin in Concert* (Columbia 31160; 1972), *Janis Joplin's Greatest Hits* (Columbia 32168; 1973), *Janis* (Columbia 33345; 1975), *Farewell Song* (Columbia 37569; 1982), *Janis* (3 CDs; Columbia 48845; 1993), and *Box of Pearls: The Janis Joplin Collection* (5 CDs; Columbia 65937; 1999).

Southern Rock

Southern rock, sometimes termed the Sound of the South, was a major commercial force in the 1970s. It blended strains of music indigenous to the region--the blues, rhythm and blues, country, and gospel--into a flexible, jam-oriented style. Although jump-started by the Allman Brothers, who were earning critical accolades and selling millions of records by the time guitarist Duane Allman died in a motorcycle crash in 1971, in the broader sense the genre represented a response to the progressive rock hybrids developed in northern cities during the late 1960s (e.g., the San Francisco Sound, Latin rock). The song lyrics--indeed, sometimes even the multicultural composition of the bands--reflected the values of the "New South"; pride in one's roots, racial harmony, etc.

Due to a strong core audience, many southern rock groups have enjoyed lengthy careers based on regular touring rather than hit singles. Continued personnel charges have brought new musical ideas to the Allmans, Lynyrd Skynyrd, and other acts without any significant loss of fan support. In the meantime, new exponents of the tradition have continued to appear, most of whom have provided innovative takes on timeworn stylistic conventions such as double (even triple) lead guitar lineups, bluegrass-rock improvisation, and redneck metal fusions. Some of the promising newcomers of the mid-1990s--most notably Government Mule, Widespread Panic, and Storyville--proved successful in siphoning off legions of deadheads in the wake of Jerry Garcia's sudden death in August 1995.

Top Artists and Their Recordings

Allman Brothers Band--*The Allman Brothers Band* (1969); *Idlewild South* (1970); *At Fillmore East* (1971); *Eat a Peach* (1972); *Brothers and Sisters* (1973); *Win, Lose or Draw* (1975); *Enlightened Rogues* (1979); *An Evening With the Allman Brothers Band* (1992)

Atlanta Rhythm Section--*Third Annual Pipe Dream* (1974); *Dog Days* (1975); *Red Tape* (1976); *A Rock and Roll Alternative* (1977); *Champagne Jam* (1978); *Underdog* (1979); *Quinella* (1981)

Black Crowes--*Shake Your Money Maker* (1990) *The Southern Harmony and Musical Companion* (1992)

Black Oak Arkansas--*Black Oak Arkansas* (1971); *Keep the Faith* (1972); *If an Angel Came to See You, Would You Make Her Feel at Home?* (1972); *Raunch 'N' Roll/Live* (1973); *High on the Hog* (1973); *Street Party* (1974); *Balls of Fire* (1976)

Charlie Daniels Band--*Honey in the Rock* (1973); *Fire on the Mountain* (1974); *Million Mile Reflections* (1979)

Lynyrd Skynyrd--*Lynyrd Skynyrd* (1973); *Second Helping* (1974); *Nuthin' Fancy* (1975); *Gimme Back My Bullets* (1976); *One More From the Road* (1976); *Street Survivors* (1977); *Lynyrd Skynyrd 1991* (1991)

Marshall Tucker Band--*The Marshall Tucker Band* (1973); *A New Life* (1974); *Where We All Belong* (1975); *Searchin' For a Rainbow* (1975); *Long Hard Ride* (1976); *Carolina Dreams* (1977); *Together Forever* (1978); *Tuckerized* (1982)

Molly Hatchet--*Molly Hatchet* (1978); *Flirtin' With Disaster* (1979); *Beatin' the Odds* (1980); *Take No Prisoners* (1981); *Double Trouble* (1985)

The Outlaws--*Outlaws* (1975); *Lady in Waiting* (1976); *Hurry Sundown* (1977); *Bring It Back Alive* (1978); *Soldiers of Fortune* (1986)

Ozark Mountain Daredevils--*The Ozark Mountain Daredevils* (1974); *It'll Shine When It Shine* (1974); *The Car Over the Lake Album* (1975); *Ozark Mountain Daredevils* (1980)

Rossington-Collins Band--*Anytime, Anyplace, Anywhere* (1980); *This Is the Way* (1981); *Love Your Man* (1988)

Sea Level--*Sea Level* (1977); *Cats on the Coast* (1978); *On the Edge* (1978); *Ball Room* (1980)
.38 Special--*.38 Special* (1977); *Rockin' Into the Night* (1980); *Wild-Eyed Southern Boys* (1981); *Special Forces* (1982); *Tour De Force* (1983); *Strength in Numbers* (1986); *Bone Against Steel* (1991)

Wet Willie--*Wet Willie* (1971); *Drippin' Wet/Live* (1973); *Keep on Smilin'* (1974); *Dixie Rock* (1975); *Which One's Willie?* (1979)

Salsa

The word means "sauce" in Spanish; however, the music bearing this name is much harder to define. Most experts agree that it is a modern arrangement of fast rhythms related to the mambo, a big-band style popular in the 1940s. These rhythms include guarachas, sones, and guanguancos, all of which originated in Cuba. Salsa can also encompass a wide range of Caribbean dance forms such as bombas and plenas from Puerto Rico, merengues from the Dominican Republic, cumbias from Columbia, and joopos from Venezuela. The form relies heavily on percussion instruments such as the congas (freestanding drums usually played in pairs), the bongos (a smaller two-drum set rested on the knees), and the timbales (a stand-mounted percussion ensemble which includes two small drums and tuned cowbells). The tipico style--a specific method of phrasing and underscoring a solo with a repeated montuno (a two or three chord phrase) riff, played on a piano or another accompanying instrument--represents a notable ingredient of salsa.

Top Artists and Their Recordings

Celia Cruz--*Mi Diario Musical*.

Eddie Palmieri--*Sentido*.

Tito Puente--*Cuban Carnival*.

Tito Rodriguez--*Carnival of the Americas*.

Mongo Santamaria--*Afro-Indio*.

HYBRID CHILDREN OF ROCK

Genealogical Outline

The legacy of aesthetic self-determination and experimentation begun during the First Wave of the British Invasion and the ensuing American Renaissance reached its culmination in the latter half of the 1960s. While more conventional sounds—most notably, the south-of-the-border-tinged pop of Herb Alpert and the Tijuana Brass, the easy listening soul of the Fifth Dimension, the bubblegum schlock exemplified by fictional groups such as the Archies, and the Vegas-styled productions of Tom Jones and Engelbert Humperdinck—continued to dominate the charts, more progressive-minded artists increasingly opted for musical eclecticism (ranging from Baroque flourishes and basso continuo rhythms to Third World instrumentation and tone colors), greater virtuosity in execution, and creative use of studio techniques like multi-tracking, feedback, and sonic collages. Song structures were expanded and turned inside-out while lyrics reflected a wider range of poetic devices and surrealistic imagery.

The example provided by the recordings of the Beatles cannot be over-estimated; the Fab Four's commercial ascendancy was firmly established by 1965, when LPs such as *Help* and *Rubber Soul* offered early glimpses of their raw talent and predisposition for creative tinkering. The public's receptivity to even the more difficult fare served up by the band convinced many rock musicians that progressive artistic growth was acceptable—even necessary—in order to achieve long-term success.

The rich diversity of the rock scene owned just as much, however, to the emergence of FM radio. Experimental programming was the order of the day as deejays attempted to discover stylistic formulas likely to generate new listening audiences. As a result, artists who would have previously been consigned either to less lucrative pop music categories (e.g., bluegrass, the blues) or to the underground found a wider form of acceptance translating into significant record sales.

Likewise, the rise of rock festivals—an offshoot of the folk and jazz festivals which had proved popular in the early 1960s—provided a viable alternative to marginal club dates and constricting packaged tours headed by media personalities like *American Bandstand* MC Dick Clark. The large audiences generated by events at Monterey, Woodstock, and the Isle of Wight not only enabled rock performers to command larger live fees, but to sell significantly larger amounts of records.

As with the socio-political trends of that era, the musical promise embodied in concept albums such as *Sgt. Pepper's Lonely Heart Club Band* and the rise of exciting new artists (e.g., Jimi Hendrix, Janis Joplin) and genres (e.g., Latin rock, big band rock) by soured by the 1970s in the face of a growing corporate ethics—reflected, on the one hand, by beer company sponsorship of tours featuring major performers—as well as the extramusic posturing which dominated heavy metal, funk, glitter rock, and other newly dominant styles.

Christian Rock/Christian Contemporary

Beyond the gospel borrowings which influenced the core composition of rock 'n' roll, the genre first appeared in the form of the Jesus rock craze in the early 1970s. Rock musicals such as *Jesus Christ Superstar* and *Godspell* played a seminal role in this new religious consciousness. However, the movement was embroiled in controversy from the outset; many clerics felt that the use of a rock beat (not to mention the dramatic liberties taken with biblical storylines) to spread the Christian message was inherently sacriligious.

The genre was revived in the early 1980s as part of the missionary zeal of the Christian right, acting in concert with the then ascendant conservative political movement. Despite concerted efforts to market major artists to the mainstream popular music audience, their impact was generally limited to Christian Contemporary radio and retail outlets (e.g., religious bookstores, chain-stores geared to small town consumers such as Wal-Mart). The genre's lack of creative spark had much to do with this state of affairs; it tended to be a bland rehash of dated rock cliches. Those CC artists achieving a modicum of mass market success--most notably, Amy Grant--did so by tempering the overtly Christian tone of their recordings.

Top Artists and Their Recordings

Code of Ethics--*Code of Ethics* (1997)

DC Talk—*Jesus Freak* (1995)

Amy Grant--*My Father's Eyes* (1979); *Never Alone* (1980); *In Concert* (1981); *In Concert, Volume Two* (1981); *Age to Age* (1982); *Straight Ahead* (1984); *Unguarded* (1985); *Lead Me On* (1988); *Heart in Motion* (1991)

Jars of Clay--"Flood" (1996)

Stryper--*The Yellow and Black Attack* (1984); *Soldiers Under Command* (1985); *To Hell With the Devil* (1986); *In God We Trust* (1988); *Against the Law* (1990)

Punk/Garage Rock

The first wave of punk rock was not about virtuousity; indeed, its finest practitioners could barely play their instruments. Rather, it reflected, according to *The Rolling Stone Illustrated History of Rock & Roll* (2nd edition), "the utopian dream of everyman an artist."

The origins of garage rock, the forerunner of mid-1960s punk, can be discerned in the instrumental groups based in California and the Pacific Northwest during the early 1960s. Within a few years a number of Mexican-American bands in southern California had begun adding vocals, most notably the Premiers ("Farmer John"; 1964), Cannibal & the Headhunters ("Land of 1,000 Dances"; 1965), and Thee Midniters ("Land of 1,000 Dances, Part 1"; 1965). By the middle of the decade, however, the creative center of the scene had shifted back to the northern Pacific coast, home base for groups such as the Sonics (Seattle), the Kingsmen, and Paul Revere & the Raiders (the latter two hailing from Portland).

The next phase, classic punk, coincided with the rise of psychedelia in 1966. New technical breakthroughs such as fuzztone and the electric twelve-string guitar enabled young musicians possessing limited playing technique to experiment with an augmented sonic vocabulary. The genre also incorporated various fads of the moment including the drug subculture and Eastern music (e.g., ragas, sitars) and philosophy. Punk bands sprang up across the nation; those cited below (categorized by locale) all had at least one moderate hit:

Boston

The Standells ("Dirty Water," "Sometimes Good Guys Don't Wear White," "Why Pick on Me"); The Remains; The Barbarians ("Are You a Boy of Are You a Girl," "Moulty")

Midwest

The Litter; Terry Knight & the Pack ("I, Who Have Nothing"); Cryan' Shames ("Sugar and Spice"); Shadows of Knight ("Gloria"); ? & the Mysterians ("96 Tears," "I Need Somebody")

South

John Fred & His Playboy Band ("Judy in Disguise"); The Hombres ("Let It Out"); The Gentrys ("Keep on Dancing"); The Swingin' Medallions ("Double Shot of My Baby's Love," "She Drives Me Out of My Mind")

Los Angeles

Count Five ("Psychotic Reaction"); Chocolate Watch Band; Syndicate of Sound ("Little Girl"); The Music Machine ("Talk Talk"); The Leaves ("Hey Joe"); The Seeds ("Pushin' Too Hard," "Can't Seem to Make You Mine")

By 1968 punk had lost its momentum, the more adventuresome bands evolving in the direction of acid rock. The remaining holdouts had no options other than heavy metal. For instance, in the Michigan area, the Amboy Dukes (fronted by gonzo guitarist Ted Nugent) took the former path, whereas Grand Funk Railroad (a spin-off of Terry Knight & the Pack), the MC5, and the Stooges (lead by Iggy Pop) opted for the latter. The rebellious element of punk attitude continued to be sustained in these stylistic offshoots, ultimately to be resurrected in the second punk wave of the mid-1970s.

Psychedelia

The psychedelic era evolved out of the social consciousness movement engendered by a commitment to civil rights, anti-war protest, the legalization of recreational drugs, and other issues on the part of the youth subculture. These issues were frequently addressed in rock song lyrics while the music itself often employed special effects geared to underscoring the message at hand. For example, the Doors' "Unknown Soldier" (1968) included a marching interlude accented by a drill sergeant's shrieked commands and the discharge of rifles. The Chicago Transit Authority's "Prologue, August 29, 1968" featured an actual recording from the 1968 Democratic National Convention which conveyed the following sequence: black militants exhorting demonstrators, "God give us the blood to keep going"; the beginning of the march; police attempting to disperse marchers; and the demonstrators chanting, "The Whole World's Watching." Pearl Before Swine's polemic on the horrors of war, *Balaklava* (1968), began with a turn of the century recording of the trumpet which was blown to commence the fabled charge of the British Light Brigade in 1856.

These spacey sound effects, however, paled in contrast to the mind expanding techniques utilized to evoke the psychedelic drug experience. Guitarist Les Paul was the spiritual godfather of studio augmentation as a result of his experiments with overdubbing and multi-tracking; his seminal 1950s recordings with vocalist Mary Ford rivaled big band and orchestral productions for fullness of sound. The unique tones he was able to coax out of his guitar within a studio environment were not equaled until Jimi Hendrix's appearance on the scene. The infancy of stereo recording in the early 1960s had witnessed a succession of sonic experiments primarily within the light pops sector. Enoch Light and the Light Brigade pioneered the spatial left-right channel ping-pong effects later employed in a spectacular manner by Hendrix in his albums, *Axis: Bold as Love* and *Electric Ladyland*. The introduction of synthesizers into the recording process by inventors such as Robert Moog in collaboration with Morton Subotnick, Walter (Wendy) Carlos, and other avant garde artists, made available another key tool for rock production wizards.

As in so many other genres, the Beatles played a pioneering role in the evolution of psychedelic effects. The group's recording engineer, George Martin, proved extremely facile at reproducing the sounds that the Lennon-McCartney songwriting team professed to have in their heads. Martin's arsenal of studio effects included tapes run backwards, filtered voices, and the inventive use of exotic instruments (e.g., the piccolo trumpet on "Penny Lane") and ambient sounds. The critical raves and commercial success of *Revolver* (1966) and *Sgt. Pepper's Lonely Hearts Club Band* (1967)--both of which reeked of psychedelic touches--spurred a tidal wave of imitators. The vast majority of rock acts insisted on (or were talked into) doing their own psychedelic projects. Even artists whose prior output appeared to be the antithesis of such studio excess--e.g., roots rocker Johnny Rivers, who was then enjoying a career revival with a series of soft ballads, and blues stylists, the Rolling Stones--were swept up by this new fad. Only Bob Dylan, who released a country-rock masterpiece, *John Wesley Harding*, at the peak of the psychedelic era, seemed able to run counter to prevailing fashion.

Psychedelia was sometimes referred to as "acid rock." The latter label was generally applied to a pounding, hard rock variant which evolved out of the mid-1960s garage punk movement. By late 1966, the Blues Magoos were calling their brand of wailing blues-rock "psychedelic" music. Although generally devoid of the studio gimmickry typifying the Beatles school of psychedelia, acid rock provided its own form of mind expansion by means of guitar pyrotechnics. Leading practitioners included the Cream, Blue Cheer, and the Amboy Dukes. When rock began turning back to softer, roots-oriented sounds in late 1968, acid rock bands mutated into heavy metal acts. Traces of the psychedelic era can still be found in the stylistic excesses of many third-generation metal groups.

Top Artists and Their Recordings

The Beatles--*Sgt. Pepper's Lonely Hearts Club Band* (1967); *Magical Mystery Tour* (1967)

The Blues Magoos--"(We Ain't Got) Nothin' Yet" (1966); *Psychedelic Lollipop* (1966); *Electric Comic Book* (1967); *Basic Blues Magoos* (1968)

The Byrds--*The Notorious Byrd Brothers* (1967); "Goin' Back" (1967); "Artificial Energy" (1968)

The Cream--*Disraeli Gears* (1967); *Wheels of Fire* (1968); "White Room" (1968)

The Doors--*Strange Days* (1967)

The Family--*Music From a Doll's House* (1968)

The Grateful Dead--*Anthem of the Sun* (1968); *Aoxomoxoa* (1969)

Jimi Hendrix (Experience)--*Are You Experienced?* (1967); "Purple Haze" (1967); "Foxey Lady" (1967/8); *Axis: Bold As Love* (1968); "All Along the Watchtower" (1968); *Electric Ladyland* (1968); "Crosstown Traffic" (1968); *Band of Gypsys* (1969); *The Cry of Love* (1970)

Iron Butterfly--*Heavy* (1967); *In a Gadda Da Vida* (1968); *Ball* (1969)

The Jefferson Airplane--*After Bathing at Baxter's* (1967)

The Lemon Pipers--"Green Tambourine" (1967/8)

The Rascals--*Once Upon a Dream* (1967); "It's Wonderful" (1967)

The Rolling Stones--*Their Satanic Majesties Request* (1967)

The Small Faces--"Itchycoo Park" (1967/8)

The Status Quo--"Pictures of Matchstick Men" (1968)

The Strawberry Alarm Clock--"Incense and Peppermints" (1967); *Incense and Peppermints* (1967); "Tomorrow" (1967/8); "Sit With the Guru" (1968); *Wake Up! It's Tomorrow* (1968); *World in a Sea Shell* (1968)

The Thirteen Floor Elevators--"You're Gonna Miss Me" (1966); *Psychedelic Sounds of the Thirteenth Floor Elevators* (1966); *Easter Everywhere* (1967); *Thirteenth Floor Elevators* (1968); *Bull of the Woods* (1969)

Bill Wyman (Rolling Stones)--"In Another Land" (1967)

Progressive Rock/Classical Rock

Progressive rock implies a particular mindset in recording and performing music, an predisposition to test established limits and boundaries. Stylistically speaking, progressive rock is all over the map. Pioneering artists, unfettered by preconceived notions of the status quo, can be found within all musical categories.

Furthermore, the means by which an artist displays "progressive" leanings may vary according to the presence of one (or more) of the following features:

(1) complex, often lengthy, compositions
(2) virtuostic performances
(3) exotic and/or eclectic instrumentation

The Beatles' release of *Sgt. Pepper's Lonely Heart Club Band*, represented a watershed development in the development of the genre. In retrospect, examples of progressive rock can be identified as existing prior to that album's appearance in June 1967, ranging from Elvis Presley's early rockabilly experiments to the Byrds' folk rock classics recorded between 1965-1967. However, post-*Sgt. Pepper* works tended to exude a seriousness of purpose (i.e., the consideration of aesthetics over the commercial marketplace) hitherto relegated to the jazz and classical music sectors. The emergence of rock journalism, largely built around young intellectuals who had grown up listening to rock 'n' roll and other popular music genres, helped to spread the gospel of highbrow rock art. The youth subculture, then preoccupied with weighty social matters such as civil rights and the anti-Vietnam War movement, wholeheartedly bought into the concept.

The concept album represented a notable subgenre within the progressive rock movement. In view of the increased profit-making potential of the long-playing twelve-inch record (which generally included ten to fourteen songs and ranged in length from thirty to fifty minutes) over forty-five r.p.m. singles, record companies concentrated their promotional efforts toward establishing the l.p. as the primary mode of aesthetic expression within the rock scene. Accordingly, rock musicians began experimenting with ways of presenting a unified thematic message (both in the music and song lyrics) within the framework of a record album. Notable concept albums produced by rock artists included:

Fairport Convention--*Babbacombe Lee* (1973)
The Kinks--*Arthur* (1968)
The Moody Blues--*Days of Future Passed* (1967); *In Search of the Lost Chord* (1968); *On the Threshold of a Dream* (1969)
Pink Floyd--*Animals* (1977); *The Wall* (1979)
The Who--*Tommy* (1969); *Quadrophenia* (1973)

After a dazzlingly creative period in the late 1960s which saw even mainstream pop artists incorporating progressive rock conventions into their work, the music business split off into an extensive array of stylistic fragments. While progressive rock was marginalized in the 1970s to the extent that its artists rarely achieved mainstream success, the genre could count on the support of a relatively substantial fan base, one that was at least the equal of funk and disco. However, the emergence of the punk movement, which viciously characterized corporate rock (many read this to mean "progressive rock") as a bloated guardian of the musical equivalent of dry rot, hastened the decline of the genre. By the 1980s, the term "new wave" was being loosely applied to all rock acts displaying progressive instincts.

Top Artists and Their Recordings

Amon Duul--*Phallus Dei* (1969); *Yeti* (1970); *Dance of the Lemmings* (1971); *Carnival in Babylon* (1972); *Wolf City* (1972); *Live in London* (1973); *Vive La Trance* (1973); *Hijack* (1974); *Made In Germany* (1975)

Aphrodite's Child--*And of the World Rain and Tears* (1970); *It's Five O'Clock* (1971); *666, Apocalypse of John* (1972)

Captain Beefheart and His Magic Band--*Safe As Milk* (1967); *Drop Out Boogie* (1967); *Strictly Personal* (1968); *Trout Mask Replica* (1969); *Lick My Decals Off* (1970); *Spotlight Kid* (1971); *Clear Spot* (1972); *Mirror Man* (1974

Camel--*Camel* (1973); *Mirage* (1974); *Snow Goose* (1975); *Moonmadness* (1976); *Rain Dances* (1977); *Breathless* (1978)

Can--*Monster Movie* (1970); *Tago Mago* (1971); *Ege Bamyasi* (1972); *Deep End* (1973); *Future Days* (1973); *Soon Over Babaluma* (1974); *Limited Edition* (1974); *Landed* (1975)

Caravan--*Caravan* (1972); *If I Could Do It All Over Again...* (1970); *In the Land of the Grey and Pink* (1971); *Waterloo Lily* (1972); *For Girls Who Grow Plump in the Night* (1973); *And the New Symphonia* (1974); *Cunning Stunts* (1975)

Curved Air--*Air Conditioning* (1970); *Second Album* (1971); *Phantasmagoria* (1971)

The Flock--*The Flock* (1969); *Dinosaur Swamps* (1971)

Genesis--*From Genesis to Revelation* (1969); *Trespass* (1970); *Nursery Cryme* (1971); *Foxtrot* (1772); *Selling England By the Pound* (1973); *Live* (1973); *The Lamb Lies Down on Broadway* (1974); *Trick of the Tail* (1976); *Wind and Wuthering* (1977)

Gentle Giant--*Gentle Giant* (1970); *Acquiring the Taste* (1971); *Three Friends* (1972); *Octopus* (1973); *In a Glass House* (1973); *The Power and the Glory* (1974); *Free Hand* (1975); *A Giant Step* (1975); *Interview* (1976); *Playing the Fool* (1976); *The Missing Piece* (1977); *Giant for a Day* (1978); *Civilian* (1980)

Gong--*The Flying Teapot* (1973); *Angels Egg* (1973); *Continental Circus* (1974); *Camembert Electrique* (1974); *You* (1974); *Shamal* (1976); *Gazeuse* (1977); *Live* (1977); *Magick Brother* (1977)

Steve Hackett--*Voyage of the Acolyte* (1975); *Please Don't Touch* (1978); *Spectral Mornings* (1979); *Defector* (1980)

Hawkwind--*Hawkwind* (1970); *A Search in Space* (1971); *Doremi Farsolatido* (1972); *Space Ritual* (1973); *Hall of the Mountain Grill* (1974); *Warrior on the Edge of Time* (1975); *Road Hawks* (1976); *Astounding Sounds* (1976); *Masters of the Universe* (1977); *Quark Strangeness and Charm* (1977)

Jethro Tull--*Time Was* (1968); *Stand Up* (1969); *Benefit* (1970); *Aqualung* (1971); *Thick as a Brick* (1972); *Living in the Past* (1973); *Passion Play* (1973); *War Child* (1974); *Minstrel in the Gallery* (1975)

Kaleidoscope--*Side Trips* (1967); *A Beacon From Mars* (1968); *The Incredible Kaleidoscope* (1969)

King Crimson--*In the Court of the Crimson King* (1969); *In the Wake of Poseidon* (1970); *Lizard* (1971); *Islands* (1971); *Earthbound* (1972); *Larks Tongues in Aspic* (1973); *Starless and Bible Black* (1974); *Red* (1974); *U.S.A.* (1975)

Spirit--*Spirit* (1968); *The Family That Plays Together* (1968); *Clear Spirit* (1969); *Twelve Dreams of Dr. Sardonicus* (1970); *Feedback* (1971); *Spirit of 76* (1975); *Son of Spirit* (1975); *Farther Along* (1976); *Future Games* (1977)

Traffic--*Mr. Fantasy* (1967); *Traffic* (1968); *Last Exit* (1969); *John Barleycorn Must Die* (1970); *Welcome to the Canteen* (1971); *Low Spark of High-Heeled Boys* (1971); *Shoot Out at the Fantasy Factory* (1973); *On the Road* (1974); *When the Eagle Flies* (1974)

United States of America--*United States of America* (1968)

Van Der Graaf Generator--*Aerosol Grey Machine* (1968); *The Least We Can Do Is Wave* (1969); *H to He Who Am the Only One* (1970); *Pawn Hearts* (1971); *Godbluff* (1975)

West Coast Pop Art Experimental Band--*Part One* (1967); *Vol. 2* (1967); *A Child's Guide to Good and Evil* (1968); *Where's My Daddy?* (1969)

Wishbone Ash--*Wishbone Ash* (1970); *Pilgrimage* (1971); *Argus* (1972); *Wishbone Four* (1973); *Live Dates* (1974); *There's the Rub* (1974)

The Youngbloods--*Elephant Mountain* (1969)

Frank Zappa (and the Mothers of Invention)--*Freak Out* (1966); *Absolutely Free* (1967); *We're Only in It For the Money* (1967); *Lumpy Gravy* (1967); *Cruisin' With Ruben and the Jets* (1968); *Uncle Meat* (1969); *Weasels Ripped My Flesh* (1970); *Chungas Revenge* (1970); *Hot Rats* (1970); *Burnt Weeny Sandwich* (1970); *Live at the Fillmore East* (1971); *200 Motels* (1971); *Just Another Band From L.A.* (1972); The Grand Wazoo (1972); *Waka Jawaka* (1972); *Overnight Sensation* (1973); *Apostrophe* (1974); *Roxy and Elsewhere* (1974); *One Size Fits All* (1974); *Bongo Fury* (1975); *Zoot Allures* (1976); *In New York* (1978); *Studio Tan* (1978); *Sheik Yerbouti* (1979); *Sleep Dirt* (1979); *Orchestral Favourites* (1979); *Joe's Garage, Act 1* (1980); *Joe's Garage, Acts 2 & 3* (1980); *Tinseltown Rebellion* (1981)

Table 74

The Band

The Band were a key force behind the back-to-the-roots trend in late 1960s rock music. Their sound represented a populist amalgam of country, folk, and rhythm and blues; its most notable feature, however, consisted of compassionate, blue collar poetry—often evoking historical themes from the standpoint of the common man—communicated by a loose vocal interplay that often had one singer begin a line of verse and another chiming in to finish it.

The Band—consisting of Arkansas native Levon Helm on drums, and four Canadians: lead guitarist Robbie Robertson, pianist Richard Manuel, keyboardist Garth Hudson, and bassist Rick Danko—came together in the early 1960s as Ronnie Hawkins' rockabilly-oriented backing group, the Hawks. They eventually drifted to the eastern seaboard, attracting attention as Bob Dylan's support band in 1965. Their work with Dylan—most notably, the 1966 Royal Albert Hall concert, and legendary Basement Tapes recorded in Woodstock, New York, while the folk-rock pioneer recuperated from a motorcycle accident—is available on countless bootlegs and official Dylan retrospectives released by Sony/Columbia.

The unadorned evocations of rural Americana in the Band's debut LP, *Music From Big Pink* (Capitol 2955; 1968; #30), recorded in 1967-1968 during the Woodstock period, drew rave reviews. They repeated this successful formula in the highly influential *The Band* (Capitol 132; 1969; #9), the reflective *Stage Fright* (Capitol 425; 1970; #5), and *Cahoots* (Capitol 651; 1971; #21).

From late 1971 until their official breakup at a gala San Francisco concert, Thanksgiving Day, 1976, the Band recorded only two more albums of original compositions, the uneven *Northern Lights/Southern Cross* (Capitol 11440; 1975; #26) and *Islands* (Capitol 11602; 1977; #64). A reunion with Dylan also led to a lackluster studio album, *Planet Waves* (Asylum 1003; 1974; #1), and competent live outing, *Before the Flood* (Asylum 201; 1974; #3), both of which sold largely on the basis of reputation. While Capitol continued to repackage older material by the group, the individual members pursued a wide range of artistic activities (including film acting and writing). They began performing again as a unit (sans Robertson) in 1983, eventually releasing three LPs of new material—*Jericho* (Pyramid; 1993), *High on the Hog* (Pyramid; 1996), and *Jubilation* (River North; 1998)—which lacked the innovative spark of their early work.

Table 75

Jeff Beck, June 24, 1944-

More than any other guitarist, Jeff Beck was responsible for defining the progressive rock genre. Combining extraordinary technique with a predisposition to expand previously defined stylistic boundaries, he blazed path in the latter half of the 1960s that would be traveled by peers such as Jimmy Page, Mick Ronson, and Paul Kossof. His innovations included the use of dissonant chords, controlled feedback, fuzztone, and sustained notes to create emotional intensity, combined with an overriding sense of compositional perspective, which precluded empty displays of virtuousity. Beck's later experiments with blues rock, heavy metal, jazz fusion and new wave rockabilly offered further evidence of his facility in an encyclopedic range of styles.

When blues guitar interpreter Eric Clapton professed dissatisfaction with the pop direction of the Yardbirds' first hit single, "For Your Love" (Epic 9790; 1965; #6), many observers of the British rock scene assumed he would be replaced by highly regarded session player Jimmy Page (later the founder of Led Zeppelin). Instead,(due in part to Page's recommendation) the group recruited the relatively unknown Beck, who immediately positioned himself in the forefront of guitar innovators, emulating the Indian sitar by filtering his guitar through a fuzzbox in "Heart Full of Soul" (Epic 9823; 1965; #9). His restrained application of then-exotic sound effects—feedback in "Shapes of Things" (Epic 10006; 1966; #11) and the dual lead interplay with Page on "Happenings Ten Years Time Ago" (Epic 10094; 1966; #30)—enabled the Yardbirds to remain commercially viable despite a pronounced experimental orientation.

Wishing to exert greater control over the creative process, he left the Yardbirds in 1967 to form the Jeff Beck Group, which featured vocalist Rod Stewart, bassist Ron Wood (Rolling Stones), drummer Mickey Waller, and keyboardist Nicky Hopkins (Quicksilver Messenger Service). While the band's two albums—*Truth* (Epic 26413; 1968; #15) and *Beck-Ola* (Epic 26478; 1969; #15)—laid the groundwork for heavy metal, internal differences spurred Stewart and Wood to join the Faces. A new edition of the band released two well executed, if predictable, LPs, *Rough and Ready* (Epic 30973; 1971; #46) and *The Jeff Beck Group* (Epic 31331; 1972; #19), before Beck joined forces with drummer Carmine Appice and bassist Tim Bogert (both formerly with Vanilla Fudge and Cactus) to form a short-lived power trio.

Beck returned to the public eye with a highly-acclaimed fusion album, *Blow By Blow* (Epic 33409; 1975; #4). He continued in much the same vein with *Wired* (Epic 33849; 1976; #16) and *Jeff Beck with the Jan Hammer Group – Live* (Epic 34433; 1977; #23), both collaborations with Hammer, the former Mahavishnu Orchestra keyboardist.

For that point onward, Beck followed an erratic career path, retiring for lengthy periods of time before resurfacing with high profile guest contributions (e.g., Mick Jagger's *Primitive Cool*, Roger Waters' *Amused to Death*) and uniformly well-received solo recordings. His LPs have included the jazz-inflected *There and Back* (Epic 35684; 1980; #21); his most polished, pop-oriented offering, *Flash* (Epic 39483; 1985; #39); "Escape" awarded the Grammy for Best Rock Instrumental), featuring Nile Rodgers' production work and bevy of vocalists; *Jeff Beck's Guitar Shop* (Epic 44313; 1989; #49), awarded the Grammy for Best Rock Instrumental Performance; *Crazy Legs* (Epic 473597; 1993), a retro tribute to Gene Vincent and his Blue Caps guitarist, Cliff Gallup; *Who Else!* (Epic 67987; 1999; #99), nominated for the Grammy for Best Rock Instrumental Performance; *You Had It Coming* (Sony; 2001); *Jeff* (2003); and *Emotion & Commotion* (2010).

Table 76

Creedence Clearwater Revival

Creedence Clearwater Revival were in the vanguard of the back-to-the-roots trend of the late 1960s, which spurred a shift in pop music's center of gravity from the progressive-psychedelic experimentation of the 1966-1968 period to a predominance of rockabilly, country and blues-based styles by 1969. Despite a career of relatively short duration, the band's recordings possess a timeless quality—with an emphasis on economical, well-crafted songs, a rock-steady rhythm section, and John Fogerty's incisive guitar riffing and soulful singing—that has helped them remain popular up to the present day.

All four band members—Fogerty, his brother, rhythm guitarist Tom Fogerty, bassist Stu Cook, and drummer Doug Clifford—were born between 1941-1945 in the San Francisco Bay area. John formed a trio with Cook and Clifford while all were in junior high school; after playing at local parties and school functions for a time, John enlisted Tom to fill out the lineup. Although both of the Fogerty brothers were multi-talented instrumentalists, capable of playing harmonica, saxophone, and a variety of string, keyboard, and percussion instruments—they developed a country-blues-rock 'n' roll amalgam based on performing during the 1959-1967 period and many hours of listening to the recordings of Chess blues masters and the 1950s Sun artists.

Several singles with the Scorpio (1965-1966) and Fantasy (1967) labels as the Golliwogs went nowhere; they are included in the retrospective anthology, *Pre-Creedence* (Fantasy 9474; 1975). When Fantasy employee Saul Zaentz purchased the company later in the year, however, he encouraged the band to try again, this time as Creedence Clearwater Revival. The funky, roots-oriented debut album, *Creedence Clearwater Revival* (Fantasy 8362; 1968; #52), released in mid-1968, seemed to run counter to the Baroque excesses of many leading rock artists of the day. The next four albums—*Bayou Country* (Fantasy 8387; 1969; #7), featuring the breakthrough pop hit, "Proud Mary" (Fantasy 619; 1969; #2), *Green River* (Fantasy 8393; 1969; #1), *Willie and the Poorboys* (Fantasy 8397; 1969; #3), and *Cosmo's Factory* (Fantasy 8402; 1970; #1)—were released in rapid succession, displaying little deviation from the band's trademark sound.

Ever mindful of critic's carping that they were a singles act (with nine Top Ten hits in less than two-and-a-half years), that their sound was simplistic and one-dimensional, the band's next LP, *Pendulum* (Fantasy 8410; 1970; #5), featured expanded instrumentation (e.g., John Fogerty's organ in "Pagan Baby") and song structures (most notably, the chromatic interlude in "Rude Awakening #2"). Flat sales did nothing to dampen disaffection within the group over John's dominant role in the songwriting, production, and performing areas. Interested in developing his own artistic identity,

Tom Fogerty departed for a solo career. The remaining members pursued a tentative three-way split of creative control on the next album. *Mardi Gras* (Fantasy 9404; 1972; #12) was an aesthetic and commercial disappointment, in part responsible for the band's breakup. Of even greater significance, Fogerty spent two decades feuding with Zaentz over financial arrangement with the label.

While John Fogerty pursued a moderately successful solo career, Fantasy—who had expanded into the jazz field in a big way thanks large to profits generated by Creedence albums—issued a steady stream of live and recycled material, including *Creedence Gold* (Fantasy 9418; 1972; #15), *More Creedence Gold* (Fantasy 9430; 1973; #61), *Live in Europe* (Fantasy 88; 1973; #143), and *Chronicle* (Fantasy 2; 1976; #100), and *The Royal Albert Hall Concert* (Fantasy 4501; 1980; #62), retitled *The Concert* when discovered that it took place at the Oakland Coliseum.

Table 77

Emerson, Lake and Palmer

Although later criticized for the pompous tone of their live and recorded work, Emerson, Lake and Palmer were perhaps unrivaled in melding classical music conventions with the intensity and rhythmic drive of rock. Seemingly unafraid to take risks, the trio's artistic successes ultimately overshadowed lapses in execution and good taste.

Formed in 1970, ELP personified the idea of a supergroup; Keith Emerson had built a considerable reputation in his native England as a keyboard virtuoso, showman, and arranger with the Nice, guitarist/vocalist Greg Lake had helped found King Crimson, and drummer Carl Palmer had been a key member of both the Crazy World of Arthur Brown and Atomic Rooster. Signing with Island Records, the band was an immediate success; their debut album, *Emerson, Lake and Palmer* (Cotillion 9040; 1970; #18), featured the pyrotechnics of Emerson and Palmer, accented by Lake's subdued acoustic guitar work and warm vocals. The next two albums—*Tarkus* (Cotillion 9900; 1971; #9) and *Pictures at an Exhibition* (Cotillion 66666; 1972; #10)—experimented with extended compositions, the latter representing a rock transcription of the famous Moussorgsky tone poem. Listener interest was maintained through continual variations in pace, color, and texture (both LPs showcased Emerson's versatility on a wide array of instruments, including piano, organ, and synthesizers).

Trilogy (Cotillion 9903; 1972; #5) and *Brain Salad Surgery* (Manticore 66669; 1973; #11) returned to a somewhat more traditional song layout, albeit with musical surprises (e.g., a rock treatment of Aaron Copland's "Hoedown") interspersed throughout. While the band took several years off to pursue individual projects, a monumental three-disc live set culled from various 1973-1974 concerts, *Welcome Back, My Friends, to the*

Show That Never Ends – Ladies and Gentlemen (Manticore 200; #4), was released in August 1974. The threesome regrouped in name to record two essentially solo albums, *Works, Volume 1* (Atlantic 7000; 1977; #12) and *Works, Volume 2* (Atlantic 19147; #37; 1977), both stylistically diversified packages ranging from Emerson's "Original Piano Concerto No. 1" to blues-inflected pieces composed by Lake and former King Crimson mate Peter Sinfield. Following an aimless studio endeavor, *Love Beach* (Atlantic 19211; 1978; #55), the live *In Concert* (Atlantic 19255; 1979; #73), and a career retrospective, *Best of Emerson, Lake and Palmer* (Atlantic 19283; 1980; #108), the band disbanded.

The relative failure of individual projects during the early 1980s led to a new collaboration between Emerson and Lake in mid-1984. Adding drummer Cozy Powell, a veteran of the Jeff Beck Group, Rainbow, and Whitesnake, they recorded *Emerson, Lake and Powell* (Polydor 829297; 1986; #23), a likeable, but undistinguished, LP. Disappointing sales led to a personnel reorganization, with Emerson, Palmer, and American bassist/songwriter Robert Berry coming together to produce *To the Power of Three* (Geffen; 1988). Its failure to chart spurred Lake's return to the fold; the resulting album, *Black Moon* (Victory 80003; 1992; #78), did better, but seemed to indicate that the band's best days were far behind them. Nevertheless, the trio soldiered on, releasing *Live at the Royal Albert Hall* (London 828933; 1993), the four-CD box set—containing old and new material—*Return of the Manticore* (London 828459; 1993), *Works Live* (London 828477; 1993), and *In the Hot Seat* (London 828554; 1994).

Table 78

Procol Harum

The roots of Procol Harum, one of leading exponents of the art rock school, lie in the Paramounts, a London band that recorded five singles between October 1963 and September 1965 and included singer/pianist Gary Brooker, guitarist Robin Trower, bassist/organist Chris Copping, and drummer B.J. Wilson. In search of a new direction, Booker was introduced to lyricist Keith Reid sometime in 1966. The two began writing songs together; several demos led to a recording contract with Deram in early 1967. Procol's first single, "A Whiter Shade of Pale" (Deram 7507; 1967)—based on the melody from Johann Sebastian Bach's *Suite No. 3 in D major*—became an international smash, selling more than four million copies overall.

In the face of heightened demand for concert engagements, the group broke up. Procol's revamped lineup—featuring Brooker, Trower, Wilson, organist Matthew Fisher, and bassist David Knights—produced three critically acclaimed albums: *Procol Harum* (Deram 18008; 1967), *Shine On Brightly* (A&M 4151; 1968), *A Salty Dog* (A&M 4179; 1969).

Artistic differences within the band, combined with disappointing sales, led to the departure of Fisher and Knights. With the addition of Copping, Procol's next two albums—*Home* (A&M 4261; 1970) *Broken Barricades* (A&M 4294; 1971)—reflected a transition from a thickly-textured keyboard sound to more guitar-based approach built around Trower's Jimi Hendrix-inspired virtuosity.

Trower's decision to embark upon a solo career led to another change in personnel: David Ball was brought in as lead guitarist and Alan Cartwright on bass, thereby enabling Copping to concentrate on organ. An offer to perform in a classical music framework led to the release of group's bestselling l.p., *Procol Harum Live in Concert with the Edmonton Symphony Orchestra* (A&M 4335; 1972). The band failed, however, to capitalize on this revival in popularity, and the next four albums showed steadily declining sales.

Procol broke up in 1977, but Brooker, Fisher, Reid, and Trower reunited to record *The Prodigal Stranger* (Zoo 72445-11011-2; 1991). Brooker, sometimes with Fisher, and hired hands would tour intermittently into the second decade of the 21st century. [Stambler. 1989]

Table 79

Spirit

Spirit recorded some of the most progressive rock music of the late 1960s. Their albums featured intelligent lyrics, innovative arrangements featuring subtly shifting sound textures, and command of an encyclopedic range of styles, including hard rock, psychedelia, folk-pop, rhythm and blues, and cool jazz. This eclecticism, combined with their reputation for straight ahead, power rock in concert, undercut efforts to achieve broad-based commercial acceptance.

Spirit was formed in 1967; original members included Ed Cassidy (born in Chicago May 4, 1924)—a veteran jazz drummer who had worked with Woody Herman, Thelonius Monk, Gerry Mulligan, Art Pepper, and Cannonball Adderley—joined stepson Randy California (then only fourteen), Jay Ferguson, and Mark Andes in 1965 as part of the short-lived Red Roosters. Cassidy and California then moved from Los Angeles to New York City for much of 1966, working recording session and with various bands. Later that year they returned to California to form Spirits Rebellious (inspired by a Kahlil Gibran book) with former acquaintance John Locke. Ferguson and Andes, who had formed Western Union in 1966, then joined, and the band decided on a slight name change.

Signed to Lou Adler's Ode label, Spirit released three critically acclaimed albums: *Spirit* (Ode 44004; 1968), *They Family That Plays Together* (Ode 44014; 1969), and *Clear Spirit* (Ode 44016; 1969). In an effort to boost sales, they opted for a greater hard rock emphasis in *The Twelve Dreams of Dr. Sardonicus* (Epic 30267; 1970). When it failed to outperform its predecessors, Andes and Ferguson left to form Jo Jo Gunne. Cassidy and Locke hooked up with Texans Chris and Al Staehely to produce the country rock-flavored *Feedback* (Epic 31175; 1971); they then departed, with the Staehelys continuing to tour under the "Spirit" moniker.

In 1974 California—who'd done session work in England and produced a solo album—re-formed the band with Cassidy. They produced a series of moderate selling LPs for Mercury during the latter 1970s—*Spirit of '76* (Mercury 804; 1975), *Son of Spirit* (Mercury 1053; 1975), *Farther Along* (Mercury 1094; 1976), and *Future Games* (Mercury 1133; 1977)—dominated by California's Jimi Hendrix-inspired ramblings. Andes and Locke briefly returned to the group in the mid-1970s; Andes would then move on to Firefall (Heart in the 1980s) while Ferguson continued his career as a solo artist and producer.

The band would continue in various configurations (recording albums for Potato, Rhino, Mercury, I.R.S., and Dolphin) into the early 1990s, always with Cassidy and California at the helm. Any hopes of further reunions were effectively dashed when California drowned off Molokai on January 2, 1997 while saving his son's life. The band's music remains widely available, however, with reissues of the most Ode/Epic and Mercury LPs now on CD as well as a compilation featuring the work of the classic lineup, *Time Circle (1968-1972)* (Sony 47363; 1991).

Table 80

Traffic

Beginning as an eclectic pop band with strong psychedelic leanings, Traffic increasingly moved toward jazz-influenced arrangements featuring extended instrumental jamming. Winwood, whose intensely soulful vocals had recently turned the Spencer Davis Group into a hit-making entity, invited woodwinds specialist Chris Wood, drummer Jim Capaldi, and guitarist Dave Mason to a countryside cottage to write material and rehearse. The resulting album, *Mr. Fantasy* (United Artists 6651; 1968), contained two Top Ten British singles, and became an FM-radio staple stateside. The artistic conflicts between Mason's pop songcraft and Winwood's jazz leanings was reflected in the stylistically divergent selections comprising *Traffic* (United Artists 6676; 1968).

Following a patchwork farewell LP in 1969 entitled *Last Exit* (United Artists 6702), Winwood joined forces Cream alumni Eric Clapton and Ginger Baker and Rick Grech (formerly of Family) to form the supergroup Blind Faith. After one album and tour followed by the brief stint with Ginger Baker's Air Force, Winwood reunited with Wood and Capaldi to record, *John Barleycorn Must Die* (United Artists 5504; 1970), Traffic's most commercially successful release, reaching number five on the pop album charts. The group's lineup was expanded to include Grech, Mason, and percussionists Reebop Kwaku Baah and Jim Gordon for the live recording, *Welcome to the Canteen* (United Artists 5550; 1971). Gordon and Grech departed after the release of the gold album, *The Low Spark of High-Heeled Boys* (Island 9306; 1971). Its laid-back, improvisational mode was continued in *Shoot Out at the Fantasy Factory* (Island 9323; 1973), which included Muscle Shoals session players bassist David Hood and drummer Roger Hawkins. Yet another Muscle Shoals musician, keyboardist Barry Beckett, was added on the live *Traffic on the Road* (Island 9323; 1973).

After *When the Eagle Flies* (Asylum 1020; 1974), which featured the Traffic's original trio plus bassist Rosco Gee, Winwood and Capaldi concentrated on solo careers. By the 1990s, Wood, Grech, and Kwaku Baah would be dead, but Winwood and Capaldi recorded one more album together under the group name, *Far From Home* (1994).

Country Rock

Country rock represented a merging of country instrumentation with rock's beat and socially conscious attitude. Its immediate precursors included rockabilly and the Nashville crossover pop of the 1960s exemplified by singers like Skeeter Davis ("End of the World"), Bobby Bare ("Detroit City"), Johnny Cash ("I Walk the Line"), Marty Robbins ("El Paso"), and Jim Reeves ("He'll Have to Go"). Country-rock was part of the backs-to-the-roots movement instigated by maturing baby boomers whose tastes were changing in favor of softer forms of pop music.

The genre's seminal artists--e.g., the Byrds, the Flying Burrito Brothers, and the Eagles--were not welcome on mainstream country radio or in the prime concert venues catering to country fans. However, many of the leading country performers coming of age in the 1980s, including Garth Brooks, Clint Black, and Brooks and Dunn, grew up listening to country rock.

Top Artists and Their Recordings

The Byrds--*Sweetheart of the Rodeo* (1968)

Charlie Daniels (Band)--*Te John, Grease and Wolfman* (1970); *Charlie Daniels* (1971); *Honey in the Rock* (1972); *Way Down Yonder* (1973); *Fire on the Mountain* (1975); *Nightrider* (1975); *Saddle Tramp* (1976); *Uneasy Rider* (1976); *High and Lonesome* (1977); *Midnight Wind* (1977); *Million Mile Reflections* (1979); *Full Moon* (1980)

The Eagles--*The Eagles* (1972); *Desperado* (1973); *On the Border* (1974); *One of These Nights* (1975); *Hotel California* (1976); *The Long Run* (1979); *Eagles Live* (1980)

Steve Earle--*Guitar Town* (1986); *Exit O* (1987); *Copperhead Road* (1988); *The Hard Way* (1989)

Joe Ely--*Joe Ely* (1977); *Honky Tonk Masquerade* (1978); *Down in the Drag* (1979); *Musta Notta Gotta Lotta* (1981); *Live Shots* (1981)

The Flying Burrito Brothers--*The Gilded Palace of Sin* (1969); *Burrito Deluxe* (1970); *The Flying Burrito Brothers* (1971); *Last of the Red Hot Burritos* (1972); *Close Up the Honky Tonks* (1974); *Flying Again* (1975); *Sleepless Nights* (1976)

Kinky Friedman (and the Texas Jewboys)--*Sold American* (1974); *Kinky Friedman* (1975); *Lasso From El Paso* (1976)

International Submarine Band--*Safe at Home* (1967)

Jason and the Scorchers--*Fervor* (1984); *Lost and Found* (1985); *Still Standing* (1986)

Kris Kristofferson--*Kristofferson* (1970); *Cisco Pete* (1970); *Silver Tongued Devil and I* (1971); *Border Lord* (1972); *Jesus Was a Capricorn* (1973); *Spooky Lady's Sideshow* (1974); *Who's to Bless and Who's to Blame* (1975); *Surreal Thing* (1976); *Songs of Kristofferson* (1977); *Easter Island* (1978); *Help Me Make It Through the Night* (1980)

Mason Proffit--*Wanted* (1969); *Moving Towards Happiness* (1970); *Rockfish Crossing* (1971); *Bareback Rider* (1972)

Michael Martin Murphey--*Geronimo's Cadillac* (1972); *Cosmic Cowboy Souvenir* (1973); *Michael Murphey* (1974); *Blue Sky Night Thunder* (1975); *Swans Against the Sun* (1975); *Flowing Free Forever* (1976); *Lone Wolf* (1978); *Peaks, Valleys, Honky-Tonks and Alleys* (1979); *Martin Martin Murphey* (1982); *The Heart Never Lies* (1983)

Anne Murray--*Snowbird* (1970); *Anne Murray* (1971); *Talk It Over in the Morning* (1971); *Anne Murray/Glen Campbell* (1971); *Annie* (1972); *Danny's Song* (1973); *Love Song* (1974); *Country* (1974); *Highly Prized Possession* (1974); *Together* (1975); *Keeping in Touch* (1976); *Let's Keep It That Way* (1978); *New Kind of Feeling* (1979); *I'll Always Love You* (1979); *A Country Collection* (1980); *Somebody's Waiting* (1980)

Mike Nesmith--*Wichita Train Whistle Sings* (1968); *Magnetic South* (1970); *Loose Salute* (1971); *Nevada Fighter* (1971); *Tantamount to Treason* (1972); *Pretty Much Your Standard Stash* (1973); *The Prison* (1975); *From the Radio Engine to Photon Wing* (1977); *Live at the Palais* (1978); *Infinite Rider on the Big Dogma* (1979)

New Riders of the Purple Sage--*New Riders of the Purple Sage* (1971); *Powerglide* (1972); *Gypsy Cowboy* (1973); *Adventures of Panama Red* (1973); *Home Home on the Road* (1974); *Brujo* (1975); *Oh What a Mighty Time* (1975); *New Riders* (1976); *Who Are These Guys* (1977); *Marin County Line* (1978)

Nitty Gritty Dirt Band--*Nitty Gritty Dirt Band* (1967); *Ricochet* (1967); *Rare Junk* (1967); *Live* (1969); *Dead and Alive* (1969); *Uncle Charlie and His Dog Teddy* (1970); *All the Good Times* (1972); *Will the Circle Be Unbroken* (1973); *Stars and Stripes Forever* (1974); *Dream* (1975); *Dirt Band* (1978); *American Dream* (1979)

Gram Parsons--GP (1973); *Grievous Angel* (1974); *Early Years* (1979)

Poco--*Pickin' Up the Pieces* (1969); *Poco* (1970); *Deliverin'* (1971); *From the Inside* (1971); *A Good Feelin' to Know* (1972); *Crazy Eyes* (1973); *Seven* (1974); *Cantamos* (1974); *Head Over Heels* (1975); *Live* (1976); *Rose of Cimarron* (1976); *Indian Summer* (1977); *Legend* (1978); *Under the Gun* (1980); *Blue and Gray* (1981); *Cowboys and Englishmen* (1982); *Ghost Town* (1982); *Inamorata* (1984); *Legacy* (1989)

Pousette-Dart Band--*Pousette-Dart Band* (1976); *Amnesia* (1977); *Pousette-Dart Band 3* (1978)

Pure Prairie League--*Bustin' Out* (1975); *Two Lane Highway* (1975); *If the Shoe Fits* (1976); *Dance* (1976); *Live!! Takin' the Stage* (1977); *Just Fly* (1978); *Can't Hold Back* (1979); *Firin' Up* (1980); *Something in the Night* (1981)

Web Wilder and the Beatnecks--*Hybrid Vigor* (1989); *Doo Dad* (1991)

Table 81

Eagles

The most successful band to emerge from the country rock genre, the Eagles gradually shifted to mainstream rock as a result of personnel moves and changes in public taste. Of greater significance, they created a body of work during the 1970s unequaled in terms of quality by any American music act.

The Eagles originated with the shared vision of guitarist Glenn Frey and drummer Don Henley when both were part of Linda Ronstadt's backup band. Two other musicians hired by Ronstadt—ex-Poco bassist Randy Meisner and lead guitarist Bernie Leadon, formerly with the Dillards and the Flying Burrito Brothers—agreed to join the enterprise and, with David Geffen serving as manager, the Eagles obtained a recording contract from Asylum.

Recorded in England with the assistance of veteran producer Glyn Johns, the debut LP, *The Eagles* (Asylum 5054; 1972; #22), exhibited a strong country rock bent built around lush vocal harmonies and Leadon's facility on a variety of string instruments. Whereas *The Eagles* succeeded largely due to three strong singles—"Take It Easy" (Asylum 11005; 1972; #12), "Witchy Woman" (Asylum 11008; 1972; #9), and "Peaceful Easy Feeling" (Asylum 11013; 1972; #22)—the follow-up LP, *Desperado* (Asylum 5068; 1973; #41), a concept album concerned with the Old West's Doolin-Dalton gang that lacked Top Forty material, was only moderately successful.

The decision to hire producer Bill Szymczyk during the recording of *On the Border* (Asylum 1004; 1974; #17; included #1 hit, "Best Of My Love," Asylum 45218)—along with the addition of guitarist Don Felder—added greater polish as well as dynamic range and texture to the outstanding melodies and intelligent lyrics typifying the band's material. *One Of These Nights* (Asylum 1039; 1975; #1)—which included the hit singles "One Of These Nights" (Asylum 45257; 1975; #1), "Lyin' Eyes" (Asylum 45279; 1975; #2), and "Take It to the Limit" (Asylum 45293; 1975; #4)—propelled the Eagles into the upper pantheon of rock stardom. The recruitment of former James Gang guitarist Joe Walsh to replace the departing Leadon resulted in a tougher rock sound on *Hotel California* (Asylum 1084; 1976; #1); the lyricism of "New Kid in Town" (Asylum 45373; 1977; #1) evoked the early Eagles sans roots references, while the extended guitar jam on the title track (Asylum 45386; 1977; #1) literally defines 1970s American rock.

Although merely consolidating earlier experiments, the final releases from the band's first phase, *The Long Run* (Asylum 52181; 1979; #1)—which included three Top Ten hits: "Heartache Tonight" (Asylum 46545; 1979; #1). "The Long Run" (Asylum 46569; 1979; #8), and "I Can't Tell You Why" (Asylum 46608; 1980; #8)—and *Eagles Live* (Asylum 705; 1980; #6), also achieved platinum success. Core members Henley and Frey opted to dissolve the Eagles at this point in order to pursue solo careers. Despite comments over the years that a reunion would never take place, Henry, Frey, Walsh, Felder, and Timothy B. Schmitt (who'd replaced Meisner in 1977) got together for a 1994 tour. The album, *Hell Freezes Over* (Geffen 24725; 1994; #1) featuring songs from an MTV performance plus four new studio tracks.

The band has continued to tour intermittently, and released a double album of original material, *Long Road Out of Eden*, on October 30, 2007.

Latin Rock

Latin rock, a stylistic hybrid built on a psychedelic foundation, but punctuated by jazz fusion and Latin elements, originated in the late 1960s along the Pacific Coast of California. Its most notable pioneer, Carlos Santana, was largely responsible for the Jimi Hendrix-inspired guitar pyrotechnics at the core of the sound. The rhythms--which were tight, metallic, and Caribbean in origin--required two or three musicians to work a standard drum kit and augmented percussion section, including timbales, congas, etc.

The genre reflected the spread of psychedelic culture to working-class and minority youth. When the energy of that movement dissipated, Santana played a major role in nudging Latin rock in the direction of jazz fusion. At points when his music appeared to have gotten too ethereal, however, Santana always could be counted on to re-explore the genre's street-based dance rhythms.

Top Artists and Their Recordings

Malo--*Malo* (1972); *Dos* (1972); *Evolution* (1973); *Ascension* (1974)

Mandrill--*Mandrill Is* (1972); *Composite Truth* (1973); *Just Outside of Town* (1975); *Solid* (1975); *Beast From the East* (1976); *Mandrilland* (1976); *Mandrill* (1977); *We Are One* (1978); *New World* (1978); *Getting in the Mood* (1980)

Santana(, Carlos)--*Santana* (1969); *Abraxas* (1970); *Carlos Santana With Buddy Miles* (1971); *Santana III* (1971); *Caravanserai* (1972); *Love Devotion Surrender* (1973); *Welcome* (1974); *Illuminations* (1974); *Borboletta* (74); *Lotus* (1975); *Amigos* (1976); *Festival* (1977); *Moonflower* (1977); *Oneness* (1979); Inner Secrets (1979); *Marathon* (1979); *Swing of Delight* (1980); *Zebop* (1981)

Jorge Santana--*Jorge Santana* (1976)

Big Band Rock

Big-band rock arose from the confluence of several musical styles in the late 1960s: progressive rock experimentation; jazz fusion, with a particular emphasis on swing era instrumentation; and the horn choirs long employed by urban blues and soul artists. The genre included the following characteristics: a rich palette of instrumental colors, with a core rock band augmented by a combination of brass (e.g., trombones, trumpets, flugelhorns) and wind (e.g., saxes, flutes) instruments; greater visceral power than was possible in most forms of rock music; and increased ensemble flexibility, which encouraged the incorporation of a more eclectic range musical styles.

Blood, Sweat and Tears' *Child Is the Father to the Moon*, released in early 1968, proved to be the pivotal big-band rock recording. The group--founded by Al Kooper, a former member of the Royal Teens ("Short Shorts"; 1957) and the Blues Project and veteran session musician who'd played on Bob Dylan's pioneering folk-rock albums--blended superb musicianship with highly innovative arrangements. The group's follow-up album, *Blood, Sweat and Tears*, effectively mixed blues, gospel, classical music, Tin Pan Alley pop, and straight-ahead rock material. One of the biggest sellers of the decade, it also included three top ten hits: "And When I Die," "Spinning Wheel," and "You Made Me So Very Happy." The group lost its momentum, though, when first Kooper, and then gravel-voiced lead singer David Clayton-Thomas, departed.

By 1970, Chicago had taken over as the most artistically and commercially successful big-band rock aggregate. In attempting to maintain its popularity in the face of changing fashions, however, Chicago evolved from a cutting-edge progressive unit to a purveyor of assembly-line soft rock.

The genre was gradually absorbed back into mainstream pop rock when it stagnated due to a lack of new talent. Experimentation with the rock band/brass lineup was limited largely to the jazz-rock sector for the next couple of decades. By the mid-1990s, however, the swing revival—spearheaded by groups like the Brian Setzer Orchestra and the Royal Crown Revue—brought brass back to the forefront of pop music.

Top Artists and Their Recordings

Audience--*Audience* (1969); *House on the Hill* (1971); *Lunch* (1972)

The Bar-Kays--"Soul Finger" (1967); *Black Rock* (1971); *Too Hot to Stop* (1976); *Flying High On Your Love* (1977); *Money Talks* (1978); *Light of Life* (1978); *Injoy* (1979); *As One* (1980); *Nightcruising* (1981); *Propositions* (1982); *Dangerous* (1984); *Banging the Wall* (1985); *Contagious* (1987)

Blood, Sweat and Tears--*Child Is the Father to the Man* (1968); *Blood, Sweat and Tears* (1969); *Blood, Sweat and Tears 3* (1970); *B, S & T: 4* (1971); *New Blood* (1972); *No Sweat* (1973); *Mirror Image* (1974); *New City* (1975); *More Than Ever* (1976)

Chase--*Chase* (1971); *Ennea* (1972); *Pure Music* (1974)

Chicago--*Chicago Transit Authority* (1969); *Chicago II* (1970); *Chicago III* (1971); *Chicago at Carnegie Hall* (1971); *Chicago V* (1972); *Chicago VI* (1973); *Chicago VII* (1974); *Chicago VIII* (1975); *Chicago X* (1976); *Chicago XI* (1977); *Hot Streets* (1978); *Chicago 13* (1979); *Chicago XIV* (1980); *Chicago 16* (1982); *Chicago 17* (1984); *Chicago 18* (1986); *19* (1988); *Twenty 1* (1991)

Don Ellis--*Electric Bath* (1967)

Lighthouse--*Peacing It All Together* (1970); *One Fine Morning* (1971); *Thoughts of Movin' On* (1972); *Lighthouse Live!* (1972); *Sunny Days* (1973)

Tower of Power--*East Bay Grease* (1971); *Bump City* (1972); *Tower of Power* (1973); *Back to Oakland* (1974); *Urban Renewal* (1975); *In the Slot* (1976); *Live and In Living Color* (1976); *Ain't*

Nothin' Stoppin' Us Now (1976); *We Came to Play!* (1978); *Back On the Streets* (1979); *Power* (1987); *Great American Soulbook* (2009)

Table 82

Blood, Sweat & Tears

Blood, Sweat & Tears were the first important big band-rock act; they attempted to fuse the stylistic and harmonic diversity possible with a swing era ensemble with the power possible with a rock rhythm section. However, the absence of a first-rate songwriter and the constantly shifting personnel lineup within the group caused a loss of the creative momentum that fueled the first few albums. By the early 1970s, the genre's innovative vanguard included Chicago, England's Audience, and Canada's Lighthouse.

The guiding light behind the formation of Blood, Sweat & Tears was Al Kooper; as a keyboardist with the Blues Project, he expressed the desire to test the stylistic limits of the blues—incorporating classical, folk and jazz influences—by means of an expanded horn section. He recruited the Blues Project's rhythm guitarist, Steve Katz, who, in turn, contacted an associate, drummer Bobby Colomby, then with folk singer Odetta. During 1967 the threesome went about pulling additional musicians into their orbit, including bassist Jim Fielder, and horn players from various New York jazz and studio aggregates: Fred Lipsius, Dick Halligan, Randy Brecker, and Jerry Weiss.

The debut album, *Child Is Father to the Man* (Columbia 9619; 1968; #47), exhibited considerable musical promise, incorporating material by Nilsson, Tim Buckley, Randy Newman, Gerry Goffin and Carole King, and Kooper himself.. Recorded after a personnel shakeup—Kooper, Brecker, and Weiss departed, and were replaced by vocalist David Clayton-Thomas, trombonist Jerry Hyman, trumpeter Chuck Winfield, and trumpeter Lew Soloff—the follow-up release, *Blood, Sweat & Tears* (Columbia 9720; 1968), reached number one, selling more than three million copies and generating three gold singles: "You've Made Me So Very Happy" (Columbia 44776; 1969; #2), "And When I Die" (Columbia 45008; 1969; #2), and "Spinning Wheel" (Columbia 44871; 1969; #2). Winning the 1969 Grammy for Album of the Year, it set an artistic and commercial standard that the band was unable to equal again.

Although the next LP, the jazz-tinged *Blood, Sweat & Tears 3* (Columbia 30090; 1970; #1), quickly achieved gold status, later releases—*B, S & T; 4* (Columbia 30590; 1971; #10), *Greatest Hits* (Columbia 31170; 1972; #19), *New Blood* (Columbia 31780; 1972; #32), *No Sweat* (Columbia 32180; 1973; #72), *Mirror Image* (Columbia 32929; 1974; #149; *New City* (Columbia 33484; 1975; #47), and *More Than Ever* (Columbia 34233; 1976; #165)—met with increasing public apathy. By the mid-1970s, BST had become a middle-of-the-road nostalgia band, performing regularly at Las Vegas and other glitzy venues. Colomby (the last original member, who left in 1976 to do A&R, but retained co-ownership of the band's name and catalog) and Clayton-Thomas would maintain control of BST, which continued to perform through the 1990s. Recording—with ABC-Paramount, LAX, and other labels—has been sporadic since the early 1980s due to the fact that none of the band's releases have charted since August 1976.

Glitter Rock

The genre, sometimes termed "glam," had its origins in the early 1970s backlash against the 1960s sexual revolution. Its chief identifying features included the glorification of sexual ambiguity and androgyny and the heightened fashion consciousness. The performers affected a decadent look typically accented by foppish and/or futuristic clothing and tons of makeup and glitter dust.

Musically, glitter came across a a slicker form of hard rock. The leading exponents ranged stylistically from punk to hard rock and greatly influenced the more theatrically inclined mainstream acts of the 1970s and 1980s, including Alice Cooper, Queen, and Joan Jett.

Glitter rock lost considerable momentum when its shock value was ultimately pre-empted by genres willing to push threatrical conventions and fashion statements further to the edge. By the latter half of the 1970s most fans had defected to either the disco or heavy metal camps. Many of the leading glitter acts went on to even greater success as mainstream artists, albeit with either progressive or hard rock leanings.

Top Artists and Their Recordings

David Bowie--*Space Oddity* (1968); *The Man Who Sold the World* (1970); *Hunky Dory* (1971); *The Rise and Fall of Ziggy Stardust and the Spiders From Mars* (1972); *Images 1966-1967* (1973); *Aladdin Sane* (1973); *Pin Ups* (1973); *Diamond Dogs* (1974); *David Live* (1974)

Gary Glitter--"Rock and Roll, Part 2" (1972); "I Didn't Know I Loved You (Till I Saw You Rock and Roll)" (1972); *Glitter* (1972)

Jobriath--*Jobriath* (1973); *Creatures of the Street* (1974)

Kiss--*Kiss* (1973); *Hotter Than Hell* (1974); *Dressed to Kill* (1975); *Alive!* (1975); *Destroyer* (1976); *Rock and Roll Over* (1976); *Love Gun* (1977); *Alive II* (1977); *Dynasty* (1979); *Kiss Unmasked* (1980); *Music From the Elder* (1981); *Creatures of the Night* (1982); Lick It Up (1983); *Animalize* (1984); *Asylum* (1985); *Crazy Nights* (1987); *Hot in the Shade* (1989); *Revenge* (1992)

New York Dolls--*New York Dolls* (1973); *Too Much Too Soon* (1974)

Roxy Music--*Roxy Music* (1972); *For Your Pleasure* (1973); *Stranded* (1974); *Country Life* (1975); *Siren* (1975); *Viva! Roxy Music* (1976); *Manifesto* (1979); *Flesh + Blood* (1980); *Avalon* (1982); *Musique/The High Road* (1983)

Slade--*Slade Alive!* (1972); *Slayed?* (1973); *Sladest* (1973); *Stomp Your Hands, Clap Your Feet* (1974); *Slade in Flame* (1975)

The Sweet--*The Sweet* (1973); *Desolation Boulevard* (1975); *Give Us a Wink* (1976); *Off the Record* (1977); *Level Headed* (1978); *Cut Above the Rest* (1979)

Tyrannosaurus Rex/T. Rex--*T. Rex* (1971); *Electric Warrior* (1971); *The Slider* (1972); *Tyrannosaurus Rex (A Beginning)* (1972); *Tanx* (1973)

Heavy Metal

Gonzo rock critic Lester Bangs, in *The Rolling Stone Illustrated History of Rock & Roll* (2nd edition), has provided one of the more colorful--and accurate--definitions of the genre:

> As its detractors have always claimed, heavy-metal rock is nothing more than a bunch of noise; it is not music, it's distortion--and that is precisely why its adherents find it appealing....it's noise is created by electric guitars, filtered through an array of warping devices from fuzztone to wah-wah, cranked several decibels past the pain threshold, loud enough to rebound off the walls of the biggest arenas anywhere. Add the aural image of a battering ram, and you've got a pretty good picture of what heavy metal sounds like.

He adds that the style also includes "brutal guitars, equally thunderous slabs of thick-thudding bass, and the obligatory extended drum solo in concert."

The British hard rock bands of the mid-1960s anticipated the genre, both its sound and attitude. Notable pioneers included the Who (e.g., "My Generation," "I Can See For Miles") and the Yardbirds alums Eric Clapton, Jeff Beck, and Jimmy Page, all masters of fuzztone-and-feedback drenched onslaughts. Jimi Hendrix provided the link between these antecedents and the earliest practitioners of the style proper via his guitar pyrotechnics and banshee vocals.

While California bands--specifically, renegades from psychedelia (e.g., Blue Cheer) and acid rock (e.g., Iron Butterfly)--were playing heavy metal, or something close to it, by early 1968, and yet another stateside group provided the name itself (Steppenwolf's line from "Born to Be Wild": "heavy metal thunder") that same year, the British scene proved more prolific at the outset of the 1970s. Three divergent movements quickly emerged there, including (1) post-psychedelic hard rock, exemplified by the cinematic guitar stylings and evocative lyric imagery of Led Zeppelin,

Black Sabbath, and Robin Trower; (2) working class rock, built on predictable heavy riffs and the cultivation of a "bad boy" image (e.g., Deep Purple, Bad Company); and (3) aristocratic Anglo-metal, featuring the glam dress of acts like Queen and Sweet.

During this time, American bands projected a distinctly working class image; e.g., Cactus, Mountain, the Frost, Aerosmith, Kiss, Grand Funk Railroad, and Bachman-Turner Overdrive (Canada). Two subdivisions grew out of this school: American revolutionary bands, who considered rock to represent an instrument of social change (e.g., MC5); and boogie bands, dedicated to simple riffing for the sake of partying (e.g., Black Oak Arkansas, ZZ Top). In reaction to these subgenres, yet another offshoot--the American Deviates--emerged. Generally inspired by the Velvet Underground, its practitioners (e.g., Iggy and the Stooges, Alice Cooper, Blue Oyster Cult) were dedicated to, in Bangs' words, "The reinforcement of whatever vestiges of primal infantalism have managed to survive into adolescence, and the glorification of adolescence as the Time of Your Life."

By the late 1970s the genre had fallen into middle-of-the-road respectability largely due to the effort of artists such as Toto, Triumph, Foreigner, Journey, Heart, Van Halen, and Ted Nugent. What little flair and freshness remained was appropriated by two newly emerging genres, speed metal and punk rock. The foremost practitioners of the former—e.g., Metallica, Megadeath, Godflesh—have remained viable throughout the 1990s, grudgingly appropriating the trappings of the more progressive hard rockers. Punk, however, proved to be the more important of the two, stripping heavy metal down, speeding it up, and providing some lyric content beyond the customary macho posturing.

The riot grrrl movement of the early 1990s also borrowed heavily from heavy metal. Notable distaff bands from the period included Bikini Kill and L7. Groups such as Luscious Jackson and Fluffy opted for a sound more closely aligned with the pop mainstream.

The late 1990s have seen a revival of the more traditional exponents of the genre. Reformed first generation bands such as Black Sabbath, Alice Cooper, and Grand Funk Railroad have again found success via both recordings and the stage; third generation copy bands such as Poison, Cinderella, Warrant, and Motley Crue have also enjoyed a commercial resurgence. In short, heavy metal has continued to thrive, a genre secure in the fact that its primary audience--teenaged males--will always derive immense sustenance from its manic energy and rebellious attitude.

Table 83

Black Sabbath

Black Sabbath will always be the quintessential heavy metal band; its members helped develop many of the genre's major conventions, including the blues-rock-derived signature riff, power chording, pronounced guitar feedback and sustain, ponderously slow tempos, wailing melismatic vocals, aggressive posturing, and escapist song lyrics. Frontman Ozzy Osbourne would become the charismatic spokesman for legions of working class youth who didn't feel comfortable with the more abstract, elitist concerns of progressive rock artists.

Black Sabbath's original members—Osbourne, guitarist Tony Iommi, bassist Terry "Geezer" Butler, and drummer Bill Ward—were all born in Aston, an industrial section of Birmingham, England. While acquainted with each other since childhood, they played in different groups until becoming aware of their musical compatibility. The foursome combined forces in the late 1960s as Earth; however, after being informed in 1969 that a more established mainstream rock act had already staked a claim to the name, they became Black Sabbath.

Steady touring, especially on the European mainland where the group first gained a large following, led to a recording contract with Vertigo. The debut album, *Black Sabbath*, was released in the U.S. by Warner Bros. (#1871; 1970; #23). It remained on the charts for sixty-five weeks, providing the needed momentum to propel the next LP, *Paranoid* (Warner Bros. 1887; 1971; #12) to triple platinum status. Although generally damned by critics for their heavy-handed approach, Black Sabbath's album continued to sell well throughout the 1970s, the following achieving platinum sales: *Master of Reality* (Warner Bros. 2562; 1971; #8), *Black Sabbath, Vol. 4* (Warner Bros. 2602; 1972; #13), *Sabbath Bloody Sabbath* (Warner Bros. 2695; 1974; #11), and *We Sold Our Soul for Rock 'n' Roll* (Warner Bros. 2923; 1976; #48).

Osbourne's decision to embark on a solo career, however, caused many of the group's fans to defect with him. The group—with Iommi and Butler continuing to co-write much of the material—limped through a transitional phase, first with American Ronnie James Dio (previously with Elf and Ritchie Blackmore's Rainbow) as lead singer between 1979-1982 (he would return from 1990-1993), followed by countless other configurations, most notably with former Deep Purple vocalist Ian Gillan (1983-1984) and a revamped lineup featuring sole original member Iommi and singer Glenn Hughes, whose resume included Trapeze, Deep Purple, and the Hughes-Thrall band (1985-1987).

After more than a year of band inactivity, Osbourne, Butler, and Iommi reunited to headline Ozzfest 1997. Ward was invited to participate in two December 1997 shows in Birmingham; the resulting live album, *Reunion* (Epic; 1998; #11) earned the group its first Grammy for Best Metal Performance ("Iron Man"). Black Sabbath continued touring through December 1999. As of mid-2001, the band was still together, working on a studio album.

Table 84

Deep Purple

Deep Purple best exemplifies the "give-the-people-what-they-want" syndrome. The core members of the band—guitarist Ritchie Blackmore and organist Jon Lord—were classically trained as well as possessing lengthy resumes as professional musicians; however, after several albums of progressive rock experimentation accompanied by spotty popularity, they opted for a stripped-down heavy metal sound, achieving a huge following in the process.

Despite the fact that all original members of the group—Blackmore, Lord, drummer Ian Paice, bassist Nick Simper, and vocalist Rod Evans—hailed from England, none of their recordings were released there through mid-1969. In the meantime, three U.S. albums—*Shades of Deep Purple* (Tetragrammaton 102; 1968; #24; including the Top Five single, "Hush," Tetragrammaton 1503), *The Book of Taliesyn* (Tetragrammaton 107; 1968; #54), and *Deep Purple* (Tetragrammaton 119; 1969; #162)—sold moderately well, blending classical motifs with hard rock (e.g., liberal borrowings from Rimsky-Korsakov's *Sheherazade* in "And the Address"/"I'm So Glad" medley). The three-part song-suite, "April," (included within the ill-fated third album, which disappeared from retail outlets shortly after release when Tetragrammaton went out of business) anticipated the band's next recording, *Deep Purple/The Royal Philharmonic Orchestra "Concerto for Group and Orchestra* (Warner Bros. 1860; 1970; #149). Although the release earned some critical raves, sales were flat; a side project by written and produced by Lord, *Gemini Suite* (Capitol 870; 1971), would be the last flirtation with the symphonic format by band members.

The band's fifth LP, *Deep Purple in Rock* (Warner Bros. 1877; 1970; #143), represented a major stylistic shift to classic heavy metal, spearheaded by lead vocalist, Ian Gillan (who'd replaced Evans in July 1969 and would attract further attention singing the lead role in the stage version of the rock opera, *Jesus Christ Superstar*). Later albums—*Fireball* (Warner Bros. 2564; 1971; #32), *Machine Head* (Warner Bros. 2607; 1972; #7), *Who Do We Think We Are?* (Warner Bros. 2678; 1973; #15), *Made In Japan* (Warner Bros. 2701; 1973; #6), *Burn* (Warner Bros. 2766; 1974; #9), and *Stormbringer* (Warner Bros. 2832; 1974; #20)—continued the formula, paying considerable financial dividends.

The band's momentum would ultimately be undermined by the loss of key personnel: Glover and Gillan departed in 1973, followed by Blackmore in 1975. Deep Purple would officially disband following the release of *Come Taste the Band* (Warner Bros. 2895; 1975; #43); the label would release *Made in Europe* (Warner Bros. 2995; 1976; #148) and various retrospective compilations in order to capitalize on lingering interest in the band.

Band members remained active in new alignments; most notably, Blackmore in Rainbow, and Lord and Paice in Whitesnake. The success of second generation metal bands, particularly those adapting to the video medium, spurred a reunion of the band's early 1970s lineup. Subsequent releases—*Perfect Strangers* (Mercury 824003; 1984; #17; *The House of Blue Light* (Mercury 831318; 1987; #34), *Nobody's Perfect* (Mercury 835897; 1988; #105, *Slaves and Masters* (RCA 2421; 1990; #87), *The Battle Rages On* (RCA 24517; 1993; #21), *Come Hell or High Water* (RCA 23416; 1994), *Purpendicular* (RCA 33802; 1996; #58), and *Abandon* (RCA 495306; 1998)—charted, albeit less dramatically the second time around.

Euro-pop/Euro-rock

"Euro-pop" denotes popular music produced by European (except the United Kingdom and Iceland) artists who have opted to employ that continent as their home base. "Euro-rock," in turn, simply refers to European material that possesses a harder edge. Although European artists have enjoyed occasional American hits throughout much of the rock era, these collective terms did not appear in music industry publications until the Swedish group, Abba, began its successful American chart run in the mid-1970s.

Although another Swedish act, Roxette, went on to achieve even greater American success beginning in the late 1980s, Abba has remained the commercial and aesthetic model for European musicians trying to gain a foothold in the largest music consumer market in the world. The group's sound was built around catchy melodies put across by soaring vocal harmonies, and backed by intricate, full-bodied production work. The straightforward lyrics were always in English so as to appeal to the American market. The overall effect was one of light, engaging pop as opposed to the more ponderous hard rock--and later, punk/new wave--styles then dominating the music industry. Furthermore, group's photogenic image, very effectively packaged in Europe by means of elaborate, lip-synched video productions, perfectly complemented the musical product. When Abba's hitmaking string ended--a combined result of internal difficulties (the dissolution of the two marriages between the four group members: Bjorn Ulvaeus to Agnetha Faltskog, and Benny Andersson to Annifrid Lyngstad) and increasingly pretentious recordings--the formula to be emulated by Europeans hopeful of stateside success was firmly in place.

Top Artists and Their Recordings

Abba--"Waterloo" (1974); "Honey Honey" (1974); "SOS" (1975); "I Do, I Do, I Do, I Do, I Do" (1976); "Mamma Mia" (1976); "Fernando" (1976); "Dancing Queen" (1976/7); "Knowing Me, Knowing You" (1977); "Money, Money, Money" (1977); "The Name of the Game" (1977/8); "Take a Chance on Me" (1978); "Does Your Mother Know" (1979); "Voulez-Vous"/"Angel Eyes" (1979); "Chiquitita" (1979/80); "The Winner Takes It All" (1980/1); "On and On and On" (1980);

"Super Trouper" (1981) "One of Us" (1981); "When All is Said and Done" (1982); "Head Over Heels" (1982); "The Visitors" (1982)

A-ha--"Take on Me" (1983)

Autograph--"Turn Up the Radio" (1984/5)

Basia--"Time and Tide" (1988); "New Day For You" (1988); "Promises" (1989); "Cruising For Bruising" (1990)

Belle Epoque--"Miss Broadway" (1978)

Boney M--"Daddy Cool" (1977); "Ma Baker" (1977); "Rivers of Babylon" (1978)

Diesel--"Sausalito Summernight" (1981)

Falco--"Der Kommissar" (1983); "Rock Me Amadeus" (1986); "Vienna Calling" (1986)

Focus--*In and Out of Focus* (1970); *Moving Waves* (1973); "Hocus Pocus" (1973); *Focus 3* (1973); "Sylvia" (1973); *Live at the Rainbow* (1973/4); *Hamburger Concerto* (1974); *Mother Focus* (1975); *Ship of Memories* (1977)

Gipsy Kings--*Gipsy Kings* (1988/9); *Mosaique* (1989/90); *Este Mundo* (1991)

Boris Grebenshikov--*Radio Silence* (1989)

Lolita (Ditta)--"Sailor (Your Home Is the Sea)" (1960); "Cowboy Jimmy Joe" (1961)

Los Bravos--"Black Is Black" (1966); "Going Nowhere" (1966); "Bring a Little Lovin'" (1968)

Nena--"99 Luftballons" (1983)

Opus--"Live Is Life" (1986)

Plastic Bertrand--"Ca Plane Pour Moi" (197)

Roxette--"Play That Funky Music" (1988); "The Look" (1989); "Dressed For Success" (1989); "Listen To Your Heart" (1989); "Dangerous" (1989); "It Must Have Been Love" (1990); "Joyride" (1991); "Fading Like a Flower" (1991); "Spending My Time" (1991); "Church of Your Heart" (1992); "How Do You Do!" (1992); "Almost Unreal" (1993)

Peter Schilling--"Major Tom (Coming Home)" (1983); "The Different Story (World of Lust and Crime)" (1989)

Shocking Blue--"Venus" (1969/70); "Mighty Joe" (1970; "Long and Lonesome Road" (1970)

The Singing Nun (Soeur Sourire)--"Dominique" (1963/4)

T'Pau--"Heart and Soul" (1987); "Only a Heartbeat" (1991)

Rock and Roll Revival

The rock and roll revival represented an attempt, in the midst of psychedelia and progressive rock experimentation, to return to the spare musical values of mid-1950s rock 'n' roll. The movement received its initial impetus in 1969-1970 from the nostalgia tour packages organized by Richard Nader, Dick Clark, and other promoters which featured original rock 'n' roll artists (albeit often with drastically altered personnel) such as the Coasters, the Drifters, Fats Domino, Little Richard, and Bill Haley and His Comets.

A contemporary retro group, the New York-based Sha Na Na, parlayed goofy stage antics with an uncanny ability to perform carbon copy renditions of classic rock 'n' roll and r & b hits to secure a weekly television program. Sha Na Na's popularity, while modest in terms of record sales, inspired the formation of many more revival acts. The more successful of these artists proved capable of augmenting oldies interpretations with first-rate original material in a retro mold.

The popularity of the movement peaked with the release of the George Lucas film, *American Graffiti*, in 1972. *American Graffiti* went on to become one of the top-grossing films of alltime, while one of its stars, Ron Howard, joined the cast of the popular TV spinoff, "Happy Days." By the mid-1970s, however, record sales of rock 'n' roll reissues and retro releases had greatly declined as the music industry turned its attention other fads.

Top Artists and Their Recordings

Mike Berry--*Drift Away* (1972); *Rocks in My Head* (1976)

Brownsville Station--*Brownsville Station* (1970); *A Night on the Town* (1972); *Yeah!* (1973); *School Punks* (1974); *Motor City Connection* (1976)

Dave Edmunds--*Rockpile* (1972); *Subtle as a Flying Mallet* (1975); *Get It* (1977); *Tracks on Wax* (1978); *Repeat When Necessary* (1979); *Twangin'* (1981); *D.E. 7th* (1982); *Information* (1983); *Riff Raff* (1984); *I Hear You Rockin'* (1987)

Flamin' Groovies--*Sneakers* (1969); *Supersnazz* (1970); *Flamingo* (1971); *Teenage Head* (1971); *Grease* (1973; EP); *More Grease* (1974; EP); *Shake Some Action* (1976); "More Grease" (1976;

EP); *Still Shakin'* (1976); *Now* (1978); *Jumpin' in the Night* (1979); *One Night Stop* (1987); *Rock Juice* (1993)

Flash Cadillac and the Continental Kids--*Flash Cadillac and the Continental Kids* (1973); *No Face Like Chrome* (1974); *Sons of Beaches* (1975); *Rock 'n' Roll Forever* (1976)

Frut--*Keep on Truckin'* (1971)

Fumble--*Fumble* (1973); *Poetry in Lotion* (1974)

Godfrey Daniel--*Godfrey Daniel* (1971)

Sha Na Na--*Sha Na Na Is Here to Stay* (1969); *Sha Na Na* (1971); *The Night Is Still Young* (1972); *Golden Age of Rock 'n' Roll* (1973); *From the Streets of New York* (1974); *Hot Sox* (1974); *Sha Na Na Now* (1975)

Showaddywaddy--*Showadywaddy* (1974); *Step Two* (1975); *Trocadero* (1976); *Showaddywaddy* (1977); *Red Star* (1977); *Crepes and Drapes* (1979); *Bright Lights* (1980)

Shakin' Stevens--*Legend* (1970); *I'm No D.J.* (1971); *Rockin' 'n' Skakin'* (1972); *Shakin' Stevens and the Sunsets* (1974); *Shakin' Stevens* (1978); *Marie Marie* (1980); *This Old House* (1981)

Blues Revival

The blues revival, which spanned the decade of the 1960s, attempted to resurrect indigenous African American music styles within a modern context; i.e., employing rock instrumentation, performing dynamics, and studio technology. The movement encompassed two different approaches, those centered in the United States and Great Britain, respectively.

In the U.S., folkies took a leadership role in the exploration of blues roots. They worshipped "authenticity," which was taken to mean an aged black man playing an acoustic instrument. Living electric interpreters such as B.B. King, Albert King, Freddie King, and Magic Sam were largely overlooked. Contemporary white performers were acknowledged only if their work focused on pre-World War II forms.

Electric blues practitioners finally began to receive recognition when white rock musicians discovered the genre in the mid-1960s. The most influential of the white artists was the Paul Butterfield Blues Band. Butterfield was an accomplished harmonica players who'd learned the craft from blues masters based in the South Side district of Chicago. The band--which also featured guitarists Michael Bloomfield (according to *The Rolling Stone Illustrated History of Rock & Roll*, the most influential performer on that instrument until the arrival of Eric Clapton) and Elvin Bishop--opened the door to mainstream acceptance for an entire generation of blues revivalists from the Allman Brothers Band to albino guitar slinger Johnny Winter.

In the United Kingdom, black American blues became available in appreciable numbers after World War II through (1) records left behind by American G.I.s and sold in secondhand stores, (2) product mail ordered by young enthusiasts, and (3) pressings leased by English jazz labels. The "trad" jazz fad of the 1950s represented a pale, but enthusiastic, attempt to recreate the Chicago and New Orleans styles popular in the 1920s (best known as "dixieland" in the United States). The best known exponent of this genre was Chris Barber; two of his sidemen, Alexis Korner and Cyril Davies, formed an r & b unit within the main band. This aggregate, Blues Incorporated, recruited another young Barber recruit, future Rolling Stones co-founder Brian Jones, and struck out on its own in 1962.

The Stones, formed in 1963, went on to become the British blues revival band both to achieve broad-based popularity and advance the genre beyond the mere imitation of old models. The Yardbirds are widely considered to have been the most accomplished of the bands to have followed in the wake of the Stones' success. Featuring the talents, in successive order, of three of the most influential rock guitarists of the rock era (Eric Clapton, Jeff Beck, and Jimmy Page, whose later installment of the band metamor- phosed into Led Zeppelin), the Yardbirds attempted a balancing act between straight blues live and progressive studio explorations (e.g., Indian raga phrasings in "Shapes of Things," electric violin in "Over Under Sideways Down," twin guitar feedback leads in "Happenings Ten Years Time Ago").

Top Artists and Their Recordings

--U.S. Artists

Mike Bloomfield/Al Kooper/Steve Stills--*Super Session* (1968)

The Blues Project--*Live at the Cafe Au Go Go* (1966); *Projections* (1966); *The Blues Project Live at Town Hall* (1967)

The Paul Butterfield Blues Band--*The Paul Butterfield Blues Band* (1965); *East-West* (1966); *The Resurrection of Pigboy Crabshaw* (1968); *In My Own Dream* (1968); *The Butterfield Blues Band/Live* (1971); *Sometimes I Just Feel Like Smilin'* (1971)

Canned Heat--*Canned Heat* (1967); *Boogie With Canned Heat* (1968); *Living the Blues* (1969); *Hallelujah* (1969); *Future Blues* (1970); *Hooker 'N Heat* (w/John Lee Hooker) (1971); *Canned Heat Concert* (1971)

The Fabulous Thunderbirds--*Butt Rockin'* (1981); *Tuff Enuff* (1984); *Hot Number* (1987); *Powerful Stuff* (1989)

J. Geils Band--*The J. Geils Band* (1970); *The Morning After* (1971); *Live - Full House* (1972); *Bloodshot* (1973); *Ladies Invited* (1973); *Nightmares...and other tales from the vinyl jungle* (1974); *Hotline* (1975); *Live - Blow Your Face Out* (1976); *Monkey Island* (1977); *Sanctuary* (1978); *Love Stinks* (1980); *Freeze-Frame* (1981); *Showtime!* (1982); *You're Gettin' Even While I'm Gettin' Odd* (1984)

Charley Musselwhite--*Ace of Harps* (1970)

Vaughan, Stevie Ray—*Texas Flood* (1983); *Couldn't Stand the Weather* (1984); *Soul To Soul* (1985)

Johnny Winter--*The Progressive Blues Experiment* (1969); *Johnny Winter* (1969); *The Johnny Winter Story* (1969); *Second Winter* (1969); *Johnny Winter And* (1970); *Live/Johnny Winter And* (1971); *Still Alive and Well* (1973); *Saints & Sinners* (1974); *John Dawson Winter III* (1974); *Captured Live!* (1976); *Together* (w/Edgar Winter) (1976)

--U.K. Artists

Chicken Shack--*Imagination Lady* (1972)

Climax Blues Band--*The Climax Chicago Blues Band Plays On* (1970); *A Lot of Bottle* (1971); *Tightly Knit* (1972); *Rich Man* (1973); *FM/Live* (1973); *Sense of Direction* (1974); *Stamp Album* (1975); "Couldn't Get It Right" (1977); "Makin' Love" (1978); "Gotta Have More Love" (1980); "I Love You" (1981)

Cream--*Fresh Cream* (1967); *Disraeli Gears* (1968); "Sunshine of Your Love"; *Wheels of Fire* (1968); "White Room" (1968); *Goodbye* (1969)

Fleetwood Mac--*English Rose* (1968); *Then Play On* (1969); *Kiln House* (1970)

Savoy Brown--*Getting to the Point* (1967); *Blue Matter* (1968); *A Step Further* (1969); *Raw Sienna* (1970); *Looking In* (1970); *Street Corner Talking* (1971); *Hellbound Train* (1972); *Lion's Share* (1972); *Jack the Toad* (1973); *Boogie Brothers* (1974); *Wire Fire* (1975)

Taste--*Taste* (1969)

Ten Years After--*Undead* (1968); *Stonedhenge* (1969); *Ssssh* (1969); *Cricklewood Green* (1970); *Watt* (1970); *A Space in Time* (1971); *Rock & Roll Music to the World* (1972); *Recorded Live* (1973); *Positive Vibrations* (1974)

The Yardbirds-- *For Your Love* (1965); *Having a Rave Up with the Yardbirds* (1965); *Over Under Sideways Down* (1966); *Little Games* (1967)

Table 85

Michael Bloomfield, July 28, 1944-February 15, 1981

Michael Bloomfield has perhaps the most gifted American guitarist within the 1960s blues revival movement. Although his later solo recordings remain relatively unknown to rank-and-file pop music enthusiasts, he can also be heard on a wide range of classic albums that helped define the emergence of progressive rock.

Although the Chicago-born Bloomfield grew up in the relatively prosperous North Shore area, he spent much time downtown observing the guitar playing techniques of the leading exponents of the Chicago blues style. While still in his teens, he graduated to performing in the local clubs. Impressed by his talent, mouth harpist Paul Butterfield invited him to be a member of the Paul Butterfield Blues Band in 1963. Bloomfield, as lead guitarist, helped distill the groundbreaking sound of the band's first two LP releases, *The Paul Butterfield Blues Band* (Elektra 7294; 1965) and *East-West* (Elektra 7315; 1966). Whereas the debut primarily updated the Chess Sound as defined by Muddy Waters, Albert King, and others, the second album stretched electric blues conventions to their limit, incorporating lengthy, jazz-influenced jamming and Indian raga flourishes.

The band's backup role for Bob Dylan's famed electric performance at the Newport Folk Festival has been released on various bootleg recordings, including *Live in Newport 1965* (Document 004; 1988). Earlier that year, Bloomfield had also played lead guitar on Dylan's critically acclaimed, *Highway 61 Revisited* (Columbia 9189; 1965), which featured the hit single, "Like a Rolling Stone" (Columbia 43346; 1965; #2).

Tired of constant touring and wanting to have more creative control, Bloomfield departed the Butterfield band to form the Electric Flag with longtime associate, singer Nick Gravenites. Put off by the massive hype surrounding his new band, he moved on again after playing on one album, *A Long Time Comin'* (Columbia 9597; 1968). For a time he seemed content to merely tread water, collaborating with Al Kooper and Stephen Stills on a couple of slapdash studio jam LPs, *Super Session* (Columbia 9701; 1968) and *The Live Adventures of Mike Bloomfield and Al Kooper* (Columbia 6; 1969).

With the exception of a couple a stabs at the commercial bigtime—*Triumvirate* (Columbia 32172; 1973), with Dr. John and John Paul Hammond, and *KGB* (MCA 2166; 1976), featuring keyboardist Barry Goldberg, bassist Rick Grech, drummer Carmine Appice, and vocalist Ray Kennedy—Bloomfield focused on solo work for the rest of his career. The results received mixed critical response; many pointed out that the creative fire of his best 1960s work was no longer in evidence. However, one release, *If You Love These Blues, Play 'Em As You Please* (Guitar Player 3002; 1976), a compendium of blues guitar licks intended as an educational tool for magazine subscribers, received a Grammy Award nomination. With his studio works failing to provide adequate financial support, he resorted for a time to scoring pornographic films, primarily for the San Francisco-based Mitchell Brothers. He died of an apparently accidental drug overdose in his parked 1971 Mercury on a San Francisco's Dewey Street.

Bubblegum Sound

Bubblegum music--the basic sound of rock minus the thread of rage, fear, and violence that has run through it since the early hits of Elvis Presley and Bill Haley--assured the spread of rock consciousness to the preteen audience. The genre appropriated the calculated innocence and (sometimes) authentic tenderness of the teen idols, adding a slice of garage band rock and the flavor of pop rock novelties (e.g., Johnny Thunder's "Loop De Loop," the Dixie Cups' "Iko Iko," and Shirley Ellis's "The Name Game"). The songs typically consisted of nursery rhymes set to simple, repetitious music. Many of the artists were fictitious entities employed as a front for a core collection of session musicians.

The immediate ancestors of bubblegum included Tommy James and the Shondells and the television sitcom stars, the Monkees. In 1966, both acts reached number one with their initial singles releases by projecting a youthful sense of fun poised at the brink of teenage angst.

These successes inspired Neil Bogert, then president of Buddah Records, to employ the production team of Jerry Kasenetz and Jeff Katz, who had attracted attention for their work with the Rare Breed ("Beg, Borrow and Steal," "Come on Down to My Boat") and the Music Explosion ("Little Bit O' Soul").

Kasenetz and Katz quickly established Buddah as a leader of the genre with hit recordings by a series of studio-only groups, including the Ohio Express, the 1910 Fruitgum Company, Crazy Elephant, the Rock and Roll Dubble Bubble Trading Card Co. of Philadelphia 19141, and Captain Groovy and His Bubblegum Army. Despite Buddah's success, the top bubblegum act--another fictitious entity called the Archies--was masterminded by Brill Building songwriter/producer Jeff Barry. The Archies, featuring the lead vocals of sessionman Ron Dante, pioneered the Saturday morning cartoon series tie-in (a frequently imitated concept).

During its prime the genre also featured a string one-shot hits by the likes of the Cuff Links (again featuring Ron Dante), Daddy Dewdrop, and the Pipkins. A number of established rock performers milked bubblegum for hit recordings, including Tommy Roe ("Dizzy," "Jam Up Jelly Tight") and the Troggs ("Hip Hip Hooray").

In the 1970s, bubblegum essentially was absorbed into the mainstream. Notable exponents included the Partridge Family, Bobby Sherman, Shaun Cassidy, Leif Garrett, Abba, and bad-girl rockers The Runaways. Kasenetz and Katz continued to mine the genre with success as late as 1977 with Ram Jam's "Black Betty," a fusion of bubblegum, heavy metal, and Leadbelly-styled folk-blues.

The concept has remained viable up through the 1990s as was proved by the chart topping run of "Mmmbop," written and recorded by Hansen, a trio of teenaged brothers, as well as a string of hits by the likes of Brittany Spears, Monica, and Brandy.

Top Artists and Their Recordings

The Archies--""Bang-Shang-A-Lang" (1968); "Sugar Sugar" (1969); "Jingle Jangle" (1969/70);""Who's Your Baby?" (1970)

The Banana Splits--"The Tra La La Song (One Banana, Two Banana)" (1960)

Crazy Elephant--"Gimme Gimme Good Lovin' (1969)

The Cuff Links--"Tracy" (1969)

Daddy Dewdrop--"Chick-A-Boom" (1971)

The Monkees--"Last Train to Clarksville" (1966); "I'm A Believer" (1966); "Pleasant Valley Sunday" (1967); "Daydream Believer: (1967); "Valleri" (1968)

1910 Fruitgum Co.--"Simon Says" (1968); "1, 2, 3, Red Light" (1968); "Goody Goody Gundrops" (1968); "Indian Giver" (1969); "Special Delivery" (1969)

Ohio Express--"Beg, Borrow and Steal" (1967); Yummy Yummy Yummy" (1968); "Down at Lulu's" (1968); "Chewy Chewy" (1968); "Mercy" (1969)

The Pipkins--"Gimme Dat Ding" (1970)

Rock and Roll Dubble Bubble Trading Card Co. of Philadelphia-19141--Bubble Gum Music (1969)

Table 86

Bell Records

Although consistently successful since the early 1960s, the Bell Records story can be divided into three distinct phases. Under the leadership of Larry Uttal, the label—along with subsidiaries such as Mala, Amy, Goldwax (Memphis), and New Voice/ Dynovoice (New York)—and the was best known in the 1960s for Southern soul artists such as Lee Dorsey, James and Bobby Purify, James Carr, early Al Green, Oscar Toney, Jr., and Mighty Sam. However, Bell also produced some of the period's best blue-eyed soul with the Box Tops and Mitch Ryder in addition to garage bands along the lines of the Syndicate of Sound.

In 1970, Bell was purchased by Columbia Pictures, who changed the label from a dark blue to silver color, and focused on Top Forty singles by adult contemporary acts like the 5th Dimension, Barry Manilow, and Melissa Manchester as well as the more bubblegum-oriented Tony Orlando & Dawn and the Partridge Family. Its U.K. division focused on the glam-rock craze, most notably, Gary Glitter, the Sweet, Suzy Quatro, and the early Bay City Rollers.

Former Columbia Records CEO Clive Davis would take control of the label in 1975 (with Uttal moving on the found Private Stock). Changing the company's name to Arista, Davis quickly built up a stable of prestige artists such as jazz-poet Gil Scott-Heron, punk high priestess Patti Smith, singer-songwriter Garland Jeffreys, and leading avant-garde jazz figures on the Freedom imprint. Nevertheless, the label's notable commercial success was largely due MOR fare by the likes of Manilow, Whitney Houston, and Kenny G.

Table 87

Buddah/Kama Sutra Records

Buddah had its origins in the establishment of the Kama Sutra label in 1965 by entrepreneurs Phil Steinberg and Hy Mizrahi and producer Artie Ripp, the force behind such hits as Doris Troy's "Just One Look" (Atlantic 2188; 1963; #10), Jay & the Americans' "Come A Little Bit Closer" (United Artists 759; 1964; #3), and the Shangri-Las' "Remember (Walkin' in the Sand)" (Red Bird 008; 1964; #5). Created as a subsidiary in 1967, the New York-based imprint quickly attracted a stable of ambitious, talented young writers and producers, including Pete Anders and Vinnie Poncia (who had provided hits for the Ronettes), Bo Gentry and Ritchie Cordell (Tommy James & the Shondells), Levine and Resnick, Elliot Chiprut, and Bobby Bloom.

Other key staff included West Coast A&R chief Bob Krasnow—responsible for signing progressive rockers Captain Beefheart & His Magic Band and Barry Goldberg—and Vice President Neil Bogart, who steered the label in the direction of bubblegum singles. His successes would include the 1910 Fruitgum Co. with "Simon Says" (Buddah 24; 1968; #4), and the Ohio Express, whose biggest hit was "Yummy Yummy Yummy" (Buddah 38; 1968; #4).

On the strength of such prepubescent fare, Buddah was the seventh-ranked label in singles sales by the time it celebrated its first anniversary in September 1968. Although later enjoying success in the pop-rock (Brooklyn Bridge, Lou Christie, Motherlode, etc.) and soul (the Impression via their Curtom subsidiary, the Isley Brothers on T-Neck) fields, the label remained saddled with the bubblegum image. The Lemon Piper's best exemplified this dilemma; fed a string of sugary material—"Green Tambourine" (Buddah 23; 1967; #1), "Rice Is Nice" (Buddah 31; 1968; #46), and "Jelly Jungle" (Buddah 41; 1968; #51)—the band attempted, unsuccessfully it turned out, to assert their hard rock side via largely ignored album releases.

Buddah's assembly-line techniques—many of its acts were studio-only concoctions like Lt. Garcia's Magic Music Box and the Rock and Roll Double Bubble Trading Card Company of Philadelphia 19141—led to an inevitable decline when its bubblegum artists fell out of favor with the public. The defection of Ripp—Billy Joel's early mentor—and Bogart, who founded Casablanca in 1973, also hurt the label. By 1983, when the company finally shut down operations, hit records had become a rare occurrence. BMG would reactivate "Buddha" as an archival label in 1999; much of the old Buddah catalog has been reissued, including material by Melanie, the Flamin' Groovies, the 1910 Fruitgum Co., and Ohio Express.

Table 88

Tommy James & the Shondells

A Dayton, Ohio native (b, 1947), Tommy James began performing with his group, the Shondells, at school dances, auditoriums, and other area venues at the age of twelve. The outfit would occasionally cut records for small companies, including a song called "Hanky Panky" for the Snap label in 1960. More than five years later, a KDKA, Pittsburgh, disc jockey played the record on his program; it quickly became the most requested single in that radio market. Roulette Records acquired the rights to "Hanky Panky" (Roulette 4686), and it reached number one on the *Billboard Hot 100* in July 1966.

James would go on to record thirty charting singles (many co-written by him and friend, Bob King)—both with the Shondells and as a solo artist—though early 1973. His Top Ten releases included "I Think We're Alone Now" (Roulette 4720; 1967), "Mirage" (Roulette 4736; 1967), "Mony Mony" (Roulette 7008; 1968), "Crimson and Clover" (Roulette 7028; 1968-1969), "Sweet Cherry Wine" (Roulette 7039; 1969), "Crystal Blue Persuasion" (Roulette 7050; 1969), and "Draggin' the Line" (Roulette 7103; 1971). His combination of romantic innocence, catchy melodies, and hook-laden refrains provided the model for the late 1960s Bubblegum genre.

The unrelenting succession of one-night stands and drug abuse led to a breakdown in 1970. After his recovery, changing public tastes made the hits harder to come by. During a brief career revival in 1980, it was estimated that he had sold over thirty million records. The 1980s also brought success for his classic songs as covered by other artists, most notably "Crimson and Clover" (number 7, Joan Jett, Boardwalk 144; 1982), "I Think We're Alone Now" (number 1, Tiffany, MCA 33147; 1987), and "Mony Mony" (number 1, Billy Idol, Chrysalis 43181; 1987). [Stambler. 1989]

Singer/Songwriter Tradition

The singer/songwriter genre flourished from the late 1960s, when popular music as a whole took on a softer cast, to the mid-1970s. These artists--generally performing their own material (Tom Rush, who interpreted the work of other contemporary singer/ songwriters, was a notable exception to this rule)--often appeared as soloists, employing either a piano or guitar for accompaniment. This spare mode of presentation helped facilitate an aura of directness which differentiated them from legions of other soft rockers.

Singer/songwriters for-the-most-part evolved out of two genres: Tin Pan Alley pop and post-Dylan folk music. The former category included Carole King, Randy Newman, Van Dyke Parks, and Laura Nyro; the latter such notables as Rush, Joni Mitchell, James Taylor, Jackson Browne, Neil Young, Leonard Cohen, and Cat Stevens. Paul Simon straddled both camps.

The appeal of these artists was largely built on the cult of personality. The most successful singer/songwriters (e.g., Young, Taylor, Browne, Simon) were able to reflect change under pressure as well as a growing awareness of inner concerns. This self-absorption stood in stark contrast to the universal idealism of the preceding era's universal idealism. Many of the folk interpreters espousing the latter perspective appeared unwilling--or unable--to evolve into the confessional realm. Many of these artists--e.g., Phil Ochs, Tom Paxton, Eric Andersen, Gordon Lightfoot--lost career momentum when folk era values no longer held the attention of the mainstream pop audience. Other artists were unable to sustain a high level of conceptual creativity regarding the expression of personal feelings. Carole King and Cat Stevens both enjoyed extraordinary success in the 1971-72 period, but suffered a severe drop-off in popularity shortly thereafter. King, in particular, remained a first-rate tunesmith; she simply appears to have lost the ability to hold the attention of many fans who'd found *Tapestry* to be full of fascinating insights.

Most of the singer/songwriters who tasted early stardom, however, retained a sufficiently large enough following to continue to release new material at regular intervals. The genre's decline in popularity during the 1970s was largely a product of the shortfall in new talent as well as new trends such as disco and the punk revolution.

Top Artists and Their Recordings

Jackson Browne--*Jackson Browne* (1972); *For Everyman* (1973); *Late For the Sky* (1974); *The Pretender* (1976)

Tim Buckley--*Tim Buckley* (1966); *Goodbye and Hello* (1967); *Happy Sad* (1969); *Lorca* (1970); *Blue Afternoon* (1970); *Starsailor* (1971); *Greeting From L.A.* (1972)

Cockburn, Bruce--*Dancing in the Dragon's Jaws* (1980); *Humans* (1980); *Stealing Fire* (1984)

Leonard, Cohen--*Songs of Leonard Cohen* (1968); *Songs From a Room* (1968); *Songs of Love and Hate* (1970)

Nick Drake--*Five Leaves Left* (1969); *Bryter Layter* (1970); *Pink Moon* (1972)

Tim Hardin--*Tim Harden 1* (1966); *Tim Harden 2* (1967); *This Is Tim Hardin* (1967); *Live in Concert* (1968); *Tim Hardin 4* (1969); *Suite for Susan Moore and Damian* (1970)

Ian, Janis--*Janis Ian* (1967); *For All the Seasons of Your Mind* (1967); *Stars* (1974); *Between the Lines* (1975)

Carole King--*Now That Everything's Been Said* (1969); *Writer* (1970); *Tapestry* (1971); *Music* (1972); *Rhymes and Reasons* (1972); *Fantasy* (1973)

Joni Mitchell--*Joni Mitchell* (1968); *Clouds* (1969); *Ladies of the Canyon* (1970); *Blue* (1971); *For the Roses* (1972); *Court and Spark* (1974)

Van Morrison--*Blowin' Your Mind* (1967); *Astral Weeks* (1968); *Moondance* (1970); *His Band and Street Choir* (1971); *Tupelo Honey* (1971); *St. Dominic's Preview* (1972); *Hard Nose the Highway* (1973)

Randy Newman--*Randy Newman* (1968); *12 Songs* (1970); *Live* (1971); *Sail Away* (1972); *Good Old Boys* (1974)

Harry Nilsson--*Harry* (1972); *Nilsson Schmilsson* (1973)

Phillips, Shawn--*Faces* (1972); *Bright White* (1973); *Furthermore* (1974)

Tom Rush--*Tom Rush* (1970); *Wrong End of the Rainbow* (1971); *Merrimack County* (1972)

Carly Simon--*Carly Simon* (1971); *Anticipation* (1971); *No Secrets* (1972); *Hotcakes* (1974); *Playing Possum* (1975)

Paul Simon--*Paul Simon* (1972); *There Goes Rhymin' Simon* (1973); *Still Crazy After All These Years* (1975)

Cat Stevens--*Matthew and Son* (1967); *New Masters* (1968); *World of Cat Stevens* (1970); *Mona Bone Jakon* (1970); *Tea for the Tillerman* (1971); *Teaser and the Firecat* (1971); *Cat Bull at Four* (1972); *Foreigner* (1973)

James Taylor--*James Taylor* (1968); *Sweet Baby James* (1970); *Mud Slide Slim* (1971); *One Man Dog* (1972)

Neil Young--*Neil Young* (1969); *Everybody Knows This Is Nowhere* (1969); *After the Goldrush* (1970); *Harvest* (1972)

Table 89

Joni Mitchell, 1943-

Joni Mitchell is the quintessential singer-songwriter; although widely recorded by other artists—Judy Collins reached number eight on the pop charts with "Both Sides Now" (Elektra 45639; 1968), Tom Rush made "The Circle Game" the title song of his third album (Elektra 74018), and three versions of "Woodstock" made the *Billboard* Hot 100—her own idiosyncratic renditions remain the definitive versions of her material. While her folk troubador origins and confessional lyrics conform to the conventions of this genre, she has avoided stylistic categorization in recording career spanning five different decades.

Born Roberta Joan Anderson in rural Saskatchewan, she studied piano and displayed a talent for composing melodies at an early age. Despite battling polio at age nine, she continued playing music (learning guitar from a Pete Seeger do-it-yourself manual) prior to starting art school in Calgary.

After a year of college, she matriculated to Toronto, working in a clothing store and trying to break into the Yorkville district's coffeehouse circuit. While there, she met and married Chuck Mitchell, a cabaret singer hailing from Detroit.

Success as a songwriter, combined with the failure of her marriage, brought Mitchell to New York in 1967. There she met longtime manager, Elliot Roberts, and David Crosby, who produced her first album, *Joni Mitchell* (Reprise 6293; 1968). In 1968 she moved to Los Angeles, producing a series of folk-inflected LPs characterized by her unusual guitar tunings, the increasingly layered use of instrumentation, and poetic treatment of themes such as sexual liberation and the search for meaning in human relationships: *Clouds* (Reprise 6341; 1969), *Ladies of the Canyon* (Reprise 6376; 1970), *Blue*

(Reprise 2038; 1971), *For the Roses* (Asylum 5057; 1972), and her pop breakthrough, *Court and Spark* (Asylum 1001; 1974).

Following the live *Miles of Aisles* (Asylum 202; 1974), Mitchell's next five albums—*The Hissing of Summer Lawns* (Asylum 1051; 1975), *Hejira* (Asylum 1087; 1976), *Don Juan's Reckless Daughter* (Asylum 701; 1977), *Mingus* (Asylum 505; 1979), and *Shadows and Light* (Asylum 704; 1980)—were strongly grounded in jazz idioms. The abstract, detached flavor of her verses and virtual absence of traditional melodies led to a gradual decline in sales.

Wild Things Run Fast (Geffen 2019; 1982), however, signaled a return to her earlier pop-rock style. Following a brief experiment with electronica and broader geopolitical themes in *Dog Eat Dog* (Geffen 24074; 1985), she has preferred to craft songs from familiar clay rather than take stylistic risks. Nevertheless, her releases continue to sell moderately well and *Turbulent Indigo* (Geffen; 1994) was awarded two Grammys. Other notable honors include *Billboard* magazine's 1995 Century Award and her 1997 induction into the Rock and Roll Hall of Fame.

Table 90

Randy Newman, November 28, 1944-

At first glance, Randy Newman would not seem a likely candidate for a mass consumption. As a composer, his work is saturated with dark humor and irony—the lyrics often portray bigoted rednecks, perverts, and other assorted losers—backed by chromatic flourishes more typical of George Gershwin than Top Forty songs. He sings with a lazy drawl accompanied by simple piano chords and subtle, impressionistic orchestra arrangements. Nevertheless, his material is widely covered by other artists and his own recordings generally sell well.

Born in New Orleans, he grew up in a musical family; his uncles, Alfred and Lionel, scored many post-World War II films. He became a staff writer for a California-based publishing company as a seventeen-year-old, dropping out of UCLA one semester short of earning a B.A. in music. A friend and staff producer at Warner Bros., Lenny Waronker, helped him secure a recording contract with the label.

Newman first gained fame as a songwriter; his songs were recorded by Judy Collins, Peggy Lee, and Three Dog Night, whose rendition of "Mama Told Me (Not to Come)" (Dunhill 4239; 1970) reached number one on the pop charts. Harry Nilsson would record an entire LP with Newman at the piano, *Nilsson Sings Newman* (RCA; 1970). Touring with Nilsson helped him develop a cult following on college campuses.

His early albums—including *Randy Newman* (Reprise 6286; 1968), *12 Songs* (Reprise 6373; 1970), *Randy Newman/Live* (Reprise 6459; 1971), *Sail Away* (Reprise 2064; 1972), *Good Old Boys* (Reprise 2193; 1974), and *Little Criminals* (Warner Bros. 3079; 1977)—were all critical successes; as a result, each release sold a bit better than its predecessor. The furor created by his first hit single, "Short People" (Warner Bros. 8492; 1977; #2)—which attacked bigotry, but was taken literally by an offended minority—made him a popular culture phenomenon. While his albums continued to sell well, he began receiving offers to compose movie soundtracks, most notably *Ragtime* (Elektra; 1979)—nominated for two Oscars (Best Song, Best Score), *Trouble in Paradise* (Warner Bros.; 1983), *The Natural* (Warner Bros.; 1984), *Three Amigos* ((Warner Bros.; 1987), *Parenthood* (Reprise; 1990), *Avalon* (Reprise; 1990), *Awakenings* (Reprise; 1991), and *The Paper* (Reprise; 1994). Although much of his time was now taken by film projects, he returned to the singles charts with "I Love L.A." (Warner Bros. 29687; 1983)—which achieved anthem status largely due to an iconic video clip directed by his cousin, Tim Newman—and "It's Money That Matters" (Reprise 7-27709; 1988).

Table 91

Neil Sedaka, March 13, 1939-

Neil Sedaka is an American institution, having achieved considerable success in two music fields—singing and songwriting—over an extended length of time. Despite widespread references to his shortcomings—a rather limited vocal technique and a tendency to graft the worst elements of formulaic Tin Pan Alley writing onto his pop-rock compositions, the sincerity and warmth communicated both by Sedaka's voice and material, further augmented in his own recordings by virtuoso production work, have resulted in an enviable recorded legacy.

Since both parents were accomplished pianists, it was inevitable that Sedaka's childhood would include musical training. Despite classical piano training at Julliard, he displayed a pronounced preference for pop material.

He began writing songs with fellow Lincoln High School (Brooklyn) student, Howard Greenfield. Their close proximity to the music publishers and record companies in Manhattan enabled them to eventually secure jobs as staff composers (Sedaka handling the music, Greenfield the lyrics) with Aldon Publishing Company. The firm's owners, Don Kirshner and Al Nevin, were successful in pitching the duo's material to emerging pop star, Connie Francis. They first supplied her "Stupid Cupid" (MGM 12683; 1958; #14), followed by "Fallin'" (MGM 12713; 1958; #30), "Frankie" (MGM 12793; 1959; #9), and "Where the Boys Are" (MGM 12971; 1961; #4).

Aldon also pedaled Sedaka to the labels as a vocalist, securing a contract with RCA (he had recorded previously with the Tokens for Melba in 1956). He immediately scored with a string of successful singles—including the Top Ten recordings, "Oh! Carol" (RCA 7595; 1959), "Stairway to Heaven" (RCA 7709; 1960), "Calendar Girl" (RCA 7829; 1960), "Happy Birthday, Sweet Sixteen" (RCA 7957; 1961), "Breaking Up Is Hard To Do" (RCA 8046; 1962; #1), and "Next Door To An Angel" (RCA 8086; 1962)—which continued up to the British Invasion. Although his singing career lost momentum, his songwriting partnership remained fruitful throughout the 1960s, resulting in hits like the 5th Dimension's "Workin' on a Groovy Thing" (Soul City 776; 1969) and "Puppet Man" (Bell 880; 1970), also a Top Thirty single for Tom Jones (Parrot 40064; 1971).

Reunited with his old boss on Kirshner Records, Sedaka attempted to revive his recording career in the early 1970s. Discouraging sales led to dissolution of his professional relationship with Greenfield; he began writing songs with lyricist Phil Cody, first testing them with the public during a concert tour of England. His warm reception there led to the release of a couple of albums, *Solitaire* (Kirshner 117; 1972) and *The Tra-La Days Are Over* (1973)

Success eluded him in the U.S., however, until the release of *Sedaka's Back* (Rocket; 1974), driven by the number one single, "Laughter in the Rain" (Rocket 40313; 1974). More hit recordings followed, including "Bad Blood" (with Elton John; Rocket 40460; 1975; #1) and "Breaking Up Is Hard to Do" (Rocket 40500; 1975), a torch-style reworking of his 1962 up-tempo teen anthem.

Although his chart successes dropped off again—a notable exception being his duet with daughter Dara, "Should've Never Let You Go" (Elektra 46615; 1980)—Sedaka remains a highly visible entertainer, both live and on television variety programs.

Table 92

Carly Simon, June 25, 1945-

One of the more popular singer/songwriters of the 1970s, Carly Simon—as opposed to Carole King's East Coast R&B leanings and the folk/jazz orientation of Joni Mitchell, two of her notable counterparts—exemplified the polished Los Angeles sound. Simon's pop instincts and rich, expressive voice have enabled her to move into film soundtrack work and Adult Contemporary playlists when no longer in mainstream fashion.

First recording in the mid-1960s as part of the folk-pop Simon Sisters with sister Lucy, Carly was signed to Elektra Records as a solo act in 1970 by producer Jac Holzman. Her debut, *Carly Simon* (Elektra 74182; 1971; #30), included the first of many hit singles, "That's the Way I've Always Heard It Should Be" (Elektra 45724; 1971; #10).

Her critical and commercial high water mark came with *No Secrets* (Elektra 75049; 1973; #1), driven largely by the success of "You're So Vain" (Elektra 45824; 1972; #1), allegedly written about film star Warren Beatty.

Marrying fellow singer/songwriter James Taylor in the mid-1970s, Simon was unable to produce anything quite approaching the quality of *No Secrets*. Nevertheless, she continued issuing solid, if uneven, albums—most notably, *Hotcakes* (Elektra 1002; 1974; #3), *Playing Possum* (Elektra 1033; 1975; #10), and *Boys in the Trees* (Elektra 128; 1978; #10)—which sold moderately well. After her last major hits—"Nobody Does It Better" (Elektra 45413; 1977; #2), from the James Bond film *The Spy Who Loved Me*, and "You Belong To Me" (Elektra 45477; 1978; #6)—Simon has appeared content to cultivate an older audience, releasing, among other things, two albums comprised of pop standards—*Torch* (Warner Bros. 3592; 1981; #50) and *My Romance* (Arista 8582; 1990; #46)—as well as a collection of material identified with the cinema, *Film Noir* (Arista 18984; 1997; #84). She has also devoted an increasing amount of time to writing, no real surprise given the fact that her father helped run the Simon and Schuster publishing house.

Soft Rock, MOR and Related Styles

In a sense, soft rock originated in the late 1950s when pop singers began employing arrangements which incorporated elements of rock 'n' roll. Andy Williams, Guy Mitchell, and Tab Hunter all achieved notable success aiming their releases at a teen audience. The genre gained more widespread recognition, however, following the rise of folk rock and the singer/songwriter tradition in the mid-1960s. These two styles, both based in the Los Angeles recording scene, ushered in a softer form of rock music which made a significant dent in the singles and album charts.

Soft rock had the following identifying features: (1) the rock beat and other abrasive coloring (e.g., intense electric guitar lines, harsh vocalizing) were de-emphasized, and (2) song lyrics tended to be upbeat and/or introspective rather than rebellious in nature. The factors guaranteeing its success included the personal music preferences of the power brokers within the music businesses, the efforts of both artists and record company executives to broaden rock's appeal, and the aging of the first generation of rock fans.

The ongoing maturation of the baby boomers--whose concert-going and record buying habits tended to remain at a much higher level than that of their parents and grandparents--ensured the long-term popularity of the various soft rock styles. Many rock artists would employ an increasingly middle-of-the-road approach as their careers evolved in direct response to the perceived shift of their core audience. Chicago, Dr. Hook, and the Doobie Brothers were all examples of artists whose music became softer and acquired greater polish over time.

Top Artists and Their Recordings

America--"A Horse With No Name" (1972); "I Need You" (1972); "Ventura Highway" (1972); "Tin Man" (1974); "Lonely People" (1974/5); "Sister Golden Hair" (1975)

The Association--"Along Comes Mary" (1966); "Cherish" (1966); "Windy" (1967); "Never My Love" (1967); "Everything That Touches You" (1968)

Bread--"Make It With You" (1970); "It Don't Matter to Me" (1970); "If" (1971); "Baby I'm-A Want You" (1971); "Everything I Own" (1972); "Diary" (1972); "The Guitar Man" (1972); "Sweet Surrender" (1972); "Aubrey" (1973); "Lost Without Your Love" (1976/7)

The Carpenters--"Close to You" (1970); "We've Only Just Begun" (1970); "For All We Know" (1971); "For All We Know" (1971); "Rainy Days and Mondays" (1971); "Superstar" (1971); "Hurting Each Other" (1972); "It's Going to Take Some Time" (1972); "Goodbye to Love" (1972); "Sin" (1973); "Yesterday Once More" (1973); "Top of the World" (1973); "I Won't Last a Day Without You" (1974); "Please Mr. Postman" (1974/5); "Only Yesterday" (1975); "Solitaire" (1975); "There's a Kind of a Hush" (1976); "Touch Me When We're Dancing" (1981)

The Cowsills--"The Rain, the Park and Other Things" (1967); "Indian Lake" (1968); "We Can Fly" (1968); "Hair" (1969)

Crosby, Stills and Nash (and Young)--"Marrakesh Express" (1969); "Suite: Judy Blue Eyes" (1969); "Woodstock" (1970); "Teach Your Children: (1970); "Ohio" (1970); "Our House" (1970); "Just a Song Before I Go" (1977); "Wasted on the Way" (1982); "Southern Cross" (1982)

Christopher Cross--"Ride Like the Wind" (1980); "Sailing" (1980); "Never Be the Same" (1980); "Say You'll Be Mine" (1981); "Arthur's Theme" (1981)

The 5th Dimension--"Go Where You Wanna Go" (1967); "Up-Up and Away" (1967); "Stoned Soul Picnic" (1968); "Sweet Blindness" (1968); "Aquarius/Let the Sunshine In" (1969); "Workin' on a Groovy Thing" (1969); "Wedding Bell Blues" (1969); "One Less Bell to Answer" (1970); "Love's Lines, Angles, and Rhymes" (1971); "Never My Love" (1971); "(Last Night) I Didn't Get to Sleep at All" (1972); "If I Could Reach You" (1972)

Art Garfunkel--"All I Know" (1973); "I Only Have Eyes For You" (1975)

Bobby Goldsboro--"See the Funny Little Clown" (1964); "Little Things" (1965); "It's Too Late" (1966); "Honey" (1968); "Autumn of My Life" (1968); "Watching Scotty Grow" (1970/1); "Summer (The First Time)" (1973)

The Grass Roots--"Where Were You When I Needed You" (1966); "Let's Live For Today" (1967); "Things I Should Have Said" (1967); "Midnight Confessions" (1968); "Bella Linda" (1968/9); "I'd

Wait a Million Years" (1969); "Heaven Knows" (1969); "Sooner or Later" (1971); "Two Divided By Love" (1971)

Harpers Bizarre--"The 59th Street Bridge Song (Feelin' Groovy)" (1967)

Nicolette Larson--"Lotta Love" (1978/9)

Little River Band--"Reminiscing" (1978); Happy Anniversary (1978)

Dave Loggins--"Please Come to Boston" (1974)

Loggins and Messina--"Your Mama Don't Dance" (1972/3); "Thinking of You" (1973); "My Music" (1973)

The Mamas and the Papas--"California Dreamin'" (1966); "Monday, Monday" (1966); "I Saw Her Again" (1966); "Look Through Any Window" (1966); "Words of Love" (1966/7); "Dedicated to the One I Love" (1967); "Creeque Alley" (1967); "Twelve Thirty" (1967); "Glad to Be Unhappy" (1967)

Gary Puckett and the Union Gap--"Woman, Woman" (1967/8); "Young Girl" (1968); "Lady Willpower" (1968); "Over You" (1968); "Don't Give In to Him" (1969); "This Girl Is a Woman Now" (1969)

Seals and Crofts--"Summer Breeze" (1972); "Hummingbird" (1973); "Diamond Girl" (1973); "We May Never Pass This Way (Again)" (1973); "I'll Play For You" (1975); "Get Closer" (1976); "My Fair Share" (1977); "You're the Love" (1978)

Three Dog Night--"Try a Little Tenderness" (1969); "One" (1969); "Easy to Be Hard" (1969); "Eli's Coming" (1969); "Celebrate" (1970); "Mama Told Me (Not to Come)" (1970); "Out in the Country" (1970); "One Man Band" (1970/1); "Joy to the World" (1971); "Liar" (1971); "An Old Fashioned Love Song" (1971); "Never Been to Spain" (1971/2); "The Family of Man" (1972); "Black and White" (1972); "Pieces of April" (1972/3); Shambala" (1973); "Let Me Serenade You" (1973); "The Show Must Go On" (1974); "Sure as I'm Sittin' Here" (1974)

Middle-of-the-Road/Adult Contemporary

While as stylistically varied as soft rock, its practitioners tended to be even more homogenized than artists within the latter category. MOR, or AC--a less prejorative term widely employed by the early 1980s--represented a particular cross-section of the radio listening audience which possessed its own clearly defined lifestyle and product loyalties (a vital consideration to brand name advertisers) combined with substantial purchasing power.

Top Artists and Their Recordings

Stephen Bishop--"Save It For a Rainy Day" (1976/7); "On and On" (1977)

Michael Bolton--"When a Man Loves a Woman" (1987)

Debby Boone--"You Light Up My Life" (1977)

Glen Campbell--"By the Time I Get to Phoenix" (1967); "Wichita Lineman" (1968/9); "Galveston" (1969); "Where's the Playground Suite" (1969); "Try a Little Kindness" (1969); "Honey Come Back" (1970); "It's Only Make Believe" (1970); "Rhinestone Cowboy" (1975); "Country Boy" (1975/6); "Don't Pull Your Love/Then You Can Tell Me Goodbye" (1976); "Southern Nights" (1977)

Rita Coolidge--"(Your Love Has Lifted Me) Higher and Higher" (1977); "We're All Alone" (1977); "The Way You Do the Things You Do" (1978); "You" (1978)

Mike Curb Congregation--"Burning Bridges" (1970/1)

Dawn (featuring Tony Orlando)--"Candida" (1970); "Knock Three Times" (1970/1); "I Play and Sing" (1971); "Tie a Yellow Ribbon Round the Ole Oak Tree" (1973); "Say, Has Anybody Seen My Sweet Gypsy Rose" (1973); "Who's in the Strawberry Patch With Sally" (1973); "Steppin' Out (Gonna Boogie Tonight)" (1974); "Look in My Eyes Pretty Woman" (1974/5); "He Don't Love You (Like I Love You)" (!975); "Mornin' Beautiful" (1975); "Cupid" (1976)

John Denver--"Take Me Home, Country Roads" (1971); "Rocky Mountain High" (1972/3); "Sunshine on My Shoulders" (1974); "Annie's Song" (1974); "Back Home Again" (1974); "Sweet Surrender" (1974/5); "Thank God I'm a Country Boy" (1975); "I'm Sorry" (1975); "Fly Away" (1975/6); "Looking For Space" (1976)

Sheena Easton--"Morning Train" (1981); "Modern Girl" (1981); "For Your Eyes Only" (1981); "You Could Have Been With Me" (1981/2); "When He Shines" (1982)

Rupert Holmes--"Escape (The Pina Colada Song)" (1979); "Him" (1980)

Mary MacGregor--"Torn Between Two Lovers" (1976/7)

Manhattan Transfer--"Operator" (1975); "Boy From New York City" (1981)

Barry Manilow--"Mandy" (1974/5); "It's a Miracle" (1975); "Could It Be Magic" (1975); "I Write the Songs" (1975/6); "Tryin' to Get the Feeling Again" (1976); "Weekend in New England" (1976/7); "Looks Like We Made It" (1977); "Can't Smile Without You" (1978); Even Now"

(1978); "Copacabana" (At the Copa)" (1978); "Ready to Take a Chance Again" (1978); "Somewhere in the Night" (1978/9); "Ships" (1979); "When I Wanted You" (1979/80); "I Made It Through the Rain" (1980/1); "The Old Songs" (1981)

Anne Murray--"Snowbird" (1970); "Danny's Song" (1973); "Love Song" (1973/4); "You Won't See Me" (1974); "You Needed Me" (1978); "I Just Fall in Love Again" (1979); "Broken Hearted Me" (1979); "Daydream Believer" (1979/80)

Olivia Newton-John--"If Not For You" (1971); "Let Me Be There" (1973/4); "If You Love Me (Let Me Know)" (1974); "I Honestly Love You" (1974); "Have You Ever Been Mellow" (1975); "Please Mr. Please" (1975); "Something Better to Do" (1975); "Come on Over" (1976); "Sam" (1977); "Hopelessly Devoted to You" (1978); "A Little More Love" (1978/9); "Deeper Than the Night" (1979); "Magic" (1980); "Physical" (1981); "Make a Move On Me" (1982); "Heart Attack" (1982)

Helen Reddy--"I Don't Know How to Love Him" (1971); "I Am Woman" (1972); "Peaceful" (1973); "Delta Dawn" (1973); "Leave Me Alone" (1973); "Keep on Singing" (1974); "You and Me Against the World" (1974); "Angie Baby" (1974); "Ain't No Way to Treat a Lady" (1975); "Somewhere in the Night" (1975/6); "You're My World" (1977)

B.J. Thomas--"I'm So Lonesome I Could Cry" (1966); "Mama" (1966); "The Eyes of a New York Woman" (1968); "Hooked on a Feeling" (1968/9); "Raindrops Keep Fallin' on My Head" 1969/70); "Everybody's Out of Town" (1970); "I Just Can't Help Believing" (1970); "No Love at All" (1971); "Rock and Roll Lullaby" (1972); "(Hey Won't You Play) Another Somebody Done Somebody Wrong Song" (1975); "Don't Worry Baby" (1977)

Bonnie Tyler--"It's a Heartache" (1978)

Pop Stylists

This subgenre owed more to the Tin Pan Alley tradition than it did to rock music. The impact of rock--both in terms of stylistic touches and performing flair--is obvious when those pop singers whose careers began after the mid-1950s are compared with their stylistic ancestors such as Frank Sinatra, Tony Bennett, and Doris Day.

Top Artists and Their Recordings

Engelbert Humperdinck--"Release Me" (1967); "There Goes My Everything" (1967); "The Last Waltz" (1967); "Am I That Easy to Forget" (1967/8); "A Man Without Love" (1968); "Winter World of Love" (1969/70); "After the Lovin'" (1976/7)

Tom Jones--"It's Not Unusual" (1965); "What's New Pussycat?" (1965); "With These Hands" (1965); "Thunderball" (1965/6); "Green, Green Grass of Home:" (1966/7); "Detroit City" (1967); "Delilah" (1968); "Love Me Tonight" (1969); "I'll Never Fall in Love Again" (1969); "Without Love" (1969/70); "Daughter of Darkness" (1970); "I (Who Have Nothing)" (1970); "Can't Stop Loving You" (1970); "She's a Lady" (1971); "Puppet Man"/"Resurrection Shuffle" (1971); "Say You'll Stay Until Tomorrow" (1977)

Bette Midler--"Do You Want to Dance?" (1972/3); "Boogie Woogie Bugle Boy" (1973); "The Rose" (1980)

Charlie Rich--"Behind Closed Doors" (1973); "The Most Beautiful Girl" (1973); "There Won't Be Anymore" (1974); "A Very Special Love Song" (1974)"; "I Love My Friend" (1974); "Every Time You Touch Me" (1975)

Barbra Streisand--"People" (1964); ""Stoney" (1970/1); "The Way We Were" (1973/4); "Evergreen" (1976/7); "My Heart Belongs to Me" (1977); "Songbird" (1978); "You Don't Bring Me Flowers" (w/Neil Diamond) (1978); "The Main Event/Fight" (1979); "No More Tears" (w/Donna Summer) (1979); "Woman in Love" (1980); "Guilty" (w/Barry Gibb) (1980/1); "What Kind of Fool" (w/Barry Gibb) (1981); "Comin' in and Out of Your Life" (1981/2)

Dionne Warwick--"Don't Make Me Over" (1962/3); "Anyone Who Had a Heart" (1963/4); "Walk on Bn" (1964); "Reach Out For Me" (1964); "Message to Michael" (1966); "Train and Boats and Planes" (1966); "I Just Don't Know What to Do With Myself" (1966); "Alfie" (1967); "I Say a Little Prayer" (1967); "(Theme From) Valley of the Dolls" (1968); "Do You Know the Way to San Jose" (1968); "Promises, Promises" (1968); "This Girl's in Love With You" (1969); "You've Lost That Lovin' Feeling" (1969); "I'll Never Fall in Love Again" (1969/70); "Then Came You" (w/The Spinners) (1974); "I'll Never Love This Way Again" (1979); "No Night So Long" (1980); "Heartbreaker" (w/Barry Gibb) (1982/3)

Andy Williams--"Canadian Sunset" (1956); "Butterfly" (1957); "I Like Your Kind of Love" (w/Peggy Powers) (1957); "Lips of Wine" (1957); "Are You Sincere" (1958); "Promise Me, Love" (1958);"The Hawaiian Wedding Song" (1958/9); "Lonely Street" (1959); "The Village of St. Bernadette" (1959/60); "Can't Get Used to Losing You" (1963); "Days of Wine and Roses" (1963); "Hopeless" (1963); "A Fool Never Learns" (1964); "On the Street Where You Live" (1964); "Dear Heart" (1964); "Happy Heart" (1969); "Love Story" (1971)

Pop Rock

These artists generally began their careers after the first wave of soft rock in the 1960s. Like such genre trailblazers as the Mamas and the Papas and the Association, rock arrangements are front-and-center. However, pop rockers also exhibit strong MOR leanings. If active in the pre-rock era, they might well have taken on more characteristics of the pop stylists.

Top Artists and Their Recordings

Toni Basil--"Mickey" (1982)

Laura Branigan--"Gloria" (1982)

The Captain and Tennille--"Love Will Keep Us Together" (1975); "The Way I Want to Touch You" (1975); "Lonely Night" (1976); "Shop Around" (1976); "Muskrat Love" (1976); "Can't Stop Dancin'" (1977); "You Never Done It Like That" (1978); "Do That to Me One More Time" (1979/80)

Mariah Carey--"Vision of Love" (1990); "Love Takes Time" (1990); "Someday" (1991); "I Don't Wanna Cry" (1991); "Emotions" (1991); "Can't Let Go" (1991/2); "Make It Happen" (1992); "I'll Be There" (1992); "Dreamlover" (1993); "Hero" (1993)

Eric Carmen--"All By Myself" (1975/6); "Never Gonna Fall in Love Again" (1976; "She Did It" (1977); "Change of Heart" (1978); "Hungry Eyes" (1987/8); "Make Me Lose Control" (1988)

Kim Carnes--"More Love" (1980); "Bette Davis Eyes" (1981); "Draw of the Cards" (1981); "Voyeur" (1982); "Crazy in the Night" (w/Kenny Rogers) (1985)

Celine Dion--"Where Does My Heart Beat Now" (1991); "Beauty and the Beast" (w/Peabo Bryson) (1992); "If You Asked Me To" (1992)

Dr. Hook (and the Medicine Show)--"Sylvia's Mother" (1972); "The Cover of 'Rolling Stone'" (1972/3); "Only Sixteen" (1976); "A Little Bit More" (1976); "Sharing the Night Together" (1978/9); "When You're in Love With a Beautiful Woman" (1979); "Better Love Next Time" (1979/80); "Sexy Eyes" (1980); "Baby Makes Her Blue Jeans Talk" (1982)

Fleetwood Mac--"Over My Head" (1975/6); "Rhiannon" (1976); "Say You Love Me" (1976); "Go Your Own Way" (1977); "Dreams" (1977); "Don't Stop" (1977); "You Make Loving Fun" (1977); "Tusk" (1979); "Sara" (1979/80); "Think About Me" (1980); "Hold Me" (1982); "Gypsy" (1982); "Love in Store" (1982/3)

Table 93

Herb Alpert (& the Tijuana Brass)

For a time in the mid-1960s, Herb Alpert's records were outselling those of the Beatles; during the week of May 21, 1966, he had five albums in the Top Twenty of the *Billboard*

Top LP's chart (including three of the top eight positions). However, he also made a significant impact with the record industry as a businessman, writing and producing many hits as well as forming A&M Records—one of the most successful artist-owned labels ever established—with Jerry Moss.

Born March 31, 1935, in Los Angeles, Alpert began his recording career with RCA as Dore Alpert shortly after a stint in the Army. He would then sign with Dot Records in 1959, again with no real success.

Teaming up with future music business mogul Lou Adler, he help write such best-selling recordings as Sam Cooke's "Wonderful World" and "Only Sixteen." The duo adopted the moniker Dante and the Evergreens to record a cover of the Hollywood Argyles' "Alley Oop" (1960). He would also produce tracks for the likes of Jan and Dean.

In 1962, Alpert combined with Moss to found A&M Records; his group, the Tijuana Brass, recorded the firm's first hit for only sixty-five dollars, "The Lonely Bull" (A&M 703; 1962). A&M would go on to be recognized as the largest independent label worldwide; by the early 1970s its roster would include such artists as Joe Cocker, the Carpenters, Free, Spooky Tooth, and Sergio Mendes.

It took a few years for Alpert's own recordings with the TJB to peak commercially. His debut release, *The Lonely Bull* (A&M 101; 1962; #24), established the group's trademark sound, a light, punchy blend of mariachi music, mainstream easy listening pop, and pre-smooth jazz. Follow-up albums—*Herb Alpert's Tiajuna Brass, Volume 2* (A&M 103; 1963; #17), *South of the Border* (A&M 108; 1965; #6), and *Whipped Cream & Ither Delights* (A&M 110; 1965; #1)—garnered increasingly greater sales. The latter LP, on the strength of the hit single, "A Taste of Honey" (A&M 775; 1965; #7), and an eye-catching cover featuring model Dolores Erickson covered only with shaving cream, elevated Alpert to the top of the pop scene. "A Taste of Honey"—with its catchy stop-and-start bass drum figure—would go on to win 1995 Grammy awards for record of the year, best non-jazz instrumental performance, best instrumental arrangement, and best-engineered record.

For the remainder of the 1960s, the TJB remained a hot commercial property, doing well with *Going Places* (A&M 112; 1966; #1), *What Now My Love* (A&M 4114; 1966; #1), *S.R.O.* (A&M 4119; 1966; #2), *Sounds Like* (A&M 4124; 1967; #1), *Herb Alpert's Ninth* (A&M 4134; 1967; #4), and *The Beat of the Brass* (A&M 4146; 1968; #1). Although public expectations limited the extent of his musical explorations, Alpert attempted some incremental variations on the group's formula, most notably the vocal ballad, "This Guy's in Love with You" (A&M 929; 1969; #1). By the late 1960s, however, his music was deemed out of step with the more serious tone of the times, and TJB albums gradually fell out of favor.

During the 1970s Alpert attempted a number of approaches to re-tool his sound, including an Afro-jazz fusion collaboration with Hugh Masekela (*Herb Alpert/Hugh Masekela*; Horizon 728; 1978; #65). After aborting a try at recording TJB hits disco style, he used the remaining studio time to explore material a jazz-pop mode more suited to his personal tastes. One of these takes, a slow-down dance song, co-written by his cousin, "Rise" (A&M 2151; 1979), reached number one on the *Billboard Hot 100*.

Alpert's subsequent releases have met with mixed success, his biggest success coming with "Diamonds" (A&M 2929; 1987; #5), which featured a guest vocal by then-emerging star Janet Jackson. Since selling A&M to PolyGram in 1990 for more than $500 million, he has turned his attention to a wide range of projects. In addition to forming a new label with Moss, Almo Sounds, in 1994, he has exhibited his expressionist paintings, co-produced Broadway musicals such as *Angels in America* and *Jelly's Last Jam*, and established a philanthropic organization, the Herb Alpert Foundation.

Table 94

Lovin' Spoonful

Founded by singer/songwriter John Sebastian and lead guitarist Zal Yanovsky, the New York-based Lovin' Spoonful evolved from jug band music to folk rock prior to its first release, the Top Ten hit "Do You Believe In Magic" (Kama Sutra 201; 1965). Due to first-rate musicianship and Sebastian's extraordinary composing skills, the band's records—dubbed "good time music" by the music press—were consistent best-sellers between 1965-1968. During that span, the Spoonful released eight hit albums—including the soundtracks to Woody Allen's *What's Up, Tiger Lily?* (Kama Sutra 8053; 1966) and Francis Ford Coppola's *You're a Big Boy Now* (Kama Sutra 8058; 1967)—and charted thirteen singles, most notably "You Didn't Have To Be So Nice" (Kama Sutra 205; 1965), "Daydream" (Kama Sutra 208; 1966), "Did You Ever Have To Make Up Your Mind?" (Kama Sutra 209; 1966), "Summer In the City" (Kama Sutra 211; 1966), and "Nashville Cats" (Kama Sutra; 1966).

Bad publicity surrounding the arrest of Yanovsky and bassist Steve Boone for drug possession in 1967 resulted in waning popularity and the dissolution of the group the following year. Drummer Joe Butler formed a new edition of the Spoonful in the late 1960s. The resulting album sold poorly, however, and Butler moved on to Broadway acting and sound editing in Hollywood.

Boosted by his Woodstock Festival performance, Sebastian enjoyed a moderately successful solo career. His "Welcome Back" (Reprise 1349; 1976), the theme song for TV's *Welcome Back Kotter*, reached number one on *Billboard's* Hot 100.

The original group members reunited to perform "Do You Believe in Magic" in the Paul Simon film, *One Trick Pony* (1980). Boone, Butler, and sometime member Jerry Yester began touring as the Spoonful in 1991. [Romanowski and George-Warren. 1995]

Power Pop

Power pop has been a commercially viable style since the late 1960s. It is a retro genre built around the merger of a hard rock sound with mainstream pop music sensibilities. The emphasis is on melodic songs, uncluttered studio arrangements, and a straightforward vocal (often featuring group harmonies) delivery. Perhaps the most notable instrumental features consists of ringing guitar chords along the lines of the catchy riff opening the Searchers' "Needles and Pins" (1964).

The chief influences behind power pop were (1) classic American rock 'n' roll as exemplified by Buddy Holly and the Crickets, Eddie Cochran, and the Everly Brothers; (2) the British Invasion bands from the 1964-1965 period, particularly the Beatles; and (3) the more melodic offerings of seminal heavy metal groups such as Black Sabbath and Deep Purple. Virtuosity is never a desirable end here; rather, the goal is tight, tuneful ensemble playing where the whole equals something far greater than the separate parts.

The style originated during the early days of progressive rock and heavy metal primarily as a nostalgic throw-back to the lighter pop sounds of the Beatles, the Kinks, and other mid-1960s hit-making bands. Early pioneers such as Badfinger and the Raspberries achieved a considerable degree of success with their singles releases. However, later waves of power pop bands found this market to be increasingly marginalized. Practitioners during the late 1970s and early 1980s found refuge under the new wave moniker; from the mid-1980s onward, they have tended to be lumped together with the alternative bands.

Top Artists and Their Recordings

Aztec Camera--*High Land, Hard Rain* (1983); *Knife* (1984); *Aztec Camera* (1985)

The Babys--*The Babys* (1977); *Broken Heart* (1977); *Head First* (1979); *Union Jacks* (1980); *On the Edge* (1980)

Badfinger--*Magic Christian Music* (1970); *No Dice* (1970); *Straight Up* (1971); *Ass* (1973); *Badfinger* (1974); *Wish You Were Here* (1974); *Airwaves* (1979); *Say No More* (1981)

Big Star--*Radio City* (1971); *Big Star* (1972); *Third Album* (1978)

The Bluebells--*Sisters* (1984)

The Bongos--*Drums Along the Hudson* (1982); *Numbers With Wings* (1983); *Beat Hotel* (1984)

Chameleons U.K.--*Strange Times* (1986)

Cheap Trick--*In Color* (1977); *Heaven Tonight* (1978); *Cheap Trick at Budokan* (1979); *Dream Police* (1979); *Found All the Parts* (1980); *All Shook Up* (1980); *One On One* (1982); *Next Position Please* (1983); *Standing On the Edge* (1985); *The Doctor* (1986); *Lap of Luxury* (1988); *Busted* (1990)

Marshall Crenshaw--*Marshall Crenshaw* (1982); *Field Day* (1983); *Downtown* (1985)

Ian Gomm--*Gomm With the Wind* (1979)

The Inmates--*First Offence* (1979)

The Knack--*Get the Knack* (1979); *But the Little Girls Understand* (1980); *Round Trip* (1981)

Nick Lowe--*Pure Pop For Now People* (1978); *Labour of Lust* (1979); *Nick the Knife* (1982); *The Abominable Showman* (1983); *Nick Lowe and his Cowboy Outfit* (1984); *The Rose of England* (1985); *Party of One* (1990)

The Members--*At the Chelsea Nightclub* (1979); *1980: The Choice Is Yours* (1980)

The Plimsouls--*The Plimsouls* (1981); *Everywhere at Once* (1983)

The Raspberries--*The Raspberries* (1972); *Fresh* (1972); *Side 3* (1973); *Starting Over* (1974)

The Records--*The Records* (1979)

The Revillos/The Rezillos--*Can't Stand the Rezillos* (1978); *Mission Accomplished* (1979); *Rev Up* (1980)

Rockpile--*Seconds of Pleasure* (1980)

The Romantics--*The Romantics* (1979); *National Breakout* (1980); *Strictly Personal* (1981); *In Heat* (1983); *Rhythm Romance* (1985)

The Rubinoos--*The Rubinoos* (1977); *Back to the Drawing Board* (1979)

Phil Seymour--*Phil Seymour* (1981)

The Shirts--*The Shirts* (1978); *Street Light Shine* (1979); *Inner Sleeve* (1980)

The Shoes--*Black Vinyl Shoes* (1978); *Present Tense* (1979); *Tongue Twister* (1980)

Smokie/Smokey--*Midnight Cafe* (1976); *Bright Lights and Back Alleys* (1977); *Montreux Album* (1978)

Sneaker--*Sneaker* (1981)

Translator--*Heartbeats and Triggers* (1982); *No Time Like Now* (1983); *Evening of the Harvest* (1984)

20/20--*20/20* (1979); *Look Out!* (1981)

Dwight Twilley (Band)--*Sincerely* (1976); *Twilley Don't Mind* (1977); *Twilley* (1979); *Scuba Divers* (1982); *Jungle* (1984)

The Undertones--*The Undertones* (1980)

Album Oriented Rock (AOR)

AOR--sometimes referred to as Album Oriented Radio--arose in the early 1970s as part of a concerted effort by FM executives--in collusion with the major record labels--to standardize playlists. Taking the Top 40 format dominating AM radio, AOR consisted of tight, scaled-down song rotations, usually one or two selections preferred by the artists themselves (or the listening audience, if the street-level verdict was unanimous in nature) from the bestselling rock albums of the day. It was geared to album, rather than 45 r.p.m. single, sales; many of the playlist selections were never released as singles.

AOR has never constituted a stylistic grouping; playlist inclusions have always been defined by radio programmer decisions. The artists enjoying heavy AOR rotation represented a wide range of musical genres. Nevertheless, some general characteristics of this have been discerned by industry observers. In his rambling survey of AOR appearing in *The Year in Rock, 1981-82*, J.D. Considine termed it "hard pop"; that is, "hard, because its sound derives from the contours of hard rock and heavy metal; pop, because its formal structure is oriented toward popsong melodicism, not the sprawling, riff-based jamming of traditional heavy metal." He adds that critics of the category dismiss it as entertainment (as opposed to "music"), whereas supporters have pointed to its propensity for selling records. AOR was also widely criticized for its tendency to bar black artists from playlists.

The genre peaked in popularity during the mid-1970s. The emergence of other commercially viable radio formats in the late 1970s and early 1980s--mostly notably disco, country pop, rock 'n' roll oldies, adult contemporary, and college radio/alternative--severely compromised its front-running status. AOR's appeal was also diminished by the decline of mainstream rock acts such as Bad Company and the Doobie Brothers. The format remains a radio fixture, albeit in a secondary role--both within radio and in relation to other media broadcast outlets--as a hit-making entity.

Top Artists and Their Recordings

Aerosmith—*Aerosmith* (1973); *Get Your Wings* (1974); *Toys in the Attic* (1975); *Rocks* (1976)

Artful Dodger--*Artful Dodger* (1975; *Honor Among Thieves* (1976); *Babes on Broadway* (1977)

Asia--*Asia* (1982)

Bachman-Turner Overdrive--*Bachman-Turner Overdrive* (1973); *Bachman-Turner Overdrive II* (1974); *Not Fragile* (1974); *Four Wheel Drive* (1975); *Head On* (1976); *Freeways* (1977); *Street Action* (1978); *Rock N' Roll Nights* (1979)

Bad Company--*Bad Company* (1974); *Straight Shooter* (1975); *Rub With the Pack* (1976); *Burning Sky* (1977); *Desolation Angels* (1979)

Pat Benatar--*In the Heat of the Night* (1979); *Crimes of Passion* (1980); *Precious Time* (1981); *Get Nervous* (1982); *Live From Earth* (1983); *Tropico* (1984)

Boston--*Boston* (1976); *Don't Look Back* (1978); *Third Stage* (1986)

Bon Jovi--*Bon Jovi* (1984); *7800 Fahrenheit* (1985); *Slippery When Wet* (1986); *New Jersey* (1988); *Blaze of Glory* (1990); *Keep the Faith* (1992)

Rocky Burnette--*The Son of Rock and Roll* (1980)

Rick Derringer--*All American Boy* (1973); *Spring Fever* (1975); *Derringer* (1976); *Sweet Evil* (1977); *Derringer Live* (1977)

The Doobie Brothers--*Toulouse Street* (1972); *The Captain and Me* (1973); *What Were Once Vices Are Now Habits* (1974); *Stampede* (1975); *Livin' on the Fault Line* (1977); *Minute By Minute* (1978); *One Step Closer* (1980)

Foreigner--*Foreigner* (1977); *Double Vision* (1978); *Head Games* (1979); *4* (1981); *Agent Provocateur* (1985); *Inside Information* (1987)

Heart--*Dreamboat Annie* (1976); *Little Queen* (1977); *Magazine* (1978); *Dog and Butterfly* (1978); *Bebe Le Strange* (1980); *Private Audition* (1982); *Passionworks* (1983); *Heart* (1985); *Bad Animals* (1987); *Brigade* (1990)

The Jefferson Starship--*Dragon Fly* (1974); *Red Octopus* (1975); *Spitfire* (1976); *Earth* (1978); *Freedom at Point Zero* (1979); *Modern Times* (1981); *Winds of Change* (1982); *Nuclear Furniture* (1984)

Joan Jett and the Blackhearts--*Bad Reputation* (1981); *I Love Rock-n-Roll* (1981); *Album* (1983); *Glorious Results of a Misspent Youth* (1984); *Good Music* (1986); *Up Your Alley* (1988); *The Hit List* (1990)

Journey--*Journey* (1975); *Look Into the Future* (1976); *Next* (1977); *Infinity* (1978); *Evolution* (1979); *Departure* (1980); *Captured* (1981); *Escape* (1981); *Frontiers* (1983); *Raised On Radio* (1986)

Greg Kihn Band--*Next of Kihn* (1978); *With the Naked Eye* (1979); *Glass House Rock* (1980); *Rockihnroll* (1981); *Kihntinued* (1982); *Kihnspiracy* (1983); *Kihntagious* (1984); *Citizen Kihn* (1985)

Meat Loaf--*Bat Out of Hell* (1977); *Dead Ringer* (1981); *Bad Attitude* (1985)

John Cougar Mellencamp--*John Cougar* (1979); *Nothin' Matters and What If It Did* (1980); *American Fool* (1982); *Uh-Huh* (1983); *Scarecrow* (1985); *The Lonesome Jubilee* (1987); *Big Daddy* (1989); *Whenever We Wanted* (1991)

Eddie Money--*Eddie Money* (1978); *Life For the Taking* (1979); *Playing For Keeps* (1980); *No Control* (1982); *Where's the Party?* (1983); *Can't Hold Back* (1986); *Nothing to Lose* (1988); *Right Here* (1992)

Orleans--*Let There Be Music* (1975); *Waking and Dreaming* (1976); *Forever* (1979)

The Outfield--*Play Deep* (1985); *Bangin'* (1987); *Voices of Babylon* (1989); *Diamond Days* (1990)

Pablo Cruise--*Pablo Cruise* (1975); *Lifeline* (1976); *A Place in the Sun* (1977); *Worlds Away* (1978); *Part of the Game* (1979); *Reflector* (1981)

Tom Petty (and the Heartbreakers)--*Tom Petty and the Heartbreakers* (1977); *You're Gonna Get It!* (1978); *Damn the Torpedoes* (1979); *Hard Promises* (1991); *Long After Dark* (1982); *Southern Accents* (1985); *Pack Up the Plantation - Live!* (1985); *Let Me Up (I've Had Enough)* 1987); *Full Moon Fever* (1889); *Into the Great Wide Open* (1991)

The Power Station--*The Power Station* (1985)

Quarterflash--*Quarterflash* (1981); *Take Another Picture* (1983); *Back Into Blue* (1985)

REO Speedwagon--*Ridin' the Storm Out* (1974); *Lost in a Dream* (1974); *This Time We Mean It* (1975); *R.E.O.* (1976); *REO Speedwagon Live/You Get What You Pay For* (1977); *You Can Tune a Piano, But You Can't Tuna Fish* (1978); *Nine Lives* (1979); *Hi Infidelity* (1980); *Good Trouble* (1982); *Wheels Are Turnin'* (1984); *Life As We Know It* (1987)

Bob Seger (and the Silver Bullet Band)--*Smokin' O.P.'s* (1972); *Back in '72* (1973); *Beautiful Loser* (1975); *"Live" Bullet* (1976); *Night Moves* (1976); *Stranger in Town* (1978); *Against the Wind* (1980); *Nine Tonight* (1981); *The Distance* (1983); *Like a Rock* (1986); *The Fire Inside* (1991)

Sniff 'n' the Tears—*Fickle Heart* (1979); *Love Action* (1981)

Bruce Springsteen (and the E Street Band)--*Greeting From Asbury Park, N.J.* (1973); *The Wild, The Innocent and the E Street Shuffle* (1973); *Born to Run* (1975); *Darkness on the Edge of Town* (1978); *The River* (1980); *Nebraska* (1982); *Born in the U.S.A.* (1984); *Bruce Springsteen and the E Street Band Live/1975-85* (1986); *Tunnel of Love* (1987); *Human Touch* (1992); *Lucky Town* (1992)

Billy Squier--*The Tale of the Tape* (1980); *Don't Say No* (1981); *Emotions in Motion* (1982); *Signs of Life* (1984); *Enough Is Enough* (1986); *Hear and Now* (1989); *Creatures of Habit* (1991)

Styx--*Styx I* (1972); *Styx II* (1973); *The Serpent Is Rising* (1974); *Man of Miracles* (1974); *Equinox* (1975); *Crystal Ball* (1976); *The Grand Illusion* (1977); *Pieces of Eight* (1978); *Cornerstone* (1979); *Paradise Theater* (1981); *Kilroy Was Here* (1983); *Caught in the Act - Live* (1984); *Edge of the Century* (1990)

Survivor--*Survivor* (1980); *Premonition* (1981); *Eye of the Tiger* (1982); *Caught in the Game* (1983); *Vital Signs* (1984); *When Seconds Count* (1986); *Too Hot to Sleep* (1988)

Tommy Tutone--*Tommy Tutone* (1980); *Tommy Tutone - 2* (1982); *National Emotion* (1983)

Toto--*Toto* (1978); *Hydra* (1979); *Turn Back* (1981); *Toto IV* (1982); *Isolation* (1984); *Dune* (1984); *Fahrenheit* (1986); *The Seventh One* (1988)

Table 95

Boston

Boston's success has defied many music business tenets; allowing considerable time to elapse between releases, with virtually no photo-ops to keep the group in the public eye, yet enjoying multi-platinum sales with a richly textured, power guitar sound that remains essentially unchanged since the release of the first album in 1976. That release, eponymously titled *Boston* (Columbia 34188), was the brainchild of guitarist

Tom Scholz. An unlikely rock star, Scholz earned a master's degree in mechanical engineering from MIT and, as a senior product designer for Polaroid Corporation, was limited to creating his music during leisure hours. His demo tapes, produced in his own twelve-track basement studio, led to a recording contract with Epic Records. These tracks formed the core of the album, although Scholz and his supporting band—including vocalist Brad Delp, guitarist Barry Goudreau, bassist Fran Sheehan, and drummer Sib Hashian—recut some of the material on the West Coast with producer John Boylan. *Boston* was a huge success, selling more than eleven million copies; in 1995, *Billboard* called it the third-best-selling LP ever, behind Michael Jackson's *Thriller* and Fleetwood Mac's *Rumours*.

The follow-up release, *Don't Look Back* (Columbia 35050; 1978), although reaching number one, sold only six million copies. Apparently concerned about a further erosion of public interest, Scholz spent eight years working on the next album. When *Third Stage* (MCA 6188) became available in 1986, Scholz and Delp—whose soaring vocals helped define the group's intricately layered sound—were the only members left from the original lineup. Driven by the number one single, "Amanda" (MCA 52756; 1986), the album topped the charts, becoming a four-million seller. At this point, Scholz's creative focus was compromised by a series of lawsuits involving former band member Goudreau and CBS Records. He also found time to invented the Rockman, a small guitar amplifier with headphones used by many musicians. With Delp having departed in 1991 to form a band called RTZ with Goudreau, Scholz was forced to dispense, once and for all, with the fiction of group collaboration. Nevertheless, utilizing a new studio built from the money won in his successful countersuit of CBS, Schloz produced a fourth album, *Walk On* (MCA), in 1994.

Table 96

Dire Straits

Dire Straits are a testament that a band can be out-of-step with prevailing fashions and still find success. Their laid-back blues-rock, accented by subtle, often sly, lyrics and Mark Knopfler's Dylanesque vocals, was nearly overwhelmed by the flood of disco and punk (later, postpunk) recordings beginning in the late 1970s. Extraordinary musicianship (highlighted by Knopfler's peerless lead guitar work) and subtle studio production work did enable the band to find commercial success, although the success of their album releases varied to a considerable degree.

The driving force behind Dire Straits was lead singer/guitarist/songwriter Knopfler, who decided to go into music full time after several years as a teacher. He assembled the band during 1976-1977; the final lineup included his brother, David, on rhythm guitar, bassist John Illsley, and drummer Pick Withers. After having their demo tapes rejected by vitually every label in England, Phonogram Records signed them in 1978 upon hearing "Sultans of Swing." Newly recorded (Warner Bros. 8736; 1978; #4 US), the single first became a hit in Holland, and then in much of Europe and the United States. With Warner Bros. acquiring their U.S. distribution rights, the band's first two LPs, *Dire Straits* (Warner Bros. 3266; 1978; #5 UK, #2 US) and *Communique* (Warner Bros. 3330; 1979; #5 UK, #11 US), were awarded gold records by the RIAA (the former ultimately selling for than eleven million copies worldwide). Furthermore, *Billboard* would designate them number one in its New LP Artists category for 1979.

With the release of *Making Movies* (Warner Bros. 3480; 1980; ##4 UK, #19 US) and *Love Over Gold* (Warner Bros. 23728; 1982; #1 UK, #19 US), the band's limitations—most notably, Knopfler's monochrome vocals and undistinguished melodies with an emphasis on minor keys—led to a decline in sales. Apparently considering new directions, the band treaded water with a couple of transitional releases, the retro EP, *Twisting by the Pool* (Warner Bros. 29800; 1983; #53 US), which celebrated Knopfler's love of the twangy rock 'n' roll popularized by the Shadows and the Ventures, and the live *Alchemy* (Warner Bros. 25085; 1984; #3 UK, #46 US).

Brothers in Arms (Warner Bros. 25264; 1985; #1 UK, #1 US) become the band's most artistically and commercially successful album, eventually selling more than twenty-six million copies on the strength of superb material—including three hit singles the MTV-friendly "Money for Nothing" (Warner Bros. 28950; 1985; #4 UK, #1 US), the Cajun-inflected "Walk of Life" (Warner Bros. 28878; 1985; #2 UK, #7 US), and reflective "So Far Away" (Warner Bros. 28729; 1986; #19 US)—pioneering digital production work tailored to the emerging compact disc medium. Perhaps recognizing the limitations of the group format as well as the futility of trying to top *Brothers in Arms*, Knopfler's decided to concentrate on outside projects, most notably, producing albums for Aztec Camera and Randy Newman, writing "Private Dancer" for Tina Turner, scoring various films (*Local Hero*, 1983; *Cal*, 1984; *Comfort and Joy*, 1984; *The Princess Bride*, 1987; and *Last Exit to Brooklyn*, 1989), session work for Joan Armatrading, a recorded collaboration with Chet Atkins—*Neck and Neck* (Columbia 45307; 1990; #41 UK; received three Grammy awards)—and a release as part of the country-oriented Notting Hillbillies, *Missing...Presumed Having a Good Time* (Warner Bros. 26147; 1990; #2 UK, #52 US).

Two more Dire Straits LPs—*On Every Street* (Warner Bros. 26680; 1991; #1 UK, #12 US), a return to the group's funky, laid-back style, and the live *On the Night* (Warner Bros. 45259; 1993; #4 UK)—would appear in the early 1990s. Perhaps due in part to the comparatively limited interest they generated, Knopfler has gone on to record a couple solo albums and compose for more films. In 2000 he would receive the Order of the British Empire medal for his contributions to the country.

Table 97

Doobie Brothers

The Doobie Brothers switched personnel and musical styles on a regular basis; the band remained popular, however, throughout these changes. Although not an innovative act, the Doobies were a case in point that high quality recorded music can be derivative, if adequate attention is placed on songcraft, tight ensemble playing, and competent production values.

The band formed in 1969 as a Northern California trio—guitarist/songwriter Tom Johnston, drummer John Hartman, and bassist Greg Murphy (replaced later that year by Dave Shogren, who in turn gave way to Tiran Porter)—named Pud. With the addition of singer/rhythm guitarist/songwriter Patrick Simmons in 1970, the Doobies began to gel. A demonstration tape led to a contract with Warner Bros., but the debut LP, *The Doobie Brothers* (Warner Bros. 1919; 1971), was only marginally successful.

Toulouse Street (Warner Bros. 2634; 1972; #21; on the charts for 119 weeks), which included the hit singles "Listen to the Music" (Warner Bros. 7619; 1972; #11) and "Jesus Is Just Alright" (Warner Bros. 7661; 1972; #35), catapulted the Doobie Brothers into the public eye. These recordings—along with the next two LPs, *The Captain and Me* (Warner Bros. 2694; 1973; #7) and *What Were Once Vices Now Are Habits* (Warner Bros. 2750; 1974; #4)—portrayed a populist, laid-back biker band. Best-selling singles such as "Long Train Runnin'" (Warner Bros. 7698; 1973; #8), "China Grove" (Warner Bros. 7728; 1973; #15), and "Black Water" (Warner Bros. 8062; 1974; #1) exuded an infectious blend of funky roots rock and smooth arrangements that made them a fixture on both AM and FM radio.

The band's sound began to evolve noticeably in the mid-1970s as talented new members were recruited. Jeff "Skunk" Baxter, a session guitarist formerly with Ultimate Spinach and Steely Dan, placed his stamp on jazz/R&B-oriented *Stampede* (Warner Bros. 2835; 1975; #4). Another Steely Dan associate, vocalist/pianist/songwriter Michael McDonald, came abroad for *Takin' It to the Streets* (Warner Bros. 2899, 1976; #8), endowing it and future releases—*Livin' on the Fault Line* (Warner Bros. 3045; 1977; #10), *Minute by Minute* (Warner Bros. 3193, 1978; #1), and *One Step Closer* (Warner Bros. 3452; 1980; #3)—with a more urbane polish and broader instrumental palette. Thoroughly dominated by McDonald, *Minute by Minute* would win four Grammys: Best Pop Vocal Performance by a Duo, Group or Chorus as well as Record of the Year, Song of the Year, and Best Arrangement Accompanying Vocalists (by McDonald) for "What a Fool Believes" (Warner Bros. 8725; 1979; #1).

Changing musical trends and other attractive career options for band members led to a breakup in 1982. Key members from both early and later editions of the Doobies reunited for selected concerts in 1987. An album, *Cycles* (Capitol 90371; 1989; #17)—which most closely approximated the early 1970s recordings and featured the hit single, "The Doctor" (Capitol 44376; 1989; #9)—was released in 1989. The band has remained active since that time, producing *Brotherhood* (Capitol 94623; 1991), *Rockin' Down the Highway: The Wildlife Concert* (Sony Legacy 484452; 1996), and *Sibling Rivalry* (Pyramid; 2000).

Table 98

John "Cougar" Mellencamp, October 7, 1951-

John Mellencamp has evolved from an AOR-friendly hard rocker in the Bob Seger-Bruce Springsteen mold to the critically-hailed exponent of country and R&B-flavored roots rock. Born in Seymour, Indiana with a form of spina bifida, he started his first band at age fourteen. After attending community college and trying a series of blue-collar jobs, he relocated in New York City in the mid-1970s with a backlog of self-penned songs with hopes of establishing a music career. There, he signed with David Bowie's manager, Tony DeFries, who assigned him the moniker "Johnny Cougar" and help secure a reported million dollar deal with Main Man. The resulting album, Chestnut Street Incident (Main Man 601; 1976), was a commercial failure, and he was dropped by parent company MCA.

Signing with Riva Records in the late 1970s (to his frustration, as John Cougar), Mellencamp began building a following through well-crafted recordings—including the hit singles "I Need a Lover" (Riva 202; 1979), "This Time" (Riva 205; 1980), and "Ain't Even Done with the Night" (Riva 207; 1981)—and constant touring. His commercial breakthrough came with American Fool (Riva 7501; 1982, #1), driven by Grammy-winning "Hurts So Good" (Riva 209; 1982; #2), "Jack and Diane" (Riva 210; 1982; #1, "Hand to Hold On To" (Riva 211; 1982), all of which were in heavy MTV rotation. The 1980s were a watershed decade for him, including the following Top Ten albums: Un-Huh (Riva 7504; 1983), Scarecrow (Riva/Mercury 824865; 1985), The Lonesome Jubilee (Mercury 832465; 1987), and Big Daddy (Mercury 838220; 1989). In addition to producing his own recordings, he was in demand to perform similar duties for other artists, including Mitch Ryder's Never Kick a Sleeping Dog (1983) and James McMurtry's Too Long in the Wasteland (1989).

He was a co-organizer of Farm Aid along with Willie Nelson and Neil Young in 1985; he wound go on to appear at Farm Aid concerts I through VI. He has given more concerts over the years to bring attention to the problems of the American farmer, and, in 1987, he testified before a congressional subcommittee. His strong political activism also extended crticism of beer- and cigarette-company sponsorship of concert tours and the refusal to allow his music to be employed in commercials.

By the 1990s, Mellencamp's recordings were less commercially successful, due in part to their more introspective tone and greater reliance on folk instrumentation. He was now moving into other fields, directing and acting in the film, Falling From Grace (1992; scripted by author Larry McMurtry), and mounting exhibitions of his paintings. He suffered a heart attack in 1994, but has continued to remain active as a performer and recording artist.

Funk

Funk was a dance-oriented offshoot of soul music which originated in the late 1960s. (The term itself had been widely used in hip urban African American circles since the early decades of the twentieth century; it carried several different off-color meanings.) Sylvester Stewart, leader of the band Sly and the Family Stone, was a notable pioneer of the genre. He developed his sound as a session musician in small San Francisco recording studios during the mid-1960s before going on to superstardom with hits such as "Everyday People" and "Dance to the Music."

By the time Sly experienced career burnout in the early 1970s, the chief features of funk were sharply delineated for the next of practitioners: (1) a strong rhythmic emphasis usually centered around a repetitious, thickly-textured bass pattern, and (2) a greater reliance on instrumental ensemble playing than had been typical of either rhythm and blues or soul. Classic exponents of the style who achieved significant success included George Clinton's Parliament/Funkadelic combine, The Ohio Players, Kool and the Gang, and Earth, Wind and Fire.

The genre dominated the black music scene throughout the 1970s, absorbing elements of disco and merging its heavy backbeat with punk's rebellious attitude to create a new stylistic offshoot, funk-punk. The innovative vanguard of funk was eventually co-opted by the growing rap movement of the 1980s.

Top Artists and Their Recordings

Bootsy's Rubber Band--*Stretchin' Out in Bootsy's Rubber Band* (1976); *Ahh...The Name Is Bootsy, Baby!* (1977); *Bootsy? Player of the Year* (1978); *This Boot Is Make For Fonk-n* (1979); *Ultra Wave* (1980)

Brass Construction--*Brass Construction* (1976); *Brass Construction II* (1976); *Brass Construction III* (1977); *Brass Construction IV* (1978); *Brass Construction 5* (1979); *Brass Construction 6* (1980); *Attitudes* (1982); *Conservations* (1983)

Brick--*Good High* (1976; *Brick* (1977); *Stoneheart* (1979); *Waiting on You* (1980); *Summer Heat* (1981)

The Brothers Johnson--*Look Out For #1* (1976); *Right on Time* (1977); *Blam!* (1978); *Light Up the Night* (1980); *Winners* (1981); *Blast!* (1983) *Out of Control* (1984)

George Clinton--*Computer Games* (1982); *You Shouldn't-Nuf Bit Fish* (1984); *Some of My Best Jokes Are Friends* (1985); *R & B Skeletons in the Closet* (1986); *The Cinderella Theory* (1989)

The Commodores--*Machine Gun* (1974); *Caught in the Act* (1975); *Movin' On* (1975); *Hot on the Tracks* (1976); *Commodores* (1977); *Commodores Live!* (1977); *Natural High* (1978); *Midnight Magic* (1979); *Heroes* (1980)

Con Funk Shun--*Secrets* (1977); *Loveshine* (1978); *Candy* (1979); *Spirit of Love* (1980); *Touch* (1980); *Con Funk Shun 7* (1981); *To the Max* (1982); *Fever* (1983); *Electric Lady* (1985); *Burnin' Love* (1986)

Earth, Wind and Fire--*Head to the Sky* (1973); *Open Our Eyes* (1974); *That's the Way of the World* (1975); *Gratitude* (1975); *Spirit* (1976); *All 'N All* (1977); *I Am* (1979); *Faces* (1980); *Raise!* (1981); *Powerlight* (1983)

Fatback--*Fired Up 'N' Kickin'* (1978); *Fatback XII* (1979); *Hot Box* (1980); *14 Karat* (1980)

Funkadelic--*Funkadelic* (1970); *Free Your Mind...And Your Ass Will Follow* (1970); *Maggot Brain* (1971); *America Eats Its Young* (1972); *Cosmic Slop* (1973); *Standing on the Verge of Getting It On* (1974); *Let's Take It to the Stage* (1975); *Tales of Kidd Funkadelic* (1976); *Hardcore Jollies* (1976); *One Nation Under a Groove* (1978); *Uncle Jam Wants You* (1978); The Electric Spanking of War Babies (1981)

The Gap Band--*The Gap Band II* (1979); *The Gap Band III* (1980); *Gap Band IV* (1982); *Gap Band V - Jammin'* (1983); *Gap Band VI* (1985)

Graham Central Station--*Graham Central Station* (1974); *Release Yourself* (1974); *Ain't No 'Bout-A-Doubt It* (1975); *Mirror* (1976); *Now Do U Wanta Dance* (1977)

Heatwave--*Too Hot to Handle* (1977); *Central Heating* (1978); *Hot Property* (1979); *Candles* (1980)

Hot Chocolate--*Cicero Park* (1975); *Hot Chocolate* (1975); *Every 1's a Winner* (1979)

Instant Funk--*Instant Funk* (1979)

Junior--*"Ji"* (1982); *Inside Lookin' Out* (1983)

Klique--*Try It Out* (1983)

Kool and the Gang--*Live at the Sex Machine* (1971); *Wild and Peaceful* (1973); *Light of Worlds* (1974); *Spirit of the Boogie* (1975); *Love & Understanding* (1976); *Ladies Night* (1979); *Celebrate!* (1980); *Something Special* (1981); *As One* (1982); *In the Heart* (1983); *Emergency* (1984); *Forever* (1986)

The Ohio Players--*Pleasure* (1973); *Ecstasy* (1973); *Skin Tight* (1974); *Fire* (1974); *Honey* (1975); *Contradiction* (1976); *Angel* (1977); *Mr. Mean* (1977); *Jass-Ay-Ly-Dee* (1978)

Parliament--*Mothership Connection* (1976); *The Clones of Dr. Funkenstein* (1976); *Parliament Live/P. Funk Earth Tour* (1977); *Funkentelechy Vs. the Placebo Syndrome* (1977); *Motor-Booty Affair* (1978)

Billy Preston--*I Wrote a Simple Song* (1972); *Music Is My Life* (1972); *The Kids & Me* (1974)

Rufus--*Rags to Rufus* (1974); *Rufusized* (1975); *Rufus featuring Chaka Khan* (1975); *Ask Rufus* (1977); *Street Player* (1978); *Masterjam* (1979)

The S.O.S. Band--*S.O.S.* (1980); *On the Rise* (1983); *Sands of Time* (1986)

Slave--*Slave* (1977); *Stone Jam* (1980); *Show Time* (1981)

War--*All Day Music* (1971); *The World Is a Ghetto* (1972); *Deliver the Word* (1973); *Why Can't We Be Friends?* (1975)

Wild Cherry--*Wild Cherry* (1976)

Zapp--*Zapp* (1980); *Zapp II* (1982); *Zapp III* (1983)

--Funk-Punk

Andre Cymone--*Survivin' in the 80's* (1983); *A.C.* (1985)

Rick James--*Come Get It!* (1978); *Bustin' Out of L Seven* (1979); *Street Songs* (1981); *Throwin' Down* (1982); *Cold Blooded* (1983)

Mary Jane Girls--*Only Four You* (1985)

Prince--*Prince* (1979); *Controversy* (1981); *Prince 1999* (1982); *Purple Rain* (1984); *Around the World in a Day* (1985); *Parade* (1986); *Sign "O" the Times* (1987); *Batman* (1989); *Diamonds and Pearls* (1991)

The Time--*What Time Is It?* (1982); *Ice Cream Castle* (1984); *Pandemonium* (1990)

Vanity 6--*Vanity 6* (1982)

Table 99

Ohio Players

Like most other notable funk acts, the Ohio Players kinetic mix of percussion, loping bass lines, and stabbing horn flourishes owed much to Sly and the Family Stone's progressive rock-soul fusion of the late 1960s. In terms of both recording productivity and career longetivity, the group was unrivaled within the funk genre.

The band was formed in 1959, in Dayton, as Greg Webster and the Ohio Untouchables. Early on, they played behind the R&B vocal group, the Falcons, appearing on recordings such as the hit, "I Found a Love" (Lupine 1003; 1962; #6 R&B). With the addition of three members from an area band, they became known as the Ohio Players.

Although they had first recorded on their own for Lupine in 1963, their stint as the studio group for Compass Records in 1967-1968 proved to be something of a breakthrough. In addition to releasing singles under their own name, they produced a number of demo tapes, one of which was released as *Observations in Time* by Capitol (#192; 1969). Moving on to Westbound Records in the early 1970s, the band enjoyed one big hit, "Funky Worm" (Westbound 214; 1973; #1 R&B, #15 pop), which revealed their penchant for tongue-in-cheek humor. They also established another tradition during this period: marketing through provocative album covers typically featuring scantily-clad women in sexually-suggestive poses.

Signing with the Mercury label in 1974, the Players began a highly successful commercial run which included the following albums: *Skin Tight* (Mercury 705; 1974; #11; featuring the single, "Skin Tight," #2 R&B, #13 pop), *Fire* (Mercury 1013; 1974; #1; featuring "Fire," #1 R&B, #1 pop), *Honey* (Mercury 1038; 1975; #2; featuring "Love Rollercoaster,: #1 R&B, #1 pop), *Contradiction* (Mercury 1088; 1976; #12), *Ohio Players Gold* (Mercury 1122; 1976; #31), and *Angel* (Mercury 3701; 1977; #41). By the time the group had switched to Arista Records in 1979, their popularity had dropped off considerably. They continued to record for a variety of labels in the 1980s—including Accord, Boardwalk, Air City, and Track—with only intermittent success. With the advent of compact discs, many of the band's classic albums were reissued (along with assorted hit collections such as PolyGram's *Funk on Fire: The Mercury Anthology*, released in 1995). Despite the death of two longtime members—saxophonist "Satch" Mitchell and trumpeter "Pee Wee" Middlebrooks—in the 1990s, the band has continued to tour up to the present day.

Table 100

War

Although early frontman Eric Burdon did not last past the debut album, War remained one of the few successful interracial funk acts well into the 1980s. Although they did not record any new material for roughly a decade beginning in the mid-1980s, the band—whose work had been covered or sampled by many R&B and alternative rock artists, including Janet Jackson, TLC, Korn, and Smash Mouth—was still releasing albums at the outset of the twenty-first century.

The band, originally billed as "Eric Burdon and War," consisted of a Los Angeles-area aggregate formerly known as Nite Shift, the former Animals vocalist, and Danish harmonica player, Lee Oskar. Following several hits featuring Burdon's keening vocals—*Eric Burdon Declares "War"* (MGM 4663; 1970; #18, *The Black-Man's Burdon* (MGM 4710; 1970; #82), and the million-selling single "Spill the Wine" (MGM 14118; 1970; #3)—the members of War decided to operate as a separate act, signing with United Artists.

Emphasizing its strong rhythmic underpinning and first-rate songwriting skills, the band released a string of trailblazing recordings, including the gold singles "Slippin' Into Darkness" (United Artists 50867; 1972; #16), "The War Is a Ghetto" (United Artists 50975; 1972; #7), "The Cisco Kid" (United Artists 163; 1973; #2) "Why Can't We Be Friends?" (United Artists 629; 1975; #6), and "Summer" (United Artists 834; 1976; #7). Their most successful albums were *All Day Music* (United Artists 5546; 1971; #16; gold record), *The War Is a Ghetto* (United Artists 5652; 1972; #1; gold record), *Deliver the Word* (United Artists 128; 1973; #6; gold record), *War Live!* (United Artists 193; 1974; #13; gold record), and *Why Can't We Be Friends?* (United Artists 441; 1975; #8; gold record).

Beset by changing fashions (most notably, the rise of disco), personnel changes and varying label support—Blue Note, MCA, RCA, Priority, Lax, Virgin, and Avenue have all released new material by the band since 1977—War has failed to match the commercial success enjoyed in the early 1970s. Nevertheless, the band—now dominated by keyboardist/vocalist Leroy Jordan and producer Jerry Goldstein—has continued to produce engaging work, ranging from film soundtrack and jazz experiments in the late 1970s to the eclectic *Peace Sign* (Avenue 76024; 1994) and Hispanic-influenced *Coleccion Latina* (Avenue; 1997), both of which featuring guest contributions from the likes of Oskar and guitarist Jose Feliciano. A competing version of War—featuring four original members of the band—began recording as Guerra ("war" in Spanish) and, later, Same Ole Band, in the late 1990s.

Disco

Disco returned dancing to the forefront of pop music, and it did so with a verve and drive fueled, at least in part, on a disregard for many of the conventions held dear by rock enthusiasts. This perceived slight on the part of rock establishment would ultimately elicit a widespread negative reaction sufficient to drive the movement back underground.

The genre emerged out of an urban subculture in the early 1970s. Discos had been quietly serving its core audience for years. They originated as settings where one could dance to recorded music. The deejay deploying two turntables, a mike, and a PA system was a fixture in black communities. Whites deployed a similar arrangement for dances featuring oldies in church basements and community centers. Discotheques such as the Peppermint Lounge helped popularize the twist and countless spin-off dances in the early 1960s. For a short time, even wealthy jet-setters found it hip to mix with the masses in New York hot spots.

By the 1970s, however, discos promised escapism and release. With music and lighting choreographed to manipulate the mood of the dancers, the experience melded 1970s self-absorption with a 1960s sense of community. Ed Ward, in *The Rolling Stone Illustrated History of Rock & Roll* (2nd edition), notes that, in this setting, who was playing the records was often more important than what the records were.

The genre appears to have received its impetus from venues such as The Loft and The 10th Floor on Fire Island and in Manhattan because gay men had trouble securing live acts to perform at their social soires. These places combined the functions of private clubs, dance parties, and avant-garde hangouts. In short, gay culture circumstances in the 1970s, partially out of the closet but still not welcome in mainstream society, played a significant role in the evolution of disco.

In light of these social forces, disco may well have the first pop music form dictated by consumers; if dancers related to a record at these venues, it was classified as disco. The style was rooted in smooth black urban pop best exemplified by Gamble and Huff's Philly Sound and the seductive raps of Barry White, Isaac Hayes, and the like. However, it also incorporated a quirky, unpredictable side: left-field oddities sometimes went on the mainstream success by way of the discos; e.g., Many Dibango's "Soul Makossa" (1973), considered by some to be he first true disco hit. By 1974 the dance club scene was regularly responsible for breaking major hits; within another year it was helping determine the way records were made. Album-sized singles were introduced to fill deejay needs; these "disco singles" became so popular that a large number of them were released commercially. In addition, many pop recordings were issued in a "Disco Version," most notably new arrangements of show-biz oldies, rock chestnuts, soul classics, classical music's greatest hits, etc.

The Disco Version's extended length, use of musical drama, and emphasis on instrumental texture rather than vocal personality or verbal complexity predisposed the genre to a strong European influence. European composers and arrangers were instrumental in freeing disco from its tendency to cannibalize the past by developing forms which were more appropriate to its dance imperatives. Rather than lengthening conventional pop songs with gimmicks, studio wizards such Munich-based Georgio Moroder developed long, structured compositions calculated to fill an entire album side with music that ebbed and flowed in one beat-driven, but melodically varied, cut. Donna Summer's "Love to Love You Baby" (1976) typified this approach with its avoidance of the widely used verse-chorus-instrumental break-verse-chorus format in favor of an extended track suggesting a compressed movie soundtrack (perhaps even a classical music work) with its different movements. This spin-off form, known as Eurodisco, could be, in Ed Ward's words, as light (or shallow) as French pop, as dramatic (or pompous) as a German symphony, as cerebral (or cold) as experimental avant-garde music, or as minimalist (or repetitive) as a chant (or ad jingle).

Disco ultimately secured mainstream acceptance through the success of *Saturday Night Fever*. Released in 1977, the film cut across all demographic lines, while the soundtrack--featuring the Bee Gees and an assortment of minor dance hits--became the best-selling LP in pop music history. Up to this point in time, the disco scene had remained outside the pop mainstream because (1) few real discos existed anywhere other than in the major urban centers, (2) music that was specifically disco (in contrast to crossover hits) continued to be boycotted by many pop radio stations, and (3) the absence of recognizable stars meant there was no handle by which less informed fans could sort through the disco section in record stores.

In the wake of disco's breakthrough, established artists (e.g., Rod Stewart, the Beach Boys, the Rolling Stones)—even new wave trendsetters, Blondie--rushed to cash in, recording in this style. Radio stations didn't just add disco cuts to their playlists, they often went <u>all</u> disco. Record companies competed to hire disco insiders and artists.

After a brief run as the top pop music genre in 1978-1979, disco began to lose its patented dance groove. In addition, its success stimulated a cultural backlash from the more reactionary elements of the white establishment. "Disco sucks" dominated bumper stickers and graffiti of the day. There were disco record bonfires and anti-disco protests that occasionally degenerated into riots (e.g., a Yankee Stadium baseball game). The rock press widely criticized the genre.

By 1980, the best dance music was again coming from its original source, black pop. Disco was absorbed back into the underground, to be resurrected in the 1980s as dance-oriented rock (DOR), alternative dance, house, go-go, electronic dance music, and, ultimately, techno. Donna Summer was the only notable disco artist to maintain past chart successes.

Top Artists and Their Recordings

The Bee Gees--"You Should Be Dancing" (1976); "Stayin' Alive" (1977/8); "Night Fever" (1978)

James Brown--"It's Too Funky in Here" (1979): a perfect marriage of funk and disco.

Cafe Creme--"Discomania" (1978): a muzak-like medley of thirty-five Beatles songs within a ten-minute time span; it removed the aura of pomposity surrounding the Fab Four, restoring them to their original condition as alluring pop music interpreters.

Cerrone--"Love in C Minor" (1977): an exponent of the Franco-Italian school.

Chic--"Le Freak" (1978); "Good Times" (1979)

Gary's Gang--"Keep on Dancin'" (1979)

Gloria Gaynor--"I Will Survive" (1979)

Thelma Houston--"Don't Leave Me This Way" (1977/8)

KC and the Sunshine Band--"Get Down Tonight" (1975); "That's the Way (I Like It)" (1975); "(Shake, Shake, Shake) Shake Your Booty" (1976); "I'm Your Boogie Man" (1976)

Kool and the Gang--"Ladies Night" (1979)

Kraftwerk--"Trans-Europe Express" (1977): provides a German focus on synthesizers and the theme of urban alienation.

Lipps Inc.--"Funky Town" (1979)

McFadden and Whitehead--"Ain't No Stoppin' Us Now" (1979)

Diana Ross--"The Boss" (1979): reveals how the genre was able to revitalize slick black acts, songwriters, and producers; for the first time since her Supremes tenure, Ross recaptured her feel for superficiality accented by eroticism.

Shalamar--"Uptown Festival" (1977): a medley of 1960s Motown hits sung by Stevie Wonder--Smokey Robinson--Diana Ross soundalikes; demonstrates how disco was able to revitalize the past by not being able to toy with it.

Sister Sledge--"He's the Greatest Dancer" (1979)

Gino Soccio--"Dancer" (1979): the Montreal native assumed Eurodisco ideas of theme variation and repetition but removed the violins and other flowery embellishments, putting new emphasis on the bass track.

Amii Stewart--"Knock on Wood" (1979)

Donna Summer--"Love to Love You Baby" (1975/6); "I Feel Love" (1977); "Last Dance" (1978); "MacArthur Park" (1978); "Heaven Knows" (1979)

A Taste of Honey--"Boogie Oogie Oogie" (1978)

Andrea True Connection--"More, More More" (1976); "What's Your Name, What's Your Number" (1978)

Village People--"Macho Man" (1978); "Y.M.C.A." (1978): best remembered as caricatures of the gay subculture.

Table 101

Donna Summer, December 31, 1948-

Donna Summer earned considerable renown as the Queen of Disco during the later 1970s; however, few were aware of her ability to interpret a wide range of material, including pop, rock, blues, soul, and gospel. In addition, her talent encompassed acting, songwriting, and record production.

Born Adrian Donna Gaines in Boston, Summer started out singing in European musicals in 1968. Her breakthrough as a recording artist came with a Giorgio Moroder-Pete Bellote production, the erotic "Love to Love You Baby" (Oasis 401; 1975; #2). Despite the predominance of disco songs in her early albums—*Love to Love You Baby* (oasis 5003; 1975; #11; gold record), *A Love Trilogy* (Oasis 5004; 1976; #21; gold record). *Four Seasons of Love* (Casablanca 7038; 1987; #29; gold record), *Once Upon A Time* (Casablanca 7078; 1977; #26; gold record), *Live and More* (Casablanca 7119; 1978; #1; platinum award), and *Bad Girls* (Casablanca 7150; 1979; #1; platinum award; featuring the hit singles "Hot Stuff" (Casablanca 978; #1; platinum award], "Bad Girls" [Casablanca 988; #1; platinum award], and "Dim All the Lights" [Casablanca2201; #2; gold record])—she revealed an inclination to try other styles; *I Remember Yesterday* (Casablanca 7056; 1977; #18; gold record) served as a case a case in point, with an all-disco side and varied material on the other, including the Jimmy Webb classic, "MacArthur Park" (Casablanca 939; 1978; #1). Among her many awards were an Oscar for best movie song in 1978 with "Last Dance" (Casablanca 926; 1978; #3) and three American Music Awards that same year (Favorite Female Vocalist – Disco, Favorite LP – Disco for *Live and More*, and Favorite Single – Disco for "Last Dance").

Wishing to make a more dramatic move away from her disco image, Summer signed with Geffen Records in 1980. Since then, her albums—most notably, *The Wanderer* (Geffen 2000; 1980; #13; gold record), *Donna Summer* (Geffen 2005; 1982; #20; gold record), *She Works Hard for the Money* (Mercury 812265; 1983; #9; gold record), *Cats*

Without Claws (Geffen 24040; 1984; #40)—have become increasingly diversified, with a particular emphasis on religious material. She won Grammy awards for Best Inspirational Performance in 1983-1984, for "He's a Rebel" and "Forgive Me," respectively.

Following a succession of disappointing LPs, Summer was relatively inactive during the 1990s. Her biggest recording success came with "Carry On," a collaboration with Moroder which won the 1997 Grammy for Best Dance Recording. She has concentrated on songwriting along with husband Bruce Sudano, particularly the country market. At the outset of the twenty-first century they were working on a musical.

Rap/Hip Hop

Rap might well be viewed as a form of musical piracy. Both its live and recorded output are built upon the sampling of existing source material with the record player and recording studio functioning as primary instruments. On the other hand, its emergence represents perhaps the most important cultural development within the rock scene over the past twenty years. Based largely on the urban black experience, it is a form of populist poetry based on the street vernacular and set to funky rhythms suited to dance venues.

The genre incubated outside of the pop mainstream during the 1970s. Hip hop pioneer, Kurtis Blow, whose recording "The Breaks" was the first rap record to go gold, credits Kool DJ Herc with being the godfather of rap (*Public News*, August 27, 1997, 10-11):

> Kool DJ Herc spun records at the Heavelow in the Bronx. His ideology became the essence of hip hop culture--of being a record collector, of finding any artist, whether jazz, rock or reggae, as long as they had a funky drum break in the middle that you could dance to. Kool DJ Herc attracted a crowd from the Bronx and Harlem who became known as B-boys....The dances the B-boys did they'd make up, cop from *Soul Train* and so on....In the beginning, around 1973-74, hip hop was strictly a black thing. Then by the late '70s, the Puerto Rican kids were getting into the game. There used to be dance contests....We were winning most of the battles but the 'Ricans went home and did their homework and came up with the power moves: windmills, backspins on one hand, flairs, which are gymnastics, turtle crawls and so on. They took it to the next level, and that's when it became known as break dancing.

Blow feels Grandmaster Flash provided the final impetus in making rap an art form, merging DJ Pete Jones' precision timing and Herc's playlist.

> You have to understand in the early days that when the breaks came in, that's when a DJ rapped or a b-boy would do his best moves....[Flash] specialized in playing just breaks and extended the break for five minutes and would then go to the next break beat. It was a definite art form, the way he played the record....Instead of mixing it softly, Flash would bang it in--bamm! That's where they get cutting from. Scratching was actually taking the beginning of the beat, holding the record with your finger and making it go backwards and forwards with your finger....He created a whole new rhythm, like a musician.

In the meantime, rap culture had spread to other urban centers, with club or street dance deejays providing the impetus by speaking over a seamless blend of recorded snippets. The Sugarhill Gang's "Rapper's Delight" (1979), the first rap record to be a hit on the pop singles charts, brought the entire scene into the mainstream. Follow-up pop successes were slow to appear over the next few years, however, as many of the pioneer rap stars (e.g., Afrika Bambaataa, Grandmaster Flash, Grandmaster Melle Mel) tended to focus on harsh social commentary.

Rap truly achieved crossover appeal when Run-DMC ushered in the "new school" with the release of its debut album in 1984. By incorporating rock rhythms and instrumentation into the genre, Run-DMC stimulated the appearance of a wide array of subgenres. These included (listed along with leading exponents):

Gangsta Rap (Dr. Dre, Ice Cube, Ice T, N.W.A., Snoop Doggy Dog, Tupac Shakur, Notorious B.I.G., 50 Cent)

Bawdy Rap (Biz Markie, 2 Live Crew)

White Rap (Beastie Boys, Snow, 3rd Bass, Vanilla Ice)

Political Rap (Boogie Down Productions, KRS-One, Public Enemy)

Jazz Rap (Digable Planets, A Tribe Called Quest, UB3)

Pop Rap (DY Jazzy Jeff and the Fresh Prince, De La Soul, Eric B. and Rakim, L.L. Cool J., M.C. Hammer, P.M. Dawn, Puff Daddy, Salt-N-Pepa, Roxanne Shante)

Alternative Hip Hop (Arrested Development, Basehead, Disposable Heroes of Hiphoprisy)

"Screw Tape" Mixes (DJ Screw, other Big Time Recordz mix-masters)

Rap's diversity would seem to hold something for everyone. Nevertheless, the genre has continued to offend mainstream sensibilities due to its blatant sexuality, off-color language, spoken lyrics devoid of traditional singing, and glorification of misogyny, lawless behavior, the use of force to settle disputes, etc. In this sense, rap appears to have much in common with early rock 'n' roll, punk, heavy metal, and other styles which have taken a strong anti-establishment stance.

Table 102

Africa Bambaataa, April 10, 1960-

While DJ Kool Herc is widely credited with creating hip-hop, Afrika Bambaataa led the way in disseminating it worldwide. His vision incorporated deejays, rappers, singers, studio producers, break dancers, and graffiti artists into one youth culture movement. Born Kevin Donovan in the Bronx, he took the name of a nineteenth-century Zulu chief meaning "affectionate leader." Known as the "Master of Records," due to his unrivaled disc collection, he experimented with recorded musical elements such as Latin rock, European disco, funk, punk, and the German electro bands such as Kraftwerk in order to create the ultimate dance environment.

Although his primary creative medium was the club and street dances, he produced many important twelve-inch singles and albums during the 1980s, most notably "Planet Rock" with Soulsonic Force (Tommy Boy 823; 1982), "Renegades of Funk" with Soulsonic Force (Tommy Boy 839, 1983), "Unity" with James Brown (Tommy Boy 847; 1984), *Planet Rock: The Album* (Tommy Boy; 1986), and *Warlock and Witches, Computer Chips, Microchips and You* (Profile; 1996). While no longer in hip-hop's innovative vanguard, he has remained in high demand as an elder statesman of the genre, working parties and raves and often making radio station appearances.

Table 103

Eazy E, September 7, 1963-March 26, 1995

Eazy-E (born Eric Wright, son of soul-funk star Charles Wright, in Los Angeles) was one of the most successful entrepreneurial artists in rock history, bar none. In addition to forming the trailblazing gangsta rap group, N.W.A., and later achieving acclaim as a solo act, in 1985 he founded his own label, Ruthless Records (allegedly with illegal profits), which became a major force in the then-emerging West Coast hip-hop scene.

Eazy-E's first album project, *N.W.A. and the Posse* (Macola/Rams Horn 5134; 1987), featured core members of N.W.A.—Dr. Dre, DJ Yella, Ice Cube—along with a supporting cast including, among others, the Doc and Arabian Prince. With the addition of MC Ren, N.W.A. released the landmark LP, *Straight Outta Compton* (Ruthless 57102; 1999; #37), which almost single-handedly launched the gangsta movement on the strength of incendiary tracks such as "F*** Tha Police" (Ruthless; issued as a CD-single and twelve-inch disc in April 1991) and "Gangsta Gangsta" (Ruthless 191; 1990; #70 UK). The album's notoriety helped propel the follow-up, *Efil4zaggin'* (Ruthless 57126; 1991; #1), to the top of the charts.

Shortly thereafter, internal differences caused N.W.A. to implode, with individual members all going on to solo careers. Eazy-E had a head start in this regard, having issued an album, *Eazy-Duz-It* (Ruthless 57100; 1988; #41), which almost predated N.W.A. His first post-N.W.A. release, the mini-CD *5150 Home For Tha Sick* (Ruthless 53815; 1993; #70), was a pedestrian affair, apparently due to the distractions of administrative duties. The next release, the mini-CD *It's On (Dr. Dre) 187 Um Killa* (Ruthless 5503; 1993; #5), revealed a greater concern for his artistic legacy; "Real Muthaphuckin G's," later released as a single (Ruthless 5508; 1994; #42), questioned Dr. Dre's role in pioneering the G-funk sound.

Shortly after collaborating with Bone Thugs-N-Harmony on "Foe Tha Love Of" (Ruthless; 1995), Eazy-E was diagnosed as having HIV; a month later he died of AIDS. He continues to be represented by posthumous releases, most notably the compilation of previously released material, *Eternal E* (Ruthless 50544; 1995; #84), and the collection of unreleased tracks, *Str8 Off Tha Streetz Of Muthaphukkin – E.W. Compton* (Ruthless5504; 1995; #3).

Table 104

Will Smith, September 25, 1968-

Philadelphia native Will Smith (aka the Fresh Prince) first found fame as a comical pop-rapper along with partner D.J. Jazzy Jeff (Jeffrey A. Townes). The duo's crossover success enabled Smith to become the first rap artist to make the transition to television success, a result of his landing the title role in the sitcom *The Fresh Prince of Bel-Air*, which ran six seasons on NBC. A string of film roles (e.g., *Bad Boys*, *Independence Day*, *Men In Black*, *Wild, Wild West*) followed, which in turn have propelled Smith back to the top of the charts as a solo act.

D.J. Jazzy Jeff and the Fresh Prince's debut album, *Rock the House* (Jive 1026; 1987; #83), attracted considerable attention due to its innovative blend of samples (ranging from James Brown to the *I Dream of Jeannie* theme) and scratching accented by the charismatic wit of Smith's humorous anecdotes. The follow-up, *He's the D.J., I'm the Rapper* (Jive 1091; 1988; #4)—driven by the hits "Parents Just Don't Understand" (Jive 1099; 1988; #12) and "A Nightmare On My Street" (Jive 1124; 1988; #15)—achieved unprecedented crossover popularity, ultimately selling more than two-and-a-half million copies. Subsequent LPs—*And In This Corner* (Jive 1188; 1989; #39; gold record award), *Homebase* (Jive 1392; 1991; #12; platinum record award; included singles

"Summertime" [Jive 1465; 1991; #4] and "Ring My Bell" [Jive 42024; 1991; #20]), and *Code Red* (Jive; 1993)—while selling well, came across as rather silly and contrived.

Although never officially disbanded, the duo hasn't recorded since 1993, apparently due to the demands of Smith's media stardom. His first solo rap recordings—two songs, including the title cut, which topped the *Billboard Hot 100*—appeared on soundtrack, *Men In Black: The Album* (Columbia 68169; 1997). The album, *Big Willie Styles* (Columbia; 1997; #1)—which included the chart-topping single, "Getting' Jiggy Wit It" (Columbia 78804; 1998)—validated efforts to place his recording career back on the front burner. The film title track, "Wild Wild West" (Overbrook 79157; 1999; #1; featuring Dru Hill and Kool Mo Dee), offered further proof that PG-rated hip-hop possesses considerable sales potential.

Black Contemporary

"Black contemporary" gained popularity with the recording industry in the 1980s as a politically correct designation for African American popular music. A direct progression beyond terms such as "race music," "sepia blues," rhythm and blues," "soul," and "funk," the genre cuts across a wide range of stylistic boundaries. It came to mean middle-of-the-road forms of music as interpreted by African Americans, particularly romantic ballads likely to be played on Top 40 AM radio stations. Black contemporary was rarely seen to include harder-edged, up-tempo styles almost exclusive identified with black artists and listeners such as rap, funk, and punk-punk (many BC acts, however, did incorporate elements of these genres). By the early 1990s, the "rhythm and blues" moniker had come back in fashion as a designation of mainstream African American pop material.

Top Artists and Their Recordings

Altantic Starr--"Circles" (1982); "Secret Lovers" (1986)

Boyz II Men--"End of the Road" (1991)

Peabo Bryson--"Tonight, I Celebrate My Love" (w/Roberta Flack) (1983); "If I Ever You're in My Arms Again" (1984)

Champagne--"How 'Bout Us" (1981); "Try Again" (1983)

Natalie Cole--"This Will Be" (1975); "Inseparable" (1976); "Sophisticated Lady" (1976); "I've Got Love on My Mind" (1977); "Our Love" (1978); "Someone That I Used to Love" (1980)

Tyrone Davis--"Can I Change My Mind" (1969); "Is It Something You've Got" (1969); "Turn Back the Hands of Time" (1970); "There It Is" (1973); "Give It Up" (1976)

DeBarge--"I Like It" (1983); "All This Love" (1983); "Time Will Reveal" (1983/4); "Rhythm of the Night" (1985); "Who's Holding Donna Now" (1985)

El DeBarge--"Who's Johnny" (1986)

Ronnie Dyson--"Why Can't I Touch You?" (1970); "One Man Band" (1973)

Richard "Dimples" Fields--"If It Ain't One Thing...It's Another" (1982)

Whitney Houston—"You Give Good Love" (1985); "Saving All My Love For You" (1985); "How Will I Know" (1986); "Greatest Love of All" (1985)

Phyllis Hyman--"Can't We Fall in Love Again" (1981)

Janet Jackson--"What Have You Done For Me Lately" (1986); "Nasty" (1986); "When I Think of You" (1986)

Michael Jackson--"Got to Be There" (1971); "Rockin' Robin" (1972); "I Wanna Be Where You Are" (1972); "Ben" (1972); "Just a Little Bit of You" (1975); "Don't Stop 'Til You Get Enough" (1979); "Rock With You" (1979); "Off the Wall" (1980); "She's Out of My Life" (1980); *Thriller* (1983); "Billie Jean" (1983)

Millie Jackson--"Ask Me What You Want" (1972); "Hurts So Good" (1973)

Quincy Jones--"Stuff Like That" (1978); "Ai No Corrida" (1981)

Kashif--"I Just Gotta Have You" (1983); "Baby Don't Break Your Baby's Heart" (1984); Love the One I'm With" (w/Melba Moore) (1986)

Chaka Khan--"I'm Every Woman" (1978); "I Feel For You" (1984)

Labelle(, Patti)--"Down the Aisle" (1963); "You'll Never Walk Alone" (1964); "Lady Marmalade" (1975); "New Attitude" (1985); "Oh, People" (1986)

Stacy Lattisaw--"Let Me Be Your Angel" (1980); "Love on a Two Way Street" (1981); "Miracle (1983)

Marie, Teena--"I Need Your Lovin'" (1981); "Lovergirl" (1985)

Stephanie Mills--"What Cha Gonna Do With My Lovin'" (1979); "Never Knew Love Like This Before" (1980)

Melba Moore--"Love's Comin' at Ya" (1982); "Livin' For Your Love" (1984); "A Little Bit More" (1986); "Falling" (1986/7); "It's Been So Long" (1987)

The New Edition--"Cool It Now" (1984/5); "Mr. Telephone Man" (1985); "Earth Angel" (1986)

Jeffrey Osborne--"I Really Don't Need No Light" (1982); "On the Wings of Love" (1982); "Don't You Get So Mad" (1983); "Stay With Me Tonight" (1983/4); "The Borderlines" (1985); "You Should Be Mine" (1986)

Ray Parker, Jr./Raydio--"Jack and Jill" (1978); "You Can't Change That" (1979); "Two Places at the Same Time" (1980); "A Woman Needs Love" (1981); "That Old Song" (1981); "The Other Woman" (1982); "Bad Boy" (1982); "I Still Can't Get Over Loving You" (1983); "Ghostbusters" (1984)

Teddy Pendergrass--"Close the Door" (1978); "Love T.K.O." (1980); "Joy" (1988)

The Pointer Sisters--"Yes We Can Can" (1973); "Fairytale" (1974); "How Long" (1975); "Fire" (1978/9); "Happiness" (1979); "He's So Shy" (1980); "Slow Hand" (1981); "Should I Do It" (1982); "American Music" (1982); "I'm So Excited" (1982; 1984)); "Automatic" (1984); "Jump" (1984); "Neutron Dance" (1984/5); "Dare Me" (1985)

Ray, Goodman and Brown--"Special Lady" (1980)

Lionel Richie/The Commodores--"Truly" (1982); "You Are" (1983); "My Love" (1983); "All Night Long" (1983); "Running With the Night" (1983/4); "Hello" (1984); "Stuck On You" (1984); "Penny Lover" (1984); "Say You, Say Me" (1985); "Dancing on the Ceiling" (1986); "Love Will Conquer All" (1986)

Patrice Rushen--"Forget Me Nots" (1982)

Tierra--"Together" (1980/1)

Luther Vandross--"Never Too Much" (1981); "'Til My Baby Comes Home" (1985); *Any Love* (1988); *Power of Love* (1991); *Never Let Me Go* (1993); *Songs* (1994); *Your Secret Love* (1996); *Luther Vandross* (2001); *Dance With My Father* (2003)

Deniece Williams--"Free" (1977); "It's Gonna Take a Miracle" (1982); "Let's Hear It For the Boy" (1984)

Yarbrough and Peoples--"Don't Stop the Music" (1981)

Table 105

Anita Baker, 1958-

An exponent of traditional rhythm and blues vocalizing, Baker's restrained intensity and subtle coloring attracted widespread media attention and pop mainstream success in the mid-1980s. Born in Toledo and raised in Detroit, she began her professional career as lead singer for the r & b group, Chapter 8, from 1976 to 1984. Her moderately successful debut album, *The Songstress* (Beverly Glen 10002; 1983) was followed by the commercial breakthrough release, *Rapture* (Elektra 60444; 1986), which included Top Ten single, "Sweet Love" (Elektra 7-69557; 1986), reputed to have sold more than four million copies. Her subsequent albums, most notably the chart-topping *Give You the Best That I've Got* (Elektra 60827; 1988) and *Compositions* (Elektra 60922; 1990), have all been bestsellers. [Romanowski and George-Warren. 1995]

Table 106

Boyz II Men

Boyz II Men have proven that a mainstream pop group emphasizing ballads is capable of outselling more trendy alternative rock and rap competitors. Their sound—a blend of doo-wop, the 1960s Motown singing groups (particularly the Temptations), and 1970s Philly Soul, accented by contemporary vocal nuances—appears unlikely to ever seem dated.

Formed in 1988 at Philadelphia's High School for the Creative and Performing Arts, the quartet—comprised of Michael McCary, Nathan Morris, Wanya Morris, and Shawn Stockman—was championed during their formative years by the New Edition's Michael Bivins. Their debut LP, *Cooleyhighharmony* (Motown 6320; 1991; #3), driven by three Top Twenty singles, ultimately sold more than nine million copies. A single from the film *Boomerang*, "End of the Road" (Motown 2178; 1992), had—for the time—the most successful chart run ever during the rock era, remaining number one on the *Billboard Hot 100* for thirteen weeks.

The group's other albums—*Christmas Interpretations* (Motown; 1993), *II* (Motown; 1994; #1 pop, #1 R&B; over thirteen million copies sold), *Remix Collection* (Motown; 1995), *Evolution* (Motown; 1997; #1 pop, #1 R&B; a Spanish-language version also released), and *Nathan Michael Shawn Wanya* (Universal; 2000)—maintained the group's hot streak, despite competition from countless imitators, most notably 'N Sync and the Backstreet Boys.

Assisted by state-of-the-art video clips and a romantic, non-threatening image, Boyz II Men have also gone on to become one of the top singles groups of all-time. According to Joel Whitburn's *The Billboard Book of Top 40 Hits*, they have recorded three of the six most successful songs since 1955: "My Sweet Day" (Columbia 78074; 1995; #1 16 weeks; with Mariah Carey—rated 1st); "I'll Make Love to You" (Motown 2257; 1994; #1 14 weeks—rated 3rd); and "End of the Road" (rated 6th). Other number hits have included "It's So Hard To Say Goodbye To Yesterday" (Motown 2136; 1991; #1 R&B), "On Bended Knee" (Motown 0244; 1994; #1 pop), "4 Seasons of Loneliness" (Motown 0684; 1997; #1 pop), and "A Song For Mama" (Motown 0720; 1997; #1 R&B).

Table 107

Luther Vandross, April 20, 1951-July 1, 2005

Vandross enjoyed a very successful career as a session singer and recording commercials prior to becoming one of the preeminent R&B stylists of his generation, widely known for his impeccable phrasing and vocal control/ Born in New York City, he began playing piano at age three. One of his compositions, "Everybody Rejoice (A Brand New Day)," was included in the Broadway musical, *The Wiz*, in 1972. He became a fixture on ad jingles, from U.S. Army to Burger King spots.

His entrée to the pop music industry came when a friend, guitarist Carlos Alomar, introduced him to David Bowie. He would contribute a song, "Fascination," and sing on Bowie's highly successful LP, *Young Americans* (RCA ; 1975), later touring with him as well. While continuing to sing jingles and cutting two obscure albums under the name Luther, he quickly became one of the busiest backing vocalists and arrangers around, recording with Bette Midler, Ringo Starr, Carly Simon, Donna Summer, Barbra Streisand, Chaka Khan, Chic, and Change.

With several labels expressing an interest in Vandross as a solo artist, he produced two demos, "Never Too Much" and "A House Is Not a Home." As a result, Epic Records signed him in 1981, granting him full creative control. Beginning with *Never Too Much* (Epic 37451; 1981; #1 R&B), he released a long string of platinum-selling albums, including *Forever, For Always, For Love* (Epic 38235; 1982), *Busy Body* (Epic 39196; 1983), *The Night I Fell In Love* (Epic 39882; 1985), *Give Me the Reason* (Epic 40415; 1986), *Any Love* (Epic 44308; 1988), *The Best of Luther Vandross…The Best of Love* (Epic 45320; 1989), and *Power of Love* (Epic 46789; 1991).

Although his singles had limited crossover appeal, they consistently reached the R&B Top Ten. Despite the demands ensuing from pop stardom, he continued to write and produce for other artists up until his death, most notably Aretha Franklin, Cheryl Lynn,

Dionne Warwick, Teddy Pendergrass, and Whitney Houston. He was also drawn to acting, making his film debut in Robert Townsend's 1993 film, *Meteor Man*.

Avant-Garde Rock

This stylistically diverse genre, ranging from eclecticism to post modern minimalism tempered by rock dynamics, has long existed on the experimental fringe of the progressive rock movement. It combined the philosophy of art for art's sake with the mass communication potentialities of the rock medium.

The pivotal development behind the rise of avant-garde rock was strong aesthetic posture adopted by the Beatles--then the most popular music act in the world--with the release of *Rubber Soul* in late 1965. The album represented a turning point in rock history. For the first time, the long-playing record was viewed as a medium for making a coherent artistic statement rather than as a mere collection of singles. Furthermore, the individual tracks displayed a heightened level of songwriting sophistication. The lyrics in songs like "In My Life" and "Norwegian Wood" revealed a maturity hitherto unprecedented in rock. The refined production work by George Martin offered a dazzling array of instrumental colors and performance dynamics.

A dedicated core of musicians--both rock scene insiders and refugees from the serious music sector seeking a larger audience-- immediately took up the baton. Their aesthetic aspirations were nurtured by a slew of newly established record labels dedicated to issuing uncompromising music within the framework of small-market economics. This ethic has remained intact for more than thirty years with the avant-garde movement continuing to be enriched by the incorporation of new conceptual ideas and stylistic influences.

Top Artists and Their Recordings

Laurie Anderson--*Big Science* (1982); *Mister Heartbreak* (1984); *United States Live* (1984); *Home of the Brave* (film soundtrack;1986); *Strange Angels* (1989); *Bright Red/Tightrope* (1994); *In Our Sleep EP* (1995); *The Ugly One With the Jewels and Other Stories* (1995)

Glenn Branca--*Lesson #1 EP* (1980); *The Ascension* (1981); *Music For the Dance "Bad Smells"* (1982); *Symphony No. 1* (1983); *Symphony No. 3* (1983); *Soundtrack for "The Belly of an Architect"* (1987); *Symphony No. 6 (Devil Choirs at the Gates of Heaven)* (1989); *The World Upside Down* (1992); *Symphony No. 2* (1992); *Symphony Nos. 8 & 10* (1994); *Symphony No. 9* (1995); *Songs '77-'70* (1996); *Symphony No. 5 (Describing Planes of an Expanding Hyperspere)* (1996)

Joseph Byrd and the Field Hippies--*The American Metphysical Circus* (1969)

A Certain Ratio--*The Graveyard and the Ballroom* (1979); *To Each* (1981); *Sextet* (1981); *I'd Like to See You Again* (1982)

(Brian) Eno--*Here Come the Warm Jets* (1973); *Taking Tiger Mountain (By Strategy)* (1974); *Another Green World* (1975); *Discreet Music* (1975); *Before and After Science* (1977); *Music For Films* (1978); *Ambient 1: Music For Airports* (1979); *Ambient 4: On Land* (1982); *Music For Films, Volume 2* (1983); *Thursday Afternoon* (video soundtrack; 1985)

Etron Fou LeLoublan--*Les Trois Fou's Perdegagnent (au pays des....)* (1977)

Robert Fripp--*Live!* (1986); *The Lady or the Tiger* (w/Toyah Willcox) (1986); *Kneeling at the Shrine* (w/Sunday All Over the World) (1991); *Show of Hands* (1991); *1999 Soundscapes Live in Argentina* (1994)

Fred Frith/Henry Cow--*Unrest* (1974); *In Praise of Learning* (1975); *Western Culture* (1978)

Philip Glass--*Einstein on the Beach* (1979); *The Photographer* (1982)

Yoko Ono--*Approximately Infinite Universe* (1973); *Season of Glass* (1981); *It's Alright (I See Rainbows)* (1982); *Starpeace* (1985); *Walking on Thin Ice* (1992); *Rising* (w/Ima) (1995); *Rising Mixes EP* (1996)

Yoko Ono/John Lennon--*Unfinished Music No. 1: Two Virgins* (1968); *Unfinished Music No. 2: Life With the Lions* (1969); *Wedding Album* (1969); *Some Time in New York City* (1972); *Double Fantasy* (1980); *Heart Play (Unfinished Dialogue)* (1983); *Milk and Honey* (1984)

Yoko Ono/Plastic Ono Band--*Live Peace in Toronto 1969* (1969); *John Lennon/Plastic Ono Band* (1970); *Fly* (1971); *Feeling the Space* (1973)

The Raincoats--*The Raincoats* (1979); *Odyshape* (1981); *The Kitchen Tapes* (1983); *Animal Rhapsody EP* (1983); *Moving* (1984); *Extended Play EP* (1994); *Fairytales* (1995); *Looking in the Shadows* (1996)

Steve Reich--*Music For 18 Musicians* (1978); *Desert Music* (1985); *Sextet/Six Marimbas* (1986); *Drumming* (1987); *Different Trains* (1989)

The Residents--*Meet The Residents* (1974); *The Residents Present the Third Reich 'n Roll* (1976); *Fingerprince* (1976); *The Residents Radio Pressure* (1977); *Not Available* (1978); *Duck Stab/Buster and Glen* (1978); *Babyfingers EP* (1979); *Eskimo* (1979); *Nibbles* (1979); *Diskomo/Goosebump EP* (1980); *The Residents' Commercial Album* (1980); *Mark of the Mole* (1981); *Intermission* (1982); *The Tunes of Two Cities* (1982); *Title In Limbo* (1983); *Residue of the Residents* (1983); *American Composer Series--Volume 1: George and James* (1984); *Whatever Happened to Vileness Fats* (1984); *Part Four of the Mole Trilogy: The Big Bubble* (1985); *The

Census Taker (1985); *PAL TV LP* (1985); *The American Composer's Series--Volume II: Stars and Hank Forever!* (1986); *The 13th Anniversary Show Live in Japan!* (1986); *Hit the Road Jack EP* (1987); *Snakeywake EP* (1987); *The Mole Show Live in Holland* (1987); *Santa Dog '88 EP* (1988); *God in Three Persons* (1988); *God in Three Pesons Soundtrack* (1988); *Double Shot o' My Baby's Love EP* (1989); *Buckaroo Blues* (1989); *The King & Eye* (1989); *Cube E: Live in Holland* (1990); *Liver Music* (1990); *Stranger Than Supper* (1990); *Freak Show* (1990; CD-ROM version, 1995); *Blowoff EP* (1992); *Gingerbread Man* (CD-ROM; 1994); *Bad Day on the Midway* (CD-ROM; 1995); *Hunters: The World of Predators and Prey* (1995); *Have a Bad Day* (1996)

Terry Riley--*In C* (1968); *A Rain bow in Curved Air* (1969); *Shri Camel* (1980); *Descending Moonshine Dervishes/Songs for the Ten Voices of the Two Prophets* (1975); *Cadenza on the Night Plain* (w/Kronos Quartet) (1986)

Savage Republic--*Tragic Figures* (1983)

Univers Zero--*Heresie* (1979); *Crawling Wind* (1980); *Heatwave* (1990); *Uzed* (1991); *1313* (1992)

John Zorn--*Pool/Hockey* (1980); *Archery* (1982); *Locus Solus* (1983); *The Big Gundown* (1986)

Table 108

Klaus Schulze, August 4, 1947-

Regarded in his native Germany as a composer/multi-instrumentalist within the classical music tradition, Klaus Schulze remains a cult figure in the United States, where the bulk of his prolific output is available only through the import bins. Despite his marginal status stateside, he is widely considered an avant garde mainstay as well as a founding father of both new age space music and the electronica genre.

Schultze first attracted attention as a member of the German progressive rock band, Tangerine Dream. Following the release of their debut LP, *Electronic Meditation* (Ohr 556 004; 1970), he departed for a solo career. His recorded work typically features extended pieces—sometimes filling an entire album—built around computer-generated synthesizers and other specially programmed electronic effects. The music itself—somewhat reminiscent of the oscillating sound loops pioneered by minimalist composers like Philip Glass—has been described as ethereal, surreal, spacey, dreamy, hypnotic, and relaxing. Since the release of the soundtrack *Body Love* (Brain 60.047; 1977), he has been in great demand as a composer/performer of European film music.

Schulze's recordings—many of which are complemented by engaging art work (e.g., the Daliesque paintings of some early 1970s titles)—include *Irrlicht* (Brain 1077; 1972), *Blackdance* (Virgin 2003; 1974), *Timewind* (Virgin 2006; 1975), *Moondawn* (Brain 1088; 1976) *Mirage* (Brain 60.040; 1977), *Dune* (Brain 0060.225; 1979), *Trancefer* (Innovative Communication 80014; 1981), *Audentity* (Brain 817-194-2; 1983; with keyboardist Rainer Bloss and percussionist Michael Schrieve), *Inter*Face* (Brain 827 673-2; 1985), *Cyborg* (A.V.I. 2002; 1986), *Mediterranean Pads* (Thunderbolt/ Magnum Music Group 2027; 1990), *Beyond Recall* (Venture/Virgin 906; 1991), and *The Dome Event* (Virgin 918; 1993; recorded live at the Cologne Cathedral).

Table 109

Tangerine Dream

Considered genre benders—part progressive rock, part avant garde—during their early years, Tangerine Dream are now viewed as forefathers of electronica, although recent work has veered dangerously close to the new age genre. The group has served as a launching pad for the solo careers of many leading experimental synthesizer artists, most notably, Klaus Schulze, Peter Baumann, Michael Hoenig, and leader Edgar Froese.

Tangerine Dream was formed in Berlin in Fall 1967 by then-art student Froese, who tried many rock and classical musicians prior to the release of the debut album, *Electronic Meditation* (Ohr 556004; 1970; reissued February 1996 on Essential 345). Pioneering keyboard-predominated electronic waves of sound, the group issued three more undergound LPs—*Alpha Centauri* (Ohr 556 012; 1971; reissued February 1996 on Essential 346), *Zeit* (Ohr 556 021; 1972; reissued February 1996 on Essential 347), and *Atem* (Ohr 556 031; 1973; reissed February 1996 on Essential 348)—before the increasing appearance of synthesizers in the pop mainstream (e.g., Mike Oldfield's *Tubular Bells*) warranted a contract with the Virgin label.

Although Tangerine Dream remained a cult staple in the U.S., their releases—featuring lush synthesizer-derived electronic washes, accented by evocative rhythmic patterns—charted regularly in Great *Britain* over the next decade, beginning with *Phaedra* (Virgin 13108; 1974; #15), *Rubycon* (Virgin 13166; 1975; #12), the live *Ricochet* (Virgin 2044; 1975; #40), and *Stratosfear* (Virgin 34427; 1976; #39). The next LP, *Sorcerer* (Virgin 2277; 1977; #25), signaled a gradual shift in the direction of movie soundtrack work, including *Thief* (Virgin/Elektra 521; 1981; #43), *Wavelength* (Elektra 81207; 1983), *Risky Business* (Virgin/Elektra 2302; 1983), *Firestarter* (MCA 3233, 1984), *Flashpoint* (Relativity 17141; 1985), *Heartbreakers* (Virgin 212-620; 1985), and *Three O'Clock High* (Relativity 47357; 1987). While continuing to produce soundtrack music, albeit largely for foreign films, Tangerine Dream has been marketed as a new age group since the early 1990s.

Table 110

John Zorn, September 12, 1953-

September 12, 1953-John Zorn is—with the possible exception of Bill Laswell—the most prolific avant garde composer/musician active today; his recordings span musique concrete, free jazz, fusion, bebop, hardcore, film soundtrack compositions, world music, and the European classical tradition. In order to document the full breadth of his eclectic experiments, Zorn has utilized a wide range of independent and European labels as well as Elektra/Nonesuch, issuing albums both as a solo artist and under various group configurations. His collaborators read like a who's who of cutting edge art music, jazz, and rock, including Laswell, Derek Bailey, George Lewis, Bill Frisell, Vernon Reid, Fred Frith, Wayne Horovitz, Bobby Previte, Albert Collins, Yamatsuka Eye, and the Kronos Quartet.

Born in Brooklyn, Zorn had developed a highly personalized approach to composition and improvisation prior to emerging as a creative force on New York's Lower East Side in the mid-1970s. While mining the free-jazz genre, he recorded his first solo albums—including *School* (1978), *Pool* (1980), and *Archery* (1981), reissued as part of the seven-CD set, *The Parachute Years* (Tzadik 7607; 1995)—all of which were initially limited to the European market. Zorn's first major label release, *The Big Gundown* (Elektra/Nonesuch 979139; 1986)—a skewed take on Ennio Marricone's cinema compositions—represented an early manifestation of his lifelong fascination with television and film.

While issuing stylistically diverse solo albums at a dizzying pace—*News for Lulu* (Hat Art 6005; 1987), a bebop tribute, would be followed three months later by *Spillane* (Elektra/Nonesuch 979172; 1986), which featured conflicting fragments of sound spliced together—he became increasingly involved in a seemingly endless array of side projects. Naked City explored postpunk styles such as grindcore; beginning with *Naked City* (Elektra/Nonesuch 979238; 1990), the band issued six LPs through 1994. Painkiller veered even closer to speed metal with *Guts of a Virgin* (Earache 045; 1991) and *Buried Secrets* (Earache 062; 1992). Masada and Bar Kokhba, two units devoted to Yiddish/ Middle Eastern music, produced more than a dozen albums between 1995-2000. Other platforms have included his Spy Vs. Spy band, dedicated to reinterpreting jazz saxophonist Ornette Coleman's work within a postmodern rock context, East Asian bar bands, and deconstruction of classical music formats such as the string quartet and piano concerto.

New Age Music

New age music evolved out of a shared consciousness among composers and performers. Their credo held that music should be based on harmony and consonance, rather than dissonance; minus the hooks and rhythmic pulse typifying popular music; employ soothing instrumental sounds (e.g., prominence of electric piano, harp, flute, bells, string ensembles); and elevate space to a key role (i.e., the electro-acoustic enhancement of instrumental tones through reverb and echo). The genre began taking form in the latter half of the 1970s (a pivotal development was William Ackerman's formation of the Windham Hill label in 1976) as baby boomers, approaching middle age and facing the full effect of career and family pressures, began exploring softer forms of pop music. A broad, amorphous category, new age includes the following subgenres:

Electronic/Computer Music. The rapidly evolving technology of modern society has placed the resources of a small orchestra within the means of most artists. This has facilitated the creation of innovative sounds hitherto impossible to achieve with traditional acoustic instruments. The key tools here are synthesizers--a large, expanding class of dissimilar instruments that often combine tape recordings, computers, and samplers--and samplers (enable a musician/programmer to blend snippets of recorded acoustic sound--e.g., a violin passage or bird songs--with electronic tones to generate new music pieces. Leading practitioners include John Adams, Carlos Alomar, Michael Amerlan, David Arkenstone, Kevin Braheney, Peter Buffet, Richard Burmer, Wendy Carlos, Suzanne Ciani, Barry Cleveland, Double Fantasy, Emerald Web, Larry Fast/Synergy, Jan Hammer, On Harriss, Michael Hoenig, Iasos, Jean-Michel Jarre, Eddie Jobson, Steve Roach, Robert Schroeder, Klaus Schulze, John Serrie, Michael Shrieve, Don Slepian, Michael Stearns, Isao Tomita, Vangelis, and Yanni.

Folk Music. Based on influences derived from traditional folk and ethnic sources (e.g., Celtic, bluegrass), this style is usually acoustic and instrumental in orientation. Divided between original compositions and classic folk material in an upbeat mode, the sound is built around such instruments as six- and twelve-string guitars, Celtic harp, flutes, and dulcimers. Notable exponents include William Ackerman, Checkfield, Malcolm Dalglish and Greg Larsen, Mark O'Connor, and Allan Stivell.

Jazz/Fusion. Representing a gentle rebellion against overly spacey new age music and frenetic jazz, this fusion style avoids the abstract dissonance typified by avant-garde jazz or classical compositions in favor of mood, texture, and flowing movement. Jazz crosses into new age territory when it avoids standard "swing" rhythms, its instrumentation is enhanced by synthesizers and the use of digital reverb, and it is not repetitious or inaccessibly intellectual. It is distinguished from other new age subgenres, especially space music, by its rhythm and identifiable melodies. Typical instrumentation includes woodwinds, horns, percussion, keyboards, and string instruments. Among the better known artists are Beaver and Krause, Peter Davison, David Friesen, Jerry Goodman, Hiroshima, Yusef Lateef, Pat Metheny, Oregon, Jean-Luc Ponty, John Renbourn, Shadowfax, Ben Sidran, John Themis, and Tim Weisberg.

Meditation Music. This style aims at expanding awareness into deeper and higher levels of consciousness. It removes negativity through careful arrangement of each note and one pattern. It isn't always serene and gentle in nature; more dynamic forms often combine drumming and pulsing music to stimulate an active response within the listener (e.g., dancing). Key practitioners include Aeoliah, Chazz, Steven Halpern, and Laraaji.

Native American/Indigenous Music. The accompaniment is provided by rattles, drums, and group chorus, depending upon the context and form of the musical presentation. The types of songs, their placement in a ceremony, and the textural form--meaningful words or vocalized sounds--reflect the world views of various tribes. Duple meter (patterns of two drum beats throughout) percussion patterns, a wide variety of tempos, and dynamic accents contribute to the distinctive quality of tribal music. The genre includes three subdivisions: sacred/ceremonial songs, social songs, and personal vocal and instrumental music. Among the notable exponents are Kevin Locke, R. Carlos Nakai, and A. Paul Ortega.

Pop Music. Of all new age genres, this one is the most energetic and accessible. It tends to be very melodic, often weaving acoustic and electronic instruments into a sonic whole. It has depth, using harmony, melody, and simple key modulations rather than creating space-like sounds. Leading artists include Bruce Becvar, Checkfield, David Darling, the Durutti Column, Michael Hedges, Eberhard Schoener, and Liz Story.

Progressive Music. This category mixes the excitement and vision of progressive and experimental music with the sensitivity and warmth of the new age genre. Largely created by state-of-the-art technology and a wide array of electronic instruments, it's cinematic in scope and imparts a feeling of momentum. Compositions deliver symphonic--sometimes psychedelic--crescendoes intended to jar the listener's perception of reality. Notable practitioners Pete Bardens, Peter Baumann, Gavin Bryars, Cusco, Patrick Gleeson, Mark Isham, Daniel Lentz, Mannheim Steamroler, Patrick Moraz, Patrick O'Hearn, and Michael Oldfield.

Solo Instrumental Music. The style serves to slow down the mind, thereby aiding in relaxation or meditation. The music often consists of long tones and is at times almost harmonically structureless. It acts as a blank canvas on which the listener can visualize personal "mind pictures." Key exponents include Philip Aaberg, Alex De Grassi, Paul Greaver, Daniel Hecht, Paul Horn, Eric Johnson, Peter Kater, Andreas Vollenweider, George Winston, and Sylvia Woods.

South Health Music. Specifically created as a tool for health and wellness, the genre attempts to either facilitate brain activity for accelerated learning or take the listener to deep places in the consciousness for meditation (via slow brain wave patterns). Many releases deal with the relationship among keynotes, colors, and the chakras; others combine vowel sounds, rhythmic pulses, drones, and different scales to resonate and affect the physical body as well as the etheric energy field. Top artists include Roger Eno, Steven Halpern, Paul Temple, and Michael Uyttebroek.

Space Music. Concerned with both inner and outer space, this style opens and creates spatial relationships. Most composers use synthesizers (sometimes exclusively) which can sustain notes timelessly or produce wholly new sounds. The balance between the rhythm track and melody line determines a great deal of the imagery and perspective of a particular piece. Leading exponents include Kevin Braheny, Mychael Danna, Peter Davison, Constance Demby, Edgar Froese, Steve Hillage, Jade Warrior, Kitaro, David Lange, Ray Lynch, Anthony Phillips, Steve Roach, Michael Stearns, and Stomu Yamashta.

Traditional Music. Contemplative rather than entertaining by nature, it is typically instrumental and incorporates sacred, meditative, and healing properties. Utilizing a structure based on ancient traditions such a Pythagorean harmonics, it transforms the vibrational level of any environment into a relaxing, inspiring, and healing atmosphere. Key practitioners include Aeolus, William Aura, D'Rachael, Dean Evenson, Steve and David Gordon, Bob Kindler, Steve Kindler, Daniel Kobialka, Penguin Cafe Orchestra, Sanford Ponder, Mike Rowland, Nancy Rumbel, Ira Stein and Russell Walder, Tim Story, Eric Tingstad, and Paul Winter.

Vocal Music. A broad-based category encompassing folk, pop, jazz, and rock. Themes covered include (1) an expanded sense of personal identity; (2) a recognition of connection with the global family; (3) a holistic awareness of the planet; (4) an awakened responsibility for one's thoughts, words, and actions; (5) an acknowledgment of the wisdom or divinity in everyone; (6) an emphasis on the healing power in relationships; (7) a recognition of the wholeness of body, mind, and spirit; and (8) an admission that there is an underlying power and intelligence called God, Love, Universal Spirit, etc., with an absence of spiritual elitism. Among the notable artists are Clannad, Eliza Gilkyson, David Hykes, Ian Matthews, Kim Robertson, Michael Stillwater, and Michael Tomlinson.

World Music. The genre spans music (1) derived solely from one culture and accepted by others; (2) created when the indigenous material of one culture is combined with the material of other cultures (e.g., melodic structures and rhythms of India fused with the impovisation of European pop music); and (3) drawn from or uniting both ancient and contemporary styles (e.g., South American flutes mixed with Spanish guitar and modern synthesizers). Key exponents include Azymuth, Patrick Ball, Spencer Brewer, Do'a, Stephan Grossman, Jan Hassell, Inti-Illimani, Stephan Micus, Popol Vuh, Shardad, and Tri Atma.

Table 111

William Ackerman, November 1949-

Although an accomplished acoustic guitarist whose solo albums incorporate elements of folk, jazz, and European classicism, his greatest impact has come from founding Windham Hill Productions. The company—which includes Lost Lake Arts Records, Magenta Records, Open Air Records, Rabbit Ears Productions, and Windham Wind Records—has dominated the new age genre since the late 1970s.

Born in Germany, Ackerman started out as a carpenter, forming Windham Hill Builders in the early 1970s. He also found time to compose guitar music for theatrical productions at nearby Stanford University; as a result, friends encouraged him to record his material. The resulting album, *The Search for the Turtle's Navel* (Windham Hill; 1976), was originally distributed privately in the Palo Alto area as a cassette.

Ackerman soon expanded his base of operations, handling business matters as well as producing other artists, including Alex de Grassi, Liz Story, and George Winston, whose *Winter* (Windham Hill 1025; 1983; #54) was the label's first big seller, spending 178 weeks on the *Billboard* album charts through 1990. Although he would relinquish CEO duties in 1986, he has remained active with the company as Artist & Repertoire head.

Although Ackerman's own LPs have not hit the mainstream pop charts, they have continued to sell moderately well over the years. His work often features only subdued steel-string guitar instrumentals; however, it is sometimes accompanied by spare violin, cello, piano, and English horn parts. His album releases—all generally cut from the same fabric—include *It Takes a Year* (Windham Hill; 1977), *Childhood and Memory* (Windham Hill; 1979), *Passage* (Windham Hill 1014; 1981), *Past Light* (Windham Hill 1028; 1983), *Conferring with the Moon* (Windham Hill 1050; 1986), *Imaginary Roads* (Windham Hill 1078; 1988), *The Opening of Doors* (Windham Hill; 1992), *Windham Hill Retrospective* (Windham Hill; 1993), *Sound of Wind-Driven Rain* (Windham Hill; 1998), and *Hearing Voices* (Windham Hill; 2001).

World Beat: Conjunto

Conjunto, like American country music, possesses rural roots and deals with traditional subjects such as drinking, cheating, lying, etc. The most notable feature of the style is its danceable 2/4 polka beat. However, many other stylistic elements can be discerned within the mix, including Mexican forms like ranchera and mariachi (the latter built around a classical instrumental ensemble--e.g., several winds, violins, guitarrons; the Germans contributed accordions, whose versatility made them comparable to today's synthesizers) and German, Polish, and Czech immigrant dances as well as other European and Mexican styles (e.g., vals, schottische, huapango, jaranas, the Spanish bolero).

The earliest recordings of accordion-based music of this type were made by Bruno Villarreal in 1928. The real pioneers of the style, however, were Narciso Martinez and Santiago Jimenez.

Tony De La Rosa, who began his career in the late 1950s, was the next big influence on the genre. Utilizing a choppy, staccato style, his accordion playing was melodic and intricate. His legacy included establishing the use of drums in the conjunto ensemble, amplifying the bajo sexto, and introducing the electric bass. Other important 1960s conjunto performers included Steve Jordan and El Conjunto Bernal.

By the 1970s, virtuoso accordion player Flaco Jiminez had introduced a rock style, along with pronounced country features, to the genre. The Texas Tornados--which included Tex-Mex singer Freddy Fender and two alumni of the Sir Douglas quintet, guitarist Doug Sahm and keyboardist Augie Meyers--became his most widely known vehicle.

Conjunto has retained a flexible, continuously-evolving core up to the present day. Modern practitioners play a wide range of styles and rhythms. The most notable styles include:

Ranchera; i.e., songs idealizing hacienda and rural life. A Mexican form of country music, its variants include norteno (northern Mexican music) whose most successful interpreter is the Los Angeles-based Los Lobos.

Corridos. Essentially ballads, they are the mainstay of most Tex-Mex bands. Usually played at a slow or moderate pace, the genre is largely comprised sad or poignant stories of struggle or controversy.

Cumbias. Part of the Tex-Mex family, they represent a simpler working-class variant of the original Colombian dance form. The genre is characterized by aggressive syncopation, percussion, and the sound of flutes and saxophones. The subject matter includes historical incidents, life stories of notorious criminals, and--like rancheras--lyrical songs about bad women, alcohol, lost love, and other struggles reflecting the social conditions of the time.

Tejano. A newer, urban-based offshoot of conjunto, the genre incorporates instruments identified with rock such as electric guitars and synthesizers. The artists tend to have a glitzy appearance, with leather, big hair, etc. Their repertoire includes rock, country, and pop material in addition to the traditional, polka-based, accordion-laced conjunto style (complete with a German oompah beat). Among the more popular artists have been Selena (Corpus Christi), Los Palominos (Los Angeles), La Mafia (Houston), and Mazz (Brownsville).

PUNK/NEW WAVE/POSTPUNK

New Wave

The British Scene

By the mid-1970s, pop music was ripe for change. Heavy metal and the progressive rock hybrids then dominating sales had turned off many listeners, exuding pretentious self-consciousness, art for art's sake, and a profit orientation that favored arena-sized audiences. At the same time, pubs had nurtured an alternative style featuring a rollicking mixture of old-style rock and roll, careening honky-tonk, and good-timey skiffle music. The "pub-rock" movement was assisted further by the formation of small labels such as Stiff Records (1976). Prime exponents included Graham Parker, Brinsley Schwarz, Dr. Feelgood, Ducks Deluxe, Kilburn and the High Roads, and Rockpile (featuring Dave Edmunds and Nick Lowe).

The new wave, in essence, represented a refinement of the punk scene. It neutralized that genre's destructive tendencies, appropriating punk's energy to revitalize traditional rock conventions. Leading artists--which included Joe Jackson, the Pretenders, Police, Wreckless Eric, Elvis Costello, and the Tom Robinson Band--also displayed a receptiveness to a wide array of stylistic influences such as reggae and jazz.

Like the pub rock and punk movements, the new wave represented a conscious reaction against the American rock industry innovations of the late 1960s, including (1) Woodstock-styled rock fests and stadium venues, (2) a dependence on mega-corporations to disseminate recordings, and (3) the view of the rock audience as a community with the artist functioning as a unifying agent (in contrast, new wave artists projected themselves as alienated loners reaching out to the loner in each of its listeners.

The American Scene

The U.S. version of the movement lacked any kind of socio-economic core. It was largely the product of youthful middle-class eccentrics motivated by the desire to leave a mark on rock history. It is notable that many of them were located far from major urban centers.

Ohio--particularly Akron and Cleveland--became a focal point for the emerging new wave ethic. These artists tended to fall into one of the following categories: (1) the arty (Pere Ubu, Tin Huey, the Human Switchboard), (2) the profane (the Bizarros, Teacher's Pet, the Dead Boys, the Rubber City Rebels), and (3) the poppy (Rachel Sweet).

Lacking the media resources available in the larger cities, local fans provided the initiative and insights necessary to generate a full-fledged movement. Where major labels weren't interested, fans managed and signed up local talent for small regional outfits. Further support was provided by mimeographed manifestos, homemade rock magazines, and an ad hoc network for the distribution of records.

By the late 1970s, the genre had finally made a substantial commercial impact at the national level when American bands such as the Cars and the Knack placed records in the upper reaches of the charts. This coincided with the first stateside breakthrough of a British new wave band, Police.

The movement remained successful into the early 1980s, fragmenting into a wide array of spinoffs, including techno-pop, the new romantics, neo-rockabilly, neo-psychedelia, goth rock, thrash, alternative dance, the ska/bluebeat revival, and indie rock.

Top Artists and Their Recordings

--The British Scene

Elvis Costello--*My Aim Is True* (1977); *This Year's Model* (1978); *Armed Forces* (1979); *Get Happy!!* (1980); *Taking Liberties* (1980); *Trust* (1981); *Almost Blue* (1981); *Imperial Bedroom* (1982); *Punch the Clock* (1983); *Goodbye Cruel World* (1984)

Joe Jackson--*Look Sharp!* (1979); *I'm the Man* (1979); *Beat Crazy* (1980); *Jumpin' Jive* (1981); *Night and Day* (1982)

Jam--*Setting Sons* (1980); *Sound Affects* (1981); *The Gift* (1982); *The Bitterest Pill* (1982); *Dig the New Breed* (1983); *Beat Surrender* (1983)

Police--*Outlandos d'Amour* (1979); *Reggatta de Blanc* (1979); *Zanyatta Mondatta* (1980); *Ghost in the Machine* (1981); *Synchronicity* (1983)

The Pretenders--*The Pretenders* (1980); *Extended Play* (1981); *Pretenders II* (1981); *Learning to Crawl* (1984); *Get Close* (1986); *packed!* (1990)

Tom Robinson Band--*Power in the Darkness* (1978); *TRB Two* (1979)

XTC--*White Music* (1977); *Go To* (1978); *Drums and Wires* (1979); *Black Sea* (1980); *English Settlement* (1982)

--The American Scene

B-52's--*The B-52's* (1979); *Wild Planet* (1980); "Rock Lobster" (1980); "Private Idaho" (1980); *Mesopotamia* (1982); *Whammy!* (1983)

Blondie--*Blondie* (1977); *Plastic Letters* (1978); *Parallel Lines* (1978); "Heart of Glass" (1979);

Eat to the Beat (1979); *Autoamerican* (1980)

The Cars--*The Cars* (1978); *Candy-O* (1979); *Shake It Up* (1981); "You Might Think" (1984)

The Knack--"My Sharona" (1979)

Pere Ubu--*The Modern Dance* (1977); *Dub Housing* (1978)

Talking Heads--*Talking Heads: 77* (1977); *More Songs About Buildings and Food* (1978); *Fear of Music* (1979); *Remain in Light* (1980); *The Name of This Band Is Talking Heads* (1982); *Speaking in Tongues* (1983); *Stop Making Sense* (1984); *Little Creatures* (1985); *True Stories* (1986); *Naked* (1988)

Table 112

The Clash

The Clash are widely recognized to have been the premier British band within the 1970s punk revolution. More politically astute than the Jam, the Buzzcocks, and other inherently pop bands, and able to sustain a high order of creativity over a comparatively long career as opposed to the incendiary Sex Pistols, the Clash supplanted the Rolling Stones as the greatest performing rock band in the minds of many critics and fans during the 1977-1986 period.

Aware of the U.S. underground punk scene espoused by bands such as the Ramones, Blondie, and the Talking Heads, the Clash—comprised of founding members Joe Strummer and Mick Jones, and shared singing and guitar roles, and later additions, bassist Paul Simonon and drummer Nicky Headon—came together in 1976. Their ability to communicate the alienation of Britain's working class youth was evident in the crudely recorded debut album, *The Clash* (CBS 82000; 1977; #12 UK), which sold well at home.

With hopes of breaking into the American market, CBS hired Sandy Pearlman (known for his work with heavy metal band, Blue Oyster Cult) to produce the second LP. *Give 'Em Enough Rope* (Epic 35543; 1978; #2 UK) earned kudos from stateside critics for its energy and intelligent lyrics, and sold moderately well due in part to a North American tour in early 1979. *The Clash*, which had previously been available stateside as an import, was released as a two-disc set—with added singles releases—on Epic (#36060), adding further luster to the band's reputation.

On the strength of increasingly sophisticated musicianship and tight studio arrangements, the Clash's recordings—the EP, *Black Market Clash* (Epic 36846; 1980;

#74 US); the albums *London Callling* (Epic 36328; 1980; #9 UK, #27 US), *Sandanista* (Epic 37037; 1981; #19 UK, #24 US), and *Combat Rock* (Epic 37689; 1982; #2 UK, #7 US); and singles " Train In Vain" (Epic 50851; 1980; #23 US), "Should I Stay or Should I Go" (Epic 03061; 1982; #45 US), and "Rock the Casbah" (Epic 03245; 1982; #8 US)—enjoyed increasing success on the American charts. Interest was further fueled by the release of the docu-film, *Rude Boy*, which spotlighted a fictionalized Clash roadie along with live footage of the band. The departure of Jones in 1983 due to musical differences with Strummer, however, led to a drop-off in quality of the band's output. While the new Jones vehicle, Big Audio Dynamite, made an immediate impact on the American charts—tt—the Clash's next album, *Cut the Crap* (Epic 40017; 1985; #16 UK, #88 US), sold poorly. Opting to disband the band in early 1986, Strummer pursued a solo career, writing film music (e.g., "Love Kills" for *Sid & Nancy*, *The Walker*), acting (*Straight to Hell*, *Lost in Space*), and performing on tour with the Pogues.

Table 113

Police

The Police were one of many conventional rock acts allowing themselves to be marketed under the New Wave banner in order to enhance their chances for commercial acceptance. Although the band's savvy blend of stripped-down guitar-driven pop, smoothed-over reggae rhythms, and bleached blonde poster boy looks connected with the public from the start, an abundance of infectious compositions and clever video clips—programmed round-the-clock by MTV and other cable TV channels—would elevate them to superstardom at the time of their breakup.

The original impetus for the Police was supplied by drummer Stewart Copeland, who provided its name and enlisted his brother, Miles, a talent agent and record executive, to manage their career. He added singer/bassist/composer Gordon Sumner (aka Sting) for his stage presence in 1976, and when the original lead guitarist left the following year, brought in Andy Summers, who was well known for session work and as a member of various British rock groups.

The band's debut album, *Outlandos D'Amour* (A&M 4753; 1978; #23), failed to catch on immediately due to BBC censorship of the initial singles releases—"Roxanne" (A&M 2096; 1979; #32) and "Can't Stand Losing You" (A&M 2147; 1979; #42 UK)—and the inability to fit established radio playlist guidelines in the U.S. Critics, however, were almost without exception, enthusiastic; *The New York Times*' John Rockwell would write that "no other rock band in recent memory has been able to combine intellectuality, progressivism, and visceral excitement so well." (April 5, 1979). When A&M decided to include "Roxanne" on the sampler LP, *No Wave*, the song entered the *Billboard Hot 100*.

With A&M providing greater studio and promotional support, the second album, *Regatta De Blanc* (A&M 4792; 1979; #25), earned a 1980 Grammy for Best Rock Instrumental Performance with the title track. The next release, *Zenyatta Mondatta* (A&M 4831; 1980; #5), did even better, going platinum and garnering two Grammys in 1981, Best Rock Performance by a Duo or Group with Vocal ("Don't Stand So Close to Me") and Best Rock Instrumental Performance ("Behind My Camel"). *Ghost in the Machine* (A&M 3730; 1981; #2), although receiving only lukewarm endorsements from the press (due in part to its darker thematic concerns), also achieved platinum sales.

The fifth LP, *Synchronicity* (A&M 3735; 1983; #1), commercially outstripped all of the Police's earlier work by a considerable margin, largely due to the widespread appeal of the Sting-composed ballad, "Every Breath You Take" (A&M 2542; 1983; #1). The work included many other gems as well, including three more hit singles: "King of Pain" (A&M 2569; 1983; #3), "Synchronicity" (A&M 2571; 1983; #16), and "Wrapped Around Your Finger" (A&M 2614; 1984; #8). *Synchronicity* would pull all of the band's earlier albums back onto the charts as well as earning two 1983 Grammys: Best Pop Vocal Performance by a Duo or Group with Vocal ("Every Breath You Take") and Best Rock Performance by a Duo or Group with Vocal.

At this point in time the band members split off to pursue various solo projects, only getting together to perform three benefit concerts for Amnesty International in summer 1986. Although demands for an official reunion for been repeatedly dashed, A&M has continued to market the Policy legacy via a steady stream of compilation releases, most notably *Every Breath You Take – The Singles* (A&M 3902; 1986; #7), *Message in a Box: The Complete Recordings* (A&M 0150; 1993; #79), and *The Police Live!* (A&M 0222; 1995; #86).

Table 114

The Ramones

The first band emerging from 1970s New York punk scene to issue an album, the Ramones established the template for the movement: frenetic tempos, terse songs—often less than two minutes in length, stripped-down arrangements featuring buzz-saw guitars, humorously moronic lyrics, and a scruffy transmogrified hippie-greaser (torn blue jeans and leather jackets) fashion sense. After touring the U.K. in mid-1976, their bash-trash-pop sound and cartoonish attitude would be copied by countless new English punk acts—indeed, the Ramones' recordings would always find a more receptive audience in Great Britain.

The Ramones' eponymous debut (Sire 7520; 1976)—released at a time when radio was ruled by corporate AOR rock, polished Top Forty singles, and the lush progressive rock of Pink Floyd, Genesis, and the like—was one of the most revolutionary albums in rock history. The band's studied primitivism would be maintained over a long string of critically lauded LPs, including *Leave Home* (Sire 7528; 1977; #45 UK), *Rocket to Russia* (Sire 6042; 1977; #60 UK, #49 US), *Road to Ruin* (Sire 6063; 1978; #32 UK), and *It's Alive* (Sire 26074; 1979; #27).

Following the band's first lineup change—with the departure of drummer Tommy Ramone (aka Tom Erdelyi), Marc Bell (aka Marky Ramone) joining mainstays lead vocalist Joey Ramone (aka Jeffrey Hyman), guitarist Johnny Ramone (John Cummings), and bassist Dee Dee Ramone (aka Douglas Colvin)—and a growing sense that the formula had grown stale, the Ramones enlisted wall-of-sound producer Phil Spector to assist in the making of the more polished *End of the Century* (Sire 6077; 1980; #14 UK, #44 US). Subsequent releases—*Pleasant Dreams* (Sire 3571; 1981; #58 US), *Subterranean Jungle* (Sire 23800; 1983; #83 US), *Too Tough to Die* (Sire 25187; 1984; #63 UK), *Animal Boy* (Sire 25433; 1986; #38 UK), *Halfway to Sanity* (Sire 25641; 1987; #78 UK), *Brain Drain* (Sire 25905; 1989; #73 UK), *Live Loco* (Sire 1901; 1991), and *Mondo Bizarro* (Radioactive 10615; 1992)—paled in comparison to the output of the leading hardcore groups of the 1980s.

Unable to capitalize on the punk revival of the early 1990s, the Ramones issued a tribute to the Sixties songs that had inspired them in the first place, *Acid Eaters* (Radioactive 10913; 1993), followed by farewell album, *Adios Amigos* (Radioactive 11273; 1995; #62 UK), and tour, documented by the live set, *We're Outta Here!* (Radioactive 11555; 1997).

No Wave

The no wave movement grew out of the coalescence of Lower Manhattan's avant-garde art and music scenes (most notably, punk rock) in the late 1970s. Its exponents were primarily unschooled musicians alienated by rock's inherent conservatism. Although appropriating punk's nihilism and raw, minimal (often using noise for noise's sake) approach, they remained wary of the genre's increasing institutionalization.

The deconstructivist inclinations of no wave were best exemplified by DNA (featuring guitarist Arto Lindsey), Mars, and Teenage Jesus and the Jerks, featuring underground poet Lydia Lunch. The Contortions were perhaps the most "musically developed" no wave group, melding atonality, free jazz, and Captain Beefheart-influenced guitar sonorities with revved-up funk rhythms. Lacking any self-perpetuating mechanism, the genre rapidly lost momentum in the early 1980s. Its most enduring performers included former Theoretical Girls member, Glenn Branca, who went on to create layered, hyper-amped guitar music with pronounced heavy metal leanings, and ex-Branca associates, Thurston Moore and Lee Ranaldo, who would found white noise pioneers, Sonic Youth.

Postpunk Music

Postpunk continued the rebellion in style and substance against mainstream rock conventions begun earlier by the 1970s punk movement. Its break from punk/new wave was precipitated by the latter's affinity with progressive rock developments and the pop mainstream in general. In contrast, postpunk was defiantly inconsequential and advanced the romantic ideals of free expression and institutional autonomy. (It continued to parallel the new wave, however, in pioneering the visual potentialities of music as well as undercutting male belligerence as a be-all.)

In actuality, postpunk was not one particular musical style, but rather a main branch of the rock ancestral tree which was further split into many smaller branches. This family would ultimately encompass a disparate array of genres, including the ska/bluebeat revival, dance-oriented rock (DOR), techno-pop, the new romantics, neo-psychedelia, the Manc Sound, neo-rockabilly, goth rock, hardcore, speed metal, grindcore, oi, the riot grrrl movement, DIY, indie rock, no wave, ambient, rave, house, techno, electronica, and trance. All of these offshoots were united by punk's essence—i.e., driving rhythms generally reinforced by aggressive vocals concerned primarily with themes of alienation and rebellion.

Although less commercially successful than mainstream formats like AOR, adult contemporary, country, rhythm and blues (referred to as "black contemporary" for a time), and the more media-friendly variants of rap/hip hop, postpunk would nevertheless greatly influence the attitude and look of popular music as a whole in the 1980s. Until the rise of grunge and, in a broader sense, alternative rock, combined with the gangsta and progressive rap schools of hip hop in the early 1990s, postpunk provided much of the creative momentum for rock.

A Survey of Postpunk Styles

--1980s

Techno-pop: Depeche Mode, Eurythmics, A Flock of Seagulls, Human League, New Order, Orchestral Manoeuvres in the Dark, Young Marble Giants.

New romantics: ABC, Adam Ant/Adam and the Ants, Culture Club, Duran Duran, Frankie Goes to Hollywood, Billy Idol, the Pet Shop Boys.

Ska/bluebeat revival: the English Beat, Madness, Selector, the Specials.

Neo-psychedelia: Echo and the Bunnymen, the Psychedelic Furs, the Teardrop Explodes.

Hardcore punk: Bad Religion, Black Flag, the Butthole Surfers, the Germs, Husker Du, the Meat Puppets, the Minutemen.

Neo-rockabilly: Stray Cats. Spin-off genre—Shockabilly: The Cramps.

Goth rock: The Cure, Gene Loves Jezebel, Siouxie and the Banshees, the Smiths.

Punk-disco: Massive Attack, Soul II Soul.

No wave: Pussy Galore, Sun City Girls, Thinking Fellers Union Local 242, John Zorn.

Indie rock: Big Black, Camper Van Beethoven, the Chills, the Mekons, My Bloody Valentine, the Pixies, R.E.M., Sebadoh.

--1990s

Electronica

Electronica refers specifically to computer based or enhanced popular music. The genre's antecedents include early efforts to integrated the synthesizer within progressive rock, 1980s techno-pop (or, as it is sometimes called, synth-rock), and 1990s techno.

Many keyboard-based progressive rock artists—most notably, Tangerine Dream, Klaus Schulze, and Eno—began moving toward ambience in the 1970s. During the next decade, ex-Be Bop Deluxe guitarist Bill Nelson, Sonic Boom, Spacemen 3, Spiritualized, and others expanded the instrumental palette of electronic ambience, incorporating treated drones, feedback-generated samples, fuzz-tone, tremelo effects, tape-manipulated Minimalism, and multi-tracked orchestration.

The urban club and hip-hop scenes also influenced the development of electronica. New York-based deejay mixers such as Grandmaster Flash and Afrika Bambaataa helped pioneer a dance-based sound built around samples and scratched beats, ultimately known as electro.

The seminal recording within this genre was "The Adventures of Grandmaster Flash on the Wheels of Steel" (Sugarhill 557; 1981; #55 R&B), which combined the bass riff from Chic's Top Ten disco hit, "Good Times" (Atlantic 3584; 1979; #1) in addition to borrowings from Blondie, Queen, and the Sugarhill Gang's "Rapper's Delight" (Sugarhill 542; 1979; #36). Afrika Bambaataa created his own brand of electronic funk in twelve-inch singles like the electronic beat collage "Planet Rock" (Tommy Boy 823; 1982; #4 R&B, #48 pop), which used Kraftwerk's "Trans-Europe Express" (Capitol 4460; 1977; #67) and "Numbers," a track from *Computer World* (Warner Bros. 3549; 1981; #72).

Although European artists and producers still dominate both the ambient and groove-oriented electronica in the 1990s, the style has retained a substantial audience in America not only in dance venues but among progressive rock followers. Despite the relative absence of radio play and print media coverage, commercial web sites such as Audiogalaxy.com (whose clients included the likes of Frail, Galaxy 7, Kinetic Daydream, LiscCrap, Poison Drinker, Sounds of Om2, and Sprocket Lunatic in 2001) have proven effective in disseminating electronica via the mp3 format.

Techno

Techno—which originated as instrumental-based electronica in 4/4 time centered around hyperactive keyboard riffing and edgy, explosive drumming—drew upon the synthesizer music of 1970s Euro-rock bands such as Kraftwerk, Faust, and Can and the postpunk industrial dance movement of the 1980s, spearheaded by Cabaret Voltaire, Throbbing Gristle, Ministry, and other largely British artists.

Although first centered in Detroit, the genre was imported by English clubs in the late 1980s. Closely aligned with house music and club raves—i.e., events characterized by lasers, mammoth sound systems, and countless dancers fueled by the designer drug Ecstasy—techno evolved from the neo-psychedelia of the Manchester-based Stone Roses and Scotland's Primal Scream into a diversity of hyphenated forms in the 1990s, including Ambient Techno and Big Beat.

The ambient school utilized samples of recording music, nature and other extraneous noises to create richly-textured, synthesizer-driven soundscapes; prime exponents included German classical composer Peter Namlook, England's Aphex Twin, and Australian avant-garde artist Paul Schutze.

Big Beat, sometimes referred to as "Rock Techno," combined pounding rhythms, synthesizer washes, and sampling within a more traditional rock format. This style owed much to the pioneering work of Prodigy, Underworld, and the Chemical Brothers, whose LPs—most notably, *Exit Planet Dust* (AstralWorks 6157; 1995; #9 UK), *Dig Your Own Hole* (AstralWorks 6180; 1997; #1 UK, #14 US), and *Surrender* (AstralWorks 47610; 1999; #1 UK, #32 US)—were instrumental in making it the best-selling recorded dance music in British history.

Trance

Trance is a broad designation for various permutations of electronically generated dance music characterized by repeated crescendos featuring Doppler effects, sequencer riffs, and propulsive bass and drum patterns. It is built primarily on three prior traditions: synthesizer-driven postpunk industrial music, Detroit-based techno disco, and early 1970s psychedelia.

Closely related to ambient, techno, and house, the genre originated in Germany during the late 1980s. Its earliest manifestation was marked by the merging of TB 303 synthesizers with mainstream dance material. Augmented by widespread use of the methamphetamine drug Ecstasy, trance spread to Goa and Thailand in the early 1990s, and then to the European club scene; most notably, Great Britain, Holland, and Italy.

From the outset, trance has continued to evolve, providing the impetus for a considerable number of subgenres, including hard trance, acid trance, trancecore (heavily influenced by 1980s hardcore), psychedelic trance, and progressive trance. The artists and deejay producers most instrumental in shaping the style have included Paul Oakenfold, BT, Sash, Robert Miles, DJ Taucher, Paul Van Dyk, Tall Paul, Vincent de Moor, Ferry Corsten, Astral Matrix, Juno Reactor, and William Orbit.

Table 115

Beggars Banquet

Beggars Banquet began in 1974 as a record store founded by London disc jockeys Martin Mills and Nick Austin in the Earl's Court district. Selling both new and used recordings, the outlet's success led to the opening of branches in Fulham and Ealing. By 1976 the company had moved into tour promotion, handling the Commodores, the Crusaders, Southside Johnny, and other artists reflecting the stores' specialties.

The rise of punk in the second half of the 1970s led to a change of emphasis; the stores began stocking the vast array of seven-inch singles being released by domestic and foreign labels, and the promotions firm focused on booking bands such as the Damned, the Stranglers, and Graham Parker. The central facility even provided rehearsal space for emerging acts.

A request by the Lurkers, a London-based punk band strongly influenced by the Ramones, for management support, led to a record label search. Failing in this regard, Beggars Banquet decided to start its own recording company. Following the debut single release, the Lurkers' "Shadow" (Beggars Banquet BEG 1; 1977), the label developed a reputation as a shrewd judge of underground talent.

As the punk movement moved closer to the pop mainstream, Beggars Banquet found commercial success. Ivor Biggun's "The Winker's Song (Misprint)" (Beggard Banquet BOP 1) brought the company its first U.K. Top Thirty hit in September 1978. Finances were placed on solid footing for good with the emergence of Doll and Gary Numan's Tubeway Army in early 1979. Numan would go on to top the British singles and album charts twice within a year—"Cars" (Beggars Banquet BEG 23/Atco 7211; 1979), "Complex" (Beggars Banquet BEG 29; 1979), *Replicas* (Beggars Banquet/Atco 117; 1979, and *The Pleasure Principle* (Beggars Banquet/Atco 120; 1980)

Success led to further expansion, most notably the launching of two subsidiary labels, 4AD in 1980, and Situation 2 in 1983. The former label, in particular, developed its own easily identifiable sound, a moody impressionistic sound characterized by colliding minor chords, swirling guitars, and swooping vocals. Key singings would include the Cocteau Twins, Dead Can Dance, X-Mal Deutschland, This Mortal Coil, Modern English, Colourbox, Wolfgang Press, and Lush. In the meantime, the parent company would maintain its own successful track record with Bauhaus, the Associates, Icicle Works, and Wah! all releasing British hits during 1982-1984. The international popularity of the Cult's "She Sells Sanctuary" (Beggars Banquet U.K./Sire 0-20407 12-inch U.S. single; 1985) helped establish Beggars Banquet as a worldwide commercial force. A long run of chart hits—both in America and Great Britain—by the likes of Bauhaus spin-off Love and Rockets, the Charlatans UK, Loop, Buffalo Tom, Mercury Rev, and Luna further cemented the label's market viability as well as its aesthetic reputation. [Thompson. 2000.]

Table 116

DIY

DIY--or "Do It Yourself"--is more a frame of mind, or approach, in creating music than any identifiable style or genre. While the term has been specifically applied to 1980s postpunk artists committed an amateurish, Everyman ethic, it has probably existed since homo sapiens first arrived at the concept of music by slapping various body parts, and experimenting with castoff bones, gourds, and sea shells.

Art music composers such as Erik Satie, intrigued with the dada movement immediately following World War I, seem to have had an affinity for DIY conventions. Certainly, it has provided an alternative perspective for the development of virtually every indigenous American popular music genre. It all but defines folk music from a purist standpoint, and has fed the populist element of rock music—that most rebellious and anti-elitist of all musical forms. The spirit of DIY literally saturates 1950s rockabilly, 1960s garage rock, and 1970s punk/new wave. It represents the missing link between the passionate rants of the Sex Pistols, the Clash, and thousands of other bands on both sides of the Atlantic who were barely able to play their instruments prior to the 1980s, and the more stripped down, incendiary, low-fi proponents of the 1990s alternative rock. Notable practitioners—and seminal recordings—of this transitional postpunk variant include the Adverts (*Crossing the Red Sea with the Adverts*; Bright 201; 1978), Swell Maps (*Collision Time*; Rough Trade; 1981), Mekons (*So Good It Hurts*; Sin 008; 1988), Television Personalities (*Mummy Your Not Watching Me*; Fire; 1982), and the Posies (*Dear 23*; DGC 24305; 1990).

Hardcore

This postpunk style retained an emphasis on the raw, hard rock basics typifying late 1970s punk. The major centers of activity during hardcore's heyday in the 1980s included London, Los Angeles, and the SST Records stable of bands in Minneapolis. It remained a force throughout the 1990s, thriving on the edges of speed metal and alternative rock (the cross-fertilization with the latter genre produced Seattle-based grunge).

Top Artists and Their Recordings

Alien Sex Fiend--*Acid Bath* (1985)

Bad Religion--*Bad Religion EP* (1981; *How Could Hell Be Any Worse?* (1982); *Into the Unknown* (1983); *Back to the Known EP* (1984); *Suffer* (1988); *No Control* (1989); *Against the Grain* (1990); *Generator* (1992); *Recipe For Hate* (1993); *Stranger Than Fiction* (1994)

Black Flag--*Nervous Breakdown EP* (1978); *Jealous Again EP* (1980); *Six Pack* (1981); *TV Party* (1982); *Everything Went Black* (1982); *My War* (1984); *Family Man* (1984); *Slip It In* (1984); *Live '84 Cassette* (1984); *Loose Nut* (1985); *Process of Weeding Out* (1985); *In My Head* (1985); *Who's Got the 10 1/2?* (1986); *Wasted...Again* (1987); *Annihilate This Week* (1987); *I Can See You EP* (1989)

Butthole Surfers--*Butthole Surfers EP* (1983); *Live PCPPEP* (1984); *Psychic...Powerless...Another Man's Sac* (1985); *Cream Corn From the Socket of Davis EP* (1985); *Rembrandt Pussyhorse* (1986); *Locust Abortion Technician* (1987); *Hairway to Steven* (1988); *Independent Worm Saloon LP* (1993)

Christian Death--*Only Theatre of Pain* (1982)

Circle Jerks--*Group Sex* (1981); *Wild in the Streets* (1982)

Dead Fucking Last--*Dead Funking Last* (199?)

Dead Kennedys--*Fresh Fruit For Rotting Vegetables* (1980); *In God We Trust, Inc.* (1981); *Plastic Surgery Disasters* (1982); *Frankenchrist* (1985); *Bedtime for Democracy* (1986); *Give Me Convenience or Give Me Death* (1987)

Flipper--*Album--Generic Flipper* (1981); *Gone Fishin'* (1984); *Blow'n Chunks* (1984); *Public Flipper Limited* (1986); *Sex Bomb Baby!* (1988); *American Grafishy* (1993)

Gwar--*America Must Be Destroyed* (1992)

Husker Du--*Land Speed Record* (1981); *Everything Falls Apart and More* (1982); *Metal Circus EP* (1983); *Zen Arcade* (1984; *New Day Rising* (1985); *Flip Your Wig* (1985); *Candy Apple Grey* (1986); *Warehouse: Songs and Stories* (1987); *The Living End* (1994)

Meat Puppets--*In a Car EP* (1981); *Meat Puppets* (1982); *Meat Puppets II* (1984); *Up on the Sun* (1985); *Out My Way EP* (1986); *Mirage* (1986); *Huevos* (1987); *Monsters* (1989); *No Strings Attached* (1990); *Forbidden Places* (1991); *Too High to Die* (1994)

Minor Threat--*Out of Step* (1983); *Minor Threat* (1984); *Complete* (1988)

Minutemen--*Paranoid Time EP* (1980); *The Punch Line EP* (1981); *Bean Spill EP* (1982); *What Makes a Man Start Fires?* (1982); *Buzz or Howl Under the Influence of Heat EP* (1983); *Double Nickels on the Dime* (1984); *The Politics of Time* (1984); *Project: Mersh EP* (1985); *3-Way Tie (For Last)* (1985); *Ballot Result* (1987)

New Model Army--*No Rest For the Wicked* (1985); *The Mark of Cain* (1986); *New Model Army EP* (1987); *Thunder and Consolation* (1989)

The Plasmatics--*Metal Priest* (1980); *Beyond the Valley of 1984* (1981)

Prong--*Primitive Origins* (1987); *Force Fed* (1989); *Beg to Differ* (1990); *Rude Awakening* (1996)

Rancid--*Rancid* (1993); *Let's Go* (1994)

Suicidal Tendencies--*Suicidal Tendencies* (1983); *Join the Army* (1987); *Suicidal for Life* (1994)

The Unforgiven--*The Unforgiven* (1986)

Table 117

Jello Biafra/Dead Kennedys

Although best known as the leader of hardcore pioneers, the Dead Kennedys, Jello Biafra is also a successful indie record label executive, spoken-word artist, and political activist. Born Eric Boucher in Boulder, Colorado, he matriculated to the San Francisco punk scene in the late 1970s. There, he formed the Dead Kennedys in 1978 along with guitarist East Bay Ray, bassist Klaus Floride, and drummer J.H. Pelligro. From the beginning, the band parlayed a rapid-fire punk sound in criticizing the Moral Majority, U.S. imperialism and fascism, America's plastic suburban lifestyle.

Although never mainstream act, a twelve-inch single, "Too Drunk To Fuck"/"The Prey"

(Cherry Red 12; 1981), reach the Top Five in Great Britain despite a radio ban. Following one album on the I.R.S. label, *Fresh Fruit for Rotting Vegetables* (SP 70014; 1981), the band formed its own record company, Alternative Tentacles, concerned with providing a mouthpiece for unsigned hardcore acts. The label was thrust into the public spotlight when the release of the Dead Kennedys' *Frankenchrist* (Alternative Tentacles VIRUS 45; 1985) led to charges of distributing pornography to minors as interpreted by newly revised U.S. obscenity statutes; the controversy centered on inclusion of a poster reproducing H.R. Giger's surrealist painting, *Landscape XX*, which depicted genetalia and various sex acts. Although a hung jury led to dismissal of the case, the protracted struggle undermined band relations, resulting in a break-up after the release of *Bedtime for Democracy* (Alternative Tentacles VIRUS 50; 1986). The Dead Kennedys would reappear in the headlines in 1993 when reissues of their first album were inadvertently included with CDs being shipped to Christian radio stations nationwide.

Biafra has continued to speak out on political issues, most notably free speech, through solo spoken-word recordings, collaborations with other artists (e.g., D.O.A., NOMEANSNO), and college lecture tours. The bulk of his energies, however, have gone into administering Alternative Tentacles, which continues to release albums by socially-conscious underground artists.

Table 118

Henry Rollins

Henry Rollins (aka Henry Garfield, born February 13, 1961, Washington, D.C.) is easily the most versatile musician to have emerged from the 1980s postpunk movement. He remains active as the leader of a hardcore band, a songwriter, a spoken-word artist, author, publisher, and an actor in films and commercials.

Rollins' multimedia career owes much to his association with the pioneering hardcore band, Black Flag, originally founded by guitarist Greg Ginn in 1977. When lead singer Keith Morris departed to form the Circle Jerks, Black Flag tried several vocalist prior to recruiting Rollins in 1981. Ginn broke up the band in 1987 in order to concentrate on running his record label, SST. Rollins made an immediate impact as a frontman in his own right, releasing a string of solo and group albums—the uncompromisingly intense debut, *Hot Animal Machine* (Texas Hotel 001; 1987), *Drive By Shooting* (Texas Hotel 03; 1987; mini-album released under pseudonym Henrietta Collins and the Wide-Beating Child Haters), the incendiary *Life Time* (Texas Hotel 065; 1988), *Do It!* (Texas Hotel 013; 1989; a mixture of live and studio tracks), and *Hard Volume* (Texas Hotel 010; 1989)—all of which featured his overtly political lyrics and aggressive vocal posturing.

He began achieving mainstream popularity after several years of constant touring capped by a headlining role in the 1991 Lollapalooza Tour (which led to a major label deal with Imago/RCA). The Rollins Band LP, *Weight* (Imago/RCA 21034; 1994; #22 UK, #33 US), was nominated for a Grammy and he became increasingly involved in the production of spoken-word recordings and videos. In mid-1996, Rollins was the center of an eight-figure lawsuit instigated by Imago for allegedly signing with DreamWorks; he argued that BMG's major distributors refused to handle his works. His next album, *Come In and Burn* (50011; 1997; #89), as well as subsequent releases, would in fact be released by DreamWorks.

In the early 1990s, he established his own press, 2.13.61, devoted to issuing his own books (most notably, the critically acclaimed collection of short stories, *Black Coffee Blues*) and those of underground writers such as Iggy Pop. He has also garnered acclaim as a versatile actor, narrating commericals for GMC trucks, the Gap, and Nike, and appearing in entertainment features ranging from gritty dramas like *Johnny Mnemonic* and *Heat*, to the family film, *Jack Frost*.

Table 119

SST

SST was started in 1980 by Greg Ginn as an outlet for distributing the recordings of his band, Black Flag. Based in Los Angeles, the record company soon became recognized as a guiding force in the newly emerging hardcore music scene. The label's early releases—which focused more on the seven-inch, 45 r.p.m. and twelve-inch, 33 1/3 r.p.m. configurations than longplaying albums—consisted largely of talent from the southwestern part of the United States, including the Minutemen, Saccharine Trust, Overkill, the Meat Puppets, the Stains, Wurm, the Dicks, and the Subhumans.

The addition of St. Paul's Husker Du to SST's roster of artists in 1983—climaxed by the release of the critically acclaimed double album set, *Zen Arcade* (SST 027; 1984)—represented a quantum leap in prestige. Ambitious bands flocked to the label from around the country. Furthermore, the break-up of Black Flag in 1986 enabled Ginn to concentrate his energies on the development on new projects. New signings during the mid-1980s included St. Vitus, Das Damen, SWA, Angest, Gone, Bad Brains, and the Leaving Trains. At this time, a market strategy seems to have been implemented by company insiders. Bands hovering on the brink of big-time commercial success—most notably, Husker Du and the Meat Puppets—would move on to major labels while SST redoubled its efforts to locate (and sign) talented unknowns performing in hardcore venues nationwide.

SST continued to expand its roster in the late 1980s, releasing materials seminal bands such as Firehose (a more ambient offshoot of the Minutemen) and Sonic Youth, one of the most influential bands of the postpunk era. In the early 1990s, the label released recordings by Pacific grunge pioneers Soundgarden and the Screaming Trees. {Thompson. 2000.]

Thrash

Thrash is a variant of hardcore distinguished by its (1) lack of a discernable melody (the vocalist usually shouts over a loud guitar buzz); (2) emphasis on crude, propulsive rhythms; (3) simple chord structures; and (4) extremely short songs, often under two minutes in length. The style, which peaked in the early 1980s, was favored by skateboarders and mosh pit denizens.

Top Artists and Their Recordings

The Germs--*(GI)* (1979); *What We Do Is Secret EP* (1981); *Germicide: Live at the Whiskey* (1981); *Lion's Share* (1985); *Rock N' Rule* (1986); *Cat's Clause* (1993)

JFA/Jodie Foster's Army--*Live 1984 Tour* (1984); *Untitled/Mad Garden* (1985)

Suicidal Tendencies--*Join the Army* (1988); *Control the Hatred/Feel Like Shit...Deja-Vu* (1989)

Oi

A sociopolitical youth movement based in Great Britain, oi arose out of the punk and skinhead cultures in the late 1970s. Its audience was working class in background; more specifically, nonconformists who were alienated from politics and establishment mores.

The music exhibited the same hardcore energy characterizing the leading punk bands of the day such as the Sex Pistols and the Clash, while the lyrics exhibited the same sense of social outrage found in 1960s protect music and Bob Marley's reggae anthems. The opening verse of "Labour Politicians Ain't Working Class" typifies the message in oi compositions:

> They talk about poverty and how fast money goes
> But how can they relate to kids in hand me down clothes
> They don't live in the East End or Glasgow
> Don't have to go to places we all have to go
> Labour politicians they ain't working class
> They eat, sleep and travel on a first class pass

Top Artists and Their Recordings

The Angelic Upstarts--*2,000,000 Voices* (1981); *Still From the Heart* (1982)

Bad Manners--*Gosh It's...* (1981); *Party Four EP* (1981); *Forging Ahead* (1982); *Mental Notes* (1985)

Blitz--*All Out Attack EP* (1981); *Never Surrender* (1982)

The Business--"Harry May"/"National Insurance Blacklist" (1981)

Case and Conflict--*The House That Man Built EP* (1982)

Cockney Rejects--*Greatest Hits Vol. I* (1980); *Greatest Hits Vol. II* (1981); *Greatest Hits Vol. III* (1982)

The Exploited--*Punks Not Dead* (1980); *On Stage* (1981); *Troops of Tomorrow* (1982)

The 4 Skins--*The Good, The Bad and the 4 Skins* (1982)

Infa Riot--*Still Out of Order* (1982)

The Last Resort--"Having Fun"/"F.U. 2" (1978)

Rose Tattoo--*Rock 'N' Roll Outlaw* (1980)

Sham 69--*Tell Us the Truth* (1978); *Hersham Boys* (1979); *The Game* (1980)

The U.K. Subs--*Another Kind of Blues* (1979); *Brand New Age* (1980); *Crash Course* (1980); *Endangered Species* (1982)

Industrial Music

Industrial music reflects--sometimes satirizing--a culture in the throes of increasing automation. It views dirty analog noise as a raison d'etre, rather than mere abstract symbolism; that is, an alternative to overbearing social order. Its musical features include abrasive sounds, machine-related repetitions sense with foreboding, innovative blends of instrumental and vocal colors, and extensive use of tape loops. The prime influences on industrial music were 1950s academic electronic music, the distortion and drone-minimalism of New York-based primitives (e.g., the Velvet Underground), the eccentric anti-style, over-amped Euro-rock improvisational bands (e.g., AMM, Faust), and Eno's then prevalent ideology of DIY anti-musicianship.

Industrial did not evolve in its own stylistic vacuum. Rather, it interacted with a number of other contemporary genres, most notably white noise, techno-pop (which blended industrial sounds with bubblegum music via an emphasis on synthesizers), and the ambient movement. The latter form consisted of atmospheric, background music in which rhythm lines--as with new age--were limited to trance dubs. Its chief proponents included Orb, Orbital, Aphex Twin, and the Art of Noise.

Top Artists and Their Recordings

Cabaret Voltaire--*Extended Play EP* (1978); *Mix Up* (1979); *Live at the YMCA 27-10-79* (1980); *Three Mantras* (1980); *The Voice of America* (1980); *3 Crepuscule Tracks EP* (1981); *2 x 45* (1982); *Hail! Live in Japan* (1982); *The Crackdown* (1983); *Johnny Yesno* (1983); *Micro-Phonies* (1984); *The Arm of the Lord* (1985); *The Drain Train EP* (1986); *Code* (1987)

Einsturzende Neubauten--*Drawings of Patient O.T.* (1983); *80-83 Strategies Against Architecture* (1984); *2 x 4* (1984); *1/2 Mensch* (1985); *Fuenf auf der Nach Oben Offenen Richterskala* (1987); *Haus der Luege* (1989); *Strategies Against Architecture II* (1991); *Interim EP* (1993); *Tabula Rosa* (1993)

Ministry--*Cold Life EP* (1981); *With Sympathy* (1983); *Twitch* (1986); *Twelve Inch Singles* (1987); *The Land of Rape and Honey* (1988); *A Mind Is a Terrible Thing to Taste* (1989); *In Case You Didn't Feel Like Showing Up* (1990); *Psalm 69: The Way to Succeed and Way to Suck Eggs* (1992)

Moby--*Moby* (1992); *Ambient* (1992); *Early Underground* (1993); *Move EP* (1993); *Everything Is Wrong* (1995)

Nine Inch Nails--*Pretty Hate Machine* (1989); *Broken EP* (1992); *Fixed EP* (1992); *The Downward Spiral* (1993); *Further Down the Spiral* (1995)

Psychic TV--*Allegory and Self* (1988); *Towards Thee Infinite Beat* (1990); *Beyond Thee Infinite Beat* (1990)

Public Image Ltd.--*First Issue* (1978); *Second Edition* (1980); *Paris au Printemps* (1980); *Flowers of Romance* (1981); *Live in Tokyo* (1983); *This Is What You Want...This Is What You Get* (1984); *Album* (1986); *Happy?* (1987); *9* (1989); *That What Is Not* (1992)

Throbbing Gristle--*Greatest Hits* (1979); *20 Jazz-Funk Greats* (1979)

White Noise and Its Stylistic Offshoots

White noise, also known as cyber-punk and post-industrial, emerged out of the postpunk movement in the early 1980s. Its artists were dedicated to the exploration of new sound clusters not traditionally viewed as "musical" in nature; this credo, combined with lyrics often inclined toward social commentary, reflects a pronounced anti-establishment stance. Still, many of the genre's prime exponents have gone on to achieve some measure of commercial success. This has not been the result of aesthetic compromise, but rather because the mainstream has incorporated elements from the genre's canon over time.

The white noise movement has produced a spin-off style, industrial dance, an abrasive music exhibiting pronounced rhythms suited for aggressive, free-form dancing. Industrial dance would rival house music as the leading dance music genres of the 1980s. House music--developed at the Warehouse, a club serving Chicago's black gay culture, by deejay Frankie Knuckles--was a mixture of speedy disco beats and latin, Philly, Salsoul, and African recordings. It combined a deep drum and bass sound with heavy reverb and urban and jungle sound effects.

When house was exported to London in the mid-1980s, deejays there began adding spaced out grooves and samples of TV chatter and other media. This hypnotic, pyschedelic variation of the Chicago style was named "acid house" by British underground music taste-maker Genesis P-Orridge.

A fad in the English pop music scene of the late 1980s, acid house combined with techno to spawn all-night psychedelic dance parties called raves. The scene, typically fueled by the mildly hallucinogenic stimulant Ecstasy, had made its way to the American West Coast by the early 1990s. Record companies took note of this phenomenon and began signing--and promoting--techno artists; by the mid-1990s the genre had entered the pop music mainstream.

Top Artists and Their Recordings

--White Noise

The Boo Radleys—*Ichabod and I (1990); Everything's Alright Forever* (1992); *Giant Steps* (1993); *C'mon Kinds* (1993)

Dinosaur, Jr.--*You're Living All Over Me* (1987); *Bug* (1989); *Green Mind* (1991); *Whatever Cool With Me* (1993)

Godflesh--*Streetcleaner* (1989)

Laibach--*Life Is Life* (1989)

Sonic Youth--*Sonic Youth EP* (1982); *Confusion Is Sex* (1983; *Sonic Death: Sonic Youth Live* (1984); *Bad Moon Rising* (1985); *Evol* (1986); *Sister* (1987); *Daydream Nation* (1988); *Goo* (1990); *Dirty* (1992)

--Industrial Dance

Hilt--*Call the Ambulence Before I Hurt Myself* (1989)

Keith LeBlanc--*Stranger Than Fiction* (1989)

Skinny Puppy--*Bites and Remission* (1984); *Cleanse Fold and Manipulate* (1987); *Rabies* (1989); *Too Dark Park* (1990)

--House/Acid House/Techno-Rave

808 State--*Newbuild EP* (1988); *Quadrastate EP* (1989); *Utd. State 90* (1990); *Ex:el* (1991); *Gorgeous* (1993)

KLF--*Chill Out* (1990); *The White Room* (1991)

The Orb--*Adventures Beyond the Ultraworld* (1990); *U.F. Orb* (1992); *Live 93* (1993); *Pomme Fritz* (1994); *Orbus Terrarum* (1995)

Orbital--*Snivelization* (1996); *The Middle of Nowhere* (1999)

Techno-Pop

Techno-pop, also termed "synth-pop" or "electro-pop," refers to a rock genre built around synthesizers (i.e., computers with musical input (e.g., keyboards)/output (e.g., amplifiers, speakers) devices. While some techno-pop artists have employed synthesizers merely for instrumental coloring (timbre), others applied them to reproduce the full range of ensemble performance from percussive effects to simulations of the human voice. Musicians make frequent use of pre-recorded tapes (or digital data stored on various types of computer software) both in the studio and for live shows.

The genre originated through the pioneering efforts of German bands such as Tangerine Dream and Kraftwerk in the early 1970s. While Tangerine Dream was, in the long term, the more influential of the two aggregates--being largely responsible for the rise of new age space music and the ambient movement--Kraftwerk provided the model for dance-beat style utilized by the first wave of techno-pop artists. The band's "Autobahn"--an early permutation of the then emerging Euro-disco sound--was a major hit in early 1975. However, Kraftwerk failed to consolidate its success due to a lack of composing talent and the inability of the members to project a telegenic image.

The movement did not reach the mainstream until 1982 when the Human League's "Don't You Want Me" reached the top of the American music charts. The record business was suddenly awash with techno-pop acts, the most successful of whom included the Eurythmics, Soft Cell, Thomas Dolby, Depeche Mode, and A Flock of Seagulls. The ascendency of the genre owed much to (1) the rise of MTV combined with the multi-media savvy of techno-pop performers, (2) advances in electronic equipment which made a wide array of sounds achievable for artists with comparatively limited resources, and (3) the fact that AOR, Top 40, and other radio friendly formats had grown stale.

The competition from other newly emerging postpunk styles in the late 1980s drove techno-pop back underground. It mutated into "electronica" during the 1990s. Yet another strain resurfaced into the commercial mainstream in late 1996, albeit with more pronounced dance rhythms. Now known as "techno," its leading acts included Orbital, Prodigy, Underworld, and the Chemical Brothers.

Top Artists and Their Recordings

Bauhaus--*In the Flat Field* (1980); *Mask* (1981); *Swing the Heartache - The BBC Sessions* (1989)

Berlin--*Pleasure Victim* (1983); *Love Life* (1984); *Count Three and Pray* (1986)

The Buggles--"Video Killed the Radio Star" (1981); *Adventures in Modern Recording* (1982)

D.A.F./Deutsch Amerikanische Treundschaft--*Alles Ist Gut* (1981); *Gold Und Liebe* (1981); *Fur immer* (1982)

Depeche Mode--*Speak & Spell* (1981); *A Broken Frame* (1982); *People Are People* (1984); *Some Great Reward* (1985); *Black Celebration* (1986); *Music For the Masses* (1987); *101* (1989); *Violator* (1990)

Thomas Dolby--*Blinded By Science* (1983); *The Golden Age of Wireless* (1983); *The Flat Earth* (1984); *Aliens Ate My Buick* (1988)

The Eurythmics--*Sweet Dreams (Are Made Of This)* (1983); *Touch* (1984); *Touch Dance* (1984); *1984* (1984); *Be Yourself Tonight* (1985); *Revenge* (1986); *Savage* (1987); *We Too Are One* (1989)

Eyeless in Gaza--*Photographs As Memories* (1981); *Pale Hands* (1982)

Fad Gadget--*Fireside Favorites* (1980)

The Fashion--*Product Perfect* (1979)

A Flock of Seagulls--*A Flock of Seagulls* (1982); "I Ran" (1982); *Listen* (1983); *The Story of a Young Heart* (1984)

The Flying Lizards--*The Flying Lizards* (1980)

Heaven 17/B.E.F.--*Heaven 17* (1983); *The Luxury Gap* (1983); *Pleasure One* (1987)

Human League--*Dare* (1982); *Love and Dancing* (1982); *Fascination!* (1983); *Hysteria* (1984); *Crash* (1986)

Human Sexual Response--*Figure 14* (1980); *In a Roman Mood* (1981)

The Human Switchboard--*Who's Landing in My Hanger?* (1981); *Coffee Break* (1982)

Industry--*Industry* (1981)

Japan--*Adolescent Sex* (1977); *Obscene Alternatives* (1979); *Tin Drum* (1981)

Men Without Hats--*Men Without Hats* (1982); "Safety Dance" (1983)

Mi-Sex--*Graffiti Crimes* (1979); *Computer Games* (1980); *Space Race* (1980)

Gary Numan--*Replicas* (1979); *The Pleasure Principle* (1980); *Telekon* (1980); *Dance* (1981)

Orchestral Manoeuvres in the Dark/OMD--*Architecture & Morality* (1982); *Dazzle Ships* (1983); *Junk Culture* (1984); *Crush* (1985); *The Pacific Age* (1986)

Our Daughter's Wedding--*The Digital Cowboy EP* (1981)

The Simple Minds--*New Gold Dream (81-82-83-84)* (1983); *Sparkle in the Rain* (1984); *Once Upon a Time* (1985); *Simple Minds Live: In the City of Light* (1987); *Street Fighting Years* (1989); *Real Life* (1991)

Soft Cell--*Non-Stop Erotic Cabaret* (1981); *Non-Stop Ecstatic Dancing* (1982); *The Art of Falling Apart* (1983)

Synergy--*Electronic Realizations for Rock Orchestra* (1975); *Sequencer* (1976); *Cords* (1978)

The System--*Sweat* (1983); *X-Periment* (1984); Don't Disturb This Groove (1987)

Talk Talk--*The Party's Over* (1982); *It's My Life* (1984); *The Colour of Spring* (1986); *Spirit of Eden* (1988)

Tears For Fears--*The Hurting* (1983); *Songs From the Big Chair* (1985); *The Seeds of Love* (1989)

Telex--*Looking For St. Tropez* (1979); *Neurovision* (1980); *Sex* (1981)

Ultravox--*Vienna* (1980); *Rage in Eden* (1981); *Quartet* (1983); *Lament* (1984)

Yaz/Yazoo--*Upstair's at Eric's* (1982); *You and Me Both* (1983)

Yello--*You Gotta Say Yes to Another Excess* (1983); *One Second* (1987); *Flag* (1989)

New Romantics

The New Romantic movement, also termed blitz, combined techno-pop elements with a glitzy fashion sense originating from the disco club scene. The continued popularity of dance-oriented rock styles in England following the disco era, combined with the heightened fashion consciousness exhibited by British youth, explains why most most blitz artists came out of that environment.

While the genre had its origins in the late 1970s, it didn't move out of the underground until late 1982. The pivotal factor proved to be MTV's receptiveness to broadcasting video clips of blitz bands. Established in the fall of 1981, the pioneering cable channel suffered from a dearth of quality product to program round the clock. The New Romantics--telegenic, sexy, and exuding a careful, fun-loving approach to life--soon dominated MTV playlists and, ultimately, radio programming and industry sales charts.

The movement had lost its momentum by the mid-1980s, however, due to competition from a wide array of postpunk styles as well as the tendency of many blitz bands to implode from within. While a considerable number of solo performers emerged from the fragmentation of these groups, none of them were able to achieve anything approaching the success they'd enjoyed the first time around.

Top Artists and Their Recordings

ABC--*The Lexicon of Love* (1982); "Look of Love" (1983); "Poison Arrow" (1983); *Beauty Stab* (1983); *How to be a...Zillionaire!* (1985); "Be Near Me" (1985); *Alphabet City* (1987)

Adam and the Ants/Adam Ant--*Kings of the Wild Frontier* (1981); *Prince Charming* (1981); *Friend or Foe* (1982); "Goody Two Shoes" (1983); *Strip* (1983); *Vive Le Rock* (1985); *Manners and Physique* (1990)

Culture Club--*Kissing to Be Clever* (1983); "Do You Really Want to Hurt Me" (1983); "Time (Clock of the Heart)" (1983); "I'll Tumble 4 Ya" (1983); *Colour By Numbers* (1983); "Karma

Chameleon" (1984); "Church of the Poison Mind" (1984); "Miss Me Blind" (1984); *Waking Up With the House on Fire* (1984); *From Luxury to Heartache* (1986)

Duran Duran--*Duran Duran* (1981); *Rio* (1982); *Carnival* (1982); "Hungry Like a Wolf" (1983); *Seven and the Ragged Tiger* (1983); "The Reflex" (1983); "Union of the Snake" (1984); "New Moon on Monday" (1984); *Arena* (1984); "Is There Something I Should Know" (1984); "Wild Boys" (1985); *Notorious* (1986); *Big Thing* (1988); *Liberty* (1990)

Haircut 100--*Pelican West* (1982)

Kajagoogoo--*White Feathers* (1983); "Too Shy" (1983); *Extra Play* (1985)

Naked Eyes--*Naked Eyes* (1983); "Always Something There to Remind Me" (1983); "Promises, Promises" (1983); *Fuel for the Fire* (1984)

Spandau Ballet--*True* (1983); *Parade* (1984)

The Thompson Twins--*In the Name of Love* (1982); *Side Kicks* (1983); *Into the Gap* (1984); "Hold Me Now" (1984); "Doctor! Doctor!" (1984); *Here's to Future Days* (1985); "Lay Your Hands on Me" (1985); "King For a Day" (1986); *Close to the Bone* (1987); *Big Trash* (1989)

Visage/Steve Strange--*Visage* (1981)

Ska/Bluebeat Revival

The ska/bluebeat revival was a retro movement concerned with recapturing the musical qualities of the 1960s Jamaican genre from a modern social and fashion perspective. The first wave emerged in Great Britain during the late 1970s. The relocation of Caribbean natives to the London area provided the initial impetus for this revived interest in ska; however, skinheads and punks also became fans of the genre. Many oi and punk groups would go on to make ska-styled records by the early 1980s.

The movement extended far beyond mere musical considerations. Like the mods and rockers who had preceded them, ska enthusiasts developed their own fashion statements. Clothing of choice included black-and-white checkered suits, skinny ties, and porkpie hats. Because the central message of ska revival songs was often one of racial unity, fans tended to exhibit a far greater degree of racial tolerance than was typically found in British society.

Although ska music could be found in major British markets throughout the 1980s, it was no longer a force within the pop music mainstream. The sole exception was the watered-down, albeit highly popular, interpretations of the genre recorded by he likes of UB40.

The second wave, which arose in the late 1980s, featured a large number of American bands, including the Mighty Mighty Bosstones and the Pietasters. Whereas the first wave of ska artists were primarily promoted through televised video clips, the latter day bands found that alternative rock radio stations were very receptive to playing their recordings. As a result, these acts have succeeded in sustaining their careers far beyond mere fad proportions.

Top Artists and Their Recordings

The English Beat-*I Just Can't Stop It* (1980); *Wha'ppen* (1981); *Special Beat Service* (1982); *What Is Beat?* (1983)

Fun Boy Three--*The Fun Boy Three* (1982); *Waiting* (1983)

General Public--*...All the Rage* (1984); *Hand to Mouth* (1985)

Madness--*One Step Beyond* (1979); *Absolutely* (1980); *Madness* (1983); *Keep Moving* (1984); *Mad Not Mad* (1985)

The Selector--*Too Much Pressure* (1980); *Celebrate the Bullet* (1981)

The Specials--*The Specials* (1979); *In the Studio* (1984)

Table 120

Mighty Mighty Bosstones

The Mighty Mighty Bosstones coined the term "ska-core" to describe their sound, a blend of the 1980s hardcore movement and England's 2-Tone craze. Although initially unable to build a strong following within either the punk or ska cultures, the band's high energy approach and willingness to experiment with the ska-core formula left them poised on the verge of superstardom by the late 1990s.

The group, initially called the Bosstones, evolved out of a Boston-based ska revival band, the Cheap Skates, in the mid-1980s. Although the Bosstones contributed tracks to at least two different ska compilations in the late 1980s, their debut album, *Devil's Night Out* (Taang! 044; reissued May 1998)—comprised of ska music filtered through a postpunk perspective—was not released until 1990. With the major 2-Tone acts—most notably, Madness, the Specials, Selector, and the English Beat—having disbanded, the Mighty Mighty Bosstones (the name decided on after finding that a 1950s Boston band been called the Bosstones) assumed leadership of the moribund ska scene almost by default. Not content to recycle timeworn bluebeat conventions, the band's early 1990s releases—*Where'd You Go EP* (Taang! 048; 1991; reissued May 1998), *More Noise and Other Disturbances* (Taang! 060; 1992; reissued May 1998), *Skacore, the Devil and More* (Mercury 514551; 1993), and *Don't Know How to Party* (Mercury 514836; 1993)—applied a hardcore-metal-rocksteady fusion to an inspired mix of new and old (e.g., Aerosmith, Bob Marley, Metallica, Minor Threat, Van Halen) material.

The next LP, *Question the Answers* (Mercury 522845; 1994; #138), represented an artistic breakthrough, featuring the production work of the Philadelphia-based Butcher Brothers (who'd previously worked with Aerosmith, Cypress Hill, and Urge Overkill), Kolderie (Hole, Radiohead), and Westwood One sound engineer, Ross Humphrey. MTV video clips, a guest spot in the hit film *Clueless* (1995), and headliner status for the 1995 Lollapalooza tour helped assure the band's commercial success as well. *Let's Face It* (Mercury 534472; 1997; #27) was even better, due largely to improved songwriting, while *Live from the Middle East* (Big Rig/Mercury 558900; 1998; #144) revealed that the Bosstones were still capable of generating raw excitement in performance.

Table 121

UB40

The multiracial, English band, UB40—the first important exponent of reggae to hail from outside Jamaica—rose to popularity in the midst of the ska/bluebeat revival craze. Although they did not address the topical concerns of West Indies reggae artists (e.g., Rastafarianism, ganja rituals, European colonialism), their songs exhibited a strong socio-political bent, addressing—among other issues, the U.K.'s unemployment problems (the band's name itself was inspired by an English unemployment form), nuclear war, and the repressive policies of former British prime minister, Margaret Thatcher.

UB40's key members—lead vocalist/guitarist Ali Campbell and lead guitarist/singer Robin Campbell—were sons of Ian Campbell, a Scottish folk interpreter popular during the early 1960s. Formed in early 1979, the band—ranging in size from eight to twelve members over the years, including core members Astro, vocals/trumpet; Michael Virtue, keyboards; Earl Ralconer, bass; Brian Travers, saxophone; Jim Brown, drums; and Norman Hassan, percussion—became a fixture on the British charts with the release of the album, *Signing Off* (Graduate 2; 1980; #2 UK). UB40's popularity spread to much of Europe in the early 1980s on the strength of LPs such as—of the which featured an augmented brass section in order to provide an authentic R&B feel to arrangements.

Until the band signed with A&M Records in 1983, their recordings had only been available in the U.S. as imports. Pushing Ali's wholesome good looks and reggae-pop treatments of rock classics such as Sonny and Cher's "I Got You Babe" (A&M 2758; 1985; #28; w/Chrissie Hynde), Neil Diamond's "Red Red Wine" (A&M 2600; 1983; #34), the Temptations' "The Way You Do the Things You Do" (Virgin 98978; 1990; #6), Al Green's "Here I Am" (Virgin 99141; 1991; #7), and Elvis Presley's "(I Can't Help) Falling in Love with You" (Virgin 12653; 1993; #1 UK, #1 US) via video clips geared to cable television and dance clubs, UB achieved considerable success in America with the following albums: *Labour of Love* (A&M 4980; 1983; #14; consisted entirely of cover versions), *Geffery Morgan* (A&M 5033; 1984; #60), *Little Baggariddim* (A&M 5090; 1985; #40), *Rat in the Kitchen* (A&M 5137; 1986; #53), *CCCP: Live in Moscow* (A&M 5168; 1987; #121), *UB40* (A&M 5213; 1988; #44), *Labour of Love II* (Virgin 91324; 1990; #30; another collection of covers), and *Promises and Lies* (Virgin 88229; 1993; #6).

Ali's departure in 1995 for a solo career disrupted the UB40's creative and commercial momentum. With his return to the fold in 1997, the band picked up where they'd off, placing recordings high on the U.K. charts—e.g., *Guns in the Ghetto* (DEP International 16; 1997; #7 UK) and *Labour of Love III* (DEP International 18; 1998; #8 UK)—albeit enjoying less success stateside.

Goth Rock

A postpunk style evolving out of the London club scene of the early 1980s, goth featured moody, typically minor-key, melodies and brooding song lyrics. Both musicians and fans reinforced the music's dark aspects by wearing black clothing, dyed black hair, and black makeup highlights set against a starkly pale foundation.

Despite a strong cult following, the genre has received comparatively little press attention. This may be due in part to its preoccupation with themes such as alienation, depression, death, and suicide. The Cure are the best known goth band; others include Nick Cave and the Bad Seeds, Joy Division, Bauhaus, Siouxsie and the Banshees, Alien Sex Fiend, Sex Gang Children, Sisters of Mercy, and Christian Death. [Romanowski and George-Warren. 1995]

Alternative Rock

Alternative rock encompassed a wide array of styles; the prime unifying feature consisted of alienation from the pretentions of 1960s art rock, an alienation that found its mouthpiece in the punk explosion. The movement was reconfigured during the postpunk era of the 1980s as an autonomous indie subculture centered around college radio and urban community clubs and broadcasting. The Athens, Georgia-based band, R.E.M., emerged in the mid-1980s as the most commercially successful exponent of indie musical values.

The grunge sound, centered in Seattle in the late 1980s, proved seminal in convincing major record labels to again promote loud rock played by youth not wearing glitter or spandex. While grunge's leading band, Nirvana, disbanded prematurely as a result of leader Kurt Cobain's 1994 suicide, the scene continued to flourish on the strength of other talented area bands such as Pearl Jam, Soundgarden, Screaming Trees, Alice in Chains, and Sunny Day Real Estate.

The alternative sound changed the essential nature of rock from a mass youth music to a particularized, anti-commercial music of bohemia, social marginals of various kinds, and the avant-garde. Not since the days of bebop jazz had pop music been so inclined to anti-pop statements.

By the mid-1990s, however, alternative rock as a whole had become increasingly mainstream in nature. Now referred to as "modern rock" on the radio and in trade publications, the genre was heavily pervaded by power pop (e.g., Teenage Fanclub, The Rembrandts), AOR hard rock (e.g., Foo Fighters, Stone Temple Pilots), and hip hop (e.g., Faith No More, Red Hot Chili Peppers).

Top Artists and Their Recordings

Archers of Loaf--*Icky Mettle* (1993); *Archers of Loaf vs. the Greatest of All Time EP* (1994); *Vee Vee* (1995)

The Descendents--*Milo Goes to College* (1982); *Bonus Fat EP* (1987); *I Don't Want to Grow Up* (1985); *Enjoy!* (1986); *All* (1987); *Liveage!* (1987); *Two Things at Once* (1987); *Hallraker* (1988); *Somery* (1991)

Faith No More--*We Care a Lot* (1985); *Introduce Yourself* (1987); *The Real Thing* (1989); *Angel Dust* (192); *Easy EP* (1992); *King For a Day, Fool For a Lifetime* (1995)

Foo Fighters--*Foo Fighters* (1995); *The Color and the Shape* (1997)

Fountains of Wayne--*Fountains of Wayne* (1996); *Utopia Parkway* (1999)

The Go-Betweens--*Send Me a Lullaby* (1981); *Very Quick on the Eye--Brisbane, 1981* (1982); *Before Hollywood* (1983); *Spring Hill Fair* (1984); *Metal and Shells* (1985); *The Able Label Singles* (1986); *Liberty Belle and the Black Diamond Express* (1986); *Tallulah* (1987); *16 Lovers Lane* (1988); *The Peel Sessions EP* (1989)

Guided By Voices--*Forever Since Breakfast EP* (1986); *Devil Between My Toes* (1987); *Sandbox* (1987); *Self Inflicted Aerial Nostalgia* (1989); *Same Place the Fly Got Smashed* (1990); *Propeller* (1992); *Vampire on Titus* (1993); *Bee Thousand* (1994); *Crying Your Knife Away* (1994); *Box* (1995)

Hole--*Pretty on the Inside* (1991); *Live Through This* (1994)

Live--*The Death of a Dictionary EP* (1991); *Mental Jewelry* (1992); *Throwing Copper* (1994)

Dave Matthews Band--*Live at Red Rocks 8.15.95* (1997); *Before These Crowded Streets* (1998)

Pavement--*Perfect Sound Forever EP* (1991); *Slanted and Enchanted* (1992); *Watery, Domestic EP* (1992); *Westing (By Musket and Sextant)* (1994); *Terror Twilight* (1999)

Primus--*Suck on This* (1990); *Frizzle Fry* (1990); *Sailing the Seas of Cheese* (1991); *Pork Soda* (1993); *Tales From the Punchbowl* (1995)

Red Hot Chili Peppers--*The Red Hot Chili Peppers* (1984); *Freaky Styley* (1985); *The Uplift Mofo Party Plan* (1987); *The Abbey Road EP* (1988); *Mother's Milk* (1988); *Blood Sugar Sex Magik* (1991); *Out in L.A.* (1994)

R.E.M.--*Chronic Town EP* (1982); *Murmur* (1983); *Reckoning* (1984); *Fables of the Reconstruction* (1985); *Life's Rich Pageant* (1986); *Dead Letter Office* (1987); *Document* (1987); *Eponymous* (1988); *Green* (1989); *Out of Time* (1991); *Automatic for the People* (1992); *Monster* (1994); *New Adventures in Hi-Fi* (1996); *Up* (1999)

Soul Asylum--*Say What You Will...EP* (1984); *Made to Be Broken* (1986); *Time's Incinerator* (1986); *While You Were Out* (1986); *Hang Time* (1988); *Clam Dip & Other Delights EP* (1988); *Soul Asylum and the Horse They Rode In On* (1990); *Grave Dancers Union* (1992)

Stereolab--*Switched on Stereolab* (1992); *Peng!* (1992); *Low Fi EP* (1993); *Space Age Batchelor Pad Music EP* (1993); *Crumb Duck EP* (1993); *Transient Random-Noise Bursts with Announcements* (1993); *Mars Audiac Quintet* (1994)

Stone Temple Pilots--*Core* (1992); *Purple* (1994); *Tiny Music...Songs From the Vatican Gift Shop* (1996)

Sugar--*Copper Blue* (1992); *Beaster EP* (1993); *File Under: Easy Listening* (1994); *Your Favorite Thing EP* (1994)

The Sugarcubes--*Life's Too Good* (1988); *Here Today, Tomorrow Next Week!* (1989); *Stick Around for Joy* (1992)

They Might Be Giants--*They Might Be Giants* (1986); *Don't Let's Start EP* (1987); *(She Was a) Hotel Detective EP* (1988); *Lincoln* (1988); *They'll Need a Crane EP* (1989); *Flood* (1990); *Istanbul (Not Constantinople)* (1990); *Apollo 18* (1992); *John Henry* (1994); *Back to Skull EP* (1994); *Factory Showroom* (1996); *Mink Car* (2001); *No!* (2002); *Here Come the ABCs* (2005); *Nanobots* (2013)

Throwing Muses--*Throwing Muses* (1986); *House Tornado* (1988); *Hunkpapa* (1989); *The Real Ramona* (1991); *Red Heaven* (1992); *University* (1995)

Urge Overkill--*Strange, I...* (1986); *Jesus Urge Superstar* (1989); *Americruiser* (1990); **Supersonic** *Storybook* (1991); *Stull EP* (1992); *Saturation* (1993)

--Grunge Sound

Alice in Chains--*Facelife* (1990); *Sap EP* (1992); *Dirt* (1992); *Jar of Flies EP* (1993); *Unplugged* (1997)

Pearl Jam--*Ten* (1991); *Vs.* (1993); *Vitalogy* (1994); *Binaural* (2000)

Screaming Trees--*Other Worlds EP* (1985); *Clairvoyance* (1986); *Even If and Especially When* (1987); *Buzz Factory* (1989); *Change Has Come EP* (1989); *Something About Today EP* (1990); *Uncle Anesthesia* (1991); *Sweet Oblivion* (1992)

Soundgarden--*Screaming Life EP* (1987); *Fopp EP* (1988); *Ultramega OK* (1988); *Louder Than Love* (1989); *Screaming Life/Fopp* (1990); *Badmotorfinger* (1991); *Superunknown* (1994)

Table 122

Beck, July 8, 1970

Postmodern rock wunderkid Beck Hansen's best years may still lie ahead, but he has already revealed a masterful grasp of songcraft and studio dynamics. His best work has fused together elements of folk-pop, roots blues, country, white noise, hip-hop, and psychedelia complemented by clever—at turns biting or surrealistic—lyrics.

Los Angeles native Beck emerged in the early 1990s with the local alternative radio hit, "Loser" (Bongload 5; 1993). The popularity of the slacker anthem led his signing with Geffen, and a newly recorded version (DGC 270; 1994; #10) became a national hit, followed by an eclectic debut album, *Mellow Gold* (DGC 24634; 1994; #13).

Possessing an open-ended contract that permitted distribution arrangements with other labels, additional Beck material flooded the market in short order. Among the more notable releases were *Stereopathic Soul Manure* (Flipside 60; 1994), a collection of home recordings from the 1988-1993 period, and the predominantly live acoustic set, *One Foot in the Grave* (K 28; 1994).

The next Geffen release, *Odelay* (DGC 24823; 1996; #16), featured his tour de force production values, shifting effortlessly from hardcore dissonance to country blues while retaining a funky rhythmic flow throughout. By now an established star, Beck further consolidated his reputation with *Mutations* (DGC15309; 1998; #13) and the decidedly darker *Midnight Vultures* (DGC 490485; 1999; #34).

The Manc Sound

The "Manc Sound"--based in Manchester, England--ensued from the onslaught of rave culture. Its audience--drawn from post- disco regulars, soccer thugs, and hippies--was most likely to congregate at the Factory Records-run Hacienda Club. Ecstasy constituted the drug of choice.

The performers were drawn from the British indie band movement. They sported baggy trousers, flowery T-shirts, and bowl haircuts. Their music consisted of hook-laden pop-rock accented by rich vocal harmonies and druggy dance beats.

In the fad-driven British trade and fan publications, the Manc Sound (also dubbed "Madchester") was quickly deemed passe. Bands such as James and Primal Scream wisely toned down the more stylized retro elements (a la Los Angeles/Strawberry Alarm Clock circa 1967) of this music and joined the alternative mainstream.

Top Artists and Their Recordings

The Farm--*Spartacus* (1991)

The Happy Mondays--*Squirrel and G-Man Twenty Four Hour Party People Plastic Face Carnt Smile (White Out)* (1987); *Bummed* (1988); *Madchester, Rave On* (1989); *Hallelujah EP* (1989); *Peel Session EP* (1990); *Pills 'n Thrills and Bellyaches* (1990); *Live* (1991); *Yes, Please!* (1992)

The Inspiral Carpets--*The Peel Sessions EP* (1989); *Cool as **** EP* (1990); *Life* (1990); *The Beast Inside* (1991); *Revenge of the Goldfish* (1992); *Devil Hopping* (1994)

James--*Shutter* (1986); *Strip-mine* (1988); *One Man Clapping* (1989); *Gold Mother* (1990); *James* (1991); *Seven* (1992); *Laid* (1993); *Wah Wah* (1994)

Primal Scream--*Sonic Flower Groove* (1987; issued in U..S. as *Volume I*); *Primal Scream* (1989); *Screamadelica* (1991); *Give Out But Don't Give Up* (1994); *Vanishing Point* (1997); *More Light* (2013)

The Soup Dragons--*Hang-Ten!* (1987); *This Is Our Art* (1988); *Lovegod* (1990); *Hotwired* (1992); *Hydrophonic* (1994)

The Stone Roses--*The Stone Roses* (1989); *Turns Into Stone* (1992); *Second Coming* (1995)

Ambient

Ambient music was first applied softer, more reflective forms of music in the 1970s, most notably new age genres and the minimalism of Philip Glass, Terry Riley, and other classically trained composers. However, the term was also applied to musicians experimenting with subtler tonal pallets in a wide array of genres embracing the avant garde, progressive rock, psychedelia, Euro-rock, free-form jazz, the postpunk styles of the 1980s, and various world music strains.

In his landmark book, *The Ambient Century*, Mark Prendergast identified two twentieth century music developments at the core of ambience:

> Firstly, music was deconstructed. Before, Western music was quite rigid. The sonata form of the Classical period had specific rules which had to be adhered to. Of course there were exceptional talents but they were constrained within a chosen form. Then the Romantics started to loosen things. Wagner's grandiose operatic orchestration and Bruckner and Mahler pushed the symphony to its limits so that by the end of the nineteenth century it began to creak under its own weight. Then along came Satie, Debussy and Ravel with a lighter touch. They wrote more accessible melodies in shorter forms which openly embraced modernity and the need to look beyond parochialism to the riches to be found in other cultures such as the Orient….As old musical ideas began to be supplanted by new, a second radical change occurred – and this was in the very way music was generated. Composers and musicians began to be fascinated by the nature of individual tones. Serialism, in its dislocative way, had thrown up an interest in the essence of a single sound. The leaders of the post-Second World War avant-garde in Europe, such as Stockhausen, Schaeffer and Varese, seized on new Electronic equipment and began to experiment with tape recorders. New qualities in sound were perceived, new tonalities divorced from any traditional acoustic instruments were realized. De Forest's invention of the valve in the 1900s had made amplification possible. This, coupled with the concept of the sound environment, made for some spectacular results.

In short, the story of ambience is reflected by the interaction of innovative musical ideas and technological changes. Technological advances tended to focus on musical instruments and the recording studio. The most notable included computer synthesizers capable of mimicking virtually any natural sounds, digital sound storage and manipulation, and audio multi-tracking.

Following decades of evolution from the classical music experiments of the early twentieth century to the progressive rock releases of the Beatles and other cutting edge pop artists of the 1960s, ambience seemed to retreat to the aesthetic and commercial fringes of the music industry. With the exception of left field hits such as Michael Oldfield's *Tubular Bells* (1973) and Enya's *Watermark* (1988), ambience – dominated by Eno, Bill Nelson, and other cult artists – exerted little influence on the pop music mainstream in the 1970s and 1980s. This situation changed dramatically with the rise of House and Techno, considered by some to be the most significant development in popular music since the heydey of progressive rock in the late sixties. Prendergast has provided the following summary of the ascendancy of these styles:

> The combination of [the hallucinogenic drug Ecstasy] with the kinetic rhythms of the new dance music exploded into a phenomenon that seemed to have no end. As the music mutated, new form were thrown up by the year. Ambient House and Ambient Techno were mind-balming responses to the intensity of club culture. Trip-Hop and Drum and Bass [or Jungle] were UK black variations of what was originally as innovation by black Americans. Rock music absorbed House and Techno, and DJs and electronicists began to tour and act like rock stars. As one century tipped into another, dance music was still a primary source of interest and creativity as Trance, a futuristic blend of technology and House and Techno, became a chart-topping, globe-girdling sensation.

The migration of these styles from dance clubs to other mass media venues (e.g., the cinema, radio, record industry) and cross-fertilization with mainstream rhythm and blues, jazz, and rock genres has further guaranteed their long-term viability.

Top Artists and Their Recordings (listed in chronological order)

Popol Vuh—*Aguirre, Wrath Of God* (1976)
Klaus Schulze—*Mirage* (1977)
This Mortal Coil—*It'll End In Tears* (1984)
Michael Brook—*Hybrid* (1985)
Spacemen 3—*The Perfect Prescription* (1987)
Bill Nelson—*Chance Encounters In The Garden Of Lights* (1988)
David Sylvian (with Holgar Czukay)—*Plight & Premonition* (1988)
Ryuichi Sakamoto—*The Sheltering Sky* (1990)
KLF—*Chill Out* (1990)
Enigma—*MCMXC A.D. (1990)*
The Orb—*Adventures Beyond The Ultraworld* (1991)
Mixmaster Morris—*Flying High* (1992)
Pete Namlook—*Air* (1993)
The Future Sound Of London—*Lifeforms* (1994)

Aphex Twin—*Selected Ambient Works, Vol. 2* (1994)
Massive Attack—*Protection* (1994)
Labradford—*A Stable Reference* (1995)
Goldie—*Timeless* (1995)
DJ Shadow—*Endtroducing...* (1996)
High Llamas—*Hawaii* (1996); *Talahomi Way* (2011)
Paul Oakenfold—*Paul Oakenfold – New York* (1998)
Paul Van Dyk—*Vorsprung Dyk Technik* (1998)
Air—*Premiers Symptomes* (1999)
Boards of Canada—*The Campfire Headphase* (2005); *Tomorrow's Harvest* (2013)

Table 123

Massive Attack

Massive Attack is widely credited with having created trip-hop, a trance-like rhythmic blend of hip-hop, deejay sampling, soulful singing, funk, and Jamaican dub music. A club scene alternative to the hyperactive energy of techno in the 1990s, trip-hop became a fixture on film soundtracks and recordings of DJ remixes.

Massive Attack evolved out of a Bristol, England-based group of DJs, rappers, singers, and sound engineers known as the Wild Bunch that functioned primarily to stage dance parties beginning in 1983. The Wild Bunch's 1986 cover of Burt Bacharach's "The Look of Love" became a major hit within the European club circuit.

Internal disputes and harassment by legal officials led to a breakup of the collective; graffiti artist/vocalist 3-D (Robert Del Naja), vocalist/keyboardist/producer Daddy G (Grant Marshall), and keyboardist/producer Andrew Vowles (better known as Mushroom) emerged out of its ashes to form Massive Attack in 1987. Generating career momentum from the release of a string of popular club singles, Massive Attack released its debut album, *Blue Lines* (Virgin 91685; #13 UK) in 1991, featuring a varied array of vocalists, including DJ Tricky, Shara Nelson, and reggae artist Horace Andy. Although the group always viewed dance singles as the ultimate art form (according to discographer Martin Strong, the hypnotic "Unfinished Sympathy" [Circa 2; 1991; #13 UK; mixed by Paul Oakenfold], is often cited as one of the most perfect singles ever crafted), their LPs—*Protection* (Virgin 3847; 1994; #14 UK), which featured jazz-pop singer Tracey Thorn and Nigerian vocalist Nicolette, among others; *No Protection: Massive Attack vs. Mad Professor* (Circa/Virgin 3; 1995; #10 UK), a remix of *Protection* with the assistance of reggae producer, Mad Professor; *Mezzanine* (Virgin 45599; 1998; #1 UK, #60 US), augmented with vocals by Andy, Cocteau Twins alumnus Elizabeth Fraser, and Sara Jay; and the eleven-CD box set of remixes, *Singles 90/98* (Virgin; 1998)—represented important summative statements of past studio experiments.

Massive Attack's future was somewhat in doubt following Mushroom's departure in mid-1999. Given public announcements of plan to continue as a duo, combined with the group's legacy of fruitful collaborations with outside talent, it appeared likely that new releases would eventually be forthcoming.

Table 124

Orb

Borrowing from a wide range of sources, including psychedelia, progressive rock, German techno, disco, and reggae dub music, the Orb are generally acknowledged as originators of the ambient dance genre. Despite copyright litigation over their heavy use of samples—most notably, Minnie Riperton's "Loving You" and Rickie Lee Jones' voice in "Fluffy Little Clouds"—they were one of the most in-demand producers/remixers of the 1990s.

The Orb—a name derived from Woody Allen's sci-fi film, *Sleepers*—was formed in South London, 1989, by synth/keyboardist Alex Paterson, then handling A&R duties for EG Records, and KLF's Jimmy Cauty. Utilizing samples from the New York radio station, Kiss FM, the duo released a twelve-inch EP, *Kiss*, on the British WAU! Mr. Modo label (#0107; 1989). Catering primarily to ambient dance clubs, they next issued the pioneering twelve-inch EP, *A Huge Ever Growing Pulsating Brain That Rules From the Centre of the Ultraworld: Lovin' You* (WAU! Mr. Moto 0177; 1989)—blending trance-like rhythms and spacey dub effects—and the ethereal single, "Fluffy Little Clouds" (Big Life 33; 1990).

Prior to the release of Orb's epic set, *Adventures Beyond the Ultraworld* (Big Life 5; #29 UK; issued 11/91 on Mercury 511034 in U.S.), in April 1991, Cauty was replaced ex-Gong guitarist Steve Hillage, Miquette Giraudy, and Andy Falconer. Combining older singles and new material, the double album almost single-handedly created a vogue for ambient club nights that nurtured artists such as Aphex Twin and Mixmaster Morris.

Collaborating with wide array of artists, Paterson—while strictly an underground phenomenon stateside—became a hot commercial property in England. Continuing to explore the stretched-out beats of ambient dance, his best-selling releases have included the twelve-inch EP, "The Blue Room" (Big Life 75; 1992; #8), *U.F. Orb* (Big Life 18/Mercury 513749; 1992; #1 UK), *Live 93* (Island 8022/Mercury 535004; 1993; #23 UK), the harder-edged *Pommefritz* (Island ORB 1/Mercury 535007; 1994; #6 UK), *Orbus Terrarum* (Island8037/Mercury 524099; 1995; #20 UK), *Oblivion* (Island 8055/Mercury 524347; 1997; #19 UK), and *U.F.Off – The Best Of* (Island 8078; 1998; #38).

Riot Grrrl Movement

The riot grrrl revolution grew out of a loose network of female rock musicians based in Olympia, Washington and Washington, D.C. Washington, D.C. was established as a leftist punk rock stronghold, while Olympia was the home of Evergreen College (long known for its strong women's studies programs) and K records, sponsor of the 1991 International Pop Underground convention, referred to as "Ground Zero for Revolution Girl Style." Devoid of any guiding dogma, the movement served a wide range of needs: (1) a conduit for finding sister musicians, (2) a safe space for processing experiences such as rape and abuse, and (3) a forum for responding to society's conservative backlash through guerrilla art and film projects and shared resources (e.g., community meetings and fanzines like *Bikini Kill, Fantastic Magazine, Girl Germs, Jigsaw,* and *Riot Grrrl*).

The underground buzz gradually spread to the mass media; although publications (e.g., *Newsweek*, *USA Today*) misinterpreted the its revolutionary leanings, the movement was nurtured by the support of mainstream artists such as Joan Jett and Sonic Youth. By the early 1990s, riot grrrl chapters had sprung up across the U.S. and abroad. Although many members have moved on to other political and social consciousness movements, the core of the movement remains the raw, punk-oriented sound of bands comprised largely of female members, including Bikini Kill, Babes in Toyland, Fifth Column, Huggy Bear, Lunachicks, Sister George, Slant 6, Sleater-Kinney, and Tribe 8. [O'Dair. 1997]

No Depression

"No Depression"--drawn from a vintage Carter Family song (and consequently became the name of an Uncle Tupelo album)--represents an extension of the alternative country rock genre which originated at the end of the 1960s with the Byrds and the Flying Burrito Brothers and was revived in the 1980s through the work of Jason and the Scorchers, Uncle Tupelo, and others. The genre melded country (particularly the twangy, honky tonk style exemplified by Hank Williams, Sr.) and punk. By the time Uncle Tupelo (a band whose influence on the scene was far greater than mere sales might suggest) split off into two new groups in 1993, Wilco and Son Volt, the No Depression movement had acquired a clear-cut identity, inspiring the publication of numerous fanzines, the establishment of countless websites thoughout the world, and a new type of radio programming known as "Americana."

Top Artists and Their Recordings

The Bottle Rockets--*The Bottle Rockets* (1993); *The Brooklyn Side* (1994)

Steve Earle--*Copperhead Road* (1988); *Shut Up and Die Like an Aviator* (1990); *The Hard Way* (1991)

The Old 97's--*Hitchhike to Rhome* (1994); *Wreck Your Life* (1995); *Fight Songs* (1999)

Son Volt--*Trace* (1995); *Straightaways* (1997); *Wide Swing Tremolo* (1999)

Vigilantes of Love--*Welcome to Struggleville* (1994); *V.O.L.* (1994)

Whiskeytown--*Strangers Almanac* (1997); *Faithless Street* (1998)

Wilco--*A.M.* (1995); *Being There* (1996); *Summerteeth* (1999)

OTHER NOTABLE TOPICS

Pop Music Video Clips

<u>Toward A Definition</u>

Pop music video clips--variously called "promo clips," "picture music," or just plain "videos"--made a substantial impact upon the public consciousness during the early 1980s. The medium, defined here to mean those several-minute filmlets accompanying pop songs as opposed to the various types of full-length video programs (e.g., extended concerts, documentaries, recapitulations of film/television appearance), acquired both its advocates and detractors in short order.

The former group included director Zbigniew Rybczynski, who won an Academy Award in 1983 for his film short, *Tango*. Rybczynski then decided that he would no longer work in the film medium because he considered it to be defunct. He began working with video clips exclusively, offering the following rationale in the January 1985 issue of *Music and Sound Output:*

> I believe now is a very interesting time. We are at the point of a big
> revolution in video. Music video is the beginning of something very
> important in culture. There is nothing more new in any other kind
> of art. Consider the (main) audience, young people. They don't
> read anymore. They have only TV screens. This is the only way
> to learn about the world or something about aesthetics. I don't think
> other art exists for a really big audience. Nobody goes to art galleries.
> This is part of the past. For the younger generation throughout the
> whole country, their only contact with art is through music video.

Critics of the medium have justified their stance with a number of arguments, most of which seem to possess questionable merit.

(1) The crass commercialism characterizing both the content of the many clips as well as the mode of presentation. The form has been subverted of skilled admen to the point where it's hard to distinguish commercial from videos on TV and other television programs. But then what medium can lay claim to being completely free of such a charge.

(2) The inclinations of a significant portion of these clips to self indulgence and plain bad taste. It would be well here to keep in mind the 95 to 5 percent radio said to characterize all art forms; that is, the majority of creations are worthless and, in the best interests of a particular genre's image, soon forgotten. To pose a rhetorical question, is it fair to blame a Dickens novel for the presence of a bevy of "penny dreadfuls" in the publishing world of that era?

(3) Their omnipresence within our society. This, of course, bears no direct correlation with correlation with the relation aesthetic (or social) merits of the pop music video clip.

(4) Perhaps the most weighty criticism has been voiced by Eric Zorn, whose main point of contention is that the medium "threatens to rob us of the special images we conjure up to go with a song." He notes that more than a majority of MTV viewers recently sampled say they "play back" the video in their minds upon hearing a particular song on the radio. The proliferation of music videos, in short, threatens to produce an entire generation of people who will overlook the sublime, extremely personal element of music." (*Newsweek*, February 13, 1984, p. 16)

In response to Zorn's argument, it should be noted that pop music videos can bring out dimensions of a song otherwise lost to the listener. It would appear that this genre is merely the most recent outgrowth of the long developing symbiotic relationship between music and the visual image. Established precedents include passion plays, opera, ballet, and incidental music for dramatic presentations.

Nevertheless, the controversy continues at fever pitch as to whether or not pop music vides are an art form or merely a clever pistache--an artiface geared to stocking the starmaking machinery of the music business. *Webster's New World Dictionary* defines art as "...creative work or its principles, making or doing of things that display form, beauty, and unusual perception...(this) includes painting, sculpture, architecture, music, literature, drama, the dance..." (Second Collegiate Edition, 1974, p. 78)

True art is often hard to distinguish from watered-down practices such as artiface (skill used as a means of trickery or deception) and craft (ingenuity in execution usually involving a comparatively lessened degree of creative thought). It could be argued that elements of all of these forms exist in pop music videos; however, a socio-historical survey of the genre would seem necessary in order to ascertain the true nature of the genre.

Historical Background

In some respects, video clips are a relatively recent development; e.g., the form's conceptual and technical sophistication, the astronomical costs of production and the burgeoning home videocassette market. If one accepts the aforementioned definition of these clips, then it can be established that they have been around far longer than the video phenomenon itself. As early as 1921, the German Oskar Fischinger started experimenting with short animated films utilizing abstract-geometrical forms dancing to jazz and classical music. He later achieved immortality for his conceptualization of the initial sequence in Walt Disney's *Fantasia* set to Bach's "Toccata and Fugue."

By the mid-1930s, visual shorts had begun incorporating plots and universally recognizable settings in order to enhance the existing musical track. Large numbers of clips were made for theatrical distribution featuring the era's big bands and other top pop artists. Michael Shore, in

The Rolling Stone Book of Rock Video, noted, "some of them are fully as imaginative and eye-catching as anything being made today."

The appearance of the video jukebox represented a further refinement in the evolution leading up to the modern day video clip. The Panoram Soundie would play musical movie shorts for a dime or quarter. Although the machine continued to be used throughout the 1940s, the majority of filmlets were produced in the early years of that decade, typically featuring simulated live performances by stars such as Louis Armstrong, Fats Waller, Cab Calloway, and Bing Crosby. However, a small percentage of them included primitive special effects as in the case of Mabel Todd's "At the Club Savoy" which employed the device of flashback to tell the story of the girl's guilt (set in a temperence hall no less!) over going on a bender the previous night.

While soundies were the victims of neglect on the part of a generation obsessed with TV and rock 'n' roll, an updated version called the Scopitone enjoyed widespread popularity in Europe during the late 1950s and early 1960s. The clips produced during this period wer gaudy and often unintentionally surreal in their attempts to visually complement the music. Neil Sedaka's "Calendar Girl" (1961) represented a case in point, featuring elaborate set and costume changes for every month of the year.

The groundwork for the present day video clip was laid in the mid-1960s as an increasing number of bands began making promotional films to send television rock shows. The rationale for the rise of this phenomenon among the pop artists of that era included (1) the lack of availability in-person, (2) the high cost--financially and physically--of constant travel (a particularly salient point of view for American acts who found a receptive market in England or their video clips via TV pop music variety programs such as *Ready Steady Go!*), (3) opposition to live performing (the Beatles--as was so often the case--set the precedent by announcing their retirement from the stage in the summer of 1966), and (4) concern with the negative implications of lip-synching as had been the modus operandi for hit artists seeking wider exposure via television since the early the early days of *American Bandstand*.

Given the experimental climate of rock music during the psychedelic period, it was inevitable that many of these prototype videos would display a high level of aesthetic creativity and technical mastery of the medium. A classic example is the 1967 clip, "Happy Jack," available on videocassette as part of the 1979 film documentary on the Who's career, *The Kids Are Alright*. The clip reveals a wealth of comic invention, casting the band members as bumbling burglars in a Chaplinesque silent-movie-style caper.

Queen's "Bohemian Rhapsody" is generally recognized as the video clip most responsible for ushering in the modern era. It is felt to represent the first case in which a video played a primary role in elevating a pop song to hit status. The clip anticipates many of the cinematic techniques achieving widespread application at a later date, including split images and widely panning stage shots.

During its infancy the video clip profited from the creative energy expended on a wide variety of fronts. Most notable sources of input were: (1) the underground art community, (2) television, (3) commercial film, and (4) dance clubs.

The Underground Art Community

Proponents within this sector were of inestimable importance in broadening the medium's aesthetic reach, incorporating elements of dramatics (e.g., acting, mime, soliloquy), contemporary art music, the graphic arts, documentary journalism, filmmaking, and animation. A San Francisco-based group of conceptual artists, The Residents, pioneered the multi-media approach to video production. The group's "Land of 1000 Dances" (1975) has been characterized by Shore as "The most utterly, exuberantly original and bizarre performance video ever." The work possesses three distinct sequences: a dreamlike pixilated opening in which the group members wheel shopping carts with pointy telephone-wire conductor- like structures attached to their fronts; a cavern club setting reveals the band perverting the 1960s dance classic for which the clip is titled in mutant tribal stomp fashion; the ending features a storm trooper zapping the unholy performers with a ray gun.

Television

Television has always been the major channel for the transmission of the video clip. Therefore, it is not surprising that a host of TV programming formats have influenced the genre, including sitcoms and serials (e.g., *Ozzie & Harriet* with Ricky Nelson, *The Donna Reed Show* with Shelly Fabares and Paul Petersen), variety shows (Elvis Presley's 1956 appearances on *The Ed Sullivan Show*, *Stage Show*, featuring Jimmy and Tommy Dorsey, and *The Steve Allen Show* remain led-in snapshots in the photo album of rock history; their ambiance was lovingly recreated by Billy Joel in his 1984 clip, "Tell Her About It.") and music concert/dance venues. The pioneering stateside shows such as *Your Hit Parade* and *American Bandstand* were duplicated in England as *Top of the Pops* and *Juke Box Jury*. The U.K.'s *Ready Steady Go!*, first broadcast in August 1963, broke new ground in allowing artist to perform without lip-synching. ABC's *Shindig* and NBC's *Hullabaloo*, both instituted in 1965, featured prerecorded, conceptual shorts such as the Beatles' "Day Tripper," which showed the band going through their typical hijinks in a railroad car set. During the 1970s, *The Midnight Special* represented the prime venue for video clips, enabling the fledging form to reach a growing audience.

The Monkees deserves at least a footnote in video clip history for its attempt to blend all of the aforementioned TV formats. Modeled after the Beatles film, *A Hard Days Night*, the program was killed by the band's lack of musical credibility at a time when progressive rock held sway as wellas the rise of pallid copied such as *The Archies* and *The Patridge Family* (the program is making a comeback in the 1980s via syndication on, ironically enough, MTV). However, as noted by director Bob Rafaelson, in *The Rolling Stone Book of Rock Video*, "Almost all the effects you see in videos today, the psychedelic solarizations, the quick cutting, are things we were doing years ago.

Commercial Films

An increasingly refined synthesis of music and plot--which became the hallmark of the conceptual video clip--evolved during the rock era. In the first true rock 'n' roll film, *Blackboard Jungle* (1955), the music functioned merely to frame the plot.

Elvis Presley, as with television, inalterably changed the course of development with his steady stream of releases between 1956 and 1968, most of which featured a half dozen or so carefully choreographed song interludes. The next advance was ushered in by the jukebox musical which starred the likes of Little Richard, Chuck Berry, Chubby Checker, and Frankie Avalon. These movies typically showcased several pop acts performing within a lame, forgettable plot. The jukebox musical mutated in the 1960s into muscle beach movies, social relevance flicks, and drug-tinged surrealism. By the time nostalgia (e.g., *American Graffiti*) and dance-oriented (e.g., *Saturday Night Fever*) films became bankable commodities in the 1970s a genuinely seamless blend of music and action had been achieved, due in large part to rock's then unassailable position as the soundtrack of life in Middle America.

Dance Clubs

By the onset of the 1980s clubs had become the outlet for the viewing of video clips. While the ascendancy of clubs to a mass preoccupation was closely linked to the disco music craze, additional factors played a key role such as the decline of radio as an innovative medium, the AOR-preoccupation of record labels and the expense of touring as a means of breaking acts. Video came to be seen by the industry as a one-time expense that could be viewed continuously, even in many places at the same time. The founding of RockAmerica by Ed Steiberg in 1980 rendered the marriage complete. Largely as a result of Steiberg's awareness of the demo tapes in abundant supply made by record companies for in-house marketing meetings, company-wide conventions, etc., RockAmerica quickly became the nation's largest video pool servicing video-equipped rock clubs.

The hegemony enjoyed by the clubs disappeared almost overnight with the institution of MTV in the fall of 1981. Within a couple of years virtually every channel in the United States possessed at least one program built around videos (see Table 1). The video clip's importance to the record industry by then transcended its original promotional uses; MTV was lending its name to sampler albums and the shorts functioned to cement the tie-in between films and soundtrack releases. On occasion, artists (e.g., Joe Jackson in 1984, Van Halen and Journey in 1986) rebelled against the make-a-clip-for-MTV syndrome. In addition, the channel's viewership leveled off in the mid-1980s (spurring the development of non-musical programming) and industry insiders such as

Dick Clark rechristened radio as the foremost arbiter in determining chart action. Nevertheless, the video clip phenomenon has remained a force within the entertainment field up to the present day.

Table 125

Video Clips On Television, 1985

A. MTV/Music Television. This cable television pioneered the Top 40 pop music concept within a video context. After losing 50 million dollars between 1981-1983, the station achieved a 8.1 million dollar profit during the first half of 1984; during the latter time span it reached 23.5 million households, up 57 percent from 1983. On January 1, 1985, its owner, Warner Amex, launched Video Hits One (VH-1), which targeted a middle-aged audience.

B. Cable Competitors

Full-time

--Discovery Music Network
--Cable Music Channel (Part of Ted Turner's communications empire, it was bought out by MTV in late 1984 after several months of lackluster impact.)

Part-time

--USA (Programs have included *Night Flight*, *Radio 1990*, and *Heart Beat City*.)
--Disney Channel (*DTV* segments, usually 15 minutes in length, several times/day.)
--BET (*Video Vibrations*)
--WTBS (*Night Tracks*)
--The Nashville Network
--Nickelodeon

C. Networks
--ABC (*ABC Rocks*)
--CBS (*Solid Gold*)
--NBC (*Friday Night Videos*; *Rock-N-America*, featuring Dick Clark)

D. Independent Stations
--*America's Top 10*, featuring Casey Kasem
--*N.Y. Hot Tracks*
--*101 Rock Place* (Channel 20, Houston, Texas)
--*Solid Gold* (syndicated reruns)

Impact Upon Society

A preoccupation with the blatantly promotional aspects of video clips as well as their vast proliferation tends to obscure the high order of aesthetic creativity characterizing a notable percentage of the available product. Additional signs of the aesthetic viability of these clips include (1) the diversified range of styles, themes, and techniques (see Table 126) developed in such a comparatively short span of time; (2) the increased involvement of first-line film directors such as Andy Warhol and Zbigniew Rybczynski with the medium; and (3) perhaps of greatest significance, the indelible mark they have left upon our society. Videos mirror, and to some degree, influence society's values, attitudes, and belief systems. Although frequently criticized as being superficial and preoccupied with sex and violence, they have employed a bold new visual vocabulary to reflect the rich diversity of life itself. The images portrayed include:

Vicarious experience. Videos offer up an exciting kaleidoscope of activities such as exotic travel (e.g., Elton John on the Riviera in "I'm Still Standing," Mike Nesmith in "Rio"), spying (e.g., Glenn Frey in a **Miami Vice** segment), and war (e.g., Pat Benatar as a fighter pilot in "Shadows of the Night").

Nostalgia. The Alan Parsons Project's "Don't Ask Me Why" parodies Depression era films, detective novels, and comic strips. Disney Television clips offer a double dose of the past--classic rock 'n' roll songs set to familiar vintage cartoon footage spliced together in montage form.

Instruction. Clips may either provide one's first awareness of an idea, issue, subject, etc., or depict it more vividly by exploiting the possibilities of the medium. "We Are the World" exhorts viewers to share their wealth with the dispossessed and starving African masses while Prince's "1999" opts for enjoying life unencumbered by Puritannical hang-ups before it's too late.

The expression of youthful rebelliousness. Targets typically include schools (e.g., Twisted Sister's "I Wanna Rock", parents (e.g., Twisted Sister's "We're Not Gonna Take It"), the law (e.g., Sammy Hagar's "I Can't Drive 55"), and a host of other institutions at the core of the Establishment.

The expression of regional pride; for example, Los Angeles is represented by Randy Newman's "I Love L.A." and Frank Sinatra's "L.A. Is My Lady."

Materialism. Chief objects of devotion include cars (e.g., ZZ Top's "Gimme All Your Lovin') and clothes (e.g., ZZ Top's "Best Dressed Man," the camp elegance of Adam Ant). Upward mobiity (e.g., Joe Jackson's "Steppin' Out") represents a major variation on this theme.

Protest. This activity is largely the province of the message video. The high profile of a spinoff school, whose seeming praise of the status quo is overlaid with a strong ironic twist (e.g., Bruce Springsteen's "Born in the USA," John Cougar Mellencamp's "Pink Houses"), attests to the artistic depth of the better video clips.

Tolerance for mild deviations in behavior. America likes to view itself as the last bastion of individuality and the skewed characterizations of some videos would appear to support this argument. Boy George, formerly with the band, Culture Club, flirted with transvestism although he made it clear that he was basically a well-adjusted, decent bloke whose father and brothers were boxers. Rod Stewart indulges in voyeurism in "Infatuation," but somehow his never-say-die attitude leaves us rooting for him to win the girl right up until the end of the clip.

In some instances video clips might be viewed as change agents within our society. Viewing clips could hasten catharsis; that is, identifying with a particular message, knowing you're not alone out there. The strong emotional and intellectual benefits of this experience could in turn stimulate the viewer to take on more of an activist role; for example, to donote food and money to the hungry in Ethiopia after viewing Band Aid's "Do They Know It's Christmas."

Summary

Perhaps the most notable feature of video clips as a recording medium is that they possess the power to evoke strong aesthetic reactions within a short time span. For many, such an experience might not signify anything other than light entertainment. However, they are capable of challenging the participant on far deeper levels, whether drawing upon other art forms (e.g., Todd Rundgren's manipulation of the visual symbols of Dali and Magritte on a more literal plane in "Time Heals") or developing the unique possibilities of the video medium itself. These possibilities include sensory overload (i.e., jamming as much information as possible within the short time span by means of increasing the rapidity of imnages, splitting the screen, etc.--a technique which has been especially influential in television ads; notable examples include Billy Joel's "We Didn't Start the Fire" and Tom Petty's "Jammin' Me"), the manipulation of predictable censoring standards (already engraved in stone for older media such as TV, the cinema, comics, radio, etc.), and dispensing with narrative demands and, thereby, encouraging figurative forms of thinking.

Table 126

Video Clip Categories

A. Live Concert. Aim: to provide an appreciation for the act as a performing unit. This represents the most cliche-ridden grouping; e.g., guitars arranged in phallanx formation, smoke bombs. A chief variant: posturing in more intimate surroundings--such as a living room or classroom--with little attempt to make it appear like the artist is really performing. Examples: Bruce Springsteen's "Glory Days"; Police's "Spirits in the Material World."

B. Dance/Theatrical Sequence. Key influence: *West Side Story*. Examples: Michael Jackson's "Beat It" and "Thriller"; Rod Stewart's "Young Turks."

C. Dramatic Action. Essence: a linear plot which may or may not conform to the song's lyrics. The visual action frequently skirts around the lyrics (they may be too vague to allow for a literal interpretation), thereby giving rise to a surrealistic frame of reference. Examples: Berlin's "No More Lies," a take-off on *Bonnie and Clyde*; Golden Earring's espionage fantasy, "Twilight Zone"; Greg Kihn's Oz parody, "Reunited."

D. Message Video. The typical approach consists of protesting the status quo. Hot topics include: class stratification, war, the environment, the complexities and pressures of modern society, unabashed hedonism, conformism, authoritarian leadership, and moral bankruptcy. Examples: Billy Joel's "Allentown"; U2's "Sunday Bloody Sunday"; Randyandy's "Living in the USA"; Devo's "Beautiful World." The latter clip, according to Shore, "may be the most powerful sociopolitical use of sustained, concentrated montage since the Odessa Steps sequence of Eisenstein's *The Battleship Potemkin*. The visuals reveal a protagonist tuning in on 1950s Americana, communicated via a quick-cut montage of images culled from newsreels and TV framed by the band's sardonic greeting-card verse. The video's progression from innocence to increasingly disturbing images constitutes the core of its dramatic thrust.

E. Conceptual. There are three major subheadings here: (1) art for art's sake; the clip glorifying technical virtuosity as its own end. Prime examples would be Missing Person's "Surrender Your Heart," which features Peter Max art endowed with breathtaking kinetic energy, and Philip Glass' "Act III," a visual depiction of the music's thematic development. (2) Art aimed at evoking an emotional reaction. The most productive style is, again, surrealism; David Bowie's "Ashes to Ashes" represents a production tour de force. Bowie is cast in three roles, that of a Pagliacci clown, high-tech junkie, and asylum inmate. The imagery is cryptic and evocative, featuring flamboyant costumes, Slavic figures in procession, a clown sinking into a lake, etc. Especially intriguing are the clip's deliberately overloaded direction (characterized by demented, horror-movie camera angles and neurotic cuts from supersaturated color to black and white) and the self-referential video-within-video motif, wherein each new sequence is introduced by Bowie holding up a postcard-sized video screen displaying the first shot of the   next sequence. (3) Anti-art art. Artists working in this category generally cultivate the cheap look, although many are of poor quality due to limited financial resources. Clips are typified by risk-taking (high degree of subjectivity, transcending the boundaries of good taste regarding the status quo, etc.) and inclinations to excess. Avant-garde artists such as Eno and Cabaret Voltaire fall within this category.

F. Humorous/Gag Presentation. Again, three main divisions exist: (1) Black humor. This form does not refer to racial subject matter but rather to a somewhat flippant treatment of the darker sides of life, often at the risk of crossing over into the realm of what a mainstream audience would consider to be bad taste. Favored themes include marital violence and fear of the bomb a la Dr. Strangelove. The Gap Band's "You Dropped a Bomb On Me" is a particularly clever variation on the latter theme, employing metaphor (i.e., love equated with a bombing raid) to achieve jarring visual--as well as literary--impact. (2) Satire. Examples abound here; Donald Fagen's "New Frontier" represents one of the more strikingly conceived contributions. The work comments playfully on 1950s mores, insecurities, and sense of aesthetic chic. The outwardly nostalgic plot reveals a teenage couple revisiting the Cold War years via a deserted bomb shelter. A less successful trend within this grouping, from an artistic standpoint, has been the self-conscious, often pretentious, attempt to spoof videomaking itself. (3) Nonsense. Utopia's "Feets Don't Fail Me Now," a product of video wunderkind Todd Rundgren, which portrays Muppet-styled cockroaches who suspect they should be involved in anything besides their present predicament, exemplifies this type.

G. The Travelogue. A prevailing strategy here seems to be the more exotic the clime the better one's chances of holding the viewer's attention. Teen stars, Duran Duran, shamefully exploit this maxim, offering the same plot from one video to another merely spread across a varying palette of locales; today a jungle in Indochina, tomorrow sailing the Caribbean, or maybe the mystical rites of the Inca past. Stop-action photography represents one of the heavily used cinematic devices within this category. Jean-Luc Ponty's "Individual Choice," Randyandy's "Living in the USA," and James Brown's "America" all feature frantically speeded-up images of Americans going about their everyday activities with liberal dollops of easily recognized physical landmarks thrown in for good measure.

TRADE PUBLICATIONS

Table 127

Billboard

Billboard has long been recognized as the leading entertainment trade weekly worldwide. Although documenting record industry developments has been its primary focus in the post-World War II era, the periodical represents a compendium of American popular culture since the late nineteenth century, covering at one time or another burlesque, the circus, fairs, medicine shows, minstrel performances, vaudeville, wild west spectacles, rodeos, zoos, Lyceum and Chautauqua, theatrical productions, musicals, motion pictures, skating rinks, bathing establishments, and coin-operated machines.

The publication, originally known as *Billboard Advertising*, was founded in Cincinnati by William H. Donaldson and James F. Hennegan. In the first issue (1894), editor Donaldson stated that it would be "devoted to the interests of the advertisers, poster printers, billposters, advertising agents, and secretaries of fairs." By 1897, the masthead title was changed to *The Billboard* (changed to simply *Billboard* in 1961) in an effort to reflect its expanding editorial concerns.

Following a period of separation from the publication due to editorial differences, Donaldson purchased Hennegan's interest in the enterprise in 1900 in order to forestall bankruptcy. He converted it from a monthly to a weekly effective May 5, 1900, thereby placing an added emphasis on the timely reporting of entertainment industry news. However, he also strengthened other types of coverage, including insightful, hard-hitting editorials and regular columns or departments concentrating on the leading show business fields. Offices were opened in New York and Chicago early in the twentieth century as a means of facilitating immediate, accurate dissemination of information.

The publication's close ties with the recording industry originated with coverage of coin-operated entertainment devices. From intermittent ads and news in 1899, *Billboard* expanded to a section entitled "Amusement Machines" in March 1932. With the jukebox an increasingly important segment of this field, the magazine inserted a "Record Buying Guide" beginning January 7, 1939 to assist in the selection process. Charting—perhaps the best known aspect of *Billboard*—first appeared as "Tunes Most Heard in Vaudeville Last Week," in the early 1900s.

With the advent of sound recordings, *Billboard* prepared weekly listings of the top sellers for the major labels. By 1938, the earliest form a national survey combining all recordings and companies appeared, the "Music Box Machine" charts, supplemented later by the "Best Sellers in Stores" (July 20, 1940-) and "Most Played by Disc Jockeys" (1945-) charts. Following World War II, the number of record charts proliferated to reflect the growing sophistication and importance of the music business, encompassing various genres (e.g., country, rhythm and blues, pop, classical, children's releases), formats (singles, LPs, radio, jukeboxes, sheet music, etc.), and locales. By 1987, *Billboard* would include eight weekly charts for albums alone: "Black," Compact Discs," "Country," "Hits of the World," "Latin," "Rock Tracks," "Spiritual," and "Pop."

The publication has incorporated a number of physical format changes in order to increase speed of publication and enhance its visual appeal. A five-column tabloid newspaper layout was introduced November 4, 1950, while coated paper was first used with the January 5, 1963 issue. The latter development opened the way to photojournalism and four-color halftone illustrations.

While *Billboard* has continued to offer a fairly consistent breakdown of features, columns, departments, reviews (generally of a descriptive, promotional nature), charts, and advertisements, augmented by regularly appearing supplements (e.g., "Billboard Campus Attractions," "Billboard International Directory of Recording Studios"), the content is constantly changing to reflect the dynamic flux of the entertainment industry.

The editorial and news material is provided largely by staff writers, with additional contributions by experts within the trade.

Billboard has further enhanced its profile by branching out into book publishing in cooperation with New York's Watson-Guptill. The long-running syndicated radio and television series, *American Top Forty*, based much of its information on the publication's chart data. Furthermore, a number of chart compilers have based developed their own reference tools from the weekly charts, most notably Joel Whitburn, owner of the Menomonee Falls, Wisconsin-based publisher, Record Research.

RECORD PRODUCERS

Table 128

Lou Adler, December 13, 1933-

As a talent manager, concert promoter, songwriter, producer, record label executive, and motion picture entrepreneur, Lou Adler was a notable tastemaker in popular music during the 1960s and 1970s. He remains best known as a major instigator of the West Coast Sound, a soft rock cutting across folk rock, surf and car songs, and the singer/songwriter tradition.

Born in Chicago, Adler grew up in the hard-scrabble Boyle Heights District of East Los Angeles. He broke into the music business as co-manager (with trumpeter Herb Alpert) of the surf-comedy duo, Jan and Dean. He and Alpert went on to form a songwriting/studio production team, working for such labels as Colpix and Dimension. Their compositions included "Only Sixteen," a hit for Sam Cooke in 1961 (Keen 2022; 1959; #28).

On his own, Adler formed Dunhill Records in 1964. The controversial protest song, Barry McGuire's "Eve of Destruction" (Dunhill 4009; 1965; #1)—penned by in-house songwriters P.F. Sloan and Steve Barri—was the label's first hit. Dunhill's long-term success was assured when the Mamas and the Papas placed a string of singles high on the charts, including "California Dreamin'" (Dunhill 4020; 1966; #4), "Monday Monday" (Dunhill 4026; 1966; #1), "I Saw Her Again" (Dunhill 4031; 1966; #5), "Words of Love" (Dunhill 4057; 1966; #5), "Dedicated to the One I Love" (Dunhill 4077; 1967; #2), and ""Creeque Alley" (Dunhill 4083; 1967; #5). He also continued work as an independent producer; his biggest success in the mid-1960s was with Johnny Rivers. He also co-wrote the number one hit, "Poor Side of Town" (Imperial 66205; 1966) with Rivers.

Selling the company to ABC-Paramount for a substantial profit, Adler was a prime mover in arranging the Monterey Pop Festival. Considered perhaps the greatest rock festival ever, from the musical standpoint, it launched the careers of Jimi Hendrix, Janis Joplin, and the Who stateside, and spurred planning for future extravaganzas. Adler's showed considerable business acumen in securing film and recording rights for the event; the profits derived from these avenues exceeded all expectations.

In the meantime, Adler founded Ode Records, which clicked immediately with Scott McKenzie's "San Francisco (Be Sure to Wear Flowers in Your Hair)" (Ode 103; 1967; #4). Later successes included progressive rock group Spirit and Brill Building songwriter Carole King. King's *Tapestry* (Ode 77009; 1971; #1 15 weeks), produced by Adler, became one of the top-selling albums of all-time, while elevating the singer/songwriter trend to a major genre.

Beginning in the 1970s, Adler shifted his emphasis to filmmaking, helping the British production, *Rocky Horror Picture Show*, become an American cult staple in the mid-1970s. He also signed Cheech and Chong to a series of comedy films. As with the Monterey Pop Festival, he placed considerable emphasis on the production of soundtrack LPs.

Table 129

Milt Gabler, May 20, 1911-July 20, 2011

Milt Gabler's musical contributions spanned many genres—most notably, jazz, rhythm and blues, and rock 'n' roll—and three distinct occupations: record retailing, ownership of a record company, and studio production. At a time when activities within the record industry were not as clearly demarcated and specialized as in the present day, he literally did it all, market analysis, contractual negotiations, talent scouting, promotional details, consulting, artist and repertoire work, and writing liner notes.

Gabler began working for the Commodore Music Shop, owned by his father, in 1926. As store manager, he was instrumental in building the enterprise into one of the leading record outlets in the New York area. By the early 1930s, he had began stocking cutout jazz and blues material, catering to musicians, songwriters, journalists, and other collectors.

He would bulk order custom pressings of deleted titles from the American Record Company, which had absorbed many bankrupt labels—including Brunswick, Columbia, Okeh, and Perfect—at the outset of the Depression to be issued as white-label Commodores. He then instituted the UHCA label (United Hot Clubs of America) as an outlet for his reissue program.

In early 1938, Commodore became the first American jazz label, recording a combo lead by Eddie Condon. Run more as a mechanism for creating the type of small-group jazz Gabler loved than as a business enterprise, Commodore continued to produce recordings through 1957. The company often served as outlet to record music which did not generate a favorable response from majors such as Columbia and Decca, including sides by Lester Young and the Kansas City Six and Billie Holiday. Holiday approached Gabler, a longtime friend, when her label, Vocalion, expressed reservations over recording "Strange Fruit," a song which addressed lynching in the South in unflinching terms. The song's flip side, a blues entitled "Fine and Mellow," would become Commodore's first hit.

Commodore's output dropped off considerably when Decca hired Gabler as a staff producer in the mid-1940s. In that capacity he worked with jazz, R&B, and pop artists, most notably, Louis Armstrong, Ella Fitzgerald, Louis Jordan, and Bill Haley and His Comets. Perhaps his most fabled recording session involved Haley at the Pythian Temple, April 12, 1954, when they produced "(We're Gonna) Rock Around the Clock" and "Thirteen Women." The release (Decca 29124), spurred by the inclusion of "Rock Around the Clock" on the soundtrack of the film, *Blackboard Jungle*, spent eight weeks at the top of the *Billboard* pop singles charts in July-August 1955, thereby ushering in the rock 'n' roll era. Gabler would continue working for Decca through the 1960s, generally with middle-of-the-road acts like Bert Kaempfert and Burl Ives.

Table 130

Bill Laswell, February 12, 1955-

Laswell has been termed a "postmodern Renaissance man," founding the Axiom label in 1988 through a partnership with Island Records, establishing Greenpoint Studio (1990), pursuing new directions in the fusion of jazz, rock, and funk both as a producer and with his own band, Material. Born in Salem, Illinois, and raised in Detroit, where he performed in funk groups, he moved to New York City in 1978. Formed at the outset to accompany former Gong frontman, Daevid Allen, on a U.S. tour, Material would become a forum for his musical experiments. Built around keyboardist Michael Beinhorn, drummer Fred Maher, and himself on bass, the group has negotiated many styles—including world music, avant garde jazz, ambient music, hip-hop, and mutant rock—and collaborated with many artists (e.g., Nona Hendryx, Sonny Sharrock, Fred Frith, Henry Threadgill, Archie Shepp, Nile Rodgers, Whitney Houston, William Burroughs). Although outside the pop mainstream, Material's recordings—*Temporary Music* (Celluloid; 1981), *American Songs EP* (Red Music; 1981), *Busting Out EP* (ZE/Island, 1981), *Memory Serves* (Celluloid/Elektra Musician 1-66042; 1982), *One Down* (Celluloid/Elektra; 1982), *Red Tracks* (Red; 1986), *Seven Souls* (Virgin 2-91360;

1989), *The Third Power* (Axiom 422-848 417-2; 1991), *Live in Japan* (Restless; 1994), and *Hallucination Engine* (Axiom; 1994)—remain required listening for adventurous listeners.

Laswell has been widely sought after both as a session player and producer. He contributed bass on Laurie Anderson's *Mr. Heartbreak* (1982) and has gone on to play with the Golden Palominos, Last Exit, the Last Poets.Brian Eno, David Byrne, Peter Gabriel, Fela Kuti, John Zorn, Bootsy Collins, and Buckethead, among others. In 1983 he cowrote and produced Herbie Hancock's hit, "Rockit" (), and won a Grammy for his work on Hancock's follow-up album, *Sound-System* (). His production of the hip-hop single "World Destruction" (), featuring Africa Bambaataa and Johnny Lydon, also garnered considerable praise. Since then, he has produced a diversified array of artists, including Sly (Dunbar) and Robbie (Shakespeare), Mick Jagger Motorhead, Iggy Pop, the Ramones, and Yellowman. [Romanowski and George-Warren. 1995]

RECORD COMPANY EXECUTIVES

Table 131

Clive Davis, April 4, 1934

Clive Davis played a key role in transforming the Columbia label into a major force within the record industry in the late 1960s. He went on to prove that this success was no fluke by working the same magic for Arista in the 1970s.

A Harvard Law School graduate destined to go far in the legal profession, Davis opted for a somewhat unconventional career path. Hired by Columbia as a contract lawyer in 1960, David gained recognition shortly thereafter by getting Bob Dylan—whose original contract had become void when the singer turned twenty-one—to renew with terms favorable to the company. His astute judgment and fair-mindedness in dealing with both associates and label clients enabled him to move up the ranks, becoming president in 1967.

Before Davis took over, Columbia had been slower than any other major label to sign—and promote—rock artists. This conservative approach had been dictated in part by Artist & Repertoire Head Mitch Miller's well-known antipathy for the genre. Davis, however, seemed free of the prejudices found in many of the musicians occupying the company's management positions; he understood that rock was entering an era of unprecedented creativity. He moved quickly to sign large numbers of talented new rock acts, including Big Brother and the Holding Company (featuring Janis Joplin), the Electric Flag, Santana, Chicago, Bruce Springsteen, and Billy Joel. The *Billboard* pop album charts tell the story of Columbia's shift in fortunes: between 1965-1967 none of its releases reached the number one position; in 1968, its releases spent twenty-four weeks at number one; in 1969, eleven weeks; and in 1970, eighteen weeks.

Despite the label's commercial success and newfound artistic credibility, many upper echelon staffers chafed at the alleged egomania displayed by Davis. An internal investigation revealed irregularities such as faked invoices and expense accounts connected with Davis, which led to his dismissal in 1973. He would later provide a different account of these developments in his autobiography, *Clive: Inside the Record Business* (New York: William Morrow, 1975).

By the mid-1970s, Davis had been hired to head the record division at Columbia Pictures. After renaming the company Arista, he signed Barry Manilow, who went on to become a major recording star. Arista's roster would eventually rival that of his former label, including the Grateful Dead, the Kinks, Eric Carmen, Graham Parker, Air Supply, Whitney Houston, and Alan Jackson.

RECORDING SESSION MUSICIANS

Table 132

Hal Blaine, February 5, 1929-

Hal Blaine may have the longest resume of any session drummer during the rock era. At a time when rock groups attempted to perpetuate the myth that they played all the instruments on their records, Blaine was used in "countless thousands of recording dates with virtually every big name in the business" [Jud Cost. Liner notes to *Deuces, "T's," Roadsters & Drums*.], including the Beach Boys, the Byrds, John Denver, Duane Eddy, Jan and Dean, Dean Martin, Elvis Presley, Paul Revere and the Raiders, Simon and Garfunkel, Frank and Nancy Sinatra, and Phil Spector's roster of artists.

Born Harold Simon Belsky in Holyoke, Massachusetts, he grew up watching Count Basie, Tommy Dorsey, Benny Goodman, and other big bands in Hartford's State Theatre across the street from where his father worked during the 1930s. When his family moved to southern California in the 1944, he began playing the drums during club jam sessions. Following a stint in the Army during the Korean War, he used the G.I. Bill to earn a degree at the Roy Knapp School of Percussion in Chicago.

Back in Los Angeles, he began performing on demos for a local deejay with songwriting aspirations. He eventually got an assignment to play on Tommy Sands' recording of "Teen-Age Crush" (Capitol 3639; 1957; #2). The record's success opened doors for other recording sessions. His ability to read music gave him a decided advantage over other studio drummers. He and the other informally dressed young turks playing the early 1960s recording sessions—including Leon Russell, Glen Campbell, and Jerry Cole—were eyed with suspicion by the older, established musicians. Hearing comments such as, "These kids are gonna wreck the business," [Cost] led Blaine to christen his cohorts the "Wrecking Crew."

Sessions with Lee Hazlewood, producer of Duane Eddy's classic singles, led a contract with RCA to record the only album in which Blaine received star billing. Recorded on October 25, 1963 and released without any promotional tour or advertising, *Deuces, "T's," Roadsters & Drums* (RCA; reissued by Sundazed 12856; 2001), by Hal Blaine and the Young Cougars, was destined for the cut-out bins. Two singles for the label—"Hawaii 1963"/"East Side Story" (RCA 8147; 1963) and "(Dance with the) Surfin' Band"/"The Drummer Plays for Me" (RCA 8223; 1963)—had been released earlier in the year, also to marginal sales. Nevertheless, Blaine's studio legacy, which has spanned some forty years, was sufficient to earn him induction into the Rock and Roll Hall of Fame in 2000.

TABLE 133

RUSS TITELMAN

Relatively unknown outside of the record industry, Russ Titelman has nevertheless been highly influential as a songwriter, session musician, and producer. He started out contributing guitar work and vocals on demos and records (e.g., the Paris Sisters, the Spectors Three) for Phil Spector. In the early 1960s, he became a staff writer for Don Kirshner's Brill Building firm, Aldon Music, collaborating with such notables as Gerry Goffin and Carole King. He went on play guitar on the television program, *Shindig*, in 1965, and found steady work as a songwriter (his credits included "Gone Dead Train," which appeared in the film, *Performance*) and studio musician.

Following his production debut on Little Feat's eponymous album (Warner Bros. 1890; 1970), Titelman was promoted to an Artist & Repertoire executive post. He would continue in that capacity until 1997, working with George Benson, Eric Clapton, Ry Cooder, Rickie Lee Jones, Ladysmith Black Mambazo, Randy Newman, Rufus, Paul Simon, James Taylor, and Steve Winwood, often co-producing with Lenny Waronker. Titelman's trademark was the ability to pack a maximum amount of music into the overall mix while making the result sound natural and effortless. According to Daniel Levitin, "Part of this is engineering, but most of it is arrangement, giving the parts the right room and space within which to breathe."

Titelman has received Grammies for Best Record with Clapton's "Tears In Heaven" (Duck/Reprise 19038; 1992; #2) and "Album of the Year" with *Unplugged* (Duck/Reprise 45024; 1992; #2). The latter's success provided the impetus for a wave of MTV "unplugged" releases. He presently serves on the Board of Governors for the New York Chapter of NARAS.

APPENDICES

I. Acoustic Era Song Lyrics

I'm Looking For The Man That Wrote *The Merry Widow Waltz*

A girlie named Lizzie,
Said, "Charlie, get busy,
And take me to see a good show."
Said he, "All right, Kiddo,
We'll go see the `Widow',
The one that's so `Merry', you know."
The `Waltz' was entrancing,
That strain set her dancing,
She's waltzed the shoes off of her feet;
There's trouble now cooking,
Says Charlie, "I'm looking,
For one that I'll brain if we meet."

CHORUS:
I'm looking for the man that wrote
"The Merry Widow Waltz!"
And if I fail to find him,
it's the greatest of my faults.
For when I think of Lizzie,
"Hop-Scotchin'" till she's dizzy;
I'm looking for the man that wrote
"The Merry Widow Waltz!"

The Janitor's squealing.
There's cracks in the ceiling,
But Lizzie goes twirling about;
The Kids' caught the fever,
The Cook and Coalheaver,
And even the dog have waltzed out.
The Hall-Boy's grown giddy,
And `sashays' with Biddy,
Each time that the Hand Organs grind;
That `Waltz' has him "going,"
Insanity's growing,
He shouts like he's losing his mind.

CHORUS:
I'm looking for the man that wrote
"The Merry Widow Waltz!"
And if I chance to find him,
he'll need more than smelling slats.
He'll never write another,
He'll think of Home and Mother;
I'm looking for the man that wrote
"The Merry Widow Waltz!"

The `Waltz' starts you shaking,
You hear it on waking,
You hear it on going to bed;
You hum it out walking,
You sing it when talking,
'Twill haunt you I'm sure till you're dead!
It oozes from cellars,
And all the Flat dwellers,
With phonographs make you a wreck;
Why, even a PARROT, way up in a garret,
Has got the WHOLE SCORE in its NECK.

CHORUS:
I'm looking for the man that wrote
"The Merry Widow Waltz!"
And the only thing can save him
Is the Sate Deposit vaults.
Chock full of lead I'll fill him,
Shout "Yes!" if I'm to kill him;
I'm looking for the man that wrote
"The Merry Widow Waltz!"

(Words by Edgar Selden and music by Seymour Furth, copyright 1907, Maurice Shapiro, New York, NY)

Over There

Johnnie get your gun, get your gun, get your gun,
Take it on the run, on the run, on the run;
Hear them calling you and me;
Ev'ry son of liberty.
Hurry right away, no delay, go today,

Make your daddy glad, to have had such a lad,
Tell your sweetheart not to pine,
To be proud her boy's in line.

CHORUS:
Over there, over there,
Send the word, send the word over there,
That the Yanks are coming,
the Yanks are coming.
The drums rum-tumming ev'ry where--
So prepare, say a pray'r,
Send the word, send the word to beware,
We'll be over, we're coming over,
And we won't come back till it's over over there.

Johnnie get your gun, get your gun, get your gun,
Johnnie show the Hun, you're a son-of-a-gun,
Hoist the flag and let her fly,
Like true heroes, do or die.
Pack your little kit, show your grit, do your bit.
Soldiers to the ranks from the towns and the tanks,
Make your mother proud of you,
And to liberty be true.

(George M. Cohan, copyright 1917, Leo Feist, Inc., New York, NY)

Bridget O'Flynn (Where've Ya Been?)

"Bridget O'Flynn?"
"Yes, Mama dear?"
"Was that you sneakin' in, come over here.
Look at the state of your Sunday clothes,
Look at your shoes and new silk hose,
You've been doin' the Charleston I suppose.
Bridget O'Flynn, just say your pray'rs,
You'll need 'em when your father comes down stairs:

CHORUS:
Bridget O'Flynn,
Where've ya been?
Bridget O'Flynn,
This is a nice time for you to come in.

The boy friend took you for a ride?
And did the car break down?
Or maybe you ran out of gas,
About ten miles from town?
Did you walk home?
Look at your shoes!
Ain't it a sin,
Faith your story and your shoes are mighty thin.
I'm tellin' you now just what to do,
If you have any friends that own a canoe,
Don't go near the water, Bridget darlin'."

"Bridget O'Flynn?"
"What is it Ma?"
"When you get out agin you'll not go far,
Faith and last night you went far enough,
You and your paint and powder puff,
Just you wait till your father does his stuff.
Bridget O'Flynn, I'd like to bet,
That you can tell who owns this cigarette:

Chorus:
Bridget O'Flynn,
Where've ya been?
Bridget O'Flynn,
This is a nice time for you to come in.
You went to see the Big Parade?
The big parade, me eye,
Sure no parade could ever take
  that long in passin' by,
Bridget O'Flynn,
Tell me the truth,
This is your chance.
There was nothin' wrong?
You just went to a dance,
Just keep away from the dancin' hall.
There's nobody there worthwhile at all,
That's where I met your father, Bridget darlin'!"

(Words by Andrew B. Sterling and music by Robert King, copyright 1926, Shapiro, Bernstein & Co., Inc., New York, NY)

II. Artist Recordings In Victor Catalog

NOVEMBER 1915*

Alda, Frances	29
Amato, Pasquale	33
American Quartet	63
Baker, Elsie	43
Burr, Henry	30
Caruso, Enrico	128
Collins and Harlan	58
De Gogorza, Emilio	45
Elman, Mischa	38
Farrar, Geraldine	58
Gadski, Johanna	40
Gluck, Alma	69
Hayden Quartet	92
Herbert's Orchestra	39
Homer, Louise	44
Jones and Murray	25
Journet, Marcel	30
Kreisler, Fritz	41
Lauder, Harry	45
Lyric Quartet	35
Macdonough, Harry	57
Marsh, Lucy Isabelle	37
McCormack, John	85
Melba, Nellie	29
Murray, Billy	84
Neapolitan Trio	26
Peerless Quartet	78
Powell, Maud	44
Ruffo, Titta	36
Schumann-Heink, Ernestine	36
Stewart, Cal	35
Tetrazzini, Luisa	32
Turner, Alan	26
Van Brunt, Walter	26
Vessella's Italian Band	40
Victor Light Opera Company	82
Werrenrath, Reinald	25
Williams, Evan	62
Witherspoon, Herbert	25

Top Artists by Number of Entries
 1. Enrico Caruso   128
 2. Hayden Quartet   92
 3. John McCormack   85
 4. Billy Murray   84
 5. Victor Light Opera Co.   82
 6. Peerless Quartet   78
 7. Alma Gluck   69
 8. American Quartet   63
 9. Evan Williams   62
10. Collins and Harlan   58
10. Geraldine Farrar   58
12. Harry Macdonough   57

Top Artists (Including Collaborations)~
 1. Billy Murray   172
 2. Harry Macdonough   149
 3. Enrico Caruso   128
 4. Henry Burr   108
~Murray's work with both the Hayden Quartet and Heidelberg Quintet not included in his total.

1925*

Artist	Entries
Alda, Frances	54; 4#
American Quartet	31
Baker, Elsie	70; 26
Benson Orchestra of Chicago	84
Bori, Lucrezia	35
Braslau, Sophie	27
Burr, Henry	65; 28
Caruso, Enrico	121; 41
Conway's Band	57
Culp, Julia	25
De Gogorza, Emilio	67
De Luca, Giuseppe	38
Ellman, Mischa	68; 6
Farrar, Geraldine	41; 24
Galli-Curci, Amelita	63
Gluck, Alma	73; 25
Golden, Billy	2; 26

Great White Way Orchestra	32
Harrison, Charles	31; 2
Heifetz, Jascha	46
Herbert's Orchestra	36
Homer, Louise	45; 8
International Novelty Orch.	67
James, Lewis	24; 18
Journet, Marcel	36
Kline, Olive	40; 23
Kreisler, Fritz	77; 2
Lauder, Harry	78
Marsh, Lucy Isabelle	49; 5
Martinelli, Giovanni	38; 2
McCormack, John	173
Murphy, Lambert	50; 4
Murray, Billy	46; 55
Neapolitan Trio	30
Paderewski, Ignace Jan	26
Peerless Quartet	74
Philadelphia Symphony Orch.	49
Pietro	40
Powell, Maud	36
Pryor's Band	129
Rachmaninoff, Sergei	26; 6
Reitz, W.H.	25
Rodeheaver, Homer	33; 6
Ruffo, Titta	42
Schumann-Heink, Ernestine	60
Shannon Quartet	34
Shaw, Elliott	11; 23
Smith's Orchestra	42
Sousa's Band	69
Stanley, Aileen	13; 13
Stewart, Cal	36
Trinity Choir	43
The Troubadours	35
Vessella's Italian Band	52
Victor Concert Orchestra	114
Victor Military Band	100
The Virginians	41
Waring's Pennsylvanians	26
Werrenrath, Reinald	80; 2
Whiteman and His Orch.	155

Williams, Evan   66
Zimbalist, Efrem   32; 4

Top Artists By Number of Entries
 1. Whiteman and His Orchestra 185
 2. John McCormack   173
 3. Enrico Caruso   162
 4. Pryor's Band   129
 5. Victor Concert Orchestra 114
 6. Billy Murray   101
 7. Victor Military Band   100
 8. Alma Gluck   98
 9. Elsie Baker   96
10. Henry Burr   93

Top Artists (Including Group Affiliations)@
 1. Whiteman and His Orchestra 185
 2. John McCormack   173
 3. Henry Burr   167
 4. Enrico Caruso   162
 5. Billy Murray   138

@Murray's work with Whiteman, the Great White Way Orchestra, the International Novelty Orchestra, and others not included in his total.

*Both listings only include artists with at least 25 entries.
#2d figure (after semi-colon) represents artist collaborations.

III. Pioneer Recording Artist Ratings

Jim Walsh's "Supreme Fifteen":

 1. Billy Murray; Henry Burr
 2. Ada Jones; Len Spencer
 3. Arthur Collins; Byron G. Harlan
 4. Harry Macdonough
 5. Albert Campbell
 6. Frank C. Stanley
 7. Steve Porter
 8. Billy Golden
 9. S.H. Dudley
10. William F. Hooley

11. Dan W. Quinn
12. Cal Stewart

Source: Walsh, Jim. "Are These the `Supreme Fifteen'?," *Hobbies*. 50 (June 1945) 16-17.

Arnold Jacobson's popularity ranking based upon requests made to his mail order cassette service since the 1960s:

1. Billy Murray
2. Henry Burr
3. Ada Jones
4. Gene Austin
5. Vernon Dalhart
6. Peerless Quartet
7. Cal Stewart
8. Collins and Harlan
9. American Quartet

Kurt Nauck's ranking of demand based upon his mail order business, Nauck's Vintage Records, instituted in the late 1980s:

1. Cal Stewart
2. Billy Murray
3. Ada Jones
4. Edward M. Favor
5. Dan Quinn
6. Russell Hunting
7. George Graham

Bill Schurk's popularity ranking based upon thirty years of record hunting as director of the Bowling Green State University Sound Recordings Archive:

1. Henry Burr
2. Billy Murray
3. Collins and Harlan
4. Frank Crumit/Al Jolson (often coupled on the Columbia label)

5. Cal Stewart
6. American Quartet

Arthur Vergara's popularity ranking based upon a lifetime of record collecting beginning around 1950:

1. Billy Murray
2. Ada Jones
3. Henry Burr
4. Collins and Harlan
5. Peerless Quartet
6. American Quartet

Printed in Great
Britain
by Amazon